College
Business
Law

ABOUT THE AUTHORS

R. Robert Rosenberg, a leading author of books on business and consumer law and business and consumer mathematics, is known to thousands of teachers throughout the 50 states and in many foreign countries. He has written over 29 books, including titles such as *Business and the Law, Outline of College Business Law, Essentials of Business Law, Business Law/30,* and *Understanding Business and Consumer Law,* all published by the McGraw-Hill Book Company. Dr. Rosenberg has taught at all educational levels—including high school, junior college, business school, and university. In addition, he has held administrative positions on the elementary, secondary, and collegiate levels and was president of Jersey City Junior College. Currently, he serves as an educational consultant at conventions and workshops. Dr. Rosenberg also contributes to professional magazines on the subjects of business law, business mathematics, and teaching methods.

William G. Ott has served as president, vice president, and director of law at Goldey Beacom College. He is the coauthor of *Business and the Law* and *Outline of College Business Law.* In addition, Mr. Ott has written numerous articles on law, credit, and school management for publications such as *Credit World, EBTA Journal, Business School Executive,* and *Creative Service.* His qualifications as an author and educator include a varied and practical background in retailing, business management, advertising, and journalism. One of the largest student law associations in the eastern United States, the William G. Ott Association, is named in his honor.

Edward E. Byers has served as editorial director and is currently editor in chief for the Gregg Division of the McGraw-Hill Book Company. In these positions he has influenced the development of many publications in the areas of general business, supervisory management, office education, and business law. He is also an author of general and specialized secretarial procedures programs as well as medical secretarial reference works. Dr. Byers has taught in both high school and college. At the business college level, he has served as an academic dean. He is also a speaker for teacher groups and contributes to professional magazines on methods of instruction and curriculum development.

College Business Law

Fifth Edition

R. Robert Rosenberg, Ed.D., C.P.A.
Educational Consultant
Former President of Jersey City Junior College

William G. Ott, A.B., LL.B.
Former Director of Law and President
Goldey Beacom College

Edward E. Byers, Ed.D.
Editor in Chief, Business, Office, and Management Publications
Gregg Division
McGraw-Hill Book Company

Legal Consultant:
David S. Cook, J.D.
Member of the New York Bar
New York City

Gregg Division/McGraw-Hill Book Company

New York   St. Louis   Dallas   San Francisco   Auckland   Bogotá
Düsseldorf   Johannesburg   London   Madrid   Mexico   Montreal   New Delhi
Panama   Paris   São Paulo   Singapore   Sydney   Tokyo   Toronto

Associate Editor: Lawrence H. Wexler
Senior Editing Supervisor: Linda Stern
Editor: Marion Bonney Castellucci
Production Supervisor: Laurence Charnow
Design Supervisor: Edwin R. Fisher
Book Designer: Barbara Bert
Cover Designer: Karen Miño

Credits: Forms on pages 50 and 51 reprinted courtesy
of Stevens-Ness Law Publishing Co.,
Portland, Oregon 97204; forms on pages 83, 503, and 535
reprinted with permission of and available from
Julius Blumberg, Inc., New York, New York 10013;
and the form on page 342 reprinted
courtesy of All-State Legal Supply Co.,
Mountainside, New Jersey 07092.

Library of Congress Cataloging in Publication Data

Rosenberg, Reuben Robert, date
    College business law.

    Includes index.
    1. Commercial law—United States. I. Ott, William
G., joint author. II. Byers, Edward Elmer, joint
author. III. Title.
KF889.3.R68   1978   346′.73′07   77-10943
ISBN 0-07-053885-9

COLLEGE BUSINESS LAW, Fifth Edition

4 5 6 7 8 9 0   DODO   8 7 6 5 4 3 2 1

Preface

Because business law is a dynamic discipline, a publication in this area benefits in usefulness and relevance through periodic updating. Legal concern for consumers and environmental protection has intensified, as reflected in new legislation and a spate of court rulings. Government regulation of business and the economy has become more pronounced, evidenced by the mushrooming reach and power of administrative agencies. The law of employment has been expanded and modified by new enactments and legal decisions, particularly regarding equal employment opportunities for minorities and women. These and other developments and their impact now and in the foreseeable future are presented in this fifth edition of *College Business Law*.

Yet this edition is more than just an integration of updatings. New chapters and many new case illustrations have been added to convey the changing attitudes of the courts, law-making agencies, and business managers and consumers. Coverage of business law fundamentals has been so modified or amplified as to make this version virtually the equivalent of a new text in the field.

RELEVANCE

This new edition offers a thorough presentation of legal principles and practices that students should understand before they enter their chosen field of work. It is written fundamentally for the business-oriented person who lacks a detailed knowledge of the law but who wants a broad knowledge of the areas of commercial law and business regulation. It is also geared to general-education and technical-industrial students who need a realistic view of the law of contracts as well as the law of employment, including right-to-work laws, workers' compensation, unemployment compensation, and social security. Continuing-education and independent-study students will find the illustrative cases to be free from complicated and often distracting procedural issues.

In a larger sense, however, the fifth edition is designed to provide all readers with:

- ☐ A basic understanding of substantive business law.
- ☐ An awareness of the legal environment in which business transactions are negotiated.
- ☐ An ability to recognize business situations that require legal counsel.
- ☐ A consciousness that business decisions must be considered and rendered in the light of their legal consequences.
- ☐ An understanding of the readers' legal rights and responsibilities as present or future business operators, workers, or consumers.
- ☐ A familiarity with the structure and workings of our legal system and with the legal remedies available under that system.

Given these objectives and their implementation, the authors consider the fifth edition to be equally appropriate for a course in traditional business law, a program emphasizing the modern environmental approach, or a course combining elements of both approaches.

NEW AND SPECIAL FEATURES

The following are the significant new and special features of this volume. Each feature helps make *College Business Law* a more effective instructional system.

Uniform Commercial Code

In this edition, UCC regulations which govern commercial transactions—that is, sales, commercial paper, bank deposits and collections, letters of credit, bulk transfers, documents of title, investment securities, and secured transactions—are presented as the "law of the land" for business. References to the code are woven directly into the text when appropriate. The practice of cluttering up the text with footnotes and citations to the UCC which have only marginal usefulness to a reader and which tend to encumber reading and comprehension has been avoided.

New Chapters and Topical Coverage

Also included in the fifth edition is coverage of subject matter that was previously omitted or lightly treated. Thus, this edition provides:

☐ Treatment of environmental law, in Chapter 1, as a distinct new source of law, with consideration given to legislative efforts to control air, water, noise, and other forms of pollution.

☐ A new chapter on consumer law (Chapter 4), emphasizing recent consumer protection laws regarding advertising, packaging and labeling, sales techniques, product quality and liability, contract rescission rights, credit card liability, and credit standing and reporting.

☐ A separate chapter on government regulation and administrative agencies (Chapter 5), focusing on statutes enacted by the legislative branch of government and executed by administrative agencies which exercise rule-making and quasi-judicial powers. Ample coverage is provided on the scope and authority of the regulatory agencies, the nature of administrative proceedings and procedures, and regulatory problems and benefits.

☐ A thoroughly revised section on agency and employment (Part 8, Chapters 26 to 29), featuring widely extended treatment of the law of employment and labor-management relations. The authors have expanded the coverage of employee rights, unfair labor practices of employers and unions, dispute-settlement procedures, workers' compensation, and laws concerned with employment discrimination. The coverage of affirmative action is particularly important because of its impact on business.

☐ Introduction of new topics such as the tort of malpractice; invasion of privacy for commercial purposes; lawyer functions, responsibilities, and fees; alternatives to court action, such as arbitration and conciliation; business taxation; Occupational Health and Safety Act regulations; pension reform; new business ventures; and updated disclosure requirements for real estate settlements.

Case Illustrations

New case illustrations, many based on decisions adjudicated within the last five years, are interspersed throughout this edition. Although used more sparingly than in the prior edition, hypothetical case illustrations are also used whenever they elucidate a legal concept more effectively than does an adjudicated case. All cases, hypothetical or otherwise, present common situations and dilemmas which people are likely to encounter in today's business world.

End-of-Chapter Exercises

The fifth edition provides a richer assortment of review and application exercises than any comparable text now offers. "Questions for Review and Discussion" serves to check students' comprehension of the chapter and to prepare the students to discuss in class pertinent subjects covered in the text. "Analyzing Cases" requires students to interpret text-related cases. "Legal Reasoning and Business Judgment" challenges students with business transactions that require them to apply principles of law presented and to determine courses of action that do not require expensive litigation. A large number of the case problems in the end-of-chapter exercises are new; others have been substantially modified and embellished in order to challenge students with current and relevant issues in business law.

Legal Terminology and Vocabulary

The authors have consciously written the text so as to minimize the use of legalese, the surfeit of which they regard as one of the primary drawbacks of other texts in the field. The current edition has been designed and illustrated to enhance readability and comprehension.

At the same time, the authors continue to believe that one of the primary objectives of any text in business law is to help the student to develop a working knowledge and understanding of the language of the law. To this end, key terms which the authors believe the student must know and comprehend are highlighted in each chapter. They appear in boldface italics. Other terms which the student ought to know are presented in light italics. A legal dictionary with over 500 briefly defined terms appears at the back of the book as still another aid to vocabulary building.

SUPPORTING MATERIALS

An *Individualized Performance Guide* accompanies this fifth edition of *College Business Law*. Its performance objectives tell the student what he or she is expected to get out of each chapter. These objectives also serve to direct student attention to business law principles and practices that make the private property system and the competitive economic system workable. Reading assignments are used to highlight the appropriate section of the text that is concerned with legal insights called for by the objectives. Additional reading suggestions are presented for the student who wishes to go beyond the confines of the text and to amplify a particular subject or point of law covered. Self-checks are provided which measure a reader's mastery of each reading assignment. A broad range of extracted cases gives students the opportunity to apply the law, analyze case decisions, and give the reason for the decisions. Answers to all Self-checks are given in a separate section of the *Individualized Performance Guide,* providing instant feedback and enabling the reader to measure his or her progress in achieving the performance objectives.

The *Instructor's Manual and Key* provides the answers for all text questions and cases that appear in the *Performance Guide.* Also included, for measurement of student progress, is a bank of test items which may be reproduced by the instructor. In addition, helpful teaching and course management suggestions are given.

R. Robert Rosenberg
William G. Ott
Edward E. Byers

Contents

College
Business
Law

Part 1
Law in a Democratic Society
Chapter 1
Sources and Categories of Law

In a world whose population consisted of only one person, there would be a state of complete harmony: no difference of opinion on any problem or issue, no act that would violate the public right of others, no wrong or injury to another's health, welfare, property, or reputation. But if the population were to increase, even by only one, there would immediately be a different situation, with potential conflicts and disagreements as to each person's individual rights. Eventually, there would have to be some agreement on rules to be observed.

Without a body of rules and principles, individuals would act to suit their own wishes or objectives. You might choose to drive your car in a manner and at a speed that endangered others, just because you enjoyed doing so. You might give in to the urge to shout "Fire!" in a crowded theater. In doing business with others, you might be inclined to be your own judge in determining your duties and in deciding whether to honor your oral or written agreements. Thus, without an accepted body of rules that state what is right and forbid what is wrong, community living would soon be reduced to a level of chaos.

JUSTICE AND THE LAW

Rules which society adopts and enforces in order to operate in an orderly way are called *laws*, and their ultimate goal is *justice*. The basic purpose of justice in a democratic society is threefold:

- [ ] Recognition of each person's human dignity and freedom and right to life, security, property, privacy, family, home, movement, beliefs, and reputation.
- [ ] Equality with respect to every person's being given the greatest possible opportunity to develop his or her potential to its utmost extent.
- [ ] Observance of responsibility so that all persons may enjoy the benefits of common purpose, interests, or pleasure in an even-handed manner.

Laws conform to social trends; laws do not determine them. As the patterns and conditions of people living together and doing business together change, laws are adapted to fit these changes. It would be impossible to achieve justice for today's citizens if we were obliged to live according to laws written fifty years ago. Similarly, laws of the nineteen-seventies—or even the nineteen-eighties—would not provide justice for the larger population projected by the year 2000.

▶ Stannus drove the family car through a town in rural Pennsylvania. She was stopped by a deputy sheriff and issued a traffic ticket for violating a local ordinance by traveling at 20 miles an hour in a 15-mile-an-hour zone. As long as the law remains unchanged, it is legally enforceable, even though current traffic control practices might suggest that this law is socially unjust.

It should be recognized that the terms *law* and *justice* are not necessarily synonymous; nor is the law an exact science. Law is created by the agents of society, such as legislatures and the courts, but each individual has a personal view of what is right or wrong. Nevertheless, in the struggle for justice, differences are generally resolved by applying the law rather than our personal views, even when we ourselves disagree with the law. Thus it is safe to say that we remain law-centered rather than justice-centered.

SOURCES OF WRITTEN LAW

The sources of written law are the federal and state constitutions, federal and state statutes, decisions of the courts, federal and state administrative agency rules and regulations, and local ordinances.

Constitutional Law

The Constitution of the United States and the constitutions of the several states are the fundamental written law. They are the foundation supporting all law in the United States. Article VI of the Constitiution states: "This Constitution, and the Laws of the United States which shall be made in Pursuance thereof; and all Treaties made, or which shall be made, under the Authority of the United States, shall be the supreme law of the Land; and the Judges in every State shall be bound thereby, any Thing in the Constitution or Laws of any State to the Contrary notwithstanding."

Both state and federal constitutions distribute the powers of government and curb governmental power in favor of individual liberties and property. The Constitution of the United States limits state and local as well as federal action. Some of its restrictions on state action are designed to leave the field clear for federal authority; other restrictions are designed to leave individuals free from state domination. For example, states may not force citizens to display mottoes or other ideological messages on auto license plates or other personal property. The federal courts and the Supreme Court have ruled that such laws violate the First Amendment's protection of freedom of expression.

▶ The Maynards, who are Jehovah's Witnesses, put tape over the motto "Live Free or Die" on their New Hampshire auto license plates to stress their disagreement with its message. They considered the motto repugnant to their moral, religious, and political beliefs and substituted a motto that pleased them better. The Maynards argued that they "wouldn't give up their life for freedom." They felt that "life was more precious than freedom." Convicted by a New Hampshire court under a mutilation statute—a misdemeanor—and for refusing to pay the fines imposed against them, the Maynards appealed to a U.S. district court and subsequently to the Supreme Court. Both courts ruled that such state laws violate the First Amendment's protection of freedom of expression.

All restrictions are interpreted and applied by courts. State courts are final authorities on the application of state constitutions to state executive and legislative action. The U.S. Supreme Court is the final authority on the application of the federal Constitution and state legislative and executive action. It has been inferred by the courts that their duty is to apply in lawsuits or advisory opinions the higher law of the Constitution against the inferior law of the legislatures whenever a conflict between the two exists. In other words, all state laws must conform to the federal Constitution as well as to the constitution of the state. Legislation enacted by cities, towns, and smaller governmental units must conform to their state constitutions. Each governmental unit—federal, state, or local—finds its authority, whether it be specifically stated (*express powers*) or derived through interpretation and implication of the express powers (*implied powers*), in the federal Constitution or a state constitution. An example of an implied constitutional power is the right of Congress to create regulative agencies such as the Interstate Commerce Commission (ICC).

Constitutional Amendments   Both the federal Constitution and the state constitutions may be changed by amendment. Amendments to the federal Constitution require approval by three-fourths of the states and the receipt by the General Services Administration of each state's official record of its action. The federal Constitution has a total of twenty-six amendments. The first ten make up the Bill of Rights and were added soon after the ratification of the Constitution by the original thirteen states. The Twenty-second Amendment, ratified in 1951, provides that no person may be elected to the office of President of the United States for more than two terms. The Twenty-third, ratified in 1961, gives citizens of the District of Columbia the right to vote for President and Vice President in national elections and allots to the District of Columbia three members in the electoral college. The Twenty-fourth forbids state or federal governments to levy a poll tax as a qualification for voting in national elections. The Twenty-fifth, ratified in 1967, provides for presidential succession in the case of the disability or death of the President. The most recent amendment, the Twenty-sixth, ratified in 1971, lowered to eighteen years the minimum voting age in local and state as well as federal elections.

Judicial Review   The judiciary has the power to review actions of the executive branch of government and to review laws passed by the legislative branch to determine whether such laws are constitutional. This principle of *judicial review* is the focal point of the idea of separation of powers. Any citizen may appeal to the courts to have a law declared invalid and unenforceable should it violate a particular freedom or in some way interfere with a constitutional right.

Courts also interpret legislation by deciding the meaning of and filling in the gaps in the statutes. The courts' interpretations, expressed in decisions, are then accepted as the law; the process is known as judicial or court decision, and the resulting law is called *case law*.

Statute Law

Enactments (laws, bills) of a federal or state legislature are known as *statutes*. Occasionally the term applies to municipal ordinances and to the rules and regulations of administrative agencies which are passed in the performance of delegated legislative duties. Because a steady stream of statutes are being passed each year by the federal Congress and by the fifty separate state legislative bodies, there are important differences in statute laws throughout the nation. This lack of similarity does not present a problem when the parties to a dispute live in the same state. However, when a buyer from state A does business with a seller in state B, a question arises as to which state's statutes control the action.

Uniform State Law The body of law known as *conflict of laws* deals with the latter question. It determines the applicable statute law in a multistate transaction or action. For instance, a court sitting in one state will generally follow its own rules or *adjective law* (matters of evidence, procedure, and appeals used in court), but it would use the substantive law of another state if the injury or wrong occurred in the other state. *Substantive law* is the law that defines the rights, duties, and liabilities of parties to an action. For example, suppose that X and Y sign a contract in New York to build a hotel in Florida. If a conflict over the terms of the contract arose, a question would arise as to which laws—New York's or Florida's—would be used to decide the issues in contention. If suit were brought in New York, the matter might be settled as follows: New York adjective law would be used in determining matters of evidence and court procedure. But Florida's substantive law as to contracts would be applied by the New York court to determine the rights and liabilities of the parties, since Florida has the most "real" contact with, and interest in, the subject matter of the contract, namely, the construction of the hotel.

Another solution to the problem is for the legislatures of all the states to adopt the same laws concerning certain business transactions. To this end, a legislative group called the National Conference of Commissioners on Uniform State Laws (NCCUSL) was created. After they are approved by the NCCUSL, proposed uniform acts are recommended to the state legislatures for adoption. The Uniform Negotiable Instruments Law (NIL) was proclaimed in this manner. The most important development in uniform state legislation has been the Uniform Commercial Code (UCC), which deals with all issues that may arise in the handling of a commercial transaction from beginning to end.

Jurisdiction of Courts Federal courts apply their own body of adjective law and their own substantive law to questions arising under the federal Constitution, statutes, codes, and treaties. Their decisions in these areas and in matters of interstate commerce are binding on state courts.

Article IV, Section 1 of the U.S. Constitution also states: "Full Faith and Credit shall be given in each State to the public Acts, Records, and Judicial Proceedings of every other State. . . ." This means that the judgments handed down in one state court shall be honored in the courts of other states.

Common Law

Common law is of judicial origin and is based on *precedent* (an occurrence of a similar incident in the past) and the doctrine of *stare decisis*, which means "to stand by the decisions and not disturb what is settled." Common law developed in three basic areas: wrongs committed against the state or society (crimes); wrongs committed against an individual's interests (torts); and individual rights created by agreement of parties (contracts). Early common-law courts using the *writ system* (an order or mandatory process in writing) developed a body of law based upon decided cases which then served as precedent for the future solution of disputes.

Stare Decisis According to the doctrine of *stare decisis*, when a court renders an opinion in a case, stating the underlying principle for its decision, that principle will be followed by that court in deciding future cases. Lower courts are also bound by the principle set forth in the decision. *Stare decisis* serves as an instrument of stability in our legal system. It assures each person equal and uniform treatment. It is a flexible principle, however, inasmuch as a court may decide that a prior decision does not come under *stare decisis* when it has lost its usefulness or when the reason for it no longer exists. Thus, courts are subject to social forces and changing conditions and deem it their responsibility to reexamine, and when necessary reverse, former precedents.

Judicial Priorities A number of legal issues are not sufficiently covered by obvious priorities such as constitutions over statutes, statutes over case law, and precedent over opinion. Often the decided cases are not in agreement, or a case involves several conflicting issues, such as whether one's property rights are superior to another's civil rights. Whenever the law needed to decide a given issue cannot be found in an existing statute, it must be created by the courts themselves. To this extent, courts have a creative job.

 A local union filed a refusal-to-bargain charge with the National Labor Relations Board (NLRB) against Airco Construction. Hearings were set, and Airco Construction asked the NLRB for permission to inspect and copy all written statements in the Board's case file. The request was denied, and Airco asked the federal district court to order the NLRB to produce the records and to suspend proceedings until the NLRB had done so. The court held that information in unfair-labor-practice cases and the sources from which it was obtained were subject to disclosure under the Freedom of Information Act. The court also held that the agency must suspend its proceedings until Airco (the employer) had a chance to obtain and study the Board's case file.

This was the first judicial interpretation of the then newly enacted Freedom of Information Act. The NLRB's claim of privacy had to be balanced against Airco's equally strong claim that disclosure was required by the act. To be sure, the court took into account the intent of Congress in passing the new law. It examined the legislative record to this end. However, the court had no judicial precedents or case law to guide it in determining how much and what type of disclosure was required under the particular circumstances presented. The court, therefore, had to "jump into the breach," so to speak, and make new law in this area by defining just how much disclosure was required. Its verdict will then serve as precedent in other similar cases presented to it or to other courts, unless the decision is subsequently overturned by a higher court.

fairness

Equity The idea of justice due to natural right, or *equity*, was introduced into courts in the United States because of the failure of the courts of law to give adequate and proper remedies in certain cases. In most states the courts of equity and courts of law are organized under a single judge. Pleadings usually indicate whether the action is legal or equitable, because in the case of equitable actions there is no right to a jury trial. Courts in equity use *maxims* (truths or rules that need no proof or argument) instead of rules of law, inasmuch as their decisions are based on moral rights and natural justice. An example of such a maxim is: "He who comes into equity must do so with clean hands." In other words, a person who is guilty of misconduct in a case is prohibited from receiving the aid of the court. Other, similar maxims are:

☐ Equity will not suffer a wrong to be without a remedy.
☐ Equity regards the substance rather than the form.
☐ Equity abhors a forfeiture.
☐ Equity aids the vigilant.

Decisions of the court in equity are called *decrees*. They are directed to the defendant, who is instructed to do or not to do something. Equity is playing an ever-increasing role in our legal system, owing to the movement toward a type of social justice that places greater dependence on maxims and less dependence on strict rules of law. Courts in equity have developed many remedies in dealing with charges of fraud, winding up a partnership, partition of property, and compelling individuals to do what they ought to have done under the terms of a contract. Among other situations that frequently require equitable remedies are the settlement of a claim which impairs the title of property, the cancellation of a contract, and the restraint of a person from committing an act.

Administrative Law

Large phases of our economic and social life today are so complicated that the courts and legislatures alone cannot deal with all the legal issues that they raise. A lawmaker or judge may simply lack the subject-matter expertise to decide a complex issue, such as whether a particular drug or consumer product is safe enough to stay on the market. Recognizing this problem, Congress and the state legislatures have empowered expert bodies, known as *administrative agencies* or *regulatory agencies*, to deal with these matters. To give the regulators "teeth," these agencies are permitted to issue orders and decrees that have the force of law and to try cases and make legal decisions in their area of expertise. Their decrees and legal decisions—the whole body of law that they generate—are known collectively as *administrative law*.

During the decade 1965–1975, particularly at the federal level, Presidents and Congresses have increased the reach and power of the administrative agencies. Since 1965 the number of regulatory agencies that produce administrative law has doubled (there are now twenty-four). They employ 105,000 persons, up from 58,455. This growth has come about as the result of public demand for cleaner air and water, for less job discrimination against ethnic minorities, women, and the elderly, and for safer autos, workplaces, consumer products, and so on. The increasing number of agencies has led to a great proliferation of acronyms—EPA, OSHA, NHTSA, which are the Environmental Protection Agency, the Occupational Safety and Health Administration, and the National Highway Traffic Safety Administration. Also widely known are the FEA, FTC, and the EEOC. In Chapter 5 you will study in greater detail the administrative agencies and administrative law, as well as the important role each plays in our national life.

Environmental Law

Congress enacted landmark legislation in the environmental field when it approved the National Environmental Policy Act (NEPA) in 1969. The measure set as national policy the goal of creating and maintaining "conditions under which man and nature can exist in productive harmony." Federal agencies were directed to consider the impact on the environment of all major activities and to include in every recommendation (*impact statement*) a written analysis of the effect of, as well as alternatives to, each proposal.

Environmental Protection Agency   All major antipollution programs dealing with air, noise, solid wastes, and pesticides were placed under the control of a single agency by the Environmental Protection Agency (EPA) legislation of 1970.

Air Quality Control   The Clean Air Act, the Air Quality Act of 1967, and the Clean Air Amendments of 1970 required the EPA to publish a list of air pollution agents for which air quality criteria would be issued. The EPA is also required to publish national primary and secondary average air quality standards for each agent cited as a pollutant. The agency is authorized to specify and set emission standards for hazardous air pollutants—those having a proven relationship to increased human death rates or serious illness. The agency is also required to publish periodically lists of the categories of new stationary pollution sources (such as utilities) and to set emission standards for them.

The EPA is authorized to set emission standards for all potentially dangerous pollutants from new motor vehicles and engines. Engines of automobiles and other light-duty vehicles must comply with standards that lower emissions of carbon monoxide, hydrocarbons, and nitrogen oxides by 90 percent within specified model years. These standards have been temporarily suspended to give automobile manufacturers more time for research.

The EPA is also authorized to seek injunctions to stop pollution sources, if local or state authorities have not acted to seek abatement. When corrective action is not taken, the EPA can issue an order requiring compliance or bring civil suits against the violator. Citizens or groups may bring suits in federal courts against alleged violators. The punishment for violations of an antipollution plan may be a fine of up to $25,000 for each day of violation and a year in jail or, for persons with prior violations, a fine of $50,000 per day and two years in jail.

Federal Water Pollution Control Early efforts by the federal government to control water pollution were limited mainly to the encouragement of both state and cooperative interstate pollution-control programs and agreements. The Water Quality Improvement Act of 1970 expanded the government's involvement in water pollution control. It was aimed primarily at oil spills. The federal government was authorized to clean up disastrous oil spills, with the polluter paying the costs. Petroleum companies were made liable for up to $14 million in cleanup. New controls were also placed on sewage coming from vessels which had fouled many of the nation's marinas, harbors, and ports.

The Federal Water Pollution Control Act Amendments of 1972 introduced a major change in the approach to controlling water pollution. Its provisions set strict limits on what could be discharged into waterways. The act set a national goal of eliminating all pollutant discharges into American waters by 1985.

A new pollutant discharge permit program, administered by the EPA, was authorized in this legislation. Violators of water quality standards and compliance schedules as well as dischargers who lack permits are subject to enforcement action. Citizens are allowed to sue polluters, the federal government, or the EPA, if they have economic or recreational interests which are adversely affected.

Noise Control The Noise Control Act of 1972 declared it national policy to protect the public health and welfare from detrimental noise. Under the provisions of this act, the EPA was given the authority to set federal noise-emission standards with the aim of limiting source noise from certain commercial products. Products specified included construction and transportation equipment, motors, engines, and electric or electronic devices. The EPA was directed to report on the adequacy of Federal Aviation Administration (FAA) flight and operational noise controls and airport noise-exposure levels. The act also required product manufacturers to warrant that new products conform to EPA regulations.

Violations of standards and EPA regulations are punishable by a $25,000 fine per day or one year in jail, or both. Federal suits are authorized against violators or the EPA or FAA for noncompliance with the mandatory provisions of the act.

Pesticides and Solid Wastes Control The examination of insecticides and other pest-control substances used in agriculture was provided for in the Federal Insecticide, Fungicide, and Rodenticide Act of 1947. The establishment of "tolerances" for chemical residues left on or in fresh fruits and vegetables was also required. Examination of chemical and color additives before they are used in foods, drugs, and cosmetics was required by subsequent amendments.

The most important recent law regarding pesticide control is the Federal Environmental Pesticide Control Act (FEPCA) of 1972. It authorizes the EPA to require testing of existing chemical substances whose manufacture, processing, use, or disposal pose an unreasonable threat to human health or the environment. The EPA can restrict the use or distribution of some chemicals, and it can also seize substances which pose an imminent hazard.

In the area of solid waste disposal, the EPA's role is mainly one of technical and financial assistance to regional, state, and local governments. The Solid Waste Disposal Act of 1965 and its 1970 amendments recognize local government responsibility to develop programs dealing with solid waste disposal such as the recycling of reusable raw materials found in solid wastes.

Commercial Law

The body of laws dealing with business transactions is commonly referred to as business or *commercial law*. Legal subjects included in this category are contracts, agency, bailments, sales, product liability, unfair competition, commercial paper, partnerships, corporations, insurance, and bankruptcy. As part of early English common law (then known as *the law merchant*), commercial law was introduced into the United States in colonial times. Starting in the nineteenth century, it was largely supplanted by the enactment of statutes in several states. Most of these statutes, which differed among the states, were based upon nineteenth-century customs of merchants which were often inadequate for twentieth-century commercial practices. To reduce the variation in statute law and its interpretation from state to state, uniform statutes (codified parts of commercial law) were introduced and adopted by the state legislatures. The first was the Uniform Negotiable Instruments Act in 1896. Other uniform statutes were adopted between 1906 and 1933. But, with the passage of time, even the uniform statutes were interpreted differently by different courts. Moreover, new types of business transactions which were not covered by the existing uniform statutes appeared. Rather than amend the separate uniform statutes one at a time, it was proposed that a code be prepared to bring commercial law up to date.

Uniform Commercial Code   The Uniform Commercial Code (UCC) was formulated in 1952 by the National Conference of Commissioners on Uniform State Laws. The conference included representatives from all states, in cooperation with the American Law Institute. The Code was offered to the state legislatures for adoption, and it has now been adopted into law by all the states except Louisiana.

The Code consists of several hundred sections and subsections grouped into ten main divisions: (1) General Provisions; (2) Sales; (3) Commercial Paper; (4) Bank Deposits and Collections; (5) Documentary Letters of Credit; (6) Bulk Transfers; (7) Warehouse Receipts, Bills of Lading and Other Documents of Title; (8) Investment Securities; (9) Secured Transactions, Sales of Accounts, Contract Rights and Chattel Paper; (10) Effective Date and Repealer.

The Code repeals the substantive provisions of many uniform statutes, including the Uniform Negotiable Instruments Law, Uniform Sales Act, Uniform Bills of Lading Act, Uniform Stock Transfer Act, Uniform Trust Receipts Act,

Uniform Conditional Sales Act, Uniform Chattel Mortgage, Uniform Warehouse Receipts Act, Bulk Sales Act, and Factors Lien Act.

The basic principles of commercial law were not drastically changed by the UCC. Nor were many areas of commercial law touched by the Code. Its purpose was to simplify, clarify, and update the law governing commercial transactions; encourage expansion of business practices through usage and agreement of parties; and make the law uniform in the separate states.

The Code holds merchants to a high standard of performance by defining what *good faith* means in a commercial setting. By defining and clarifying often misunderstood business and legal terms, it helps the parties to construct their contracts and aids the courts in interpreting and enforcing them. It declares that contract terms which are clearly unfair and unreasonable ("unconscionable") may be unenforceable. It provides rules that state what business people may or may not do. For example, shippers of goods may not contractually exempt themselves from liability for inaccurately counting packages received for shipment; and a warehouse may not write a contract so as to limit its own liability for converting the goods of others for its own use.

Questions for Review and Discussion

To the student: A separate Individualized Performance Guide *provides important performance objectives for each chapter and an enriched selection of case problems that call for the application of points of law introduced in each text chapter.*

1. Name and discuss the three fundamental purposes of justice.

2. What is meant by the statement "Laws conform to social trends; laws do not determine them"?

3. Why do we remain law-centered rather than justice-centered?

4. What is the basic difference between the way

the federal Constitution and the various state constitutions limit governmental power?

5. What is the doctrine that is central to the concept of separation of powers?

6. Should the power of courts over legislation be limited to the doctrine of judicial review?

7. Explain why the Uniform Commercial Code is considered to be the most significant development for business in the field of uniform state legislation.

8. What is the meaning of *stare decisis*?

9. Distinguish common law from statute law.

10. Give reasons for the large number of governmental administrative agencies.

Analyzing Cases

1. Lipka has been charged with breach of a simple contract in a common-law action. Before the trial begins in the state court, Lipka's lawyer

finds that the provisions of the Uniform Commercial Code adopted by the state legislature cover contract breach. How will the UCC statute affect Lipka's case? • See also *Lux* v. *Higgins*, 69 Cal. 255.[1]

2. The state legislature enacted a law prohibiting the driving of automobiles more than ten years old on the public highways. Chung was arrested and fined for driving his antique Model A Ford on the state thruway. He appealed the decision to a higher court, claiming that the statute enacted by the state legislature was unconstitutional. Does Chung have the right to have the state statute declared void? Explain. • See also *Frost* v. *Railroad Commission of State of California*, 46 Sup. Ct. 605, 271 U.S. 583.

Judicial review

3. At a railroad crossing Dobbs observed a sign which read "Stop, Look, and Listen!" She stopped her car, walked to the crossing, looked in both directions, and listened for any approaching trains. She was arrested on a charge of obstructing traffic and taken before a magistrate. Dobbs pleaded that she was doing only what the sign directed. What would be the outcome of her case? Explain. • See also *People* v. *Bird*, 300 P. 23.

4. Wolski, the owner of a small farm, discovered that at common law he was deemed to have property rights that ran down to the center of the earth and up to the heavens. He sued to stop the regular flights of an airplane over his farm at a height of 30,000 feet, claiming trespass. Will Wolski win his case? Explain. • See also *U.S.* v. *Causby*, 328 U.S. 56.

5. While walking on the sidewalk, Froelich was stopped by a man who refused to let her pass. She was compelled to obtain the aid of a police officer in order to continue her walk. What constitutional right was denied Froelich by the man who stopped her on the street without her consent? Explain. • See also U.S. Constitution, Fifth Amendment.

6. Labow found employment in Washington, D.C., and moved his family there from Texas, where they had lived for ten years. Several weeks before the Presidential election, Labow decided to register to vote. A co-worker informed him that residents of the District of Columbia had no voting rights and that it would be a waste of time to attempt to register for the November election. Was Labow correctly advised? Explain. • See also U.S. Constitution, Twenty-third Amendment.

Legal Reasoning and Business Judgment

At the end of each chapter several situations will be presented to test your legal reasoning and your business judgment. In dealing with these situations, weigh the desirability of seeking a legal remedy in coming to a settlement against what might be advantageous to your company. You might decide that a friendly settlement would be more effective in building company goodwill and financial strength than a favorable court decision would be.

Analyze the legal aspects of these business problems. Suggest possible solutions.

1. The legislature in the state adjoining the one in which Diamond International has its offices passed a statute prohibiting out-of-state manufacturers from selling their products within the state's borders. Two salespersons representing Diamond are arrested and arraigned for violation of this new law. What would you suggest (a) as a solution that would protect Diamond's commerce rights and (b) as a defense for its sales representatives?

2. O'Connell is a homeowner in Milwaukee. The Hacker Building & Supply Co., located

[1] The legal cases cited here and elsewhere in this text represent valuable reference material for the student and can be found in most law libraries or large public libraries. Decisions in the cases cited are based upon the same points of law covered in the legal situation described in the text case. In this case, for example, the number *69* preceding the abbreviation *Cal*. refers to volume 69 of the California reports on legal decisions on cases heard in California courts. The figure *255* is the page number on which the decision can be found.

nearby, burns trash regularly in an open area. The smoke and fly ash from the fires have settled on the O'Connell house and grounds and on the property of others in the immediate area. O'Connell wants relief and seeks information on whether he can ask for an injunction to stop the practice and to recover the damages for the harm which has been caused to the paint on his home and to his lawn furniture. What is the law?

3. The medical officer of your company has received notice from the state health department that it intends to make periodic inspections of all plants located in the state to uncover conditions that might affect the health of employees or the residents of the community. The medical officer, having studied the state constitution, claims that the state has no authority to make such inspections, since he has found no provision in the constitution authorizing the creation of a public health department or the right of an inspector to enter private property for such inspections. Is the medical officer correct in his interpretation of the law? Explain.

Chapter 2
Torts and Crimes

A *tort* is a legal wrong against ~~private wrong~~ person or property, independent of contract. A *crime* is an act in violation of a public law or a breach of a public right or duty due the whole community. When the wrong is a tort, the injured party must sue to recover compensation for damages suffered. Thus the purpose of tort law is to compensate the injured party, not punish the offender. When a crime is committed, the state brings the legal action to enforce punishment or exact a prescribed penalty. The purpose of criminal law is the punishment of the accused by fine or imprisonment based on public policy. One act may be both a crime and a tort, however, when both society and the victim are wronged.

> With reckless disregard for the safety of others, Peddicord intentionally drove through a stoplight at a high speed and seriously injured Rudnick following an argument at a local bar. Peddicord's wrongful act (assault and battery) is both a wrong against society (a crime) and a wrong against Rudnick (a tort). Society can punish Peddicord, and Rudnick can sue him for injuries.

TORTS

Tortious harm or injury may result (1) *intentionally*, if the act that is unlawful is performed with the intent to cause harm; (2) *willfully*, if the act is reckless and it should have been known that harm would result; or (3) *negligently*, if the act results from failure to exercise due care. Negligence is the theory of fault upon which most claims for personal injury are based. Included in this fault category are automobile accidents, malpractice, and injuries to pedestrians. Product liability resulting from injuries caused by manufactured goods, foods, and drugs is a growing field of torts. Another category is the invasion of the right of privacy resulting from the use of electronic devices. Some of the most common torts are discussed and illustrated below.

Negligence

The word *negligence* means a failure to use reasonable care. Judgment in such cases is influenced by the nature of the act, the role of the parties, and the attendant circumstances. Each action for negligence is based on a breach of some duty on the part of one person to protect another against injury. The injured person may collect damages if it can be proved that the person causing the injuries had a duty to exercise care, there was failure in that duty, and the injuries or damages resulted from that failure.

> ▶ Fire swept Mirenda's warehouse, gutting the interior and destroying furniture stored for pickup and delivery to dealers. A fire investigation indicated that the fire started near the fuse boxes. The dealers sued Mirenda, stressing that the building's electrical wiring was old and faulty and that this represented careless handling of their goods. Mirenda argued that reasonable care had been exerted and that this is the extent of the duty owed by a warehouse owner to his customers. He pointed out that the cause of the fire could not be conclusively determined. He noted that in his three years of ownership the warehouse had had no electrical problems or fires. There were manual fire extinguishers, and no smoking was allowed in the warehouse area. Goods were stacked away from electrical wiring. The jury decided that Mirenda had satisfied the duty of reasonable care and could not be held negligent and responsible for the loss.

"Reasonable Man" Standard In a tort action, the *reasonable man (person) standard* is a composite behavior pattern in the minds of the jurors. The phrase does not apply to a person's ability to reason; rather it refers to "those qualities of attention . . . and judgment which society requires for protection of [its] own interest and the interests of others." It does not outline in any case what should have been done. This flexibility is desirable inasmuch as it is not possible to keep a behavior code up to date or to foresee what the hypothetical reasonable person would do as a result of the variations in both facts and conditions that might take place.

Contributory Negligence When it can be shown that the party asking for damages because of another's negligence was partly to blame for the injuries or damages through his or her own negligence, recovery will be denied or proportionately reduced. Tort lawyers often use the *contributory negligence* argument as a defense in negligence torts involving more than one person.

> ▶ While crossing the street, Bussey was struck by a car driven by Budwig. Bussey proved that Budwig was not exercising reasonable care at the time of the accident. Budwig's lawyer produced a witness who testified that Bussey was glancing at a newspaper and crossing the street against the traffic signal when he was struck. Being partly to blame for the accident, Bussey might not recover all or a portion of the damages that would otherwise be awarded.

Society has taken the position that contributory negligence between employee and employer is undesirable as a matter of public policy. Laws known as workers' compensation laws have been enacted.[1] These statutes balance the

---

[1]The Government Printing Office uses the term *workers' compensation* in reference to both federal and state statutes in this area. The term *workmen's compensation* continues to be the official one in a majority of states, although several states, such as New Jersey, have adopted the term *workers' compensation* in order to eliminate possible sexist connotations. *Workers' compensation* will be used throughout this text in lieu of *workmen's compensation* and in reference to compensation laws, benefits, and other related aspects of the law in this area.

interest of employees and employers by creating liability without fault and by creating specific and detailed schedules of amounts due for various injuries. At the federal level, the Federal Employer's Liability Act (FELA) obtains similar results for businesses engaged in interstate and foreign commerce. These statutes require proof of negligence, but they do not limit the amount of recovery.

Under a related doctrine, that of *last clear chance*, a defendant may be held liable in a negligence action if it is shown that he or she had the last chance to avoid injury, even though the plaintiff was negligent.

Malpractice   Malpractice suits, torts involving misconduct, unreasonable lack of skill, or illegal or immoral conduct, have increased enormously in recent years. Such actions frequently involve professionals such as corporate officers and directors, public officials, physicians, lawyers, and sometimes teachers. Owing to ignorance, carelessness, disregard of established rules, or malicious intent, unnecessary suffering or personal injury is caused by failure to perform a service in accordance with acceptable standards.

Malpractice suits against doctors and lawyers have multiplied tenfold in the last fifteen years. In the area of medical malpractice, this increase stems from the public expectation that medicine should have a cure for every ill and from the increased capability of patients, lawyers, and jurors in ferreting out instances of medical negligence. As a result, errors of omission, as well as errors of commission, are brought into court. To deal with the problem, some states are enacting laws that set maximum amounts that may be recovered in malpractice suits. Other states are opting for "no-fault" personal injury payment systems.

The crucial issue is how the word *malpractice* is defined. Even when terms like breach of contract, misrepresentation, breach of warranty, or negligence are substituted, the results are the same: Someone is personally hurt, or a business in which the person is interested is badly hurt. If, as a result of another's carelessness, a person suffers damage, then liability exists. Like most legal formulations, however, this one is complex in practice. Both carelessness and injury must be established in a court of law. Generally, it is within the framework of a jury trial that the connection between carelessness and injury can be either established or rejected.

 Pizor entered the hospital for treatment of an infection in his arm. A doctor gave the arm a cursory examination and cleansed the wound with an antiseptic solution, assuring Pizor no other treatment would be required. Later Pizor was hospitalized and almost lost the use of the arm. The doctor had failed to discover that blood poisoning had set in, a conclusion that he could have reached had he given Pizor a thorough examination. The doctor would no doubt be subject to a suit for negligence, or malpractice, and would be held responsible for all damages suffered by Pizor because of the doctor's gross negligence.

Bodily Harm

Invasions of the law resulting from bodily harm or fear of bodily harm or from impairment of movement are called assault, battery, and false imprisonment or arrest.

Assault Threatening to harm or to strike another person, with the apparent ability or power to carry out the threat, is considered to be an *assault*. Contact is unnecessary. The harm is the awareness and fear of the impending battery.

Battery The unlawful application of force on the body, regardless of its degree, is *battery*. Any touching of another, however slight, or of the person's clothing or anything attached to the person, if done in an unlawful, willful, or angry manner, is a battery. A surgical operation performed unlawfully without the patient's consent may constitute battery. Spitting in the face or on a person is also a battery, as is hitting someone with a rock or throwing acid on the clothing or skin of a person. Battery can also take place when someone who is unconscious is touched or struck.

 Siegel, in a fit of rage, threw a rock at his neighbor Valenta but failed to hit him. Valenta was frightened by the act and developed a facial twitch after the incident. This attempt to commit a battery, even though it was not completed, remains an assault for which Siegel may be prosecuted. Valenta may recover money damages in a civil lawsuit.

Had Siegel in his state of rage made menacing or threatening gestures at Valenta with the rock in hand, the court would generally hold that this behavior was sufficient to constitute assault. An object of the law is to prevent the threat of battery as well as any actual assault upon an individual.

False Imprisonment or Arrest Depriving another of his or her freedom and liberty when one does not have the right to do so can be construed as *false imprisonment* or *false arrest*. Any form of detention which prevents a person from going about his or her business constitutes imprisonment. An officer making an arrest without reasonable grounds or suspicion is liable for any loss, injury, or anguish caused the arrested party. In fact, any action or threat of force that compels a person to remain where he or she does not wish to remain or to go where he or she does not wish to go is an imprisonment. Anyone who takes away another's liberty may be sued for this tort.

 Spano was shopping when a store security officer arrested her as a shoplifter as she was leaving the store. The officer did not see her taking merchandise; nor did anyone else. An examination of the bag she carried revealed that she had paid for its contents. Spano can sue the officer for money damages in civil court. The court would probably rule that the arrest was made without reasonable cause. In cases of this kind, the employer of the officer is often joined in the suit for damages.

Injury to Property

Invasions or injury to property interests are referred to as *trespass to personal property* and *trespass to land*.

Trespass to Personal Property A *trespass to personal property* is the unlawful interference by one person with the control and possession of the goods of another. It arises when goods are removed or damaged, and it can be committed even when there is no intention to deprive the owner permanently of the goods.

Conversion is a trespass involving the wrongful disposition and detention of the personal property of one person by another. Personal property includes possessions such as a car, clothing, jewelry, or stocks and bonds. The most common forms of conversion arise when someone wrongfully either sells goods which belong to another or refuses to return goods to their rightful owner. It would be conversion for the person who rents an automobile to try to sell it to someone else, or to refuse to return it when the rental period ends.

Another form of conversion is the unauthorized use of property or the unlawful destruction or alteration of property owned by another.

> Pendexter has 140 linear feet of cedar rails and fifteen posts in his garage. He plans to erect a two-rail fence. While he is away, an unfriendly neighbor enters the garage and cuts the rails and posts into smaller lengths suitable for burning as firewood. This alteration of the identity of Pendexter's property renders the neighbor liable for the wrongful conversion of the fence rails and posts.

Conversion also occurs when a person disposes of property without the owner's consent. Should you borrow a friend's motorbike and then without the owner's permission give it to a third party, you are liable for converting the motorbike to your own use.

Trespass to Land   Traditionally, the individual enjoys the right to own and use land without interference. Even the simplest form of entry upon private property without the owner's consent, even if the property is unharmed, constitutes *trespass*. Examples include the intrusion of animals on one's property, the throwing of something on someone's land, or using private property as a shortcut. More serious trespass results when the land or its owner is damaged. It is trespass to use land for an unauthorized purpose, to remain on land when permission to be there is denied, or to dump or abandon things on another's land. Land includes the surface and any buildings on it, the space above, and the ground beneath.

A sales representative has the implied right to go onto land or to enter a business establishment in the hope of selling without committing trespass, but he or she must depart if asked to do so. Police officers have specific powers of entry, as do public health and fire inspectors, to enter certain premises.

Interference with a person's use or enjoyment of land is indirect trespass and may be classified as *private nuisance*. Creating a noise that disturbs another is an example. Blocking a right of way or taking away a right of light can also be a nuisance. Annoyances that affect the public generally constitute a *public nuisance*. Although a public nuisance is primarily a crime and not a tort against land, an action in tort can result if an affected person suffers a loss over and above that suffered by the public as a whole.

Defamation

Any slanderous communication that defames another or injures another's reputation may constitute *defamation*. The statement must stand the test of whether in consequence of its being made people might regard the recipient with ridicule, contempt, or hatred. Defamation in a temporary form such as speech is *slander*; in a permanent form, such as writing, it is *libel*.

Slander The use of spoken defamatory words which injure the reputation of another person is *slander*. Generally, it is actionable if the complaining party proves that the statements caused financial loss. Loss need not be proved, however, when allegations are made that a person in an office, a trade, or a profession is unfit to hold the position or practice the trade.

 Kinsella was angry with Joyner, a realtor, because Joyner had insisted on being paid the full commission on a real estate sale that she had made for Kinsella. Kinsella spread the word that Joyner was "a cheating, lying chiseler." Joyner would be permitted an action against Kinsella for damages to her reputation on the tort of slander.

Libel Defamation in writing is *libel*. Unlike slander, it is actionable even without financial loss. Such statements must clearly refer to the plaintiff either expressly or by implication. The statement must also be published to a third party, inasmuch as a person's reputation depends upon the opinion of others. A newspaper, magazine, or other periodical publishing such false statements, even though the editors may believe that the statements are true, is subject to action for damages, as is the person who originated the libel.

A defendant can show unintentional defamation by apologizing or publishing a suitable correction. In the interests of free speech and criticism, opinions rendered on matters of public concern may be defended when they represent "fair comment" and are made in good faith. Statements in court and in legislative sessions are privileged and are completely protected. There is protection in the absence of malice where a publisher has a duty to make a statement and the recipient has an interest in receiving it.

 An editor published statements to the effect that a public official was accepting bribes. The official sued the editor for damages, claiming that her reputation had been injured. Although the editor could not prove the truth of the written statements, he contended that they had been expressed by trustworthy persons. The editor's defense would be acceptable if he could show that the statements were comments on a matter of public interest and were made in good faith and in the absence of malice.

Interference With the Right of Privacy

The Fourth Amendment to the Constitution states: "The right of the people to be secure in their persons, houses, papers, and effects, against unreasonable searches and seizures, shall not be violated, and no Warrants shall issue, but upon probable cause, supported by Oath or affirmation, and particularly describing the place to be searched, and the persons or things to be seized." One might safely conclude that the right of privacy is protected by the government. But the framers of the Bill of Rights were concerned with protection from police invasion of privacy and not with invasion of privacy by a private citizen. A "peeping tom," for example, could not use the Fourth Amendment as a shield to avoid criminal liability for invading another's privacy.

The law is generally responsive to the wishes of the people at a given period. Thus, there are only such legal rights of privacy as the people through the legal system elect to recognize. And such rights can be modified when circumstances arise that menace our national life.

Invasion of Privacy for Commercial Purposes   Early common law did not afford a remedy for invasion of privacy. As previously stated, however, the strength of the common law, upon which our present legal system is based, is its capacity to expand and adapt to the social, economic, and political changes inherent in a dynamic human society. Thus, for example, the courts do recognize the right not to have one's name and picture used without permission as part of an advertising campaign, and remedies are now available when this right is violated.

> Muir, an attractive young woman, discovered that her picture had been used on the box cover design for Purity Flour without her prior knowledge and consent. A photographer who had taken pictures of her had sold one to the flour manufacturer for commercial purposes. Muir sued for $30,000 in damages, claiming humiliation, annoyance, and embarrassment as the result of the public exposure. The court would hold that the appropriation of name or picture for commercial purposes was a cause of action for invasion of the rights of privacy.

Electronic Eavesdropping   Federal statutes prohibit the tapping or interception of telephone conversations in most circumstances even when such surveillance is authorized by state law. Evidence of illegally heard conversation may not be admitted in state or federal courts. Title III of the Omnibus Crime Control and Safe Streets Act of 1968 specifies that electronic eavesdropping and wiretapping by both officers of the law without court warrant and private persons are federal crimes. A judge may not issue an eavesdrop authorization unless he or she has been shown "probable cause" that someone is committing a crime (which would be in itself sufficient cause for an arrest). Damages may be recovered by a person whose communications are intercepted, disclosed, or used.

Privacy Act   The Privacy Act of 1975 sets up specific guidelines for government agencies on the maintenance and disclosure of personal records. A review of the Privacy Act reveals that most people think highly of their privacy and want it to be protected.

An individual's mailing address may not be sold or rented by a government agency, unless such action is authorized by law.

Government agencies are forbidden to make disclosures of material in an individual's record without that individual's consent. Exceptions for criminal law purposes must be supported by a record that satisfactorily answers the questions What? When? To whom? Why?

The collection and retention of information by a government agency are limited to what is relevant and necessary to the legal purpose of the agency. When gathering data, an agency must make known under what authority the data is sought and how it is to be used.

An individual may not be penalized by a federal, state, or local government for refusing to give his or her social security number, unless required by law to do so in specific instances.

An individual has the right to see personal records and to demand correction of inaccurate information. A statement of disagreement may be included in the individual's record if the agency refuses to make a correction. The government agency must give the individual a reason if access to records is denied.

Privacy Protection Study Commission   A seven-member Privacy Protection Study Commission has a mandate to probe the impact on personal privacy of recordkeeping, not merely by the government but also by private organizations. The commission is empowered to investigate data banks, automated data processing programs, and information systems of governmental, regional, and private organizations. It is also empowered to recommend extensions of the law in an effort to remedy abuses in the collection of personal information (Pub. L. No. 93-579). With subpoena power, the commission is expected to hold hearings in four areas: *Credit cards*—Is the information collected from applicants necessary? Is it sold? Can it be corrected? *Mailing lists*—Should they be sold? Can an individual have his or her name removed from a list? *Travel and hotel reservation systems*—How long is information kept? Who has access to this information? *Insurance companies*—What do they do with information? Are third-party reports verified?

Interference With Business Relationships

Persons conducting businesses have a duty not to injure others. Conduct that induces breach of contract or infringes on trademarks or trade names violates the trust placed in them. Other torts that serve to invalidate business contracts, including mistakes, deceit, duress, and undue influence, are presented in Chapter 7, "Offer and Acceptance."

Unfair Competition   Some business torts amount to unfair methods of competition. Those that belittle or slander the goods or services of another and bring about a breach of contract or trespass on trademarks and trade names entitle the person wronged to damages. Unfair competition also arises when false claims or statements are made by others with respect to the quality of goods or services offered. When such false claims cause a person to break a contract in order to be free to make another, a tort is committed.

> Cole accepted an offer by Nor-West Auto to sell a three-year-old Toyota and made a $20 deposit. On the way home Cole stopped at New Hope Motors. Cole told Dorfman, the New Hope salesperson, that he had agreed to purchase a car from Nor-West. Dorfman actively persuaded Cole that Nor-West "laundered" the odometers of their cars so that they appeared to be less used and more valuable. Cole confronted Nor-West with the accusation made by the New Hope salesperson and announced his decision not to purchase the Toyota. Dorfman's unproved

charge of fraud was a deliberate inducement for Cole to break his contract with
Nor-West. It constitutes an unfair method of competition and would entitle
Nor-West to an injunction against a repetition of such statements and an action
for damages.

Another form of unfair competition involves the unlawful use of another's
trademark—the word, name, symbol, or device used to distinguish the goods of a
producer. The first user has an exclusive right to use a trademark, and others may
not use or substantially copy it. Geographical names that suggest a location of
origin are in the public domain and cannot be designated as technical
trademarks. The same is true of proper names, since every person has a right to
make use of his or her name in connection with a business. Terms or marks which
describe origin, style, or quality of an article are considered common or generic
terms and cannot be protected by trademark.

> Educational Development Corporation brought suit against Economy Company
> in federal court for using the term *Continuous Progress* in a spelling program. EDC
> had used the term to identify some of its products and had been successful in
> securing a trademark. The U.S. district judge ruled in favor of Economy Com-
> pany. EDC's registration of the trademark was held invalid because it was a
> generic term.

A trademark is protected against infringement on goods of the same character. The courts apply three tests to determine whether goods are of the same type.
Are the items used together—such as records and record players? Can the items
be substituted for each other, such as aluminum combination doors and wood
storm and screen doors? Does one item call the other to mind, or are they
associated together in retail stores? This test could be applied, for example, to
shirts and ties.

> Procter & Gamble Company (P & G) registered the trademark *Mr. Clean* for its
> liquid detergent and later registered *Mr. Clear, Mr. Sheen, Lady Clean,* and *Mrs.
> Clean*. Certified Chemical & Equipment Company filed to register *Mister Stain* for
> a stain-removing compound. P & G opposed the registration. The U.S. Court of
> Customs and Patent Appeals ruled that P & G had a right to bar registrations of a
> mark using the courtesy title *Mr.* or *Mister* in association with words designating
> a cleaning compound that would be sold through the same retail outlets to the
> same class of consumers.

The user of a trademark in interstate commerce may have the trademark
registered with the U.S. Patent Office for a period of twenty years. The first user
of an established trademark is protected, however, regardless of registration, and
can bring a common-law action for unfair competition in the state courts against
the user of a similar, later mark.

CRIMES

A *crime* is a wrong against society for which the law prescribes punishment by
death, imprisonment, fine, or removal from office. The state or federal govern-

ment institutes an action against any person who (1) commits a criminal act or (2) refrains from performing a duty prescribed by statutory law. At common law, crimes are dealt with in order of seriousness—treason, felonies, and misdemeanors. Most states, however, divide offenses into only felonies and misdemeanors; some list *infractions* as a third category of crime.

Crimes Against the State and Public Order

Crimes directed against the state and public order may be classified as treason, espionage, and the bribery of a public officer. Usually, the commission of these acts constitutes the offense, and there is no need to prove wrongful intent.

Treason   In Article III, Section 3 of the U.S. Constitution, *treason* is defined as the levying of war against the United States or giving aid and comfort to the nation's enemies. Therefore, any citizen who starts a rebellion or aids and abets alien enemies would be subject to the charge of treason. No person shall be convicted of treason unless on the testimony of two witnesses to the same overt act, or on confession in open court.

 Cognetta, an army officer, helped a foreign agent purchase classified government papers, provided him room and board for a period of ten days, and helped the agent obtain a job as a cover for sabotage activities. The testimony of two witnesses regarding this aid and comfort would be held sufficient for conviction.

Espionage   Federal statutes define *espionage* as the gathering or transmitting of information relating to the national defense of the United States for the political or military use of any foreign nation. Such spying upon war production or upon scientific advances in military programs is under the investigative authority of the FBI, or under military jurisdiction when the accused is a member of the armed forces. Federal statutes also prohibit the photographing or sketching of military installations.

Bribery of a Public Officer   The crime of *bribery* involves a corrupt agreement induced by an offer of reward. Central to the offense is the offering, giving, receiving, or soliciting of something of value to influence official action or the discharge of legal or public duty. Whether the recipient knows that a bribe is being offered, or whether the recipient accepts or rejects it, does not void the offense. Bribery taints a wide range of official conduct. It has been used to obtain political preference in appointments to public office. Company executives have used corporate funds to affect action on pending legislation or to block the calling of a strike. A city works commissioner who awarded a waste-removal contract to a hauling firm without competitive bidding, after receiving a $5,000 cash payment, would be guilty of bribe acceptance.

Felonies Against the Person

Crimes that are punishable by death or imprisonment for a term exceeding one year are defined as *felonies* under federal law. Many states follow the federal definition, but some specify that the place of imprisonment must be a state prison; others treat certain criminal acts as either a felony or a less serious category. Crimes most often spoken of as felonies are homicide and manslaughter, burglary and arson, robbery, and maiming and kidnapping.

Homicide and Manslaughter   *Homicide*—the killing of any human being—is not always a crime. It is, however, a necessary ingredient of the crimes of murder and manslaughter. When it is done in self-defense or in the lawful execution of a judicial sentence, the term merely describes the act and does not result in a judgment. Homicide is recognized as justifiable or excusable when the killing is caused by or is the result of misfortune, accident, duty, or self-defense. Both *manslaughter* and *murder*, on the other hand, are degrees of wrongful homicide. Involved is the killing of a human being without justification or excuse in law.

 Santoro intentionally drove her car into the one driven by Garcia, whom she had on several occasions threatened to kill if the opportunity ever presented itself. Santoro could be charged with murder if Garcia died as a result of the deliberate act.

Murder is the unlawful killing of a human being by another with *malice aforethought* (intent), either express or implied. Manslaughter, in contrast, is the unlawful killing of another in a sudden heat of emotion (voluntary manslaughter) or in the absence of proper caution (involuntary manslaughter).

Burglary and Arson   *Burglary* consists of a break-in of a home or building for the purpose of committing a felony. Entry through an open window or door is not considered breaking in. The slightest forced entry, such as turning a doorknob or inserting a stick through a window while remaining outside, constitutes burglary.

Arson involves a deliberate and unjustified burning of another's building that is enclosed with walls and covered by a roof. Thus, the burning of a house by accident or negligence is not arson. The burning of automobiles and personal property is covered by arson statutes in some states. In most states, setting fire to one's own property to obtain insurance money is also considered arson.

 Stanke, believing that he had been defrauded by Cogswell in a business deal, set fire to Cogswell's garage. The fire was quickly extinguished, and only a small amount of burn damage resulted. Stanke was guilty of the crime of arson even though the garage was not seriously damaged or destroyed.

Robbery   The crime of *robbery* is the act of taking personal property in the presence of another against that person's will by means of force or fear.

By intimidation, Breuner determined where DeLucca kept her jewelry. He left her bound in one room while he took possession of her property in another room of the house. The court would hold that Breuner's actions constituted robbery.

Maiming and Kidnapping Maiming and kidnapping are among the most serious crimes committed against the person. *Maiming* includes acts done with the intent to injure or disfigure the victim's person—for example, cutting off part of the body or inflicting a wound that breaks the skin, whether by some kind of instrument or by corrosive acid.

Gorski, a meat inspector, was angered by a newspaper article Loter had written in which he accused Gorski of taking bribes. He decided to teach Loter a lesson. Preparing a strong caustic solution, Gorski went to Loter's home and threw the solution in his face. Loter suffered severe facial disfigurement and the loss of sight in one eye. Because of his cowardly and premeditated act Gorski would be found guilty of maiming.

Kidnapping is the unlawful abduction of a person against his or her will. It constitutes false imprisonment, with the additional element of removal of the victim to another place. Most state laws distinguish between simple kidnapping and the more serious offense involving demands for ransom or child stealing.

Crimes Against Property

Larceny, embezzlement, and obtaining property by false pretenses are crimes in which the wrongdoer seeks to obtain possession of the property or money of another.

Larceny A person who unlawfully takes possession of goods or money belonging to another person and carries them away with the intention of converting such property to his or her own use is guilty of *larceny*. The value of the property taken—$50 in many states, as high as $200 in others—determines whether the theft is grand larceny and a felony or petty larceny and a misdemeanor.

Basso removed a leisure suit from a department store display rack, put it on, and left the store without paying for it. He obviously had no intention of either returning the suit or paying for it later. Basso would be guilty of the crime of larceny.

Embezzlement A person who wrongfully takes the property of another for his or her own use, for example, through a breach of one's employer's trust, has committed the crime of *embezzlement*. In contrast with the crime of larceny, in which the offender comes into possession of property unlawfully, the embezzler comes into possession of the property or the money by legitimate means in the ordinary course of business.

Du Bois, the cashier for Haig Jewelers, removed $500 from the store safe after entering a false credit to the account of a customer. When an audit uncovered the illegal transaction, Du Bois would be convicted of criminal embezzlement in most states even though she might have intended to borrow the money for a short time.

Obtaining Property by False Pretenses A person who, by making untrue claims of fact, obtains the property or money of another with intent to defraud the owner is guilty of obtaining property by *false pretenses*. Examples are obtaining goods on credit by presenting a false financial statement, obtaining a down payment from a customer in a business transaction by presenting a false financial statement, or obtaining a down payment from a customer in a business transaction by falsely representing oneself as the agent of another. Only a narrow distinction exists between the crime of false pretenses and larceny. In the latter, the victim has no intention to part with title to and possession of the property taken; in the crime of false pretenses, the victim does intend to pass on ownership, but the change of ownership is accomplished by fraud.

▶️ Kolbe presented a false financial statement to Citizens Savings Bank for the purpose of obtaining a car loan. The bank subsequently learned that the financial statement was fraudulent and filed a complaint with the district attorney. It would be recognized that Kolbe obtained money under false pretenses, a punishable crime.

Misdemeanors and Ordinance Violations

Crimes that are not as serious as felonies are commonly spoken of as misdemeanors or ordinance violations.

Misdemeanors Crimes not punishable by death or imprisonment in state prisons are frequently called *misdemeanors*. Included in the category of lesser crimes against society are offenses such as disorderly conduct, drunkenness, exceeding speed limits, and simple assault. These breaches of the law may be prosecuted on complaints filed before local magistrates.

▶️ Chidsey was stopped by a police officer for exceeding the posted speed limit and for failure to signal a left-hand turn. She will be fined on each charge. If Chidsey is a regular visitor to the court on similar charges, she may receive a jail sentence, or she may lose all driving privileges for a period of time, or both penalties may be imposed.

Ordinance Violations Laws adopted by city, town, or village officials for the protection of public health, morals, safety, and welfare are known as *ordinances*. These laws protect the community from fire hazards and nuisances and regulate such activities as home and building construction, billboard advertising, sidewalk use, and parking. Although violations of such laws are sometimes classified as petty offenses or public torts rather than crimes, the person charged may be fined, jailed, or both.

Arrest and Rights of the Accused

Any *unlawful* interference with a fundamental right of personal liberty may be grounds for complaint against a police officer or anyone else.

Arrest Without Warrant   Generally, a party has the right to be free from arrests not supported by a warrant issued by an impartial magistrate and those not supported by probable or reasonable cause. A police officer may make an arrest without a warrant, however, when he or she has *reasonable suspicion* that the person being arrested is responsible for a crime. An officer in hot pursuit of a suspect may follow the person into a dwelling without a warrant.

Use of Unwarranted Force   A police officer may not use any more force than is reasonably necessary to overcome the resistance of the person being arrested. Use of unwarranted force during an arrest or after a suspect is in custody constitutes assault and battery. Anyone so charged can be prosecuted under federal civil rights statutes or appropriate assault and battery statutes.

Writ of Habeas Corpus   The Constitution provides the accused or imprisoned with the right to use the *writ of habeas corpus*. The writ directs the custodial official to bring the person who is alleged to be unlawfully held before a court in order to determine the legality of the imprisonment. People held in jails, mental institutions, or any other legal place of confinement may be released when sufficient grounds justify the use of the writ.

Questions for Review and Discussion

1. Distinguish between torts and crimes.

2. A person made a false statement that injured the reputation of another. The statement was made during conversations with friends and also in a letter written to friends out of town. What are the torts committed?

3. What is the *last-clear-chance* doctrine? Explain.

4. Under what conditions may a person collect damages for injuries resulting from the negligent acts of another?

5. What is the distinction between assault and battery?

6. How does a misdemeanor differ from a felony?

7. For a person to be found guilty of the crime of larceny, what must be proved?

8. What is meant by the doctrine of contributory negligence?

9. Into what three general classes are crimes divided?

10. What are the torts that interfere with business relationships?

Analyzing Cases

1. While driving her car along a busy thoroughfare, Silberg turned her head to look at her two children in the rear seat because they were being unruly. At the same instant, another car pulling out of a driveway struck Silberg's car in the middle of the left side, causing considerable damage to both cars. Will Silberg recover damages from the driver of the other car in a tort action? Explain. • See also *Wichita Falls Traction Co.* v. *Hibbs,* 211 S.W. 287. Contributory negligence

2. Leete Drugs, Inc., operated a chain of stores in New Jersey, which has a statute banning the use of lie-detector tests by private employers. Having experienced considerable losses from theft, store management requested that job applicants take lie-detector tests after signing a consent form stating that "Leete Drugs, Inc., has not influenced, requested, or required me to take this lie-detector test or submit to a lie-detector test as a condition of employment or continued employment." Suzuki was hired, and after taking the test she was fired on the basis of the test results. Would this use of a lie-detector test represent an invasion of Suzuki's privacy? Explain. • See also *State* v. *Community Distributors, Inc.,* 317 A.2d 697. yes

3. The Kings had a large church wedding and a hotel reception. A photographer was hired to take pictures of the wedding and reception. A few weeks later they saw several of their wedding pictures in a store window, advertising the photographer's special wedding services. What action, if any, may the Kings take against the photographer? • See also *Frazen* v. *Shenk,* 221 Pac. 932. invasion of privacy

4. Sterling operated a drugstore in close competition with a cut-rate store on the same block. The cut-rate store, in an effort to injure Sterling's business, brought a charge against Sterling of selling prohibited drugs to persons suspected of being narcotic addicts. The charge was without foundation and was dropped without the case's being brought to trial. Sterling brought an action against the cut-rate store for $75,000 damages to his reputation. Will Sterling succeed? Explain. • See also *Empire Guano Co.,* 201 Ala. 77; 78 S. 53. unfair competition

5. A disgruntled patient wrote a damaging letter to Dr. Jones, pointing out to him what a poor physician he was and how anyone accepting his services would be taking his life in his own hands. The doctor read the letter and angrily instituted a legal action to recover damages because of the patient's alleged libel. Will Dr. Jones recover damages from the writer of the letter? Explain. • See also *Washington Times Co.* v. *Bonner,* 86 F.2d 836, 66 App. D.C. 280. no one else read the letter.

6. Stoopes became enraged over a neighbor's negligence in permitting his dog to enter Stoopes's yard, where it dug up several expensive plants. Stoopes leaned over the fence separating the two properties and tried to hit his neighbor, who kept several feet away from Stoopes at all times. The neighbor sued Stoopes for assault. Will he succeed? Why? • See also *State* v. *Johnson,* 20 So.2d 741, 207 La. 161. no, he didn't have the ability for assault

Legal Reasoning and Business Judgment

Analyze the legal aspects of these business problems. Suggest possible solutions.

1. Putnam bought a car on time. The dealer assigned the security agreement for the balance due to an automobile finance company which was to receive the monthly installment payments. After paying as required for fifteen months, Putnam received a visit from the finance company's representative, who told him that their computer record indicated he was delinquent in his payments. He showed his cancelled checks to prove that he was not. The same thing happened two months later and again several months after that. The third time Putnam refused to produce his records, and his car was repossessed by the finance company while parked at his place of work. What action can Putnam take? conversion

false pretense

2. Fromme was suffering from dizzy spells, and his doctor decided to hospitalize him for tests. His absence from work prompted his employer to determine the reason. The company doctor

contacted Fromme's physician, who turned over all the hospital records, including a psychiatric report. Fromme lost his job as a result. What legal steps can Fromme take to remedy the invasion of his privacy as a patient? *invasion of privacy* *due process*

3. A plant guard reported that he had been struck by a discharged employee. The guard was forced to report to the company doctor for treatment and was not able to return to work for several days. A conference with the firm's lawyers was held, at which the legal positions of the guard, the company, and the discharged employee were discussed. What legal steps might be taken? *battery*

Chapter 3
Courts and Court Procedures

Law is a system of rules and precedent that members of a society establish as a standard of conduct so that they can live together in reasonable harmony. It attempts to regulate the relations of individuals to the government, those of the government to the individual, and those among individuals. If there is a conflict in these relations, the law also provides a court system through which individuals or the government or both may seek relief in the form of a decision. The court may give the injured person or government relief, or it may not. In either case a decision is made.

THE COURT SYSTEM

The laws of this country are enforced and interpreted by a federal court system and state court systems. Three sources are responsible for the creation and governing of operation of these two systems: (1) constitutional law, which provides for the general structure of the court system; (2) substantive law, which creates, defines, and regulates the legal rights and obligations of individuals; and (3) adjective law, which prescribes the method by which a person obtains relief in court and the rules of procedure which the courts are to follow in adjudicating cases.

The court system operates through the work of lawyers, judges, and juries. Lawyers who are officers of the court serve as counselors, advocates, and public servants. It is the lawyer's role to present the client's complaint or defense to a court. Judges are the public officials who preside over a court and administer the law. They control the court proceedings whereby a right is acquired or a remedy is enforced. Included in this process are all the possible steps in an action, from its commencement to the execution of a judgment. The jurors' sworn duty is to inquire of matters of fact and declare the truth upon evidence laid before them. In criminal cases, most states require that the jury's decision be unanimous; some states permit less than unanimous agreement. Civil cases can be decided by a majority vote of the jury.

Jurisdiction of the Courts

The authority of a court to hear cases is called its *jurisdiction*, which is fixed by law and is limited as to territory and type of case. Courts having *original jurisdiction* hear a case when it is first brought into court. Courts having power to review cases exercise what is called *appellate jurisdiction*. Courts exercise *general jurisdiction* if they have the power to hear any type of case. Other courts have only limited jurisdiction.

State Courts

The courts of each state are organized according to the provisions of its constitution. Despite differences from state to state, such as the names for similar types of courts, there are basic similarities. The chart on page 31 (Fig. 3-1) illustrates the legal authority and organization of the several reviewing and trial courts in a typical state.

Trial Courts The general jurisdiction *trial court* has the power to hear any type of case. It is often known as the *circuit court*, the *court of common pleas*, or the *superior court*. In a few states, trial courts are divided into two parts—a *court of law* and a *court of equity* or chancery. In most states the equity courts and law courts are organized under a single judge, who has two dockets. Whether the case is in equity or in law is determined by the remedy desired. When the action is equitable rather than legal, there is no right to a jury trial. The judge passes upon questions of both law and fact, and he or she decides the case upon the pleadings (the parties' written statements of their claims and defenses) without the introduction of oral testimony. There are no legal rights in equity, for the decision is based on moral rights and natural justice. The *maxims of equity* discussed in Chapter 1 serve as guides to the judge in rendering the decision of the court, which is called a *decree*. In contrast to a judgment in a court of law, which is measured in damages, a decree of a court of equity is directed to the defendant, who is given instructions regarding some *specific performance*; that is, the defendant is ordered to do or not to do something. Contracts for sale of real estate, patented items, heirlooms, rare movable property, and other goods or property not readily obtainable on the market may be enforced by specific performance. Another form of decree is known as an *injunction*. The defendant is directed to "cease and desist" from what he or she might be doing to the detriment and injury of the complaining party.

> Klaas, an expert in art restoration, sold his business to Bieder and agreed not to open a similar business in the city for three years. In less than one year Klaas violated the contract by starting an art-restoring business six blocks from Bieder's shop. Bieder can apply to a court of equity for an injunction restraining Klaas from continuing his competitive business. An award of damages only would be inadequate; with a court-ordered injunction, however, Bieder's losses from Klaas's competitive business can be halted promptly.

In addition to general jurisdiction trial courts, there are other courts having original jurisdiction over specific areas or types of cases. For instance, courts with

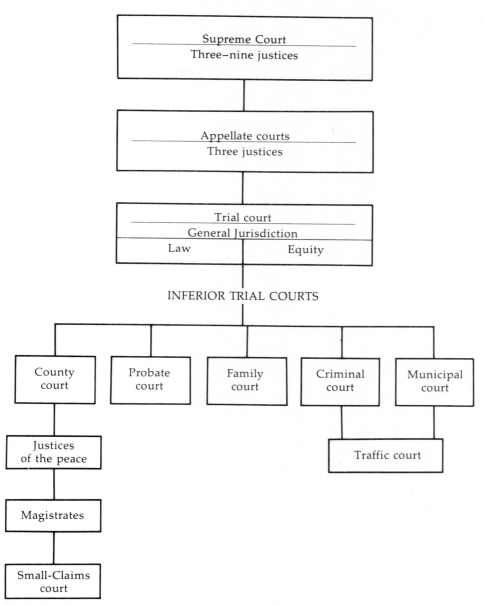

Fig. 3-1.   State court system

jurisdiction limited to a county or a city are often called *county courts* or *municipal courts*. A *probate court* deals with wills and estates of deceased persons. A *family court* handles divorces, family relations, juveniles, and the mentally incompetent. Violators of state laws and municipal ordinances are tried in a *criminal court*.

minimum. $1,000 limit

Small-Claims Courts The courts of original jurisdiction in minor cases are known as *traffic courts, magistrates' courts,* and *justice of the peace courts*. They handle a large number of cases such as traffic violations, collection of small debts, and enforcement of some contracts. The magistrate or justice of the peace may be elected, appointed by the mayor or other municipal authority, or appointed by the governor subject to confirmation by the state legislature. The authority of such officials in civil actions is limited to small claims where the amount in question does not exceed a limited sum of money, such as $750. Criminal authority is limited to misdemeanors. The procedure in all such courts is informal, without a jury, and an appeal may be taken to a county court or another appropriate trial court. In a criminal case, the state may not appeal if the verdict is not guilty.

> While driving through a town, you are stopped by a traffic officer on a charge of exceeding the posted speed limit. At a hearing before a local magistrate you are found guilty and fined. If you feel that you have not received a fair trial with an opportunity to present all the evidence on your side, you may, by posting a bond, appeal the decision.

The small-claims courts are a recent development in the court system. Their purpose is equal justice for rich and poor in the handling of cases that have personal importance but involve little money. A qualified judge presides over small-claims court proceedings. Instead of the usual court costs, which sometimes exceed the sum involved, there is only a nominal filing fee of several dollars. The persons involved need not consult a lawyer. The person who starts the action merely describes the basis of the claim against the defendant in ordinary language. The judge and the defendant then ask questions. The defendant then tells his or her side of the story and answers questions directed by the judge and the person making the claim. After hearing both sides, the judge makes a determination according to the rules of substantive law.

Appellate Courts The court of final authority in the state system is the *appeals court*. It does not hear witnesses but examines the records of proceedings before the trial court to determine whether there was error of law. Attorneys for the parties file arguments and make their statements orally before the court. The appellate court may agree with the judgment of the trial court, in which case the losing party must comply with the judgment. If the appellate court does not agree with the application of law made by the trial court, it may set aside or modify the action of the trial court and enter such judgment as it concluded the trial court should have taken. It can also send the case back to the trial court with directions to hold a new trial.

> Suppose you appeared in the county court for a traffic violation in which another person was injured. The jury brings in an unfavorable decision, but your lawyer believes that certain procedural rules were violated during the proceedings. Your lawyer could file for a review of the findings and rulings of the trial court in the appropriate appellate court on questions of fact as well as questions of law. It

would there be determined whether the trial court's decision should stand or be
revised.

In states with two levels of reviewing courts, appeals are generally taken to the
lower or "intermediate" appellate court rather than to the court of last resort or
supreme court of appeals. Although a person is entitled to one trial and one
appeal, he or she may obtain a second review if the higher court agrees to such a
review. The decision of the state supreme court of appeals is final, unless a case
involves an interpretation of the U.S. Constitution and can be taken to the
Supreme Court of the United States.

> Jordan was arrested by a police officer, who entered her home without a warrant.
> She was tried and convicted on a criminal charge. Jordan then appealed her case
> through the state courts, claiming that the initial arrest had been illegal and the
> conviction secured without regard to her constitutional rights. Should the state
> courts refuse to accept her arguments relating to the arrest, she would be permit-
> ted to appeal to the United States courts on the grounds that her rights as a citizen
> under the federal Constitution were disregarded to her legal injury.

Federal Courts

Article III of the U.S. Constitution provides: "The judicial Power of the United
States, shall be vested in one supreme Court, and in such inferior Courts as the
Congress may from time to time ordain and establish. . . ." The present system of
federal courts, established by Congress, includes the U.S. Supreme Court, eleven
U.S. courts of appeal, the U.S. district courts (at least one for each state), and
others such as the Court of Customs and Patent Appeals, the Court of Claims, and
the Tax Court. The chart shown in Fig. 3-2 illustrates the federal court system,
including the administrative agencies.

Federal courts have jurisdiction over cases involving (1) wrongs covered by
federal statutes or by constitutional guarantees, (2) citizens of different states,
(3) actions between states, (4) actions between states and the federal government,
and (5) treaties. Judges of federal courts are appointed by the President subject to
confirmation by the Senate.

District Courts   Every state constitutes at least one judicial district with one
district court. These courts are trial courts which try all cases involving the federal
Constitution or federally enacted laws. They also have jurisdiction over all cases
involving a controversy between citizens of different states and criminal cases
involving federal statutes. They hear all matters involving important subjects
such as bankruptcy, internal revenue, interstate commerce, national banks,
patents, copyrights, trademarks, and admiralty when the amount in controversy
exceeds the sum of $10,000, exclusive of interests and costs.

> An agent of the FBI was wounded by a fugitive who was attempting to avoid
> arrest. The perpetrator was apprehended by the state police and jailed to await
> arraignment and trial. The federal district court will claim jurisdiction. The

perpetrator will be given over to the federal district court, since the offense was
committed against an employee of a federal agency.

Special Courts   Congress has created special courts—such as the Court of Customs and Patent Appeals, the Court of Claims, the Tax Court —which handle the
subjects indicated by the name of the court.

Courts of Appeals   In most cases, an appeal is taken from a U.S. district court to
a *U.S. Court of Appeals* of the circuit in which the district court lies. These courts
cannot review, re-try, or correct the judicial errors of a state court. State cases
must be appealed to the U.S. Supreme Court when they come within the federal
jurisdiction.

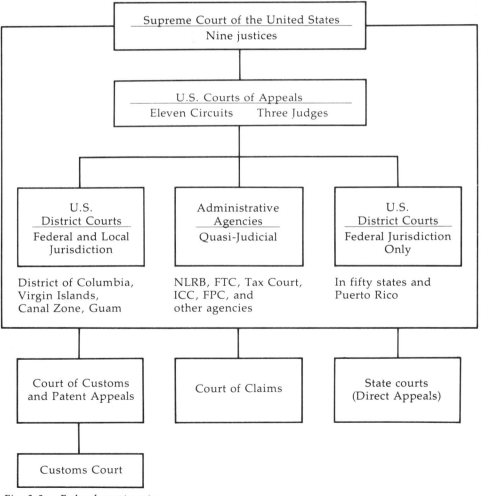

Fig. 3-2.   Federal court system

> After conviction in a district court, the offender in the previous case could appeal the decision should he or she have grounds. A reversal by the Courts of Appeals would require that the perpetrator be given a new trial in the district court before a new jury.

Certiorari   A *writ of certiorari* is a means of gaining appellate review. It is issued by a court to an inferior tribunal or an administrative agency for the purpose of correcting errors in law. It is used when an immediate review is justified to determine whether erroneous or unwarranted acts or proceedings occurred and, rarely, to determine whether the decision rendered was correct.

The Supreme Court   The *U.S. Supreme Court* was established as the court of final jurisdiction in all cases appealed from the U.S. district courts and in cases sent by the state supreme courts. It also has original jurisdiction in all cases affecting ambassadors or other public ministers and consuls, and in cases in which a state is a party.

The Supreme Court consists of nine judges. The presiding judge is the Chief Justice of the United States. A decision is handed down by the Court by a majority opinion of the nine judges. Both a majority opinion and any dissenting opinion, that is, one which presents the position of the justices opposed to the majority opinion, are rendered. Both opinions are available for publication and study.

> An electric power and light company had high-voltage lines running through several states. In extending these lines, it encountered resistance from private landowners in getting needed rights-of-way. The state trial court upheld the company's right of eminent domain. When the case was appealed to the U.S. Supreme Court, five judges affirmed (upheld) the decision of the state court, and four dissented. As a result of the majority opinion, the decision of the state court stood.

Review of Orders Issued by Administrative Agencies   The federal administrative agencies are not officially part of the federal court system. Their rulings may be appealed to a U.S. Court of Appeals, which may enforce, modify, or set aside orders by such agencies as the Federal Trade Commission or Interstate Commerce Commission. It should be recognized that judicial review of administrative agency actions is limited. Legislatures have delegated authority to agencies because of their expertise, and courts usually exercise restraint and resolve doubtful issues in favor of the agency. Judicial responsibility is limited to maintaining consistency with statutes and determining that a fair hearing is not denied to a party in an administrative hearing.

ARBITRATION

Arbitration is a means of settling disputes other than by court action. It takes place when one or more persons are appointed to hear arguments presented by the parties and to give a decision or award which is accepted as final. The rules followed are either set by law or agreed upon in the arbitration agreement.

Parties are given notice of the time and place of the hearing. The procedure is quite simple. Testimony is received by the arbitrators, who then weigh the considerations and render a decision without giving the reason for it. There are no formal pleadings or motions, and strict rules of evidence are usually not followed.

The advantages of arbitration as a substitute for court action are several. It is quicker and less expensive than prosecuting or defending a cause in court. Arbitration also allows the parties to continue their business relationship while the dispute is being decided. Another advantage is that complex issues can be submitted to an expert for decision. For example, an architect may serve as arbitrator when building construction is the issue. Other specialists, such as educators and certified public accountants, may decide issues relating to finances and labor relations.

Various approaches to arbitration have been taken by the states. In a few states, the principles of common law apply. At common law, at any time prior to the rendering of a final award, either or both parties may cancel the agreement to arbitrate, since the continued consent of the parties is required. Other states have laws which cover only the enforcement of arbitrated awards. In these states, the agreement to arbitrate may also be canceled prior to the final award, but once the award is handed down, quick and effective means for enforcing it are available. Most states, however, have adopted arbitration statutes that cover all phases of referring an issue for arbitration, the award, and its enforcement. In states which recognize the statutory method exclusively, the arbitration agreement may not be canceled, and awards are enforceable. In states which recognize both the common-law and statutory method, the agreement may be canceled if common-law arbitration is used, but not if the statutory method is utilized. The Uniform Arbitration Act of 1955 has been adopted by fourteen states. The Federal Arbitration Act also covers businesses engaged in maritime and interstate commerce.

Most statutes that authorize arbitration require a written agreement to arbitrate. They also require a referral of an issue for arbitration within a certain period of time after a dispute arises—usually six months. Both federal and state laws are being widely used to enforce arbitration agreements in labor disputes. In most states, the decision in a workers' compensation dispute between an employer and employee is made by an arbitrator. Many commercial contracts (such as insurance policies) contain a clause providing for arbitration in settling disputes. Compulsory arbitration laws are being considered as a partial solution to problems involving strikes by public employees (such as police and firefighters) and strikes in industries affecting the public interest. An arbitration clause is usually a part of coverage provided under compulsory laws concerning uninsured motorists. Such policies provide the insured motorist recovery from the insurance carrier of up to a specified amount for bodily injuries.

In out-of-court determinations of disputes, arbitration must be distinguished from *mediation*. The purpose of mediation is to provide fair input into negotiations, to seek a compromise or to encourage conciliation. In contrast with the arbitrator, who has the authority to impose a binding solution, the mediator's decision is nonbinding on the parties.

LEGAL PROCEEDINGS

Judicial procedure is concerned with the legal mechanism by which a lawsuit is presented to the court for decision. The whole process of bringing suit in a court is called *litigation*. The injured party who begins a legal proceeding is called the *plaintiff*, or complainant, and the person against whom the proceeding is brought is called the *defendant*, or respondent.

Procedure for litigation is prescribed by statute, and it varies in details from state to state. A review of the rules common to many states and to federal courts will provide a meaningful understanding of the method followed in the courts. *Criminal procedure* is the method established by law for the apprehension, trial, prosecution, and fixing of the punishment of persons who have broken the law. *Civil procedure* refers to the rules that are followed in any personal action at law involving individual rights.

Filing a Complaint

To obtain legal relief the plaintiff must, with or without a lawyer, file a complaint with the clerk of the court having jurisdiction to hear and decide the controversy. The *complaint* is a written pleading or petition which sets forth the cause of the action.

The clerk of the court issues a *summons*—a written legal order—which, together with a copy of the complaint, is served personally on the defendant. In some states, the summons may be left with an adult member of the defendant's family, and a copy is mailed to the defendant. Notice by mail or by publication is also used when the address of the defendant is unknown, when the defendant is a nonresident of the state, or when the defendant hides to avoid personal serving of the summons. The summons contains the date by which the complaint must be answered or some other action attacking the complaint must be taken.

Pleadings

The parties define the issues in a lawsuit by a procedure known as *pleading*. This is accomplished by each party's making charges of fact and the other party's either admitting or denying them. In this manner the parties identify the facts of the case, the evidence that is available to prove the facts, and the rules of law that apply to the facts. If a defendant who is subject to the jurisdiction of the court fails to file an *answer* to the plaintiff's complaint, or if the plaintiff fails to file an answer to the defendant's *counterclaims*, the court may enter a default judgment against the offender. If the court finds that the complaint fails to state facts sufficient to give the plaintiff a cause of action against the defendant, the court will either permit the filing of an amended complaint or dismiss the suit. If either party fails to appear in court on the day set for trial, the other party is entitled to a judgment by default. All pleadings are submitted to the court in writing. Copies are given to the other party in the case.

Discovery Procedures

The law provides for pretrial *discovery procedures*, which are designed to help guarantee that the results of lawsuits are based on the merits of the complaint, rather than on the skill or lack of skill of lawyers. Discovery practices blunt the efforts of a lawyer to win a lawsuit by surprise rather than on the basis of the facts of law. Discovery procedures include taking the statements of witnesses, serving interrogatories (questions) to be answered by the opposition, and ordering for inspection any items involved in the pending action, such as exhibits, documents, and photographs. In addition to the primary purpose of keeping each side fully aware of all facts involved in the case, discovery procedures also encourage settlement of suits and the avoidance of trial.

Trial

If the case is in equity, or if no jury demand has been made, the judge decides the case without a trial. In criminal or civil cases in which the issues are questions of fact and one of the parties has requested a jury trial, the trial is set and a jury is enrolled.

Jury Selection   Once it is decided that the issues of the controversy and the redress for the wrong are to be determined by a jury, jury selection begins. In the selection process, each side has the right to examine prospective jurors. If it is found that a prospective juror is not entirely impartial or is connected in some way with the disputants or their witnesses, that person may be *challenged for cause* by either side. In addition to challenges for cause, which are unlimited in number, each side is allowed a certain number of *peremptory challenges* for which no cause need be stated. The number of such arbitrary challenges varies according to state and the type of court.

Opening Statements   After the jury has been selected, the attorneys for the plaintiff and the defendant make their opening statements. These statements, which are not argumentative, are generally restricted to the bare exposition of the issues involved and the evidence which each side expects to present and prove.

Witnesses   Following the opening statements, the trial proceeds with the taking of testimony. The witnesses for both sides are sworn in and testify. After giving direct testimony, in response to questions asked by the lawyer who called the witness, the witness is subjected to cross-examination. That is, the witness answers the cross-questions of the opposing lawyer. Then, when all the plaintiff's testimony and evidence have been presented, the defendant's lawyer usually moves to dismiss the case on the grounds that, at law, the plaintiff failed to prove his or her cause of action. If the motion is denied, the defendant's lawyer proceeds to call witnesses and to furnish evidence.

Closing Statements   After all evidence is in, either party may request the judge to rule that a claim has not been proved or a defense has been inadequate and that the jury be directed to render a verdict to that effect. If this motion is overruled, the attorneys summarize their cases. The defendant's lawyer, and then the plaintiff's lawyer, sums up the evidence and attempts to persuade the jury to bring in a favorable verdict for his or her client. This process is called the *presentation of oral arguments*, and the summary is known as a ***summation***. The judge then instructs the jury as to the rules of law relating to the case.

> A typical jury instruction in a case in which negligence resulted in injury and the party injured is seeking to recover money to pay medical expenses might be as follows: "The court instructs the jury that the plaintiff has alleged that she was injured because of the negligence of the defendant and that she, the plaintiff, exercised due care and caution for her own safety. If you find from the evidence that the plaintiff was guilty of contributory negligence which caused the injury, then your verdict will be for the defendant. On the other hand, if you find that the plaintiff was not negligent, your verdict will be for the plaintiff in this case."

Verdict and Judgment

After the judge has instructed the jury, the jury retires to deliberate upon its verdict. In privacy, the jury studies the evidence in order to isolate the facts and attempts to apply the law as instructed by the judge. A unanimous vote of the jurors is usually required for a verdict. Some states accept a three-fourths majority decision. Failure of the jury to agree results in their discharge by the court. A new trial may then be ordered.

Upon reaching a verdict, the jury returns to the court and announces its verdict. The verdict is entered by the judge in the court records, and the case is now said to be decided, or adjudicated. By the terms of the judgment, the defeated party is required to pay the amount specified or to do a specific thing. Court costs, but not legal fees, are usually assessed against the loser.

Execution

A judgment of a definite amount acts as a lien on the loser's property. If he or she does not pay the judgment, the court will order the loser's property to be sold by the sheriff to satisfy the judgment. This order by the court is known as a ***writ of execution***. Any excess from the sale must be returned to the loser. If the verdict is in favor of the defendant, his or her lawyer obtains a judgment dismissing the complaint.

Execution may also be issued against any income due the loser, such as wages, salaries, or dividends. This is known as *execution against income*, or ***garnishment***, and the proceedings are known as *garnishee proceedings*. By law, only a limited percentage of wages or salaries, usually 10 percent, can be garnished. Checking accounts in a bank are also subject to garnishment.

If the plaintiff suspects that the defendant is planning to leave the jurisdiction of the court or to conceal his or her assets by converting them into cash, the plaintiff may request the court to issue a ***writ of attachment***, a special remedy sometimes granted in a lawsuit. This court order authorizes a police officer to seize and hold a defendant's property until the case is decided.

To protect the defendant against malicious action, the court usually requires the plaintiff to post bonds to ensure compensation to the defendant if the seizure should prove to be unwarranted or unjustified.

Appeal

On alleging certain errors, a party defeated in a trial may appeal a judgment to a higher court (appellate court) which reviews the law followed by the lower court. It either affirms the decision or orders a new trial.

The most common grounds of appeal involve questions of law, and these questions vary. It may be claimed the verdict was excessive or inadequate or not supported by the evidence. Evidence which should have been admitted may have been rejected. Sometimes, questions were disallowed which should have been allowed. In some cases, the judge may have refused to instruct the jury as requested and as it should have been instructed; or the judge may have instructed the jury in an incorrect or inappropriate manner.

If a judgment is appealed on the basis of alleged errors of fact, the appellant must show that the errors were not minor ones. An appellate court will not reverse a lower court decision on frivolous grounds. An appellant must present a strong case to show that the errors were substantive and that the resulting judgment was clearly against the weight of the evidence.

An appeal in an appellate court is an expensive proceeding. All of the case records and most of the evidence must be reproduced. The written arguments (briefs) of the opposing attorneys must be copied and filed before the case can be placed on the appeal docket. In due time the case is heard. Attorneys for each side appear and present short oral arguments. The case is then taken under advisement until the judges have reached a decision. An opinion explaining the reasons for the court's decision is then prepared.

LAWYERS

Attorneys-at-law are lawyers who are qualified by training to advise others on legal matters and to prepare, manage, and try cases in court. They should not be confused with *attorneys-in-fact*, who are agents authorized to act in another's place. The latter's authority is conferred by an instrument in writing called a *power of attorney*. In addition, every lawyer is an *advocate* and *negotiator*. As advocate, the lawyer defends, maintains, or recommends a cause or proposal of a client to other attorneys and their clients. As negotiators, lawyers seek compromise and mutually acceptable alternatives to court action.

Responsibilities of Lawyers

The principles which govern lawyers in the practice of their profession are a part of the oath of admission to the bar. A lawyer's responsibilities are:
- ☐ To support the U.S. Constitution and the state constitutions.
- ☐ To respect the courts of justice and the officers of the court.
- ☐ To provide unqualified counsel and defense in any suit that is honest and debatable under the laws of the land.
- ☐ To preserve the confidence and secrets of a client.

☐ To avoid professional impropriety in protecting the client's interests and reputation.

☐ To provide competent legal counsel when and where it is needed.

Alleged violations of the lawyer's duties sworn on admission to the bar are investigated by grievance agencies of the state and local bar associations. When a lawyer is formally charged with a violation of the oath of admission, the matter is referred by the bar association to the state courts. The highest court in the state then hears the case and determines whether the lawyer is fit to continue the practice of law.

The Ingredients of Good Legal Advice

Good legal advice is the product of knowledge of the pertinent legal principles and the relevant facts involved in a legal action (litigation). Since the client has the best knowledge about the dispute, this information must be disclosed to the lawyer, who is pledged to protect confidences. Since good advice is derived from knowledge of all essential facts, full disclosure is a must if legal counsel is to be sound. It is also beneficial if the client has some understanding of the legal process, the lawyer's function, and the law relating to the proposed action. In short, high-quality legal support tends to result when the client understands the legal advice offered.

Compensation

Legal advice can be very costly. Setting a fee is often a matter of judgment, and it should be discussed before any service is rendered. There are several factors that enter into the fee-setting process. These include:

☐ Agreement to pay a fixed fee or customary charges of the bar. This is often the practice in routine cases such as handling an uncontested divorce or a no-asset bankruptcy or drafting a simple will.

☐ Contingent fee that is paid if there is a recovery. The lawyer will charge more in such a case than he or she would if there were a contingent fee with a fixed minimum agreed upon.

☐ Fixed rate per hour based on the number of hours spent working on a case. This method is usual with complicated and lengthy court action involving large sums of money.

☐ In some states, local court rules regulate the fee schedule in negligence and wrongful death actions. A fee in excess requires court approval.

Questions for Review and Discussion

1. Explain how substantive law differs from adjective law.

2. What is a decree in a court of equity? How does it differ from a verdict in a court of law?

3. Explain the term *general jurisdiction* and its importance to trial courts and inferior courts in the state court system.

4. Ellis owes Wolfe $50, which she refuses to

pay. Court costs and legal fees make it impractical for Wolfe to take legal action against Ellis. What can Wolfe do to avoid bearing the loss?

5. Over what cases do the federal courts have jurisdiction?

6. Under what circumstances is it possible to transfer from the state court to the federal court system or to appeal from a decision of the highest court of a state to a federal court?

7. Contrast the role of the arbitrator with that of the mediator in settling disputes other than by court action.

8. Identify the advantages of arbitration as a substitute for court action.

9. What are pleadings in a lawsuit, and how are they implemented?

10. What are the responsibilities of lawyers?

Analyzing Cases

1. Each day on their way to work, several people living in the neighborhood elected to walk across McKenzie's property. Despite a number of instructions not to continue the practice and not to make a path across the property, the practice was continued. To what court should McKenzie go for relief? • See also *Ill. C.R. v. Ill. C.C.*, 56 N.E.2d 432. small claims - damages court of equity - injunction

2. A conflict involved improvements on land purchased by Midkiff from a developer in another state. A decision handed down by the state trial court was appealed to the highest court of the state and then to the U.S. Supreme Court. Midkiff's request for specific performance was upheld by five assenting justices. A dissenting opinion was written by four justices. Would the land developer have the right to challenge the decision due to the closeness of the assenting and dissenting votes? • See also *Boyd* v. *U.S.*, 116 U.S., 616. no, need a majority

3. The California Bar filed a petition charging Fabrizi with unauthorized practice of law in the formation of corporations. Fabrizi was not a lawyer, but he was experienced in business as a broker and business consultant. Fabrizi formed two corporations for friends and family without charging a fee for his services. Fabrizi argued that as a broker and business consultant he had prepared listing agreements, agreements of sale in the form of deposit receipts, bills of sale, general affidavits, and other documents. Would Fabrizi's actions constitute unauthorized practice of the law? • See also *The Florida Bar* v. *Keehley*, 190 So.2d 173. yes, not certified

4. Salander Galleries, Inc., sold Whalen two antique goblets made of cranberry glass. Prior to their delivery to Whalen's home, she was notified by the manager of Salander Galleries that the two goblets were no longer for sale. Whalen wanted the goblets to complete a set that she had been collecting for ten years. What legal action should Whalen take? • See also *Waddle* v. *Cabana*, 220 N.Y. 18, 114 N.E. 1054. equity - goblets   small claims - money back

5. Peake was arrested on a charge of speeding and taken before a magistrate for a hearing. Peake felt that the magistrate was untrained and thus poorly qualified to preside over the proceedings. What might Peake do to protect his rights in this matter? • See also *Sevy* v. *Swick Piano Co.*, 4 App. Div. 615, 39 N.Y.S. 409. writ of certiorari

6. Bosak filed a complaint against Elliott for injuries received in a fall in Elliott's home during a visit there. Elliott failed to seek legal advice. When no answer was filed to the complaint made by Bosak, the trial court entered a default judgment for the amount sought in the claim. Elliott argued that the judgment was illegal and invalid as she did not have the opportunity to defend herself in the court. Is Elliott correct? • See also *State* v. *Delk*, 194 S.E. 194, 212 N.C. 631.

Legal Reasoning and Business Judgment

Analyze the legal aspects of these business problems. Suggest possible solutions.

1. The credit department of Tek Bearing, Inc., has received a forged check through the mail from a customer who ordered and received some of the company's products. As the forger lives in a distant state, legal action against him will involve a great deal of expense and time on the part of Tek Bearing's attorneys. Suggestions are sought for the most practical means of recovering from the forger or possibly having him imprisoned for his criminal act. In what court should the action be brought? Discuss fully.

2. An adjoining landowner is in the process of erecting a dam across a stream from which Milford Fabricating has always drawn water for manufacturing use. Milford Fabricating complains to the landowner, who replies, "Sue me and see how much money you will get!" The company is not interested in the recovery of money damages but, rather, in the continuance of the flow of water to its property, because the loss of the water rights will cause an interruption of operation. What course of action should the company take? To which court should the company go for the relief sought?

3. Stolfi, Inc., is involved in litigation in another state in which the sympathetic interests of the judge are in favor of the opposing party. In selecting the jury and in rendering several decisions on matters of procedure during the trial, the judge was openly and obviously biased against Stolfi. The jury returns a verdict for the other party. Can you suggest any rights that Stolfi might have in this obviously unfair handling of the case?

Part 2
Government Regulation and Consumer Protection

Chapter 4
Consumer Law

Recent years have seen a marked growth and interest in *consumer law*—the movement to protect the legal rights and interests of consumers in the marketplace. Despite the interest behind the consumer movement and its doctrine of *caveat venditor*—that is, responsibility for product defects or deficiencies lies with the seller of goods—there are problems in determining the real goals underlying consumer law. Legal relief on behalf of the consumer comes in a variety of forms, but not all of this relief is equally effective or even consistent, namely, in:

- ☐ Providing help to the poor and low-income person.
- ☐ Helping to end racial injustice.
- ☐ Improving distribution and the quality of products.
- ☐ Increasing the availability of scarce goods and credit.
- ☐ Strengthening governmental control and regulation.

Nevertheless, some very useful and positive legal approaches have developed and have been applied in consumer law reform. There is a growing recognition that buyer-borrowers have little real choice in determining sales and financing terms. Their only practical choice is to either buy the goods on the credit terms offered them or not buy the goods at all. The trend in the law is to consider this choice unsatisfactory. Since 1930, in fact, this trend has been reinforced by a marked change in the rulings of the courts. The once paramount doctrine of *freedom of contract*, which assumes bargaining between two parties who are relatively well informed, free and equal in power, has been whittled down by rules relating to public health, safety, morals, security, and contentment.

Section 2-302 of the Uniform Commercial Code provides that if the court finds a contract to be *unconscionable* at the time it was made (based on unfair sales techniques or terms), the court may refuse to enforce the contract or may void the result or results of the unconscionable contract. In addition, there is a body of common law which deals with standard-form contracts and with take-it-or-leave-it contracts that include ***disclaimers*** (denial of an interest, right, or property) contained on tickets and checkroom and luggage receipts, which are referred to as ***contracts of adhesion.*** The courts generally hold that unbargained or printed disclaimer clauses do not effectively disclaim express warranties which are part of the agreement of sale.

The doctrine of ***caveat emptor***—"let the buyer beware or take care"—is being steadily weakened by implied warranties and the introduction of legal blocks to disclaimer and limitation clauses. A seller or manufacturer must warrant the safety and reasonable fitness of a product; and his or her warranty may not be written so as to disclaim or limit liability for an unsafe or unfit good. In short, the trend has been to create a more favorable legal balance for the consumer. To a large degree, the creation of this balance is the prime object of consumer law.

The legal categories which are central to consumer law are those dealing with the sale of goods and the provision of credit to the purchaser of goods. Thus the primary emphasis to date in the developing body of consumer law has involved such problems as:

☐ Regulation of advertising.
☐ Control of sales techniques and methods.
☐ Door-to-door sales.
☐ Scope, interpretation, contents of the sales contract and security agreement.
☐ Quality of the product, including title, packaging, and labeling requirements.
☐ Rescission rights of the buyer.
☐ Restrictions on repossession and collection procedures available to the seller.
☐ Setting of maximum interest charges.
☐ Circumscribing the rights of the holder in due course in consumer credit.
☐ Restrictions on freedom of contract through the doctrine of unconscionability.

ADVERTISING

Legislation in most states provides that advertising must be truthful and honest. Furthermore, the business owner must provide in reasonable amounts the goods advertised as being a "special" or reduced in price. Communications such as catalogs, circulars, and advertisements must be worded so as not to be offers. These communications are generally considered to be preliminary in nature and are sent for the purpose of inviting the person reading them to respond with an offer. The same principle is applied to merchandise that is displayed with price tags in stores or store windows. In a similar manner, a "For Sale" ad in a newspaper is merely an offer to sell and is not a proposal to make a contract which can be accepted.

> Juarez instructed the *Roanoke Times* to run an ad for the sale of a 1976 VW Rabbit for $3,290. The price appeared as $2,390, because of a composing error. Festo agreed to purchase the car at the price stated in the newspaper and wrote a letter confirming the acceptance. When Juarez refused to sell, Festo began a suit for breach of contract. The court would rule that Juarez's ad was merely an invitation to trade and not an offer that could be accepted by a willing buyer.

The regulation of advertising is for the most part entrusted to the Federal Trade Commission (FTC). Its power to declare trade practices unfair is found in the Federal Trade Commission Act and in the Wheeler-Lea Amendment of 1938. The latter declared unlawful any unfair or deceptive acts or practices; outlawed false advertising of foods, drugs, devices, or cosmetics; made it a misdemeanor to use false advertising about a product which might be injurious to health; and allowed the FTC to forbid advertisement of foods, drugs, or cosmetics that it reasonably believes to be false.

Deception

It is unlawful for an advertiser to claim that one brand of a product is superior to another when in fact all such brands of the product are basically the same in respect to ingredients and food value. Advertisers must keep a file of data that supports advertising statements and must produce the evidence when requested by the FTC.

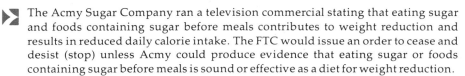

The Acmy Sugar Company ran a television commercial stating that eating sugar and foods containing sugar before meals contributes to weight reduction and results in reduced daily calorie intake. The FTC would issue an order to cease and desist (stop) unless Acmy could produce evidence that eating sugar or foods containing sugar before meals is sound or effective as a diet for weight reduction.

Any advertiser who willfully and knowingly gives false or inaccurate information, or fails to provide information requested, is subject to criminal liability punishable by a fine of up to $5,000 or one year in jail, or both.

Corrective Advertising

In ordering an advertiser to cease and desist from continuing deceptive advertising, the FTC may also order the advertiser to engage in corrective advertising. A new advertisement can be ordered in which the former false or deceptive statements are contradicted and the truth stated. An alternative order is not to advertise at all until the influences gained through deceptive advertising have faded.

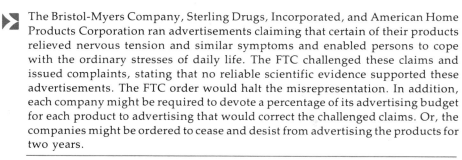

The Bristol-Myers Company, Sterling Drugs, Incorporated, and American Home Products Corporation ran advertisements claiming that certain of their products relieved nervous tension and similar symptoms and enabled persons to cope with the ordinary stresses of daily life. The FTC challenged these claims and issued complaints, stating that no reliable scientific evidence supported these advertisements. The FTC order would halt the misrepresentation. In addition, each company might be required to devote a percentage of its advertising budget for each product to advertising that would correct the challenged claims. Or, the companies might be ordered to cease and desist from advertising the products for two years.

PACKAGING AND LABELING

Among the federal laws that protect the consumer from being misled by labels or by packaging methods are the Fair Packaging and Labeling Act of 1966, the Wool Products Labeling Act, the Fur Products Labeling Act, the Textile Products Identification Act, and the Cigarette Labeling and Advertising Act.

The Fair Packaging and Labeling Act (FPLA) deals with consumer goods and requires that the product bear a label informing the consumer (1) who made the product, (2) what is in the package, (3) how much the package contains, and (4) the net quantity of one serving if the number of servings is given. The FPLA requires that package labels include both ounces and larger units of weight or measure. The use of qualifying words such as *jumbo* or *super* along with statements of net quantity of contents is prohibited.

Econ Home Products, Inc., included on the label of its detergent the statement "12 jumbo ounces of detergent." Under the provisions of the FPLA, the Federal Trade Commission would issue cease and desist orders to Econ Home Products for noncompliance with the prohibition of the addition of qualifying words or phrases to the net content statement. Had the label read "12 ounces of fast-acting detergent," it would have been allowed.

Unit pricing (cents per pound of various brands of goods) is not required by the FPLA. Authority to regulate standards of size (large, medium, small), cents-off promotions, additional-ingredients information, and nonfunctional slack filling of a package is limited to requesting that manufacturers and packers participate in developing "voluntary" product standards. Thus, a "small" package of potato chips can differ greatly in net quantity from a "small" bottle of hair shampoo.

SALES TECHNIQUES

The Truth-in-Lending provisions of the Consumer Credit Protection Act (CCPA) were passed by Congress in 1968. Truth-in-Lending requires that certain disclosures and notice be made by lenders and merchants who sell goods or provide services on credit about the cost of the credit. Its purpose is to provide disclosure of terms so that a consumer can compare the various credit terms available and avoid the uninformed use of credit.

Regulation Z

Under the CCPA, the Federal Reserve Board developed *Regulation Z.* The regulation details how credit terms to be stated are figured and the exact words to be used in written disclosures which inform customers (buyers, borrowers, or debtors) of their credit terms. Regulation Z divides all transactions to which the CCPA applies into two general classifications: (1) open-end credit and (2) other-than-open-end credit. gives you the right of recission

Open-End Credit   This form of credit applies to plans under which the creditor (seller, lender, or secured party) may permit the customer to make purchases or obtain loans from time to time. The customer has the privilege of paying the balance in full or in installments. A finance charge or the cost of the credit may be figured by the creditor from time to time on an outstanding unpaid balance. Under an open-end credit account plan, it is contemplated that there will or may be repetitive transactions on a revolving basis. Department-store charge accounts and credit card purchases are examples of open-end credit.

Other-Than-Open-End Credit   All credit transactions other than open-end are defined as other-than-open-end. Regulation Z divides this type of consumer credit into three subclassifications: (1) sales of personal property, (2) sales of real property, and (3) nonsale credit. The third classification includes liens and mortgages on real and personal property and loans. A *lien* is a charge, hold, or claim upon the property of another as security for some debt or charge.

Finance Charge and the Annual Percentage Rate

The *finance charge* and the *annual percentage rate* are the two most important disclosures required by Regulation Z.

Finance Charge   Briefly stated, *finance charge* means the cost of the credit on any given transaction stated in terms of dollars. It is the sum of all charges payable directly or indirectly by the customer and imposed directly or indirectly by the creditor as a condition of the extension of credit. Numerous types of charges are included, such as interest, time-price differential, discounts, service, transaction or carrying charges, loan fees, points, or finder's fees, as well as fees for appraisal, investigation and credit reporting, and insurance premiums.

Annual Percentage Rate   The *annual percentage rate* is the cost of credit on any given transaction stated as an annual percentage. It is not interest, although the interest included in the finance charge is one of the factors reflected in its computation. In common transactions involving equal monthly payments on declining balances, the rate is based on (1) the total finance charge, (2) the amount financed, and (3) the number of payments scheduled to repay the debt. The rate is the annual cost of the credit extended in a particular consumer credit transaction in terms of a percentage. Even though the rate exceeds the highest lawful interest rate, the transaction is in no sense usurious.

Accuracy   The annual percentage rate must be stated with an accuracy to the nearest one-quarter of 1 percent. The rate is determined by the actuarial method, and its computation is a very complicated matter. The Federal Reserve Board has compiled two volumes giving rates on various amounts in regular monthly and weekly installments over various periods of time. These volumes can be purchased at small cost from the Board of Governors of the Federal Reserve System, Washington, District of Columbia 20551, or from the Federal Reserve Bank of San Francisco, 400 Sansome Street, San Francisco, California 94120.

Disclosures

There are certain disclosures which when applicable must be made in all other-than-open-end consumer credit transactions. Briefly, the basic disclosures are:

☐ The date on which the finance charge begins to accrue, if it differs from the date of the transaction.

☐ The finance charge and the annual percentage rate, except on small credit transactions when the amount financed does not exceed $75.

☐ The number of payments, their total, and the respective amounts and due dates of the installments scheduled to repay the indebtedness.

> Healy financed a new car with National Finance Company. He was told before the agreement was signed that repayment of the $2,000 loan would be spread over a period of 36 months and that small regular payments would be required plus several substantially larger payments along the way. National Finance Company would not be in violation of Regulation Z as long as it gave Healy the number of installments and the amount and due date for each installment payment, as well as his obligation for default or late payment. Some states have laws that provide for a right of refinancing should the larger or "balloon payments" prove too much for the consumer when due.

☐ The amount or method of computing default, delinquency, or similar late payment charges.

☐ A description of any secured interest held or to be acquired by the creditor and on what property.

☐ The method of computing penalty charges, if any, for prepayment.

☐ Identification of the method of computing unearned finance charges which may be refunded, credited, or abated if prepayment is made.

A disclosure form for a consumer credit transaction is illustrated in Fig. 4-1. It shows an unsecured loan of $1,000, repayable in fourteen equal monthly installments of $75 each. The interest rate is 8 percent per year, payable monthly. Interest is included in the $75 installment payment. In the disclosure form, the date on which the finance charge begins is the date of the transaction, January 2.

Rescission Provision

The *right of rescission* is given to consumers in connection with certain real property transactions. Rescission is the right to back out of any transaction and to cancel and escape from all liability, notwithstanding the fact that the individual has become obligated in writing to perform. The right is given by the CCPA with respect to consumer sales of real property and consumer loans secured by real property, if the real property involved is used or expected to be used as the principal residence of the buyer or mortgagor.

When such right exists, the creditor is required to give notice of that fact to the buyer by delivering to him or her two copies of a notice exactly in the form set forth in Regulation Z, printed in 12-point boldface type on one side of a separate statement which identifies the transaction to which it relates. Also required at the foot of the notice are the printed words *I hereby cancel this transaction*, with a

DISCLOSURES (Installment Notes)

(NOTICE: If this is a consumer credit transaction as defined by the Truth-in-Lending Act and Regulation Z, federal law requires that the creditor, lender or payee MUST make disclosures to the borrower or maker, for which purpose the following or equivalent must be used; if this is not a consumer credit transaction, a note form similar to that below, but without printed disclosures, is available.)

1. Proceeds $1,000.00
2. ______________ $--------
   ______________ $--------
   Other charges not part of line 4—itemize
3. Amount financed (1 + 2) . . $1,000.00

4. **FINANCE CHARGE;** interest $50.00
   Other ______________ $----- total $ 50.00
5. Number of payments 14 ; Total of payments 3 + 4 $1,050.00
6. **ANNUAL PERCENTAGE RATE** 8 %

If note is prepaid, no part of **FINANCE CHARGE** will be refunded, but pre-computed interest, then unearned, will be abated; (if, in the note below, interest is payable **in addition** to regular equal principal payments, make the following additional disclosures); each payment on principal, $______; amount of **FINANCE CHARGE** in first scheduled payment, $______, and in last scheduled payment, $______.

I/We acknowledge receipt of a copy of the (1) note below and (2) above disclosures before signing the note.

______________ Maker-Borrower James Geddes Maker-Borrower

$1,000.00 Stamford, Connecticut , January 2 , 19--

I (or if more than one maker) we, jointly and severally, promise to pay to the order of XYZ State Bank

at Stamford, Connecticut

One Thousand--*DOLLARS,*

with interest thereon at the rate of 8 *percent per annum from* date *until paid, payable in* monthly *installments of not less than* $75.00 *in any one payment; interest shall be paid* monthly *and* ~~*in addition to~~ **is included in the minimum payments above required; the first payment to be made on the* 1st *day of* February, *19--* , *and a like payment on the* 1st *day of* each month *thereafter, until the whole sum, principal and interest has been paid; if any of said installments is not so paid, all principal and interest to become immediately due and collectible at the option of the holder of this note. If this note is placed in the hands of an attorney for collection, I/we promise and agree to pay holder's reasonable attorney's fees and collection costs, even though no suit or action is filed hereon; however, if a suit or an action is filed, the amount of such reasonable attorney's fees shall be fixed by the court, or courts in which the suit or action, including any appeal therein, is tried, heard or decided.*

* Strike words not applicable.

James Geddes

FORM No. 1317—Truth-in-Lending Series—INSTALLMENT NOTE. TB — Stevens-Ness Law Publishing Co., Portland, Ore.

Fig. 4-1. Disclosure form for an installment note

date-line and a space for the buyer's signature, should he or she decide to cancel (see Fig. 4-2).

To exercise the right of rescission, the buyer signs and dates one copy of the notice delivered by the creditor and mails or delivers it to the creditor's place of business before midnight of the third business day following the transaction, or following the date of the delivery of the required disclosure of notice of right to rescind, whichever is later. Oral notice of rescission is wholly ineffective. During the rescission period, no money may be disbursed, except in escrow. ***Escrow*** refers to the delivery of funds or some document, such as a deed, to a neutral third party to be held until performance of some act or some event occurs.

Porter signed a security agreement with Willett Sales Company in which she pledged her car as security for payment of any debt created by the installation of a central air-conditioning system. Two days later Porter discovered that she could have the same installation done for much less money by another dealer. Porter may rescind the agreement without further obligation by merely mailing the rescission form provided her before midnight of the third day after signing the security agreement.

3 business days to cancel any home sale

FORM No. 1301—TRUTH-IN-LENDING SERIES.
Stevens-Ness Law Publishing Co.
Portland, Oregon 97204 SN

1301

NOTICE OF RIGHT OF RESCISSION

Identify: Real property sold by contract or covered by mortgage or trust deed; materials, work or services contracted for, or other transaction which may result in a lien; show the type of the transaction with names of contracting parties.

Motor Vehicle Contract, Loan No. 2114, dated January 26, 19--, of ALICE PORTER, 190 Grove Road, Jamaica, NY 11400, as security for installation of an air-conditioning system at her home at the above address, by WILLET SALES COMPANY, 1300 Crossbay Blvd., Jamaica, NY 11400.

*Identification of Transaction

NOTICE TO CUSTOMER REQUIRED BY FEDERAL LAW

Date of consummation of contract

You have entered into a transaction on January 26, 19--, which may result in a lien, mortgage, or other security interest on your home. You have a legal right under federal law to cancel this transaction, if you desire to do so, without any penalty or obligation, within three business days from the above date or any later date on which all material disclosures required under the Truth-in-Lending Act have been given to you. If you so cancel the transaction, any lien, mortgage, or other security interest on your home arising from this transaction is automatically void. You are also entitled to receive a refund of any down payment or other consideration if you cancel. If you decide to cancel this transaction, you may do so by notifying

NAME OF CREDITOR AND ADDRESS OF CREDITOR'S PLACE OF BUSINESS

Willet Sales Company
1300 Crossbay Blvd.
Jamaica, NY 11400

Date within which customer may rescind (three days after consummation)

by mail or telegram sent not later than midnight of January 29, 19--. You may also use any other form of written notice identifying the transaction if it is delivered to the above address not later than that time. This notice may be used for that purpose by dating and signing below.

I hereby cancel this transaction.

(Date) (Customer's signature)

Important Information About Your Right of Rescission.

EFFECT OF RESCISSION. When a customer exercises his right to rescind under paragraph (a) of this section, he is not liable for any finance or other charge, and any security interest becomes void upon such a rescission. Within 10 days after receipt of a notice of rescission, the creditor shall return to the customer any money or property given as earnest money, down payment, or otherwise, and shall take any action necessary or appropriate to reflect the termination of any security interest created under the transaction. If the creditor has delivered any property to the customer, the customer may retain possession of it. Upon the performance of the creditor's obligations under this section, the customer shall tender the property to the creditor, except that if return of the property in kind would be impracticable or inequitable, the customer shall tender its reasonable value. Tender shall be made at the location of the property or at the residence of the customer, at the option of the customer. If the creditor does not take possession of the property within 10 days after tender by the customer, ownership of the property vests in the customer without obligation on his part to pay for it.

Receipt of two copies of the foregoing notice is acknowledged.

DATED: January 26, 19--. Alice Porter Customer

Customer's signature acknowledging receipt of two copies of notice

*For exceptions, see Sec. 226.9(g) of Regulation Z; for waivers see Sec. 226.9(e).

Where there are two or more customers, each of whom is a party to the above transaction, an original and duplicate copy of the above notice must be given to **each of them**, and a receipt taken from **each**. Regulation Z, Section 226.9 (b), 226.9 (j), 226.902.

ORIGINAL AND DUPLICATE TO CUSTOMER; OTHER COPIES TO CREDITOR.

Fig. 4-2. Notice of Right of Rescission

Real Estate Truth-in-Lending Practices

The Federal Trade Commission is responsible for the enforcement of the Truth-in-Lending provisions insofar as most real estate licensees are concerned. The Federal Home Loan Bank Board enforces Truth-in-Lending as it applies to savings and loan associations. In making loans in conjunction with the sale of real estate, proper disclosure must be made to the lender, as pointed out in connection with other types of consumer credit transactions. And in addition to becoming criminally liable, an individual may become civilly liable to the borrower. A fine amounting to as much as twice the finance charge—but not less than $100 or more than $1,000 plus court costs and reasonable attorneys' fees—may be collected.

CREDIT CARDS

Congress amended the Truth-in-Lending Act in 1970 to include dealing with credit cards. The most important section from the point of view of consumer protection is the limiting of the liability of a credit card holder to only $50 for the unauthorized use of the card. For any liability to attach, moreover, the issuer must give notice to the cardholder of the potential liability and must provide a self-addressed, prepaid notification to be mailed in the event of card loss or theft. The issuer must also provide a method to identify the user of the card, such as a signature, photograph, or some electronic or mechanical confirmation. Also prohibited is the distribution of unsolicited credit cards; no credit card, except renewals, shall be issued except in response to a request or application.

 Pike's wallet, containing his American Express credit card, was stolen. He immediately notified American Express by mail that the card had been lost. In spite of Pike's prompt notice, the thief used the card for purchases totaling $980. Pike would be liable for $50 of the unauthorized use of his credit card if the use occurred before American Express received notice that the card had been stolen.

PRODUCT QUALITY AND RELIABILITY RISK

How safe does the consumer have a right to be? Suppose he or she is careless or ignorant about how to use a product safely? Should the consumer be protected against making mistakes or prevented from doing something risky that he or she freely chooses to do? The National Commission on Product Safety considers a risk unreasonable if consumers:

- ☐ Do not know that a risk exists.
- ☐ Cannot determine the likelihood and severity of the risk.
- ☐ Do not know how to deal with the risk.
- ☐ Would pay the cost of risk reduction or elimination if given the choice.

Consumer Product Safety Act

In 1972 the Consumer Product Safety Act (CPSA) created an independent regulatory commission with broad powers:

- ☐ To protect the public against unreasonable risks of injury associated with consumer products.
- ☐ To assist consumers in evaluating the comparative safety of consumer products.

☐ To develop uniform safety standards for consumer products and to minimize conflicting state and local regulations.

☐ To promote research and investigation into the causes and prevention of product-related deaths, illnesses, and injuries.

The act has a direct influence on anyone living in the United States who makes, imports, distributes, sells, or uses what is defined as a consumer product. These are the items that are sold to and used by consumers in their homes, schools, and at play.

The act gives anyone the right to file a lawsuit in any federal court to force compliance with the act by anyone covered by the act. In effect, this right is the consumer's equivalent of a "citizen's arrest," since neither the person filing the suit nor his or her property needs to have been harmed in order to recover. As part of the lawsuit, the winning party is awarded attorneys' fees plus the costs of the suit. Needless to say, these fees can be substantial, and by holding out the possibility that the manufacturer may have to pay them, the act seemingly promotes and encourages the filing of many such suits.

In addition to its own powers to devise standards, safety rules, and sanctions, the act grants to the commission the right to obtain an injunction in any federal court. An *injunction*, issued by a court, requires the person to whom it is directed to do or refrain from doing a particular thing. Under the act, this injunction, if granted, prohibits the distribution of a product in the stream of commerce.

The act imposes civil penalties for its violation of up to $500,000, plus criminal penalties of up to a $50,000 fine and one year's imprisonment. Most important, the act gives to an injured person a separate right to sue for damages, the costs of suit, and reasonable attorney's fees. This is in addition to the right to sue under the common law in one's own state for injuries. This right, in effect, gives the injured person opportunity for recovering double damages or more.

▷ Dichter's daughter was injured while riding a bicycle down a steep hill with a friend behind her on the seat. Although she attempted to reduce the speed of the bike, the front wheel struck a curb with considerable force. She catapulted over the handlebars and injured her chin. In a suit alleging that the manufacturer had installed defective brakes and which he filed in his home state court, Dichter recovered a $5,000 verdict. He could also file an additional action in federal court and recover an additional $5,000.

A manufacturer can no longer take the position that it was not known that a product was unsafe. With the CPSA, the manufacturer must have documentation proving that the product is adequately tested, that the quality and reliability of the product are monitored before it is shipped out of the plant, and that action is taken by the manufacturer on any valid complaints made by users. The capability to recall the product at any time must be maintained should the need arise.

▷ One evening the Cochrans had vichyssoise for dinner, a cold potato soup made by Bon Vivant, Inc. The couple did not eat much because the soup tasted spoiled. The next morning Mr. Cochran felt ill. He began seeing double and had difficulty speaking. He was admitted to the hospital and by evening was dead. Mrs. Cochran was later admitted to the same hospital, totally paralyzed. Investigation soon revealed that the Cochrans were victims of botulism—deadly botulin toxin. As a result, the Food and Drug Administration went to court to obtain orders to seize and hold all Bon Vivant products. Bon Vivant also went to court—to file for bankruptcy.

Federal Food, Drug, and Cosmetic Act

The Federal Food, Drug, and Cosmetic Act (FFDCA), administered by the Food and Drug Administration, prohibits the manufacture or introduction into interstate commerce of any food, drug, medical device, or cosmetic that is adulterated or misbranded. A series of 1958 amendments to the FFDCA prohibited the use in food of additives which have not been adequately tested to establish their safety. Deep in the fine print of Section 409(c)(3)(A) is the Delaney Clause. It states, "No additive shall be deemed to be safe if it is found to induce cancer when ingested by man or animal, or if it is found, after tests which are appropriate for the evaluation of the safety of food additives, to induce cancer in man or animals."

The legislation was viewed as a logical method of providing the FDA with added legal muscle to prevent hazardous substances from entering the human food chain. Since passage of the amendments, the FDA has invoked either the spirit of the clause or the clause itself in twelve cases where a substance was deemed harmful, including such cases as Red Dye No. 2 and cyclamate, an artificial sweetener.

FAIR CREDIT LAWS

Two laws are now in effect which are designed to provide credit card holders and women seeking credit with broad protection against unfair billing practices and discrimination.

Equal Credit Opportunity Act

Designed primarily to aid women, the Equal Credit Opportunity Act forbids discrimination on the basis of sex or marital status. Practices such as refusing to allow a married woman to open an account in her maiden name and requiring new applications from women whose marital status has changed are prohibited by this law.

The act provides that creditors must open separate accounts for spouses on request, when both have enough income to qualify separately. Creditors must keep accounts in both names and make reports to credit bureaus in both names to allow the woman to establish her own credit history. Creditors must also recognize income from a part-time job and refrain from asking about birth-control or child-bearing plans.

Fair Credit Billing Act

The companion legislation, the Fair Credit Billing Act, provides uniform complaint procedures for credit card holders. It requires credit companies to acknowledge complaints within thirty days and give an explanation within ninety days. Special information forms that are required by the law are distributed in monthly billings.

Under the terms of the billing act, if a complaint is made in writing within sixty days after mailing of the bill, a credit card holder need not pay for the item until the matter is resolved. However, if no mistake has been made, accrued finance charges will have to be paid. If the credit-issuing company makes a mistake in the complaint process, it may not collect the first $50 of the charge (including finance charges), even if the charge is correct. Failure to comply with the complaint provisions can cost the company between $100 and $1,000 in the case of an individual and as much as $100,000 in a *class action*—a court action brought on behalf of other persons similarly situated. Other provisions of the law require prompt attention by the creditor to credit balances, payments, and changes of address.

Before a complaint can be lodged by a cardholder, the amount in dispute must exceed $50. Several other formal requirements must also be met. These are discussed in greater detail in Chapter 23.

GARNISHMENT RESTRICTIONS

Federal restrictions on garnishment, a part of Title III of the Consumer Credit Protection Act, took effect in 1970. Under federal law, *garnishment* is a legal procedure, following a court action, through which earnings of a person are required to be withheld by an employer for the payment of a debt.

Disposable Earnings

Under the act, garnishment is restricted by an employee's disposable earnings—which may be different from a worker's take-home pay. As defined by law, *disposable earnings* are those remaining after certain amounts have been taken out from wages or salary, such as withholding for federal income tax, state and city income taxes, and social security payments. Not included as deductions from overall earnings in arriving at the disposable-earnings figure are those voluntarily authorized by the employee. In this category are such withheld amounts as payroll savings, union dues, and purchases of stock in the employer's company.

The basic rule in determining how much can be taken in a garnishment action is that the total cannot exceed the lesser of the following amounts: either 25 percent of an employee's disposable earnings in one week, or the amount by which these earnings exceed thirty times the federal minimum hourly wage.

> Haley earned a weekly salary of $115, which, after income tax and social security deductions, amounted to disposable earnings of $100. When she fell behind $150 in payments on an automatic dishwasher which she had purchased from Mayfair Appliance Company, garnishment proceedings were brought against her. In her situation, the largest amount of money available for garnishment would be $25 a week—25 percent of her disposable earnings.

For employees paid once a month, wages are protected up to $299. The corresponding figure of protection for those paid on a semimonthly basis is up to $149.50. Employees paid every two weeks are protected up to $138. An important point to remember is that state law takes precedence if it calls for a smaller garnishment than that provided by the federal regulations.

Restriction on Collections

Garnishment is usually restricted to the collection of overdue accounts which have resulted from the purchase of goods and services related to the maintenance and operation of a home. Food, furniture, fuel, utilities, and home appliances all come within this description. Some courts have been very liberal in the definition of this restriction, permitting garnishment in unusual situations.

> Reybold was sued on a debt in connection with the purchase of a four-channel stereo/quadraphonic receiver. Following judgment, the seller garnished Reybold's wages. Although the equipment purchased could hardly be termed necessary to the operation of the home, many courts would allow the creditor the right to garnishment in similar cases.

Employment Discharge Restriction

The Consumer Credit Protection Act not only limits the amount that can be taken out of an employee's paycheck to satisfy a debt but also prohibits an employer from discharging any employee for a single garnishment.

Violation of the act is a crime which can bring a fine of up to $1,000 and imprisonment for up to a year. The possibility of a private action for damages and reinstatement can also be implied.

> Tubbs filed a private suit against the Continental Insurance Company when they fired her for her first garnishment. The appellate court held that the law's criminal penalties were not sufficient to protect a discharged worker against the resulting hardship. Put another way, the court held that the criminal penalties expressed in the law failed to compensate the jobless and credit-stricken victim.

FREEDOM OF CONTRACT

The Uniform Commercial Code attempts to establish minimum standards of good faith, reasonableness, and fairness in all business transactions. If vigorously applied, these requirements of business morality would limit the scope of freedom of contract and the right of parties to make a contract on such terms as they choose. To date, however, the courts have almost exclusively limited these "morality" remedies to the consumer and have not allowed them as a defense in cases in which both parties to the contract are business persons.

Unconscionability

The most important "reasonableness" provision of the UCC is Section 2-302, which deals with unconscionability. Its function is to prevent gross injustice which may result from breakdowns in the bargaining process or the total absence of real bargaining in consumer transactions. *Unconscionability* has been defined by the courts as unfair and fraudulent sales techniques, concealment, misleading language, and other unfair procedures in making a contract. There is no provision in the UCC for the recovery of money damages. The only remedies available are rescission and correction of the contract.

The cases which so far have dealt with unconscionability have been judged on factors and situations involving low education level, low economic status and lack of bargaining power, and inability of Spanish-speaking people to read and understand a contract written only in English. The existence of a meaningful choice is an important consideration—that is, can the same product be obtained from another available source without the objectionable provision or term? Many courts would also hold that an unreasonably excessive price in a consumer case constitutes unconscionability.

▶▶ Gonzales signed a contract with Park Ridge Books, Inc., believing that he was to receive a set of encyclopedias for his children for only $29. He was later sued on the agreement, which, in fact, stated that he had agreed to pay $29 a month for 36 months for the set of encyclopedias. Gonzales, who was unable to speak or understand English, was represented at the hearing by an interpreter. The court found the contract to have been unconscionable at the time it was made. Gonzales was unable to read and understand it, since it was written only in English, and the encyclopedia salesperson took advantage of an obvious gross difference in bargaining power.

Cooling-Off Period

A Federal Trade Commission rule gives consumers a three-day *cooling-off period* if they buy merchandise costing more than $25 from door-to-door salespersons. All contracts for door-to-door sales which exceed $25 must carry a notice to the buyer that he or she may cancel the contract within three days from the date of the agreement.

It is unlawful for the seller to fail to honor any valid notice of cancellation by the buyer. Within ten business days after receiving a notice, the seller must refund all payments made under the contract, return any goods or property traded in by the buyer, and cancel and return the contract made in connection with the sale.

Consideration of the door-to-door rule was given as a result of many complaints about the activities of some sales personnel. Consumer complaints regarding door-to-door sales fall into four basic categories.

Deceptions Salespersons sometimes say that they are conducting a survey or are engaged in a brand identification promotion program to gain entrance to a home. Once inside, they begin the sales pitch.

High-Pressure Sales Tactics Sales tactics generally include varying degrees of persistent and offensive pressure.

Misrepresentation In many cases, the consumer does not see the product before he or she is convinced to buy it. In all such instances, the consumer must take the word of the salesperson as to the quality and characteristics of the merchandise.

High Price for Low Quality   Because the sale is made in the home, the consumer does not have the opportunity to shop comparatively before making a decision to buy. Thus, merchandise sold at home is sometimes of relatively lower quality while bearing a very inflated price.

> Conetta received an uninvited salesperson into her apartment. The salesperson represented a nationally advertised dance studio. She was impressed with his sales pitch, which promised her self-confidence on the dance floor. After some urging, Conetta signed an agreement whereby she made a first payment of $45 against a total cost of $350 for lessons at a specified dance studio located twenty miles from her residence. The following day Conetta called a local dance studio and learned that she could obtain similar instruction for $150. She may cancel the agreement by notifying the dance studio prior to midnight of the third business day after receiving the contract. Within ten business days, the dance studio must return the $45 advance payment made by Conetta.

Assignment of Wages

Many consumer credit arrangements contain a provision whereby the consumer assigns future wages to a creditor in the event of a default in payments. A wage assignment requires no court action by the creditor and thus differs from a garnishment. The creditor merely notifies the consumer's employer of the assignment and requests that wages be turned over to satisfy the debt.

In some states, wage assignments are not permitted for certain types of transactions, such as credit sales. In many states, and under the Federal Consumer Protection Act, there is a limitation on the amount that may be deducted from an individual's wages during any pay period.

The wage assignment must be a separate document and not part of any sales contract or other instrument. It must be headed by the words *Wage Assignment* printed or written in boldface letters not less than ¼ inch in height. A copy of the document must be given to the wage earner at the time the sales contract is executed. A wage assignment remains in effect even when a change in employment occurs. If an employee executes more than one assignment, all the assignments are collectible, subject to the requirement that the total amount must not exceed 15 percent of the employee's gross wages. Wage assignments are not valid for any purpose after three years from the date of execution.

CREDIT STANDING AND REPORTING

Consumers who have a charge account, a mortgage on their home, or life insurance or who have applied for a personal loan or job almost certainly have a "file" existing somewhere. It may simply be a few inches of computer tape with coded data about bill-paying habits. Or it may be a manila folder with much more: interviews with former employers, extracts from police and court records, even a rundown on what neighbors say about the person's drinking habits, his or her morals, and how well the children are handled.

The companies that gather and sell such information to creditors, insurers, employers, and other businesses are called *consumer reporting agencies*. The legal term for the report is a *consumer's report*. If, in addition to containing credit information, the report involves interviews with a third person about a person's character, reputation, or manner of living, it is referred to as an *investigative consumer report*.

Fair Credit Reporting Act

The Fair Credit Reporting Act (FCRA) became law in 1971 and is administered by the Federal Trade Commission. It was passed by Congress to protect consumers against the circulation of inaccurate or obsolete information and to ensure that consumer-reporting agencies exercise their responsibilities in a manner that is fair and equitable to consumers. Under this law, a person can find out from the reporting agency why he or she has been denied credit, insurance, or employment. The provisions of the FCRA do not, however, apply when commercial credit or business insurance is requested.

Credit Disclosure Rights

On any application for credit or insurance, there is usually a line buried somewhere on the form that says, "A routine review of your credit and mode of living may be made," or something similar; it can easily pass unnoticed. The reasons for collecting all this personal data vary. Insurance companies, for example, argue that those with stable incomes and conformist life-styles make better drivers, or better court witnesses in case of an accident and lawsuit, than do those with debt difficulties and nonconforming life-styles. Like it or not, the credit dossier exists, but you can demand disclosure.

If you are just curious, you can call the local credit bureaus to see whether they have a file on you. If you have been denied an economic benefit such as credit, the disclosure is free. If you are just being cautious, the agency can charge a nominal fee, usually $5. Disclosure is usually oral on anything except straight credit data. The credit reporting agency need not let you see or hold your file, and usually the agencies do not.

You may not hear about or see everything in your file. Many reports contain detailed medical information, gathered on behalf of your insurance company from your doctor and hospital. The credit investigators are also allowed to keep the sources of their information secret, except in court. Therefore, you will not learn who called you a drunk. Those who want to defend themselves against an inaccurate credit report have additional rights, as follows:

- ☐ To take anyone along when visiting the consumer reporting agency to check the file.
- ☐ To obtain all entitled information free of charge within thirty days of an interview when denied credit, insurance, or employment.
- ☐ To be told who has received a consumer report within the preceding six months, or within the preceding two years if the report was furnished for employment purposes.
- ☐ To have incomplete or incorrect information reinvestigated, unless the request is frivolous; and, if the information is found to be inaccurate or cannot be verified, to have such information removed from the file.

☐ To have the agency notify, at no personal expense, those named who have previously received incorrect or incomplete information that this information has been deleted from the file.

☐ To have another version of information placed in the file and included in future consumer reports, when a dispute between the person and the reporting agency about information in the file cannot be resolved.

☐ To request that the reporting agency send the added version of the disputed information to certain businesses for a reasonable fee.

☐ To have a consumer report withheld from anyone who under the law does not have legitimate business need for the information.

☐ To sue a reporting agency for damages if it willfully or negligently violates the law; and, if the suit is successful, to collect attorney's fees and court costs.

☐ Not to have adverse information reported after seven years. The major exception is bankruptcy, which may be reported for fourteen years.

☐ To be notified that a business is seeking information that would constitute an investigative consumer report.

☐ To discover the nature and substance but not the source of information that was collected for an investigative consumer report.

Krebs applied to the Home Insurance Companies for life insurance, and a request for a consumer report was sent to Confidential Research Associates, Inc. The report incorrectly indicated that Krebs was a drug user, and he was refused life insurance. Krebs sued Confidential Research Associates for damages, claiming that they negligently violated the law. Unless CRA exercised reasonable care in obtaining its information, its protection from liability would be lost. Krebs has the right, of course, to have CRA notify those he names who previously received the incorrect information that it has been deleted from his file.

Questions for Review and Discussion

1. Explain what is meant by the doctrine of freedom of contract.

2. What is the general function of the unconscionability section of the UCC?

3. May disclaimer and limitation clauses, oral or written, be used by a seller of consumer goods and services or by a manufacturer to exclude or modify any implied warranties of fitness for a particular purpose or to void any remedies for breach of warranty?

4. Identify the unfair or deceptive acts or practices declared unlawful by the Wheeler-Lea Amendment administered by the Federal Trade Commission.

5. What must an advertiser do in support of its advertising statements before it may safely claim that its product brand is superior to another? To what criminal liability is the advertiser subject?

6. Under the Fair Packaging and Labeling Act, what product information must the label on a consumer good bear?

7. Explain the finance charge and the annual percentage rate, the two most important disclosures required by Regulation Z.

8. Explain what is meant by the right of rescission, and indicate the category of consumer sales to which it is applicable.

9. Describe the scope of the Consumer Product Safety Act and the powers of the administering commission.

10. May garnishment be used for the collection of all debts? Explain.

Analyzing Cases

1. Carlucci applied for and received a Chevron credit card from the Chevron Oil Company. Shortly after the card was received, it was stolen and used for the unauthorized purchase of gasoline, tires, and a battery, totaling $274.49. Carlucci refused to pay Chevron for the merchandise purchased with the stolen card, although his responsibility was set forth in the notice received when the card was delivered by mail. Is Carlucci responsible for the unauthorized purchases that were made on the stolen card? Explain.• See also *Union Oil Co. of Cal.* v. *Lull*, 349 P. 2d 243.

he has to pay #50

2. Studwell signed a contract for the installation of a central air-conditioning system in her home. It was agreed that Studwell would contact friends and make appointments for the sales representative to present the same offer to them. For each sale made to one of the referrals, Studwell would have her own payments reduced. Studwell was dissatisfied with the performance of the air-conditioning system and brought an action to rescind the agreement. Will she succeed? Explain.• See also *Lefkowitz* v. *ITM, Inc.*, 52 Misc. 2d 39, 275 N.Y.S. 2d 303. *If within 3 days*

implied warranty

3. Mestres entered into an agreement with Frozen Food, Inc., for the purchase of a 23.2-cubic-foot chest freezer and food plan. Although she was Spanish-speaking and had little knowledge of English, she signed the sales agreement, written in English, that was provided by the sales representative. She soon discovered that the cost of the freezer and food plan was much higher than she had understood and that she would be unable to make the payments called for in the sales agreement. May Mestres rescind this agreement? Why?• See also *Frostifresh Corp.* v. *Reynoso*, 274 N.Y.S. 2d 757. *yes, unconscionability*

4. Prang signed a note in payment for a set of ovenware, tableware, and cutlery purchased from Custom House in anticipation of her marriage. The merchandise was shipped and arrived three weeks after she had received notice from Commercial Finance, Inc., that they had purchased her note and that all payments must be made to them. Upon receipt of the merchandise, Prang found it to be shoddy and inferior in quality to that which had been displayed and demonstrated by the Custom House sales representative. Investigation disclosed that all notes secured by Custom House in the sale of its merchandise were sold to Commercial Finance, Inc. The finance company had received many complaints from dissatisfied consumers during the previous year. May Prang refuse to pay her note? Explain.• See also *Nassau Discount Corp.* v. *Allen*, 44 Misc. 2d 1007, 262 N.Y.S. 2d 967.

high price - low quality deception

5. Romano signed a contract for the purchase of a $2,000 above-ground pool and accessories sold to him by a sales representative who visited all the homes in the neighborhood. Romano made a $300 down payment and agreed to pay the balance in monthly installments of $112. After the sales representative departed, Romano realized that the monthly payments were more than he could safely afford. The following morning Romano wrote the supplier and stated that he wished to cancel the agreement. May this contract be canceled? Explain.• Rule 4, *CCH Trade Reg. Rep.* par. 38,029. *yes 3 day cooling-off*

6. Community Furniture Company sold Renshaw a new stove, refrigerator, and television set. At the time of the sale, the salesperson learned that Renshaw was dependent for her income on welfare payments and that she was already in debt for other home purchases. When Renshaw defaulted in payment on the stove, refrigerator, and TV, an action was started to attach Renshaw's personal property. Can the seller succeed in holding Renshaw responsible on the contract? Explain.• See also *Williams* v. *Walker-Thomas Furniture Co.*, 350 F. 2d 445.

unconscionability

Legal Reasoning and Business Judgment

Analyze the legal aspects of these business problems. Suggest possible solutions.

1. You are the personnel manager of the Esco Corporation and friendly with Dr. Foote, who has occasionally treated employees of Esco. Foote phones you to say that Millard, an Esco employee, owes him $175 for past-due rent. Dr. Foote asks you to help him collect it, and you agree. You send an interoffice memo to Millard, with copies to his supervisor and the personnel file, saying that you received a letter from Dr. Foote threatening garnishment if Millard does not pay the $175 owed. The memo goes on to say that disciplinary action will be forthcoming unless Millard takes care of the matter immediately. Millard takes care of the matter by filing suit against Esco Corporation and you for libel, asking for general damages and punitive damages. Were you correct in aiding in the collection of a debt from an employee before a garnishment order arrived?

2. As advertising manager for Porter Tools, Inc., you launch an extensive national and local advertising campaign on TV and in magazines, trade journals, and brochures depicting the results of comparison tests of Porter drills and jigsaws and those of Skil Tools Company. In the ads, statements are made concerning the qualities of Porter products and those of Skil. What defense would you offer if Skil went into federal district court charging that "false, misleading, deceptive, and incomplete" statements about their products had been made in the ads?

3. Drucker, a patient of Dr. Ratner, died without paying a balance of $250 for the physician's medical services. The patient's estate moved to dismiss the action brought by the doctor to obtain the balance due, on the basis that the litigation emanated from a consumer credit transaction and the summons was not bilingual. What consideration would you give to the estate's defense? Note: Drucker, a German, knew English.

Chapter 5
Government Regulation and Administrative Agencies

There is little limitation to the power of state and federal government in the regulation of business, provided the regulation is applied fairly. The regulatory activities of state governments are based on a state's *police powers*—its right and authority to restrict private rights in order to promote and maintain public health, safety, and morals—that is, the general welfare. (The term *police power* as used here is not to be confused with any powers used or exercised by state or local police departments.) The power of the federal government to regulate business is rooted in Article I, Section 8 of the Constitution. "Congress shall have Power . . . to regulate Commerce with foreign Nations, and among the several States. . . ." In defining the power, the Supreme Court said, "It is the power to regulate; that is, to prescribe the rules by which commerce is to be governed."

It is often uncertain whether a federal statute should be regarded as being of such a nature as to exclude state action. The Supreme Court attempts to uphold the standard that it is undesirable to permit state action in addition to federal action when the state statute on the subject would interfere with the operation of the federal statute. The situation is frequently complicated by the fact that business problems are not respecters of city or state boundaries. City problems reach out beyond the city limits into neighboring suburbs and metropolitan areas. Many social and economic problems have assumed national significance. Business operations have become national and international in scope. Thus the trend in the regulation of business has been toward national legislation, reflecting the nationalization of the economy.

As the social and economic problems that stem from the complexity of business and industry have multiplied, governments have authorized administrative agencies in order to reduce the load of problem solving and decision making carried by the executive branch, legislative bodies, and courts. These government commissions or boards are given authority to regulate particular business activities. They create and enforce most of the laws which regulate business transactions. On the federal level alone, over a hundred agencies exercise some degree of control over private business enterprise.

GOVERNMENT REGULATION

The federal government has exclusive power to regulate all aspects of foreign trade. State or local laws regulating or interfering with federal regulations of commerce with foreign nations are unconstitutional.

 San Francisco lawmakers passed a city ordinance requiring that all goods sold at retail that had not been produced in the United States or by a Common Market nation be so labeled. This law would be unconstitutional. A state or local law may not distinguish between goods from different sources in such a way as to deny some of the goods equal consideration.

Interstate Commerce

Under the commerce power, the federal government may regulate interstate transportation and communication. In defining the power of the federal government to regulate commerce among the several states—interstate trade—the Supreme Court ruled that "among" may be restricted to commerce which concerns more than one state. The commerce of a state which is completely internal—intrastate—may therefore be regulated by the state itself.

 The state of Arizona passed a law limiting the length of passenger and freight trains entering or leaving that state. It was passed under its police power as a safety measure. The railroad challenged the constitutionality of the law. The courts would rule that the Arizona law imposed a burden on interstate commerce conducted by the railroad. It interfered with the movement of trains through the state as well as with the adequate, economical, and efficient operation of the trains. The need for such a regulation, if any, must be outlined by the appropriate nationwide authority. Arizona would have the right to make such a requirement for trains operating intrastate.

Crossing a State Line Any crossing of a state line of persons or goods is considered interstate commerce. A person walking across a state line, as well as persons or goods moving across a state line by land, water, or in the air, moves in interstate commerce. Thus all forms of communication, including radio, television, telegraph, and wireless, are interstate commerce.

Orr cut a stand of trees on his property in New Hampshire. The logs were frozen in the river within the boundaries of the town of Groveton, awaiting the spring thaw and a float down the Connecticut River to Greenfield, Massachusetts. The Groveton tax collector taxed Orr for the logs. Orr appealed, claiming that his preparation of the logs for export to another state exempted them from taxation. The court ruled that products from farm or forest that are collected for export are not yet exports nor in the process of exportation until assigned to a common carrier for transportation out of state. Orr was required to pay the tax on the logs.

Carriers

All rail, land, water, and air carriers are regulated by the federal government and to some extent by state governments.

Rail Carriers The authority of the Interstate Commerce Commission (ICC) extends over interstate railroads as well as bridges, ferries, interstate bus and motor truck transports, pipelines (except water and natural gas), shipments partly by water and partly by other means, and freight forwarders.

The ICC regulates the services of railroads. It prohibits rebates and other discriminatory practices. A public railroad can neither expand nor abandon any part or all of its operations without ICC approval. The Commission also must place a value on railroads, set rates, and prescribe uniform accounting methods. The ICC also ensures that railroads conform to safety appliance requirements. Significantly, the ICC prepares plans for the consolidation of existing rail lines into a smaller number of larger lines under a national railway system.

Motor Carriers The authority of the ICC over the types of motor carriers is not the same as that over railroads, because of certain distinctions. Some motor carriers, such as passenger buses, offer their services to any member of the public able to pay his or her fare. On the other hand, the contract carrier, such as a moving van company, may refuse to carry goods as it chooses. In addition to these carriers, there are private carriers (companies with a fleet of trucks) which carry only company merchandise. In the case of a common carrier, the ICC will not permit an interstate common carrier to operate unless it can show that the services rendered by existing carriers are inadequate and that it has the ability to deliver the services needed. Contract carriers must obtain a permit which is granted when the carrier shows that it is fit to perform the services in question. The ICC may fix minimum and maximum rates for common carriers, but only minimum rates for contract carriers.

> Arrow Carrier Corporation applied to the ICC for a certificate authorizing it to carry sheet steel between certain states. Arrow showed that it could provide this service at a lower rate than that charged by the competing railroad. The certificate was refused on the grounds that there was adequate rail service between the points indicated. Arrow appealed the ruling. The court held that a rejection of Arrow's application on the finding that existing rail service was adequate, without regard to the advantages of the proposed service, was contrary to the national transportation policy.

Water Carriers The power of the ICC to regulate water transportation is similar to its power to regulate motor carriers. Its powers extend deeper into the states, however, because of Congress's power over navigable waters in addition to its commerce powers. With the exception of water transportation between the United States and foreign countries or U.S. possessions and that of bulk carriers (such as tankers) carrying three or fewer classes of commodities, the ICC has authority over water transportation.

Air Carriers Control of air commerce is under the power of the Civil Aeronautics Board (CAB). It requires that all planes be licensed as airworthy and that all pilots be licensed as qualified operators. Common air carriers operating on scheduled runs, but not other air carriers, must also obtain certificates of convenience and necessity. The CAB prescribes rates between air carriers and has the power to eliminate discrimination.

Communications

All interstate communications—wire and wireless—are regulated by the Federal Communications Commission (FCC). It tries to maintain telephone and telegraph rates at a just and reasonable level. Approval for extensions or abandonment of lines must be given by the FCC.

Because of the nature of radio and television communication, there are a number of special regulations. A federal license must be obtained before interstate broadcasting is begun. It must be established that the granting of the license will benefit the public interest, necessity, or convenience. Such licenses are granted for a limited period, and a renewal at the end of that period is not automatic. The FCC determines the location of broadcasting stations, the frequency bands assigned, the services to be furnished by the station, and the qualifications of station operators. The Commission cannot serve as a censor of what is said over the air, but it does ban improper language. The FCC also controls competition among broadcasters by refusing to allow owners to operate more than one station in a service area.

> The *Inquirer*, a regional newspaper, applied for a federal license to build a radio broadcasting station. The request was opposed by a licensed station that had operated in the area for several years. The licensed station showed that it had operated at a loss and that an additional station would only add to its economic injury. The FCC would rule that economic injury to a competitor is not sufficient ground for refusing a broadcasting license. In short, the *Inquirer* would be granted a federal license if there was an available frequency over which it could broadcast without interference with others and if it could demonstrate competency, adequacy of equipment, and financial ability to make good use of the assigned frequency.

Monopolies

The Sherman Antitrust Act was passed by Congress in 1890 to promote competition in interstate commerce. The act is based upon the power of Congress to regulate interstate commerce. It deals with two forms of business behavior. Section 1 declares illegal every contract, combination in the form of trust, or conspiracy in restraint of trade or commerce among the states or with foreign nations. Illegal are contracts that fix prices, divide territories, corner commodities, or limit production in restraint of trade.

Section 2 deals with monopoly, the attempt to monopolize, or conspiring with other persons to monopolize any part of the trade or commerce among the several states. Persons are deemed guilty of monopolizing if they have the power of controlling prices or excluding competition. In judging the offense of monopoly, the court differentiates between willful gaining of that power and growth due to business shrewdness or a superior product. Any persons or corporations found guilty of antitrust activities are liable to punishment by heavy fines, contract voiding, termination of corporate entities, and shedding of assets acquired through illegal actions.

▶▶ An action for an injunction under the Sherman Antitrust Act was brought against seventy-one corporations in nine states, including the Standard Oil Company of New Jersey. They were charged with conspiring to restrain the trade and commerce in petroleum among the several states. It was charged that the defendants entered into agreements for the purpose of price-fixing, limiting production, and controlling the transportation of oil and its products. It was also charged that the defendants, operating through Standard Oil Company of New Jersey as a holding corporation, caused that company to acquire a majority of the stocks of other corporations engaged in the oil business and to control those corporations in violation of the act. The trial court found Standard Oil Company of New Jersey and thirty-seven of its corporate subsidiaries guilty under the Sherman Act of forming a combination in restraint of trade and of attempting to monopolize. The court enjoined Standard Oil Company from voting stocks or otherwise controlling the thirty-seven subsidiaries.

Bigness by Acquisition

The Clayton Act, which was designed to make the Sherman Act more specific, deals with "bigness" as a violation of the antitrust law. Under its provisions, no corporation that deals in or manufactures products that move in interstate commerce shall acquire the assets of another corporation, when the effect of such acquisition may substantially reduce competition or create a monopoly in any section of the country or in any line of commerce.

▶▶ The second-largest producer of metal containers acquired the assets of the third-largest producer of glass containers by exchanging stock and assuming the liabilities of the glass container producer. Under Section 7 of the Clayton Act, an order was sought to require the metal container company to divest itself of the stock of the glass container company. The metal container company argued that the types of containers produced by the two companies were for the most part not in competition with each other. The competition that existed between glass and metal in the packaging of baby foods, soft drinks, and food generally was examined by the court. The district court ruled that the merger was a move by a dominant company to make an acquisition that improved its market power and the effectiveness of its competitive efforts by the elimination of a potential competitor.

Tie-In Sales

The Clayton Act outlaws the *tie-in sale* or *lease agreement* in which the person buying or renting goods agrees to use with these goods only other materials sold by the other party. These exclusive dealer arrangements are prohibited when the agreement involves a machine or equipment that will also operate satisfactorily with materials furnished by any other competitor.

▶▶ A radio and television tube manufacturer distributed tubes throughout the country and licensed other manufacturers to use its patented circuits, but specified that the latter must buy their tubes exclusively. If the nature of the patented circuits furnished were such that the circuits would not operate with tubes furnished by other competitors, the restriction would be lawful. If, on the other hand, tubes furnished by other competitors could be used, the restriction would be ruled an unfair trade practice and a violation of the Clayton Act.

Price-Fixing

The courts condemn price-fixing agreements under Section 1 of the Sherman Antitrust Act. Any combination of persons formed for the purpose and with the effect of raising, depressing, or fixing the price of goods in interstate or foreign commerce is considered illegal. Since the result of such agreements is the elimination of some form of competition, the courts hold that, even when reasonably administered, they involve the power to control the market.

 Ten manufacturers of bathroom fixtures (in control of about 80 percent of the manufacture and distribution of these products in the United States) entered into an agreement to fix and maintain uniform prices—just low enough to discourage competition. Thus, consumers paid more than they would have paid had prices been fixed by competition. The manufacturers argued that they did not have a complete monopoly and that their prices were reasonable. Their agreement would be void under Section 1 of the Sherman Antitrust Act.

BUSINESS TAXATION

The U.S. Constitution and various state constitutions establish the government's authority to levy and collect taxes, whether on the national, state, or local level. In order to raise money to offset the cost of its operations, the government levies taxes for specific reasons on persons, property, or privileges. Income, excise, and sales taxes are typical of those affecting persons doing business. Real property taxes are collected on land and buildings attached to land, and personal property taxes are generally collected on items such as machinery, furniture, and fixtures. Corporations pay a franchise tax for the privilege of doing business.

Taxes may be classified according to whether they are levied under federal taxing authority or under state and local taxing authority.

Federal Taxing Authority

Constitutional provisions pertaining to federal taxing authority are found in Article I, Section 7: "All bills for raising Revenue shall originate in the House of Representatives; but the Senate may propose to concur with Amendments as on other Bills"; and in Section 8: "The Congress shall have the Power to lay and collect Taxes, Duties, Imposts and Excises, to pay the Debts and provide for the common Defense and general Welfare of the United States; but all Duties, Imposts and Excises shall be uniform throughout the United States."

The courts interpret this taxing power broadly. Thus, a variety of federal taxes exist, including the following:

☐ Manufacturers' excise taxes—applied to consumer goods such as automobiles, tires, and appliances.

☐ Retailers' excise taxes—collected on the sale of cosmetics and furs.

☐ Taxes levied on safe deposit boxes, the transportation of persons, and telephone, telegraph, and cable services.

☐ Taxes levied on the conveying of property following death, such as estate, inheritance, or legacy taxes.

☐ Taxes levied on the privilege of employing workers, i.e., social security taxes.

☐ Taxes levied on cigarettes, cigars, and snuff.

☐ Taxes levied on those doing business as importers of drugs and firearms manufacturers and importers.

☐ Taxes collected on distilled spirits and gasoline.

Much of the federal government revenue results from income tax on individuals and corporations. The power to levy this tax is found in the Sixteenth Amendment to the Constitution: "The Congress shall have power to lay and collect taxes on incomes, from whatever source derived, without apportionment among the several states, and without regard to any census or enumeration." Laws governing the federal income tax are found in the Internal Revenue Code, which is enforced by the Internal Revenue Service, a division of the Treasury Department. Taxpayers' returns are subject to three levels of review and appeal: audit by a revenue agent; the District Conference, Appellate Division; and a district court.

State and Local Taxing Authority

States and their political subdivisions levy taxes to the extent permitted by their state constitutions and by the Constitution. Some state taxing authority derives from the Tenth Amendment: "The powers not delegated to the United States by the Constitution, nor prohibited by it to the States, are reserved to the States respectively, or to the people." Article I, Section 10, however, limits state taxing power: "No state shall, without the consent of Congress, lay any Imposts or Duties on Imports or Exports, except what may be absolutely necessary for executing its inspection laws. . . ."

Courts often must rule on whether a state or locality has exceeded its taxing power. Courts consider the taxing authority granted in the state constitution or, if interstate commerce is involved, in the U.S. Constitution. Whether legal violations exist depends on the answer to constitutional issues such as: (1) Is the tax fairly apportioned among the states? (2) Is there sufficient business activity to justify the tax? (3) Does the tax discriminate against interstate commerce? and (4) Does the tax unjustly burden interstate commerce?

▶ An Atlanta, Georgia, corporation with its principal place of business in Columbia, South Carolina, is a common carrier of petroleum products. It owns and operates a pipeline system extending from Dallas, Texas, to Pittsburgh, Pennsylvania. Approximately 148 miles of the pipeline are located in Kentucky, and over this distance the corporation owns and operates several pumping stations and tank storage facilities and employs 40 workers. The corporation does not have administrative offices in Kentucky, nor does it conduct intrastate business in petroleum products. The corporation contested the imposition of a fairly apportioned corporation franchise tax by the state of Kentucky under the Commerce Clause. The court would sustain the validity of the tax by reasoning that the tax was not imposed merely or solely for the privilege of doing interstate business in Kentucky. It was a fairly apportioned means of requiring the corporation to pay its just share of the cost of state government, upon which the corporation relied and by which it was furnished protection and benefits.

Nexus and Apportionment

The commerce clause (Article I, Section 8, Clause 3 of the Constitution) places limits on the power of state and local governments to tax businesses conducting interstate commerce. The state may, however, tax such business income when it can be shown that the business receives benefits from the state or local government. This linkage with the taxing state is known as *nexus.*

 Coast Industries, Inc., a South Carolina company, produces modular office panel systems for use in new and remodeled office areas. They sell and ship to customers in Ohio but do not maintain an office or regular sales force in the state. Ohio residents sell the panels, and they are paid commissions on the sales. Coast Industries objects to the Ohio requirement that a tax be paid on the modular panels purchased in Ohio. The court would very likely rule that nexus exists, and Ohio would be permitted to levy a fair tax on the panel systems.

In most cases, states have the power to levy a use, property, or income tax on businesses conducting interstate commerce. The tax must be *apportioned* (proportionally divided and distributed), however, in accordance with the scope of the business operation and the volume of business conducted within the state. In this manner, a business operating in two or more states is not subject to the burdens of multiple taxation, and thus violations of the commerce clause are avoided. Apportionment formulas are established to assure that a state does not discriminate against a business enterprise or impose an unreasonable burden on it.

ADMINISTRATIVE AGENCIES

The breadth and depth of the administrative process cause major problems for the business community. During the past decade, the reach and power of regulating agencies have vastly increased. Large areas of our economic and social lives are controlled by appointed and civil servants known as *regulators*. Although nobody in the federal government keeps track of all the forms sent out to individuals and businesses by these agencies, one survey revealed that more than 9,800 different types of forms exist. An estimated 556 million responses are returned every year, with hundreds of millions of hours needed to gather the data and complete the forms. Every rule-making agency publishes its rules, but there are so many that no one person, company, or law firm can gather them all together to examine them, let alone know what they contain. The Code of Federal Regulations, containing only the basic, standing rules set down by the agencies, already fills a shelf 15 feet long with 60,000 book-size pages of fine print. These appointed officials and civil servants now make more rules than the elected members of Congress do. A Library of Congress study found that in a given year the federal bureaus churn out about 7,500 new or amended regulations—roughly eighteen regulations for every law. Most of these regulations carry the force of law; that is, violators of these regulations are subject to fines or jail.

Federal Administrative Procedures Act

Every agency must separately state and publish in the Federal Register the administrative regulations adopted. Under the terms of the Federal Register Act, filing such documents with the administrator in charge of the Federal Register is sufficient to give notice of the contents of such documents to any person subject thereto or affected thereby. Every five years, each agency of the national government is required to file a complete codification of all documents which have general applicability and legal effect and which are in force at the time.

Agency Powers

Administrative agencies have the power to make the laws that regulate the industry or business behavior when substantial technical or specialized knowledge is required. The real source of this power can be summed up in one word: *necessity*. Elected officials in the several branches of government simply cannot deal with all the problems of a complex industrial society. They would have little time to perform their primary functions were they required to have expertise in fields as diverse and complex as communications, energy, transportation, and agriculture. Thus, it has become a matter of expedience to establish administrative agencies to exercise combined executive, legislative, and judicial functions in fields such as these, with broad powers to grant licenses, prohibit unfair methods of competition, adjust prices, prevent profiteering, and otherwise regulate many areas of the nation's economy.

To carry out their mandate and authority, legislatures are increasingly giving the agencies additional powers as well. Thus, agency administrators have the power to investigate their area of control in order to obtain facts regarding alleged violations of regulations and to determine whether there is need for additional rules. Persons may be required to appear as witnesses, and corporations or associations can be compelled to produce information to determine whether there is sufficient ground to bring suit against the business being investigated.

A number of administrative agencies have also been given the power to sit as a court and to rule on whether a violation of the law or of the regulations of the agency has occurred. Although this judicial power is firmly established, agencies generally favor the use of informal settlements. For example, the wrongdoer agrees to change the practice or conduct voluntarily or by a *consent decree*, which sets forth the terms of the agreement that will end the proscribed activity.

> The Federal Trade Commission announced that it had accepted an agreement containing a consent order prohibiting Cape Enterprises, Ltd., of New York City from making false and misleading statements and engaging in deceptive practices to sell distributorships. The complaint that led to the consent order alleged

that Cape Enterprises misrepresented that persons who purchased a distributor-ship could earn sums ranging from $600 a month to $100,000 a year; said that such earnings were made by a significant number of persons who had purchased and operated such distributorships; and held that Cape Enterprises would secure established, sales-producing accounts or locations for purchasers of their distributorships. In addition to ordering Cape Enterprises to stop these misrepresentations, the consent order required a disclosure statement to be given to any prospective distributor indicating the rights and obligations of the parties under the agreement, the financial history of Cape Enterprises, the number of distributorships presently operating, and the fact that the agreement could be canceled within ten business days of its execution.

All such consent agreements are for settlement purposes only and do not represent an admission by the alleged offender that they have violated the law.

When issued by the administrative agency on a final basis, however, a consent order carries the force of law with respect to future actions. A violation of such an order may result in a fine of up to $10,000 per violation.

Administrative Agency Proceedings

Except in cases requiring prompt action, such as the sending of obscene matter through the mails, the enforcement of tax laws, and the exercise of police power in protecting public health and safety, the need for immediate action by an administrative agency is rare. As a rule, some notice is given to those who will be affected, and some form of hearing is held, at which time the alleged violators may present their case.

Serving a Complaint Either a private person damaged by the conduct of another or the agency on its own initiative may present a complaint. The complaint is served on the alleged violator, and time is provided to file an answer.

Rules of Procedure The rules used in these hearings are made by the administrative agencies themselves. The hearings are more informal in character than court trials are. On the whole, however, they follow the general pattern set by courts. The rules of evidence are not strictly followed, because the hearing examiner may not have legal training. This is not to say that agencies can ignore all rules. They cannot, for example, refuse to permit any cross-examination.

The hearing examiner or arbitrator receives the evidence, submits findings of the facts, and makes recommendations to the board or commission regarding the disposition to be made. The board or commission studies the report and issues its orders as the law in the case demands.

A major difference between an administrative agency hearing and a court hearing is that there is no right of trial by jury in the former. Another difference is that the hearing examiner may be authorized to make a decision first and then hold a hearing to confirm his or her position. Protection against self-incrimination is also limited. It cannot be employed in respect to records which by law must be kept by the persons subject to the investigation.

▷ National Oil sold gasoline retail in its own service stations, as well as to independently owned service stations. In selling gasoline to its independently owned stations, National Oil gave price-cutting permission in return for a tie-in sales agreement covering other petroleum products. National Oil was prosecuted for making illegal tie-in sales and for unfair methods of competition under the provisions of the Clayton Act. The evidence on which the case was based was obtained from information found in the business records that National Oil had been required to produce. National Oil claimed immunity from prosecution for any matter arising out of its business records on the grounds that the constitutional guarantee against unreasonable search and seizure had been violated. The protection provided against self-incrimination does not apply when an agency obtains information by compulsion and when the records by law must be kept by the person subject to investigation.

Regulatory Problems

For various reasons, governing bodies create new agencies and more regulations every year. As their numbers increase, the number of hearings and court actions increases, even though few agency decisions are actually reviewed. Neither legislatures nor Presidents have been effective in checking agency performance or in correcting failings. It is argued that some regulations become more burdensome than the problems they were intended to solve.

▷ The idea of recycling waste paper for ecological purposes has sometimes backfired. The energy consumed in cleaning a street littered with paper that has not been picked up on schedule can far exceed the energy saved by the recycling process.

Agencies are accused of favoring certain industries and contributing to inflation and inefficiency. It has been charged that the most-regulated industries have become federal dependents, carrying on business in a comfortable cost-plus world. The major problems, however, are associated with personnel, costs, delays, and procedures.

Personnel   Sometimes it is charged that appointments to agency jobs are made in payment of political debts rather than on the basis of ability and experience. It has been shown that agencies can be rendered toothless when manageable commissioners are deliberately chosen.

▷ Presidential appointments to the FCC have included a former congresswoman whose experience in communication was limited to singing on the radio for several years. A college roommate and best man at the President's wedding was appointed to the ICC.

It has also been charged that some agencies, especially those that set rates, are captives of the industries they are supposed to supervise. This can be true when commissioners and key staff are specialists drafted from the ranks of the regulated industries.

High Costs   There is simply no accurate way to measure the cost effectiveness of regulatory agencies or the impact of this cost on the taxpayers and the business community. Direct costs can be estimated. In 1965 the twelve major agencies spent $860 million. The proposed budget for 1976 listed $3.8 billion for the twenty-four major agencies. These figures suggest that the cost of regulatory law increased from $4.30 per person to about $10.36, adjusted for inflation, during an eleven-year period. But this is only a part of the concern. The aides in the Office of Management and Budget estimate regulation costs to be at least $130 billion a year in inflated prices, additional costs to business, and lost productivity. A growing number of people both inside and outside government service are accusing the agencies of being inefficient and ineffective in balancing the cost of regulatory programs with their potential benefits. Evidence suggests that some agencies, principally the older ones, contribute to limiting free competition and keeping prices high in the industries they regulate.

> The Civil Aeronautics Board (CAB) had refused to let Laker Airways (a British airline) charge less than $300 for regularly scheduled New York-to-London flights. Airlines scheduling the same round-trip flight were charging over $600 for an economy-class ticket. Later, the CAB ruling was overturned.

One agency's rules sometimes clash with those of another.

> OSHA job safety rules called for protective railing around blood pits in meat-packing plants. Agriculture Department inspectors disapproved of the railings because they became encrusted and unsanitary. OSHA compromised by allowing employees to use safety harnesses to prevent their falling into the pits.

Outright mistakes are made.

> The Consumer Products Safety Commission (CPSC) erroneously banned as unsafe a plastic toy ball manufactured by Martin Toy Products, Inc. The Commission later admitted the error, but the company estimated that it lost $1.2 million in canceled orders and forced layoff of all but ten of its eighty-five employees. Congress authorized payment of damages to Martin, with the amount to be set by a claims court.

Delays   Most federal administrative agencies have been accused of failing to act to reduce the months and even years of delay that plague the regulatory process. The Administrative Conference, an agency created by Congress to reduce inefficiency and unfairness in government, reported that despite a request that agencies keep time logs on the number of cases decided by administrative law judges, only a handful of the agencies had complied. Of the thirty agencies that conduct formal administrative proceedings, only four or five statistically monitor and publicly report time intervals occurring between key steps in proceedings.

> The FDA went through nine years of hearings, proposals, and comment periods before deciding that any product labeled "peanut butter" must contain at least 90 percent peanuts.

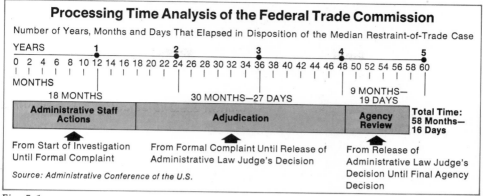

Fig. 5-1

Estimates by the Administrative Conference showed that restraint-of-trade cases within the Federal Trade Commission averaged 58 months 16 days—almost five years from start to finish. Deceptive-practice cases in the same agency averaged 34 months 4 days, or almost three years (see Fig. 5-1). Pipeline certificate cases in the Federal Power Commission normally require just under two years.

Procedures   In order to give those asserting their rights a full and fair hearing in administrative hearings, Congress has required procedures that are more parallel to established judicial proceedings. This requirement has resulted in the inability of many agencies to settle issues without long delays. The frequent use of the consent order (in which an alleged violator agrees not to continue doing an act without admitting or denying it) is often questioned on the basis that it does not serve justice. The use of advisory groups consisting of experts and citizens from outside government is a matter of growing concern to those being regulated. Many of these meetings are secret, and no transcript of their proceedings is available. The members of most of these advisory groups come from lobbying groups, trade associations, and the business interest groups being regulated. Another very serious concern about the agency process is the amount of unchecked power placed in the hands of bureau administrators.

 Thanks to its sweeping powers, the FCC alone clears new domestic communications services. Instead of encouraging development of new services and equipment, however, the FCC has been charged with regarding telephones and telegraphs as the only feasible services. Thus the first international communications satellite was launched in 1964, whereas the first domestic satellite was not launched until 1974.

Regulatory Benefits

There is movement in Congress aimed at reviewing the regulators' powers. But changes require legislation, and Congress moves slowly. More to the point, however, is the obvious fact that the day-to-day legal impact of local, state, and federal administrative rules and regulations is so broad and complex that courts and legislative bodies alone cannot possibly deal with all the issues and questions these regulations generate.

Much of the federal and state regulation is carried on without complaint, or in fact with the strong support of the persons being regulated; and sometimes there are calls for more regulation instead of less. More than 3,400 people with savings accounts at a Houston bank did not lose their money when the bank closed its doors—the Federal Deposit Insurance Corporation (FDIC) paid them. The Food and Drug Administration got a court order to seize imported boar-bristle brushes from a Los Angeles importer because the brushes were contaminated with lice eggs. And the air is measurably cleaner since EPA began work. Even the auto manufacturers reluctantly concede that federal auto safety regulations save motorists' lives by the thousands. Federal job safety inspectors fined a New York girdle maker $500 for locking the emergency exit fire doors. The auto safety officials pressed California, Utah, and Illinois to force motorcyclists to wear approved crash helmets. Pollution officials are moving to outlaw traditional marine toilets on even small cruising boats, requiring either waste-treatment devices or inexpensive but inconvenient tanks that hold waste on board. Thus, even though the faults of the administrative process make it difficult to live with, even its most vocal critics concede that a good many agency regulations are necessary.

Questions for Review and Discussion

1. What is the source of authority and power that enables the federal government and the states to regulate business and commercial activity?

2. What trends are evident with respect to government regulation of business when state governments and the federal government have concurrent powers?

3. When are goods or passengers deemed to be "in interstate commerce"?

4. What is the present national policy toward the regulation of carriers by rail, highway, water, and air?

5. What is the constitutional basis for the Sherman Antitrust Act?

6. Does it make any difference if the person reselling an article practices price-fixing in order to compete with a larger competitor? Explain.

7. What are four constitutional problems that must be considered by courts faced with the task of determining whether a state has exceeded its power to tax businesses engaged in interstate commerce?

8. What is meant by the following: "A state may impose an apportioned, nondiscriminatory tax on businesses engaged in interstate commerce when there is sufficient *nexus*"?

9. How are the regulations by administrative rule-making authorities brought to the attention of the persons who are to obey them?

10. How does a legal proceeding conducted by an administrative agency differ from proceedings in the regular courts?

Analyzing Cases

1. The Federal Power Commission ruled that a proposed natural gas rate increase was too high and ordered lower rates to be instituted. The Commission came to this conclusion without using any formulas to determine rates. Could a court overrule the Commission's order based on this failure to weigh different formulas? • See *Federal Power Commission* v. *Natural Gas Pipeline Co.*, 315 U.S. 575. yes arbitrary

2. United Fuel piped gas from West Virginia to Ohio. It sold to Portsmouth Gas, which sold gas at retail in Portsmouth, Ohio. The Ohio Public Utilities Commission commenced a proceeding to regulate the rates of Portsmouth Gas as well as the rate at which United sold its gas to Portsmouth Gas. It ordered United Fuel to produce its books. Would United Fuel be successful in an effort to seek an injunction against this order? •See *Ohio P.U.C.* v. *United Fuel Gas Co.*, 317 U.S. 456. yes, the federal gov't regulates it

3. After a proper hearing, the Interstate Commerce Commission established the maximum rate railway carriers could charge. Then the ICC considered new evidence and, declaring that its own findings had been in error, concluded that the maximum rate it had established was too high. Could a carrier be held liable for reparations based on the difference between what it had charged and the new, lower rate? • See *Arizona Grocery* v. *Atchison, Topeka & Santa Fe Railway*, 284 U.S. 370. no.

4. A class action was brought against a manufacturer of aspirin. The plaintiffs' claim was based primarily on Federal Trade Commission Act provisions which prohibit unfair or deceptive trade practices and false advertising. The plaintiffs alleged that the aspirin company had made false statements in claiming that its aspirin product was more than twice as fast-acting as competitors' products. Could the plaintiffs properly bring this action? • See *Holloway* v. *Bristol-Myers Corp.*, 327 F. Supp. 17.

5. Prior to a proceeding before the FTC, a libel proceeding was brought in the federal courts claiming that a company's product, "Gizzard Capsules," was misbranded in violation of the Food and Drug Act, in that the manufacturer falsely claimed that the product could cure worm infections in poultry. The defendant company won the suit. The FTC then found that the claims were false and brought an action claiming that their use constituted an unfair method of competition within the meaning of the Federal Trade Commission Act. Could the FTC finding stand, or was it bound by the judgment in the first suit? •See *George H. Lee Co.* v. *F.T.C.*, 113 F. 2d 583.

6. Section 310 of the Packers and Stockyards Act made it necessary that a hearing be held before the Secretary of Agriculture could fix rates for market agencies. Is an order of the Secretary of Agriculture fixing rates for market agencies under the act invalid if the evidence and arguments were heard and considered by an assistant to the Secretary rather than by the Secretary himself? •See *Morgan* v. *U.S.*, 298 U.S. 468.

Legal Reasoning and Business Judgment

Analyze the legal aspects of these business problems. Suggest possible solutions.

1. You are president of an interstate bus company. The ICC has found your corporation guilty of improper conduct for using substandard emission-control devices. Its ruling requires the corporation to replace these devices at an approximate cost of $300,000. Counsel has informed you that the likelihood of success if the ruling is taken to court is very good, but that the estimated legal fees will be in the neighborhood of $250,000. Should your corporation go to court or comply with the Commission's ruling? What factors should you consider? *comply because if you lose you would lose much more.*

2. The Civil Aeronautics Board has jurisdiction over rates and regulations concerning the airline industry. The President wants to appoint a former executive of a major domestic airline to the Board. Is this action advisable? Should the appointee accept?

3. A railroad applies to the ICC for an increase in its interstate rates. After a proper hearing, the ICC rejects the rate increase proposal. The railroad appeals. The judge disagrees with the Commission's ruling, but because the decision was not capricious or arbitrary, the judge is forced to sustain the Commission. Will an appeal to a higher court be likely to succeed? *no.*

A *contract* is an agreement between two or more competent parties, based on mutual promises, to do or to refrain from doing some particular thing which is neither illegal nor impossible. The agreement results in a legally enforceable obligation.

▶ Calivito went into a department store and purchased an electric blanket for $65. She paid $10 down and promised to pay the balance when the blanket was delivered. This agreement resulted in a contract enforceable at law because the parties mutually assented to the terms and conditions of a legally enforceable transaction.

Persons who enter into a contract are said to be *in privity*; that is, they have direct rights and obligations arising from the contract as opposed to those who are only indirectly affected by it. The various kinds of contracts are explained below.

TYPES OF CONTRACTS

Business agreements are based upon contracts made in anticipation of the acceptance by persons or businesses of obligations for mutual benefit of all parties concerned. The law has been careful to classify the many types of contracts into convenient areas, each of which has its own special and peculiar requirements. However, *all* contracts must follow definite requisites common to the types presented in this chapter.

Oral Contracts

To be enforceable, a contract need not be in writing. In fact, the greatest number of contracts made are *oral contracts*, which are legally enforceable.

▶ Kravitz called Herald Square Beauticians, making an appointment for Friday afternoon at 3:45 P.M. Kravitz and the manager made arrangements for certain services to be given at that time. The oral agreement between Kravitz and the

Part 3
Contracts
Chapter 6
Nature and Classes of Contracts

1. agreement
2. competent parties
3. mutual promises
4. to do or refrain from something
5. legally enforceable

79

shop created legal obligations for both parties which neither could later disregard.

Written Contracts

A *written contract* may consist of letters, signed sales slips, notes, or other writings as long as the intentions of the parties are clearly stated. "Written" or "writing" includes printing, typewriting, or any other reduction of the parties' intentions to some tangible form. The law does not specify a particular form or language to be followed. The words used will be interpreted in their usual sense and as used in usual commercial transactions.

> Elliott wrote a short letter to Lakeside Pools, offering to work as a lifeguard for the months of June, July, and August at a salary of $450 a month. Lakeside Pools wrote to Elliott, informing her that she had the job. The two letters constitute a written agreement or contract.

It is advisable to use written contracts for all agreements of a complex nature and for those to be performed at a much later date. In this way future misunderstanding can be avoided because the terms of a written contract may not be changed without the written consent of both parties.

> Suppose you are responsible for engaging a "name" band to play at your college dance several months from now. A written contract with the bandleader or with his or her booking agent would provide definite assurance of performance. Such a contract would also make it easier for you to sue for damages should the band fail to keep the engagement.

Tape-Recorded Agreements   Electronic tapes and recordings have been upheld as sufficient to prove agreements between contracting parties. When such devices are used, the parties must be aware that the tapes are being made and consent to the recording. They should also initial the cassette or tape label for future reference, attesting that the voices so recorded are actually theirs. Tapes and recordings can, if properly evidenced, be even more acceptable proof of a contract than written memoranda are.

> Picillo discussed with Padgett Roofing Company the details of work to be done on the Picillo Building. Their discussions, as well as the agreement and conditions of work to be done and money to be paid, were recorded on Padgett's cassette recorder by mutual consent. Copies of the recording were given to both parties and properly initialed and identified for future reference. Courts in many jurisdictions would admit the recording as evidence to prove the existence of the Picillo-Padgett contract and its terms.

Implied Contracts

A gesture or even an expression of willingness on the part of one person to accept another's acts making it possible for one person to benefit at the expense of another, can constitute an *implied contract*. In such cases, it is acts by the persons involved, rather than their words, that creates the binding agreement. Picking up a newspaper and dropping the required change on the newsstand; placing a dime in a vending machine for chewing gum; and stepping onto a bus and depositing the fare in a coin box illustrate such implied contracts.

There are two kinds of implied contracts: (1) those implied in fact and (2) those implied in law.

Implied in Fact   If parties by their actions directly or indirectly imply that they intend to be contractually bound, their acts serve to create agreements that are *implied in fact*. For this type of agreement to be enforceable, it must be shown that one party provided benefits that the other willingly accepted and knew required payment in kind. For example, an act that is done for one's parents would be implied to have been done out of love and affection rather than in expectation of payment; hence, such an act would not create a contract implied in fact. By contrast, if the action was undertaken for some payment (not necessarily money), a contract that is implied in fact would result.

> Meadow Gold Dairy left a quart of milk at Lopez's home each day. Lopez took the milk into the house, used it, and returned the empty bottle to the porch. This continued for an entire month, Lopez taking in the milk and returning the bottle to its accustomed place on the porch. Lopez's willingness to accept and use the milk implied a contract relationship with Meadow Gold Dairy. Lopez would be obligated to pay for the milk.

Silence may also result in an enforceable implied contract. Watching another who mistakenly performs services which benefit you creates a burden upon you to point out the mistake to the one making it.

> Three people enter your yard and plant several fruit trees. You watch them work, knowing that they are supposed to do the work elsewhere. If you have no reason to believe that the work is being done gratuitously, you have an obligation to pay the reasonable value of the service and materials.

Implied in Law   Sometimes the court will impose contract obligations on a person who neither *knew of* nor *sought* the services of another. This is a second type of implied contract: *implied in law*.

> An unconscious woman was found on the road by a passerby who arranged to have her taken to a hospital for medical attention. When the injured woman regained consciousness, she denied any obligation to pay for the treatment, claiming that she had never entered into an agreement with the hospital.

The court may rule that an obligation exists through a *quasi contract*. A quasi contract, though not actually a contract, results from circumstances wherein a court concludes that one party is being unjustly benefited at the expense of another whose services were given in an emergency. The injured woman in the above case should be required to pay for her treatment, even though she was unconscious, as the expenses might otherwise fall upon the one who arranged for the hospital treatment.

However, while the quasi contract is designed to protect the "good Samaritan," as in the above example, it may not be used by a "do-gooder" to force payment for an act that one simply feels *should be done*.

> ▶▶ Klein, during a neighbor's absence, saw the need for cutting grass and cleaning up the absent neighbor's property. She billed the neighbor $50 for all work done. Such acts may not be justified under the concept of quasi contract.

Formal Contracts

State laws, in specific situations, require *formal contracts* if the parties are to be bound. For example, transactions for the sale of real property must be carried out through terms of a formal contract. The requirements of formality vary from state to state.

> ▶▶ Kovach signed an agreement to buy ten acres of woodland located in the Adirondack Mountains. The seller found another interested buyer who would pay a higher price for the land. Kovach had signed the sales agreement without including any representation of the SEAL. Kovach would be helpless in attempting to enforce the contract in a state that required such a formality in real estate agreements.

Originally a formal agreement was one in writing, signed and witnessed and containing the seal of both parties. A person's seal may be any mark or sign placed after the signature, intended to be the signer's seal. It does not require an impression in the document made by a ring or other mechanical device. In states that still require the seal on formal contracts, it is sufficient to write the word *SEAL* after the signature. It is also acceptable to write the letters *L.S.* after the signature; this stands for the words *locus sigilli* ("place of the seal").

Formal agreements are usually prepared by attorneys or from model forms found in reference legal guides. Technical legal language is used which may be difficult for the average person to understand. However, formal agreements need not be written in this fashion; simple, understandable English may be used. In fact, some states have passed legislation requiring all contracts to be written in language that the ordinary person may comprehend. In most cases it is the requirement of the seal that makes a contract formal, not the language used. See Fig. 6-1 for an illustration of a formal contract.

Entire, or Indivisible, Contracts

Entire contracts are those in which each part of the agreement is dependent upon the other parts for satisfactory performance. Entire contracts are not performed until all the terms of the agreement have been executed.

> ▶▶ A young man placed an order with his tailor for a new suit. The tailor called him when only the trousers were finished, demanding payment before starting to make the coat. The making of a suit is an entire contract, and the tailor may not demand payment until the suit is finished and ready for delivery.

Contracts for the purchase of sets or suites that are not usually sold as separate units are also said to be *indivisible contracts*.

A newly married couple ordered a dining-room table and six matching chairs from a furniture showroom. A few days later the dealer appeared at the door to deliver the table and only four matching chairs. The dealer explained that these were the last four chairs that were left and that identical chairs were no longer obtainable from the factory. Was the couple obligated to accept the shipment, since the dealer was acting in good faith? Were they obligated to accept the table anyway? Or might they have refused to be bound at all?

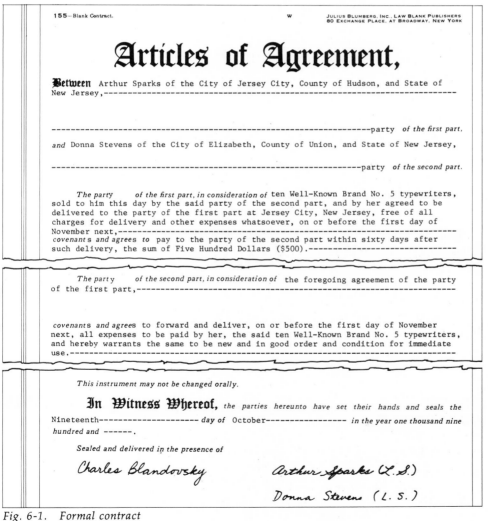

155—Blank Contract.   W   JULIUS BLUMBERG, INC., LAW BLANK PUBLISHERS
                                                                                  80 EXCHANGE PLACE, AT BROADWAY, NEW YORK

Articles of Agreement,

Between Arthur Sparks of the City of Jersey City, County of Hudson, and State of New Jersey,---

---party *of the first part,*

and Donna Stevens of the City of Elizabeth, County of Union, and State of New Jersey,

---party *of the second part.*

The party   *of the first part, in consideration of* ten Well-Known Brand No. 5 typewriters, sold to him this day by the said party of the second part, and by her agreed to be delivered to the party of the first part at Jersey City, New Jersey, free of all charges for delivery and other expenses whatsoever, on or before the first day of November next,--- *covenants and agrees to* pay to the party of the second part within sixty days after such delivery, the sum of Five Hundred Dollars ($500).------------------------------

The part*y*   *of the second part, in consideration of* the foregoing agreement of the party of the first part,---

covenants and agrees to forward and deliver, on or before the first day of November next, all expenses to be paid by her, the said ten Well-Known Brand No. 5 typewriters, and hereby warrants the same to be new and in good order and condition for immediate use.---

This instrument may not be changed orally.

In Witness Whereof, *the parties hereunto have set their hands and seals the* Nineteenth-------------------- *day of* October----------------- *in the year one thousand nine hundred and* ------.

Sealed and delivered in the presence of

Charles Blandovsky   Arthur Sparks (L.S.)

                                      Donna Stevens (L.S.)

Fig. 6-1.   Formal contract

The seller's failure to deliver all six chairs resulted in cancellation of the entire agreement. When a contract stipulates that the goods stated in the contract are to be tendered in a single delivery, payment is due only when such tender is made.

▶ The Swansons placed an order with a furniture store for the delivery of a three-piece living-room suite consisting of a sofa and two overstuffed chairs. Later, the store attempted to deliver the sofa and only one chair. The Swansons refused to accept the partial shipment on the grounds that a full suite was required to complete their home decoration plans. The Swansons were within their rights.

Another type of entire, or indivisible, contract arises when the agreement covers merchandise to be used with other related merchandise.

▶ Mason ordered a spray-gun outfit consisting of a gun and a compressor unit. The supplier delivered the compressor unit but no spray gun. Since the compressor is of no use without the gun, Mason would be legally justified in canceling the entire agreement.

Divisible Contracts

Divisible contracts contain acts or promises not dependent upon one another for satisfactory performance. Demand for payment may be made for the completed parts even though other parts have not been completed. Partial performance is permissible.

▶ The Browns ordered a living-room chair from a department store. On the same day and in the same store, they ordered a set of matched golf clubs to be sent out in the same shipment. Are the Browns obligated to pay if the store delivers the clubs but not the chair?

Contracts covering two or more independent items, each of which may stand alone, are called *divisible contracts*. One who has satisfactorily executed one part of a divisible contract may demand payment for what has been done, although other parts may still be unexecuted. The failure of the store to deliver the chair would not excuse Brown from the obligation to pay for the golf clubs. The Browns would, nevertheless, have a legal right to complain about the failure of the seller to deliver the chair and would be within their right in seeking damages in a complaint based on the terms of their contract.

Unilateral and Bilateral Contracts

If only one party to a contract is bound by a promise, the contract is referred to as a *unilateral contract*. Such a contract results when an article is to be delivered on the payment of a fixed sum of money. The promise of delivery binds the promisor to the performance of the act on payment by the promisee. A binding agreement is then in force, and the promisor may not then revoke his or her promise.

▶ Tom Simpers promised Mary Angelini $35 if Angelini would photograph a house which Simpers had for sale. No promise of performance was exacted from

Angelini, and until she started work there would be no obligation on the part of Simpers.

When both the parties to a contract are bound by the promises that they have made, the contract is referred to as a *bilateral contract*. Such a contract results when a promise is made to deliver an article at a fixed price in return for a promise to pay the price agreed on.

 Suppose, in the previous illustration, Angelini had *promised* to take the photographs in return for Simpers's promise to pay her $35. This agreement would have then consisted of *two* promises and would therefore be a bilateral contract, a promise for a promise.

STATUS OF CONTRACTS

At any certain moment, contracts may be completed, partially completed, or awaiting initial action.

 Russell's co-worker Tompkins agreed to obtain an expensive fishing rod for Russell at a special discount from a friend in the sporting goods business. Russell gave Tompkins a check for the price of the rod. What type of contract is this? Is the contract completed, or are there further acts to be performed by one or both of the parties?

Executory Contracts

The *present status* of a contract is either executory or executed. Contracts which have not yet been fully performed by the parties are called *executory contracts*. They may be completely executory, in which case nothing has been done; or they may be partly executory, in which case the contract is partially complete.

 Valdez contracted with the Atlantic Boat Works for the painting and calking of a powerboat. The firm completed the work satisfactorily and delivered the boat to Valdez. A bill for the work was mailed to him. This contract is executory on the part of Valdez and executed on the part of the boat works. The contract will remain executory until Valdez has paid the bill.

Executed Contracts

Contracts whose terms have been completely and satisfactorily carried out by both parties are *executed contracts*. Such contracts are no longer active agreements and are valuable only if a dispute about the agreement occurs at a later time.

 Palmero hired a mechanic to install a spotlight on a new car. The mechanic was paid when the job was completed. This contract is now executed, with no part remaining uncompleted.

ENFORCEABILITY OF CONTRACTS

Valid Contracts

With respect to enforceability, a contract may be *voidable, void,* or *valid*. A *valid contract* is one that meets all legal requirements for the type of agreement involved. Such a contract is fully enforceable by either party.

> Feldman made her application for health and accident insurance. A policy was issued and premiums paid. Six months later she was confined to the hospital for surgery. Since she held a valid agreement with the insurance company, payments would be made to her according to schedules established in the policy. Refusal to make payments could result in a complaint to the state insurance commission as well as a civil action for damages.

Voidable Contracts

The law provides for contracts which contain contestable features but are otherwise legal in subject matter and operation. Contracts in this category are considered valid until the injured party declares them to be otherwise. Only the injured party has the right to cancel a *voidable* agreement.

> Rice left her car at a service station to have a set of heavy plastic seat covers installed. When she returned to pick up the car, she found that a set of less expensive cloth covers had been installed instead.

The law would permit Rice to void the original agreement and insist on the removal of the unwanted covers; or she may accept the cloth covers with a suitable price adjustment. This contract is voidable.

> Watkins offers to sell you a used typewriter for $25, assuring you that it is in good operating condition. You accept the offer and take the typewriter home. After you use the machine awhile, you find it does not operate satisfactorily and needs considerable repair work to make it usable.

The same principle of law as in the Rice case permits you to cancel your agreement with Watkins for the purchase of the typewriter. The machine does not work as represented; you are the injured party and can cancel this voidable contract. Or you may choose to keep the typewriter if Watkins adjusts the price or has the machine repaired to your satisfaction.

> Fulmer sold Jackson a car on which he received a down payment. No additional payments were made to Fulmer over a period of three years, although numerous requests and threats of suit had been made in an effort to collect the debt. State law gave Jackson a defense against payment in that the statute of limitations for collections of open accounts outlawed such debts after three years had passed. Thus, what was originally a valid enforceable agreement has now been rendered unenforceable due to a state law and the passing of time.

(handwritten in margin:) when one or more of the parties can get out of the contract it is voidable (numerous)

Void Contracts

Unlike a voidable contract, a contract that is void is illegal or unenforceable from its inception. Usually this is the case where the contract lacks one or more requisites of a valid contract—mutual assent, capable parties, consideration, and legal subject matter. These are discussed further in the following chapters.

Unconscionable Agreements

Under the Uniform Commercial Code, a court may now declare a contract to be voidable as unconscionable (see Chapter 4). An *unconscionable agreement* is one in which the terms are so clearly unreasonable and contrary to the interests of a contracting party as to render the contract void and unenforceable. Taking unfair advantage of a person's inability to speak English or of someone's clearly inferior bargaining position could come within the UCC definition of "unconscionable."

Questions for Review and Discussion

1. What are the two kinds of implied contracts? Give an example of each.

2. (*a*) What is a seal? (*b*) What kind of contract requires a seal? (*c*) How would you make a seal on an instrument that you were required to sign and seal?

3. What is a contract?

4. How are the terms of an agreement in an implied contract ascertained? In an express contract?

5. What is the difference between the following contracts: (*a*) executory contract and executed contract, (*b*) formal contract and simple contract?

6. (*a*) What is a voidable contract? (*b*) Who has the right to decide the status of a voidable contract?

7. (*a*) What is meant by writing when used in relation to a contract? (*b*) Must legal terms be used in a contract?

8. What is a divisible contract? An entire contract? Give an example of each.

9. How does a quasi contract differ from a contract in the ordinary sense?

10. Under what two conditions should a contract be in writing rather than oral?

Analyzing Cases

1. While the Johnsons were at home, an oil truck drove into their driveway and delivered 275 gallons of oil into their oil tank. Mr. Johnson permitted the driver to complete the delivery and then went outside and said, "Thanks, old man, for the gift of the oil." Actually, the driver had made a mistake. The delivery was to have been made at another house on the same street. Will the oil company be successful in an action against Johnson for the price of the oil? Explain.
• See also *Spencer* v. *Spencer*, 181 Mass. 471.

yes, implied in fact

2. Mr. Cain ordered a suit and a topcoat. When the garments were delivered, the trousers did not match the jacket of the suit. However, the topcoat was the one Cain had ordered. Must Cain pay for both the suit and the topcoat; either one of them; or neither? Explain. • See also *Hjorth* v. *Albert Lea Machinery Co.*, 142 Minn. 387. *just topcoat, divisible contract*

3. Mr. Strong buys a new car but cannot pay cash for it. The finance company agrees to accept Strong's note and allows him to pay for the car in eighteen installments. The car dealer holds the title to the car until the payments are completed. Is this an executed or an executory contract? Explain. • See also *Trapani* v. *Universal Credit Co.*, 151 Kan. 715 *when it is paid for it is executed.*

4. A color television set was delivered to Olsen by TV Specialties, Inc. The bill was marked "Paid In Full." Olsen had the set brought into the house, signing the delivery receipt. The set was supposed to have been delivered to another Olsen who lived in the same apartment building. What is Olsen's responsibility to the TV Specialties Company? Explain. • See also *Moser* v. *Milner Hotels*, 6 N.J. 278. *to take reasonable care of the tv until the other Olsen gets it*

5. Rothstein found an injured person lying unconscious on the street late one evening. Rothstein called a physician who ordered an ambulance and had the injured person taken to the hospital. Medical and hospital bills over a three-day period totaled $1,100. Is Rothstein or the patient responsible for the bills submitted? Explain. *patient, implied in law (quasi contract)*

6. Morea ordered a new Mercedes from European Imports, Inc. The agreement was oral, due to the long-time association of Morea with European Imports. Morea selected the body style, color of paint, transmission option, leather upholstery, and other options available at added cost. When the car was delivered, it lacked several of the accessories and options Morea had ordered. What kind of contract should Morea have had with European Imports? Why? *written*

Legal Reasoning and Business Judgment

Analyze the legal aspects of these business problems. Suggest possible solutions.

1. The purchasing department of your company ordered five leather chairs and other matching pieces to be installed in the president's office. The furniture was to be billed as one complete order, totaling $4,100. When it was delivered, only four chairs were available, and it was explained that it would take another three months before the other chair could be obtained. What would you recommend to the purchasing department as a solution to this problem?

2. During a visit by prospective customers to the salesroom of your firm, one of the visitors was struck by an illness that rendered her unconscious. A quick discussion ensued as to what responsibilities the company would have in ordering a physician and sending the guest to the hospital for treatment. Would the firm be legally responsible for these expenses? *no, unless they caused the illness.*

3. Carpenters arrived at your company's plant and started immediately to remove a high fence that management had previously decided to replace with a metal web fence. The crew went about their work for several days with the full knowledge of the plant manager, who did not disturb them. It later developed that a mistake had been made, and the crew was supposed to have been working at a different plant site. What responsibilities, if any, would your firm have to the workers who made such extensive repairs? *reasonable value or full cost implied in fact*

Chapter 7
Offer
and
Acceptance

People may agree on almost any matter without incurring legal obligations to one another. They may agree that a certain person is attractive, that a new car has excellent design features, or that one school is better than another. This type of simple agreement is not a contract. Even though the parties reach faulty conclusions, no legal injury is done for which damages may be sought.

A contract not only contains an agreement but also has legally enforceable obligations. These obligations are willingly accepted in return for some benefit to be enjoyed.

> The O'Keefes had invited three couples to their home for dinner. They made careful and expensive preparations for the dinner party, but the guests never arrived, nor did they offer any apologies or explanations.
>
> The Pilgrim Dining Room had accepted a reservation for a party of three couples who ordered a special dinner to be served. The management made extensive preparations for the guests, but they neither arrived nor canceled the reservation.

These two situations have much in common. Are they contracts? Social engagements are usually considered to be simple agreements without legal obligation. The O'Keefes had arranged a social engagement that involved no legal responsibilities on either side. However, the Pilgrim Dining Room is operating a business, and the reservation would be considered a legally enforceable agreement, or contract.

The ability to recognize a contract is important in the management of a business, a home, or one's personal life. To be legally enforceable, a contract must contain the following four requisites:

☐ Mutual assent or agreement
☐ Competent parties
☐ Consideration
☐ Valid subject matter

A court will not enforce any agreement that does not contain these four essential elements, to be discussed in this chapter and the other chapters in this section.

MUTUAL ASSENT

Before two or more people conclude the terms of an agreement, much discussion and haggling may take place. The final conclusion upon which both agree is the basis of any contract and is called their *mutual assent*. A contract for sale of goods may be made in any manner sufficient to show agreement, including conduct by both parties which recognizes the existence of such a contract. Proposals, counterproposals, and spirited bargaining gradually lead both parties to a satisfactory, acceptable position. Reaching a mutually acceptable agreement may take several weeks or but a few minutes. The agreement may be written, oral, or implied.

For the mutual assent to exist:

- ☐ There must be an offer.
- ☐ There must be an acceptance of the offer.

The Offer

An *offer* is a proposal made by one party to another indicating a willingness to enter into a contract. The one making the offer is the *offeror*; the one to whom it is made is the *offeree*.

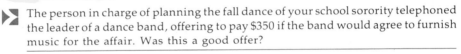 The person in charge of planning the fall dance of your school sorority telephoned the leader of a dance band, offering to pay $350 if the band would agree to furnish music for the affair. Was this a good offer?

Yes. It contained all the requisites:

- ☐ Communication
- ☐ Serious intent
- ☐ Clarity

Communication   The proposal must be conveyed by the offeror and received by the offeree. Communication may be by telephone, letter, telegram, or the like. Communication may also be implied by the acts of the offeror, such as depositing a coin in a vending machine. The language or acts of the offeror must be such that they are understood by the other party.

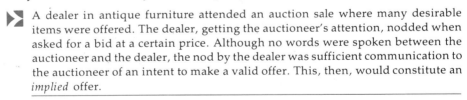 A dealer in antique furniture attended an auction sale where many desirable items were offered. The dealer, getting the auctioneer's attention, nodded when asked for a bid at a certain price. Although no words were spoken between the auctioneer and the dealer, the nod by the dealer was sufficient communication to the auctioneer of an intent to make a valid offer. This, then, would constitute an *implied* offer.

A person signing a contract is *presumed* to have read and understood all its contents. He or she is therefore obligated by all its terms. A *presumption* is a fact that the courts accept as true until proved otherwise.

Toledano received an invitation to become a member of a book club. She signed a membership card that stated she would receive a free book. She was later required by the club to buy four other books. This obligation was contained on the signed membership card, which Toledano did not bother to read. Must she buy the four books?

She would be. Under such circumstances, the law is realistic, recognizing that it would be much too difficult for the offeror (the book club) to prove that the offeree (Toledano) had actually read all the conditions of membership recited in the membership card. A court will simply *presume* that she had read all the terms and would hold her liable for the payments.

Serious Intent   Offers made in jest, in anger or rage, or in other ways indicating a lack of seriousness or reason are not valid.

> Professor Allen was very much annoyed that a favorite reference book was missing from her office library. In the presence of several students, she said, "I'll give $1,000 to find out who always borrows that book just when I want to use it." Was this a good offer? If one of the students learns who the borrower was, must the professor pay the promised reward?

The fact that the professor was emotionally upset prevented her from expressing her real intent in regard to finding the student who borrowed the book. Thus, no true meeting of the minds could have resulted, and there was no valid offer.

Lack of serious intent does not invalidate an offer unless such a condition is apparent to both the offeror and the offeree.

> Luther, intending to play a joke, offered his expensive watch to Alvarez for $10. Alvarez did not realize that Luther was joking and accepted the offer, tendering $10 to Luther. Luther will not be permitted to avoid the consequences of this properly communicated and seemingly serious offer.

Had Alvarez been aware of Luther's joke, would a contract have arisen? No. When both parties enter an agreement in the spirit of fun, mutual assent has not been reached.

Clarity   Unless both parties have sufficient information to make the proposal clear and understandable, there is no valid offer.

> A college student said to a friend, "I'm running short of funds this term. I think I'll have to sell my car. Do you know anyone who'd like to buy it?" "Sure, I'll buy it!" the friend replied.

In the above case no mention was made of price, terms, delivery, or other conditions vital to the sale. As a general rule, remember that an offer should include points similar to those covered in the lead of a good newspaper story—*who, what, when, where, how much*—if it is to be clear, definite, and certain.

In certain instances an offer is valid even though the price is not included if the agreement pertains to matters that would enable the court to fix a reasonable price in view of all surrounding circumstances.

> A large poultry farm contracted to sell 1,500 dozen eggs to a local supermarket, delivery to be made on October 29. The parties neglected to include the price in their agreement. A court could declare the offer to be valid, setting the price at the wholesale price in the market on October 29.

In other cases the parties may agree to be bound to an agreement in which they knowingly neglect to include the price or have not determined this matter at the time the agreement was made:

> Husfelt signed an agreement reserving a room in a college dormitory for the September term. The dorm fees had not been determined or published at the time the reservation was made, but both Husfelt and the college agreed that the contract would be binding.

Although lacking in definiteness, the agreement would be enforceable. However, if the room charge represented an unreasonable increase over the dormitory room fee charged the previous term, the agreement could be voided.

When it is agreed that the parties are not to be bound until after the price is fixed, neither party is bound until that is done. If, in anticipation of a satisfactory price, some goods are delivered to the buyer and accepted, he or she must return them if not satisfied with the price that is subsequently established. If it is impossible to return them, the buyer must pay a price determined by the court to be reasonable.

Offers to Collective Groups   A valid offer may be made either to an individual or to a group acting as an organized body.

> A sales representative met with the fifty members of a college history club. The representative offered the group a special price on a set of encyclopedias to be used in the club's reference library. After a contract had been made, the club attempted to void its obligation on the ground that an offer had not been made. The court held that the proposal made to the club as a unit did constitute an offer, making the contract enforceable.

In this case it was particularly fitting that the offer be made to the collective group, since the purchase was to be made for the common use of all members and not for any one individual in the assembled group.

Bids or Estimates   Calls for bids or estimates for work to be done or materials to be furnished do not bind the person calling for the bids to give the work to the contractor submitting the lowest bid. Such calls for bids are not offers but rather represent requests for offers, to be accepted or rejected by the caller. The caller usually reserves the right to determine whether the lowest bidder has the necessary ability, skills, and financial stability to carry out the proposed agreement and to reject a low bid if this is not the case. Statutes in some states, however, require that if a bid on a public contract is accepted, the bid or offer of the lowest and best bidder must be the one accepted.

Printed Notices   Printed notices on steamship and railroad tickets, parking lot claim checks, insurance policies, telegraph blanks, and similar forms are considered to be part of the communicated offer, even if they are not read. The stipulations on baggage checks, however, must be called to the attention of the holders; and the printed statements on the letter paper on which an offer is written must be referred to in the body of the offer to be considered as having been communicated. Notices on parking lot claim tickets are considered part of the contract only if written or printed in a conspicuous manner.

A wholesale stationery company wrote all contracts with supply houses and made all offers to retailers on letter paper on which there was printed, in small type at the bottom of the paper, the following statement: "This company reserves the right to cancel the above offer, or contract, any time within five days from the date made, because of changing markets and demands."

It was held that statements such as this have no legal effect unless specifically referred to in the body of the writing of the contract or offer.

Invitations to Trade   Offers made by individuals and groups to one another are not to be confused with advertising, which is meant to attract persons who may be interested in the sale or purchase of goods and services.

Abramowitz heard a television announcement in which a nearby store advertised electric razors for $15. He went to the store and offered to buy a razor, tendering his money to the clerk. He was told that the price had been increased to $35. Was the store obligated to sell Abramowitz the razor at the advertised price?

The typical television announcement, as well as other common forms of advertising, such as the sale advertised in the newspaper, the circular letter, and the mail-order catalog is merely an invitation to trade. The potential customer is invited to come in and do business. He or she is the one who actually takes the first legal step toward the sale. He or she makes an offer to buy at the advertised price. Abramowitz, therefore, has made no contract with the store. He merely made it an offer to purchase the razor for $15, which the store did not accept. Many states have enacted laws which make it a misdemeanor to make intentionally misleading or false statements in advertising of any kind.

Public Offers   Attempts to communicate proposals to persons of unknown identify through advertising are held to be valid offers.

Klein, an attorney, lost a briefcase containing many valuable documents. She advertised in the *Evening News*, offering a reward of $25 to the person who would return the briefcase and contents to her. Is Klein making a valid offer when her proposal is being communicated to the 35,000 readers of the *Evening News*?

Although Klein's offer may be read by 35,000 people, the purpose of the advertisement is to seek out only one person—the one who found the briefcase. Therefore it is a valid offer. Because the identity of the offeree is not known, such offers can be made in no other way and are effective in creating mutual assent.

Acceptance of the Offer

The second major element in establishing mutual assent is acceptance of the offer. Acceptance is fully achieved when the offer has been accepted by the offeree. It requires communication of such intent to the offeror and, except as provided by the Uniform Commercial Code, total agreement with the terms of the offer as made.

Communication of Acceptance   Communication of acceptance of an offer may be either expressed or implied. In an *expressed acceptance* the offeree may use any method of communication that he or she chooses, unless the offer states that acceptance must be made in a particular manner. A stipulation such as "Reply by Western Union" or "Reply by return mail" included in the offer constitutes the prescribed manner of acceptance. Communication of acceptance to the offeror completes the agreement and thereby binds the parties to a contract.

> The Electronic Development Corporation sent a telegram to the New England Battery Company offering to purchase 100 high-amperage batteries at a quoted price of $105 per unit. The battery firm accepted this offer in a letter mailed the same day the offer was received. Use of the mail in communicating the acceptance conforms to the Uniform Commercial Code and to general custom.

When the acceptance is communicated by the offeree through the same agency that was used in communicating the offer, an agreement is said to have been completed as soon as the acceptance was sent. In the above case, had the acceptance been communicated by a telegram, it would have been completed as soon as the offeree filed the telegram with the telegraph company. In situations like this it is good practice to request a receipt from the communicating agent, whether it be the telegraph company, the postal system, or any other agency. The receipt should show the date and exact time of delivery of the acceptance to such an agent. Such evidence may be valuable if a misunderstanding later arises between the parties as to when the acceptance was sent and the agreement completed.

> Kowalski mailed an offer to Clark in which he proposed to sell Clark valuable surplus machinery at a special price of $35,000. Clark immediately wrote and mailed his acceptance to Kowalski, obtaining a receipt from the postal clerk indicating the date and time of the mailing. Should the acceptance letter be lost or delayed, Clark would suffer no loss because his acceptance was complete when it was delivered to the post office.

The question of the status of an acceptance in cases in which the offeree successfully recovers his or her letter from the post office *before it is delivered* has received much consideration in the courts. The courts have reached no firm conclusion in cases decided so far. Postal laws and regulations also fail to provide a clear answer to this problem. It has been held that even though the offeree intercepts the letter, an acceptance deposited in the mail is nevertheless effective. The acceptance may not then, therefore, be invalidated by the offeree. Some courts, however, have taken an opposite view.

Should the offeree select a different means of communicating his or her acceptance than was used by the offeror, no mutual agreement would be reached until the acceptance reached the offeror in person, or the offeror's home or office.

▶ Suppose, in the above case, Clark decided to send his acceptance by telegram. The acceptance would have no effect until received by Kowalski. Clark has by this change of agency assumed all risks involved in any failure of communications resulting in loss or delay of his message of acceptance.

To secure uniformity in the acceptance of offers and to avoid confusion in the minds of the parties, it is now customary to conclude the written offer with the following stipulation: "The acceptance of this offer will not take effect until the acceptance has been received at the office of the offeror." Such a statement in the offer protects the offeror in the event that an acceptance is properly sent but is lost or delayed in delivery.

A qualified or a conditional acceptance acts as a rejection of the offer. This type of reply may be treated as a *counteroffer*, but it will not bind the parties to an agreement based upon the original offer.

▶ A dealer offered to sell Benson a television set for $435, delivered and installed. Benson replied that he would take the set if the dealer would repair his damaged antenna as part of the free installation service. Does this action result in mutual agreement?

Benson's acceptance was conditional and qualified, resulting in the rejection of the original offer. Benson is actually making another offer, or a counteroffer, and the dealer is free to accept or reject it as he or she chooses.

However, in transactions *between merchants* counteroffers may be made without the effect of invalidating or rejecting the original offer. By *merchants* is meant parties other than those purchasing from a retail outlet; thus, transactions between business people and other business people, wholesalers and retailers, and the like are transactions between merchants. Additional terms proposed by the offeree in such cases become a part of the contract, unless (1) the original offer expressly limits acceptance to the terms of the offer, (2) the additional terms materially alter the original offer, or (3) notification of objection to them has already been given or is given within a reasonable time after notice of them is received.

▶ American Plastics Company made on offer to sell a special type of plastic mold at a price of 20 cents each in lots of 5,000. The offer contained the following: "The terms of this offer are final and not open to negotiation or alteration." Any proposed change would have no effect upon American Plastics' proposal.

A person may also indicate acceptance of a valid offer by his or her actions. This is known as an *implied acceptance*.

▶ While sitting on her front porch, Criscioni watched three men paint a fence on her property. The men later learned that they had made a mistake. The fence they were to have painted was in the next block. Did a contract arise between Criscioni and the painters?

Criscioni, by her toleration of the trespassers and by her failure to protest, implied acceptance of obligation for the work done. She will be required to pay the reasonable value of the work and the materials used.

► Suppose, in the above case, Criscioni had not been at home, and she did not discover that the fence had been painted until she returned in the evening. Would Criscioni have had an obligation to pay the painters for their work under these circumstances?

Criscioni would not be obligated in this situation. She did not learn of the benefits bestowed until after they had been completed. There had been no communication of the painters' offer and no expressed or implied acceptance by Criscioni of the work done.

Silence as a Means of Acceptance   Silence may indicate assent, provided both parties understand and agree that this is to be the means of acceptance.

► A vacuum cleaner sales representative demonstrated one of the latest-model cleaners at Brown's house. Brown said that she was interested in buying the cleaner but would have to consult her husband before deciding. The representative then offered to leave the machine with Brown, saying, "I'll leave it here so that you can show it to your husband. If I don't hear from you by the end of the month, I'll send you a bill for the machine." She agreed. A month passed, and the representative's bill arrived. Is Brown obligated for the price of the vacuum cleaner?

By her silence Brown accepted the sales representative's offer and would be liable under the agreement discussed with the representative. Both parties had agreed that continued silence would be the manner of acceptance.

However, silence as an indication of approval may not be imposed without the consent of both parties.

► Brown received a letter that said, "If we do not hear from you within ten days, we will ship the vacuum cleaner described in the enclosed folder and bill you for $140." In this case Brown would have no obligation either to buy the cleaner or to communicate with the seller, because the shipment was made without her previous consent.

Unordered Merchandise   The delivery of merchandise not ordered represents nothing more than an offer. Under existing postal regulations, the receiver of unordered merchandise may treat such goods as a gift; that is, the receiver has the right to dispose of the merchandise without fear of legal reprisal. If such goods are delivered by a private parcel service, however, postal regulations do not apply. In that case, the receiver may keep the goods for a reasonable time and then pay for them or dispose of them as desired. What constitutes a reasonable time depends on the type of goods involved.

► Daniels received a box of greeting cards in the mail from a firm in Georgia. Enclosed in the box was a letter stating, "You may either mail $5 for the cards or return them to the sender within ten days." Under postal regulations, Daniels is not obligated to do either of these things. The cards are considered to be a gift, which Daniels may use in any way desired. She may even destroy the cards if she wishes.

Termination of the Offer

What happens to an offer if it is not accepted by the offeree? Does it remain in force indefinitely? Does the offeror have any further control over the offer that he or she has made once it has been communicated? The offeror *does* have a continuing control, which may be exercised in the event that the offeree does not directly refuse the proposal.

Rejection of Offer   The refusal of an offer by the one to whom it is directed and communicated is a *rejection*. Once an offer has been rejected by the offeree, he or she cannot attempt to accept it later. Rejection terminates for all time the existence of an offer.

> Dr. Baker offered a partnership in his private practice to Dr. Kline, a young surgeon. Kline, hoping to secure a more favorable opportunity, declined Baker's offer. He later wrote to Baker, saying that he had reconsidered the matter and was now accepting the offer previously made. Did a contract arise? The answer is no, as Kline's rejection ended the offer, and the acceptance letter had no validity.

Counteroffer   A qualified or conditional acceptance of another's offer acts as a rejection and is a *counteroffer*.

> A friend offered to sell Fernandez a typewriter for $185 in cash. Fernandez replied, saying, "I'll pay you $35 now and give you the balance at the end of the month." The conditions of payment added by Fernandez constitute a counteroffer, thus invalidating the original offer and replacing it with a new one made by him.

Exceptions to this rule have been covered previously in the treatment of acceptance of an offer.

Revocation of Offer   An offer that has been neither accepted nor rejected can be *revoked* or *withdrawn* by the offeror. After an offer is revoked, it may not be acted upon by the offeree. *The offeror always has the right to withdraw his or her offer at any time up until the time it is accepted.* Offers may be revoked in any one of four ways:

- [ ] By communication
- [ ] Automatically
- [ ] By passing of more than a reasonable time
- [ ] Through the death or insanity of the offeror

Revocation by Communication   The offeror may revoke his or her offer at any time merely *by communication* of that intention to the other party. However, the communication must be completed before the other party has accepted; otherwise, it will have no effect upon the offer already accepted. Communication may occur through direct notice to the offeree or through information which may reach the offeree in any other manner. It is important only that the offeree know that the offer no longer is held out.

▶ You are offered a position as lifeguard for the summer. Before giving an answer, you wish to think about the offer for a few days. You finally make up your mind to accept, but a few minutes before you notify the resort manager, you receive a postal card telling you that another individual has been given the job.

The manager was within his or her rights in withdrawing the original offer. Notice of revocation reached you before you had accepted the offer. Therefore, no legal basis for complaint could be shown by the loss of your right to the job.

Automatic Revocation   An offer is terminated *automatically* by expiration of the time limit if one is specified.

▶ Mears selected an expensive formal gown which the manager of a fashionable shop agreed to hold for her until she decided to make the purchase. The agreement provided that the shop would give Mears until Wednesday afternoon to make up her mind.

The shop would have no further obligation to *communicate* with Mears. Unless she accepted the offer within the time specified, it would automatically revoke itself according to its own terms. Even though a specific time period was stipulated, the offeror is permitted to revoke an offer at will at any time. To do this, however, the offeror must communicate his or her intended revocation.

▶ On Tuesday afternoon the shop had the opportunity to sell to Jarvis the gown being held for Mears. Jarvis was prepared to pay cash and close the deal at once. The manager of the shop called Mears and informed her that the shop was revoking its offer to her. Suppose Mears objected, saying that she had until Wednesday afternoon to make up her mind?

An offeror, again, has the right to revoke an offer *any time up until the time the offer is accepted*. The manager, therefore, had the legal right to revoke the offer through communication.

An exception to this rule occurs when the offeree ''binds the bargain'' by giving the offeror money or something of value for the offeror's promise to keep an offer open. This is known as an *option*, as distinguished from a simple offer. If money is given to the offeror in this type of transaction, it is known as *earnest money*.

▶ Bettmann, an auto mechanic, was offered a high-grade compression gauge for $15. Before saying yes, Bettmann wanted to check other gauges available at competing stores. To assure that the first offer would still be available, he gave the owner $3 to keep the offer open. Thus, the offer became a binding agreement between the two parties, pending the outcome of the buyer's decision.

A seller has no legal responsibility to return the earnest money should the buyer decide not to make a purchase. For the sake of goodwill, however, a merchant often returns the buyer's money or gives a credit slip in the amount on deposit.

Revocation by Passing of Time   As a general rule, offers do not continue in effect very long after they have been made. When a definite time period has not

[handwritten margin note: the offer is revoked when it is recieved / the offer is accepted when it is sent]

been stated or when no option has been given, an offer will terminate *after a reasonable time has elapsed*.

> Three days before the opening of the new term, Kahn offered to sell a set of used books to Jones, who would need them in her courses. Jones was not sure that she wanted the books, and Kahn said, "Think the matter over and let me know whether you want them." Jones did not announce her acceptance until the first day of the new term. In the meantime Kahn had sold the books to another student. Was the offer to Jones still in effect when she informed the offeror of her intention to buy?

In deciding what is a reasonable amount of time, time is considered as being relative, depending upon all the circumstances of the offer. Experience and transactions between the parties, the subject matter of the offer, its perishable qualities, anticipated price fluctuations, intended usage, and other factors will be considered in the determination of what would be a reasonable time.

What about the used books? Obviously, Jones would have had to make some reply before the first day of the new term. She had received an offer three days earlier. Because of the time element and the limited opportunity to sell used books, Kahn would not be expected to continue her offer indefinitely. Jones's acceptance was made too late. The offer had lapsed owing to the passage of more than a reasonable time.

A *unilateral offer* is conditioned upon the actual commencement of a task within a reasonable period of time. It is *accepted by the act of the offeree's commencing performance* of the work or service desired by the offeror. Unless performance is started within a reasonable period of time or if the offeror has not received notice of the acceptance, the offeror may treat the offer as having lapsed prior to acceptance.

> Willis said to Burns, "I will pay you $350 if you will survey my property and prepare an accurate plan suitable for filing in the office of the registrar of deeds." Burns replied, saying, "I am busy at present, but if I have the opportunity I will do the job for you." Nearly four months later Burns went to the Willis property and started the survey. Willis may treat the offer as having been revoked, and Burns's belated acceptance will not bind Willis.

Revocation by Death or Insanity   Because an offer is the property of the one who makes it, it is revoked immediately upon the death of the offeror.

> Fakuda offered to sell his house to Sullivan in a letter containing a description of the property and the terms of the sale. Sullivan was very much interested and planned to accept the offer. However, prior to actual acceptance by Sullivan, Fakuda was killed in an auto accident. The offer lapsed when Fakuda was killed. A contract could not now result from Sullivan's acceptance.

The offer ceased to exist at the moment of Fakuda's death because it would have been impossible to achieve mutual assent. Acceptance of an offer must be communicated to an offeror. Death precludes this possibility, and the offer is automatically revoked. Revocation occurs at the moment of death, and it is not necessary that the fact be communicated to the offeree.

Insanity, which robs a person of his or her reason, also revokes offers that may have been previously made. A person declared insane is incompetent to make contracts of any kind. All legal matters must be handled for incompetents by a duly appointed guardian.

Irrevocable Offers *Irrevocable offers* or so-called "firm offers" are those made by a merchant "in a signed writing which by its terms gives assurance that [the offer] will be held open." *Dealings between merchants* under the Uniform Commercial Code are firm offers. A wholesale house may not revoke at will offers made to dealers when and if retailers are dependent on such offers in developing marketing plans for store merchandise. The rationale for the concept of irrevocable offers derives from the respected legal doctrine of *promissory estoppel*: One who has made an offer may not rescind it at the expense of another who acts, relies upon, and makes commitments on the basis of such offers.

 Schmitt, owner of a clothing store, received an offer from Modern Shirt Company, offering oxford-cloth shirts at $2.10 each in dozen lots. Schmitt went ahead with plans for a sale, using advertising about the shirts as "leaders" to draw customers into the store.

The shirt company is obligated to hold the offer open for a reasonable length of time and may not revoke the offer without consideration of Schmitt's position. Nor may Schmitt delay action in accepting the company's offer beyond a reasonable time.

ILLEGAL ASSENT OF CONTRACTING PARTIES

After mutual assent has been achieved, does the law protect the contracting parties in their contractual relationship? If one or the other party discovers that he or she has been cheated or discovers that a mistake has placed him or her at a great disadvantage, must that party continue to be bound by the terms of the agreement?

Each party to a contract is protected from the chicanery of the other or from the mistakes that may have crept into their agreements. Six defects involving mutual assent are recognized by the courts, and those suffering under any of these defects will be given protection from the demands made by the other party to an agreement. The defects which may void mutual agreement are fraud, misrepresentation, mistake, undue influence, and duress. Under certain circumstances, a contract is also voidable on the grounds of unconscionability (see Chapter 4).

Fraud

Fraud is either a wrongful statement or a concealment pertinent to the subject matter of a contract knowingly and intentionally made to the damage of the other party. Fraud, if proved, invalidates any contract and makes the wrongdoer liable to the injured party for all losses plus damages.

To dissolve mutual assent on the claim of fraud, the complaining party must prove:

- ☐ That the other party made a false statement.
- ☐ That the false statement was intentionally and knowingly made.
- ☐ That he or she made the false statement with the intent that the other party rely on it.
- ☐ That the complaining party did rely on the false statement.
- ☐ That the complaining party was damaged by the false statement.

> ►► The Murphys, a young married couple, purchased a new dining-room suite from a furniture store. While showing them a suite, the salesperson said, "This furniture is constructed of genuine New England maple and is handmade." Shortly after the Murphys bought the set, they discovered that the pieces were of a soft wood with a laminated New England maple appearance. They also discovered that the furniture had been mass-produced. Were the Murphys bound by their agreement with the furniture store?

In this case, it is clear that (1) the salesperson made a false statement in representing the dining-room set as solid New England maple and handmade, (2) he was in a position to know that these statements were not true, (3) he made the statements with the intent that the Murphys might rely upon them, (4) the young couple did rely upon the salesperson's statements, and (5) they suffered damages. The agreement, therefore is voidable, and the Murphys may demand return of all money paid as well as payment for other damages they may have suffered as a result of the seller's fraudulent statements and acts.

Statements of opinion, or a sales representative's "puffing," are not considered to be material statements of fact, which are required in proving fraud.

> ►► In describing the dining-room set the salesperson also said, "This is the finest buy in town and could not be duplicated elsewhere for twice the price. It is sold especially to those who must get the most for their money and are still aware of style and value."

Although statements such as these probably influence a buyer, they are considered to be nothing more than persuasive statements; in and of themselves they will not destroy mutual assent. Moreover, if a buyer makes his or her own investigation of the seller's claims and does not rely upon them, fraud cannot be proved.

> ►► Suppose the Murphys had paid a cabinetmaker $5 to visit the furniture store and examine the furniture. If, after learning of the true quality of the merchandise, the Murphys still made the purchase, could they recover their money by claiming fraud?

Since in this case the Murphys clearly *did not rely* on the seller's statements, any action brought by them to dissolve the contract on the basis of fraud would fail.

The *intentional concealment* of known defects or undesirable features of merchandise by the seller is considered as fraudulent as the making of a false statement.

 While the young couple were examining the dining-room furniture, the salesperson covered up a deep scratch on the tabletop by placing a sales pad over it. Such an intentional concealment of an obvious defect would create grounds for the dissolution of the agreement on the grounds of fraud.

In actions based on fraud, the complaining party is able to use all legal remedies available in actions for nonfraudulent breach. The complaining party's right to a claim for damages is not weakened or dismissed by the action of rejecting or returning the goods nor by the rescinding of the sales contract for any goods in question.

Misrepresentation

When one party makes a false statement, *believing it to be true*, and the other party is injured thereby, the contract may be dissolved on the ground of *misrepresentation*. In misrepresentation, there is nothing to indicate any intentional wrong by the one making the statement.

 While at the furniture store, Murphy bought a table radio. "This is a ten-transistor model," the salesperson told him. Later, at home, Murphy discovered that the set had only six transistors. Upon investigation, it was found that a stock clerk had accidentally attached the wrong price tag and specifications sheet to the radio when it was placed on the salesroom floor. May Murphy sue the store on a claim of fraud?

No. In the case above, the salesperson actually believed that the radio was a ten-transistor model. The salesperson and the store, however, may be held liable for misrepresentation. The successful complainant in a contract action based on misrepresentation will receive no damage award. The court merely returns both parties to their original positions, one returning the money paid and the other returning the merchandise sold.

Undue Influence

Undue influence is the use of a position of superiority or control over another as a means of coercing that person into entering into an agreement. The coercion in such situations is entirely mental, and no physical force or threats are used. The relationship between employer and employee, teacher and student, and doctor and patient could create situations involving undue influence.

 Gomez received a visit from his supervisor one evening. "I always like to know that my men are well covered by life insurance," the supervisor said, "and I have made it a practice to sell them sizable policies after they have started working for the company. I have found that the men who take policies from me are the ones who really get ahead with the firm." Because of these statements, Gomez thought it best to buy a policy from his supervisor, and he applied for a $10,000 policy,

suggested as the minimum that he should carry. May this agreement be rescinded by Gomez should he desire to do so?

The sale of the insurance was accomplished through the use of the favored
position the supervisor had in relation to Gomez's employment and future
career. Any agreement made under such conditions could not be said to have
been freely entered into, and the complaining party would have the right to have
the contract obligation dissolved. Undue influence always involves the use of
mental coercion.

Duress

The use of the threat of force against a person or his or her family or property is
known as *duress*. When such acts are used to cause a party to enter into a
contractual agreement, the agreement may be dissolved on the grounds that there
had never been a free and willing meeting of the minds between the two parties.

▶︎ The owner of a shopping mall was asked to buy insurance to cover possible
breakage of the large plate-glass windows throughout the mall. The premium
quoted was exorbitant. After the owner had turned down the offer, the agent
predicted that much glass damage might occur in the area if the owner was not
insured. Such a threat would constitute duress and would justify a request to
police authorities to investigate the agent offering the insurance.

Mistake

To dissolve mutual assent on the grounds of a mistake, the law requires that the
mistake be mutual, or that it concern both parties.

▶︎ The Murphys visited the sample room of an interior decorator to select material
for drapes. They asked the clerk to show them a dark blue material, which they
bought and took with them. When they examined the material in daylight, they
found that it was black and not the dark blue that they thought they had bought.
Both the clerk and the young couple had made the same mistake. May they return
the material and demand the return of their money?

In the above case, both the seller and the young couple had been mistaken as
to the correct color of the material purchased. There had never been a true and
complete meeting of the minds, and no mutual assent was actually achieved. The
Murphys would be entitled to return the material and to demand a refund of the
money. This is known as a *bilateral mistake*.

A *unilateral mistake* is one that involves but one of the parties, and it will not
excuse that party from the obligation entered into with the other.

▶︎ Suppose, in the preceding case, the clerk had told the Murphys to pick out the
material they desired and then call him. They chose the black material, thinking it
was a dark blue. They later discovered their mistake and attempted to return the
material. Will they succeed in their demand against the store?

The mistake made by the buyers in this case was unilateral, or one-sided. The seller did not know of the mistake, nor did he in any way take advantage of the selection of a wrong color. No recovery would be permitted under such conditions, and the contract would be entirely valid and enforceable.

Failure of one of the parties to understand the meaning of commonly used terms included in the written agreement will not excuse the party who will suffer from having made the mistake.

 Tobin purchased a prefabricated house from a Michigan manufacturer, agreeing to a price of $18,500 f.o.b. Battle Creek, Michigan. When the prefab was delivered to the building site, Tobin was given a bill which included freight from Battle Creek to his lot located in New Jersey. Tobin protested, claiming that he thought the terms "f.o.b. Battle Creek" meant that the seller would pay all freight charges. Tobin is not excused for this unilateral mistake of not understanding the meaning of a commonly used business term.

Questions for Review and Discussion

1. Name the four essentials of every good contract.

2. Explain revocation and name four ways in which an offer may be revoked.

3. (a) What is a counteroffer? (b) What effect does it have upon an offer?

4. Name five situations, any one of which may invalidate mutual assent.

5. (a) What five points must one prove in order to dissolve mutual assent on the ground of fraud? (b) How does fraud differ from misrepresentation in the relief given the complaining party?

6. What is the difference between duress and undue influence? Give an example of each.

7. (a) What is meant by "a mutual mistake"? (b) Give an example of a unilateral mistake in a contract.

8. Discuss the various methods of communication of acceptance by the offeror's agent; by the offeree's agent.

9. Describe the provision of the Uniform Commercial Code regarding the failure of parties to state the price in their agreement.

10. What does the Uniform Commercial Code say about the medium used by an offeree in accepting an offer?

Analyzing Cases

1. Two months before Christmas, Harkness received a box of greeting cards from a mail order company in a distant state. The package contained a letter instructing Harkness to send one dollar for the cards or to return them to the sender. Must she follow the instructions of the card company? Explain. • See also *Martwick* v. *Selover*, 197 Wis. 627. no, it was unordered mail

2. On January 10, Berkowitz received through the mail a letter from Pontolucci in which he offered to sell Berkowitz a set of valuable books for $85. Berkowitz mailed a letter of acceptance to Pontolucci the same day. The next day Berkowitz received a telegram from Pontolucci stating that he was revoking his offer. What relationship now exists between Pontolucci and

Berkowitz? Explain. • See also *Geary* v. *Great At. & Pac. Tea Co.*, 366 Ill. 625.

3. Campbell saw a sign in a store window advertising a new fur-trimmed coat for $25. She entered the store, tendered her $25, and demanded the coat. The manager refused to sell the coat, saying that a mistake had been made in printing the price, which should have read $250. Campbell sued the store for failure to deliver the coat after she had accepted their offer. Will she recover? Explain. • See also *Keller* v. *Holderman*, 11 Mich. 248; and *Meridian Star* v. *Kay*, 207 Miss. 78.

4. Wong had a valuable hunting dog that frequently accompanied him into the woods. On one of the walks the dog disappeared, and Wong advertised a reward for its return. A friend of Wong's found the dog and returned it to him without having read or heard of the advertised reward. Must Wong pay the reward if the finder later claims it after seeing the advertisement?

Give reasons for your decision. • See also *Summes* v. *Frazier*, 6 Mass. 344.

5. A representative of the Merchants Protective Association visited the Marks Furniture Store and offered an insurance policy to the owner to protect him against breakage of his large plate-glass display windows. He pointed out that by pure coincidence the merchants who had not taken the policy had suffered glass breakage by gangs of hoodlums. Marks agreed to take the policy. Is this contract voidable? Explain. • See also *Inland Empire Refineries Inc.* v. *Jones et al.*, 69 Idaho 335.

6. National Plastics Company offered HobbyArt, a model and art supplies retail outlet, 100 dozen make-it-yourself plastic jewel boxes at $32 a dozen. The offer was to remain open for ten days. Three days later HobbyArt received a letter withdrawing the offer. HobbyArt brought suit claiming that the proposal was a firm offer and not subject to withdrawal. Is the offeree correct in its claim? Explain.

Legal Reasoning and Business Judgment

Analyze the legal aspects of these business problems. Suggest possible solutions.

1. The advertising manager of your company placed a full-page announcement of a discount sale in the local paper. By mistake she used the terms "65 percent discount" when she meant "35 percent discount." Calls started coming into the sales department from buyers demanding that their orders be accepted. Is the firm legally obligated to accept orders at the discount in the advertisement?

2. One of the secretaries was asked by the head of the personnel department to buy ten tickets to a club dance in which he was privately interested. He told her that her promotion would depend to a great degree on the manner in which she cooperated with department heads like himself. She promised to take the tickets but is now afraid she will not be able to pay for them. How should she be advised?

3. An offer is received by the purchasing department of your company, in which a neighboring firm offers to sell 1,500 pounds of nails which it has on hand and would like to dispose of. The purchasing agent has a request for nails from one of the departments of the company. However, as no price was mentioned in the offer, the purchasing agent questions its validity. What is involved in this matter, and what would you advise?

Chapter 8
Capacity
of
Parties

May a teenager make an enforceable contract? May a seller of goods and services demand that a teenage buyer carry out the obligations contained in their agreement?

The law has always placed a protective screen about those persons who, because of immaturity, might be exploited by others in the making of business agreements. The contract of a youth under legal age is *voidable*. He or she may declare the contract void, or he or she may force the other party to carry out the promises made. This is the minor's right—and the minor's alone. The other party, if competent to contract, must abide by all the terms of the agreement as long as the youth wishes that party to do so.

> Columbo, who is a minor, bought a powerboat from the Sea Spray Boat Company. He paid the seller $500 in cash and signed a note for $2,500, to be paid at the end of two years. After using the boat for two months, he tied it up at the Sea Spray Company's dock and requested the return of his $500. He also disclaimed any further responsibility for the note that he had signed. May the boat company refuse Columbo's demand for the money and sue him on the note?

Columbo may rightfully demand the return of the money he has already paid, and he will not be required to honor the note for $2,500 held by the Sea Spray Company. However, some courts now permit the seller to deduct from the amount paid a reasonable sum to cover the use of the seller's property while in the youth's possession.

CONTRACTS OF MINORS

A move has been under way to place more responsibility on minors who have reached their eighteenth birthday. Across the United States, state legislatures have changed their statutory law to comply with the Twenty-sixth Amendment to the Constitution, ratified in 1971. This amendment lowered to eighteen years the minimum voting age in local and state elections as well as in federal elections. The impact of this new right to vote has not stopped at the ballot box. States have found it difficult to limit eighteen- to twenty-year-olds in other areas relating to legal maturity. Age limits on business arrangements such as making a contract, owning property, borrowing money, and the right to sue and be sued have been revised in many states.

Many states now permit women to marry without consent of parents after their eighteenth birthday. In almost all jurisdictions, however, the minor's contract remains voidable. Exceptions to this rule have been made in contracts made by minors engaged in some business enterprise or where minors have definitely used their position to take advantage of another.

> Porter, a minor, purchased a train ticket and made a trip from New York to Los Angeles. After having reached her destination, Porter demanded the return of her money on the claim that she was a minor. Porter had taken advantage of her rights under the contract and could be charged for her trip regardless of her age.

It is a well-established doctrine, however, that still gives minors the right to avoid their agreements.

Statutory law in each state should be studied to ascertain the *age of majority*, or *legal age*, whether it be eighteen, twenty-one, or some other age. To establish uniformity in determining the precise moment when a person's age changes, the legal birthday comes at 12:01 A.M. of the day preceding the day on which one would ordinarily celebrate a birthday. This rule is based upon the last day of one's present year rather than the first day of the next year.

> Stone, seventeen years old, has his birthday on November 5. A general election will be held on November 4, and all persons eighteen years of age and older on that date may vote. As his legal birthday is declared to be at 12:01 A.M. of November 4, Stone will be eligible to vote in the election.

Affirmance of Minor's Contracts

If a minor makes a payment or indicates in any other way, expressed or implied, an intention to be bound by an agreement after reaching his or her age of majority, the minor is said to have affirmed the agreement and will be held liable for all its terms.

> Suppose Columbo had continued to operate the powerboat after reaching the age of majority or had made a payment on the note. By these two acts he would have indicated a continuity of obligation after reaching his majority. He has thereby affirmed the contract and will not be permitted to avoid it thereafter.

Avoidance of Minor's Contracts

When a minor's contract is made with a competent person, *only the minor* has the right to avoid the obligation. The other party is bound as long as the minor is willing to be bound.

If minors are engaged in their own business, some states by statute require them to respect their obligations under contracts related to the business. The minor's liability will not extend beyond the assets of the business itself.

> Phillips, who is a minor, operated a student lunchroom. Because of poor management the business failed, and creditors demanded full payment of bills amounting to $1,275. The total assets of the business amounted to less than $500.

The creditors threatened to levy against Phillips' automobile and her other personal property to make up the difference. The court would permit the sale of the business assets toward the settlement of Phillips' bills, but would not allow the creditors any rights against Phillips' car and other belongings.

The right to avoid a minor's contract is a personal privilege granted by law to the minor or *his or her guardian*. With the exception of the minor's guardian, no other person may avoid the contract on the minor's behalf.

> Martin, a minor, purchased a gold watch for $75, to be delivered by the jeweler the following week. Martin's uncle, believing that the watch was unnecessary, notified the jeweler not to deliver the watch. Unless the uncle was Martin's legally appointed guardian, he had no right to cancel Martin's contract.

Minor's Right to Recover Property Sold   A minor who sells personal property to another who knows him or her to be a minor may demand the return of what has been transferred. The minor may not, however, recover his or her property from third parties who may have purchased the articles in good faith.

> Logue, a minor, sold a ring to DeFalco, for which he received a fair price. DeFalco knew Logue was a minor. DeFalco later sold the ring to O'Brien. Logue later attempted to recover his ring from O'Brien but was unsuccessful, as his only right of action would have been with the original purchaser, DeFalco.

Contracts Enforceable Against Minors

Contracts made by minors for merchandise and services considered necessary to their health, education, and welfare are said to be contracts for necessities. A minor may not void obligations entered into for such purchases. He or she will be held *personally liable* for their cost unless the subject matter of the contract has already been provided by his or her parents or other responsible persons or agencies. Necessities include food, shelter, clothing, medical expenses, education, and other items in an amount and at a cost deemed proper in consideration of the minor's individual needs and social and financial status.

> Morgan is a minor in very modest circumstances. She is taking a course in business administration, for which she ordered several books required in her studies. The books purchased are necessary to the furtherance of her education. Even though she is a minor in modest financial circumstances, she will be obligated to fulfill her contract.
>
> Thompson, another minor whose family is wealthy, ordered an expensive dress for formal wear. Although such a dress would not be considered a necessity for Morgan, in the previous case, Thompson's social position and wealth would make it an ordinary need, and she would be required to fulfill her contract.

Both Morgan's and Thompson's purchases were for things not already provided. Had they been already provided, these purchases would no longer have been deemed necessary but only duplications of things already owned or promised.

It has also been held that the tuition and fees related to taking courses that prepare one for employment are necessaries, whereas a liberal arts program would not be included in the definition of what constitutes necessaries.

Emancipation or Abandonment of Minor's Rights The term *emancipation*, when applied to the contracting capacity of a minor, relates to those situations in which parents have given up their rights to the care, custody, and earnings of the minor and have made a complete disavowal of parental duties. Abandonment, likewise, refers to the parents' intentions and actions wherein they have withdrawn or neglected parental claims to a minor child. A minor who has been emancipated and abandoned would be accepted as an adult under the law.

▶▶ Mitchell, a minor, married and left her parents' home in order to establish a home for her new family.

Hernandez, also a minor, left his parental home to accept a position in a distant city. Hernandez made clear that he no longer wished to be dependent upon his family and requested that they not send him any help, financial or otherwise.

Will the youths in these two cases be permitted to void all agreements that they make in the future if the agreements do not cover necessities? The decision in both cases will be negative. Mitchell, who married before reaching the age of majority, is said to have been *emancipated* from her parental ties, and she will thereafter be treated as an adult in all legal matters. Hernandez also will be considered an adult in his business agreements because of his *abandonment* of any further rights as a minor in relation to his parents.

To decide otherwise would place such persons in most unfavorable positions should they attempt to make purchases for things not considered necessities. Emancipation and abandonment place adult responsibilities upon minors. The law recognizes that without such obligations responsible parties would not be willing to contract with them.

Although the minor under the doctrine of emancipation and abandonment is considered an adult in his or her responsibilities on contracts, it is an exceptional situation wherein merchants and others accept such a person's signature and promise without adding the signature of one above the age of majority.

▶▶ Parseghian ran away from home at the age of eighteen, leaving behind him a note telling his parents he never intended to return. Both parents accepted the young man's decision and made no attempt to locate him. Parseghian attempted to purchase a car in his own name and to pay for it in monthly payments over a period of twelve months. Although emancipated, Parseghian was not able to complete the sales agreement without the signature of a friend who at the time was twenty-five years old.

Minor's Torts A minor is not permitted to avoid responsibility for damages to persons or property resulting from his or her own willful, negligent, and wrongful acts.

▶▶ Columbo failed to observe the ordinary rules of safety while operating his powerboat near a congested dock area. Owing to his negligence, he collided with another boat. The boat sank, and one of its passengers was seriously injured. Is Columbo liable to the owner of the other boat and to the injured person for the financial losses due to his negligent acts?

Minors will be held *personally responsible* for injuries resulting from their own torts. Damages to property and to persons will be chargeable to them personally and *not to their parents* unless the latter either have instructed such minors to act or have condoned their acts. The privilege of avoiding contract obligations is not extended to the torts of a minor.

Although the parents are not responsible in most cases, some states have passed legislation making them liable, usually up to $300, for *malicious* damage caused by minor children. These laws have been passed to place greater responsibility on parents in disciplining their children.

Most contracts prepared today will contain a concluding statement signed by the buyer stating that he or she has reached the age of majority. One under the age of majority who signs such an acknowledgment may be held liable under the tort action of *deceit*. Even so, many courts hold that the entire agreement is voidable and the tort action would fail.

Minor's Crimes A child below the age of seven years, known as the "tender years," is not recognized as having the mental capacity to plan a criminal act. From the ages of seven to fourteen, there is a strong presumption favoring a minor's innocence of criminal intent required for conviction. With few exceptions, persons fourteen years of age and older are fully responsible for their crimes, the same as adults.

> A group of teenagers, ranging in age from fifteen to nineteen years, set fire to a barn as a prank. They were discovered and held on an indictment for the crime of arson. They could not offer their ages as a defense of the crime committed and will be required to stand trial for the offense. In many states persons of these ages will be tried in separate courts provided for the prosecution of juveniles.

CONTRACTS OF MENTALLY INCOMPETENT PERSONS

Contracts made by persons legally declared mentally incompetent are void.

> Milstein, declared mentally incompetent by a court-appointed psychiatrist, signed a contract for the sale of his house and other property. Is this contract enforceable against Milstein?

Having been declared mentally incompetent by a court-appointed psychiatrist, Milstein is incompetent to make even the simplest contract. Only those contracts made for him by a legally appointed guardian may be enforced. Therefore, the contract he made is void from its inception.

Another group of persons whose contracts are either void or voidable are those who have temporarily or permanently lost their powers of reasoning.

Persons suffering from mental disease but not declared insane are permitted to make contracts for necessities. All other contracts made by these persons are void. Other disturbed persons who have recurring periods of normalcy are considered to be fully competent during such lucid periods, and all contracts made or affirmed by them at those times are enforceable.

▶ Marovich has recurring periods of mental blackout, during which times she remembers nothing that she has done. Following each attack, she is normal for periods of from two to three weeks. Then she experiences renewed attacks of her mental illness, which usually last for several days. Any contracts made by Marovich during her periods of mental stress and illness would be voidable. Those made during her "good days," or affirmed at that time, would be valid and enforceable.

CONTRACTS OF INTOXICATED PERSONS

Intoxication, to a degree that deprives a person of his or her power to reason and understand, renders a person incompetent to contract. He or she has the right to void any contracts made while in that condition.

▶ While attending an anniversary party, Baxter became intoxicated. Another guest, taking advantage of the situation, offered Baxter $25 for a ring that he had unsuccessfully tried to buy many times before. Baxter accepted the $25 and gave his ring to the other man. May Baxter demand the return of the ring when he realizes what he has done?

Since Baxter did not comprehend the meaning of his acts when he sold the ring, he could demand that his property be returned upon his offer to return the $25 he received. While the courts do not condone intoxication, they recognize it as a real obstacle in reaching mutual assent.

Reversing the situation, persons who make a purchase while intoxicated may later demand the return of their money. In order to make such a demand, however, they must tender to the seller the merchandise they purchased while intoxicated.

The recent increase in the use of depressive drugs and narcotics which seriously impair the user's powers of reasoning has given rise to contract defenses similar to those now used by persons intoxicated by alcohol.

CONTRACTS OF MARRIED WOMEN

A married woman has the same legal rights in contracts and property ownership as any other adult.

▶ Jacoby, a legal secretary who had her own bank account and had established her own credit in the community, placed an order for the purchase of a new automobile to be registered in her own name. After the order was placed, the agency returned the contract, saying that the contract was not valid without her husband's signature. Under modern statutes, a court would rule that the contract was valid and enforceable as originally executed and that the signature of her husband was not required.

CONTRACTS OF CORPORATIONS

A *corporation* is a legal entity (an artificial person) created by statute, with an existence of its own, separate and distinct from that of the individual members. It has the right to sue, to be sued, and to act in its own name within the boundaries of the rights permitted under it corporate charter.

Corporations are considered as competent parties to make contracts with other corporations, partnerships, individuals, or government authorities. It has been held in the past that a corporation is competent to make only such contracts as come within the scope of its created corporate authority. Recent decisions have enforced contracts outside of the corporation's authority, particularly when such contracts have been partly executed by either party.

> Road Builders, Inc., was incorporated with the intent and with the right to build roads and perform other acts directly related to the road-building business. The board of directors authorized the president to contract for the building of a ten-story office building adjacent to a new highway they were building. Work was started immediately on the new building. Road Builders, Inc., and the other contracting party could now enforce completion of the agreement, although it was not within the express or implied charter rights of Road Builders, Inc., to do other than build roads.

ONE-PARTY CONTRACTS

A person may not contract with himself or herself. The basic element of a contract is *mutual assent*, which requires a meeting of the minds between two or more persons.

> Sandra Parks formed the Sandra Parks Corporation, to which she transferred title to all her real property, securities, and bank accounts. Parks formed the corporation as a holding company to hold title to her property in the event that she is sued at some future time. May a creditor to whom Parks is indebted obtain a judgment against her and in satisfaction of the judgment attach the property held by the corporation?

Although Parks did sell her property to a corporation, the corporation was owned entirely by her and it could not rightfully be said that two parties had participated in the transaction. Such an arrangement, created for the sole purpose of defrauding creditors, may usually be set aside, with the return of the property to the true owner (in this case Sandra Parks) for the benefit of her creditors.

CONTRACTS WITH ENEMY ALIENS

Any person who owes allegiance to a country with whom the United States is at war is considered an *enemy alien*. Contracts made by a citizen of the United States with an enemy alien that result in giving aid or comfort to the enemy or involve the safety of the United States are *void*.

> The American Electronic Development Corporation contracted with a research scientist to work on the development of advanced rocketry circuits and controls to

be used in national defense. The scientist was a refugee from a European country and had not yet become a citizen of the United States. The United States dropped all diplomatic relations with the other country, after which the electronic corporation terminated its agreement with the scientist. Any action on this contract by the former employee would be decided in favor of the employer, who would be permitted to discharge the man on grounds of national security and the common good.

Questions for Review and Discussion

1. (*a*) What is the rule for determining a person's legal birthday? (*b*) Using this rule, explain how you would figure your next legal birthday.

2. What contracts made by a minor may not be voided by the minor on the grounds of incapacity to contract?

3. How does the law differentiate among various types of insane persons and their right to declare their contracts void?

4. (*a*) What effect does intoxication have upon enforceability of contracts? (*b*) Why do courts recognize intoxication as grounds for dissolving a contract? Explain.

5. (*a*) When are the parents of a minor responsible for the minor's torts? (*b*) What legislation is now being introduced in some states relating to liability for children's torts?

6. (*a*) What is meant by "affirming one's contract"? (*b*) When must this be done?

7. What rights does a corporation have in making contracts?

8. Are minors excused from liability on contracts in connection with business ventures in which they are engaged?

9. Do married women have the same contract and property rights as their husbands? Explain.

10. Under what conditions may a contract made by a citizen of the United States with an enemy alien be voided?

Analyzing Cases

1. Seltzer, a minor aged eighteen, purchased an expensive fur coat and signed an installment contract agreeing to make payments over a period of eighteen months. After making several payments and wearing the coat during the winter months, Seltzer returned it to the store and demanded the return of her money and the cancellation of the contract. The store refused to do so and sued Seltzer for the balance owed on the installment contract. Will the store succeed? Give reasons for your answer. *See also *Weeks* v. *Berschaver*, 140 Kan. 244. *yes, it was a necessity*

2. During a period of mental depression, Giles entered a men's shop and purchased $800 worth of expensive suits. In his work as a truck driver, Giles had little or no use for suits like these. When the clothes were delivered to his home, he refused to accept them, stating that he was not his real self on the day he bought them. How will the court determine whether or not Giles must pay for the suits? *See also *Perper* v. *Edell et al.*, 160 Fla. 477.

3. Turner, while intoxicated, agreed to sell his diamond ring, worth $350, to Murton for $50. The next day Turner changed his mind and refused to carry out the agreement. Murton brought suit against Turner for damages. Judgment should favor whom, and why? *See also *Anderson* v. *Hicks*, 134 N.Y.S. 1018.

4. Tom Shockley, a wealthy minor who was twenty, ordered his tailor to make him a suit at a cost of $225. When his suit was ready, Shockley informed the tailor that he had changed his mind and was avoiding their agreement. Could the tailor force Shockley to pay for the suit even though he was only twenty years old? • See also *O'Donniley* v. *Kinley,* 220 Mo. App. 284.

5. Greer decided to take a trip to California on a jet plane. After arriving in California from New York, he demanded the return of his money on the ground that he was only a minor and that the trip was in no way a necessity to him. What would the court decide in this case? Explain. • See also *Merchants' Credit Bureau* v. *Kouri Akiyama,* 64 Utah 364.

6. Burell, a minor, sold certain property to Noyes at a reasonable price. Two years after reaching his majority, Burell demanded the return of his property and offered to return the money received for it. Noyes refused. What can Burell do about it? Explain. • See also *Ruehle* v. *Lange,* 223 Mich. 690.

Legal Reasoning and Business Judgment

Analyze the legal aspects of these business problems. Suggest possible solutions.

1. Your boss's daughter is on a pleasure trip through the Southwest, and several bills have come to him for souvenirs and clothes that she has bought and charged to her father. She is seventeen. Because these bills seem excessive, your boss is concerned about his responsibility for them and wonders whether he is obligated to pay the bills. What is his legal responsibility for his daughter's purchases?

2. The credit department of your company has a problem that concerns a long-overdue account for merchandise sold to two young men who operate the University Shop. Information obtained by the company indicates that the business in question is failing. It is the opinion of the credit executives that since both partners are minors, the account should be written off as a total loss. Would you offer any suggestion that might benefit your company's position in this matter?

3. A young married couple visits the Massey Department Store and makes a contract for the purchase of a living-room suite and wall-to-wall carpeting for three rooms of their apartment. Due to their youthfulness, you question them as to their ages and learn that the husband is twenty and his wife eighteen. The credit department seeks your advice in the matter of (*a*) accepting the couple as competent to contract and (*b*) the enforceability of any agreement made with them. What do you suggest?

Chapter 9
Consideration

A third element essential to any valid contract is the mutual exchange of benefits and sacrifices between the parties. This exchange is called *consideration*. It is the service or merchandise which one contracts to give in exchange for money or some other thing of value.

> ▶ Jefferson bought a corsage for his fiancée. By this act, he entered into a legally enforceable contract with the florist. In return for the payment of money, the florist gave the flowers to Jefferson. Consideration was exchanged, and a valid contract was created.
>
> Jefferson took the corsage to his fiancée. By doing so, he gave up ownership of the flowers. In this situation there was no exchange of benefits and sacrifices. Jefferson sacrificed ownership by an outright gift, which imposed no obligation on his fiancée. There was no consideration; therefore, no contract.

REQUISITES OF CONSIDERATION

Consideration need not always take the form of money. Any of these exchanges of values is sufficient to constitute an enforceable agreement:

☐ Doing, or promising to do, a legal act or service that yields pleasure or benefit to the other party when one is under no legal obligation to do this act is consideration.

In the case above, if Jefferson had agreed to type the florist's monthly bills in exchange for the flowers, his work would have constituted valid consideration.

☐ Refraining, or promising to refrain, from doing something that one is otherwise free to do and has a legal right to do is consideration. This act of refraining is called *forbearance*.

Suppose Jefferson had been growing flowers during the summer and had sold some of his better blooms to people in his neighborhood. If he agreed to stop selling flowers in return for a promise from the florist to supply him with seeds and young plants, this exchange of promises would be satisfactory consideration.

Any legal agreement containing the mutual exchange of benefits and sacrifices will be acceptable as consideration in proving a contract.

> ▶ Emerson said to Stuart, her nephew, who was eighteen years old, "I will give you $100 when you become of age (twenty-one years old) if, in the meantime, you will not smoke."

Stuart refrained from smoking and demanded the $100 when he became twenty-one. Emerson refused to pay the money, claiming that Stuart had not given consideration for his promise, just as she had not received any benefit from Stuart's good conduct.

It was held that refraining from doing something one is otherwise free to do and has a legal right to do constitutes sufficient valid consideration for a promise. Stuart had a legal right to smoke. Even though he, rather than Emerson, was benefited by the agreement, by refraining from smoking at her request, he was giving sufficient consideration for the promise.

Third-Party Benefits

The benefits agreed upon in a contract need not accrue to the contracting parties themselves. If the benefits are bestowed upon others at the request of either party, the consideration is valid.

> Your parents made a contract with an automobile sales agency for the purchase of a sedan, which is to be registered in your name and delivered to you on your birthday. Your parents have reserved no rights in the car. Delivery of the car to you will be consideration to your parents for their promise to pay the dealer. The dealer's sacrifice was his or her obligation to carry out a promise made to your parents.

Another common example involving third-party benefit is a promise made by a parent to pay tuition and other expenses to a school that has agreed to accept his son or daughter as a student.

LEGALITY OF CONSIDERATION

Unless the benefits and sacrifices named in an agreement are lawful, the contract involving them will be void and unenforceable.

> Lipski made an agreement with a friend to drive the friend's unlicensed car to another town during the late evening hours when the police would not see her. Lipski was to receive $25 for driving the car. The agreement is not enforceable by either Lipski or her friend, since the consideration constituted an illegal act by Lipski.

A more complete study of illegal contracts will be discussed in the next section covering *valid subject matter*.

ADEQUACY OF CONSIDERATION

Persons who willingly enter into a contract will be held bound by its terms, even though the benefits exchanged may seem to be inequitable and unfair.

> O'Shea needs cash immediately and offers his typewriter for $50; you accept the offer. Several days later he demands the return of the typewriter, claiming that its real value is $150. Did the agreement contain valid consideration?

Although $50 may seem an inadequate price for a good typewriter, both parties agreed that the figure was satisfactory when the contract was made. The courts have not been willing to sit in judgment on the equality of a bargain. Profits gained through skillful bargaining are considered to be the basis of free trade and competition.

Barren Promises

A promise to do that which one is already bound to do either by law or by contract is called a *barren promise*. Because of lack of acceptance of any additional sacrifices, such promises do not constitute valid consideration. The three most frequent types of barren promises are discussed below.

☐ A promise to do something that one is legally required to do is unenforceable.

> Velez promised her twenty-year-old son that she would buy him a new car on his twenty-first birthday if he would observe all traffic laws while driving the family car during the next year. Velez would have no legal obligation to carry out this promise, as the son has agreed to do nothing more than he is required to do by law.

☐ Promises of the kind exacted by the parent in the above case are barren promises. In all such cases one party has accepted a new obligation in return for the other's promise merely to carry out an already existing one.

☐ A promise to do nothing more than one has already pledged to do is unenforceable.

> Murphy, a police officer, read a notice of a reward for the capture of a felon who had escaped from the state prison. He successfully traced the wanted man to a hideout, made the arrest, and delivered the man to the authorities. Must those who advertised the reward now pay Officer Murphy?

☐ By the very nature of his employment, a police officer is obligated to investigate and arrest lawbreakers during off-duty as well as on-duty hours. Murphy's sacrifice was only a barren act and unenforceable because of lack of valid consideration.

☐ A promise to pay any part of an existing debt is a promise to do nothing more than the debtor is already obligated to do.

> Levy owed the Acme Printing Company $50 on an overdue account. He received a letter stating that the company was willing to cancel the entire debt if Levy would send $25. After paying the $25, Levy received a demand for the balance of the account.

☐ Levy offered nothing to the Acme Printing Company in return for its promise to reduce the amount owed by the payment of the $25. This promise was not, therefore, supported by consideration and may not be enforced by Levy.

> Suppose the account was not yet due, and Levy had until the twenty-fifth of the month for payment. The Acme Company offers to reduce the account by one-half if Levy will pay $25 today, the tenth of the month.

☐ The sacrifice of time by early payment would constitute valid consideration to the printing company, and Levy would be released from paying the balance of the account.

Payment in Goods or Services

A claim against a debtor is considered to be discharged if the creditor accepts payment, either wholly or partly, in goods or services instead of money. This practice holds whether or not the claim is disputed and regardless of the actual value of the goods or the services offered. Services performed before they are required to be performed, or payments made before they are due under the original obligation or made at some place other than that at which they were to be made, constitute additional satisfactory consideration for the discharge of a debt.

 Hearnes, who owed Lehr $500, offered her $100 cash and a gold ring in full payment of the debt. Lehr accepted the offer. Later, Lehr brought suit for $375, submitting evidence to prove that the ring was not worth more than $25.

It was held that the debt was discharged, regardless of the actual value of the ring. (See Adequacy of Consideration, page 116.)

Accord and Satisfaction

Would part payment of a bill rendered for the installing of new brakes, for example, act as full payment? If the cost of the brake repair job is conspicuously displayed, the bill rendered is for an *undisputed amount*, and a part payment would not be sufficient to cancel the charge.

The acceptance of payment when signified as full payment on a *disputed amount* is known as *accord and satisfaction*. This occurs when the parties do not come to an agreement as to the cost of goods or services on a contract between them. In contrast, an undisputed amount is one in which the parties definitely agree to all charges before the contract is performed or executed.

If the cost of a brake job is not displayed, the charges for the job might involve a disputed amount. Assume that the owner of the car did not know what the job would cost because no price was shown and no agreement was made before the work was started. Would part payment then satisfy full payment of the bill?

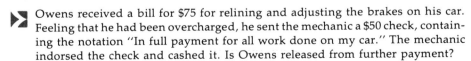 Owens received a bill for $75 for relining and adjusting the brakes on his car. Feeling that he had been overcharged, he sent the mechanic a $50 check, containing the notation "In full payment for all work done on my car." The mechanic indorsed the check and cashed it. Is Owens released from further payment?

By indorsing and cashing Owens's check, the mechanic showed a willingness to accept the lesser sum of a *disputed amount*. This is known as an *accord* and a *satisfaction*. The accord is the expressed or implied agreement of the creditor to accept less than the amount demanded; the satisfaction is the payment by the debtor of that amount.

```
                        October 15, 19--

The Acme Printing Company hereby releases Sandra
Benedito from all obligations on her account as of
this date.

                        ACME PRINTING COMPANY

                        Walter King (L.S.)
                        President
```

Fig. 9-1. A general release

Consideration in a General Release

In practically all states, debts may be canceled without consideration when the creditor gives the other party a statement in writing releasing him or her from the debt. Had Levy (see above) received a statement similar to the one in Fig. 9-1, he could not have been called on for further payment.

The law provides that "any claim or right arising out of an alleged breach can be discharged in whole or in part without consideration by a written waiver or renunciation signed and delivered by the aggrieved party."

Promises Not to Sue

A settlement involving a promise not to sue is binding on both parties.

Calloway was injured when timbers fell upon her from a roof which was undergoing repairs. The sidewalk had not been blocked off, and the contractor, accepting responsibility for the negligence of his employees, agreed to pay Calloway $750 in full settlement of any claims she might have. Calloway accepted the $750, signed a release, and discharged the contractor from any further liability to her. Calloway later learned that she could have recovered much more than the $750 she received. In an action for an additional amount Calloway would fail because of her previous promise, supported by the consideration of $750.

In such cases the rights of the parties are frozen if it is later learned that the injured party might have been entitled to more damages or if the one making payment discovers that he or she has paid too much. The acceptance of the amount agreed upon terminates the future rights and liabilities of the parties toward one another in the event of a subsequent dispute on the same issue.

Options

An *option* is the giving of consideration to support an offeror's promise to hold open an offer for a stated or reasonable length of time. In the case of a merchant offeror, consideration is not required if he or she gives a written and signed offer containing the promise. The time on such written promises is limited to no more than three months. An offer by a merchant exceeding the three-month limit would be like any other offer and would require consideration to support the promise.

Modification of Sales Agreements

A modification by mutual agreement of an existing sales contract does not require additional consideration to support the modification.

> Mark contracted to buy a refrigerator-freezer from a discount sales outlet. All terms were agreed upon by both parties. The day after the agreement was made, Mark called the seller, requesting that the unit be delivered to his house, a matter that was not mentioned previously. The seller agreed to deliver the unit to the buyer's house without additional charge. The promise is binding upon the seller without the necessity of further consideration from Mark.

SEAL IN CONSIDERATION

Historically, a *seal*, when made a part of a written agreement, gave the contract the *presumption of consideration*. Hence the party affixing his or her seal to the instrument did not have the burden of proving that consideration was given. The seal has now been outlawed in many states and no longer has the universal respect it once held.

In the case of contracts for sale of goods, the use of seals is unnecessary and inoperative. The law provides that "the affixing of a seal to a writing evidencing a contract for sale or an offer to buy or sell goods does not constitute the writing of a sealed instrument, and the law with respect to sealed instruments does not apply to such a contract or offer."

SUBSCRIPTIONS AND PLEDGES

May a freewill pledge of funds to a private or a public cause be enforced, in view of the requirements of consideration? Are such pledges enforceable as contracts?

> The civic leaders in your community propose a plan for the building of a neighborhood swimming pool for all the children in the area. Construction costs are to be met through pledges made by public-spirited citizens. You sign a card pledging to give $100 as your share in the undertaking. Does your pledge carry a legally enforceable obligation to pay the $100?

The courts recognize a pledge like this one as an enforceable agreement, supported by consideration. The benefit accruing in return for the promise to give $100 is the construction of the pool. This is valid consideration, supporting the promise made by you. Should either the original plans be altered or the project be canceled, the pledge would be unenforceable.

> A welfare fund is launched by a group of people interested in doing work among the underprivileged children in your town. Five hundred adults subscribe $10

each for the establishment of the fund. Are these subscriptions supported by valid consideration?

In the interest of public welfare, the courts have ruled that the consideration to the donors consists of the promises made by all the others who have made pledges. This concept of consideration is used in support of all promises of money to be used for undefined causes.

GIFTS

A promise to make a gift or to perform some gratuitous service at some time in the future is not enforceable.

▶▶ A neighbor promised to lend you her car over the weekend. Relying on this promise, you made an appointment with an important prospective customer.
When you called for the car you were told that your friend had changed her mind and had taken a trip in the car. May you now demand damages from your neighbor for her failure to carry out her promise to you?

Promises of gifts, either of property or services, to be made in the future contain no consideration and for that reason are not enforceable under the law of contracts. In the above case, because no consideration had been offered for the use of the car, the agreement was unenforceable. However, if one actually transfers property or performs some gratuitous service, the act is executed and no consideration may be demanded as a reward; nor may the donor of the gift demand its return.

PAST CONSIDERATION

A subsequent promise to give something of value for that which already has been done is known as *past consideration*. Past consideration is not valid consideration and is not enforceable.

▶▶ Suppose, in the preceding case, your neighbor had lent you her car as promised. When you returned it, you promised to give her $10 the next day as an expression of your appreciation. Would this promise be enforceable at law?

Since the money promised is supported only by past consideration and not by any promised future act, it may not be collected.

MORAL CONSIDERATION

Demands of the conscience in tribute to the good deeds of others constitute *moral consideration*. Promises supported by allegiance, friendship, or honor will not be enforced as contracts for lack of legal consideration.

▶▶ A classmate had given Perlo hours of his time in an effort to help him pass the final examinations. After passing the exams, Perlo promised to buy his friend a fountain pen as an expression of his appreciation. This promise was based only on moral consideration and could not be enforced by the classmate.

Questions for Review and Discussion

1. What is the meaning of benefits and sacrifices in the study of consideration?

2. Will the courts review the agreements of parties to determine whether the consideration named was adequate and sufficient for both parties?

3. Explain the meaning of an undisputed amount and a disputed amount.

4. (a) Explain consideration and its application to pledges and subscriptions. (b) Is a pledge of money for the building a church enforceable? Explain.

5. (a) What is past consideration? (b) How does it affect the enforceability of an agreement for payment of money?

6. Is the promise of a gift to be presented in the future enforceable? Explain.

7. (a) Give an example of moral consideration. (b) Will the courts recognize moral consideration in the enforcement of a contract?

8. (a) Give two examples of barren promises. (b) Explain why such promises will not support another's promise on a contract.

9. (a) What is a seal? (b) What is its importance in the matter of consideration?

10. Is a promise not to sue acceptable as valid consideration in a contract? Give an example of this type of agreement.

Analyzing Cases

1. O'Neill, a police officer, agreed to pay special attention to Arnold's home while Arnold was on vacation. Arnold's property was on O'Neill's regular beat, and Arnold agreed to pay O'Neill $50 for the protection given. If Arnold fails to pay the $50, may O'Neill collect the promised payment through court action? Explain. •See also *Vanderbilt* v. *Schreyer*, 91 N.Y. 392.

2. Lynch received a bill from Dr. Richards for surgery and postoperative treatment rendered during Lynch's recent illness. The bill was for $1,500, which Lynch thought excessive for the services rendered. No agreement had been made between Lynch and the surgeon prior to Lynch's admission to the hospital. Lynch mailed Richards a check for $900 with the following indorsement on the back of the check: "Accepted in full payment for all professional services rendered." After Richards indorsed the check and deposited it, a second bill was received by Lynch for the balance of the account, or $600. Is Lynch legally responsible for payment of this balance? Explain. •See also 97 U. of Pa. Law Review 99.

3. Sanders assisted two elderly ladies whose car had been stranded in a snowbank during a blizzard. More than an hour was required to get the car back on the highway. "Young man, we appreciate your great kindness. We promise that we will mail you a check for $25 for your work and time." May Sanders enforce this promise if the check is not sent? Explain. •See also *Fender* v. *McCain*, 144 Neb. 58.

4. Shannon agreed, after many requests from her parents, to be more careful in her housekeeping of the pleasant room used for a bedroom and study. The parents promised an increase in Shannon's allowance in the amount of $25 more each month if this task were done. Does Shannon have a legally enforceable agreement with her parents? Explain. •See also *Katherine Lane* v. *David D. Sullivan*, 302 Mass. 213.

5. Bleyer bought three dresses from the Mod Shop for a total price of $145. Two weeks before her bill was payable, Bleyer received an urgent call from Mod Shop's credit manager, suggesting that if payment were made at once the shop

would accept $100 in full payment. Bleyer agreed and made payment of $100, but she was later billed for the balance of $45. May Mod Shop collect the $45 through legal action? Explain.
• See also *Bice v. Silver,* 170 Ia. 255.

6. Chenowitz agreed to sell a used typewriter to

Poole for $35. A few days later, but before the $35 was paid and the machine delivered, Poole asked Chenowitz to guarantee the typewriter. Chenowitz agreed to guarantee the machine for sixty days. Is this new promise enforceable in absence of any new consideration to support it? Explain.

Legal Reasoning and Business Judgment

Analyze the legal aspects of these business problems. Suggest possible solutions.

1. A fund-raising project, seeking public subscription for a new sports arena, has been launched in your city. You have received a request from the public relations director of the project to come into your plant to talk with employees at a meeting during their lunch break. The rank and file of the workers do not have any background in law. How would you handle this request? If you granted it, would you also make any comments to employees before or after the presentation by one of the fund raisers?

2. The purchasing agent of your firm received a letter offering a 10,000-watt standby generator for sale for only $500. The letter states that the machine is in excellent condition and has had less than ten hours' use. The usual cost of this unit would have been at least ten times the quoted price in the letter. The purchasing agent seeks your advice in the matter, asking for some legal guidance in the enforceability of the agreement if accepted. What is your advice?

3. One of your employees had been promised the gift of an antique chest by a grandparent. The chest was quite valuable and was dated 1722 by the craftsman who made it. The employee tells you that it is now rumored in the family that the relative is about to give the chest to another granddaughter. What advice can you give your employee as to the enforceability of the earlier promise?

Chapter 10
Validity
of
Subject Matter

The fourth element required of an enforceable contract is *valid subject matter*. This term refers to the legality of the goods or services covered by the agreement, and the purpose of it. Both the goods or services and the manner and purpose of execution of the contract must be acceptable under the law if the contract is to be enforceable.

LEGALITY OF SUBJECT MATTER

A young person purchases a set of hubcaps from a reputable automobile accessories store. There is nothing illegal either in the nature of the goods bought or in the manner in which they were sold. The contract is a good one, and if the hubcaps are not as represented, the purchaser may seek damages from the seller.

Now suppose that the youngster had bought the hubcaps from a person who had stolen them. Both the stealing of the caps and the unauthorized sale would make the contract of sale invalid. If the purchaser should find the caps unsuited for his or her purpose, he or she would have neither the right nor the opportunity to get satisfaction from the seller.

ILLEGALITY OF SUBJECT MATTER

There are three general types of acts which render contracts void because of illegality of subject matter. They are:

☐ Acts contrary to the common law.
☐ Acts contrary to statutes and local ordinances.
☐ Acts opposed to the welfare and security of the public at large.

These are known as "acts against public policy and good morals." The sale of the stolen hubcaps would represent all three types.

Although any agreement containing illegal subject matter is void and may not be enforced, protection is often given to persons who have at times placed themselves in unfavorable positions by spending considerable time and money in carrying out agreements that are not *obviously* illegal or harmful to other persons.

124

> A regulation of the Interstate Commerce Commission prohibits a driver engaged in interstate commerce from working continuously for more than eight hours. It imposes a penalty upon companies who are guilty of thus requiring their drivers to work. Even though a driver violated the provision, he would be permitted to recover the value of services rendered to the company.

Had the driver in such a case knowingly hauled a cargo of smuggled goods, however, he would have been engaged in an obviously illegal operation and would have no rights in any demands made for services rendered.

The Uniform Commercial Code does not directly provide direction in interpretation of contracts under the qualifications of legality. There would be continuing conflict in setting up uniform guidelines due to the great differences in statutes and ordinances in each state and individual local incorporated community.

Illegality in Divisible Contracts

If a contract is divisible and the illegal acts are confined to an unimportant segment of the duties, the other parts of the contract remain enforceable.

> You accept a position as an accountant with a small construction company. On two occasions your employer has you drive a company station wagon to transport a group of carpenters to their job. You do not have a chauffeur's license, which is required of persons who drive for hire. Would your entire employment contract be void because you are driving illegally?

The driving of the station wagon is not an important part of your position and is in no way related to your employment as an accountant. The contract would be enforceable since it refers to your work as an accountant, not as the driver of the station wagon.

Rule of *in Pari Delicto*   When both parties to an illegal agreement are equally wrong in the knowledge of the operation and effect of their contract, they are said to be *in pari delicto* (in equal fault). In such cases no aid will be given to either party in an action against the other, and the court will award no damages to either. When the parties are not *in pari delicto*, relief will often be allowed if sought by the more innocent of the two. While this rule is not applicable where one may be less guilty of premeditation and intent to achieve a gain through known illegal acts, it may be applied when one party is not aware that a law is being broken and where there is no intent to do a wrong.

> Haines agreed to remodel Kronski's house so that it might be used as a public restaurant. Haines accepted $500, with Kronski's promise to pay an additional $2,000 when the job was done. Haines was aware that zoning laws would not permit commercial use of any property in the area. Kronski was not aware of this fact, and in an action against Haines the court would rule that Kronski might recover his $500 as the parties were not *in pari delicto*.

Sunday Agreements

The making and performance of contracts on Sunday is regulated by state statutes and local ordinances. Changes in the laws relating to Sunday observance have been brought about in many localities during the past several years either by popular referendum or by statute. When laws restrict business dealings on Sunday, the following two rules should be observed:

☐ Contracts made on Sunday or any other day stating that the work is to be done on Sunday are void. Contracts related to the health and welfare of the community are exempted from this provision.

> A group of young people made a contract with a theater for a theater party to be held on a Sunday evening. Only the members of the group and their friends would be present, by invitation. This contract is void and unenforceable under the above rule. In those areas, however, where Sunday observance is no longer in force, the contract would be valid and enforceable by both parties.

☐ Contracts made on Sunday in which the work is to be done on a business day are valid and enforceable. In some states these contracts must be affirmed on a business day to make them enforceable.

> On Sunday evening, Torres made arrangements with a painter to have her car painted the following day. Since the work was to be done on a business day, the contract would be valid except in those communities and states requiring later affirmation.

Many of the present laws restricting business and other activity on Sunday were passed by the state legislatures in the early history of this country. They have been labeled *Sunday blue laws* by those seeking their change or removal. These laws vary widely from state to state as well as from county to county in the same state. Different attitudes generally associated with urban and rural areas have brought about this conflict of law. Pressures of commercialism have reduced Sunday regulation either through state statutes, local laws, or constitutional interpretation.

Legal Holidays

Legal holidays have never received the same close attention as Sundays in the matter of contracts. Generally, contracts entered into or to be performed on legal holidays are valid and enforceable. If the payment of money or the performance of certain acts is to be made on a holiday, the courts will permit such payments to be made and such acts to be performed on the next regular business day following. Suppose you signed a promissory note dated April 4, payable in three months. Since the date of payment falls on July 4, a national holiday, payment may be made on July 5 or the next business day following July 4.

Some contracts, by their very nature, are enforceable if they are to be performed on legal holidays, and failure to perform will result in an action for damages.

▶▶ The First Regiment Band made a contract with the Centerville Independence Day Committee to furnish music for a celebration to be held on July 4 in the city square. This contract is enforceable and must be executed on the date named.

Legal holidays in any state or community are those days specified by the national, state, or local governing bodies. Religious holidays and days of celebration set aside by fraternal orders are not included in the meaning of the term.

Gambling and Wagering Agreements

Any act or promise based upon a wager or gambling is an unenforceable agreement. Only in certain jurisdictions where wagers are permitted by law are such contracts valid and enforceable.

▶▶ You attend the motorcycle races with several friends. State law permits the placing of bets through state-supervised betting windows, where a tax is collected on all bets made. If one of your friends offered to bet with you on the outcome of the race, could this agreement be enforced?

No. Wagers made in defiance of a statute and not under the provisions specified by the law would be held invalid. The winner would have no contractual rights against the other party and would be unsuccessful in any attempt to obtain his or her winnings through legal action.

▶▶ If, in the above case, the racetrack was situated in a state whose laws permitted racing according to statute and provided state-supervised agencies for the placing of bets, wagers placed through what is called the parimutuel system would be valid and enforceable.

Insurance Contracts   When insurance was first introduced, contracts written on the life or property of others were looked upon as a kind of wagering agreement. Today, however, such contracts are upheld in view of the great benefits to be derived through the spreading of individual losses over large groups of policyholders. The dictates of public policy show that such agreements are in the public interest.

▶▶ The Dickinson School District purchased insurance covering all schools in the district against loss by fire. Although a return from this agreement with the insurance company would depend upon the outcome of an uncertain event (that is, a possible fire), the policy is valid in that it is in the public interest and for the common good.

Stock and Commodity Transactions   Agreements made for the sale and purchase of shares of stock or commodities are valid only when it is intended that the actual shares and commodities are to be delivered to the purchaser. Otherwise the agreement is considered only as a wagering contract and would be held invalid.

▶ Massey entered into an agreement with a commodity speculator for the purchase of 100,000 bushels of wheat at the price to be quoted on September 15, three months in the future. The usual terms of delivery were not included in the agreement. Is the contract enforceable?

Since the parties did nothing more than bet on the price of wheat as it might be on September 15, the agreement is void, and neither party can enforce performance.

Agreements for the purchase of securities without intention of delivery of the certificates of ownership are known as *bucket-shop transactions*. They are legally unenforceable and are not approved by members of the security trade. These transactions, moreover, have no effect upon the actual market quotations, since they are made outside regular channels.

Illegal Interest Rates

The practice of charging more than the amount of interest allowed by law is called *usury*. To protect borrowers from excessive interest charges, each state has passed laws which specify the rate of interest that may be charged in lending money. The legal interest rates vary from state to state. The obvious intent is to set a rate that will be equitable for both the borrower and the lender.

▶ A man who borrowed $100 from a loan shark agreed to repay the loan in a week at 10 percent interest. Another individual borrowed the same amount from a commercial bank at the legal rate of interest. Are both agreements enforceable and legal?

In the first example, the man is being charged 10 percent interest a week, which amounts to an annual rate of 520 percent for the use of the money! This agreement would be void because the interest rate is illegal. The borrower in the second example has entered into a valid and enforceable contract, since the agreement is to pay only the legal yearly rate on the loan, usually 6 percent.

The legal interest rate is the amount of interest that will be applied in those cases wherein the loan agreement does not specify the amount of interest charged. The *maximum rate* may be greater than what is called the *legal rate*. Special statutes provide higher interest rates for small loan companies, pawnshops, and other lending agencies accepting high-risk applicants for credit. Revolving charge accounts in consumer sales often permit 1 to 1½ percent per month on any unpaid balance. Under separate legislation, corporations are also permitted to charge higher interest rates than those allowed in consumer loans.

Penalties for Usury Laws relating to usury provide penalties for those who charge interest over the legal limits. Among the penalties fixed by the statutes of the several states are the following:

☐ Forfeiture by the lender of any interest in excess of the legal rate.
☐ Forfeiture of all interest payments.
☐ Forfeiture of both the interest and the principal.

Contracts which on the surface may appear free of usury may be found invalid for that very reason. A seller and buyer may agree on an inflated price for merchandise sold, thereby assuring the seller of an amount greater than the regular price plus interest would have netted him or her. Other schemes include dating a security instrument back several months, thereby increasing the actual interest to be paid for money borrowed for a relatively shorter period of time.

▶ Lefkowitz borrowed $500 from Burns on September 10, at 7 percent interest, for a period of six months. The note prepared by Burns and signed by Lefkowitz stated that the loan was made in June, to be paid in December. Thus, the interest to be paid was actually double the 7 percent stated. This, of course, would be a usurious note if it could be proved.

Interest Charges on Overdue Debts   Interest at the prevailing legal rate may be added to debts which have become overdue. Interest will be computed from the date agreed upon for the payment of the debt to the date on which it is finally paid.

▶ Brown bought two dresses for $125; terms, 30 days. She did not pay the account when it was due, and on its next statement the store added interest for one month at the prevailing legal rate. The charge is legal, although many business houses do not follow the practice because of their desire to retain the goodwill of their customers.

Agreements to Commit Crimes

Any agreement to commit a crime in return for a promise of money is void. Crimes include both misdemeanors and felonies. Acts may be considered illegal either by common law or by statute.

▶ Cerrutta lives in a state where the sale, transportation, or use of fireworks without a permit is illegal. He asked Markowitz, who was making a trip into another state, to bring back $25 worth of fireworks for him. When Markowitz returned, Cerrutta refused to reimburse him for the fireworks.

The agreement between the two parties involved the commission of an illegal act. Any action by Markowitz against the other party would fail because of the illegality of the subject matter of their contract.

Unlicensed Transactions

Certain businesses and professions are required to be licensed to:

☐ Provide a source of income, a part of which will be used in the supervision of the business or profession being licensed.
☐ Provide supervision and regulation of businesses and professions that might otherwise inflict harm upon the general public if allowed to operate without controls.

Contractors, undertakers, doctors, dentists, restaurateurs, and others in public service must be closely supervised and controlled for the protection of the general public. Services rendered and goods sold in the absence of a required license result in invalid contracts. Such contracts are not enforceable.

> Two college students opened a roadside stand as a summer venture, selling cold drinks and sandwiches. The state board of health required all food dispensers to secure licenses and to take health examinations. The youths had not complied with either of these requirements. Would contracts made by them in this business be enforceable?

No. Any agreement relating to the business of these youths would not be legally enforceable. The same ruling would apply to beauty shops, barbershops, and other businesses requiring sanitary conditions and regular inspection.

Agreements Against Public Policy

Certain agreements made between individuals may be harmful to the public good. Such agreements are said to be *contrary to public policy*. An actual injury to the public need not be proved if the intent of the agreement is other than good. Many agreements come within this group, the most important of which are summarized below.

Agreements to Obstruct Justice   In this group are included the following agreements: to protect another from arrest, not to prosecute a criminal, to suppress evidence, not to serve as a witness in a trial, to encourage lawsuits (known as *champerty*), to give false testimony, to bribe a juror. These acts are not only sufficient to render a contract void but they also usually carry penalties because they are considered criminal offenses.

> Anderson was a witness to an accident involving two cars. One of the drivers paid Anderson $50 in return for her promise to forget all that she had seen. Anderson later changed her mind and testified truthfully about the facts concerning the accident. Is she responsible for damages resulting from her breach of the agreement to remain silent?

The contract Anderson made with the driver is void because it is considered against public policy, and any effort to hold her to it will be unsuccessful.

Agreements in Restraint of Marriage   The law has always regarded marriage as a sacred institution and as the privilege of all persons, not to be denied by private contract with other persons. Promises not to marry in return for some benefit will not be enforceable by either party.

> Johnson's father wished her to remain single and offered her $50,000 if she would not marry. The agreement is void. She would be permitted to marry at any time even though she has agreed to her father's request. Even if Johnson did keep her promise, her father would have no legal obligation to pay the money promised.
>
> Suppose Johnson had agreed to a request made by her father not to marry an undesirable young man with whom she had been keeping steady company. This

contract would be valid and enforceable. In this case she had not given up the right of marriage, but had agreed not to marry a particular person (which constitutes valid subject matter).

Agreements with Enemy Aliens   Agreements that result in giving aid or comfort to the enemy are void.

A naval base was located within an area inhabited by citizens of an unfriendly foreign power who had migrated into the area. To relieve naval personnel from arduous labor, workers were chosen from among civilians living within the area. Should hostilities break out between the two governments, the employment of these civilian workers would be considered contrary to the public good, and hence invalid and improper, because of financial aid and intelligence that might thereby be made available to the enemy.

Agreements Interfering with Public Service   Contracts in this group include agreements to bribe or interfere with public officials, to obtain political preference in appointments to office, to pay an officer for signing a pardon, requiring one of the parties to the agreement to break a law or commit a tort, and to influence a lawmaking body to seek personal gain.

Benjamin entered into an agreement with the state highway engineer in which the engineer agreed to use his influence to have the new state highway run adjacent to Benjamin's farm. Benjamin paid the engineer $5,000 for his promise to attempt to grant this request. This agreement is void and may not be enforced. The failure of the engineer to exert his influence would give Benjamin no rights in seeking the return of the $5,000 paid.

Agreements to Defraud   Such agreements are deemed invalid and therefore unenforceable.

Dillon, the owner of a large piece of property located in mountainous country, promised to pay Leonard $500 to tell a visitor that the land contained rich deposits of valuable ore. Dillon's plan was then to approach the visitor and sell the property at a large profit. This agreement constitutes an invalid contract and may not be enforced by either Dillon or Leonard.

Agreements to Pay Officers to Perform Acts Within Their Duties

A property owner promised to pay two firefighters $5,000 if they would make a special effort to rescue a relative believed trapped in his blazing home. This contract is not enforceable because the firefighters are pledged to save lives and property from fire.

Agreements to Suppress Competition   Such agreements may be made at public sales or in connection with the letting of contracts.

Three new schools were to be built in a certain rural district. Only three contractors were available for the bidding. They agreed to bid on all three jobs but arranged the amounts of the bids among themselves so that each would be awarded one of the construction jobs. This agreement is not enforceable.

Agreements to Induce Parties to Breach Their Contracts

The Smith Oil Company had a contract to supply oil for one year to the public schools in a certain town. Brown, the owner of another firm, offered to pay the purchasing agent $500 if he would break the contract and give the business to Brown's firm. This agreement is unenforceable because it is contrary to public policy.

Agreements Contrary to Good Morals   An example of such an agreement is a conspiracy to commit a theft and divide the spoils.

Agreements to Defraud Creditors by Selling One's Property

Billings anticipated the loss of his business to creditors. He made an agreement to sell his business to Jenkins at a very low price on the promise that after his debts had been cleared through bankruptcy proceedings, he would buy back the business from Jenkins at the same low price. This agreement is void and unenforceable.

Contracts in Restraint of Trade

The law is a constant protector of the rights of persons to make a living and to do business freely in a competitive market. If persons enter into contracts that take away these rights, the rights will be restored to them by declaring such contracts void. Agreements which have the effect of removing competition or denying to the public services they would otherwise have, or which result in higher prices and resulting hardship, will be declared void.

The three major building contractors in a certain locality agreed to build no new homes under $40,000 within a 20-mile radius of their town. This agreement is void on the ground that it interferes with and restrains competition and free trade. Any attempt to enforce the agreement upon one who might build less expensive houses would fail.

Business and professional persons have a right to provide protection for themselves when they purchase a going business or practice. These agreements are valid when made with the former owner if their provisions are not too broad. If the restrictive features are too broad, they will be declared void, but the other features of the contract will remain in force. For example, the seller's right to make a living in the same business or profession in another community or in the same community in later years may not be taken away.

Lawrence successfully passed her examination for admission to the bar. She was anxious to establish herself in a practice in a small upstate town. After careful investigation, she found an older man with a legal practice which she offered to purchase. The contract of sale specified that the seller would not enter into the legal profession in the same town for a period of two years.

This agreement would be enforceable, since it did not take away the former owner's right to continue his profession. Had the agreement restrained the seller from entering law practice anywhere within the state for a period of ten years, the restriction could have been declared void and unenforceable. The reasonableness of the restraint determines the legality and enforceability of the agreement.

Monopolies   *Monopolies* are business agreements that result in the restraint of competition and free trade. Monopolies result when a contract or an agreement among manufacturers, producers, or dealers (1) divides territories within which they shall confine their operations, or (2) seeks to eliminate or restrain competition. These agreements often cause consumer prices to soar by restricting output or by fixing or controlling prices. Monopolies of this type are illegal and void.

> Three television and radio dealers enter into a contract whereby each agrees to respect the territory in which the others operate their business. Each one agrees not to accept service calls or sell sets to persons living within the areas assigned to the other two. This agreement restricts free trade, creates a hardship on the consumers in all three areas, and is against public policy. In any action brought on this agreement, the court would declare it unenforceable.

Legal Monopolies   All monopolies are not illegal. Public policy recognizes that in certain circumstances a monopoly may be a valuable instrument which gives incentive to talented persons and enterprises and benefits society as a whole. The law grants recognition to the following categories of monopolistic agreements.

Patents   **Patents** are valid enforceable monopolies granted by the federal government to inventors, who are given exclusive rights to their inventions, usually for a period of seventeen years. *Ordinary patents* give protective coverage to inventors of processes, machines, chemical formulas, and articles of manufacture. *Design patents* cover "any new original and ornamental design for an article of manufacture," such as a newly designed toy. Design patents, unlike ordinary patents, may be granted for a period of less than seventeen years. The use of a patent without the owner's permission gives the patent holder the right to demand all profits from the unauthorized use of the patent. All patents are registered for a fee with the U.S. Patent Office in Washington, D.C.

Copyrights   **Copyrights** protect the writings of authors, the works of artists, painters, and sculptors, and the musical scores of composers from unauthorized reproduction, republication, and sale. Under the Copyright Revision Act which took effect on January 1, 1978, a work created after that date is protected for the duration of the creator's life plus fifty years. Works created prior to that date are protected for seventy-five years from the date the work was first copyrighted. Under the previous law, a copyright extended for a period of twenty-eight years, with the option of renewal for an additional twenty-eight years. Copyrights are registered with the Library of Congress, also located in Washington, D.C.

Trademarks   These consist of unusual and unique symbols and trade names that are distinctive and novel and are adopted for goods sold in more than one state. The registration of a *trademark* or trade name with the U.S. Patent Office establishes the priority of its use and gives the owner its exclusive use for twenty years. A further discussion of the legal effects of trademarking may be found in Chapter 2.

Franchises   **Franchises** are legally protected public or private business ventures operated with the authorization of the state, federal, or local government or under agreement with a privately owned parent company. If franchised by public authority, such ventures are called *public franchises*. A public utility, such as an electric or telephone company, illustrates this type of venture. Typically, a public service commission oversees the public franchise and has approval or veto power over the rates it may charge consumers and over other related activities. Other types of franchises, unregulated by governmental authority, are called *private franchises*. Both types of franchises protect investors from competition of sorts within a specified territory as stated in the franchising agreement creating them. For a more complete study of private franchise ventures, see Chapter 31.

Trade Secrets and Employment Contracts   The most valuable assets of many large business houses are the secret methods of production and the formulas used in the manufacture of highly competitive consumer goods. The success of certain advertised soft drinks, cleaning fluids, chemicals, and automotive equipment depends upon keeping production methods confidential. Such companies must protect themselves from the loss of trade secrets through persons in their employ. An employee may be required to sign a contract which restrains him or her from working for competitors for a reasonable time after leaving his or her present job. The employee may also be required to assign to an employer all patents taken out during his or her term of employment and for a period of some years thereafter if the patents in any way relate to the work of the employer. Contracts for the protection of trade secrets, while in restraint of trade, are valid if reasonable. They serve to encourage and protect firms engaged in research and development which result in ultimate public good.

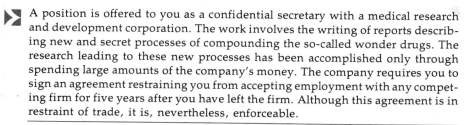

A position is offered to you as a confidential secretary with a medical research and development corporation. The work involves the writing of reports describing new and secret processes of compounding the so-called wonder drugs. The research leading to these new processes has been accomplished only through spending large amounts of the company's money. The company requires you to sign an agreement restraining you from accepting employment with any competing firm for five years after you have left the firm. Although this agreement is in restraint of trade, it is, nevertheless, enforceable.

Questions for Review and Discussion

1. What are the three types of acts which may render a contract void because of illegal subject matter?

2. (*a*) How is a monopoly created? (*b*) Name four kinds of legal monopolies.

3. When is a contract entered into on a Sunday valid?

4. Are agreements in restraint of trade ever valid? Explain.

5. (*a*) What is usury? (*b*) What are the three usual

penalties imposed on persons guilty of charging excessive interest rates?

6. Distinguish between an ordinary patent and a design patent.

7. What is the rule of *in pari delicto*? Give an example of its use.

8. (*a*) Why are public utilities granted monopoly

rights? (*b*) Do you approve of the creation of such monopolies?

9. A professional person who had not complied with a licensing statute rendered services in connection with his occupation. What is the legal effect of such a transaction? Explain.

10. What is a franchise? Distinguish between a public franchise and a private franchise.

Analyzing Cases

1. McCabe was engaged and had plans to be married two weeks after graduation from college. His parents disapproved of the marriage and offered McCabe a new car and money for a trip if the wedding plans were canceled. Following these suggestions, McCabe canceled the wedding plans. The parents then refused to give McCabe the promised car and money. May they be sued for breach of this agreement? Explain. • See also *Attridge* v. *Pembroke*, 235 N.Y. App. Div. 101.

2. Egbert was a witness to an accident in which three persons were seriously injured. The driver of the car at fault gave Egbert $100 in return for Egbert's promise not to come forth as a witness or to testify against this driver in any subsequent lawsuit. Egbert later offered the injured parties' attorney assistance in proving their case. Will this subject Egbert to legal action for breach of contract? Explain. • See also *Board of Education* v. *Angel*, 75 W.Va. 747.

3. Lanfranchi sold a sporting goods store to Reed for $35,000. Lanfranchi had made hundreds of friends over the years through good treatment of customers. At Reed's request Lanfranchi agreed, in writing, not to open another sporting goods store for ten years within a radius of 50 miles of the present store. Is this condition of the sale enforceable if Lanfranchi

opens another store? Explain. • See also *Hill* v. *Central West Pub. Service Co.*, 37 F. 2d 451.

4. Guttierez, a city building inspector, agreed to approve improper concrete work that had been done on the Hightower Building. Owners of the Hightower Building promised to appoint Guttierez to the position of manager of the building, which paid a much higher salary than the inspector's post he held. Are the Hightower people obligated to carry through with this promise?• See also *Allen* v. *City of Lawrence*, 318 Mass. 210, 61 N.E. 2d 133.

5. Olson borrowed $300, in an emergency, from Faithful Loan Company. The loan was for ten weeks, with interest at 7 percent per week. Olson had difficulty in meeting the interest payments and was not able to pay the principal at the end of the ten weeks. Would Olson have any grounds for complaint on this loan? Explain.

6. Roberts specialized in chemical research for Hughes Chemical Company. Roberts had access to all secret materials that had resulted from research in this area by the company over a ten-year period. In her employment contract, Roberts had agreed not to accept employment with a competing firm for ten years after the Hughes contract expired. Is this employment contract an illegal restraint of trade? Explain.

Legal Reasoning and Business Judgment

Analyze the legal aspects of these business problems. Suggest possible solutions.

1. A representative of a competing firm approached the president of your company at a social affair. He suggested that the two companies get together on a price policy to be introduced with new machine models about to be offered to the public. The suggested plan would ensure greater profits to both companies, reduce advertising expenses, and create a better atmosphere of overall cooperation between the two organizations. What advice would you offer your firm if consulted on the proposal? *turn them down*

2. You are employed by a frozen food processing company engaged in packing sweet corn and lima beans. The advertising department prepared new labels for packaging. One of the artists came up with the name "A-Corn" for the new labels. Your firm was advised to secure a copyright on this name. Is this the proper advice? Why or why not? *no, it's not worth it*

3. The credit department of your company devised a plan whereby it appeared possible to realize greater profits from credit contracts than from the actual profits on goods sold. Customers were to be charged 5 percent per month on all unpaid balances of their 30-day charge accounts. Customers would be encouraged to take their time in settlement of current bills. What reaction would you have to this plan if your advice were sought? *illegal interest*

Chapter 11
Form
of
Agreement

To be enforceable, must a contract be in writing? May parties enter into agreements which are partly oral and partly written? Would you advise a person to make only written contracts?

In discussing the four requirements of contracts we have examined numerous contract situations. Some of the agreements were written, some oral, and some only implied. The validity of the contracts did not always depend upon their being written. You might have concluded, therefore, that a valid contract need not necessarily be in writing. The exception to this rule is that certain contracts are *required* by law to be in writing. Moreover, a written agreement is desirable, but not required, under the following circumstances.

☐ When the agreement is executory and is not to be performed at the time it is made.

> You visit a store and order clothes to be made to your measurements. A week later, the store informs you that your clothes are ready, but when you call for the order, you find that the items are different from the ones you thought you had ordered. The clerk maintains that they are the right clothes. Without a written memorandum of some sort, neither party would have a clear record of facts if the contract were to be enforced through legal action.

☐ When the agreement contains many details and specifications which may confuse the parties before performance is completed.

> A decorator is hired to paper and repaint the inside of your nine-room house. Several patterns are selected, a different one for each room. When the work is finished, you refuse to pay, claiming that the decorator used the wrong paper in two of the rooms. A written contract, although not required, would have made the position of both parties clear, and, in the event of an action on the contract, a proper decision could be made by the court.

THE PAROL-EVIDENCE RULE

When a contract is put in writing after its proposed terms have been discussed orally, only those rights and obligations mentioned in the written agreement may be enforced. Oral evidence may not be presented which will in any way conflict with that which is written. This is known as the *parol-evidence rule*.

137

Suppose, in the preceding case, the decorator had orally promised to repair plaster cracks in the hallway, which was not to be papered. Had the rest of the agreement been written, this additional obligation would not be enforceable. Any attempt to seek damages for nonperformance of the entire contract would fail. The parties could have included this among the terms of the written agreement, had they desired.

Oral Evidence

Oral evidence may be introduced if its sole purpose is to clarify some point in a written agreement. Such evidence is acceptable only when the written agreement is not clear by its own terms and expressions. The Uniform Commercial Code provides that "... terms as are included therein may not be contradicted by evidence of any prior agreement or of any contemporaneous oral agreement but may be explained or supplemented."

 The sellers of a radio included in their written agreement a 60-day guaranty of the instrument. Within the guaranty period, two tubes burned out, and the purchaser seeks their replacement under the guaranty. The sellers refuse, claiming that the guaranty covers only the set, not the tubes.

Oral evidence may be introduced in an attempt to determine whether the written guaranty covered both the set and the tubes or only the set. The general practice of persons engaged in the sale of radios may be introduced to indicate the *custom of the marketplace*. If it is found that the custom of the business is to guarantee only the set, the tubes would not be covered.

The Code provides that the express terms of the agreement as well as any course of dealing and usage of trade shall govern; but when express terms and trade usage are not considered, then the express terms shall control the course of performance.

THE STATUTE OF FRAUDS

While the parties to a contract may decide for themselves whether their agreements shall be written, oral, or merely implied, the statute of frauds specifies that certain agreements, to be enforceable, require written contracts. The written agreement in these situations becomes important only if the parties disagree and attempt court action. Unless a written agreement is produced, the courts will not recognize the contractual relationship. While there are some minor differences in the interpretation of the statute in the several states, uniformity does exist in its most important phases. The statute specifically outlines six types of contracts that *must* be written if they are to be enforceable.

Executory Contracts

Parties seeking protection under the statute of frauds must first meet the requirements of the statute.

▶ Chung guaranteed a personal debt of one of her business associates. The agreement was oral, although the statute of frauds required that it be in writing. Chung's associate failed to pay the debt when it became due. Is Chung liable on her promise of guarantee?

Inability to produce a written agreement will bar the creditor from any recovery against the guarantor. Thus, the statute of frauds provides Chung with a complete defense in any demand made against her for payment of the other's debt.

▶ Suppose, in the above case, Chung had carried out her promise. When she learned that she had been under no *legal* obligation to do so, she demanded the return of the money paid to the creditors. Would the courts return the parties to their original positions because Chung's promise had not been in writing?

The courts would not consider such a request. The statute of frauds applies only to *executory* contracts. The fulfillment of the promises made by both parties would terminate the contract, and the statute of frauds would no longer apply to the agreement.

What Is Meant by "Writing"

A sales slip, a letter, a memorandum—any one of these may constitute a contract; so also do formal deeds, mortgages, and leases. Which group is enforceable? Does either group satisfy the statute of frauds definition of a *written contract*? Do both groups satisfy the definition? Just what is meant when the statute states that "the agreement must be in writing"?

The statute requires only that the *agreement be in writing*—nothing more! A pen, a pencil, a typewriter, or any other mechanical device comes within this definition. The writing should be intelligible. It may be embodied in letters sent between the parties; it may be written on any surface suitable for the purpose of recording the intention of the parties.

To be complete, the written agreement, or memorandum, as it is often called, should contain the following information: (1) terms of the agreement; (2) identification of the subject matter; (3) statement of the consideration promised; (4) names and identities of the persons to be obligated; and (5) signatures of the parties to the contract.

▶ You order a new tennis racket from a sporting goods store. The clerk writes the order on the regular sales slip, noting the model, manufacturer's name, and price. You sign your name to the sales slip. This memorandum would be satisfactory under the requirements of the statute of frauds.

While the above description of a "writing" is preferred to ensure clarity in the event of a suit at law, the writing may be acceptable even though it omits or does not correctly state some term agreed upon by the contracting parties. Such written agreements may be enforced even though material terms are omitted. The court may supply omitted terms, including the price, terms and place of payment, terms of delivery, and other factors, *but not the quantity*. To be enforceable, only the following must be shown in the writing: proof of contract intent, the quantity ordered, the names of the parties, and their signatures.

Oral agreements are often made in which the parties state that the oral agreement will be reduced to writing and signed, to comply with the statute. Such promises are not enforceable, as only the written contract itself is valid.

 The Wohlmans talked with Rascowski and agreed to sell their house and lot for a price agreed upon. It was orally agreed that they all would meet at the Wohlmans' home the following day to draw up and sign a written agreement. The agreement to create the written contract for land is not enforceable, and the parties are without legal rights in the matter.

Types of Contracts Under the Statute

The statute of frauds specifies the following six types of contracts *that must be in writing* to be valid and enforceable.

Executor's Debts Agreements by executor or administrator to pay debts of deceased out of his or her own personal estate must be committed to writing. An *executor* may be either a person or a corporation named in a will to oversee the distribution of the deceased's estate according to the provisions contained in a will. An *administrator* is one named by a court to do the work of an executor if none is named in the will or if the executor either refuses to perform or is incapable of performing the duties. Persons having the responsibility of executor or administrator often make promises for the protection of the survivors, under emotional stress. Such promises must be in writing to be enforceable, thus removing the possibility of enforcing unintentional or ill-advised oral statements.

 You are named as the executor of your brother's estate. A creditor demands the payment of $500 owed by the deceased. To protect your brother's wife from the claim, you promise to pay the bill yourself. This promise would not be enforceable against you unless it were reduced to a written agreement.

Guaranty of Payment A promise to pay another's bills or to settle for any of his or her wrongful acts, *if he or she does not settle them personally,* is an obligation that must be in writing if it is to be valid and enforceable. This is a *guaranty of payment*. A guaranty is thus distinguished from a suretyship, which is a primary obligation and which would be enforceable even though made orally. A *surety* is liable with the principal debtor on the original contract.

 Friends call you long-distance from a garage that is fifty miles away to say that they must have a new tire for their car to get back home. The garage agrees to give your friends the tire if you guarantee the payment. Any oral guaranty of payment over the telephone would be unenforceable under this section of the statute. But suppose that you had said to the manager of the garage, "Give them the tire, and I will pay for it." Would this statement be enforceable?

In the second instance the promise was not one of guaranty, but one in which you made yourself *directly and primarily* responsible for the amount of credit extended. Thus you made your own contract with the garage; you were not guaranteeing another's obligation. The oral promise was binding on you. This type of agreement is known as a *surety* as compared with a *guaranty*.

A promise to pay the debt of another is not required to be in writing to be enforceable if the main purpose of the person who is making the promise is to gain some advantage of his or her own. This is known as the ***leading-object rule***.

▶ Coleman purchased a large quantity of canned goods from Indiero. Before receiving delivery of the goods, he contracted to sell part of the purchase to Fried. Because Fried needed the canned goods for his trade, he visited Indiero and asked her to make immediate shipment to Coleman. He promised Indiero that if Coleman failed to pay, he would do so. Indiero did as Fried requested and, when Coleman did not pay for the purchase, attempted to hold Fried to his promise.

It was held that Fried's promise was binding, even though made orally. The main purpose of Fried's promise was not merely to secure the debt of Coleman but to gain a business advantage of his own.

Contracts Taking More Than One Year to Complete From Date Made　If the terms of an executory agreement make it impossible to complete the agreement within one year of the date of the agreement, the contract must be in writing.

▶ You are offered a position as a salesperson for a firm that desires your services in calling on all prospective customers in the fifteen counties of the state. It is planned that you are to spend one month in each county. When you report for work, the manager informs you that the position is no longer open to you, although you had accepted the offer. Any action against the company would fail in that the contract could not be completed within one year and there had been no written agreement.

The time period regarded by the statute starts from *the date on which the contract is entered into* by the parties, not from the date on which the contract is to be placed in operation. An agreement entered into on Wednesday in which a person agrees to start working the following Monday for one year would therefore have to be in writing.

Had a position been offered to you that *could* possibly be completed within one year, the agreement would have been enforceable even though oral.

▶ Suppose, in the previous case, the employer had said, "We want you to cover the fifteen counties of the state, and the job must be completed within fifteen months." The contract need not be in writing, since the fifteen months is merely a time period during which the work must be completed. There is no restriction whereby the work could not be completed in twelve months or even less.

It is generally held that a contract of employment intended to continue for the life of an employee need not be in writing. It is possible that such a contract may be completed within one year of its beginning. Some states, however, have enacted statutes which require *lifetime agreements* to be in writing, taking into consideration the apparent intent of both parties that the contract is to last longer than one year.

Contracts in Consideration of Marriage   Agreements made *in consideration of marriage* must be in writing. This section does not relate to the *marriage contract* itself, which in almost all cases is oral. It refers to those promises made by parties prior to marriage in which they accept additional obligations not ordinarily included in the implied obligations of marriage itself. Such promises are enforceable only if they are in writing and are agreed upon prior to the marriage.

> ▶ A young woman owns a large amount of real property, free and clear of any encumbrances. She is about to be married in a state whose laws specify that real property owned by the wife at the time of her marriage will be jointly owned by both husband and wife after marriage. The husband is asked to sign an agreement that he will give up this right in his wife's property and that his wife may operate or sell her holdings with no interference from him.

This agreement is one made *in consideration of marriage*. It is in writing, agreed to before marriage, and signed by the man the woman intends to marry. It is enforceable under the statute of frauds. Because the agreement concerns interest in real property, many states would require that it be under seal as well.

Sale of Real Property   All contracts for the transfer or sale of any interest in real property must be in writing. In many states in which the seal is still in use, these contracts must be under seal. Real-property transactions have always been looked upon as formal and of a most serious nature because of the finality of transfer of rights irreplaceable by the owner. A lease for the renting of another's real property must be in writing unless it is for a period of less than one year.

> ▶ After searching for months, a young married couple found a house which fitted their needs perfectly. The location, size, price, sale terms, proximity to church, school, and shopping centers were all they had been looking for. After thorough discussion with the owner, they agreed to buy the house and sealed the agreement with a handshake. Did this oral agreement result in an enforceable contract?

No. The agreement is not enforceable by either party. If all parties accepted and carried out their obligations, the law would not interfere, nor would their contract actions be void. However, if either party refused to perform, the agreement could not be enforced.

Experienced real estate salespeople and brokers eliminate the possibility of loss of sales and commissions by carrying with them convenient contract forms which create enforceable obligations until such time as more formal agreements may be drawn up at the real estate office.

Sale of Personal Property Over Given Limit   Agreements for sale of personal property the price of which exceeds the amount set by statute must be set down in writing. So numerous are the sales of personal property that the UCC provisions require a written agreement only when the purchase price is $500 or more. The Uniform Commercial Code provides that a contract for the sale of goods for the price of $500 or more is not enforceable unless there is some writing sufficient to indicate that such a contract has been made between the parties and signed by the party against whom enforcement is sought or by an authorized agent or broker.

▶ A young person entered into an oral contract to buy a diamond engagement ring for $800. The jeweler put the ring aside for the customer, but two days later the youth called and canceled the sale. Although there had been mutual agreement, serious intent, consideration, and valid subject matter, the agreement is not enforceable for lack of a written contract.

If there has been either a part payment by the buyer or a part delivery of merchandise by the seller as the result of the oral contract, the oral contract is enforceable only to the extent of goods delivered or money paid.

▶ Hetzler purchased a boat and an outboard motor for $1,900. It was agreed that the price of the motor was $750 and the boat $1,150. At the time of the sale Hetzler paid for the motor, promising to return the next week to pay for and accept delivery of the boat. Any attempt to enforce the entire oral contract would be unsuccessful due to the requirements of the statute of frauds under the Uniform Commercial Code.

Sale of Securities A contract for the sale of securities is not enforceable by way of action or defense unless there is some writing signed by the party against whom enforcement is sought. The writing must be sufficient to show that a contract has been made for sale of a stated quantity of described securities at a stated price.

▶ Fulmer agreed to sell Jackson ten shares of a certain stock for $89. Although they had every intention of carrying out the agreement, neither Fulmer nor Jackson could enforce the sale in the absence of the required written agreement.

If the party against whom enforcement is sought admits in court that a contract was made for sale of a stated quantity of described securities at a fixed price, the contract is enforceable.

A contract for the sale of such personal property as a right under a bilateral contract, royalty claims, patents, and the like must be evidenced by a signed written agreement if the price involved is in excess of $5,000. This rule does not apply to contracts for the sale of goods or securities or to security agreements.

Auction Sales In auction sales the purchaser is not required to enter into a written agreement for the purchase of personal property exceeding the $500 limit set by the Uniform Commercial Code. The notation made by the clerk of the auction in the sales sheet, initialed by the purchaser, is sufficient.

▶ A collector, seeking an antique table, attended an auction. She purchased the desired table with the closing bid of $575. Although a latecomer to the sale might offer a much higher bid for the table, neither the auctioneer nor the seller could declare the previous sale unenforceable because of the lack of the usual written and signed agreement.

In an auction sale the sale is complete when the auctioneer announces this fact by the fall of the hammer or in some other customary manner. When a bid is made while the hammer is falling in acceptance of a prior bid, the auctioneer may in his or her discretion reopen the bidding or declare the goods sold under the bid on which the hammer was falling.

Work, Labor, and Service Contracts

The sale of personal property covered by the statute refers to those things available for sale without alteration or special manufacture. Agreements for the purchase of items requiring special manufacture or not available for sale to the trade are not within the statute. They do not require written agreements to make them enforceable. Oral agreements, if proved, will be satisfactory.

 Suppose a hunter ordered for the protection of his valuable gun a special carrying case made of cordovan leather. This type of case must be made to special order. This contract would be one for work, labor, and service, and it does not come within the statute. Even though the price charged exceeds the statutory limit for personal property sales, it will not apply to this situation.

SPECIAL STATUTES REQUIRING WRITTEN CONTRACTS

The statute of frauds is the most important of the laws relating to written contracts. Other special contracts required by other laws to be written include the release of debt, covered in an earlier section, and the resumption of obligations after bankruptcy.

 A close friend borrowed money from you a few years ago but, because of business reverses, has not been able to repay you. As a gesture of friendship, you agree to cancel the existing debt. This is a release of debt, and most states require that it be in writing and under seal to be enforceable.

THE STATUTE OF LIMITATIONS

The law provides a time limit covering the period in which certain actions must be taken in contract, tort, and crimes. The statute of limitations may be used as a defense against a tardy creditor unless he or she is able to produce evidence of either of the following conditions:

☐ A written promise by the debtor, signed by the debtor and reaffirming his or her promise to pay, after the time has passed during which the account ordinarily could have been collected.

As a lawyer for a retail store, you seek to collect a debt which has been outlawed by the running of the statute of limitations. You write to the debtor informing her that she owes $50 and asking her to verify the amount. She writes back, stating that it is correct. This serves as a reaffirmation of the debt and renews the right of your firm to enforce the collection of the debt.

☐   A part payment of the debt, or of interest accrued on the debt, after the time covered by the statute has passed.

> You offer to settle the account in the above case if the debtor will pay $5 of the $50 she owes. Should she pay, the debt is thereby reaffirmed in its entirety, since part payment of an undisputed amount cannot act as payment of the full amount without a release under seal. After paying the $5, the debtor may no longer use the statute of limitations as her defense.

FORMAL CONTRACT REQUIREMENTS

A *formal contract* is one which is in writing, is signed by the party or parties obligated, and contains their seals if state law so requires. This type of contract is used for the purchase of another's interest or ownership in real property. Bills of sale, mortgages, deeds, leases, and municipal and corporation contracts are also included in this group of formal contracts.

Signatures

A written agreement should be signed by both parties. If, because of illness or for some other good reason, one of the parties is unable to sign the agreement, it may be signed by another for that party. The signature should be followed by a statement similar to the one in Fig. 11-1 and should be signed by a witness.

If one of the parties to a contract cannot write his or her name, he or she may make a mark (an X or other symbol), which should be followed by a statement by a witness, as in Fig. 11-2.

Witnesses

In a few cases when witnesses are required, the statement "Signed in the presence of" should by placed at the left of the names of the parties to the contract, and below this phrase should appear the names of the witnesses.

Signature: *Thomas Stewart*

WITNESS: I hereby attest that Thomas Stewart was physically unable to sign his name and that his name was signed by me in his presence and at his request.

Ronald Paul

Fig. 11-1.   Signature for an incapacitated person

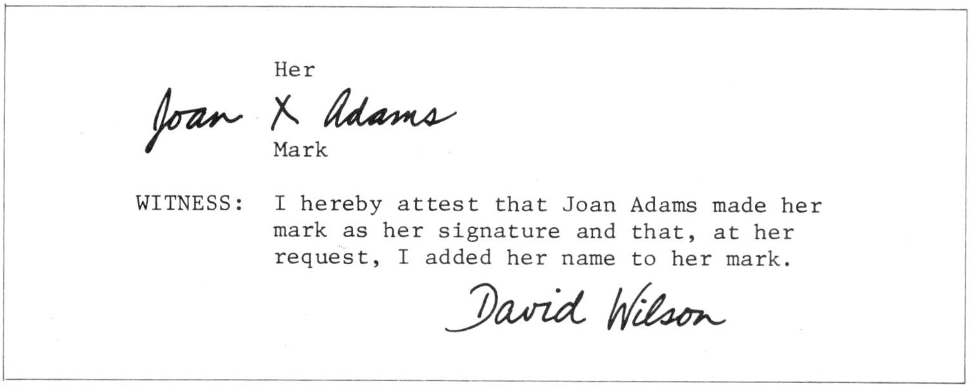

Her
Joan X Adams
Mark

WITNESS: I hereby attest that Joan Adams made her mark as her signature and that, at her request, I added her name to her mark.

David Wilson

Fig. 11-2. Signature of a person who does not know how to write

Acknowledgment

The ***acknowledgment*** of a contract is the witnessing of its signing by a notary public or some other competent court officer with this authority. The parties to the agreement declare, in the presence of the officer, that this is their contract, thus avoiding the necessity of proving signatures and seals at any later time if the contract is involved in a dispute. The notary or officer then affixes his or her seal and signature to the instrument as witness to the acknowledgment by the parties. *Notaries sometimes insist on reading the documents being acknowledged. They have no legal right to do so, and the parties may refuse such invasion of privacy.*

Questions for Review and Discussion

1. Should all contracts be in writing? Explain.

2. What is the parol-evidence rule? Give an example applying the rule.

3. Name the contracts that must be in writing under the statute of frauds.

4. What is meant by a written contract as covered by the statute of frauds?

5. Are contracts that come under the provisions of the statute of frauds illegal if they are not in writing? Explain.

6. (*a*) What is meant by the statute of limitations? (*b*) Explain how its provisions affect the collection of debts.

7. (*a*) What is meant by contracts for work, labor, and service? (*b*) How do these contracts compare with contracts for the sale of goods?

8. (*a*) What is a contract in consideration of marriage? (*b*) What are the differences between a contract to marry, a contract of marriage, and a contract in consideration of marriage?

9. What is an executor? an administrator?

10. How does a person sign a contract if he or she is unable to write (*a*) because of illness? (*b*) because he or she is illiterate?

Analyzing Cases

1. Hastings is engaged to a young woman who has an excellent position as secretary to the president of a large corporation. She tells Hastings that she has decided to work for two more years before getting married. Hastings offers her $1,500 if she will give up the idea and marry him at once. She accepts his offer, but after they are married he refuses to pay her the money promised. Does the wife have a right of action against her husband? Explain. • See also *Weld* v. *Weld*, 71 Kan. 622. *it must be in writing*

2. On May 15, Young is offered a position as an accountant with the Universal Housing Corporation to work for two years, starting June 1. Young accepts the offer, resigning from another position which he has held for several years. When he reports for work, Young finds that the position has already been filled by the owner's nephew. Young brings an action against the company for damages resulting from the breach. Will he recover? Explain. • See also *Warner* v. *Texas & Pac. Ry. Co.*, 164 U.S. 418. *no it has to be in writing*

3. Gretto was named administrator of Hall's estate. In defense of Hall's widow, who was threatened with suit unless certain of Hall's bills were paid immediately, Gretto said, "Leave my sister-in-law be. You will get your money. If things get worse, I'll pay the bills myself." In consideration of this promise, the creditors withdrew their threats. If the accounts are not settled by the estate, may Gretto be charged for the creditor's losses? Explain. • See also *Makin* v. *Dwyer*, 205 Mass. 472. *no it has to be in writing*

4. Gap Auto Sales sold Stoltzfus a used Dodge.

The salesperson guaranteed the car for 60 days, promising to replace all defective parts with no charges for labor or parts. Stoltzfus signed the sales agreement for $750 and took delivery of the car. Two weeks later the car's automatic transmission had to be replaced. Stoltzfus discovered that there was nothing in the written contract about the guarantee. Who would be responsible for payment for the new transmission and its installation? *Stoltzfus*

5. Dahl was offered a position as administrative secretary in a leading law firm. Salary was set at $190 a week. Other benefits were a $5,000 life insurance policy, a four-week vacation with full pay, Blue Cross and Blue Shield insurance paid by the firm, as well as tuition and books paid for paralegal courses at a nearby college. Discuss this contract and whether it must be in writing to be enforced by either Dahl or the legal firm. Should Dahl ask that the contract conditions be included in a written agreement? Explain. • See also *Dykema* v. *Story & Clark Piano Co.*, 190 N.W. 638. *yes.*

6. Moore, an avid lover of good music, had Denver Music Company design and install a stereophonic music system in his cathedral-ceilinged living room. The firm agreed to supply all parts and installation for $4,780, to which Moore orally agreed. After the job was completed, Moore hesitated to pay the bill. One defense given was that the contract was unenforceable because it was not in writing. Do you agree with Moore's defense? Explain. • See also *Heintz* v. *Burkhard*, 29 Ore. 55. *no, especially contract doesn't need to be written.*

Legal Reasoning and Business Judgment

Analyze the legal aspects of these business problems. Suggest possible solutions.

1. As personnel manager of an office machines

firm, you have been looking for an experienced computer technician to service machines out on lease from your firm. One applicant for the job had better-than-average qualifications, excellent references, and unequaled knowledge of all new computer schematic wiring and repair. There were other available jobs, but the applicant showed an interest in joining your company. How would you "firm up" this future employee's agreement to start work the following month?

2. Your company is interested in acquiring a piece of property adjacent to its Liberty River plant location. You invite the owner to talk over the matter at lunch in the Stevens Hotel. According to reports, the attractive offer you will make to the owner may be snapped up because of his immediate need of money to cover mounting obligations. How will you prepare yourself for this crucial meeting during which you hope to make a deal for the company?

3. One of your older employees is called to the office to discuss a new pension plan. Employees entering the plan are required to accept a payroll deduction as co-contributor to the payments made to an insurance company that is going to administer the pension. This particular employee, although valuable and skillful, has never learned to write. What would you do in getting this employee's signature on the pension agreement so it is legally acceptable?

Chapter 12

Operation of Contracts

When parties enter into a contract, they assume certain obligations and duties. Parties are discharged from these commitments only when they have done what they promised to do under the contract or are released from their responsibilities by the other party. Of course the other party is still bound if he or she still has something to do.

As a general principle of law, only the parties to a contract incur obligations and acquire rights under the contract. A person cannot voluntarily pay another's debts and so take the place of the original creditor.

PERFORMANCE

Each party to a contract looks to the other for perfect and complete execution of all promises made. Anything less is not satisfactory performance and may lead to financial losses and possible legal action. The actions which an injured party may take are determined to a great extent by the seriousness of the other's failure to perform.

> A couple contracted with a builder for the construction of a house. After partly completing it, the builder stopped work and showed no intention of returning to the job.

This case is one of almost complete failure to give satisfactory performance. The builder has breached, or failed, in that promise, and the couple may rescind their agreement. In doing this, they would be relieved of all obligations to the builder for the value of the work already done and for the materials that were used on the incomplete house.

> Suppose the builder had conscientiously performed his obligations and the house was complete except for a few feet of molding that he had neglected to place around a door. Would the couple be permitted to rescind their agreement and be released of all obligations to pay, as they were in the first case?

This breach would be less damaging than the other. There has been *substantial performance* of the contract, and the builder may demand payment of the agreed price, with a deduction allowed for the small detail left unfinished. Whether substantial performance has been achieved depends on the amount of work done in relation to the entire agreement.

Third-Party Referees

When parties to a contract anticipate possible disagreement on performance, they may select a disinterested outside party as final judge.

 The couple and the builder select an architect who, they agree, will be the sole judge of whether the contract is satisfactorily completed. The builder will not be released from his obligation and the couple will not be required to pay until the architect has approved the work and has issued what is known as a *certificate of performance*.

When Time Is of the Essence

In certain contracts the time element, as well as performance, is of utmost importance.

 A young woman orders a taxi to take her to the airport to meet a plane which she plans to take to Chicago at 10 A.M. The taxi is late in picking up the young woman, and she misses connections for the flight.

In this contract the time element is as important as performance itself. In agreements of this kind, it is said that "time is of the essence." The trip to the airport is useless if it is not completed in time for the passenger to board the plane.

 Suppose the young woman had taken a taxi to her home. The time element is not nearly so important in this instance. Should the taxi arrive a few minutes late, the contract would still be enforceable.

Joint Liability

Joint contracts are those usually preceded by the words "We promise to. . . ." They are agreements in which two or more persons, acting as one, contract with another party and are said to be *jointly liable*. Joint parties are usually sued together, although more modern decisions indicate that they may be sued individually.

 O'Connor and Green enter into an agreement with Cohen, in which they say, "We promise to deliver 10 tons of coal to you on December 15." This is a joint contract, and failure to deliver the coal would permit Cohen to sue both O'Connor and Green.

Judgments by a court against persons with joint liability may be collected from all the parties, share and share alike, or they may be collected from only one of them. When the damages are collected from only one, a *contribution* may be sought by that individual from the others for their proportionate share of the judgment.

 Suppose, in the action by Cohen against O'Connor and Green, the court awarded a judgment in favor of Cohen, who collected the entire amount from O'Connor. O'Connor, in turn, may demand from Green a share of one-half the judgment.

Several Liability

When two or more persons acting on one side of an agreement hold themselves out as *individually responsible*, they are said to be *severally liable*. This type of agreement usually reads, "I promise...." or "Either of us promises...." The injured party in this type of agreement has the right to sue the others individually. Since each one has complete liability on the agreement, a release of one will not release the other.

 If O'Connor and Green had made an agreement with Cohen in which they had accepted several liability, Cohen could have sued either O'Connor or Green. If O'Connor had been sued, then Green, the one released from liability in the suit, would be liable to O'Connor for a proportionate share of any judgment obtained against him.

Joint and Several Liability

When two or more persons sign a contract using the expression "We jointly and severally agree and promise...," they are jointly and severally liable. They may be sued collectively or individually, at the option of the injured party. Payments by the ones not joined in the suit may be demanded by the one against whom the judgment is collected.

 O'Connor and Green enter into an agreement with Marcello in which they state, "We jointly and severally agree and promise to pay Marcello $600 when he delivers to us one used 3-ton truck." Failure to pay could result in an action against either O'Connor or Green or against the two of them at the same time.

Third-Party Beneficiaries

Third parties are persons or corporations who may in some way be affected by a contract but who are not one of the contracting parties. Early legal decisions gave these parties, often called *outside parties*, no rights in the agreements made by others. In recent years recognition has been given to the third party, who may under certain conditions enforce his or her rights under another's contract.

When a contract is made for the express benefit of a third party, he or she may demand damages for failure of performance.

 A father makes arrangements with the head of a private school for entering his daughter as a student. The resulting contract is made expressly for the benefit of the young woman. Although she is a third party, she would have the right to enforce the agreement if the school subsequently refused to admit her.

Two qualifications are necessary to permit a person to claim the rights of a *third-party beneficiary*.

☐ The contract must have been created for the purpose of benefiting the third party.
☐ One of the parties making the agreement must owe money or be under some duty or obligation to the third party at the time the contract is made.

The daughter in the previous case qualifies as a third-party beneficiary under both rules.

It is not necessary that the person benefited know of the contract at the time it is made. He or she may adopt the promise and its benefits whenever he or she learns about them. Before adoption of the benefits, the original parties may cancel their agreement if they wish to do so.

> ▶ Hernandez, the mother of a twelve-year-old boy, entered into an agreement with Kane under which Kane would care for the boy should anything happen to Hernandez. In consideration of the promise, Hernandez deeded a valuable property to Kane. In the event of Hernandez's death, the son would have the right to enforce this agreement when he received notice of it.

Incidental Beneficiaries   Contracts often result in benefits to third parties as an indirect consequence of the contract. The contract is not created for their benefit, and they are merely looked upon as *incidental beneficiaries*. They have none of the usual rights granted to the direct beneficiaries in the previous cases.

> ▶ A large mail order house contracted with a printer for the production of 100,000 copies of a catalog. The contract stated that the printer should use "only ink manufactured and supplied by the Midnight Ink Company." The printer used another manufacturer's ink. May the ink company named in the contract seek damages from the printer as a third-party beneficiary?

The ink company was a mere incidental beneficiary and could not enforce any agreement made with the printing firm in its position as an outside party.

Third-Party Interference   Persons who intentionally interfere with the performance of a contract made by others may be held responsible for any resulting damages. The action against such *third-party intermeddlers* is a tort.

> ▶ An outside party discourages a party to a contract from continuing his contract with a builder. If the acts of this outside third party result in a disruption of the contract in force between the builder and the other person, the builder may seek damages from the third party.

ASSIGNMENT OF CONTRACT RIGHTS

As a basic rule of law, most contracts may be assigned. A contract right is a property right and may be of greater value to an outside third party than to the one who possesses its rights to benefits. Often a party may realize greater profits from the sale of a contract right than by exercising the right himself or herself.

> ▶ O'Hara bought an option on a large farm in the Texas oil country for $10,000. The Big Barrell Oil Company offers O'Hara $85,000 for an option to buy the land. The profit to O'Hara from the sale of the option could give him an immediate return on his investment.

Delegation of Duties

It is a basic principle of law that only rights, not duties, may be assigned. A duty may, however, be delegated to a third person if the performance is not one which requires the special skill or talent of the original contracting party.

> Golman contracted to build a riding stable for King. Golman was engaged, at the time, in many other building projects and anticipated difficulty in completing King's job within the time agreed upon. Golman chose McCall to do this work in his stead, being responsible to King for complete and proper performance of all work done by McCall.

Parties may assign their rights under a contract, but they are not permitted to transfer their obligations. The one transferring the contract right is known as the *assignor*.

> Suppose you contract to purchase a new sports car, specifying that you are to pay for the car in eighteen equal monthly installments. After six payments, you find you cannot continue. A friend offers to buy the contract from you. The obligation to make the monthly payments may not be assigned. The dealer has a private right to determine who his or her debtors will be, basing the decision on individual credit ratings and financial reliability.

The code provides that an assignment of "the contract" or of "all my rights under the contract" is an assignment of rights. Unless the language or the circumstances (as in an assignment for security) indicate the contrary, it is a delegation of performance of the duties of the assignor, and its acceptance by the assignee constitutes a promise by him or her to perform those duties. This promise is enforceable by either the assignor or the other party to the original contract.

Form of Assignment

An assignment may be either written or oral. If the original contract was required to be in writing under the statute of frauds, the assignment must also be in writing. If the original contract required a sealed contract, the assignment also must be under seal.

Notice of Assignment

A party to a contract will not be obligated by any assignment until he or she receives notice of the assignment. Communication of the notice must be made by the one to whom the assignment has been made, known as the *assignee*.

> Morris owes Martinez $50 for work he performed on her car. Martinez assigns the right to the $50 to Allen, one of his creditors.

It is Allen's responsibility to give notice of the assignment to Morris. If she pays the $50 to Martinez before receiving notice, Allen, the assignee, will have no right of action against her. Allen may, however, seek payment from Martinez, because of Martinez's wrongful acceptance of the money that he had already knowingly assigned. Had Morris paid the money to Martinez after receiving notice of the assignment, she would be liable to Allen and would be required to pay him also.

Right to Investigate Assignment   After notice of assignment is made, the party receiving such communication may demand a reasonable time in which to investigate the validity of the assignment. Since assignments are not always in writing, this precaution may be particularly important before paying out funds to a stranger who claims an assignment.

> Suppose, in the above case, Allen gave oral notice to Morris that the right to collect the $50 had been assigned to him. With no more certainty than Allen's word, Morris is given the right to contact the assignor, Martinez, before meeting the demand.

Subsequent Assignments

Should the assignor of a right make a second or a third assignment of the same right to different persons, the first one giving notice to the other party will be accorded the superior right to the claim.

> Seltzer was indebted to Miller for $350. Moreno accepted an assignment of this claim, for which she gave Miller $350, less $25 as her profit from the transaction. Before Moreno gave notice to Seltzer of the assignment, Miller again assigned the same claim to Hoffman for an equal amount. Hoffman gave Seltzer immediate notice of the assignment. In the subsequent claim made by Moreno against Seltzer, Moreno will have no rights due to her failure to give notice. She would, however, have a right of action against Miller, who remains as a guarantor of payment of the debt.

Consideration in Assignments

A party to a contract may not refuse to honor an assignment on the ground that the assignor had transferred his rights without consideration from the assignee. Only the assignor may rescind or declare the assignment void for lack of consideration before the rights have been enforced.

> Ruther assigned to Stover a contract to install a heating system in the Norris Building. Stover gave nothing to Ruther in consideration of the assignment. Until Stover begins the work or has given notice of the assignment to the owners of the Norris Building, Ruther can rescind the assignment. However, the building owners may not complain if Ruther has seen fit to make a gift of this contract right to a third party.

Contracts That May Not Be Assigned

There are three exceptions to the rule that contracts may be assigned.

Contracts Restricting Assignment by Their Own Terms When the offeror and the offeree include in the terms of their contract an agreement that the contract may not be assigned, both parties will be restrained from making any assignments.

> McGraw contracted to build a garage for Pitt. The contract stipulated that McGraw would do the work himself and that he would not assign the contract to any outside third party. Although such a contract could, under ordinary circumstances, be assigned to another competent builder, the restricting clause would invalidate any attempt to do so.

The law provides that a prohibition of assignment of "the contract" is to be construed as barring only the delegation to the assignee of the assignor's performance.

Contracts Not Assignable by Law or Public Policy Some state and federal statutes have been enacted making the assignment of public contract rights illegal and invalid. For example, members of the Armed Forces are not permitted to assign their wages to any person other than dependents. Many state and city governments prohibit the assignment of wages and salaries of public officials. Contractors engaged in the construction of public buildings and public works are usually prohibited by statute from assigning the income to be received from such projects.

Contracts Requiring Personal Service Personal-service contracts may not be assigned if they are dependent on one's singular talent or if they are made by a member of a profession. Doctors, musicians, artists, athletes, and members of the other arts and professions may not assign their contracts. Tradespeople are not included in this classification. Their skills are regarded as being standardized, with little difference resulting if the work is done by any skilled person in the same trade.

> An artist is engaged to paint a mural in the reception room of a new medical center. This particular artist was chosen because of her interpretive abilities in pictures of the type desired. This is a personal-service contract, and, because of the special talent of the artist, it may not be assigned. The contract need not contain the usual restrictive clause against assignment.
>
> Suppose the medical center had contracted with plasterers to prepare the surfaces of the reception room walls for the artist's work. Although this contract is for personal service, it may be assigned because it is related to a trade and not to a profession or an art.

In the matter of ordinary contracts for services not involving a talent, the law provides that a party may perform his or her duty through a delegate unless otherwise agreed, or unless the other party has a substantial interest in having the original promisor perform or control the acts required by the contract. By delegating performance, a person is not relieved of any duty to perform or any liability for breach.

An *employment contract* is a personal-service contract that may not be assigned when an employer sells his or her business to another. An employer has no right to assign to the new owner the contracts still in force with members of his or her staff. The employees may not be restricted in their choice of an employer and may consider their obligations terminated upon the sale of the business.

> ▶ You are employed as a cost accountant under a three-year contract with a publishing company operated by partners Fisher and Berry. The owners sell their rights in the business to another firm in a nearby city, assigning to the new owners all executory contracts of employment then in effect. Neither you nor any of the employees will be bound by this assignment. The new employer may offer employment to the previous owners' employees, who may or may not accept the offers made.

A different view is held in the case of a corporation transferring its employment contracts when the company is sold to new owners. The contract of employment is held by the corporation, not by the stockholders, and as long as the corporation continues as such the contracts are enforceable.

> ▶ Suppose the publishing firm in the preceding case had been a corporation and the new owners had gained control by the purchase of a majority stockholding. This would not constitute an assignment, although to all practical purposes ownership had changed.

The Assignor's Guaranty

The assignors of a contract right, by their act, become guarantors of the work or promises that have been assigned to another. They likewise become guarantors of payment to the assignee from the other party to the original contract. As stated earlier, a person is not relieved of any duty to perform or any liability for breach on the grounds that performance was delegated to another.

> ▶ Acme Contracting Company agreed to construct a large building for Held and Company. Acme assigned the contract for the plumbing to Doakes, a local contractor. Acme, by this assignment, makes itself liable for the work done by Doakes and also guarantees to Doakes that Held and Company will pay the amount due for the plumbing work done. The guaranty will remain in force until both sides of the agreement have been fully executed.

Assignment by Operation of Law

The law will sometimes provide for the assignment of rights. Assignments of this type will be enforced even in the absence of any agreements between the parties concerned. The two most important of these assignments are discussed below.

Death of a Contracting Party Death brings about the automatic assignment of all contract rights of the deceased to either an executor or an administrator of the estate. The assignment is effected by law and covers all executory contracts with the exception of personal-service contracts. All rights to collection of money, to demand performance, and to the sale or purchase of real estate or personal property would be assignable by law immediately at death.

> Fairfax entered into a written agreement with Dodge to sell Dodge a building for $75,000. Three days before the date of settlement, Dodge was killed in an accident. The right to purchase the building is assigned by law to Dodge's executor, who may enforce the agreement in the same manner as could be done by any other assignee of the contract right.

> Suppose Dodge had agreed to teach a real estate course at a local college. Neither the college nor Dodge's executor would have any rights under the agreement, which requires Dodge's personal services.

Bankruptcy of a Contracting Party   The Federal Bankruptcy Act provides that when one is declared bankrupt through proper court action, the assets of the insolvent person or company will be assigned to an officer known as a *trustee*. The bankrupt's property will then be liquidated by the trustee for the benefit of the creditors. All contract rights held by the bankrupt party will be included among the assignments made under the provision of the law.

> Sikorsky, an automobile dealer, was declared bankrupt through bankruptcy proceedings instituted by his creditors. A large number of outstanding accounts receivable and notes receivable are found on Sikorsky's books. All these rights will be assigned to the trustee in bankruptcy for collection for the benefit of the creditors.

Rights of an Assignee

"The assignee steps into the shoes of the assignor." This is an accepted legal maxim used in explaining the rights of an assignee to a contract right. What the assignor may have done himself or herself, the assignee may likewise do. Any benefits denied the assignor may be denied the assignee. Should the other party to the contract have any defenses against the assignor, these same defenses may be used against any claims brought by the assignee.

> Thompson Brothers painted the Merchant's Bank Building for an agreed price of $7,800. After completing the work, Thompson Brothers assigned its claim against the bank to the Wholesale Paint Company, its largest creditor. The bank refused to pay the Wholesale Paint Company, claiming that the work done by Thompson Brothers was not satisfactory and therefore unacceptable by them. This defense is as effective against the Wholesale Paint Company, the assignee, as against Thompson Brothers, the assignor.

In cases like this, the assignee is permitted to enforce the original claim of its account against the assignor. The latter remains a guarantor of the assignment until it has been satisfied.

NOVATIONS

When two contracting parties agree to some material change in their executory agreements, the change creates what is known as a *novation*. The change may relate to the parties themselves, the consideration, the subject matter, or any other provision of their original agreement. A novation is actually a new contract, based upon a former one but containing one or more significant changes.

> ▶▶ Kemp has a two-year contract with the Smith Electric Company as credit manager. Kemp wishes to accept a position in another state. He introduces another competent credit manager to Smith, the president of the firm. Smith then agrees to release Kemp if this new person will take over Kemp's contract for the rest of the two-year period. This is a novation, and the release of Kemp creates a complete separation of the parties.

Novations differ from assignments in the following four ways:

☐ Assignments may be made without the mutual consent of both contracting parties. Novations, on the other hand, require the mutual assent of both the original offeror and the offeree.

> Rugg, a painting contractor, contracted to paint the offices of the Johnson Electric Company. He now finds that he has undertaken more contract obligations than his firm can handle. If he decides to assign this contract to another reputable painter, he would not be required to have the Johnson Company's permission. He may also seek to have the contract turned over to the other firm with the consent of the Johnson Company. In the first case, Rugg would remain a guarantor; in the second, he would be fully released because, by the company's consent, a novation had taken place.

☐ Assignments may not release the assignor of his or her obligations to an existing contract. Assignors may assign only their rights. Novations transfer *all rights and obligations*, giving the replaced party complete freedom from the contract of which he or she was formerly an active part.

☐ In an assignment the "assignee steps into the shoes of the assignor." This is not true in a novation. The new member of the contract has a new agreement with the other party, and it does not necessarily carry all the obligations previously in force.

> Had the Rugg painting contract in the above case been assigned, the rights of the assignee would have been exactly the same as Rugg's; also the responsibilities would not have changed. Had there been a novation, the Johnson Electric Company and the substituted painting contractor might decide on far different terms from those in the Rugg agreement.

☐ The assignor of an executory contract is never fully released until the contract is executed. In a novation the former party steps out free of any and all obligations on the original agreement.

> Vandegrift had a maintenance contract with the Larkin Company to do all adjustments and repairs to its electric motors over a five-year period. After two years, Vandegrift assigned this contract to the Johnson Electric Company. Although the assignment has been made and all parties are in agreement, Vandegrift will remain a guarantor of all work done by the Johnson Electric Company for the three years that the contract still has to run.

Questions for Review and Discussion

1. Distinguish between a novation and an assignment.

2. What are the three exceptions to the rule that all contracts may be assigned?

3. Explain the axiom, "An assignee steps into the shoes of the assignor."

4. Discuss the meaning of substantial performance as related to operation of contracts.

5. Discuss the assignor's guarantees.

6. Distinguish between the rights of a third-party beneficiary and an incidental beneficiary.

7. Under what conditions may there be assignment by operation of law?

8. May both rights and duties be assigned?

9. Analyze the restriction that prevents the assignment of certain types of personal-service agreements.

10. Distinguish between joint liability and several liability.

Analyzing Cases

1. Anderson agreed to make tapes for commercial announcements in which his easily recognized delivery would be used. Anderson's written employment agreement was for one year. No restrictions against assignment were included in the written agreement, although this was discussed during negotiations with management. Anderson attempted to assign the job to another well-known performer when the agreement had been only partially executed. Did Anderson have this right? Explain. • See also *Kauffman* v. *Raeder*, 108 Fed. 171, 179. no personal service

2. Nichols overhauled Harrington's foreign car. When the car was delivered back to Harrington, close inspection showed that Nichols had neglected to replace one of the eight spark plugs in the ignition system. Harrington angrily declared that Nichols had breached the contract and refused to honor the bill of $238. Did Harrington have this right? Explain. • See also *Spalding* v. *Rosa*, 71 N.Y. 40.

3. Kovados Painters contracted with the state of Delaware to repaint the Delaware Memorial Bridge for an agreed price of $2,500,000. Agreements were signed, and performance was to commence in April. Kovados attempted to assign the agreement to another firm that had other work in the same geographic area. Would the assignment be valid if made?

4. Taylor Real Estate Company agreed to sell Arnold's farm on the regular commission arrangement. Contracts between Taylor and Arnold were signed and sealed, as required in their state for all real estate transactions. Taylor then assigned the right to sell the property to Market Realtors, by letter without seal signed by Taylor. Market Realtors secured a buyer, but Arnold refused to accept the deal. What defense does Arnold have to any legal action brought by Market Realtors? Explain. • See also *Hofferberth* v. *Duckett*, 175 N.Y. App. Div. 480.

5. Dr. Gravers, an obstetrician, accepted Mrs. O'Leary as a patient during her pregnancy through delivery of the child. Eight months later, Gravers informed Mrs. O'Leary of his intention to take a vacation in Bermuda. She was told that her case was being assigned to a Dr. Bones, an equally skillful and reputable obstetrician. What are the rights and obligations of the doctor and the patient? Explain. • See also *Johnson* v. *Vickers*, 139 Wisc. 145.

6. Chou, through negligence, wrecked Howard's truck. Chou contracted with King Cars, Inc., for work required in rebuilding the truck body and other repairs needed in the engine and steering system. King Cars later attempted to rescind the agreement, and Howard entered suit against the firm. King Cars' attorney objected to

Howard's intervention in the matter, claiming that there was no privity of contract between King Cars, Inc., and Howard. Was this a proper defense? Explain.

Legal Reasoning and Business Judgment

Analyze the legal aspects of these business problems. Suggest possible solutions.

1. A contractor agreed to build a power plant to be used for supplying electricity to your company's Silverside Plant. One month after the contract was awarded, your firm learned that the contractor was making plans to assign the agreement to another company. There was a rumor that a novation might also be executed before long. If asked for guidance, would you suggest a novation, or would you prefer that the original contractor assign the agreement to another responsible firm?

2. Country Bumpkins, a popular musical and vocal trio, were engaged to play for your company's annual outdoor picnic at Brandywine Park. A few days before the day of the picnic, you were informed that the job had been passed along to Fiddlers Three, an equally popular and capable group of entertainers. As organizer of the picnic, what would you plan to do about this shifting of entertainers? Legally, what could you do?

3. An employee brought you the following problem and sought your guidance. An artist had been secured by members of the family to do a portrait of your employee's maternal grandfather. He had been in public life for years and had an outstanding reputation, and the family wished to honor him in this way. The artist, without giving any notice, had asked another artist to do the job. In fact, the contract had been assigned to this second artist, whose work was not acceptable to those contributing to the cost of the painting. What advice could you give this employee?

Chapter 13
Discharge
of
Contracts

Although some contracts continue in effect for years, the law does not look upon a contract as being effective permanently or forever. Even the so-called "perpetual-care agreements" given with lots sold in a cemetery are subject to possible termination if circumstances or conditions require it. Termination occurs (1) when either party to an agreement concludes the contract according to its terms, or (2) when the law intervenes, making the agreement inoperative. The law differentiates between *termination* and *cancellation*. Cancellation results from one party's failure to perform, giving the other the right to put an end to the agreement. The cancelling party has the right to seek damages against the other for the breach of agreement. On the other hand, when a contract is *terminated*, there is no resulting recognizable suit for damages by either of the parties.

The termination of contracts is quite as important as their formation and operation. A contract may be terminated for any of the following causes.

TERMINATION BY MUTUAL AGREEMENT

A contract may be terminated under the terms contained in the initial agreement. Such terms anticipate the time, conditions, and so on, which would constitute completion of the obligations of the parties to one another.

> Suppose a woman was hired for six months to assist in the introduction of new office procedures. When the agreement was made, she was told that her employment would last for six months. Termination, therefore, would result from the mutual agreement of employer and employee at the inception of their contract.

The parties to a contract may also terminate their agreement by a subsequent meeting of the minds on the same matter. An existing agreement may be mutually rescinded by both parties who agree on its termination.

> Suppose the woman in the preceding example had asked the company to release her from her temporary assignment so that she might accept a career position elsewhere. A willingness on the part of the employer would result in a friendly termination by mutual agreement.

TERMINATION BY PERFORMANCE

Complete and satisfactory performance of the terms of an agreement will effect its termination. Provision for termination is not necessary when the agreement calls for the performance of one specific act or a series of such acts. An example of termination of performance is the delivery of merchandise.

▶▶ Bronski placed an order for equipment to be used in conjunction with his teaching of reading comprehension and speed reading. He mailed a certified check with his order. Several days later the equipment was delivered in good condition, thereby completing and terminating the contract. Had different equipment or damaged equipment been delivered, or any omission been made in the order, the contract would not then have been *terminated*.

Substantial Performance

If the greater part of an agreement has been carried out and only a small part has not been completed, the contract is said to have been ***substantially performed***. A failure to perform an important part of the agreement may result in a complete rescission of the agreement, whereas a substantially performed contract will permit only a proportionate reduction in the amount of money to be paid.

▶▶ You order a suit from a tailor, and he does everything possible to satisfy your tastes in the finished garment. He neglects, however, to sew two buttons on the sleeve. The contract has been substantially performed, and you would not be permitted to declare it rescinded on the ground that the tailor has not delivered a finished suit. You do have the right, however, to deduct from the agreed price the cost to you of completing the work that the tailor was to have done.

Satisfactory Performance

It is often stated in contracts that payment need not be made if the parties are not satisfied with the results. Several interpretations are placed on the meaning of this statement.

Satisfaction to One's Personal Taste Many articles and services are of such a nature that only the one buying them will be permitted to determine what is meant by *satisfaction*. Services rendered in a beauty salon or barbershop, photographs taken at a studio, and portraits painted by an artist are in this classification. Regardless of the skill and application of the person doing the work, the customer may, on the basis of his or her personal judgment and satisfaction, refuse payment.

▶▶ Betty Montalvo made an appointment with a reliable beauty salon to have her very expensive wig trimmed and styled. The manager told her that unless she was satisfied with the results of their work she would not have to pay them for their services. The customer's personal taste and judgment alone will be the determining factor as to satisfaction in this case.

Satisfaction Unrelated to Personal Taste   Satisfactory performance of contracts for those goods and services not involving *personal taste* does not permit the arbitrary judgment of the parties in ruling on the matter of satisfaction. Contracts for the sale of mechanical devices and services offered by tradespeople are of this type. Both parties may introduce expert witnesses in determining whether or not satisfaction has been achieved. Since even the expert witnesses may disagree on satisfaction, a jury is often required to make the final decision after sifting the opinions offered on both sides of a case.

> You purchase a fountain pen. The seller tells you that if the pen is not satisfactory, you may return it and receive a refund. Satisfaction in this case will be satisfaction as applied to the operation of the fountain pen within the limits of its expected normal performance.

Satisfaction Determined by Outside Parties   As pointed out in the previous section, contracting parties may delegate the decision as to satisfactory performance to an unbiased, disinterested, but competent outside party. Architects, engineers, lawyers, and other professional persons are often called upon to act in this capacity.

> The chief engineer of the state highway department and a road contractor mutually agreed upon the appointment of Engineers Associated, Inc., as arbitrator in disputes concerning satisfactory completion of bridges and roads under contract. All decisions of the third party must be accepted as final unless it can be shown that the third party was obviously favoring one or the other party.

Performance by Payment of Money

Contracts requiring the payment of money are not complete until the amount agreed upon has been paid. Unless the agreement provides that payment may be made by check or some other means, *payment in cash is implied*. When payment is permitted by check, note, or some other means, it is considered to be only a conditional payment. The purchaser is not finally released until the credit instrument has been honored by the bank or the persons on whom it was drawn.

> O'Grady contracted with the Northern Fur Company for the purchase of a $500 mink jacket. When O'Grady called for the jacket, she offered the cashier her check for $500 as payment. The store would not be obligated to accept the check unless they had agreed to do so at the time of the sale. Payment in cash would otherwise be implied.

Tender of Performance   To *tender* means to offer. A ***tender of performance*** is an act or overture of a party showing that he or she is ready, willing, and able to perform his or her obligation. Tender may relate to the payment of money, the performance of a promised act, or any other matter stipulated in the terms of an agreement. The tender must be unconditional, without reservation, and without qualification.

▶ Tender of a check in the preceding illustration did not constitute a valid tender, as the check offered was but a conditional payment of the $500 promised.

Effect of Tender When money is tendered in payment of a debt and it is refused by the creditor, the debt is not extinguished. The debtor, however, will be relieved from payment of any interest on the debt from the date of tender. Costs of collection from a debtor may not then be added to his or her account. The refusal of tender of goods or services releases the one making tender from any further obligation and gives that person the right to sue the other party for breach of contract.

▶ The Allens signed a lease for an apartment to which they were to be given possession on October 25. On that date the landlord offered them the key to the apartment, which they refused to accept. This refusal releases the landlord from any further obligation to the Allens and gives him the right to sue for their breach of contract of rental.

Legal Tender *Legal tender* is money that Congress has declared must be accepted if offered in payment of a debt. Examination of our paper currency will show the imprint, "This certificate is legal tender for all debts, public and private," or words to this effect. At one time the law provided that only a limited number of coins could be used in the payment of a debt. This was changed in 1933 in the Agricultural Adjustment Act, which states that "all coins and currencies of the United States (including reserve notes and circulating notes of Federal Reserve Banks and national banking associations) heretofore or hereafter coined or issued shall be legal tender for all debts, public and private." This is in agreement with Section 462 of Title 31 of the United States Code. Legal tender has also been differently defined by state statutes, which of course relate to payment of intrastate accounts only.

▶ Phillips owed Matthews $200 on a current bill for merchandise. Just before Matthews closed her store, Phillips stopped and offered two $100 bills in payment of this bill. Matthews did not have a safe and refused to accept the cash, asking Phillips to return the next day to make payment. Although the bill is not paid, Phillips is relieved of any further obligation to make tender of payment. It will now be the responsibility of Matthews to call for and collect the account. Such tender of *legal tender* also relieves Phillips of any obligation to pay interest on this bill should it not be collected by Matthews during a period of several months.

Conditions of Valid Tender When tender is made for the payment of a debt, certain conditions must be observed by the debtor.

☐ Tender must be made in the manner required by the contract, at the proper time and place, and to the proper person.

Couzens purchased an automobile from the Allen Motor Company to be used by him on a one-month trip across the country commencing August 1. A provision of the contract provided for delivery on or before July 31. The automobile was delivered September 1, and Couzens refused it. The company sued, claiming due tender. The court ruled that Couzens was not bound by the contract because the tender was not good. It was not made at the proper time.

☐ When tender of money is made, it must be for the exact amount due and in legal tender of the country.

Harrington ordered a snow-removal machine for use on his sidewalk and driveway. The price of the machine was $189. When the machine was delivered, Harrington offered a personal check in payment. The seller refused to accept the check and declared the sale terminated by Harrington's failure to live up to his agreement to pay him $189 cash. Did the dealer have this right against Harrington's contract?

When money is mentioned in a contract, the law implies this to mean payment in legal tender. To be otherwise, the parties must have agreed and expressed themselves in their contract. While the acceptance of checks is quite normal in today's business, it is the final right of sellers to insist on payment in cash and to treat the contract as breached unless the buyer complies. In refusing Harrington's personal check, the seller was exercising a legal right.

☐ If tender of goods is made, the contract must require goods instead of money; and the goods so tendered must meet the requirements of the contract.
☐ Present ability to perform must be shown by an actual offer of the money or goods due. A mere expression of willingness to pay the amount due is not sufficient.

You owe a bill at a lumberyard where you receive a discount of 2 percent if the bill is paid ten days after delivery of the supplies ordered. Within this period you call at the office and give them your note for the amount less 2 percent discount. Although you are acting in good faith, you have not made valid tender as required in order to take advantage of the discount. The cash discount is earned only when payment is made in cash, not by a promissory note.

☐ The offer of payment of a past-due debt must include the interest from the due date to the date of the tender of payment.

Suppose in the last case you delayed payment of the amount owed the lumberyard three months from the date on which you received your first statement. An offer to pay the amount indicated on the statement, without interest added, would not be valid tender. The lumberyard would be within its rights in demanding that the interest be added to the amount of the original statement.

TERMINATION THROUGH IMPOSSIBILITY OF PERFORMANCE

If, at the time of making an agreement, circumstances are such that performance is impossible, the contract will be declared void from its very beginning. Whether the impossibility is known or unknown to the parties is immaterial. The result would be the same, and the parties would be discharged.

At 9 A.M. you offer to sell your hunting dog for $50 to a business associate. The associate accepts the offer, pays the money, and promises to call for the dog the next afternoon. You learn later in the day that your dog had been killed at 8:30 that same morning. The contract is void, having been rendered impossible of performance. The money you received would have to be returned to the other party.

Acts of God

The common law at one time permitted discharge when impossibility was caused by an "act of God." Today an act of God will discharge the parties only if that provision is included in their original agreement.

> Bernstein contracted with Carlin for the purchase of 10,000 bushels of wheat located in a grain elevator. A few hours before delivery was to have been made, the elevator was struck by lightning and all the wheat was destroyed. The provision covering acts of God was not included in the agreement. Carlin is not excused from his obligation to deliver 10,000 bushels of wheat. It would be his obligation to secure wheat from some other source and tender that wheat in performance of his agreement.

Statute law in most states now provides interpretation of termination through acts of God. Courts in those states have repeatedly held that, when substantial performance of a contract is possible, the impossibility of precise performance due to an act of God does not excuse either party to the contract.

> American Builders contracted with the Stewart Lumber Company for 1 million board feet of No. 2 dressed white pine. Prior to delivery, Stewart Lumber Company's lumberyard was destroyed by a hurricane. Although an act of God would seem to have made performance impossible, the lumber company would be obligated to secure lumber elsewhere, which may be done through proper negotiation. Stewart must deliver the lumber to American Builders under their agreement.

"Frustration-of-Purpose" Doctrine

Special attention is given to a type of contract whose performance is possible but unnecessary because the purpose of and reason for the contract no longer exists. Such contracts may be terminated without damages when the purposeful object of the agreement has itself been eliminated through no fault or intent of either party. Such contracts must have been made with both parties having full awareness of the intended purpose involved. This rule is known as the *frustration-of-purpose* doctrine.

> National Enterprises, Inc., leased a ball park for the express purpose of presenting a regional football league championship series. Three days before the scheduled date of the first game, ten members of one team were hospitalized with dangerously contagious hepatitis. The series had to be canceled, and ticket refunds were made. Under the frustration-of-purpose doctrine, National Enterprises, Inc., would be free of any obligations under the lease.

TERMINATION BY ALTERATION

Any alteration of a contract which changes the rights or obligations of the parties is known as a *material alteration*. When a material alteration is made with the intent to defraud the other party, the contract may be voided by that party. If the alteration was unintentional and resulted from a mistake, the contract will be considered as originally agreed upon by the parties. In some states a material alteration with intent to defraud may also lead to criminal prosecution.

> Stern signed a contract for a television set. Included with the contract was Stern's promissory note for $200, the price named in the contract. The seller changed both the note and the contract to $300. This is a material alteration with the intent to defraud Stern. Stern may consider both the note and the contract void and unenforceable.

An alteration which in no way changes the parties' agreement but only adds to its clarity and is made without fraudulent intent will not give grounds for termination. It is not good practice, however, to make even this type of alteration without the consent and initialing of the change by both parties.

> Bonnice signed a contract for the rental of a summer cottage at Revere Beach. At the time of signing, it was believed that the instrument had been completely prepared. Bonnice later discovered that in one of the three places designating the termination date of the lease the other party had not inserted the date. Bonnice wrote in the date at the proper place, not changing the intent or purpose of the lease in any way. Bonnice's act would not make the lease contract invalid.

TERMINATION BY DEATH OR DISABILITY OF A PARTY

Death or a disabling sickness or accident will terminate the obligation of performance of a *personal-service contract*. Termination will not be permitted, however, if the service to be performed is of the type that could be done equally well by another. This provision applies to those services requiring a special talent.

> A magazine publisher made a contract with an artist for the creation of a cover design for the fall issue. When the artist had only partly finished the work, he became ill with a muscular disease which made it impossible for him to continue. The artist will be excused from the contract, and his obligation will be terminated because of impossibility of performance. His skill is of a singular type and cannot be replaced by the introduction of another party to do his work.
>
> Shaeffer entered into an agreement to construct an industrial building for the Keys Motor Company. While engaged in the performance of the agreement, Shaeffer was killed by a falling steel beam. The contract was declared terminated by Shaeffer's heirs, and the Keys Motor Company brought action against the estate. The court held that the contract was still subject to complete performance and was the responsibility of Shaeffer's estate. This contract did not contain the qualities of a personal-service agreement, which would have demanded personal performance by Shaeffer, as was true in the previous case.

TERMINATION BY OPERATION OF LAW

If a law prohibits the performance of the terms of an agreement, the parties will be discharged and the agreement terminated. Such termination refers to laws already in effect and to those passed after the contract has been made.

➤ An importer entered into contracts with several large department stores for the delivery of a shipment of songbirds from a tropical area. Sometime later, before the birds could be brought into the country, the U.S. Department of Agriculture prohibited the entry of the birds to prevent the spread of a tropical disease. The importer would be released from the contracts with the department stores because of impossibility of performance resulting from the new regulation.

The passing of laws increasing the cost of performance on a contract will not release or change the original agreement.

➤ Suppose, in the above case, a tax was placed on the importation of the birds which increased by 50 percent the cost of delivery. The seller would not be relieved of his or her initial obligation to the stores, even though this added cost would represent a substantial loss.

TERMINATION BY BREACH OF CONTRACT

When a party refuses to fulfill his or her obligations either by failure to carry them out or by performing them in a negligent and unsatisfactory manner, he or she is said to have breached the contract. Contracts are usually breached in one of three ways, and the injured party has the right to demand damages.

Anticipatory Breach

When parties to a contract announce their intention of renouncing their liability, they are said to have made an *anticipatory breach*. They have, in other words, breached their agreement even before they have been required to act. Modern decisions permit the injured party to bring an action for damages at once rather than waiting until the date of performance has arrived and passed.

➤ Oliver made a contract with a painter to paint the Oliver house and garage. The painter was to begin work on April 1, but on March 15 he called Oliver and said that he would not do the job as agreed. Oliver now has the right to bring an action for damages against the painter for an anticipatory breach.

The wronged party in cases of anticipatory breach is guided by the following three rules. The wronged party may (1) for a commercially reasonable time await performance by the repudiating party; or (2) resort to any remedy for breach, even after notifying the repudiating party that he or she will await the latter's performance and after urging retraction; and (3) in either case suspend his or her own performance or proceed in accordance with the seller's right to identify goods to the contract notwithstanding breach or to salvage unfinished goods.

Thus, once a party has received notice of cancellation of an agreement by the other, that party is not permitted to continue with the execution of work or service covered by their agreement. To do so would only add to the amount of damages resulting from the other's breach.

➤ A publisher was in the process of printing a run of 100,000 booklets to be used in the introduction of a new product. The product manufacturer ordered cancellation of the contract after only 35,000 of the booklets had been completed. Continued production of the other 65,000 booklets would be at the publisher's risk. Damages available to him would be determined by the costs already incurred plus the profits he would have made had he been permitted to execute the entire agreement.

Deliberate or Negligent Acts

If parties to a contract intentionally create situations which make performance impossible, they have breached their agreement. Gross negligence in the treatment of the subject matter could bring the same result. Thus, a contract is breached if the owner of a horse that is being sold permits the animal to stray near a railroad crossing, where it is killed. Also, if one party prevents the other from carrying out his or her obligation, such an act of prevention is considered to be a breach.

 McCarthy entered into a contract to rewire Santillo's house. When McCarthy arrived to start work, Santillo prevented him from entering the house. Santillo breached this contract by his own act of making performance impossible.

In those cases involving the sale of goods where a loss does not result from the deliberate or negligent acts of either party, where the risk of loss has not yet passed to the buyer, but where the goods were in existence and identified by the buyer prior to their loss, two rules of law apply: (1) If the loss is total the contract is avoided; and (2) if the loss is partial or the goods have so deteriorated as no longer to conform to the contract, the buyer may nevertheless demand inspection. At his or her option, the buyer may either treat the contract as avoided or accept the goods with due allowance from the contract price for the deterioration or the deficiency in quantity, but without further right against the seller.

 Custom Builders ordered all the steel required for the construction of a modern motel and lounge. A fire wrecked the plant of the steel company where the finished and prefabricated steel members were ready for delivery to the job. To expedite the completion of the job, Custom Builders elected to take delivery of all the steel it deemed undamaged. By so doing they waived all future action for nonperformance against the other party.

Failure to Perform an Obligation

The failure of a party to perform his or her obligations, either in part or in entirety, constitutes a breach of contract. Failure may be complete, in which case the contract is entirely invalidated; or it may be partial, which in some cases requires the injured party to pay for work already completed. This type of breach is often related to the doctrine of *abandonment*. Intentional abandonment of one's obligations for a long period of time, even though a major part of a contract has been performed, may relieve the other party of any obligation of payment or performance.

▶ Conway left her car with McClure Motors on their promise that they would overhaul the engine and repaint the body for a total cost of $435. After the car had been repainted, work was started on the motor job. After getting about half finished, McClure Motors pushed the job aside and did no further work on it. After four weeks of waiting, Conway demanded the return of the car in its unfinished condition. Conway will be required to pay for the painting of the car but owes nothing for work started and not completed on the motor.

A demand of adequate assurance of performance may be made when reasonable grounds of insecurity are apparent. When a demand for some assurance of performance in writing has been made and it is not given within thirty days, there has been a repudiation of the contract.

Damages for Breach

How much should a person seek from the one who has breached an agreement? May one seek an arbitrary figure? Are there certain formulas that will guide the injured party in determining what he or she will be allowed?

In all claims for breach of contract, the party bringing the suit must prove and justify the amount of damages in terms of money. Actions for breach of contract result in money *damages*, which are fixed according to the losses suffered by the injured party.

Actual Damages   In actions for breach of contract, the injured party is permitted to recover only the *actual damage* caused by the other's failure of performance.

▶ You make a contract with a bookstore for the purchase of a set of law books offered to you for $65. The store fails to deliver the books as agreed. Upon investigation, you find that the same set of books will cost you $100 elsewhere. You may, therefore, sue for your actual damage, which is the difference between $65 and $100, or $35, the amount you will actually lose by having to buy the books from another source.

The amount of damages resulting from a seller's refusal to deliver is the difference between the market price at the time of notice of repudiation and the price as agreed upon in the contract. The wronged party may also demand any other damages resulting from the other's breach. If, however, the buyer is able to reduce the expenses in consequence of the breach, such allowances must be made.

▶ Takeo purchased a piano from the Delaware Piano Company for $950. He agreed to pay the seller an additional $50 for delivery to his home. The piano company later refused to carry out its agreement, and Takeo was able to purchase the same instrument from another dealer for $1,100. The second dealer agreed to deliver the piano without cost. Takeo would recover the difference between the two prices quoted, or $150. From this amount he would be required to deduct the $50 which he realized in saving the cost of delivery from the second company.

Incidental Damages   In addition to the damages computed above, *incidental damages* are allowed. These include such expenses as are reasonably incurred in connection with the inspection, receipt, care, and custody of goods rightfully rejected as well as commissions and other expenses reasonably related to the breached agreement and resulting in the wronged party's loss.

Punitive Damages   If a wrongdoer's acts are notoriously willful and malicious, a jury may impose *punitive damages* upon him or her. These are damages above and beyond what is normally awarded an injured party. They are designed to punish the wrongdoer and to make an example of him or her so that like acts are not repeated by others.

Speculative Damages   Damages computed on the basis of what are called *hopeful rewards* (not based upon provable facts) and such gains as one might contemplate making from unassured future successes are said to be *speculative damages*. Such damages are not allowed.

> Ramirez entered into a contract with a vacuum cleaner company to work as a door-to-door salesperson. After only three days' work, he was discharged. Ramirez sued the company for $1,500, claiming that this was the amount he would have made in commissions in one month had the company permitted him to continue on his job. These are speculative damages, with no actual performance record to verify Ramirez's claim of loss. Damages will not be allowed.

Nominal Damages   So-called "test cases," involving little or no actual financial loss or damage, are sometimes taken before the courts. The person bringing such action is primarily interested in a legal decision to set forth his or her rights in future similar situations. If the complainant is successful in such an action, only *nominal damages* are awarded against the other party. By common law, nominal damages are usually 6 cents, but the amount awarded will vary, often being $1.

> A property owner has a neighbor who insists on walking over her land. After asking the man several times, without success, to stop trespassing, she sued him. No damages could be shown, but the court would give a judgment in favor of the complainant, awarding nominal damages to her.

Liquidated Damages   Parties will sometimes include in their contract a statement of agreed damages should either one or the other breach the contract. They agree that these will be the damages paid in the event that a suit is brought on the contract. The damages must be realistic and in proportion to the losses that might occur. If they are otherwise, the court will disregard them and leave the matter of setting damages to the jury.

To be enforceable, liquidated damages must be reasonable. Reasonableness is determined in the light of the anticipated or actual harm caused by the breach, the difficulty of otherwise proving the loss, and the inconvenience of seeking other remedies. Fixing unreasonably large liquidated damages is prohibited.

> The Hill Manufacturing Company ordered a machine for its new plant being constructed in Atlanta. The machine was a vital link in the production of a new product, and the Hill Company had inserted in its contract with the seller the following terms: "The Hill Company will be paid $200 each day beyond the date agreed upon for delivery of said machine." Considering the profits that might be

lost through delay in delivery, the penalty clause would no doubt be considered reasonable and proper.

Minimizing the Damages An injured party must take all available steps to minimize the damages that might accrue from the other party's failure of performance. At all times he or she will be obliged to protect the other party from any unnecessary losses.

 Lister contracted to deliver 1,000 baskets of tomatoes from his farm to a cannery. When he attempted to deliver the tomatoes, the canner refused them. Lister would have an obligation to make an attempt to sell the tomatoes to another buyer. He would then be allowed to demand payment for the difference between what he was able to get for his produce and what the canner had contracted to pay.

Specific Performance

Up to this point, all the situations discussed have concerned actions for damages taken before a court of law. In actions on contracts, courts of law award only money damages. But money damages do not always satisfy the one who is damaged. A party's satisfaction might be found only in the performance of an existing agreement. He or she would then seek a *decree of specific performance* in a court of equity. Specific performance may be decreed where the goods are unique, or in other proper circumstances—for example, where goods are available to the public through only one source, as when manufactured and sold by only one firm holding entire restrictive rights as to a specific product. A decree of specific performance from a court of equity, or chancery as it is sometimes called, is a demand by the court that the agreement be carried out and performed as agreed upon by the parties, without attention to money damages.

 Ross purchased an oil painting in a secondhand shop for $100, making a $10 deposit on the painting and agreeing to return the next day with the balance of the money. When she returned and tendered the $90 balance, the owner of the shop refused to give her the picture. As it would be impossible to have the painting duplicated, Ross would have a right to seek specific performance of the contract, requiring the owner to sell her the painting according to their agreement.

If the subject matter of a contract may be secured elsewhere, specific performance will not be granted. The injured party may then seek only money damages in a court of law. Had the picture been only a print, a copy of which might be bought in another shop, specific performance would have been denied.

Injunctions

Injunctions are another form of relief granted by courts of equity. Whereas a decree of specific performance applies to property rights, injunctions apply to actions of persons.

Restraining Injunctions   A *restraining injunction* prevents a person from doing some specific act. If the party so restrained fails to abide by the court's orders, the court will fine the party for contempt of court or put him or her in jail. An injunction of this type is granted against a person who may have agreed to perform specific acts and then refused to carry out his or her promise. Although the injured party is not permitted to force the offender to carry out the promised act, the injured party may restrain the offender from doing the same things elsewhere for the duration of the agreement.

▶▶ Kelley signed a contract to play ball with a professional club for an entire season. On the date of the first game, Kelley refused to report and stated that he was canceling his agreement. Although the club could not force Kelley to play, they could seek a restraining injunction against him, which would bar him from playing with any other club during the season. In cases of this type, the equity court may also assess the party with damages resulting from failure of performance.

Mandatory Injunctions   A *mandatory injunction* is one which requires a party to *do* certain things left undone, except acts involving personal services. Performances by prizefighters, musicians, TV performers, and other professionals may not be enforced under a mandatory injunction.

▶▶ A contract was made with a firm to landscape a large area to be used as a summer camp. After the completion of the work, the contractors left several pieces of heavy machinery on the camp property, refusing to remove them. The owners of the camp could seek a mandatory injunction requiring the contractors to remove their equipment.

Questions for Review and Discussion

1. Discuss nominal damages and when nominal damages are awarded.

2. Explain the meaning of specific performance and penalties levied in event performance is not carried out.

3. Distinguish between awards made in a court of law and awards made in a court of equity.

4. Are speculative damages awarded in some contract cases?

5. Discuss the difference between termination and cancellation of contracts.

6. Distinguish satisfactory performance in personal-service contracts compared with satisfaction in contracts related to mechanical devices and the like.

7. What is legal tender? Is there a limitation on the number of coins that may be tendered in payment of a bill?

8. Explain tender of performance.

9. Does an act of God always excuse a party from obligation to perform promises contained in an executory contract?

10. Under what condition is a contract terminated through additions made to a written agreement after its acceptance by both parties?

Analyzing Cases

1. Jordan Products Company agreed to supply All Strings Instruments, Inc., with steel strings for guitars to be delivered to the wholesale distributors. All Strings' entire sales operation depended on regular delivery of strings. Floods shorted out motors and other equipment at the Jordan plant. The firm declared the contract terminated due to an act of God. Is the Jordan Company relieved of obligation to All Strings Instruments, Inc.? • See also *Booth* v. *Spuyten Duyvil Rolling Mill Co.,* 60 N.Y. 487.

2. Ward signed a lease contract, giving Weaver possession of an apartment for a period of five years, at a rental of $225 a month. Ward died during the term of the lease. Heirs of Ward declared the lease terminated due to death of the lessor. Weaver argued that the lease gave full use of the apartment for the entire lease period. Who was right in this dispute? Explain. • See also *Lloyd* v. *Murphy,* 142 Pac. 939.

3. Turner agreed to build a swimming pool for Rabel, to be ready for use by May 1. Unexpected delays required more time for completion of the pool. It was not ready until May 15. Rabel refused to honor Turner's bill, claiming that the agreement had been breached. Was Rabel correct in this reasoning? Explain. • See also *Roos* v. *Lassiter,* 188 F. 427 (C.C.A.).

4. Crouch and Company installed an oil burner in the Engineers Club Building. Crouch guaran-

teed satisfaction in the written agreement for the job. After the installation was in full operation, the Engineers Club refused to pay Crouch. Members expressed judgment of dissatisfaction due to the discovery of small scratches on the housing of the furnace, a quiet humming of the motors and pumps, and failure to install a safety switch in a manner required by the electrical code. Discuss these complaints. Do they justify refusal of payment?• See also *Pattry* v. *Berick,* 50 R.I. 435.

5. General Manufacturers made a part delivery of goods to Harcum Company, under an oral agreement that called for total delivery of $5,000 worth of personal property. Harcum Company refused acceptance of additional goods, claiming that it was protected under the statute of frauds. General Manufacturers brought suit against Harcum. The main reason for the suit was to establish a precedent in decisions related to this section of the statute of frauds. General succeeded in its suit but did not prove damages. Might the court award damages anyway? If so, what would they be?

6. Drake contracted to deliver a new living-room suite to Watts for $850. Watts made a deposit of $50, but two days before delivery was scheduled, she called and canceled the sale. What kind of breach is this? What are Drake's rights?• See also *White* v. *Metropolitan Merchandise Mart,* 48 Del. 526, 107 A. 2d 892.

Legal Reasoning and Business Judgment

Analyze the legal aspects of these business problems. Suggest possible solutions.

1. One of the dump trucks used in your contracting business developed leakage in the hydraulic lift. Kirkwood Garage agreed to make repairs and get the truck back into service within one week. Six weeks passed, and the truck was still

not ready. A visit to the garage disclosed that the lift was partly disassembled but that no actual work had been done. You must rent a truck from Truck Rentals, Inc., while this one is being repaired. How would you settle this matter?

2. A sales representative was hired by your company on a two-year contract. The job required travel over four states, visiting prospective customers for the firm's products. You discovered that this employee was spending most of the time watching television in motels or patronizing local racetracks. Lack of work was showing up in plummeting sales figures. You discharged the employee, who has now lodged a suit against the company for $25,000. This is the amount of commissions the representative contends would have been earned had the job continued. How serious is this problem, and what should be done to avoid a money judgment against the firm?

3. One of your difficult accounts has owed $187 for many months, with no indication that the bill will soon be settled. You now threaten the party with a lawsuit if payment is not made at once. This has brought action and the delivery of 1,870 dimes, together with a demand for a receipt for the debt. What should be done in the face of this embarrassing situation witnessed by other customers?

Part 4
Sales
Chapter 14
The
Sales
Contract

There is no area in the study of law that relates more to the law of contracts than does the law of sales of personal property. Very few businesses, organizations, or individuals can look back over twenty-four hours without recognizing that they have been involved in one way or another in a sale, either as the seller or the purchaser. Without thinking of the legal implications, millions of people each day purchase food, clothing, shelter, newspapers, and countless other items. An understanding of sales law will enable buyers or sellers to better meet their valid obligations and responsibilities and to avail themselves of the benefits to which they may be entitled resulting from an exchange of money for property.

The law of sales confines itself to the transfer of rights to personal property. Real property transactions are so different from the rules relating to personal property that the law treats real property as a special study.

GOODS

Personal property includes all movable objects, both tangible and intangible. It also includes those things which, while not movable, are not intended by the owner to be a part of realty. The determination of one's intentions may result in expensive litigation between buyer and seller when the intention of the parties is not expressed.

▶ Harrigan sold his home, which contained many items that the buyer assumed would go with the property. When the buyer took possession of the property, he found that Harrigan had removed shelves, an intercom system, and a large mirror which had been installed over the fireplace. The seller assumed the removed articles to be personal property; the buyer thought that they went with the house. Only by the application of well-defined legal guidelines may a court now determine which party has the right to the items in contest.

Property which is perceptible to the senses, which is material, and which may be moved about is called *tangible property*. Automobiles, furniture, ships, and television sets are examples of this kind of property. *Chattel* is another term for tangible property. Tangibles such as machinery, equipment, and merchandise are *choses in being*. The law of sales is specifically limited to choses in being, that is, to tangible property.

Property which is not perceptible to the touch or sight is ***intangible property***. This includes items generally looked upon as *rights*. In this classification are stocks, bonds, mortgages, patents, copyrights, and rights guaranteed under certain types of contracts. The real value of intangible property does not exist in the certificate of ownership to such rights but in the rights themselves.

A share of stock, for example, carries with it an intangible property right. The stock certificate is nothing more than a printed agreement, but it gives its owner definite rights in the corporation named on the certificate.

Goods which are not yet in existence or under the control of man are called ***future goods***. They include fish in the sea, minerals in the ground, and goods not yet manufactured.

 A fisherman made a contract with a West Coast cannery for the sale and delivery of 25 tons of salmon which he proposed to catch within the next week. Although the fish actually exist, they are said to be future goods until they have been taken from the water and landed in the boat.

UNIFORM REGULATION OF SALES

The great majority of all contracts today have to do with the sale of goods. Consider each item of food in the supermarket, each car on the sales lot, each newspaper, each book, and each magazine on the newsstand. Then contemplate the millions of items sold at the variety stores. So great is the importance of the sale of personal property that special laws have been enacted by the various states for the regulation of such sales.

The sale of personal property often involves the laws of more than one state. Many years ago the legal problems arising from sales involving more than one state were so complicated that people hesitated to make such contracts. To overcome this difficulty, a uniform code of laws covering sales contracts has been adopted by practically all the states and has brought about uniformity of customs and practices in sales contracts. This body of law is known as the Uniform Commercial Code (UCC).

THE SALES CONTRACT

A *sale*, as defined by the Uniform Commercial Code, is "the passing of title (of goods) from the seller to the buyer for a price." If title is to pass at some future time, the agreement is not a sale but a contract to sell.

Sales contracts, like other contracts, require proof of the four essentials that make agreements valid and legally enforceable: mutual assent, capable parties, consideration, and valid subject matter.

 Columbo offered to sell his car to Wong for $2,000. Wong accepted and paid Columbo the sum named.

This is a sale because it contains the four essentials of a valid contract.

Mutual Assent

Mutual assent was achieved by Wong's acceptance of an offer made by Columbo. The offer is clear, definite, and certain; it was communicated; and it was seriously intended. The offer was made to Wong alone, and Wong communicated an acceptance in the same manner in which the offer was made.

In agreements wherein a *merchant* makes a signed, written offer to buy or sell goods with the *promise* that the offer will remain open for either a reasonable or a specific period of time, such an offer is irrevocable, even though no consideration has been given to support it. In no event, however, may such period of irrevocability exceed three months.

Capable Parties

Neither Columbo nor Wong is known to be incapable. Parties to a contract are presumed to be capable until they are shown to be otherwise.

Consideration

The consideration in any contract consists of an exchange of benefits and sacrifices between the parties. Each of the parties has promised to give a benefit in return for a benefit.

Valid Subject Matter

Valid subject matter means that the object of the transaction is legal and is not against public policy. Nothing indicates that the subject matter of this agreement is in any way illegal or against public policy.

All sales contracts analyzed in this chapter should be carefully considered in the light of these four requisites.

TITLE, OR OWNERSHIP

A sales agreement transfers the ownership (title) from the seller to the buyer. Valuable merchandise is usually accompanied, when sold, by some evidence of title. This could be the title certificate of an automobile, a sales slip, a bill of sale, or some other documentation. The evidence of title, it must be pointed out, is not the true title. Title is really an intangible right evidenced by the certificate of title. Jewelry, objets d'art, motor vehicles, expensive home appliances, and the like are sold with some evidence of title from the buyer.

 Polands Jewelers sold a 1.5-carat ring to Doyle. When the ring was delivered, Doyle received a certificate of ownership. The certificate showed the names of seller and buyer, an exact description of the ring and diamond, and the price paid. The certificate was made out in duplicate, one copy being kept by the store.

A title certificate is invaluable to an owner should a claim be made to an insurance company for reasons of fire or theft. It is also useful in situations where another may claim title to the same property.

How does one prove title to goods of less value—goods to which one may not have a document of ownership? A party claiming title to goods in another's possession must show the right of ownership. Thus, an owner may be called on to defend a right of ownership in a hat, a pair of shoes, a coat, or other goods that may have fallen into the hands of a finder or an impostor. The owner may introduce witnesses to testify as to the owner's rights through association with the owner and the goods in question. A sales slip, a cleaner's ticket, a repair ticket, or the like could be useful in establishing ownership. It would be impossible to file title documents for all of one's personal property. The owner may anticipate such need, however, and keep a list of serial numbers and other identifying marks that would assist a court in giving judgment as to the real owner.

Title in Contracts of Sale

A *contract of sale* is an agreement between seller and buyer for the immediate transfer of title, together with possession or the right of possession. The transfer is made in consideration of a price paid by the buyer. According to the Uniform Commercial Code, "Unless otherwise explicitly agreed, title passes at the time and place at which the seller completes his performance with reference to the physical delivery of the goods... even though a document of title is to be delivered at a different time or place."

> Rubenstein bought a new car from Boulevard Chevrolet. Payment was made, Rubenstein signed a delivery receipt, and Boulevard delivered the car. Rubenstein was assured by the salesperson that the title certificate would be mailed as soon as transferred by the Department of Motor Vehicles. The fact that Rubenstein did not obtain the title certificate at the time of the sale does not mean that title had not passed to the buyer.

Title in Contracts to Sell

An agreement that either states or implies that title is to pass at some later time is a *contract to sell.* In some sales, possession is given the buyer at the time of the sale, but it is understood that the seller remains the owner until all money is paid. Until conditions of passing of title are executed, the buyer has only possession.

> Harrah bought a living-room suite under an installment contract. Twelve payments were due the seller. The contract stated that title would not pass until Harrah had made all twelve payments. This is a *contract to sell.*

In order to pass title, goods must be in existence and identifiable. Future goods, then, can be sold only under a contract to sell. After the goods are produced or are identifiable as goods (not future goods), title will pass and the agreement would be a contract of sale.

> Petticoat Stables made an agreement with Hutchins for the sale of a colt yet unborn. The mare had carried the colt for many months, and birth was expected in six weeks. Was this a contract of sale or a contract to sell?

In the above case the existence of the colt, though it is still unborn, can be proved by medical means; therefore, the transaction is a *contract of sale*. Were the foal to be stillborn, the loss would fall on the buyer, Hutchins. However, an agreement to sell a colt that "might" be born to a presently unbred mare would be nothing more than a *contract to sell*.

Ownership rights to personal property may be passed to a buyer without money payment. Numerous credit sales are made each day in which title is transferred to a buyer at the time of the sale. The consideration, in these cases, is the *promise to pay*. The sale made on an ordinary charge account would imply the passing of title at the time of the sale.

 Henshaw bought a suit from a store where she had established good credit through years of trading. Ownership of the suit passed to Henshaw at the time of the sale, without the necessity of payment until perhaps thirty days later.

Failure to satisfy the payment of money owed on a charge account does not give sellers a right to reclaim the merchandise, except when special state statutes give them that right. However, a seller may sue a buyer for the money promised and due.

ORAL AND WRITTEN CONTRACTS

Of the millions of sales contracts made every day, by far the greatest number are oral or implied. Sales through vending machines, self-service counters, and the like are implied; sales made by clerks over the counter are usually oral. In some situations a written memorandum of the sale is desirable to avoid future misunderstanding.

 Shockley agreed to buy a set of the *Encyclopaedia Britannica* from State Book Stores. The salesperson described the set to be of "a recent edition." Shockley took this to mean they were of the current edition. When the books were delivered, it was found that they were of a former edition. A written agreement that named the edition in exact terms would have resolved the dispute that followed between Shockley and the seller.

Statute of Frauds

All sales of personal property the price of which is $500 or more must be evidenced by a satisfactory written agreement between the seller and the buyer. An executed contract where possession and title pass at the time of the sale would not come within this requirement. Contracts to sell where title and possession are to be transferred at some future time and contracts for sale of future goods the price of which is $500 or more must be in writing to be enforceable.

 Auto Electric Stores agreed to purchase surplus batteries owned by Perry's Electric Specialty Shop. The agreement was oral and called for cash payment of $750 upon delivery of the batteries thirty days from date of agreement. In the absence of any written agreement, the sale may be voided by either party.

Sales Between Merchants   An exception to this general rule is made when the sale is made *between merchants*. If either merchant delivers a confirmation of the oral agreement to the other within a reasonable length of time and if the receiver is aware of the contents of the correspondence, this will satisfy the requirements of a written contract. The receiver, however, may avoid any commitment or obligation by giving written notice of any objection to the contents of the confirming letter within ten days of its receipt.

> Suppose, in the previous illustration, Auto Electric had written a confirmation of the order and delivered it to Perry's Electric Specialty Shop two days later. Unless Perry's communicated a written objection to Auto Electric's confirmation within ten days, the agreement would be construed as a valid enforceable agreement.

An informal note or memorandum in writing would satisfy the writing requirements. The writing must contain the names of the parties, the price agreed upon, a description of the goods sold, and the signatures of the parties or their agents.

> Gannon agreed to sell Manifold three electric guitars and a powerful amplification system for $675. Delivery was to be made in ten days, at which time Manifold agreed to have the money ready for payment. Gannon noted these facts on the back of an envelope which both he and Manifold signed.
>
> The memorandum was sufficient to satisfy the requirements of a written agreement, thereby obligating both parties to a contract to sell.

Voidable Agreements   When the parties carry out their agreement in a satisfactory manner, the law will not render the transaction invalid for want of an agreement in writing. Executed contracts need not be in writing; the writing requirements apply only to contracts which are *executory*.

If there has been a part payment or a part delivery in conformance with the contract terms, the law will consider valid only that portion of the agreement that has been performed.

> If Gannon, in the previous case, did not have a written agreement but had delivered one of the three guitars to Manifold, the court would enforce payment for that one instrument. Part delivery would not, as was the case under the statute of frauds prior to the adoption of the code, make the entire sales agreement enforceable.

Constructive Delivery   The delivery of the ignition key to an automobile or the executed title certificate to a car, motorcycle, or other chattel is said to be a *constructive delivery*, as contrasted to a *part delivery*. Constructive delivery is considered a token delivery of the entire chattel, not merely a part of it. This would permit the enforcement of the seller's entire agreement if such delivery was accepted by the buyer.

> McIntosh agreed to sell Toumey all the silver flatware that was contained in a silver chest in McIntosh's office. Toumey accepted the key to the chest, promising to return the next day and pay the $900 price agreed upon. The delivery and

acceptance of the key will be construed as an *entire* delivery of the chest and its contents, making both parties liable in an enforceable contract of sale.

ENTIRE AND DIVISIBLE CONTRACTS

When a number of separate articles are purchased under an agreement in which it is indicated that the sale is to be treated as a single transaction, this is held to be an *entire* contract in the interpretation of the statute of frauds. The total amount of all the articles, not the cost of each one, determines whether a written contract is required.

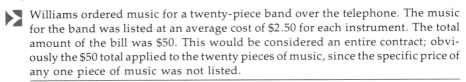 Williams ordered music for a twenty-piece band over the telephone. The music for the band was listed at an average cost of $2.50 for each instrument. The total amount of the bill was $50. This would be considered an entire contract; obviously the $50 total applied to the twenty pieces of music, since the specific price of any one piece of music was not listed.

Clearly divisible contracts, on the other hand, would be treated differently under the statute. A purchase of many different items to be shipped at different times, or under separate invoices, when unrelated to each other, would be considered a divisible contract. This contract is enforceable if oral, even though the sum of the combined purchase price might exceed the statutory or code limit.

▶ Suppose Williams ordered a series of new marches which were to be published over a period of several months. He agreed to pay $35 for each of twenty marches to be mailed to him. Failure to enter into a written agreement would not affect this agreement. Each march and each payment is a separate act, unrelated to the one before or after.

LABOR AND SERVICE CONTRACTS

A contract entered into for the manufacture of specific personal property conforming to a special description and design is said to be a *contract for labor and materials*. This does not come within the requirements of the statute of frauds or the Uniform Commercial Code as to value. Such agreements do not have to be in writing, regardless of the contract price agreed upon.

▶ A special arrangement of a series of light classics was prepared for Williams. The arrangement and scores for each individual instrument were to be prepared and bound in a folio. The contracted price for the arrangement was set at $875 by the publisher and writer. Because of the special treatment required, this agreement would be enforceable although no written contract was written and signed.

Interpretation of whether an agreement is for labor and materials or a sales agreement depends somewhat on the individual characteristics of the chattels produced and the lack of a demand for them in the general market.

The New York rule, followed by some states, agrees in general with the rule just given with one exception: If the goods ordered are not in existence at the time the contract is made, the contract is one for labor and services, even though the goods might be suitable for the trade in the ordinary course of business.

▶ Alberts orally agreed to print 10,000 copies of a book of mathematical formulas of general use in business offices, to be sold to persons in accounting and clerical work. The completed books were to be of a type that might be offered for sale to thousands of prospective buyers. When the books were finished, the buyer refused to make payment, claiming that the contract was oral and therefore not enforceable under the statute of frauds. Under the New York rule, the contract would be interpreted as one for labor and services, and a written contract would not be required.

REQUIREMENTS OF THE BULK SALES LAW

Merchants have occasionally made sales of their entire inventory to one buyer for the purpose of defrauding the wholesale firms with which they do business. Although all bulk sales are not made with this intent, creditors' rights are protected under the provisions of the Uniform Bulk Sales Act and the Uniform Commercial Code. "A *bulk transfer* is any transfer in bulk and not in the ordinary course of the transferor's business of a major part of the materials, supplies, merchandise, or other inventory of an enterprise."

Buyers under a bulk sale may lose all ownership rights in the goods purchased if they do not abide by the provisions of the act and the code. Creditors who have suffered damage may demand the return of all goods bought, with no obligation to reimburse the purchaser.

There are four requisites of the bulk sales law:

☐ At least ten days before the sale is made, the seller shall give the buyer a detailed inventory of the merchandise, including cost price.

☐ The seller shall give the buyer a written list of the names and addresses of his or her creditors, together with the amount owing to each, sworn to by the seller as correct and complete.

☐ The buyer shall keep the inventory of merchandise and the list of creditors for ninety days. This rule has been modified under the code to read as follows: "The transferee preserves the list and schedule for six months next following the transfer and permits inspection of either or both and copying therefrom at all reasonable hours by any creditor of the transferor, or files the list and schedule in (a public office to be identified)."

☐ The buyer shall notify each of the seller's creditors (either by registered mail or personally) of the proposed sale and the terms of the sale at least ten days before taking possession of the goods or paying for them. The buyer must give notice to any party who is known to him or her to have any claim against the seller, even though this party is not included in the list of creditors supplied by the seller.

After observing these four requisites, the buyer may pay for and take title and possession of the inventory. Creditors who have not, to that time, taken any action to interrupt the sale have lost their right to do so.

▶ Jenkins advertised a radio and television store for sale. The sale was to include all furniture, fixtures, and inventory. Griffin, without heed to the provisions of the bulk sales law, purchased the business. An inventory of goods valued at $25,000 was included in the sale. One week after Griffin had taken title and possession, and had paid Jenkins, five major creditors sought to attach the inventory to cover Jenkins's indebtedness.

Had Griffin followed the regulations of the bulk sales act, and had no creditors made claims during the presale period, he would have had complete rights to the inventory purchased. As it is, the entire inventory may be taken by the five creditors as a means of recovering money owed by Jenkins's business.

The bulk sales law is applicable to businesses whose principal activity is to sell merchandise from stock. It also includes firms which manufacture the goods they sell.

Questions for Review and Discussion

1. Distinguish between the terms *title* and *certificate of title*.

2. Explain in what way a contract of sale is different from a contract to sell.

3. In what way has the Uniform Commercial Code assisted in reducing confusion in sales agreements?

4. Discuss the reason for the Uniform Bulk Sales Act. What does this law require?

5. How does constructive delivery differ from delivery? Give an example of constructive delivery.

6. Is it possible to transfer title to goods without the buyer's paying money? Explain.

7. How do contracts for labor and service differ from sales contracts?

8. Explain how the statute of frauds regulates executory sales agreements.

9. Explain the importance of both seller and buyer signing a sales contract.

10. What is the New York rule pertaining to contracts for labor and materials?

Analyzing Cases

1. Stewart selected a new motorcycle at Harry's Cycle Shop. The sales price was $897. The sales representative promised delivery the following afternoon, and Stewart agreed to make payment in full at that time. After the cycle was made ready for delivery, Stewart called the shop and said the deal was off. Does Harry's Cycle Shop have any legal right to damages? Explain. • See also *Trainman* v. *Rappaport*, 41 F. 2d 336.

2. Porter ordered new kitchen cabinets for a house being purchased. Due to the unusual dimensions of the kitchen, the cabinets had to be made to order according to patterns supplied by the cabinet company. The cost of the cabinets came to $975. Without a written agreement, Por-ter refused to make payment, claiming the defense of the statute of frauds. Was Porter correct in this issue? Explain. • See also *Eddleman* v. *Myers*, 98 Ind. App. 394.

3. Harrington Manufacturing Company, located in Michigan, ordered 250 tons of soft coal from Allegheny Mining Company, a Pennsylvania firm. The coal was to be delivered and paid for at Harrington's plant located in Ohio. How would the Uniform Commercial Code assist in interpretation and enforcement of this agreement if there were any dispute over the sale in the three states in which the transaction occurred? Explain.

4. Beaver Hardware Store sold its entire inven-

tory to Higgins Outlet. As required, Beaver supplied Higgins with a complete listing of all his creditors and the amount owed to each. Following the requirements of the bulk sales law, Higgins notified the creditors of the sale prior to the date on which transfer of title was to be made. Higgins neglected to notify one creditor, to whom Beaver Hardware owed $3,900. What are the rights of this creditor after the Beaver-Higgins agreement is executed and Higgins has taken title and possession of Beaver's inventory?
• See also Uniform Commercial Code, art. 6, sec. 6-104–107, and *Goldberg* v. *Martin,* 203 La. 70, 13 So. 2d 465.

5. Greensboro Produce Company contracted with Thornton for 20 tons of green beans to be grown on Thornton's farm and delivered when ready for canning. At the time of their agreement, the seed had not yet been planted. Was this a valid contract of sale? Explain.

6. Clothier agreed to sell Scott a power cruiser that was tied up in a marina 250 miles away. Scott had seen the craft and knew that it was a good buy at $7,800. There was no written agreement, but Scott paid Clothier with a check for the full amount, and Clothier gave Scott the keys to the boat. Clothier later found another buyer who would give a thousand dollars more for the boat. He attempted to set the sale aside under the provisions of the statute of frauds. May Scott defend the agreement as being final? Explain.
• See also *Pinkham* v. *Mattox,* 53 N.H. 600.

Legal Reasoning and Business Judgment

Analyze the legal aspects of these business problems. Suggest possible solutions.

1. A sales representative calls from a distant city with the following information. He has noticed that one of the firm's customers is in the process of loading the store's inventory into a truck belonging to a competitor. Your representative had no knowledge of this intended big sale of merchandise. Investigation in the accounting department shows that the store in question owes your company $3,289. What course of action is indicated for your company in this situation?

2. The purchasing department placed a telephone order with Diamond Press for $1,200 worth of forms to be used in the sales and shipping departments. The job was well under way when a sales representative of another printing plant stopped by and offered to do the same job for $850. One of the employees (who is taking a business law course) suggested that the agreement made with the first printer be rescinded. The employee stated that the statute of frauds required a written agreement for contracts of this kind when over $500. What advice would you offer to the purchasing department on this matter?

3. Sterling Auto Sales offered to sell a truck, in good condition, to your company for less than half of its current market value. You wanted to take advantage of the offer but had no checks with you; neither did you feel that the seller would appreciate your suggesting a written promise. How would you bind Sterling Auto Sales to this agreement in the absence of a down payment or delivery of the truck at the time?

Chapter 15

Title and Risk

A person who has just bought a piece of jewelry is robbed of the jewelry while leaving the store. A car dealer signs over to a customer the title certificate to a new car. In each case, has title passed to the buyer of the merchandise? Must the purchaser of the jewelry suffer a loss because of the robbery, even before he or she reaches the street?

Title to personal property passes *when the parties intend it to pass*. This is one of the accepted doctrines of the law of sales. In the first example, the customer made the purchase, and the package was wrapped, accepted, and paid for. Therefore, title had passed to the customer before the robbery, and he or she must bear the loss. The second example is much clearer in the determination of passing of title. The seller has clearly expressed an intent by signing the title certificate, which gives the other party the rights of ownership.

ACQUIRING TITLE

Title (ownership) of goods may be acquired in many different ways. Although sales agreements are the most common means of transferring title to goods, there are other methods.

Finding Goods

A finder does not get title to another's lost property. An effort must be made to discover the identity of the real owner. State laws provide, however, that if a reasonable effort is made to locate the owner, without success, the finder may claim ownership of the goods. Different states have different time limits beyond which the finder will be recognized as the actual owner.

Gifts

Title may be transferred by a gift. To do this, the *donor* (the one giving the gift) must have had the intent to pass title, and the *donee* (the one receiving it) must have taken possession of the goods. Either real or constructive possession is sufficient. Thus an owner handing a friend the keys to his car and saying "Take my car as a gift" will pass title. It is not necessary that a certificate of title be transferred at that moment.

Inheritance

Title to goods may be transferred by a will, or by law when the deceased dies without a will. Title passes immediately on the owner's death, although possession may be delayed until the settlement of the estate.

Court Judgment

A court may award title to goods owned by one against whom there is an unpaid judgment on file. Through a court order, a debtor's goods may be sold to satisfy such judgments. A court of equity may issue a decree of specific performance ordering a party to transfer title to goods which have been sold but to which the seller has denied the buyer both title and possession.

 Langus bought an eighteenth-century blanket chest from Olde Towne Shop. Payment was to be made in 30 days, as permitted under Langus's charge account. When Langus returned to get the chest, Olde Towne's owner rescinded the sale. Langus may seek a decree in specific performance, requiring the owner to give up title and possession of the chest as agreed to in the contract.

Original Production

Ownership may derive from one's efforts in writing a book, painting a picture, inventing a new gadget, and the like. The one who creates an original product or work may have title to it protected under the copyright or trademark laws. (See Chapter 10.)

Accession

The offspring of animals, the proliferation of growing plants, and so on are owned by the person who has title to parent animals or plants. The owner of goods also takes title to their *accessions*—i.e., any additions to or modification of presently owned goods.

Confusion

Negligent or intentional confusion of goods with goods belonging to another may transfer title. Making it impossible to separate and identify the property belonging to each gives the innocent party title to the combined mass of goods.

 Union Stamp and Coin Company loaned coins to Stabler. The coins were then mixed with other coins owned by Stabler. It was impossible to then determine which were Stabler's coins and which belonged to Union Stamp and Coin.

Unless the coins could be separated according to their real owners, Union Stamp and Coin would be permitted to claim all the coins.

Adverse Possession

Title may be acquired by adverse possession of another's property. *Adverse possession* occurs when one has the property without permission of the owner for a period longer than that required by law. The one in possession must treat the property as his or her own. Possession must be open and notorious, not concealed. It makes no difference that the one in possession is aware that the property belongs to someone else. After the lapse of a period of time set by statute, the one in possession is permitted to claim title.

> ▶ Lawrence found a fishing rod and reel on a beach frequented by many fishermen. Each day thereafter, Lawrence returned to do surf fishing. Other fishermen saw and admired Lawrence's fishing rod and reel. There was no attempt made to either conceal or camouflage what had been found.

After the lapse of time set by law, Lawrence could claim title.

SINGLE OR MULTIPLE TITLE

Title may be transferred to one or more new owners. Rights and obligations, whether of one or several persons, depend on the definition of the type of ownership accepted. Many of the following general classifications of single or multiple ownership apply to real property as well as personal property. (Real property ownership will be discussed in Part 10 of this book.)

Severalty Ownership

Ownership by one person alone is known as *severalty ownership*. Title is not shared with any other person.

Joint Tenancy

Persons owning equal shares in personal property are joint tenants, and they have *joint tenancy*. Each individual has an *undivided interest* in the entire chattel, or property. Death of a joint owner (tenant) transfers that individual's title right to the surviving joint tenant(s).

> ▶ Jevins, Cantwell, and Swift were members of a flying club, and together they bought a Piper Comanche. Title to the aircraft was put in all three names as joint owners. Neither one, then, had complete ownership of any specific part of the aircraft. Each member had an undivided interest in the entire plane.

Tenancy in Common

Tenancy in common differs from joint ownership only in the right of survivors. Death of one of the co-owners passes title to that one person's share to his or her beneficiaries named in a will or to his or her heirs if there is no will.

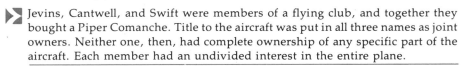

> ▶ Clark and Tatman purchased two CB transceivers and a base station. They owned them as tenants in common. Should either Clark or Tatman die, that co-owner's

share would not go to the other owner. It would go to person(s) named in the will
of the deceased or to their heirs.

Tenancy by the Entireties

Tenancy by the entireties is a special type of joint tenancy. Whereas in an ordinary
joint tenancy ownership may be held by *two or more* persons, tenancy by entireties is restricted to spouses: a husband and a wife.

Tenancy in Common with Right of Survivorship

In an effort to remove confusion, many states have passed legislation to remove
the use of tenancy by entireties. In those states, ownership between husband and
wife does not require the special classification. Ownership is under the definition of tenancy in common. Addition of the words *with right of survivorship*
removes any doubt that ownership might have been a joint tenancy. Death of
either husband or wife, if a joint tenancy, would pass title rights to heirs of either
the husband or wife, rather than to the other spouse.

Community Property

Eight states have legislation with regard to ***community property*** rights. These
give each spouse a one-half title interest in personal property owned by the other.
Excepted from this right are goods owned by either party prior to marriage or
property acquired by gift or inheritance during marriage.

> Prior to marriage Jarrell owned a car, sewing machine, fur coat, and valuable
> jewelry. Her husband owned a motorcycle, a complete set of mechanic's tools,
> and tenancy in common, with others, in an airplane. After marriage, individually
> and together, they made numerous purchases for the home and for themselves
> personally. Only those things purchased after marriage are included in their
> community property.

When "big-ticket" items are purchased by two or more persons, attention should
be given to the type of ownership the parties have agreed to, and a memorandum
should be signed specifying that agreement. Failure to do this may lead to bitter
argument and dispute.

> Rothmeyer and Leger together bought office furniture to be used in their partner-
> ship business. They spent $2,500 on this purchase. Weeks later, Leger was killed
> in an accident. No records showed whether title to the furniture was taken as a
> joint tenancy or a tenancy in common. Both Rothmeyer's and Leger's beneficia-
> ries claimed the furniture.

The terms used in describing joint ownership and tenancy in common are very
similar. Attorneys generally use the expression *with right of survivorship* if joint
ownership is intended. When courts are unable to determine whether ownership
is *joint* or *in common*, there will be a presumption in favor of tenancy in common.
This assures the surviving heirs, rather than an outsider, of receiving complete
title to the deceased's personal property.

OWNERSHIP OF GOODS

Stolen Goods

Although a presumption of title to goods usually follows possession of them, it is possible for a person to have possession of goods without having title, just as it is possible for a person to have title without having possession. Thus, a thief acquires no title to goods that are stolen and, therefore, cannot convey a good title. The true owner never relinquished title to the goods, and even an innocent purchaser, who acquired the goods in good faith and for value, would be obliged to return the goods to the owner. Title to stolen goods never left the true owner, and possession can always be regained by that owner if the goods can be found, no matter in whose possession they may be at the time.

 Lane purchased a typewriter from Jarvis, paying a fair price for it. Later, Tyron demanded that Lane return the typewriter to him, claiming that Jarvis had stolen the machine from him. Tyron proved ownership by a bill of sale.

It was held that Lane must return the typewriter to Tyron. Lane can acquire no better title than Jarvis had. Jarvis could not convey title to Lane, for he had no title himself.

Lost Goods

The finder of a lost article has a good title against claims by everybody except the true owner who lost the article. Thus, a person who buys an article from someone who found it acquires no better title than the finder had. If the true owner learns that the article is in the possession of the buyer, the buyer will be obliged to surrender it or to pay its value to the owner, even though he or she acquired the goods from the finder in good faith and for fair value.

Estoppel

When the real owner of goods vests another with the appearance of ownership and the latter sells the goods to an innocent purchaser for value, then the purchaser acquires a title that is valid even against the real owner. This is in keeping with a principle of law known as *estoppel*. This principle holds that, as between two innocent parties, the one who makes a fraud possible must bear the loss resulting from such fraud. He or she is estopped from denying that the facts on which the innocent party acted were not as represented by the person perpetrating the fraud. (Estoppel will be treated in more detail in the next chapter.)

INTENT TO PASS TITLE

If the parties in a sales contract state when title is to pass, no conflict will be encountered in proving ownership. It is doubtful whether you have ever clearly expressed such an intent in any purchase or sale you have made. Most persons give this matter little or no thought. Even in written contracts, title is rarely mentioned unless the agreement is prepared by persons well versed in the law.

Contracts for the sale of expensive merchandise on credit terms are a common exception.

> Suppose the purchaser of a car made arrangements to pay for it over a period of two years. Arrangements would be made with a bank or finance company for such a sale. The installment contract usually stipulates that "title will not pass to the purchaser until all payments have been made."

Such careful expression of intent removes the possibility of a dispute between the seller and the buyer at some later date, should the buyer default on the obligation to make payments. Although the buyer does not have title until all payments have been made, the contract will state that he or she has full and complete responsibility for the car for the entire time it is in the buyer's possession and will be liable for all payments due, even though the car may be destroyed before all payments are made. For this reason, the seller requires the buyer to show proof of insurance that will protect the seller's, or the bank's, financial interest.

The Uniform Commercial Code provides that a buyer obtain "a special property and an insurable interest" in the goods as soon as they are identified to the contract, and that "the seller retains an insurable interest in goods so long as title to or any security interest in the goods remains in him."

Specific Time or Condition

Title to goods does not pass gradually. It passes at one precise moment or on the completion of certain conditions contained in the sales agreement. To assist in setting the time when title passes, the Uniform Sales Act provides guideposts in determining intent when it is not actually expressed. Fundamentally, title always passes when parties have agreed to an *unconditional contract* to sell *specific goods* in a *deliverable state*.

> Kennedy picked out a new coat at Arthur's Style Center. No alterations were necessary. The price was acceptable. Kennedy agreed to take the coat as he had found it, paid for it, and left the store. There is no question that title passed to Kennedy at the time of the sale.

Conditional Promises

When a contract contains conditions that must be met either by the buyer or the seller, title will not pass until those conditions have been fulfilled. Changes, adjustments, delivery, or other stipulations, if included in the sales contract, must be carried out before the title passes to the buyer.

> Suppose, in the previous case, Kennedy was not pleased with the sleeve length. The store manager said, "We make alterations without charge. Our tailor will fit the sleeves, and you may pick up the coat anytime tomorrow." The agreement now contains a condition. Title will not pass to Kennedy until the alterations have been made.

Should the coat be damaged, for any reason, before all conditions have been met, the loss must be borne by the seller.

TYPES OF GOODS

Specific Goods

Goods must be ascertained and identified before title passes to the buyer. Selection of specific property is required of the buyer. Although buyers themselves usually make this selection, they may delegate the responsibility to the seller or an agent.

 Before purchasing a piano, Bromberg was shown three identical instruments. She did not select any specific one but said, "I'll take one of these pianos," paying her money at the same time. Since Bromberg did not indicate which of the three she desired, title would not pass to any one of them.

If, before final selection was made, any or all of the instruments were destroyed, Bromberg would not suffer any loss. She did not have title to any of them.

The buyer may appoint the seller as his or her agent for the purpose of selecting specific goods when it is considered more convenient or desirable to do so. The seller must act in good faith in making the selection. Failure to do so will void the agreement, and title will not pass.

 Because Bromberg was not familiar with tonal qualities, she requested the seller to select one of the three pianos for her. If the seller put a "sold" tag on one of the instruments that he had had difficulty in selling to more discriminating buyers, would title pass?

Title would not pass in this situation because the seller did not act in good faith. Bromberg would not be responsible on her contract, and should the piano be damaged, the seller would have to bear the loss that always goes with ownership.

The goods must be in proper order, and all adjustments, alterations, and preparations must be made before title passes. The conditioning of a new car, the alteration of a dress or suit, or the timing of an expensive watch are illustrations of acts required to place goods in a *deliverable state*.

 One of the three pianos was finally selected, and the seller told Bromberg that she could have the instrument after it was polished and tuned by the store. These two acts would place the piano in a deliverable state, and only then would title pass.

Future Goods

A contract for the sale of future goods is a ***contract to sell***, since it would not be possible to pass title at the time the agreement is made. Future goods are not capable of being ascertained and identified, as required for passing of title. Until such time as they have been specifically appropriated to a particular buyer's contract, they are known as ***unascertained goods***. Title to future goods passes only after they have come into existence. Before any interest in the goods can pass from seller to buyer, the goods must be both in existence and identifiable. If not in existence and identifiable, they are ***future goods***. Any sale of future goods, therefore, can be only a contract to sell—not a sale. In the determination of when title does pass to future goods, the following three conditions must have been met:

☐ The goods must have been completed and made ready for the purchaser, with no conditions remaining to be performed.
☐ The goods must have been selected either by the buyer or by the buyer's agent.
☐ The goods must have been *appropriated to the contract* by such acts of the seller as marking, setting aside, or consigning to shipment.

> Harvard Shoe Stores, Inc., ordered 15,000 pairs of a certain style of boot from Grant Leather Manufacturing Company. The contract provided that the manufacturer buy, label, and create the boots for shipment to Harvard. Harvard agreed to accept delivery from the manufacturer's loading platform within 24 hours' notice of completion of each 5,000 pairs.

No obligation of ownership exists in the purchaser until all the above conditions have been fulfilled. Any damage to the goods before these three conditions are complied with must be borne by the seller.

Fungible Goods

Goods usually sold by weight or measure are known as *fungible goods*. The characteristics of each individual particle in such goods would be so similar to all others that identification would be impossible and useless. Wheat, flour, sugar, and liquids of various kinds are examples of fungible goods.

The following two rules apply to the passing of title to fungible goods.

☐ When fungible goods are ordered and it is not specified from which particular grain elevator, storage lot, or tank they are to come, the general rule applying to similar goods must be observed. The goods must be set aside, they must be specific goods, and they must be in a deliverable state. *There may be a sale of a part interest in existing identified goods.*

> Johnson placed an order with the Western Grain Company for 10,000 bushels of wheat. Johnson's truck was to pick up the wheat at the grain company's storage depot. During the night, all the wheat on the company's premises was completely destroyed by fire. As the wheat for Johnson had not yet been separated from the company's wheat and as it had not been designated from which lot it was to come, title had not yet passed. The grain company would have to absorb the loss.

☐ When fungible goods are sold from a specific lot or mass, title to the purchaser's portion will pass without the necessity of separating it from the entire mass. The Uniform Commercial Code provides that "an undivided share of an identified bulk of fungible goods is sufficiently identified to be sold although the quantity of the bulk is not determined. Any agreed proportion of such a bulk or *any quantity thereof* agreed upon by number, weight or other measure may to the extent of the seller's interest in the bulk be sold to the buyer who then becomes an owner in common."

Suppose Johnson's wheat was to be drawn from the wheat stored in Elevator No. 3 and that elevator had been partially destroyed by fire. Title to the wheat in this case would have passed at the time of making the agreement, and Johnson would be required to accept a proportionate loss in the wheat contained in the elevator. If only half of the wheat was destroyed, Johnson's loss would have been 5,000 bushels, half of the amount he owned in the elevator at the time of the fire.

SALES WITH RIGHT OF RETURN

Because of competition and a desire to give satisfaction, sellers of goods often give buyers a right to return merchandise if it is found unsatisfactory. Determination of ownership while the merchandise is in the buyer's possession is important in the event of losses not attributed to the negligence of the buyer. Sales with the right of return are of two kinds.

Sales on Approval

When goods are sold *on approval,* they remain the property of the seller until the buyer has expressed his or her approval. The approval may be indicated by the oral or written consent of the buyer or by the buyer's act of retaining the goods for more than a reasonable time. Using the goods in a reasonable and expected manner on a trial basis will not imply an acceptance. Grossly careless use and a failure to inform the seller of the buyer's intent to return, however, could constitute an acceptance.

 Pasterewski did not wish to be obligated for the purchase of a new piano before trying it out at home. The seller agreed to rent the piano to Pasterewski for a month. If he decided to keep it, the rental paid would apply to the purchase price.

Pasterewski had agreed to a sale on approval. At the end of the month, he would have an implied obligation to communicate with the seller and announce his final decision. Failure to communicate within a reasonable time after the month had passed could result in his implied consent, title thereby passing to Pasterewski.

Sale or Return

Sales of merchandise are also made with the understanding that the purchaser take title to the goods, with the right to revest title in the seller after a specified or reasonable time. In such cases the purchaser must accept all the obligations of ownership while the goods are in his or her possession.

While in the buyer's possession, the goods must be cared for and used in a reasonable manner, anticipating their possible return in the same condition as when received, after making allowance for ordinary wear and tear. Also, the goods must be returned at the buyer's risk and expense.

 Hayden shopped the shelves at Discount Drugs. She was seeking a satisfactory product for tinting her hair. "Rainbow All" displayed a coupon on its package which read: "If for any reason you are not satisfied with this product, return the unused portion for a full return of money paid. Please retain receipt for identifica-

tion of purchase." This was a sale-or-return condition. Hayden would receive
both possession and title, with a right to return both to the seller.

There are advantages to be gained through use of either the sale-on-approval or
the sale-or-return type of agreement. Realizing that greater risk is given to one
having title, a sale on approval would be best for a buyer. For the same reason, a
seller is best protected under the conditions provided by sale or return.

SPECIAL TYPES OF SALES

The law applies different rules to special types of sales that present situations
other than those usually met in the marketplace. Three of the most common of
these are presented here.

Auction Sales

In *auction sales* the auctioneer presents goods for sale, which is similar to an
invitation to trade. Bidders in the crowd respond with their *offers*. The highest bid
(offer) is accepted by the auctioneer, usually by the drop of the hammer together
with the auctioneer's calling out "Sold."

   If, while the hammer is falling, a higher bid comes from those in the crowd,
the auctioneer has two options: (1) declare the goods sold, or (2) reopen the
bidding.

   By custom the sale must either be advertised as an absolute sale or a sale with
reserve. In an *absolute sale*, the goods must be sold to the highest bidder,
regardless of how little an item might bring. In a *sale with reserve*, goods may be
withdrawn from auction if bids do not meet the expectations of their owner. If
terms have not been advertised or announced by the auctioneer as to the type of
sale, it will be assumed to be a sale with reserve.

Stoltzfuss, an auctioneer, announced that a sale would be *with reserve*. A
latecomer bid $2,000 on a 1926 English MG roadster. Stoltzfuss refused to sell the
car at that figure. The latecomer demanded that the $2,000 bid be accepted.
Stoltzfuss, by announced terms of the sale, was justified in withdrawing the car
from auction.

Statute of Frauds   In auction sales, the code makes an exception to the
requirement of a written agreement when price of goods exceeds $500. In auction
sales, an appointed clerk keeps written records of all final bids and sales. By the
UCC provisions, the clerk's record replaces the need of a written agreement.

Suppose, in the previous example, Stoltzfuss had accepted the $2,000 bid. Would
the bidder be bound if careful examination of the car disclosed that it was not
worth the money offered? The bidder would be bound by the accepted bid as
entered in and evidenced by the auction clerk's record of the sale.

By-Bidding   *By-bidding* is the practice of planting persons in the crowd for the
purpose of raising bids made by innocent purchasers. By-bidding is both un-

ethical and illegal. If it is proved, an accepted bid developed in this way may be declared void. Auctioneers are licensed in most states only after passing examinations and being carefully investigated in matters of character and reputation. It is rare, today, that an auctioneer would permit by-bidding, proof of which would result in cancellation of his or her license.

Conditional Sales

Sales agreements which contain terms to be met before or after passing of title are *conditional sales*. A condition that must be carried out prior to the passing of title is a *condition precedent*. Conditions effecting title rights after the transfer of title are *conditions subsequent*. Conditions may relate to the goods, to payment, or to anything else agreed to between seller and buyer. Sales on approval and sale-or-return agreements illustrate the conditions precedent and conditions subsequent.

Sales With a Lien Reserved

Sales in which it is agreed that the buyer takes title but the seller retains possession are *sales with a lien reserved*. The seller in this case must take ordinary care to protect the buyer's goods in his or her possession. A popular type of sale in this category is the highly advertised layaway sale.

 Mary's Gift Shoppe sold a pressed-glass punchbowl to Blackman for $135. Blackman paid $50, and the shop retained possession of the bowl until such time as Blackman would return and pay the $85 owed. The bowl was tagged, identifying it as Blackman's property.

This was a typical sale with a lien reserved. Should the bowl be damaged before Blackman took delivery, it would be Blackman's bowl that was damaged. If damage came through negligence or lack of ordinary care by the shop, it would be their responsibility. In such case the shop would have to return Blackman's $50, or replace the bowl.

SECURITY AGREEMENTS

Sales on credit in which the buyer takes possession but the seller retains title are *security agreements*. Security agreements are carefully regulated by the provisions written into the Uniform Commercial Code. A security agreement gives a creditor certain rights in taking and selling a debtor's property in event of a default in payment.

DELIVERY OF GOODS

The delivery of goods has a definite relationship to the passing of title. It may be agreed that title will pass at the time of the sale when the buyer picks up the goods at the seller's place of business. Or there may be a condition precedent, requiring delivery of goods to the buyer's place of business or home prior to passing of title.

Delivery by Private Carrier

Delivery by the seller's vehicle or by a vehicle hired by the seller implies that title will not pass until goods are received by the buyer at his or her address.

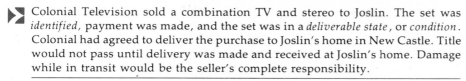 Colonial Television sold a combination TV and stereo to Joslin. The set was *identified,* payment was made, and the set was in a *deliverable state*, or *condition*. Colonial had agreed to deliver the purchase to Joslin's home in New Castle. Title would not pass until delivery was made and received at Joslin's home. Damage while in transit would be the seller's complete responsibility.

Delivery by Common Carrier

Delivery by common carrier includes delivery by air and railway express, railway freight, truck lines, steamship lines, and other agencies operating under public franchise. (See Common Carriers, Chapter 20.) Title to goods shipped by common carrier passes according to terms included in the bill of lading. These are what are called *free on board* or *f.o.b.* terms.

Sales "f.o.b. Shipping Point"   These terms indicate that the buyer will pay all shipping charges. More important to this study, it indicates that title to the goods passes at the point of origin. Delivery to the carrier by the seller and acceptance by the carrier complete the transfer of title. The carrier's acceptance is evidenced by the carrier signing the bill of lading. Thus the buyer accepts full responsibility as owner during transit of the goods.

▶ Goods were shipped to Harlan Brothers, Memphis, Tennessee, by Marcus Manufacturing. Terms of shipment were f.o.b. shipping point. During shipment the goods were destroyed by fire. Harlan Brothers, not Marcus, would be obligated to pay the shipper for the goods shipped. Likewise, Harlan Brothers would place a claim against the carrier in its obligation as insurer of goods accepted for shipment.

Sales "f.o.b. Destination"   Goods shipped under these terms belong to the shipper until they have been delivered to the destination shown on the bill of lading. Destination, for purpose of passing title, requires that (1) the goods arrive at the place named in the bill of lading, (2) the consignee is given notice of their arrival, and (3) a reasonable time is allowed for the consignee to pick up the goods from the carrier.

▶ Suppose, in the previous example, the shipment to Harlan Brothers had been made under terms of *f.o.b. Memphis, Tennessee.* Title to the goods would not have passed at the shipping point. The shipper would have had to suffer the loss, and Harlan Brothers would have had no obligation for payment.

The terms used are not always mutually agreed to by the seller and buyer. Certain goods are shipped according to the accepted *custom of the market place.* As an example, it is common practice for automobiles to be shipped f.o.b. Detroit. Buyers of foreign cars are normally quoted prices as f.o.b. point of entry. The buyer is charged freight from the point where a new car is unloaded from a ship to the showroom where the car was purchased.

Sales "f.o.b., c.o.d." When terms of shipment do not specify *shipping point* or *destination,* it is assumed to be *f.o.b. shipping point.* Adding the term *c.o.d.* (cash on delivery) instructs the carrier to retain *possession* until the carrier has collected the cost of goods. Thus, this is another example of a *sale with a lien reserved.*

C.i.f. and c.f. Terms By c.i.f. terms the carrier is instructed to collect *all* charges and fees in one lump sum. These include cost of goods shipped, insurance, and freight charges to the point of destination. C.f. terms do not include insurance.

cost insurance freight

CONSUMER PROTECTION LEGISLATION

Greater attention has been given consumer protection laws over the past decade than ever before. Federal, state, and local lawmaking bodies are giving careful attention to consumer demands seeking protection from shoddy merchandise, unenforceable guarantees, hazardous products, and the like. In the face of high-pressure sales tactics and deceptive sales and advertising practices, consumer rights are being reviewed and strengthened where possible. The federal government has also been considering the creation of an Agency for Consumer Advocacy. Such an agency would protect the legal rights of consumers in the courts and before governmental agencies. Many states and local governments have already established consumer protection agencies to address consumer complaints.

"Cooling-Off Period" Statutes

Federal and state legislation now gives consumers the right to rescind sales agreements of certain kinds without giving reason for cancellation. Three days are given for terminating door-to-door sales agreements when the money involved exceeds $25. Sales representatives are required to inform buyers of these rights and to supply them with self-addressed envelopes if notice is to be given.

Truth-in-Lending Act

Regulation Z of the Truth-in-Lending Act regulates lenders and merchants in their relation with borrowers and buyers on credit. Credit terms must be expressed clearly and without concealment. Failure to make complete and understandable disclosure of credit charges may subject the creditor to prosecution and the voiding of a sales agreement.

> Merchandise Mart sold Madison a dishwasher on an installment sales plan. The agreement, as presented to Madison, disclosed nothing more than the amount of monthly payments.

This agreement could be declared void on grounds that it did not conform to the requirements of the Truth-in-Lending Act. It should have shown the interest charges at a per annum percentage rate, the number of months payments were to be made, and the cash price before adding credit charges.

The cooling-off statutes and the Truth-in-Lending Act are discussed in greater detail in Chapter 4, along with other important consumer-protection legislation relating to sales contracts.

Questions for Review and Discussion

1. Mention five ways one can acquire title to goods other than by a sales agreement.

2. How do future goods differ from other goods?

3. Discuss the general rules that determine when title passes.

4. Explain title as it refers to fungible goods.

5. Give an example of a sale with an undivided interest.

6. Distinguish between a sale with a lien reserved and a conditional sale.

7. When does title pass in each of the following? (*a*) f.o.b. shipping point; (*b*) f.o.b. destination; (*c*) f.o.b., c.o.d.

8. Discuss the rights of husband and wife in states that have community property. Are all goods covered by these rights?

9. In auction sales, is the offer made by the auctioneer or the bidder? Explain.

10. Distinguish between a sale-or-return and a sale on approval.

Analyzing Cases

1. Peters and Adams bought a power cruiser, which they anchored in Chesapeake Bay. They each used the boat on alternate weekends. During a weekend when Adams was using the cruiser, the bow of the boat was damaged when it scraped an unmarked jetty. Adams claimed that the part of the boat damaged belonged to Peters. Was Adams correct in this reasoning? • See also *Counts* v. *Metzger*, 228 S.W. 2d 395.

2. Sanchez made a bid of $800 on a violin being sold at auction. Before the end of the sale, she decided not to take the violin. The auctioneer was told to cancel the bid, giving the statute of frauds as a legal reason. Was Sanchez able to disregard the sale for reasons given? Explain. • See also *Stanhope State Bank* v. *Peterson*, 205 Iowa 578.

3. Ward ordered heavy machinery from a company in Moline, Illinois. The machinery was shipped to Ward, terms f.o.b. Moline. En route to its destination in Los Angeles the machinery was destroyed when the freight train derailed and caught fire. Ward refused to honor the bill for the machinery. Will he be required to pay for it? Explain. • See also *Smith Co.* v. *Moschlades*, 183 N.Y.S. 500.

4. Polaski found a valuable first edition that someone had dropped on the street. She took the book home, placing it with others in a collection of other first editions. The owner's name could not be found in the lost book, and Polaski made no effort to locate the owner. Does she now have title to the book? Explain.

5. Picillo bought a car from Broad Motors, who agreed to change the oil, tune up the motor, and give the car a polish and wax job before delivery. After the oil had been changed but the other work had not been finished, the car was stolen from the seller's garage. Broad insisted on payment for the car, claiming that it belonged to

Picillo when stolen. Was the seller correct? Explain your decision. • See also *Bates* v. *Smith*, 47 N.W. 249.

6. Cohen bought a raincoat but had some doubts as to its weatherproof qualities. The sales clerk assured her, "If that coat doesn't keep you dry, just bring it in and you'll get your money back." Rain did seep through the coat onto her other clothing. Did Cohen have title to the coat when purchased? What kind of sale was this? • See also *Walker* v. *Houston*, 215 Cal. 742.

Legal Reasoning and Business Judgment

Analyze the legal aspects of these business problems. Suggest possible solutions.

1. The store where you work sold a television set to a customer, giving him the right to return the set if not satisfactory. Money was paid, and the set was delivered to the customer's residence. A thief entered the house one evening, taking the television and other valuables. The customer asked for the money back, claiming that this was a sale on approval. How would you have interpreted this sale if asked for guidance by the sales department of the store?

2. Your company and another one bought a truck that was to be shared by the two firms. Each company had its own experienced and competent drivers. While being used by the other firm, the truck was damaged by a rock slide over which the driver had no control or warning. Your employer seeks advice as to responsibility for repairs. Would cost of repairs be borne entirely by the other firm, or would the cost be divided?

3. You have been asked by a friend for advice concerning rights to property bought since marriage and used in the house rented by your friend and his spouse. They are about to separate, and there are arguments about a television, a freezer, a living-room suite, and an electric organ that were bought and paid for by one of them. They are living in a community property state. What advice could you give your friend about these acquisitions?

Chapter 16
Rights and Remedies of Parties

May an owner of goods pass title? Always—or almost always. How about a neighbor who borrows your lawnmower? Could he or she sell your lawnmower to an unsuspecting buyer and pass title? And what happens when a thief sells the television stolen from your house? Does the innocent buyer have the right to keep the television? These are all logical questions that arise when two parties claim ownership to the same property. At times they are easily answered. In other cases the decision comes only after the court and jury review exhaustive testimony from both claimants.

Essentially, only the owner, or one representing the owner, has the right to pass title. However, even then a *remote party* or an outside party may interrupt an owner's attempt to pass title. Consider the creditor who has recorded a lien against property in your home. A so-called innocent purchaser will be in trouble and must satisfy the lien before claiming real and complete ownership.

This chapter considers the rights, remedies, and liabilities of:

☐ Rightful owners of goods who pass title to others unintentionally by what is known as *estoppel*.
☐ Rightful owners of goods wrongfully possessed by others, as by theft.
☐ Buyers and sellers, if there is breach of contract.

PASSING OF TITLE BY ESTOPPEL

The Uniform Sales Act recognizes seven situations in which title will pass to a remote party although the owner did not intend to sell. Title in these cases is said to pass by *estoppel*. Estoppel results when a person or persons by their conduct lead others to believe that certain facts are true when they are untrue, and the others act on the assertion or representations to their injury. Thus, when one acts in such a way as to lead others to believe that another is one's agent when in fact he or she is not, one is prevented (estopped) from denying the authority of that agent.

In order to claim good title to another's goods under the doctrine of estoppel, a remote party must be able to prove the following facts:

- ☐ The purchase was made from one in *rightful possession.*
- ☐ The purchase was made in *good faith,* the buyer believing the seller to be the real owner or the one appointed to sell for the real owner.
- ☐ The buyer must have *given value* for that to which he or she now claims ownership under estoppel.

The following seven estoppel situations are enforceable when each of the above facts is proved.

By Transfer of Money or Negotiable Instrument

When the owner of cash or negotiable instruments made out to bearer entrusts possession of the property to another, a transfer to a third party for value will terminate the real owner's title to them.

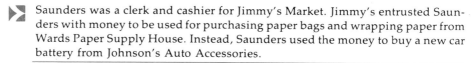

Saunders was a clerk and cashier for Jimmy's Market. Jimmy's entrusted Saunders with money to be used for purchasing paper bags and wrapping paper from Wards Paper Supply House. Instead, Saunders used the money to buy a new car battery from Johnson's Auto Accessories.

Johnson was not aware that the money used by Saunders belonged to Jimmy's Market. One has a right to believe that a person in possession of cash is the owner. Jimmy's Market would be estopped from making any claim against the auto accessory store. Of course, Jimmy's could enter a complaint of embezzlement against Saunders. They could also sue Saunders for the return of money used. They might even demand title and possession of the car battery, which could be resold to recover the loss.

When Seller Deals in Same Type of Goods

When the owner of goods gives up possession of property to another who sells the same type of property and when that person sells the property to an innocent purchaser for value, title to the goods passes by estoppel. The owner made the sale possible by leaving the goods where he or she did. Entrusting the goods to a merchant would imply that he or she had given the merchant the right to sell the goods.

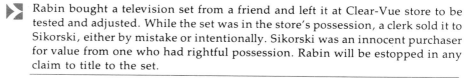

Rabin bought a television set from a friend and left it at Clear-Vue store to be tested and adjusted. While the set was in the store's possession, a clerk sold it to Sikorski, either by mistake or intentionally. Sikorski was an innocent purchaser for value from one who had rightful possession. Rabin will be estopped in any claim to title to the set.

In all such cases the real owner has the right to seek damages from the one who sells his or her goods without permission.

When Seller Is Permitted to Present Self as Real Owner

When the owner of goods gives up rightful possession to another and permits that party to act as the real owner, a sale to an innocent purchaser will estop the real owner's future claim of title.

> Romano loaned McCarthy a typewriter, which McCarthy kept for several months. Chu Teh, a frequent visitor to McCarthy's apartment, asked to buy the typewriter, and McCarthy agreed. Chu Teh had every right to believe that the typewriter belonged to McCarthy.

Although Romano was the real owner, Chu Teh would be permitted to keep the machine. Romano had never intended to pass title, but had given rightful possession to McCarthy. Through that act, Chu Teh was able to view McCarthy as the real owner. Obviously, Romano could demand from McCarthy the reasonable value of the typewriter and could bring legal action to recover any damages.

When Person Is Entrusted With Proof of Ownership

Estoppel denies the real owner title to goods sold by one to whom *indicia of title* have been entrusted. Indicia of title include certificates of title, bills of lading, bills of sale, and similar title documents.

> Reisler, an employee of Apex TV, was given a negotiable bill of lading and instructed to pick up ten crates of television receivers at a freight depot. Reisler sold the bill of lading to an innocent purchaser who had been convinced of Reisler's right to make the sale. Apex TV would be unsuccessful in attempting to recover the shipment from the innocent purchaser, but it would have the right to bring criminal and civil action against the dishonest employee.

When Buyer Is Innocent Purchaser of Goods Sold to Another Under Conditional Sale

When goods are sold on installment contracts, the seller usually includes a condition precedent for the passing of title. This condition states that title to goods sold will not pass until all payments have been completed. A purchase by a remote party of goods sold under such an agreement would estop the real owner if the purchaser had not been aware of the condition precedent.

> Murphy bought a color television set for $500, terms $100 down and the balance in twelve equal monthly installments. The contract stated that Clear-Vue would transfer title to the set when all payments were made. A sale of the set by Murphy to an innocent purchaser for value would terminate Clear-Vue's title rights, and Clear-Vue would be estopped in any claim made against the third party.

Remedies Against Estoppel in Conditional Sales   Sellers may protect themselves from loss of title in one of two ways. The seller may record the title in a public office, or the seller may conspicuously mark the property as a warning that the one having possession is not the actual owner.

> Bergstrom bought an expensive watch from Morris Jewelers, making a $25 cash payment at the time of purchase. The balance of $150 was to be paid in twelve monthly installments. Morris Jewelers had the sale recorded in the county recorder's office. The record showed that title to the watch would not pass until all payments were made.

Any person buying the watch would not be considered an innocent purchaser. The recording of the sale gave *constructive notice* to all persons that the watch still belonged to Morris Jewelers. Although persons purchasing used merchandise should always check public records, in actual practice they rarely do so. Failure to check, however, does not weaken the real owner's right to demand the return of the merchandise from the "innocent" purchaser.

When Seller Has Only Voidable Title

Anyone who obtains property through fraud, misrepresentation, mistake, undue influence, or duress, or from one not capable of contracting, holds only a voidable title to the goods. The seller has the right to *void the sale* and demand the return of the property. However, should an innocent purchaser buy the property before the sale has been voided, the former owner would be estopped in any attempt to retrieve the property from the innocent buyer.

> Reed bought an expensive television set from Clear-Vue on a 30-day charge account. In making the purchase, Reed made several fraudulent statements to Clear-Vue's credit department. Although the set was bought by fraudulent means, a resale by Reed to an innocent purchaser for value would cut off the right of Clear-Vue to demand the return of its former property.

As in the other situations, the seller may always bring an action on the contract against the original purchaser for any loss.

When Property Is Already Sold

When goods are sold and the buyer leaves them in possession of the seller, a second sale of the same goods to an innocent purchaser will estop the first buyer in any further claim of ownership. (See paragraph headed "When Seller Deals in Same Type of Goods" on page 202.)

> Chandler bought a new television set from Clear-Vue, paying for it at the time of the sale. As it was to be a holiday gift, Chandler requested the right to leave it at the store for two weeks. A sale of the set by the store to another party would terminate Chandler's ownership rights in it. Chandler would, however, have the right to sue the store for the unpermitted sale of the set.

SALES BY PERSONS HAVING WRONGFUL POSSESSION

Possession of personal property secured through the use of force, cunning, or theft is wrongful possession. Unlike all the situations in estoppel, where possession was willingly given by the owner, wrongful possession is always without either implied or express permission of the owner. The real owner is *never estopped* in a claim of title when goods are sold to a remote innocent party by one having wrongful possession.

> A thief entered Clear-Vue's Center City store and stole a hi-fi speaker, which he later sold to an innocent purchaser who believed the thief to be the real owner.

Clear-Vue would have the legal right to demand the return of the speaker if the purchaser were ever located. The purchaser's only chance of recovery would be in an action against the thief for the money paid to him, if the thief is caught.

The continued sale of the stolen property through several innocent buyers would not, however, in any way defeat the real owner's right in the property.

▶ Suppose the person who purchased the speaker from the thief later sold it to another television store, which in turn sold it to another innocent purchaser. Estoppel would not operate to the disadvantage of Clear-Vue, from whom the speaker was originally stolen.

The rights of possession and title of successive buyers of stolen property can never be any better than the rights of the thief. The criminal responsibilities, of course, are not to be compared. The later buyers are usually innocent.

What remedies does a rightful owner have against one who has wrongful possession of his or her goods? In most states three actions are possible: *replevin*, *trover*, and *trespass*. **Replevin** is an action whereby a court of law commands an offender to return wrongfully held goods to their real owner. **Trover** is a common-law action permitting the owner of goods to demand payment for the value of his or her property from a wrongful possessor. And an action of **trespass** permits the owner of property to recover the value of the goods together with all profits and gains that the other party may have received through unpermitted use or resale. (These three actions are explained further in Chapter 18, "Nature of Bailments.")

CONTRACT BREACH AND SELLER REMEDIES

The legal remedies described above apply to one who has wrongful possession and title to personal property or goods. But what happens if one has *rightful* possession and one of the parties breaches the contract? A **breach of contract** occurs when one or both of the parties—buyer and/or seller—breaks or cancels the contract or fails to carry out his or her contractual obligations.

In this section are discussed the remedies that are available when there is a breach: first, of the seller against the buyer and second, of the buyer against the seller.

In the event of a breach of contract of sale or a contract to sell, the seller has several remedies against the other party. Each remedy has a particular use and application, depending (1) upon the way in which the contract was breached and (2) upon the recovery desired by the seller under the circumstances.

When Buyer Refuses to Accept Goods Tendered

It is the duty of a buyer in a sales contract to accept the goods and pay for them when delivered. A refusal to accept delivery gives the seller three remedies:

☐ The seller may store the goods for the buyer and sue the buyer for the purchase price if the goods are not readily resalable to another customer.

☐ The seller may resell the goods immediately if they are of a perishable nature or if they might depreciate rapidly in market value. Automobiles, clothing, and the like decrease in value when new models appear. After the sale, the injured party may sue the other for the difference between what the property brought on resale and the price the buyer had agreed to pay in his or her contract.

> Owens Motors sold a new car to Hudson three weeks before the announcement of new models. Hudson refused to take delivery when the car was ready. In anticipation of a decrease in price when new models appeared, Owens Motors sold the car to another interested buyer. The second deal, however, brought $200 less than would have been realized had Hudson not breached the contract.

Owens Motors could have demanded $200 from Hudson to cover its proved loss. In situations like this, the seller must act in good faith in making the second sale. If Owens Motors, to benefit a friend, had sold the car at a ridiculously low price, Hudson would not have been obligated to make up the difference. The price at which goods are resold should be within a range considered proper in comparison with prices then being charged by other dealers for the same merchandise.

☐ The seller may retain the merchandise and sue the buyer for the difference between the contract price and the market price at the time the buyer breached the sales agreement.

When Buyer Refuses to Pay

A seller has a right of action against a buyer who refuses to make payment according to terms of a sales agreement. The seller's rights vary depending on which party has possession of goods at the time of the buyer's breach.

When Seller Has Possession   The seller has a right to retain possession when the buyer has refused payment prior to transfer of possession. This is true whether or not title may have already passed to the buyer. If payment is not made within a reasonable time of the buyer's demand, the seller may sell the goods and demand damages caused by the buyer's breach.

 Martin bought a coat, suit, and dress from the Blue and Gold Shop. The three items were put on layaway after Martin made a $5 payment. It was agreed that the merchandise would be picked up on March 1, and $100 due would be tendered at that time. Martin did not return. The goods bought declined in price due to an unseasonable weather change. The Blue and Gold Shop finally sold the three items for only $50.

Martin could be held liable for the store's $50 loss. Had the seller anticipated the unexpected decline in price, the goods would have been sold sooner when Martin did not respond to the store's demand for payment.

When Buyer Has Possession   When possession has been transferred to the buyer, the seller may sue for the purchase price. If title has not passed, as in an installment sale, the seller has the right to demand the return of goods, resell them, and charge the original buyer with any loss originating from the buyer's breach.

> General Appliance Stores sold an electric stove to Furjanic. The sales contract included installment payments over a period of twelve months. The seller retained title until all payments would be made. Furjanic was given possession of the seller's stove, to be used during the twelve-month period.

Failure to meet installment payments gives the seller two choices of action. Furjanic may be sued for the entire balance still owed, or General Appliance may repossess the stove, sell it as used merchandise, and charge Furjanic for any loss resulting from such a forced sale.

Right of Stoppage in Transit

Stoppage in transit is a special right permitted a seller when he or she discovers the insolvency of the buyer after the shipment of goods has been started over the lines of a common carrier and before the goods have been delivered to the buyer. This right is available on both f.o.b. shipping point and f.o.b. destination shipments. The seller must satisfy the carrier that the buyer is insolvent and must accept all responsibility for any damage that may result to the carrier if shipment of goods is interrupted. Should this action be taken against a buyer's goods, both the seller and the carrier may be subjected to a suit for damages if the insolvency information is unfounded.

Right of Rescission

An unpaid seller who has transferred title to but not possession of goods may rescind the sales contract if the purchaser repudiates the contract or does some act that shows he or she is unable to perform or is in default of payment for an unreasonable time. Notice of rescission of the transfer of title must be given to the buyer by the seller. A seller who has partly performed is excused from further performance under these same conditions.

A rescinded contract is always treated as if it had never been made. For that reason, no action for damages can result therefrom on the demand of either party. However, if partial delivery has been made on a contract and one of the parties fails to meet his or her obligations, the injured party may treat the remainder of the contract as rescinded and sue for damages for the part completed.

CONTRACT BREACH AND BUYER REMEDIES

A buyer has many remedies available either by action at law or, in some cases, in equity. The buyer's *legal rights* in event of the seller's breach are discussed here.

Delivery of Different Quantity Than Ordered

The seller must deliver the exact quantity of goods as agreed to in the contract. Delivery of a smaller quantity than ordered gives the buyer the right to reject the goods delivered and demand damages for a breach of contract.

▶ Missouri Grocers Exchange contracted with Sunbright Soap Company for 500 cases of laundry detergent at $18 a case. When the goods were delivered, the receiving department counted only 470 cases. The market price for the detergent had dropped to $16.50 a case between the date of the contract and the date of delivery.

The buyer would gain here by rejecting the entire shipment. The seller would no doubt prefer to renegotiate and give Missouri Grocers Exchange the benefit of the new price rather than having the 470 cases shipped back. Unless a compromise could be reached, future goodwill between the two parties would be severely damaged.

If a buyer receives a larger quantity than the sales contract specified, three remedies are available.

☐ The buyer may reject the entire shipment.
☐ The buyer may accept only what was ordered and reject the rest.
☐ The buyer may accept the entire shipment, paying for all goods received at the contract price.

▶ During an inflationary market, Harmon Manufacturing Company delivered one hundred window air conditioners to Alexander Supply Company. Alexander's order called for only seventy-five units. Inflation had caused a price increase of 16 percent since the contract for the seventy-five units had been made.

With a rising price trend at hand, the buyer would no doubt elect to accept the entire shipment. Alexander could then realize a savings by buying the twenty-five additional air conditioners at the old price.

Delivery of Unsatisfactory Goods

When goods do not compare with the sample and description of goods ordered, the buyer has a choice of two remedies.

Return Goods and Demand Refund   Return of goods and demand of a refund is permitted as a buyer's remedy in all states. Some states also allow a suit for breach of warranty. If the seller refuses to accept merchandise returned, or fails to make a refund of money already paid, the buyer may hold the goods *in the name of the seller* and sue for the purchase price, as well as for any damages caused by the seller's breach.

▶ Caravan Motel ordered ten dozen bath towels from samples shown by Fleming Towel Company's representative. Caravan paid the Fleming agent 50 percent of the price with the order. The towels delivered were inferior to those shown to Caravan at the time the order was given.

Caravan would have the right to return the towels and to ask for refund of the money already paid. In the event of a legal action, Caravan could also demand damages that would be sufficient for the motel to buy the type of towels which were shown by the firm's representative but not delivered.

Retain Goods and Demand Money Damages   When goods are sufficiently satisfactory, the buyer may retain the goods and demand money damages. Damages would be an amount that would represent the difference between the value of the goods ordered and the value of those received.

 In the previous case, Caravan Motel could have negotiated to accept the towels delivered. The buyer would demand a price adjustment considered fair in return for accepting the inferior-quality towels.

Nondelivery of Goods

The buyer's rights against a seller who fails to deliver ordered goods are conditioned by determination of which party has title. The buyer's right to damages for breach depends, however, on whether or not title has passed.

Where *title has not passed,* a refusal to deliver ordered goods permits a buyer to sue for breach of contract. Damages sought would be the difference between the contract price and the price of the same goods in the marketplace on the date of the breach. The buyer may also claim incidental or consequential damages resulting from nondelivery.

 Acme Restaurants ordered four sides of choice beef from Haldas Wholesale Butchers. Haldas failed to deliver the beef when promised. The quoted wholesale price on choice beef had advanced 9 cents a pound since the date of contract. Acme Restaurants would be justified in demanding damages of 9 cents a pound for the weight of beef not delivered. Any other incidental damages could be added to the claim.

On the other hand, a buyer is given additional rights when the seller fails to deliver goods to which *title has already passed* to the purchaser. In addition to the right to sue for breach of contract, the buyer may bring other actions related to the seller's obligation to respect the buyer's title rights. Two remedies open to the buyer are discussed here.

Tort Action of Conversion   A seller who refuses to deliver goods owned by the buyer is considered in wrongful possession. The buyer may institute a tort action of *conversion* as a remedy against the seller's interruption of the buyer's title rights. The amount of damages allowed would be the value of the goods at the time of the conversion.

 Stevens Company bought a truck scale from Atkinson Scale Company. Their agreement was an unconditional contract of sale of specific goods, in a deliverable state. Stevens Company agreed to pick up their scale on March 14. Subsequently, Atkinson sold the same scale to another buyer at a price $500 higher than the price quoted to Stevens.

Stevens had title to the scale by terms of the contract. The buyer may demand damages equal to the price of the scale *at the time of the breach.* Stevens, in an action of conversion, may demand $500 plus the return of any money already paid on the sales contract.

Demanding Possession Through Replevin   An owner of personal property may use an action of *replevin* to recover goods in the possession of the seller. A court-ordered writ of replevin would require the seller to convey the goods to the purchaser, who has valid title to them.

> ▶ Northeast Seafood Company sold a quantity of lobsters to the Hotel Commodore, accepting the hotel's check for $485. When someone came for the lobsters, Northeast refused to release the crates that had been set aside for the hotel. Lobsters were in short supply, and the hotel had need for the lobsters which were rightfully theirs.

An action of replevin would be appropriate as a means of getting possession of the lobsters. The agreement between Northeast and the hotel was a contract of sale, of specific goods, in a deliverable state. Title had passed, and the seafood company could only hold the lobsters for the hotel's convenience.

Actions in Equity   A buyer may demand performance of a sales agreement through an action in a court of equity. A decree of specific performance, if granted by the court, would require the seller to deliver the goods described in the sales agreement. An action in equity is permitted only when money damages do not satisfy. If the goods described are generally available in the marketplace, an equity decree will be denied. Objets d'art, rare gems, antiques, and goods described as one-of-a-kind come within the jurisdiction of the equity courts.

> ▶ Ramsdale signed an agreement to purchase a 1909 automobile offered for sale by Antique Cars, Inc. The price was $28,000, and the seller agreed to take care of the car until Ramsdale made arrangements for its transport to Ohio. When Ramsdale notified the seller that arrangements had been made, Antique Cars informed the buyer that the sale was off. A court of equity would grant a decree of specific performance.

This was a one-of-a-kind sale. Ramsdale would not find it possible to go into the marketplace and purchase another 1909 car of the same make and model.

> ▶ Gregson signed an agreement to purchase a Dodge Dart. Money was paid and contracts signed. The seller had certain work to do on the car before delivery. Gregson was later informed that the seller would not make delivery, and the money paid would be returned.

This was not a sale of unique merchandise. Cars of the kind purchased by Gregson were available at other car agencies, ready for sale and delivery. Money damages, if there was damage, would satisfy. Damages would be the difference between the amount of money Gregson paid the breaching party and the amount that would be charged for the same car elsewhere.

ASSESSING DAMAGES

Damages owed to either seller or buyer are determined by arbitration, negotiation, compromise, or a jury trial. Damages must be actual, not speculative. At times they may be nominal, or, when intentional damage is indicated, they may be punitive. (See Chapter 13.)

Questions for Review and Discussion

1. Who has the right to transfer title to personal property?

2. Name the various situations in which a buyer becomes owner through estoppel.

3. Discuss the two ways in which a seller retains the right of ownership of goods sold under a conditional sales agreement.

4. Name two remedies that a buyer may use to regain property held by a seller before title has passed to the buyer.

5. What are the three remedies permitted a buyer to whom the seller delivers more goods than called for in the sales contract?

6. Discuss the rights of an innocent purchaser of stolen goods.

7. Under what conditions would a seller institute stoppage-in-transit rights?

8. Distinguish between a buyer's rights in a court of law and in a court of equity in claims made against a seller.

9. Under what conditions would a buyer institute an action of conversion against a seller?

10. When may a seller recover goods to which the buyer had no more than a voidable title?

Analyzing Cases

1. Plummer purchased a refrigerator under a conditional sales agreement. The seller retained title subject to final payment. Plummer moved out of the state. Before moving, a neighbor bought the refrigerator at a bargain price. $175 was still owed the appliance dealer under the conditional sales agreement. Under what conditions may the seller take possession of the refrigerator from its new "owner"? Explain. • See also *Lawrence* v. *Worcester Lunch C. & C. Mfg. Co.*, 300 Mass. 543.

2. Landers's stereo was stolen from a dormitory room. After she reported the theft, the police located the stereo in a local pawnshop, where the thief had used it to make a loan. The manager of the pawnshop refused to give up possession of the set, claiming that he had been an innocent victim and had given money to one who appeared to be the real owner. Does Landers have the right to recover the set? Explain. • See also *Doyle* v. *State*, 77 Ga. 513.

3. Classic Book Company sold a set of valuable books to Gomez. The publisher agreed to a sale-or-return condition as a part of the sale.
While in Gomez's home, the books were damaged by his dog. May Gomez now return the books as being unsatisfactory? Will his money be refunded? Explain.

4. Stern worked as a collector for Credit Furniture Company. He took $75 of the collections and bought a target pistol from Grahm's Sporting Goods Store. Credit Furniture, learning of the misuse of its funds, demanded that Grahm return the $75. Will Credit Furniture recover the $75 from the sporting goods store? Explain. • See also *Eatonville State Bank* v. *Marshall*, 170 Wash. 503, 17 P.2d 14.

5. Arnold purchased a socket wrench set from Thurber Tool Supply on their layaway plan. Arnold did not return and pick up the set on April 15, as agreed. Thurber sold the same set to another customer on May 15. Would Thurber be liable to Arnold on an action of conversion? Explain.

6. Monroe stole goods from Central Department Store, her employer. The goods were then sold to an innocent purchaser, who had every reason to believe that Monroe had proper title to the goods. The store manager, realizing Monroe was a thief, traced the sale and sought recovery of the merchandise from the new buyer. Will the store recover its property? Explain. • See also *Snyder* v. *Lincoln*, 150 Neb. 581, 35 N.W.2d 483.

Legal Reasoning and Business Judgment

Analyze the legal aspects of these business problems. Suggest possible solutions.

1. Your firm sold 10,000 bushels of wheat to Stillman Flour Mills, delivery to be taken on August 15. Stillman called on July 15, stated that the demand for white flour had dropped, and canceled the order for the 10,000 bushels. The price of wheat had dropped 15 cents a bushel between the dates of the contract and Stillman's cancellation. What would you suggest be done about this matter?

2. During a business trip through New Mexico, one of your firm's representatives sold sales samples to a customer. The samples were specially packed, and due to their special manufacture they were quite valuable. The buyer recognized the samples as goods that a sales representative would not usually sell when contacting customers. It is important that your firm recover the samples. What problems may be met, and how would you solve them?

3. A buyer in the purchasing department located parts for machines being used in your plants—a valuable find, as the machines in question had been built more than forty years ago. The purchasing agent made the owner an offer. It was accepted and later confirmed by the seller's letter. Now the seller has decided not to sell the parts as agreed, hoping to find another buyer who would offer more money. What should be done here to protect the company's interest?

Chapter 17
Warranties and Product Liability

To most purchasers, nothing (except perhaps price) is quite as persuasive as a seller's warranty or guarantee; as a sale becomes more difficult, the seller often adds on warranties to a point where the buyer cannot resist. Yet nothing is quite so difficult to interpret and understand as the terms of a cleverly written warranty. In fact, so much confusion has existed that the Federal Trade Commission now requires manufacturers and sellers to be explicit and clear in all guarantees and warranties made to consumers.

The FTC and the courts have also held that statements made in advertising which induce consumers to buy may be interpreted as warranties. In some circumstances, therefore, a published advertisement may be considered more than an invitation to trade.

> ▶▶ Twentieth Century Auto Polish was advertised as a safe, noncorrosive polish, manufactured to the highest standards required of finishes. Rankin bought a can of the polish, and it ruined the finish of her new car. Rankin could seek damages against the manufacturer, claiming that the advertised statements were warranties made to any prospective purchaser.

Warranties are either express or implied by law. *Implied warranties* are enforceable by the terms of the Uniform Commercial Code; they do not result from agreements made between the seller and buyer. *Express warranties*, however, are those agreed by the parties to a contract of sale. They may include any guarantees acceptable to the parties.

EXPRESS WARRANTIES

A warranty made by the seller, either in writing or orally, at the time of the sale will be enforceable by the buyer according to its terms. Any statement of fact or promise made by the seller that relates to the goods being sold and becomes part of the agreement between seller and buyer is said to have created an express warranty that the goods will be as described or explained to the buyer.

> ▶▶ Clarke visited the Kirkwood Tire Mart and discussed tires at some length with the owner. After much deliberation, Clarke decided to take four tires. With the tires,

Clarke received the following printed warranty: "This tire is unconditionally guaranteed for 5,000 miles. If damaged for any reason whatsoever, including road hazards, it will be repaired or replaced by the seller without charge. The seller-manufacturer further agrees to reimburse the buyer for any emergency road service should the tire prove defective."

This is an express warranty, and its terms are sufficiently inclusive to cover damage from broken glass, nails, sharp curbing, or other road hazards which could hardly be blamed on manufacturing defects. Most guarantees, however, are not so generous and would not grant so many rights to the buyer.

A seller-manufacturer typically includes certain limiting statements or disclaimers in an express warranty. The statement usually reads, "No other warranties, either express or implied, are to be construed as being part of this contract and warranty." In recent years, federal agencies have been successful in getting some manufacturers to exclude such disclaimers from implied warranties. These same manufacturers, however, are not barred from excluding disclaimers that were not originally part of the written warranty statement from express warranties. A sales agency—as distinguished from the manufacturer—may agree to include additional implied warranties in their sales agreement with a buyer. Commonly, also, special warranties given by a supplier of parts are included in the buyer's more complete protection.

 Kerslake purchased a new car from a General Motors dealer. Shortly after he took delivery, one of the new tires blew out. The tires, battery, and radio were covered by special warranties given by the manufacturer of those parts of the new car. The tire would be replaced under the warranty given by the tire manufacturer, not by General Motors.

Parol-Evidence Rule

The *parol-evidence rule* provides that when written contracts are made between parties, the only terms that will be enforced are the terms included in the written agreement. This means that if the seller makes statements of great importance on which a buyer depends but these statements are not included in the signed agreement, they are not considered part of the sales contract and cannot be enforced by the buyer.

 Rabel purchased an electronic calculator to assist in teaching advanced math courses. In addition to the written warranty, the clerk orally assured Rabel, "Don't worry about that guarantee. We stand behind everything we sell. I don't care what goes wrong with it. We'll either fix it or replace it over a full twelve months." The printed warranty was for only six months. Any complaint by Rabel after six months would not come within the warranty regardless of the clerk's oral statements.

A certain freedom is given in the application of the parol-evidence rule in relation to oral statements made by a seller which clarify the meaning of the written agreement. Written guarantees are at times vague as to the meaning of some of the terms contained. These may be clarified by oral evidence which thereby becomes a part of the warranty unless expressly excluded by the written agreement.

> ▶ Turkel's new television set included a written manufacturer's warranty. The warranty read, "Warranted for six months from date of delivery." Four months later, the picture tube stopped functioning. Turkel demanded a replacement under the warranty. The seller claimed that the warranty did not include the picture tube.

The written warranty in the above case is such that a court would permit the introduction of oral evidence to clarify whether the guarantee would cover the picture tube. The "custom of the marketplace," or what a warranty would normally cover in the case of a television sale, would be decisive in determining the court's verdict. Expert witnesses, those professionally acquainted with such custom and use, might be called by the seller and buyer to give their views of what the warranty might reasonably mean in a situation such as the one discussed above.

Opinion and "Puffing"

Warranties are based on statements of fact—nothing else. Opinions of salespersons, exaggerated and persuasive statements, and the like are not included. Courts have long recognized the temptation of salespersons to indulge in "puffing," or extolling their wares beyond the point of fact. Buyers must use good judgment in separating a seller's statements of fact from those statements that are only opinion or puffing.

> ▶ A sales representative demonstrated a vacuum cleaner. "This is the finest and most dependable cleaner on the market. It is far ahead of all competitors' models in design and performance. Why, it has a ⅔ horsepower motor and a bag capacity of 1½ cubic feet. If you can find anything better at the price, please buy me one and I'll give you double what you paid for it."

The only statements of fact here were the ones concerning the motor and the size of the bag. The others are nothing more than talk, puffing, and opinion. Such statements do not qualify as warranties. Neither would they be actionable in a suit for fraud or misrepresentation.

Professional and Expert Opinion   The expression of opinion by recognized experts and professionals may be accepted as fact. Buyers frequently seek advice of sellers known for their reputation and expertise in a particular field. Although the expert's statements may be prefaced by "in my opinion," they are still accepted as warranties.

> ▶ A transatlantic airline pilot sought a watch that would be dependable in connection with operating schedules. A reputable horologist was contacted in the watch department of a fine jewelry store. The horologist chose a watch for the pilot, saying, "In my opinion this is the finest timepiece you could buy for the demanding use to which it will be put."

The horologist's *opinion* represents more than just talk or puffing. Under the circumstances, and given the horologist's position, it was tantamount to a statement of fact. Should the watch prove to be of poor quality and not meet the buyer's demands, a breach of warranty might be claimed.

Exaggerated Statements   Statements made to impress a buyer as being factually true, but which a reasonably prudent person would recognize as exaggeration, are not interpreted as warranties.

> ▶ Central Tire sold a set of radial tires to Hershall. Central's manager said, "These tires are the last you will buy for that car. I guarantee that they will outlive the life of your car." Hershall's car was a late model with but a few miles on the odometer.

Statements of this kind are not accepted by ordinary persons as statements of fact to be depended on. They are mere exaggerations that the buyer might optimistically accept, although he or she is not likely to believe they are true.

IMPLIED WARRANTIES

Implied warranties are guarantees given buyers by operation of law. The seller may, in most cases, avoid these warranties only by an agreement or a notice given to the purchaser at the time of the sale. The "no other warranties express or implied" statement would be sufficient to protect the seller from most implied warranties. The prudent buyer should be careful about accepting merchandise in which the implied warranties have been removed by such a notice.

Implied warranties are either implied warranties of title or implied warranties of quality.

Title

The owner of the title rights in the goods bought is protected by three *implied warranties of title*. These enable buyers to seek recovery from sellers if their title rights are lost. Sellers may not relieve themselves of the implied warranties of title. The three implied warranties are as follows:

- ☐ The seller warrants to be the real owner.
- ☐ The seller warrants to have the right to sell.
- ☐ The seller warrants that the buyer will not be interrupted in the quiet enjoyment of the goods purchased. By *enjoyment* the law means that the buyer will be assured that there are no hidden claims, liens, or encumbrances of any kind against the property which might later cause loss of title to another person.

> ▶ Murphy purchased a television set from a neighbor who was moving to a distant part of the country. She paid $400 less than the original price, although the set was only six weeks old. Two months after buying the television, Murphy had it taken from her by the Clear-Vue Television Stores, who had recorded the original sale as a conditional sale, with more than $500 owed them by the original purchaser. Murphy sued her former neighbor for her loss by using the three implied warranties of title, all of which were breached in this sale.

The implied warranties of title apply to most situations, but it should be noted that they do not protect a buyer at an auction or a sheriff's sale. Such sales transfer no better rights than are vested in the one for whom the sale has been made.

> A judgment was entered against Murphy after a trial over an automobile accident in which she had run into the other car. The sheriff confiscated Murphy's personal property, including a television set, and sold all the property to cover the judgment. The purchaser of the television set later lost it to Clear-Vue because of its rights under the recorded conditional sales contract. The purchaser may not hold the sheriff responsible for this loss by using the implied warranties of title.

Quality

Of greater importance to most buyers are the ***implied warranties of quality***. These warranties relate to the goods themselves and to their intended use.

Sale by Description   When a sale is accompanied by a description of the goods to be delivered, there is an implied warranty that the goods will be as described. When exact and technical specifications are used, such descriptions are regarded as final. They displace inconsistent samples or models or general language of description.

> Salem University ordered textbooks to be used in a psychology course. The publisher's descriptive literature showed the text to be ideal for second-year college classes. Sample copies were not made available for inspection. When delivered, the book proved to be for the high school level and not applicable to Salem's psychology course.

The publisher's description constituted an implied warranty. The books were purchased as a result of that description, which proved to be inaccurate. Salem University may enforce its warranty rights by rescinding the contract and returning the books to the seller.

Sale by Sample   A sale of goods may be made with the understanding that the goods delivered will be the same as a sample. Under the implied warranty, the purchaser has the right to refuse the merchandise if it differs from the sample. A sample taken from an existing bulk displaces inconsistent general language or description.

> Consumer Electronics examined current models of CB transceivers submitted for approval by five different manufacturers. After exhaustive tests, it was decided to purchase a hundred sets available through Mid-West Radio Corporation. A sampling of the hundred sets received indicated that their performance was inferior to that of the sample set tested. Consumer Electronics may return the sets to Mid-West Radio.

Sale by Description and Sample   When a sale is made through the use of both samples and description, the sale carries a double warranty that the merchandise will conform to both the description and the sample. This type of warranty has the weight of an *express warranty* when made part of the basis of the bargain. It warrants that the whole of the goods shall conform to the description and the sample or model. Failure to conform to both gives the buyer the right to rescind the sales agreement on grounds of breach of warranty.

Merchantability of Goods The Uniform Commercial Code provides that, unless excluded or modified, a warranty that the goods shall be merchantable is implied in a contract for their sale if the seller is a merchant with respect to goods of that kind. Under the code, the serving for value of food or drink to be consumed either on the premises or elsewhere is a warranted sale.

The code further provides that, unless excluded or modified, other implied warranties may arise in the course of dealing or from usage of the trade.

Fitness for Purpose Sold When a seller is informed of the intended use of goods that are being sold, there is an implied warranty that the goods will be suitable for that use.

> Arundel Apartments purchased a carton of 15-ampere fuses. They were to be used in each apartment's individual lighting circuit. However, the fuses were incapable of carrying the 15-amp load. When tested, they were found to be only 10-amp fuses mislabeled by the manufacturer. This represents a breach of implied warranty of fitness. Arundel may return the fuses and demand the proper fuses or a refund.

The enforceability of this implied warranty, however, will depend to some extent on whether selection of goods was made by the buyer alone or by the seller. An implied warranty will always cover the use for which the goods were manufactured, regardless of who makes the choice. Thus, in the above case there would be an implied warranty covering the fuses' electrical capacity, even though a buyer might select the wrong fuse for a particular installation.

Buyer's Choice When a buyer makes his or her own independent selection from available merchandise, there is no warranty of fitness other than a general warranty.

> Carson, office manager for Willow Home Products Company, ordered five dozen typewriter ribbons for use by office personnel. The seller suggested a commercial ribbon that assured longer use in a business office. Carson rejected the suggestion and insisted on buying the cheaper ribbons. The ribbons did not hold up, having to be replaced after less than four weeks' use.

The ribbons purchased were fit for home use, not commercial use; they were not sold or represented as being suitable for office use. There was no breach of an implied warranty of fitness on the seller's part.

When a seller realizes that a buyer is making an obvious mistake, he or she is obligated to point out the mistake. Carson, in the illustration, made a mistake which the sales representative cautioned against. By failing to observe the seller's advice, the buyer lost the warranty of fitness for the ribbons purchased.

Seller's Choice The implied warranty of fitness is strictly applied in cases where the buyer relies on the seller's choice of goods for use in a particular application.

▶ Suppose, in the previous example, Carson said, "You know more about ribbons than I do. What do you recommend for use by our employees?" The salesperson suggested the commercial ribbon. After only four weeks the ribbon in each typewriter had to be replaced.

Under ordinary commercial use there has been a breach of the implied warranty of fitness. Although each office application might be somewhat different, the seller's representation in this case was such as to make Carson believe the ribbons would last much longer than noncommercial ribbons.

RULE OF CAVEAT EMPTOR

Caveat emptor, meaning "let the buyer beware," is an expression frequently used in sales transactions. This common-law principle states that when buyers of goods have the opportunity to examine the goods and do not do so, or if they do examine the goods and fail to take notice of obvious defects, they will not be permitted to have the sale set aside on either the express or implied warranties of quality or for reasons of fraud or misrepresentation, which an examination should have revealed.

▶ Clear-Vue offered Blaustein a floor-model stereo set at a greatly reduced price. Blaustein was told to look the set over carefully before making up her mind. After a hasty inspection, she accepted Clear-Vue's offer. A short time after the delivery of the set, Blaustein attempted to rescind the contract on the ground that there was a large scratch across the top of the mahogany cabinet. Unless the scratch was made after her inspection, the doctrine of *caveat emptor* would operate as a bar to any claim Blaustein might make to have the contract set aside.

Hidden Defects

Caveat emptor will not shield the seller from an action for damages if the defects complained of are such that a reasonable examination would not uncover them.

▶ Suppose Blaustein carefully examined the stereo set but did not discover that the speaker was only a 6-inch model instead of the 12-inch model that this set was advertised to contain. The speaker cabinet was covered with a tapestry that made close inspection almost impossible. Blaustein would have a right to claim a breach of warranty by description. *Caveat emptor* would not apply, because it would be impossible to determine the defect by ordinary examination.

To Whom the Rule Applies A difference in knowledge among buyers will determine to some degree the application of the rule of *caveat emptor*. The expert and the novice, the jeweler and the buyer of the diamond ring, the electronics specialist and the average buyer—the difference in skill and knowledge between one and the other places a greater burden upon the one with more understanding of what is being bought. The greater a buyer's knowledge, the more pronounced will be the application of *caveat emptor*.

▶ D'Angelo, an automobile mechanic, bought a used car from a second-hand dealer. D'Angelo examined the car very carefully and after much deliberation accepted the seller's offer. Only after driving the car home did he find that it was a six-cylinder model and not an eight, as he had supposed it to be. D'Angelo will have to live with this mistake, as the matter would have been obvious to anyone with even an ordinary knowledge of automobiles. Even though the seller had stated it to be an "eight," D'Angelo, because of his professional knowledge and his examination of the car, would not be permitted damages.

"As Is" Sales

A common practice in the sale of used cars, lawnmowers, electrical appliances, and similar merchandise is for the seller to stipulate that the goods are being sold *"as is."* The use of such expressions as "as is," "with all faults," and others clearly indicates that all implied warranties are excluded.

▶ Cruz bought a used electric generator from an acquaintance who had not used it for several years. The seller said, "Take the outfit as it is and you can have it for $125." The usual price for such a generator would have been three times the price offered. Cruz later complained that it cost $100 to put the machine in running order and sued the seller on the basis of an implied warranty of fitness. No recovery will be allowed.

Implication of Patent or Trade Names

No warranty exists that goods sold under a patent or trade name will correspond to the performance or qualities indicated by the name used. Buyers are required to protect themselves by examination and by reading the accompanying labels and instructions.

▶ National Soap and Detergent Company advertised a new product called "Everclean." It was a fairly good detergent but no better than scores of others being marketed at the time. No inference would be drawn from the name as to the performance capabilities of this product.

The Federal Trade Commission is now demanding that product names may not camouflage the effectiveness of the product. Increasingly, manufacturers are policing themselves, with the aim of giving names to their products which reasonably describe their quality and effectiveness.

ASSIGNMENT OF EXPRESS WARRANTIES

Implied warranties are valid only between a seller and buyer. They may not be assigned to a third party. Express warranties, however, may be assigned unless the original buyer is restricted from making an assignment. The warranty, then, would contain such terms as, "This warranty valid only between manufacturer and original buyer. It may not be assigned."

Nichols responded to a classified ad that read: "Almost-new garden tractor for sale. Guaranteed for two years. Only three months old." Nichols bought the tractor, believing that the manufacturer's warranty would continue for another 21 months. When difficulties developed, Nichols took the tractor to the dealer. The dealer pointed out that conditions in the warranty prohibited its assignment.

It is an exception, rather than the rule, to find printed warranties that do not contain restriction of assignment. However, competition among automobile manufacturers has led to the introduction of assignable warranties in that industry. The auto manufacturer's warranty usually continues in force for the benefit of subsequent owners for a time or mileage limitation specified in the warranty.

 McGrath took delivery of a new car, warranted for five years. The warranty required the buyer to return the car to the original dealer or another authorized agency every 1,000 miles for inspection and service. There was no restriction against assignment of the warranty to any person owning the car during the five-year period. As part of advertising and sales plans, assignable warranties generally have given consumers more respect for and confidence in motor-vehicle manufacturers and sellers.

WHO IS PROTECTED

By law, warranties and their protection are extended to members of the buyer's family, household, and guests. Persons injured because of defects in goods purchased may seek damages against the manufacturer-seller. A seller may not disclaim this responsibility.

 General Heating Services installed a gas furnace in Payne's house. The furnace was warranted against defects which might cause circulation of unburned gas into the living areas of the house. Payne's family and weekend guests were made ill from escaping gas that filled the bedrooms during the night. The seller's warranty would provide protection to Payne, his family, servants, friends, and guests.

WARRANTIES UNDER STATUTES OF LIMITATIONS

Actions at law on either a sales contract or a warranty may be barred after a certain period of time by statutes of limitations which are in force in all states. Time limits within which an action must be commenced are not uniform in all states, but with some exceptions, four years is the usual time period.

 Suppose Payne, in the previous illustration, complained of illness after exposure to the leaking gas. A doctor advised him to see an attorney, but nothing was done. Five years later Payne succumbed to a serious illness attributed to weakness caused by the gas inhalation. It is now too late for Payne to start an action against General Heating Services.

PRODUCT LIABILITY

Court decisions and recent legislation have developed the doctrine of ***product liability***. The law at one time restricted damage actions on contracts and torts to persons who were in privity, or had a direct relationship through a contract, with the other party. Today, a manufacturer or seller may be liable to consumers with whom the manufacturer has had little or no contact. Injuries to persons or damage to property caused by defects in design and manufacture give consumers a right to seek recovery under the law of product liability.

Obligations under product liability go beyond implied or express warranties. Liability is extended to the manufacturer, the seller, and all others in the normal marketing chain. It extends to the retail store or seller, to manufacturers, growers, packers, and all others engaged in the marketing process. In addition, it extends to all users and others who might be injured by another's use of a product.

 O'Daniel purchased a new car from Boulevard Motors. The car operated without any problem for six months. At that time the right front wheel collapsed. The car turned over, injuring O'Daniel, two passengers, and a pedestrian and wrecking a parked car.

Proof of defective construction would give all of the injured parties a right to seek damages from the manufacturer and Boulevard Motors. The owner of the wrecked car could also seek recovery under product liability. In a legal action, it would be normal procedure to name both the manufacturer and the seller as joint defendants.

Obligation to Give Notice of Hazards

The manufacturer or seller is obliged to give buyers notice of hazards related to goods purchased. Failure to give proper instructions regarding use, safety precautions, and danger warnings may make the seller and manufacturer liable for damage to buyers and others. Neglecting to enclose moving parts inside protective guards may be further grounds for damages if injury is caused thereby.

 Calhoun purchased a power saw from a local hardware store. To keep costs down, the manufacturer did not include the customary protective guard over the saw blade. Calhoun lost a thumb, an injury that could not have happened had a guard been in place. Calhoun may seek damages from the hardware store and the manufacturer.

Actions under product liability generally derive from negligence, misrepresentation, or a breach of warranty.

Negligence   Persons may seek damages on grounds of ***negligence*** as related to product liability. Negligence may be discovered in preparation of frozen, canned, or fresh foods or in the manufacture and assembly of consumer products.

Fink bought a rotary mower from Kojak's Hardware Store. Instructions contained the usual warnings about proper use and handling of the mower. Warranty

statements were also provided. Fink's sixteen-year-old son lost his left foot when
the whirling blade detached itself from the motor shaft.

Mechanical, scientific, and engineering tests will determine the cause of the
mower's defect. If negligence in manufacture, design, or assembly caused the
accident, the seller and manufacturer may be held responsible under the law of
product liability.

Misrepresentation   Misrepresentation in advertising and sales promotion, giving consumers false security, may give one grounds for suit in product liability.
Announcements that tend to draw a buyer's attention from hazards of use are
actionable as intentional concealments of possible hazards. Manufacturers spend
millions in exhaustive research before releasing products to the public. Before
marketing a new detergent, drug, cosmetic, synthetic fiber, food additive, brake
system, or other product, nearly every safety test conceivable is run by the
manufacturer. Nonetheless injuries sometimes result. Product liability is designed to protect the normal, ordinary person; injuries to a "one-in-a-million"
victim are not subject to damage actions.

> Arnold Chemical Company developed and perfected a synthetic leather.
> Thousands of pairs of experimental shoes were distributed to men, women, and
> children who were tested under controlled supervision. Out of 500,000 super-
> vised tests, the synthetic leather had minor and negative reactions on only three
> persons. With such test results as support, Arnold Chemical Company would be
> safe in marketing the shoes without fear of charges of negligence or misrepresen-
> tation.

Breach of Warranty   Further liability may be traced to a ***breach of warranty***. The
advertising of a product has been judged an express warranty that the product is
fit for use if illustrations and statements suggest that the product is safe for a
particular use.

> A plastic manufacturer advertised a new type of nursing bottle. The advertise-
> ment implied that the bottle was safer than others on the market. The bottle was
> advertised to be "danger-free" even when the mother was not present during
> feeding. Suppose several babies were strangled while drinking from this newly
> marketed bottle? Could action be brought against the manufacturer?

Unless there had been exhaustive research and supervised testing, the manufacturer and sellers would be strictly liable for breach of warranty in the above
example.

Strict Liability

Two-thirds of the states now apply the doctrine of ***strict tort liability***—that is, the
liability of manufacturer and seller extends to all persons who may be injured by
any marketed product. Injured bystanders, guests, or others who have no relationship with the product, the seller, manufacturer, owner, or renter may seek
damages caused by defects in the offending product.

▶▶ Ryder Truck Rental rented a truck to Jackson. While he was waiting for a light to change, the truck moved forward due to a faulty brake system. Martin, in another car, was injured when the truck hit her car. The Delaware Supreme Court ruled, on an appeal, that Ryder could be held liable even without proof of its negligence. It was only necessary for the injured party to prove that the truck had a defect which caused personal injury or property damage to the plaintiffs.

Under the doctrine of strict tort liability in cases of product liability, an injured party no longer need base a claim strictly on negligence, misrepresentation, or breach of warranty. An injured bystander need only prove that (1) the product was defective, (2) the defect was the proximate cause of the injury, and (3) the defect made the product unreasonably dangerous. All three qualifications were evident in the Ryder illustration.

For further discussion of liability and damages under the law of product liability, particularly under the Federal Consumer Product Safety Act, see the discussion headed "Product Quality and Reliability Risk" in Chapter 4.

Questions for Review and Discussion

1. Enumerate the implied warranties of title.

2. Discuss rules regulating the assignment of express warranties.

3. Have all states adopted the doctrine of strict tort liability?

4. Distinguish between statements of fact and puffing, as related to express warranties.

5. Why are auction and sheriff sales excluded from requirement of the implied warranties of title?

6. What is the purpose of today's product liability laws and decisions?

7. List the implied warranties of quality.

8. May a seller's opinion ever be claimed as a warranty? Explain.

9. Distinguish the warranty of fitness under seller's choice and buyer's choice.

10. What are the three causes from which product liability cases are derived?

Analyzing Cases

1. Centerville Appliance Mart sold Banning an electric mixer. At the time of purchase, the mixer was examined by Banning but was not tried out by connecting it to an electric outlet. When she turned it on at home, it did not work. Will Banning recover on grounds of breach of implied and express warranties? How does *caveat emptor* relate to this sale? •See also *Gregg* v. *Page Belting Company*, 46 At. 26.

2. Daniels, a dairy owner, purchased an insec-ticide advertised to protect dairy cows from deer flies. Use of the chemical brought sickness to the herd and a serious loss in milk production. May Daniels recover damages from the manufacturer of the insecticide? Explain. •See also *Dobias* v. *Western Farmers Assoc.*, 491 Pac.2d 1346.

3. Salvatore bought a gallon of paint which was used on the exterior of his garage. A heavy rain washed off the paint, which necessitated a lengthy clean-up and another paint job. Salvatore had sought no advice in selecting the paint. The paint, by manufacturer's instructions, was for indoor use. May Salvatore recover damages for breach of warranty of fitness? Explain. • See also *Standard Oil Co.* v. *Daniel N. Cooperage Co.,* 77 N.E.2d 526.

4. Vasquez contracted with Acme Heating Company for installation of a new gas-burning furnace. Vasquez selected the furnace desired, accepting no suggestions from Acme's heating engineer. The furnace operated as it was supposed to by the standards of the heating industry. It did not, however, heat the house. A larger furnace would have been satisfactory. Vasquez sued Acme Heating Company for breach of warranty of fitness. Will she succeed in this action? Explain. • See also *Wisconsin Red Pressed Brick Co.* v. *Hood,* 54 Minn. 543.

5. Passengers on a bus were injured when the brake system failed and the bus went over an embankment. The bus was fitted with electric brakes. Investigation proved that there were defects in the design that caused the malfunction. Against whom, and on what grounds, may the passengers seek damages for injuries received? Explain.

6. Belli purchased a bottle of hair spray. Instructions warned the buyer to make a spot test before using the preparation. Persons allergic to the chemical were told to return the unused bottle for a full refund. Belli disregarded these instructions and used the spray, bringing on a skin ailment that was difficult to cure. Belli sued the manufacturer on grounds of product liability. Will she succeed in this action? Explain.

Legal Reasoning and Business Judgment

Analyze the legal aspects of these business problems. Suggest possible solutions.

1. Your company produces a custom-built machine according to blueprints and specifications supplied by the buyer. A complaint is now received that the machine will not perform functions for which it was designed. Your engineering department informs you that the machine was built exactly as ordered according to all specifications. The buyer refuses to pay for the machine, contending that there was a breach of warranty of fitness for the purpose for which it was sold. How would you settle this matter to the advantage of your employer?

2. A buyer purchased raw materials your firm had stocked but no longer needed. The buyer's representative visited your plant, inspected the material, and took samples. The samples were tested and approved by the buyer's chemist and engineer. The buyer now refuses to pay for the raw material, claiming that it is not suitable for the purpose for which it was sold. What steps should be taken on behalf of your company?

3. Your company is engaged in the manufacture and sale of cosmetics and hair products. A research chemist in your laboratory reported the discovery of a new formula that will restore the growth of new hair for bald persons. The product was tried by several employees, who were very happy with the results. The firm's board of directors appropriated $3 million for the final development and marketing of this long-awaited consumer product. The sales division is anxious to get started and to introduce this new product before a competitor comes out with a similar item. What problems do you anticipate, and what suggestions would you like to see carried out before this hair restorer is marketed for human use?

Part 5
Bailments
Chapter 18
Nature of Bailments

A student rents a typewriter. A pedestrian finds a briefcase. A neighbor borrows a friend's ladder. How do these situations differ from the ones you have studied under the law of sales? In what respects are they similar?

In each of the three situations, possession of tangible personal property has been given to someone other than the owner, but in no case was there an intent to give title. Each situation illustrates a transaction known as a bailment.

A *bailment* is the transfer of possession of personal property by the owner, known as the *bailor*, to another person, called the *bailee*. In a bailment neither the bailor nor the bailee intends that title to the property should pass. The bailee has an obligation to return the same property to the bailor at a later time or on demand.

▶ Rent-A-Car leased a station wagon to Harper. Harper signed a rental agreement that listed rights and obligations of Rent-A-Car and Harper, the bailee. Harper paid a security deposit and a fee for insurance, and he agreed to return the car in 48 hours. Through the lease, these two parties created a bailment.

CHARACTERISTICS OF A BAILMENT

Bailments are distinguished from other agreements by several characteristics.

Possession

A bailment is created at any time a bailee takes rightful possession of another's personal property. Good judgment must be exercised by the bailee in the care, use, and preservation of the other person's goods. Possession should not be confused with custody. One who has the physical control of another's goods, but is under the constant supervision of the owner in their use and care, has only *custody*. *Possession*, in a bailment relationship, implies that the bailee not only has physical control of another's goods, but also has the responsibility of personal supervision and care as well.

▶ Whann agreed to drive Gabrilowiscz's car during a trip they were making together. Gabrilowiscz sat beside the driver during the trip, making decisions on routes to be taken, speeds traveled, and stops made. Whann was not a bailee. Gabrilowiscz had possession; Whann had nothing more than custody.

Suppose, at the end of the first day, Gabrilowiscz asked Whann to take the car to a service station to get gas and an oil change. Whann went alone. This is now a bailment. Whann, as bailee, had physical control of the car and had to make decisions as to its care and protection.

Delivery and Acceptance

Bailments require a delivery of goods by the bailor and acceptance by the bailee. Only when the goods are accepted is a bailment actually created. Delivery and acceptance also imply *offer* and *acceptance*, the requisites of mutual assent. This is important in establishing a bailment contract, and it is necessary if a bailee is to be obligated to the bailor in any way.

 Walker carried many packages during a shopping spree prior to the holidays. A clerk in one store was willing to look after Walker's packages. Delivery of the packages to the clerk and the clerk's acceptance of them created a bailment. The two acts also implied offer and acceptance, creating *mutual assent*.

Obligation to Return Goods

Another requirement is that, when the bailment relationship ends, the bailee return to the bailor the same goods as were delivered and accepted. Goods must be returned in their *original form* or in an *altered form*, depending on the conditions of the bailment agreement.

 The typewriter in your office needs to be repaired and adjusted. The Typewriter Service Company agrees to do the work and takes the machine to its workshop. It is the intent of both parties that the same typewriter be returned, but in a different condition than when it was removed by the Typewriter Service Company.

Not to be confused with a bailment is a ***mutuum***. When the owner of property loans goods to another with the intention that the goods may be used and later replaced with an equal quantity of the same quality of goods, there is no bailment. A transaction of this kind is known as a *mutuum*.

 Lefelt's Stationers borrowed six typewriter ribbons from the Typewriter Service Company. It was agreed that Lefelt's would replace the ribbons with six others when their order was received from the manufacturer. In this case, Typewriter Service Company gave up both possession and title to their six ribbons. This was a mutuum, not a bailment transaction.

Retention of Title

The owner of bailed property *never passes title* to a bailee. Agreements by which title does pass from one person to another would come within the law of sales, gifts, exchanges, and the like.

▶ Scotto was a guest at a friend's farm, where they both hunted quail. After two days of unsuccessful hunting, Scotto departed, saying, "I'll leave my gun here. It won't do me much good from now on. You may have better luck with it than I have had."

A situation like this could lead to a serious dispute in the future. What did Scotto mean with those parting words? Did the friend receive title to Scotto's gun? Or was it Scotto's intent merely to leave the gun until a return visit? If Scotto intended to offer the friend the gun as a gift, then there was no bailment. If Scotto expected to pick up the gun during a return visit, then a bailment was created, for the friend then would have an obligation to take care of the weapon and return it to Scotto undamaged. Perhaps only a jury could determine whether Scotto's intention was to pass title or merely possession. A clear expression of intention would eliminate problems of this kind.

THE BAILMENT CONTRACT

Bailments are contracts which, to be legally enforceable, must contain all the elements of any valid contract: (1) mutual assent, (2) capable parties, (3) consideration, and (4) valid subject matter.

▶ Heller loaned a .38 revolver to Alberts, who planned to carry it while taking a large sum of money to the bank for deposit. Alberts bought Heller a box of .38-caliber bullets in return for use of the gun. Heller had a permit to carry a concealed deadly weapon; Alberts did not.

Was the Heller-Alberts agreement a valid bailment contract? On analysis, we find that all the elements of a valid agreement were present except one.

☐ There was a meeting of the minds, or *mutual assent*, created through the acceptance of the offer made.
☐ Both Heller and Alberts were *capable parties*. As with other agreements, this contract would be voidable if either party were proved incapable—if either were a minor or were insane.
☐ The agreement was supported by *consideration*. The exchange of the box of bullets for the gun represented that consideration—the mutual exchange of benefits and sacrifices by the parties.
☐ The agreement was unenforceable, however, because it lacked the fourth element of any legal contract: *valid subject matter*. Lending a deadly weapon, to be carried in public, to one without a permit is illegal. If Alberts had had a permit to carry the gun, all the requisites of an enforceable agreement would have been present, and a valid bailment would have been created. But this was not the case in the example.

GRATUITOUS BAILMENTS

In *gratuitous bailments*, property is transferred to another person without either party's giving or demanding payment of any kind. Such bailments lack consideration; therefore, they may be rescinded at any time by either party. Parties to such agreements usually consider them only as favors. In reality, however, definite legal responsibilities are placed upon both the bailor and the bailee. There are two kinds of gratuitous bailments: (1) bailments for the sole benefit of the bailor and (2) bailments for the sole benefit of the bailee.

Bailments for Sole Benefit of Bailor

When possession of personal property is transferred to another for purposes that will benefit only the bailor, a *bailment for the sole benefit of the bailor* results.

 Baxendall agreed to deliver Higgins's watch to a jewelry shop which she would pass on the way to work. Higgins gave her the watch, and she placed it in a briefcase with other valuables. Baxendall was promised no reward for this act. It was a favor. It was also a bailment for the sole benefit of the bailor.

Bailee's Obligation of Care   In this type of bailment, the bailee is required to use *slight* care in the protection of the bailor's property. Any damage to the property caused by the bailee's *gross negligence* will make the bailee liable to the bailor. *Slight care* is defined as the degree of care that a person of ordinary prudence would exercise in the same situation. Suppose that Baxendall, in the previous illustration, was grossly negligent and put Higgins's watch in a place where it could easily be stolen or lost. This is something which a person of ordinary prudence normally would not do. If the watch were stolen or lost, Baxendall could be held liable to Higgins for damages. Whether a bailee in fact exercised slight care or was grossly negligent is usually a matter to be decided by a jury in any particular case.

Use of Bailor's Property   The bailee has no implied right to use the bailor's property. Use without permission is technically a tort of *conversion* on the part of the bailee; it would make the bailee fully liable for any damages that might result, even if he or she had used great care and was not guilty of negligence. (Conversion, you may recall, is the civil wrong that arises when one unlawfully treats another's property as one's own.)

 Lindstrom agreed to care for Holbart's car while Holbart was absent from the city. Although permission to use the car had not been given, Lindstrom drove the car many times to save having to walk.

Should Lindstrom become involved in an accident as a result of the unauthorized use of Holbart's car, he would be fully and indefensibly liable to Holbart for damages. In a case like this, it is not even necessary that the bailor prove lack of care by the bailee.

Some property, however, requires use or exercise to maintain its value. If the property is of a type that might depreciate from nonuse, the bailee would have an implied obligation to perform the services necessary to maintain the property in proper condition.

> O'Toole agreed to care for Armstrong's Chesapeake Bay retriever during the latter's absence on a trip to Ireland. O'Toole took the dog on a hunting trip, thinking that the best way to keep the animal in good condition. The dog was lost and never recovered by O'Toole.

Was O'Toole exercising the animal to keep it in good condition, or was it pressed into service for O'Toole's own pleasure and benefit? If a jury believed that the latter was true, O'Toole would be guilty of conversion and liable for damages. If the jury ruled that he was trying to exercise the dog, however, he would have met all the obligations of a bailee under this type of bailment relationship.

Duty of Bailor   In bailments for one's sole benefit, the bailor has two obligations implied by law. Failure to observe these obligations may make the bailor responsible to the bailee for any resulting damages.

Delivery of a Safe Chattel   The bailor must deliver a safe chattel to the bailee. If the property is dangerous or harmful in ways that would not be noticed on casual observation, the bailor must give notice of such dangers to the bailee.

> Rogers knew that her car dripped oil from the engine. Shannon was not told of this condition, and the painted surface of the cement floor of Shannon's garage was ruined. Rogers would be responsible for the expense of cleaning and repainting the floor.

If the dangers would be obvious to the bailee, the bailor would *not* be held liable for damages.

> A biology professor asked a college student to care for two rattlesnakes during the professor's attendance at a scientific meeting in another state. The student removed the snakes and container to a dormitory room. One of the snakes struck the student while it was being fed.

The student was obviously aware of the dangers involved in taking care of the snakes. It is doubtful that the owner would be responsible if a claim were made based on delivery of an unsafe chattel.

Reimbursement for Necessary Expenses   The bailor has a duty to reimburse the bailee for any expenses the bailee might have in the care of his or her property. The bailee has a corresponding duty to keep such expenses within a reasonable amount, depending upon the circumstances.

> Rogers took care of Hawthorne's boat while Hawthorne was on vacation. A sudden storm damaged the hull of the boat, which required immediate repair to keep it from sinking. The repairs by the marina cost $350. Hawthorne would be obligated to reimburse Rogers for the $350 spent in the necessary preservation of the damaged craft.

Suppose, in this case, Rogers had decided to have the entire hull scraped and painted when the boat was out of the water. Could Rogers hold Hawthorne responsible for that expense? No, because the extra work was neither necessary nor authorized by the owner.

Title to Increases and Profits   The bailor is entitled to any increases or profits accruing to bailed property while it is in the bailee's possession. At the termination of the bailment, the bailor is entitled to receive a careful and complete accounting of such increases or profits from the bailee.

 Harvell, a farmer, cared for Anderson's beagle hunting dog after the hunting season. The dog gave birth to a litter of puppies. The puppies are Anderson's property by right as the bailor-owner.

Termination of Bailment   Either party may terminate a gratuitous bailment. Lacking consideration, the bailment agreement is not enforceable. Should the bailee terminate the bailment, he or she must then return the property to its owner at a proper time and place. Termination by the bailor requires the giving of notice of such intention of termination and a request that the property be returned.

 Sobocinski agreed to store Sawyer's stereo system in his home while Sawyer's house was being remodeled. Finding it inconvenient to continue storing all of this equipment, Sobocinski loaded it in a station wagon and left it in Sawyer's unfinished and unlocked house without giving any prior notice.

While Sobocinski certainly had a right to terminate the above bailment, the manner in which it was done would make him liable for any loss or damage that might result. If the equipment were stolen from the unoccupied house, it would be Sobocinski's duty as bailee to compensate Sawyer for any damages.

Bailments for Sole Benefit of Bailee

Transactions in which the possession of personal property is transferred for purposes that will benefit only the bailee are gratuitous bailments for the *sole benefit of the bailee*.

 Matthews asked Rogers if she might use the latter's car for a trip she planned to make to Kansas City. Rogers agreed to lend the car, asking nothing in return for this favor. The bailment was created for the sole benefit of the bailee, Matthews.

Bailee's Obligation of Care   Bailments for the sole benefit of the bailee place a far greater responsibility upon the bailee than those previously studied. The bailee must exercise *great care* and is liable for any damage resulting from even *slight negligence*.

 Matthews took her 500-mile trip in Rogers's car. At no time during the entire trip did she check the oil in the engine. This carelessness resulted in some damage to the motor. Matthews did not exercise necessary care, and she will be responsible for any repairs resulting from her negligence.

In bailments for the sole benefit of the bailee, the bailee is not an insurer of another's goods, that is, the bailee does not accept *full and complete* responsibility. The bailee is responsible for damages only when they result from lack of proper care.

Use of Bailor's Property The bailee has the right to use the property for the purposes for which the bailment was created. Use for other purposes or use over a longer time than provided for in the agreement will make the bailee responsible for any damages that may result to the property, regardless of the amount of care exercised.

> Robbins used Castro's chain saw to cut up a small tree that fell during a storm. The cutting of the tree was all that Castro had agreed to allow Robbins to do with the saw. Robbins decided to cut up other timber awaiting the fireplace. The saw's engine caught fire. Even though Robbins was in no way responsible for the fire, he is obligated to reimburse Castro for the damage.

Any *ordinary* and *expected expense* incurred in the use of another's property must be borne by the bailee.

On the other hand, repairs and adjustments not caused by ordinary use or damages not attributed to the bailee's negligence become the responsibility of the bailor. The bailee is not obligated to replace parts which break down because of the gradual use and depreciation of the other's property over a long period.

> Swanson, with Oberly's permission, took Oberly's motorcycle on a trial ride. Every precaution was taken to avoid damage. Nevertheless, on the way home, the front tire blew, and Swanson found it necessary to buy a new tire. The old tire had been badly worn in many places. The blowout was not caused by Swanson's negligent use. Oberly, the bailor, would be responsible for any *unusual* and *unexpected* expenses resulting from the tire blowout.

Duty of Bailor The bailor must deliver a safe chattel to the bailee. If the chattel is not safe and if the dangerous conditions are not apparent upon ordinary examination, the bailor has an obligation to call such facts to the bailee's attention.

> While driving down a long hill, Swanson applied the brakes. The brakes failed, the motorcycle was damaged, and Swanson was injured. Oberly had a responsibility either to deliver a motorcycle with safe brakes or to point out the hazard to Swanson if he knew about it. Failure to give warning makes Oberly responsible for any personal injuries to Swanson as well as for all repairs to the motorcycle.

Termination of Bailment Bailments for sole benefit of bailee are ended when the bailee concludes the use for which the other's property was loaned. As with other gratuitous bailments, the bailment may end at any time as long as this does not cause injury or damage to the other party. Death or insanity of either party results in termination by operation of law. If the bailment is created for a specific length of time, however, death of the bailor does not terminate the bailee's right to continued possession for the agreed-upon uses of the bailed property.

> Sweigert loaned an electric sander to Kilby for the two weeks that it would take to sand Kilby's power cruiser. Sweigert died before the two weeks ended and before Kilby had finished the job. The executor demanded the drill returned at once. Kilby is not obligated to return the drill until the end of the second week.

MUTUAL-BENEFIT BAILMENTS

When personal property is transferred to a bailee with the intent that both parties will benefit, a *mutual-benefit bailment* results. The ordinary bailments involving business transactions are usually mutual-benefit bailments.

 In preparing for a trip to Detroit, Cameron left a suit at the Valet Shop to be cleaned and pressed. The agreed-upon price for these services was $2.50. Both Cameron and the Valet Shop will benefit from the transaction. This is a mutual-benefit bailment.

Duty of Bailee

The bailee is required to use *ordinary care* and will be responsible for damages resulting from his or her own negligence. The bailee is not an insurer. He or she will not be responsible for damages caused by the willful misconduct of third parties or by acts of God.

 The Valet Shop completed cleaning and pressing Cameron's suit and placed it on the rack with other finished work. Before Cameron called for the suit, a burglar stole it. The store had not been negligent, and the loss was not due to lack of ordinary care. Cameron will have no rightful claim against the Valet Shop for the loss suffered.

Ordinary Care Ordinary care is the amount of care that a reasonable person would use under the same circumstances. This is not the amount of care that one always uses in the protection of one's own possessions. If a loss occurs, the bailee will not be excused from liability by claiming, "I used the same amount of care with Jones's property as I would use with my own."

 Cameron's suit was damaged during the cleaning process. As a defense, the cleaner said, "I had one of my own suits in the same cleaning operation with yours. What is good enough for my things is good enough for my customers'!" Such reasoning would not excuse the Valet Shop if negligence were found.

Use of Bailed Property The bailee must use the bailed property only for the express purposes permitted by the bailor as provided for in the contract of bailment. The rental of a car, tools, or formal wear, for example, implies the right of reasonable use. Failing to use the property as agreed makes the bailee responsible for any damages that might result, regardless of the degree of care that was exercised.

 Smith rented a formal suit from the Valet Shop. While wearing it, he crawled under a friend's car to make an adjustment to the brakes. Smith was liable to the Valet Shop for the resulting damage to the suit. The bailed property had not been used for the purposes permitted by the bailor.

Duty of Bailor

In a mutual-benefit bailment, the bailor must respect the bailee's contracted right of possession. Bailments of this type contain consideration and may not be terminated without mutual agreement. Right of possession may be interrupted, however, if the bailee has exceeded his or her rights in the property or is not exercising proper care in its use.

Safe Chattels   The bailor must warn the bailee of any defects in the bailed property which are not known to the bailee; which, because of their character, would not become known to the bailee on a casual inspection; which might result in injury to the bailee; or which might interfere with the use or purpose for which the article was delivered to the bailee.

Termination of Bailment

The parties may anticipate termination of mutual-benefit bailments in their original agreement. They can specify the length of time the bailment is to extend or for what purpose the property is to be used. The parties may also end their agreement by mutual assent at any later time.

Kinds of Mutual-Benefit Bailments

Four basic kinds of mutual-benefit bailments exist. These are (1) pledge, or pawn; (2) contract for use of chattels; (3) contract for custody of chattels; and (4) contract for work or service on chattels. In addition, a bailment by necessity, also described below, may be implied by law.

Pledge, or Pawn   A person wishing to borrow money must often give the lender possession of personal property as security for repayment of the debt. The property thus left as security is called the *pledge*, or *pawn*. The borrower, or debtor, is the *pledgor*, or bailor. The lender, or creditor, is the *pledgee*, or bailee. The pledgee may be a bank, a loan company, a credit union, a pawnbroker, or another person.

Bloom needed $50 to buy new textbooks for college. Rogers agreed to lend her the money if he could have her typewriter as security for the repayment of the $50. Rogers thereby became a bailee of Bloom's typewriter, pledged as security for the loan.

Rights and Duties of Pledgor   The owner, or pledgor, gives an implied warranty of title of property pledged as security. This warranty of title also applies to a bailment of property pledged as security for the repayment of a debt. The pledgor has the right to redeem his or her property upon settlement of the debt or other promise so secured. A failure to return the property gives the pledgor the right (1) to bring an action to recover his or her property or (2) to bring an action to recover the present value of the goods or to sue for trespass and ask for the damages resulting from the pledgee's refusal to return the property.

▶ Repayment of the $50 loan to Rogers gave Bloom the right to the return of her
typewriter. If Rogers refused to return it, Bloom would have the right either to sue
Rogers to get it back or to sue him for damages for the value of the pledged article.

Rights and Duties of Pledgee   The pledgee's obligations are similar to those in
other mutual-benefit bailments. These obligations are described here.

☐ The pledgee must take ordinary care of the property. He or she is not an
insurer unless he or she accepts that additional responsibility by agreement.

☐ All profits and increases must be turned over to the pledgor or their total
deducted from the outstanding debt.

☐ The pledgee must return the identical article pledged when the loan is paid.

☐ The pledgee has no right to use the pledged property, unless express permission is given or use is necessary for the proper care of the article.

> Nelson pawned a double bass at a local pawnshop, receiving $90 as a 30-day loan,
> with interest. Brown, the shop owner, rented the instrument to a musician who
> was playing that evening at a nearby hotel. Renting Nelson's bass fiddle was a
> breach of the pawnbroker's duties. Nelson could demand the return of the
> instrument and the money received by the pawnbroker for rental of the instrument.

☐ The pledgee may keep the property and refuse to return it until the secured
debt has been settled in full. The pledgee need not surrender the property
even if the pledgor obtained the article by fraud (if the pledgee had no
knowledge of the fraud).

☐ If the article pledged is stolen goods, the pledgee will be required to give up
the article to the real owner without the owner's reimbursing the pledgee.

Surrender of the pledged property by the pledgee before he or she receives
payment of the loan does not cancel the debt.

If the pledged property was destroyed or stolen and the pledgee was in no way
negligent, the pledgor would not be released from the debt.

▶ Northrop pledged a watch with a pawnbroker as security for the repayment of a
loan. The pawnbroker put the watch in a seemingly secure safe. The safe was
robbed and the watch stolen.

> It was held that the pledgee (the pawnbroker) was required to exercise only
> ordinary care and was liable only for ordinary negligence. The pawnbroker was
> not liable for the loss and would not be barred in an action against Northrop on
> the debt.

Contracts for Use of Chattels   A mutual-benefit bailment results when an
agreement is made for renting a chattel for a fixed sum or at a definite rate.
Examples are borrowing a book from a rental library and hiring a horse from a
riding academy or an automobile from a drive-it-yourself firm.

The bailee has the *right* to the exclusive possession and use of the article
during the period of the contract. The bailee must exercise *ordinary care* in the use
and protection of the property. Damages resulting from causes outside the

bailee's control will not make the bailee liable. However, damage or destruction caused by his or her use of the article in a way different from that agreed upon makes a bailee absolutely liable to the bailor.

Contracts for Custody of Chattels   Contracts for the storage of property are mutual-benefit bailments when a fee is charged. Garages, warehouses, grain elevators, and similar businesses are engaged in bailments of this kind.

The bailee, except by special agreement, is not an insurer. The bailee must exercise *ordinary care*. He or she has no implied authority to use the bailed property unless use is necessary to maintain the property's value.

> Zerke boarded a valuable racehorse at Hamilton Stables. Hamilton had full responsibility for the care of the horse during Zerke's absence. The horse was not taken from its stall over a period of three weeks, and lack of exercise crippled it. Ordinary care, in this case, required that the animal be exercised. (Exercise does not necessarily mean use.)
>
> Suppose Hamilton Stables had entered Zerke's horse in a race at the county fair grounds. If the horse won a purse, the money would belong to Zerke. If the horse were injured, Zerke could hold the stable responsible as an insurer, having exceeded its rights as bailee.

The bailee's promise to store property in a specific place (room, garage, barn, etc.) restricts the bailee from moving it elsewhere. To move the property elsewhere is a breach of the bailment contract, making the bailee an insurer. This makes the bailee fully responsible regardless of the cause of damage to the property. Commercial bailees, anticipating the need for movement of property, include that right in a bailment contract.

> Rodney's Warehouse accepted goods, including a davenport, from Jackson. The items were to be stored in two numbered lockers on the fifth floor of the warehouse. Jackson's receipt showed the numbers and location of the lockers being used. When the goods were taken from the warehouse, Jackson noted that they had been moved to a third-floor location. Her expensive davenport had been ruined by rats on the third floor.

The warehouse obligated itself as an insurer by moving Jackson's property without permission. She may demand damages without the need to prove the bailee negligent.

Parking Lots and Garages   In early cases concerning the owners of cars left in garages and parking lots, the operator of the parking facility was generally regarded as a bailee, with the obligations outlined above. However, operators of lots and garages today issue parking receipts which clearly state that the arrangement *is not a bailment*. The card given to the customer defines the contract as one between a lessor and a lessee, the fee paid for care of the car being called *rent*. As will be learned in the study of real property in a later chapter, the operator of a garage or lot reduces his or her responsibility to a great degree in this manner.

> Your car is parked in a garage which claims itself to be a lessor of space for the storage of your car. While in the garage it is stolen. It is unlikely that you will

recover damages from the operator if it can be proved that there actually was a lessor-lessee relationship.

Safe-Deposit Boxes   A bank operating a safe-deposit-box service has the possession of both the customer's box and its contents. Even though a bailment relationship was maintained for many years in this situation, today's safety-deposit contracts speak of the bank as the renter and the other party as the lessee. Under this arrangement, it is argued, the bank does not take *possession* of the property. The bank maintains that a person renting the box is in the same relationship as one renting an apartment from a landlord. The landlord is not responsible for the furniture and other articles kept in one's apartment.

Contracts for Work or Service on Chattels

Agreements in which property is transferred to another for work, repairs, or other service—for which the owner agrees to pay a fee—are mutual-benefit bailments. Cleaners, repair shops, and persons developing photographic film, for example, are engaged in bailment transactions of this kind. The bailee is not an insurer, but he or she must exercise ordinary care. Losses by fire, theft, or other causes beyond the control of the bailee do not excuse the bailor from paying for the bailee's services if the work is completed prior to the time of loss and if the bailor is notified that the property is ready for delivery.

 Rogers left a car at Modern Paint Shop for a new paint job. When the car was ready to be picked up, she was notified. Two days later, before she took delivery of the car, the shop was burned out, together with the newly painted car. The fire resulted when burglars entered an adjoining building, where they started a fire.

Modern Paint Shop has no obligation to compensate Rogers for the loss. This was a bailment requiring ordinary care. The loss did not result from lack of care or negligence on the part of Modern Paint Shop.

Bailments by Necessity

A common type of mutual-benefit bailment, implied by law, is the ***bailment by necessity***. This arises when one purchases a suit or dress and is required to give up possession of one's own property while being fitted; when one receives services in a barber or beauty shop, where one must give up possession of a hat or other articles of apparel; and in other similar situations which require a customer to give up possession of property for the benefit of both parties. In such cases the bailee is required to accept the other's property and to exercise ordinary care in its protection.

 Carson had an appointment at a hairdresser's. The day was cold and rainy, and she wore a heavy coat, overshoes, and a storm hat. The operator asked Carson to put her things on a rack outside the booth, which was out of sight. There was no other place to leave them.

This is a typical bailment by necessity. It would have been inconvenient, improper, and perhaps impossible for Carson to have remained clothed in her rainwear while being served by the shop. Even though the shop had placed a sign "Not Responsible for Articles Left Here" over the rack, it did not remove the shop's responsibility as a bailee of her things.

EXCEPTIONAL TYPES OF BAILMENTS

The law recognizes two types of bailments where the obligation of the bailee is imposed by law rather than by mutual agreement of the parties. In these situations, the bailee must exercise the same degree of care as in other bailments for the sole benefit of the bailor. (See the earlier discussion in this chapter.)

Involuntary Bailments

In an *involuntary bailment*, personal property is delivered to a stranger through some agency beyond the control of either party, as by an act of God. The law implies delivery of the property to the one who comes into possession.

 During a hurricane, personal property of many kinds was blown onto Smith's land. An involuntary bailment resulted, and Smith had the implied obligation to give some care, though slight, to the property until the real owners were located and the property returned.

Lost Property

By implication, the finder of lost property becomes the bailee of the article if he or she takes it into his or her possession. The rights and duties of the finder are those of a bailee. Thus, the finder of a purse or of any other property acquires an ownership that is second only to the real owner's right to the property. The finder is considered to be the bailee of the property, holding it for the true owner until he or she can be located. The situation is the same when someone comes into possession of property by mistake.

Misplaced Property   There is an exception to the rule that the finder holds the property until the true owner can be found. If the lost property is found on the counter of a store, on a table in a restaurant or hotel, on a chair in a washroom, or in some similar public or semipublic place, it is considered not to be *lost* but to have been *misplaced*. It is reasonable to suppose that the owner will remember leaving it there and return for it. For this reason, the finder may not keep the article in his or her possession but must leave it with the proprietor or manager to hold for the owner. If the property is found on the floor or in the corridor or any other place that would indicate that it was not placed there intentionally, the finder may retain possession of the article. In this case, it is not likely that the owner would recall where he or she lost it.

 Drew, a customer, found a purse on a small shelf in a fitting room of the Vogue Dress Shop. She gave the purse to the owner of the store, but later, when she learned that it had not been claimed, she sued the store for its return.

Drew could not regain possession of the purse. It was found in an area used only by customers of the shop. The proprietor owed his customers a duty of guarding any property that was left there. He was therefore entitled to retain possession of the purse.

Responsibility of Finder The finder of lost property has a legal responsibility, usually fixed by statute, to make an effort to learn the identity of the owner and return the property to that person. Advertising the property in a general-circulation newspaper is usually evidence of the finder's honest effort to locate the owner. Statutes in many states provide that, if the finder of lost property has made an effort to locate the owner and has not been successful within a period specified by law, the property then belongs to the finder.

> While on a hike through a wooded area, Blackstone kicked a cardboard box which broke open and disclosed a bundle of currency of various denominations. Blackstone picked up the box, examined its contents, and discovered a bank deposit slip made out in the name of a local merchant. As soon as he took possession of the box containing the currency, the finder became the bailee and accepted the legal responsibility of taking care of the money and returning it to its rightful owner.

> Suppose the bank deposit slip had not been in the box and Blackstone was unsuccessful in an attempt to find the rightful owner. After making a sincere effort to locate the real owner, and after a period of time set by statute, Blackstone would become the owner of this find.

Escheat of Lost and Abandoned Property When property is found and turned over to officials of a state, without any claim registered by the finder, the property becomes the property of the state after a period of time set by statute. The same rule applies to bank deposits and other claims which have been abandoned by persons in whose names such claims were registered. In these latter instances, a period of up to twenty years is usually required to establish the right of the state to take title.

Offer of Reward The finder of lost property is entitled to any reward offered if he or she has not surrendered possession of the property before learning of the reward. If the finder learns about a reward *after* returning a lost article, he or she cannot legally enforce payment of the reward—having returned the article without expecting any. But if the finder learns about a reward *before* returning the property, he or she need not surrender possession until the reward is paid. If a reward has not been offered, the finder is entitled to be reimbursed for any expenses that he or she may have incurred in connection with the possession of the property.

> Shannon's dog broke loose and ran away. She advertised a reward of $25 for its return. A boy found the dog and returned it to Shannon in response to the advertisement. If she refused to pay the $25 offered, the boy could rightfully retain possession of the dog and not return it until the money was paid.

TORTIOUS BAILEES

Persons who have *wrongful possession* of another's property are said to be **tortious bailees**. There are four types of tortious bailees:

☐ One in possession of stolen property.
☐ One wrongfully retaining possession of the lost property of another.

> Bradshaw found a wallet belonging to Compton. Intentionally and knowingly, he refused to either return the wallet or contact Compton about the matter. Bradshaw placed himself in a vulnerable position because of his failure to return Compton's property; he would be fully responsible for the wallet and contents, regardless of the circumstances under which Bradshaw himself might have lost it. Such failure to act would also make him criminally liable on a complaint made to the police.

☐ One using a bailed article for a purpose other than agreed upon.
☐ One refusing to return property at the termination of the bailment.

Tortious bailees are fully and unconditionally responsible for any and all damage that results to property in their possession, regardless of the degree of care that they might exercise or the cause of the damage.

LAWFUL RECOVERY OF PROPERTY

An owner of personal property, when deprived of its possession, may not recover possession by "taking the law in his or her own hands." Lawful means are available through either civil or criminal complaints filed with the proper courts. Even in cases where a tortious bailee refuses to give up possession, it is not the owner's right to use force or any other illegal means to recover what is rightfully his or hers.

 Walker loaned Pennington a snow blower after a heavy snow. Instead of returning the machine when finished with it, Pennington locked it in his garage. Walker demanded its return, but Pennington refused. He said that it had not stopped snowing and that the machine would be returned when he was good and ready.

Walker has no right, by law, to enter the garage and recover the snow blower. To do so would open the bailor to an action of trespass, breaking and entering, or other criminal charges. The owner instead should seek a writ through a court of law to have the machine returned.

When a person is deprived of the right of possession by a tortious bailee, he or she may seek one of three actions against the offender.

Replevin

Replevin is a common-law action used to get recovery of personal property that is wrongfully held by the one in possession. Replevin commands the bailee to return property to the owner. The action is taken through a court of law. The proper name, used by the courts, is a ***writ of replevin***. This action is always used when the owner seeks the return of the property, rather than its value.

 The University Library loaned books to Keaveny. They were first editions, and part of a set that had been out of print for a hundred years or more. It would have been impossible to replace the volumes without making a search throughout the country for volumes in the same good condition.

The University Library would seek a writ of replevin, to be served against Keaveny, demanding the return of the books.

Trover

Trover is an action used when the bailor prefers to recover the *value* of property held by a tortious bailee rather than the property itself. The value awarded is the value of the goods at the time the bailment was created, not the value at the time that the action is taken.

 Whittington, who owned many fine horses, loaned a saddle horse to Charles for the afternoon. Charles did not return the horse, but stabled it in his own barn and made no move to call Whittington or to indicate an intention to return it later. Whittington learned that the horse had been injured while being ridden by Charles.

The owner would be better rewarded by demanding the value of the horse according to its worth at the time it was delivered to the bailee. The condition of the animal would not encourage Whittington to seek its return. Charles would be liable for all damages as well as for the animal's value.

Trespass

An action of ***trespass*** permits the owner to recover the value of wrongfully held property together with profits the tortious bailee may have realized through the unpermitted use or sale of the property.

 Scriber borrowed Henry's 35-foot power launch for a weekend of sailing and fishing. Scriber used the boat to take a party out fishing on the bay, charging each guest $25 for the day's outing. The boat was damaged from Scriber's negligent handling, and repairs would have cost Henry more than $1,100.

The owner might rather seek an action of trespass against the bailee. Henry would recover the value of the boat, as of the time of loaning it, together with all money collected by Scriber from the people who had been on the trip.

Questions for Review and Discussion

1. Distinguish between the words *possession* and *custody*. Which one is associated with bailment?

2. How much care is *ordinary care* in a mutual-benefit bailment?

3. Discuss tortious bailees. Generally, what three common-law actions may an owner bring against a tortious bailee having possession of the bailor's property?

4. How do bailments differ from sales?

5. Explain the relationship between a bank and one keeping valuables in a safety deposit box; between the owner of a car parked in a parking lot and the owner of the lot.

6. Under what conditions may a bailee use property belonging to the bailor?

7. Distinguish between termination of gratuitous bailments and that of mutual-benefit bailments.

8. Discuss the requisites of a bailment contract.

9. Give an example of (*a*) a bailment by necessity and (*b*) an involuntary bailment.

10. List the different types of mutual-benefit bailments in commercial use.

Analyzing Cases

1. Mueller attended the Army-Navy football game in Philadelphia. Kovich loaned Mueller a pair of binoculars to make the game more interesting. The binoculars were stolen when Mueller left them on a vacant seat during half-time. What are Mueller's obligations to Kovich, if any? • See also *Lazar* v. *Cohen,* 127 N.J. Law, 310.

2. Kinkaid asked permission to put a car in Anderson's two-car garage during a heavy snowstorm. After Kinkaid ran the car in, Anderson locked the garage door, taking the key into the house. Kinkaid's car was stolen from the garage, but Anderson's was left untouched by the thieves. Is Anderson liable to Kinkaid for the loss of the car? • See also *Wells* v. *West,* 212 N.C. 656.

3. Martin borrowed Steen's car for a drive in the country. Although he drove very carefully, the car was wrecked when struck by an unexpected rock slide. Steen brought suit against Martin, demanding money damages to replace the car. Will Steen succeed in this action? Explain. • See also *Siegel* v. *Spear & Company,* 234 N.Y. 79.

4. Harris rented a boat from Dukes for a trip to an island located two miles offshore. Since it was a good day for sailing, Harris continued the trip all the way across the bay. During that part of the trip, the boat struck a submerged piling, ripping out the bottom and ruining the craft. Harris proved, in court, that the accident did not result from any lack of care, nor was it caused by any negligent act. Do these defenses free Harris of liability to Dukes? Explain. • See also *Lane* v. *Cameron,* 38 Wis. 603.

5. Julian loaned a television set to Bleyer a week before the beginning of the World Series in October, then asked for it to be returned so that his own family could watch the Series games. Bleyer refused to give it back, saying this would upset his plans to watch the games. What are Julian's rights in this situation? • See also *Baer* v. *Slater,* 158 N.E. 328.

6. Turner stored a friend's furniture in a vacant room in her house. She did this as a favor, charging the friend nothing for storage. Turner decided to shift the furniture to another room, wishing to redecorate and put to use the room containing the furniture. Would Turner have any obligation to the friend if the furniture were destroyed due to no negligence on her part? • See also *Hargis* v. *Spencer,* 244 Ky. 297.

Legal Reasoning and Business Judgment

Analyze the legal aspects of these business problems. Suggest possible solutions.

1. A service representative of your firm borrowed a car from an acquaintance to make calls to customers. As was the representative's practice, the keys were left in the ignition lock during a service call in a suburb of the city. The car was stolen. Who is responsible for the loss of the car?

2. Your firm plans to open a parking lot for the employees. They will be charged a small sum for maintenance of the lot. You have the job of drawing up an agreement which will be signed by all persons using the lot. As a representative of management, what would you include in this agreement?

3. Your firm rented a computer to help perform a cost analysis of plant operations. One day during lunch break, a plant electrician started the machine to see how it worked. Since he knew nothing about its operation, he jammed the machine and caused much damage. The owner of the computer billed your firm for the expensive repairs and replacement of damaged parts. Discuss this case and the liabilities of all parties concerned.

Chapter 19
Responsibilities
of
Hotelkeepers

Among facilities available to those who travel or live away from home are hotels and convenient roadside motels. Dormitories are available to college students. An important function performed by those operating such facilities is the safekeeping of a guest's or resident's property. Thus, the responsibilities of hotelkeepers come within the study of bailments. The legal duties and rights of those owning and operating such facilities will vary depending on whether the particular facility is classified as (1) a private accommodation or (2) a public accommodation.

PRIVATE ACCOMMODATIONS

Dormitories, rooming or lodging houses, and clubs that offer living facilities on a contract basis are *private accommodations*. They are not regulated under the same laws provided for hotels and motels. In private accommodations, owners are given the right to select guests, and they may require contracts covering a week, a month, or longer periods. The owner or manager has an obligation to exercise ordinary care in protection of the guest's personal property. A mutual-benefit bailment relationship exists between the guest and the one operating such a facility.

> Students living in dormitories at Hallstead College signed contracts obligating them to a full semester's residence. Rooms were assigned by the resident director. Typewriters, clothing, and other personal property of the students which they left in their rooms established a mutual-benefit bailment with the college. Ordinary care by the resident director would require that security services be installed to restrict strangers from entering rooms of students.

Negligence on the part of management makes the owner of private accommodations liable for losses of a guest's personal property. Open entrances, unguarded hallways, or unrestricted movement of strangers through the facility could be regarded as negligence.

PUBLIC ACCOMMODATIONS

Public accommodations are those that hold themselves out to the public as willing to accept transients for unspecified periods of residence. Historically, under English common law, the inn was regarded as a public-service venture.

Where there was no protection for the night, from highwaymen, robbers, and the like, it was the innkeeper's legal obligation to accept all guests who might apply at the door of the inn. The law governing hotelkeepers in the United States has not changed in this respect. Public accommodations may not select their guests, and they may not require long-term contracts of residence. Their guests are *transients*, persons whose length of stay is not regulated by contract. Although a transient may remain for one, two, ten, or more days, the obligation may be terminated at will by the guest.

Included in the category of public accommodations are hotels and motels, which have rights and responsibilities respecting guests, lodgers, licensees, and business guests.

Guests and Lodgers

A *guest* is a transient who enters a hotel in proper condition and is willing and able to pay for accommodations. The hotelkeeper has an insurer-like liability for property brought into the hotel by a guest. Statutes generally allow the hotelkeeper to limit this liability, reducing the hotelkeeper's basic duty as an insurer. Dollar limits may be placed on the hotel's liability, and notice may be posted directing guests to deposit valuables in the hotel safe. A *lodger*, on the other hand, is one who is a permanent resident. A lodger's living accommodations are usually referred to as a *boarding house*. While the hotelkeeper has common-law liability for luggage and other property brought into the hotel by a guest, the boarding house keeper's liability with boarders is limited to ordinary care of property.

 Sefcik was able to obtain a comfortable room at the Morely Hotel. After three days' residence, she decided that the Morely was ideally located for her business. Accordingly, she made arrangements to rent the room for eight months at a special discount rate. While Sefcik was originally a transient guest, the new arrangement changed her status to that of a lodger. The Morely now had a duty to provide ordinary care for Sefcik's property. It ceases being an insurer.

Licensees and Business Guests

Persons not living at a hotel but entering it to enjoy the other facilities offered to the public are either business guests or licensees. A **business guest** is one coming on the premises with the intention of transacting some business with the hotel or its occupants.

 Sefcik arranged a dinner party at the Morely Hotel for purchasing agents of firms trading with her company. While in the dining room, the group would be considered business guests. The Morely would be obligated to provide safe surroundings for such persons.

Other persons coming on the hotel premises for their own convenience and without invitation are *licensees*. To such persons the management owes only the minimum degree of care.

▶ During a sudden rainstorm, several passersby entered the Morely Hotel and sat in the lobby until the storm had passed. Such persons would be considered licensees only.

The presence of licensees in a lobby, waiting room, or rest room is *permitted but not encouraged*. One who takes unfair advantage of this permitted right may be classed as a trespasser. A hotelkeeper's main duty to a licensee, or trespasser, is to refrain from inflicting intentional injury. The hotelkeeper would be obliged to inform the licensee of any dangers that might cause him or her injury, but there is no legal duty requiring the hotelkeeper to remove those dangers, as is the case with a hotel guest or business guest.

RIGHTS AND OBLIGATIONS OF HOTELKEEPERS

The hotelkeeper's obligations to a guest and the guest's property are imposed by common law and state statute. The obligations and rights are not by contract with the guest.

Obligation to Accept All Transients

A hotelkeeper is required to accept all guests who apply for accommodation. By the Civil Rights Act of 1964, and other federal and state legislation, the hotel may not discriminate in selection of guests for reasons of race, creed, color, sex, or ethnic background.

▶ Harrison sought accommodations at the Atlantis Hotel. The clerk refused accommodations, saying that the hotel catered only to members of the medical and legal professions and their families. Excluding Harrison as a guest made the hotel liable to Harrison for any damages he might prove resulting from the hotel's actions.

The hotelkeeper is permitted two exceptions from the obligation to accept all who might apply.

☐ A hotelkeeper may refuse accommodations to persons whose presence might imperil the health, welfare, or safety of other guests, or of the hotel itself.

Suppose Harrison, in the previous example, entered the Atlantis Hotel in an intoxicated condition. Harrison was boisterous and threatened a guest who stood in his way at the hotel desk. Harrison's condition and actions would warrant the hotel clerk's refusal to admit him as a guest.

☐ Would-be guests may be turned away when all rooms are occupied or reserved.

State laws which gave public accommodations other rights of refusal in past years were invalidated completely by the Civil Rights Act of 1964. Unless accommodations are refused for one of the two reasons given above, the hotelkeeper is subject to liability on a complaint made by a would-be guest.

Duty of Care Owed to Guest's Person

A hotelkeeper must exercise *reasonable care* in protecting its guests. Guests may claim damages resulting from a lack of care or from negligence on the part of the hotel or its employees.

> ▶ Chalmers occupied a room as a guest of the Central Hotel. During the night an intruder entered her room, closed the door, and assaulted and raped her. Chalmers suffered both physical and mental injury from the experience. The hotel was negligent in permitting strangers to use an elevator that took them to the sleeping floors. No security guards were employed, and the elevator operators were not required to ask for identification of those going to the upper floors of the hotel.

The hotel was grossly negligent and failed to exercise reasonable care toward the safety of the guests. Chalmers would recover damages attributed to the hotel's disregard of its duties to the guests, particularly Chalmers.

A hotelkeeper must respect and guard the guest's *right of privacy*. Guests are guaranteed, by law, exclusive and undisturbed privacy of rooms assigned by the hotel. Interruption of the guest's privacy through unpermitted entry by hotel employees or other guests, or through negligence, creates a liability under a tort action for *invasion of privacy*.

> ▶ Velez occupied a room in the Lakeside Hotel. While he was watching television, a stranger opened the door and entered the room. The hotel clerk had negligently assigned the occupied room to this late guest. Velez may seek damages against the hotel for invasion of privacy.

As a practical matter, guests rarely sue a hotel in cases of this kind. An understanding is generally worked out whereby the hotel agrees to dispense with charges for the guest's accommodations and meals for the duration of his or her stay at the hotel.

Duty of Care Owed to Guest's Property

A hotelkeeper has a greater duty of care toward a guest's property than is imposed in the usual mutual-benefit bailment. Hotelkeepers are held by law to be *insurers* of the guest's property. The insured property includes all chattels (personal property) brought into the hotel for the *convenience* and *purpose* of the guest's stay. In the event of loss, the hotelkeeper may be held liable, regardless of the amount of care exercised in the protection of the guest's property.

> ▶ Thieves entered rooms on the twentieth floor of the Glenmore Hotel. Entrance was made through locked doors. Burglar alarms had been disconnected by the professionals who planned the robbery. Even though every protection had been provided against burglary, the hotel remained an insurer of the guest's property. The hotel is liable for any losses its guests reported.

Limitations of Hotelkeeper's Liability as Insurer

As protection to hotelkeepers, the common law has provided exceptions to the rule that the hotelkeeper is an insurer. Each exception to the rule relates to a situation in which the hotelkeeper is denied the privilege of giving protection, or the guests themselves are at fault. It would be unfair to make hotelkeepers insurers under any of the following exceptions.

Contributory Negligence of Guest   The negligence of guests toward their own property, when locks and other safety devices are provided for their use, relieves the hotelkeeper of liability in the event of a loss.

> Locks were installed on all sleeping rooms in the Mainline Hotel. Bellhops instructed guests in the use of the locks, and they were advised to lock their doors whenever leaving their rooms. Hardesty left the hotel without locking the room door, and property was stolen from his room. The hotel is not liable for this loss.

Acts of God   Losses to the guest's property due to so-called acts of God do not come within the liability of the hotelkeeper as an insurer. Acts of God include floods, tornadoes, cyclones, earthquakes, and other unpredictable natural phenomena.

> A hurricane struck Centerville, breaking several windows in the upper floors of the Morely Hotel. The accompanying rains caused considerable damage to property belonging to Sefcik and the other guests. Losses were the direct result of an act of God, and the Morely will not be obligated to reimburse the guests for the damages claimed.

Damage caused by acts of God is actionable if the bailee-hotelkeeper could have anticipated the onrush of a hurricane, flood, high winds, or other natural events. If it can be shown that the hotelkeeper knew of the impending disaster and could have protected the guest and the guest's property by taking usual precautions, the damage is then said to have been due to negligence rather than an act of God.

> A motel in Florida was equipped with special protective window sashes that were to be installed in the event of a hurricane warning. The motel manager received several warnings of an impending hurricane but did not install the protective sashes, saying: "I have been fooled before and will not do all that work for nothing this time." The storm did hit the area, windows were blown in, and much damage resulted to guests' property. The manager could not, in this case, claim exemption from damages due to losses resulting from an act of God.

Acts of Public Enemy   Persons or groups whose activities are directed at an attempt to overthrow the government are considered the *public enemy*. Thieves, arsonists, murderers, and other criminals are not included in this definition unless their activities are combined with an intent to overthrow the government. Hotelkeepers are not responsible for losses of guests' property resulting from acts of the public enemy.

During an extended business trip, Muller stopped at a hotel close to the border of a neighboring country. During her stay, a group of insurgents came into the town, raised their country's flag, and stormed the public buildings and Muller's hotel. Although Muller would ordinarily have had a claim against the hotel for her losses, she was barred from any recovery since those making the raid were recognized as the public enemy, *attempting to overthrow the recognized government*.

Accidental Fire   The loss of property due to accidental fire, in which no negligence may be attributed to the hotelkeeper, is another exception to the hotelkeeper's liability as an insurer. This provision also includes fires caused by other guests staying at the hotel at the same time. Such persons, even though on other floors, are called *fellow guests*.

A fire broke out on the seventh floor of the Royal Hotel. Although the fire was confined to that floor, several guests on other floors reported losses to their property due to fire and water. The hotel was able to prove that the fire had started from a cigarette dropped on a bed by one of the guests. Such careless smoking violated both a city ordinance and a rule of the hotel. The hotelkeeper would not be responsible for the losses caused by the fire.

Inherent Nature of Goods   The hotelkeeper is not obligated for damages arising out of characteristics of the property that cause its own deterioration. Damage of such property from other causes, however, will not exempt the hotelkeeper as an insurer.

Wood's sales samples included many highly polished metal parts that would rust if not kept in a low-humidity area. Because of a heavy storm and sultry weather, his hotel room became damp and musty. Wood's samples were ruined because of deposits of rust caused by weather conditions. The hotel would not be responsible as an insurer of Wood's samples. They were damaged through the inherent nature of the goods, not by the hotelkeeper's lack of care.

Statutory Limitations to Hotelkeeper's Liability

In most states, hotelkeepers are further protected by laws limiting the amount of claim any guest may make for a single loss. The limit is usually $500 or less, depending upon the state in which a hotel is located. These laws also give the hotelkeeper the right to provide a safe or vault for the better protection of the guests' valuables. A guest who does not use the safe provided for his or her valuables will be personally responsible for losses and may not seek recovery from the hotelkeeper. The hotel gives notice to guests of the prevailing statutes by posting copies of the statutes in each room.

Presley, a professional photographer, was assigned to cover a national political convention. Many cameras, valuable lenses, and flash equipment were stored in his room. One evening a thief entered the room and removed cameras and lenses valued at $3,500. Under most state laws, the hotel is liable for no more than $500 of the loss reported.

A reasonable interpretation of the law permits a guest to keep in his or her room those valuables that one would ordinarily have on or about one's person at all times. These would include a watch, cufflinks, rings worn, and a reasonable amount of cash.

Hotelkeeper's Right of Lien

Hotelkeepers are permitted a right of lien on the property of a guest. If a guest cannot pay his or her bill, the hotelkeeper is permitted to take possession of the guest's property as security for payment at some later date. Payment of the bill releases the property and terminates the right of lien.

> When Smith completed her hotel stay, she discovered that she did not have sufficient cash to pay her bill at the Park Hotel. The hotel would not accept her check and took possession of her luggage as security until the bill was paid. After cash was wired to Smith by her firm, she paid the bill. This terminated the hotel's right of lien on her property.

Some courts have recently held that before a hotelkeeper may make claim to a guest's luggage or property, the guest must have a hearing before a magistrate. In such cases, the magistrate reviews the available evidence. If it is warranted, the magistrate issues a writ permitting the hotel to exercise its right of lien.

Questions for Review and Discussion

1. Define (a) hotel guest, (b) transient, (c) lodger, (d) licensee, and (e) business guest.

2. Enumerate and discuss the exceptions to a hotelkeeper's obligation to accept all persons.

3. Distinguish between a hotelkeeper's duty of care toward a guest and toward a licensee.

4. Under the law governing hotelkeepers, what is meant by the term *public enemy*? Give an example of a situation involving the public enemy in the case of hotelkeepers.

5. How has the federal Civil Rights Act of 1964 affected a hotelkeeper's obligations to accept persons for accommodations?

6. What are the two obligations owed by a hotel to a guest's person?

7. Enumerate the common-law exceptions to a hotelkeeper's obligation to act as the insurer of a guest's property.

8. Under what conditions does the law bar a hotelkeeper from using the defense of act of God?

9. Compare the duty of care owed by a hotel to a guest with that owed by a lodging house to a lodger.

10. Explain the statutory limitations on the hotelkeeper's obligation as insurer of a guest's property.

Analyzing Cases

1. Harrigan, a known criminal, demanded accommodations at the Derby House Hotel. The clerk recognized Harrigan and refused to make a room assignment, although there were rooms available in the hotel. Harrigan threatened legal action against the hotel on a charge of discrimination in selecting its guests. Was the clerk within legal bounds in denying Harrigan a room? Explain. • See also *Benedict* v. *Eppley Hotel Co.,* 159 Neb. 23, 65 N.W.2d 224.

2. Tower Hotel rented Chou a three-room suite during the winter months, when it was more convenient for him to live in the center-city area. Chou paid for lodging under a special plan permitting long-term guests. He sought to recover the value of a suit that was stolen from the suite, basing his claim on the hotel's obligation as insurer of guest's property. Would Chou succeed in this claim? Explain. • See also *Hancock* v. *Rand,* 92 N.Y. 10.

3. Lerner entered the Chambers House Hotel to buy a magazine. As she was walking toward the newsstand, a section of decorative plaster fell from the ceiling, injuring her. The hotel denied any liability, claiming that Lerner was a trespasser, not having registered as a guest of the hotel. Will Lerner recover damages against the hotel? Explain. • See also *Smith* v. *Smith,* 136 Ga. 531.

4. Members of Lakeville College basketball team were guests at the Winston Arms Motel. The team was on its annual winter tour, playing other colleges in the area. During the night a fire in the motel destroyed the team's basketball uniforms, balls, and other equipment. The fire was caused by sparks dropping to the roof from a nearby factory chimney. Is the motelkeeper liable to the team for its loss? Explain. • See also *Holstein* v. *Phillips,* 59 S.E. 1037.

5. Fields agreed to meet an acquaintance in the lobby of the Harrigan House. He was not registered at the hotel. During their meeting Fields walked across a marble floor, fell, and was injured. A sign was posted near where Fields fell, stating "Floor Recently Waxed. Be Careful." Fields claimed damages for injuries, arguing that the hotel had an obligation to make the premises safe for its guests. Would Fields recover damages on these grounds? Explain. • See also *Moody* v. *Kenny,* 153 La. 1007, 97 So. 21; and *Wagner* v. *Baker,* 126 Ga. 532, 55 N.E. 181.

6. Lefeber was severely burned when using a sunlamp provided for guests in their hotel rooms. The burn was the result of a defect in an automatic timer that was supposed to turn off the lamp at a time set by the user. Lefeber sought to claim damages from the hotel for injuries received. Is the hotel liable? Explain. • See also *Benedict* v. *Eppley Hotel Co.,* 159 Neb. 23, 65 N.W.2d 224.

Legal Reasoning and Business Judgment

Analyze the legal aspects of these business problems. Suggest possible solutions.

1. As organizer for an employees' luncheon, you reserve a private dining room at the Parrot Hotel. During the luncheon, a waiter spills hot soup on one of the employees, causing the latter to require medical attention. The hotel denies any liability, arguing that it has no obligation to persons merely entering the premises for a luncheon. How would you respond if you wanted the hotel to defray the costs of the employee's medical treatment and purchase of a new suit?

2. While attending a convention in a distant city, you were injured in a fall in the hotel hallway. Examination of the carpet showed that a seam had broken and your toe had caught in the tear, which caused the fall. The hotel management denied liability, placing the blame on you. What argument would you present in an attempt to recover damages for your injuries and inconvenience?

3. One of your sales representatives called the main office about samples stolen from a hotel room. The representative had observed every precaution when leaving the room—locking the door and windows and locking the valuables in their cases. A thief had entered during the employee's absence and removed the sample cases. The hotel manager denied any liability, claiming that sales samples would not satisfy the definition of guest's luggage, as stated in the law. Would your representative and the firm be able to recover for this loss under the hotel's obligation as insurer?

Chapter 20
Regulation of Common Carriers

Individuals, partnerships, and corporations in the business of transporting goods and passengers are known as *carriers*. Carriers are either *private carriers for hire* or *common carriers*. The carrier of goods is a bailee of the personal property that it transports. The carrier of passengers is a bailee only of the passenger's luggage given into its possession. Both are bailees of goods belonging to another, but the obligations, rights, and responsibilities of the two types are very different. What kind of carrier is the moving company that you hire to transport your household goods to your new home? What obligations does a railroad assume for shipping cartons of TV sets for a local manufacturer? How are railroads, airlines, and telephone companies regulated?

PRIVATE CARRIERS

Persons and firms engaged in the transport of goods and passengers under private contract arrangements are known as *private*, or *contract, carriers*. They are permitted by law to select those with whom they want to do business. They do not operate on regular schedules and are not regulated by state or federal authority as to rates charged and services offered. The acceptance of merchandise by them creates a bailment for mutual benefit. They are required to exercise ordinary care, as in all other mutual-benefit bailments, and are responsible for any losses arising from their negligence. They are not considered to be insurers of the goods that they ship.

> Maris moved to a different apartment after the expiration of his current lease. Larimore Moving and Storage Company contracted to move Maris's furniture and belongings. The charge for the van and a four-man crew was $35 an hour. As a private carrier, Larimore was entitled to adjust its rates depending on the nature of each job accepted. Any damage to Maris's belongings, if due to the negligence of the company's work crew, would be Larimore's responsibility entirely.

COMMON CARRIERS

Common carriers of passengers and freight are public-service ventures operating under government-granted franchises. Their rate schedules and operations are regulated and inspected by federal, state, or local public authority. Interstate carriers have double scrutiny, from both federal and state commissions. All rate and schedule changes require approval by the public authority before being placed in effect. Common carriers are a kind of quasi-public operation. *Quasi-public businesses* must satisfy strict rules promulgated by public officials while at the same time operating for a profit through private investment.

> Red Ball Taxi Company operated under a franchise granted by the city of Ashton. It served the public, maintaining cab stands at railroad stations, leading hotels, and the municipal airport. The franchise gave Red Ball exclusive rights to operate a taxi service within the city of Ashton.

In consideration of the special privileges allowed under the franchise, a common carrier must accept all persons seeking transportation. It may not, as with a private carrier, select its own passengers, make its own rate schedules, and use its own discretion in determining where to operate and provide services.

COMMON CARRIERS OF FREIGHT

Railroads, trucking companies, boat and steamship lines, and air carriers are all franchised as common carriers of freight. If a common carrier does all of its business within the boundaries of one state, it is an *intrastate carrier*. Such carriers are franchised by state authority, usually a public service commission. *Interstate carriers*, those operating between states, receive their franchises from a federal agency, the Interstate Commerce Commission (ICC). Regulation of air carriers and the granting of franchises for airline service come under the jurisdiction of the Civil Aeronautics Board (CAB). (See Chapter 5.)

Duties of Carriers

Common carriers of freight must accept *without discrimination* all goods offered to them for shipment. Discrimination either through the selection of customers or through the use of preferential rates is illegal. Exceptions to the rule against discrimination are as follows:

☐ A common carrier is not required to accept goods of a type it is not equipped to carry.

An oil company contacted the Northern Railroad about shipping fuel oil over its lines. The Northern had never carried fuel oil in bulk, and no cars were available for that type of freight. The Northern would not be required to buy special cars to provide the service demanded by this shipper.

☐ The carrier may refuse goods which are inherently dangerous and which would create hazards beyond the control of the carrier's usual safety facilities.

Jet Engines, Inc., was interested in experimental work being done on a new type of jet-propulsion fuel. The fuel was exceedingly dangerous to handle. Jet Engines demanded that the Northern Railroad transport a quantity of the fuel to its test center 200 miles from the home plant. The Northern would be within its rights in refusing to accept the fuel, owing to its inherently dangerous characteristics.

☐ The common carrier may refuse goods that it does not represent itself as hauling.

> The Lehigh and Southern Railroad Company operated a line adjacent to the Northern. All equipment was designed for the sole purpose of carrying ore to blast furnaces located far from the mines. The carrier accepted shipments of ore from various shippers. Any requests from shippers of other types of raw materials or goods would not have to be honored, and the carrier would not be subject to discipline or suit from the Interstate Commerce Commission or the courts.

☐ The carrier may refuse goods that are improperly packed. Proper packaging is determined by the type of goods being shipped, the length of the haul, and the usual custom of the trade.

> Ten aircraft engines were made ready for shipment to a European buyer. Jet Engines, Inc., delivered them to the Oceanic Steamship Lines for transatlantic shipment. The engines had not been treated against damage from salt air, required in all overseas shipments. The steamship company would have no obligation to the shipper if it refused to accept the shipment.

☐ The carrier may refuse goods that are not delivered at the proper place and time.

Rights and Liabilities of Carriers

A common carrier has two rights which it may enforce against shippers of goods:

☐ The right to the payment of fees agreed upon for the shipment of the goods.
☐ The right of lien on all goods shipped for the amount of the shipping charges due. This right of lien is terminated when payment is received by the carrier. Should the *consignee* (the one receiving the goods) fail to pay the charges, the shipper has the right to sell the goods at public sale, placing the receipts from the sale to the credit of the consignee.

> Hanlon Book Company ordered paper from Maine Paper Company. The paper was shipped from Bangor, Maine, under terms that transferred title to the paper when delivered to the carrier. Hanlon Book Company refused to pay shipping costs when informed of the arrival of the shipment. Notice was finally given to both firms of the carrier's intention to sell the paper to recover shipping charges. At a public sale, the paper brought a high bid of $237. The carrier deducted shipping costs and turned over the balance to the Hanlon Book Company.

Duty of Care Common carriers of goods are obliged as *insurers of all goods accepted for shipment*. The obligation here is similar to that placed upon a hotel-keeper in relation to the guest's property. The Uniform Commercial Code has adopted the philosophy of the "reasonably prudent man (person)" and the care he or she would ordinarily give under the same circumstances. This has not changed the law of any state, however, that imposes upon the carrier the common-law responsibility of an insurer. The carrier, therefore, is responsible as an insurer regardless of whether he or she has or has not been negligent.

▶▶ Plyboard was shipped from Salem, Oregon, to St. Louis. Title to the plyboard, by terms of shipment, passed to the buyer when shipped. When it arrived at St. Louis, the buyer inspected the shipment. The plyboard had been ruined by heavy rains that leaked into the faulty car. The railroad attempted to prove that roof damage to the car was not their fault and that the carrier had exercised extreme care in protecting the plyboard from damage.

The carrier was an insurer. Even successful proof that extreme care had been given would not alter the carrier's liability for damage to the plyboard.

Exceptions to Carrier's Liability Because of the great amount of freight transported by common carriers, the law has provided relief to the carrier from strict adherence to its liability as an insurer. If the damage claimed resulted from any of the causes described below, the carrier will be relieved of its obligation to the shipper or the consignee.

Acts of God and Acts of the Public Enemy These two exceptions would be interpreted in the same manner as those presented in Chapter 19, "Responsibilities of Hotelkeepers."

▶▶ The Northern Railroad maintained a freight yard adjacent to the Mackinack River. Warnings were issued that the river would gradually rise to flood stage over the next twenty-four hours. Although it had the opportunity to move all cars out of the yard, the railroad did nothing, and the contents of all cars were ruined by the flooding waters. Although the railroad denied responsibility, using the act of God defense, it was held that the loss was due to the carrier's negligence and failure to act rather than to an act of God. The railroad would be held liable to its shippers for all losses incurred by them.

Acts of Public Authorities If goods are seized by an inspector or a legal agency owing to illegality, unsanitary conditions, or similar justifiable reasons, the carrier is no longer liable for failure to deliver the goods shipped.

▶▶ Landers Air Freight accepted a carton of drugs for shipment to a San Francisco medical center. The Food and Drug Administration ruled that drugs of the type shipped were unsafe. FDA agents were ordered to confiscate all shipments of the drug before delivery to buyers. The shipment was taken by FDA agents who awaited arrival of Landers's flight at San Francisco.

Landers Air Freight has no liability to the shipper or receiver. The acts of a public authority supersede a carrier's obligation as insurer of a shipper's goods.

Acts of the Shipper Contributing acts of the shipper which cause or add to the loss will exempt the carrier from liability for damage. Mistakes in addressing and labeling and in improper packaging come within this category.

▶▶ Jet Engines, Inc., had contracted to send aircraft engines to Europe with Oceanic Lines. The shipping department neglected to fasten one of the engines with the bolts provided in the special crates used in the shipment. As a result of this oversight, the engine was badly damaged when a crane lifted the crate from the pier to the ship's deck. Because of the negligence of Jet Engines, Inc., no recovery would be allowed against the steamship lines.

Inherent Nature of the Goods   Perishable goods, evaporating and fermenting liquids, diseased animals, and articles of similar nature do not come within the insurable obligations of common carriers when such inherent qualities are the cause of damage.

Bills of Lading

The written contract between a common carrier and the shipper is called a *bill of lading*. The shipper usually makes out the bill of lading on forms supplied by the carrier. When the goods are accepted by the carrier, its agent signs triplicate copies, giving evidence of receipt of the goods. One copy of the bill of lading is kept by the carrier. The other two are for the shipper and the consignee, respectively. A bill of lading may be used as proof of ownership by the shipper or buyer, depending on the terms of the contract. One who has a bill of lading has the right to demand delivery of the goods from the carrier after the goods reach their destination.

Straight Bill of Lading

The party shipping goods under a bill of lading is known as the *consignor*; the one to whom it is shipped is the *consignee*. When the bill of lading does not contain the words "to the order of," it is consigned to one specific person and it is not negotiable. The consignee, however, may *assign* the bill of lading to another person.

When an assignment is made by the consignee of a straight bill of lading, it is then the obligation of the assignee to inform the carrier of the assignment. If such notice is not given, the carrier would be free of any liability if he or she delivered the goods to the original consignee named in the bill.

> Modern Machine Company shipped three cases of machine parts to Talley over the CB & Q Railroad. A copy of the straight bill of lading was promptly mailed to Talley. Talley assigned the shipment to Rembaugh Machine Shop for value received; he did not give Rembaugh the bill of lading, however. As the consignee, Talley was given notice of the arrival of the three cases. He went to the freight depot, showed the bill of lading, and was given possession of the entire shipment. Rembaugh may not make complaint to the CB & Q Railroad. His only avenue for recovery would be a suit against Talley.

Order Bill of Lading

A bill of lading on which the words *to the order of* precede the consignee's name is an *order bill of lading*. It is similar to a negotiable bank check and may be transferred from one party to another by indorsement and delivery. This transfers ownership of the goods described in the bill of lading. A carrier is liable should goods be delivered to the consignee rather than to the person to whom the bill of lading has been transferred. The carrier's agent must examine a bill of lading to determine whether there has been an indorsement before delivering the goods. The carrier is never excused if delivery is made to one who does not present an order bill of lading.

> An order bill of lading was attached to a draft and sent to a bank located near Jet Engines, Inc. The transaction represented the shipment of specially milled brass fittings required in Jet Engines' manufacturing process. A freight clerk at the

carrier's freight depot delivered the shipment to one of the consignee's truck drivers, who picked up other shipments at the same time, without receiving the bill of lading. Should any difficulties arise from this unauthorized act of giving up possession of the shipment without the bill of lading, the carrier would be liable to the shipper for all losses incurred.

The Interstate Commerce Commission has approved a standard bill of lading for use in all interstate shipments. It contains all the conditions under which the carrier undertakes the movement of the goods, and there is a presumption that the shipper has read and is familiar with all its terms. Intrastate shipments may be contracted for under a different type of bill of lading, which permits a carrier to exempt itself from losses caused by the negligence of its own employees. This exemption is not permitted in interstate shipments.

> Jet Engines, Inc., shipped a box of parts to a dealer in its own state. The shipment was carried by a local freight line, and a bill of lading was duly issued and signed by the carrier. Later in the day Jet Engines was informed that the shipment had been destroyed by a fire caused by the negligence of one of the carrier's truck drivers. On examination of the bill of lading, it was found that the carrier had exempted itself from liability for such loss. The carrier was within its rights, and no recovery for the loss could be claimed by Jet Engines, Inc.

If an employee of a common carrier issued a bill of lading without actually receiving the goods described in the bill, the carrier would be completely liable to any innocent third party who might have given value to the fraudulent holder. The one giving value for the bill of lading has a right to depend upon the carrier's position in issuing a bill that would from all intents and appearances give the impression of being genuine.

> Colonial Appliances shipped eight freezers to Johnson Stores over the Rio Grande and Eastern Railroad. The bill of lading called for ten freezers. The freight agent accepting the order signed the document without checking the number of crates. If the order bill of lading were sold to a buyer in the belief that there were ten freezers en route, the carrier would be liable for the two missing freezers.

Limitation of Carrier's Liability   Carriers may limit the amount of their liability by the terms of a bill of lading. Federal agencies give approval of such limitation in bills of lading used in interstate shipments. The Interstate Commerce Commission has such authority, as granted by the Federal Bill of Lading Act. State commissions have similar powers in regulating intrastate shipments. A shipper may increase the limits stated in the bill of lading by paying an additional fee to the carrier.

Although a carrier may limit its liability, it may not avoid claims that are attributed to negligence. In intrastate shipments, the Uniform Commercial Code states, "A carrier who issues a bill of lading . . . must exercise the degree of care in relation to the goods which a reasonably careful man would exercise under like circumstances."

▶ Heath Motor Company shipped a rebuilt Porsche motor from its plant in Kansas City, Missouri, to Sports Cars, Ltd., in St. Louis. The bill of lading limited the carrier's obligation as insurer to $100. Through the negligence of the carrier's employees, the motor was dropped from a freight platform, landing on an underpass thirty feet below. The motor had to be rebuilt, causing a loss of $350. The $100 limitation would not apply to this intrastate shipment.

The limitation agreement, in interstate shipments, is also governed by the Interstate Commerce Act (USCA, title 49, chap. 1, sec. 20.11): "No contract, receipt, rule, regulation or other limitation of any character whatsoever shall exempt such common carrier, railroad, or transportation company (receiving property for *interstate* transportation) from . . . liability . . . for the full actual loss, damage, or injury to such property caused by it."

The Civil Aeronautics Act (USCA, title 49, chap. 9, sec. 483), provides, among other things, the right of the carrier to limit its liability to the value of goods, and also its liability for flight cancellation, rerouting, and transshipment.

▶ Diamond Press had to stop all operations due to breakage of a drive shaft essential for powering its large presses. Stringer Machine Company, of Albany, specialized in this type of machinery. It was arranged that a replacement shaft be shipped immediately by Eastern Air Freight. *Because of bad weather conditions,* the plane carrying the shaft was rerouted to another airport 200 miles away from Diamond Press's location.

Eastern Air Freight will not be liable for the loss to Diamond Press resulting from the delay and continued shutdown of its printing plant. Since the rerouting was due to circumstances beyond the carrier's control, the USCA will exempt Eastern from liability in this case. Had it been within Eastern's power to deliver the shaft to the designated point, the outcome would have been different.

Carrier's Implied Obligations

The carrier must supply the required transportation facilities and storage facilities for goods awaiting shipment or delivery. The carrier is also required to ship the goods by the proper route and to protect them during shipment.

Common carriers will not be excused from liability for losses due to strikes, mob violence, fire, and similar causes. Losses from damage to perishable goods delayed in shipment due to strikes become the carrier's liability. Recent labor legislation, however, has come to the assistance of common carriers in these matters. Labor unions are now required to give notice of impending strikes weeks in advance of the strike dates. Armed with such notice, the carrier may reject shipments that might be damaged by delays caused by such strikes.

▶ Service Trucking Company, a common carrier, was notified by its union that a strike was called for March 15 because of labor-management problems. Plant Growers, Inc., delivered crates containing two million Marglobe tomato plants to Service's freight depot on March 13. In light of its liability, and with knowledge of the impending strike, Service would be justified in refusing this shipment of perishable plants.

Wrongful Delivery If goods are delivered to the wrong person because of the shipper's negligence or mistakes in making out the bill of lading and shipping labels, the carrier is relieved of liability. If, however, the mistake or negligence is the carrier's, the carrier is liable.

Connecting Carriers

Common carriers often accept goods for shipment to points beyond the terminus of their own lines. The goods are then transferred to *connecting carriers* in order to complete delivery. Losses during shipment over the facilities of the connecting carriers will be determined according to the following rules.

Interstate Shipments The initial carrier will be responsible for damages while the goods are in the custody of connecting carriers if the shipment is an *interstate shipment*—one that goes beyond the borders of the state in which it originated.

> Red Lion Luggage Corporation of Chicago shipped ten cartons of goods to Riverside, Louisiana. The cartons were transferred to a riverboat line for final delivery after the initial carrier deposited them in a freight depot in New Orleans. Since this is an interstate shipment, the initial carrier continues as the insurer of Red Lion's goods until they are safely delivered to the consignee in Riverside.

Intrastate Shipments Shipments made to points within the same state are called *intrastate shipments*. The initial carrier is relieved of any liability for losses that may occur while the goods are in the possession of connecting carriers.

> Sportswear, Inc., located in Spokane, Washington, shipped an order of winter sportswear to a dealer located in Olympia, Washington. Rawlins Truck Lines carried the cartons to Everett, Washington, where they were transferred to Western Pacific Lines, a connecting carrier. Any damage to the goods while in the possession of Western Pacific Lines may not be charged to the initial carrier.
>
> The liability of Rawlins Truck Lines was terminated when the goods were delivered to the connecting carrier.

If the initial carrier fails to use good judgment in the selection of connecting carriers, it may be held liable for losses even in intrastate shipments. Suppose, in the previous case, Rawlins Truck Lines had transferred the Sportswear shipment to an inexperienced and poorly equipped connecting carrier. The lack of good judgment in selecting a more efficient carrier would subject Rawlins Truck Lines to any action that might result from loss or damage incurred by Sportswear, Inc.

Termination of Carrier's Liability as Insurer

A common carrier ceases to be an insurer of goods after they have been delivered to their destination. The bill of lading, which is the carrier's contract, usually states that forty-eight hours after the goods have arrived at their destination and the consignee has been notified of their arrival, the carrier's status will be reduced to that of a mutual-benefit bailee. This change reduces the carrier's liability from that of an insurer to one required to exercise ordinary care. A delay by the consignee beyond the forty-eight-hour limit also permits the carrier to charge additional fees for the storage of the goods still remaining in its possession. This fee is known as a *demurrage charge*.

Door-to-Door Delivery   Many carriers are willing to contract for what is called *door-to-door delivery*. Under these terms the carrier continues to be an insurer until the goods have been deposited at the street address or plant of the consignee.

COMMON CARRIERS OF PASSENGERS

Common carriers offering passenger service include buses, railroads, airlines, and taxicabs.

A *passenger* is a person who enters the premises of a common carrier with the intention of buying a ticket for a trip. One continues to be a passenger as long as he or she continues the trip. This relationship is terminated after one has reached the destination printed on the ticket and left the premises of the carrier.

 Kelley, an engineering representative of Jet Engines, Inc., purchased a first-class reservation on Western Airlines for a flight into Chicago. Because of unforeseen difficulties and a difficult weather problem, the plane was one hour late in departing. During the time that Kelley remained in the passengers' lounge waiting flight departure, he would be considered a passenger, subject to all rights and privileges of airline passengers.

Duties of Carrier

A common carrier has an obligation to accept all persons who may seek passage over its lines. Carriers, like hotelkeepers, may not discriminate in the selection of passengers. There are, however, exceptions to this general rule.

☐ Common carriers may refuse passengers when all available space is occupied or reserved.

   The Twentieth-Century Limited out of New York to Chicago was fully reserved by persons en route to a political convention in Chicago. Hundreds of others demanded tickets but were refused. Charges of discrimination were brought against the carrier. Proof that there were no reservations available cleared the carrier of liability.

☐ Passengers may be refused if they are disorderly, intoxicated, insane, or infected with a contagious disease. To accept such persons would be to endanger the health and welfare of the other passengers. If these persons were accepted for passage, the carrier would be liable for any resulting injuries to the other passengers.

   Two intoxicated passengers were allowed to board a scheduled airline flight. Both held valid tickets that had been issued hours before. During the flight they became boisterous and unruly. By order of the flight captain, they were removed from the flight at the first stop.

The captain, as an agent of the airline, acted within legal limits in having the two passengers deplaned. They were a threat to other passengers and to the safety of the flight itself.

Obligations to Passengers

A carrier must exercise reasonable care in the protection of passengers. Injuries resulting from a carrier's negligence give a passenger the right to sue for damages. Carriers spend millions of dollars annually on the installation and improvement of safety systems to ensure safe travel for passengers. Airlines are continually doing research for better application of radar and other scientific navigational inventions for the safer operation of their planes.

> As an airplane made its approach for landing at Chicago, the "Fasten Seat Belts" warning was not given by either the captain or the stewardess. As the plane touched ground, several passengers were thrown from their seats and injured. The airline would be liable for all injuries and resulting damages caused by the aircraft crew's negligence in not giving warning as required in the airline's regulations.

Obligation of Carrier for Baggage

In conjunction with the carrying of passengers, a carrier is obliged to accept a reasonable amount of baggage. Baggage includes those things necessary for the comfort of the passenger and for the purpose of the trip. Excess baggage may be shipped by a passenger on payment of additional fees. Personal luggage carried aboard an airline and kept at one's seat does not generally come within the weight limits permitted each passenger.

When a baggage car or baggage compartment is available for checking luggage, the carrier is considered an insurer of the luggage checked by the passengers and left in these places. Property kept by passengers at their seats or in overhead compartments places upon the carrier the obligation of exercising ordinary care for its safety. The Camack Amendment to the Interstate Commerce Act expressly permits the common carrier to limit its liability in connection with baggage carried in interstate commerce.

> Canaris kept in her possession, during the flight, a briefcase containing many valuable papers and company directives for her trip. When she left the plane at Chicago, she discovered she had forgotten to pick up the briefcase, which was on the seat beside her. Investigation did not disclose the whereabouts of the case. Loss was due to Canaris's own negligence, and the airline is not responsible to Canaris or her firm.
>
> Had Canaris checked the briefcase with her other luggage in the baggage compartment of the plane, the airline would have been an insurer, and she would have been able to recover her loss.

The carrier is excused from liability for losses when the loss results from the passenger's negligence.

Compensation for Overbooking

The Civil Aeronautics Board requires an air carrier to offer a specified amount of compensation to passengers holding confirmed reservations for a particular flight who have been denied boarding because that flight has been oversold. The regulation applies only to regularly scheduled *interstate* flights. The amount of compensation ranges from a minimum of $25 to a maximum of $200.

Refusing Compensation   A "bumped" passenger is not obligated to accept the compensation offered. If a sum is offered and accepted, however, the compensation is said to represent liquidated damages, and the case is closed. A passenger whose damages are reasonably greater than the $200 limit may seek a recovery through litigation and proof of loss occasioned by being bumped.

> Hughes was scheduled to appear on a television show to be taped in California. The producer contracted to pay Hughes $10,000 for appearing on the show. Hughes was "bumped" from a reserved seat on a flight that would have reached California in time for her appearance. The air carrier knew the importance of the flight to Hughes but made no exception. Hughes refused to accept the compensation offered by the carrier and commenced a suit for damages of $10,000 plus punitive damages because of the carrier's failure to abide by the confirmed reservation.

Flight Delays and Cancellations   Like other common carriers, air carriers do not guarantee their operating schedules. Schedules as published cannot take into account such factors as adverse weather conditions, airport repairs, or mechanical breakdowns. When necessary, the carrier provides overnight lodging and meals and limited ground transportation to passengers so inconvenienced. Carriers also have undertaken the moral obligation to reroute stranded passengers by means of other airlines.

Chartered Buses

Private groups often charter, or rent, buses or other equipment from common carriers for special occasions. The carrier in such a case is considered a contract, or private, carrier. As such, the carrier would have an obligation of exercising reasonable care for the safety of all passengers transported.

> The annual picnic for all workers at Jet Engines, Inc., was scheduled to be held at Pine Lake. The local bus line contracted with the company to furnish three buses for the transportation of the employees. One of the employees was injured when a bus operator started the bus without properly warning the passengers. The bus company would be liable for the passenger's injury resulting from negligence and lack of reasonable care.

Car Pools

Persons who form an organized *car pool* for commuting purposes from home to school, home to work, and the like are not considered to be common carriers. But the expansion of cooperative groups into commercial ventures could result in a complaint to the public service commission by those corporations holding franchises for providing public transportation. This would be true only where regular fares are being charged and the service is offered on a somewhat regular schedule.

Members of car pools are obligated to give reasonable care to the passengers being carried. Damages arising from negligent upkeep of the car or careless driving can result in tort actions against the owner-driver of the vehicle. When arranging a car pool, the owners of the cars involved are advised to consult with their auto insurance coverers to determine what risks and liabilities they might encounter in case of an accident.

 Shilling owned a Volkswagen bus, which was used on family vacation trips. By arrangement with seven others in the neighborhood, Shilling agreed to provide daily transportation to and from their jobs in the city. Each member of the car pool agreed to pay $10 a week for this transportation.

If an accident occurred, Shilling's insurance company might refuse responsibility for damages. Shilling used the bus for commercial purposes. The risk assumed by the insurer in the above case covered only noncommercial uses. A different premium for the insurance might have to be paid if the coverage were to be extended to include commercial uses of the van.

INTERSTATE COMMERCE COMMISSION

The Interstate Commerce Commission, referred to as the ICC, is a federal agency responsible for the regulation and inspection of interstate common carriers. All common carriers must file schedules of rates for passengers and freight with the commission. The ICC scrutinizes all rates as a protection for the public from discriminatory or unfair practices by the carriers. Rate changes, whether for passenger or freight service, must have the approval of the ICC before being put into effect. If schedules filed by the carriers are ignored, the carrier may be called before the commission for a hearing on a complaint, resulting either in a penalty or in a dismissal of the charge.

 Miller planned to leave Richmond on a regular flight to Jacksonville. Inquiry at the reservation counter revealed that the flight had been removed from the airline schedule that afternoon. Curtailment of the Richmond-Jacksonville schedule had been approved by the Interstate Commerce Commission, signs were posted, and new timetables were being printed. Miller would have no grounds for complaint to the ICC.

The ICC also has jurisdiction over the regulation of trucks operating between states as common carriers. The drivers of such equipment must carry logbooks in their truck cabs. These show the number of hours they have been driving, points of departure and destination, the trips made, and other information pertinent to operation and safety of heavy truck movement.

STATE COMMISSIONS

Almost all states have set up commissions for the regulation of intrastate common carriers. Bus companies, short-line railroads, pipelines, toll bridges, and other public carriers come within the jurisdiction of the state commissions' rulings. Rulings of both the Interstate Commerce Commission and the state commissions may be appealed to the courts if they do not satisfy the complainants or the carriers.

> Daily schedules provided commuters living in the Pike Creek Valley area with transportation into the city. Buses operated seven days a week. A survey of use showed that only five persons regularly used the bus service on weekends. As a result the bus company was showing a loss in operation on those two days.

The bus company would be permitted to submit income and expense studies to the state commission, seeking termination of weekend service to Pike Creek Valley. If the request were reasonable, as here, it would no doubt be granted.

Questions for Review and Discussion

1. How does the Interstate Commerce Commission regulate carriers?

2. Distinguish between private and common carriers.

3. Discuss the amount of care required of a common carrier in event of damage to freight. What degree of care must a carrier use in protecting passengers from injury?

4. How does an order bill of lading differ from a straight bill of lading?

5. At what point does a person become a passenger? When does that relationship terminate?

6. Discuss the initial carrier's liability for damage to goods in custody of a connecting carrier in (*a*) interstate shipments, (*b*) intrastate shipments.

7. Distinguish between common carriers of passengers and car pools.

8. Enumerate the exceptions to the rule that a common carrier must accept all persons as passengers.

9. Are common carriers required to accept all goods delivered for shipment? What exceptions, if any, are allowed?

10. List the exceptions to a common carrier's liability as insurer of freight accepted for shipment.

Analyzing Cases

1. Brown, an airline passenger, was killed along with others when the aircraft collided with an unidentified object. Investigation by government authorities disclosed no negligence on the part of the carrier. The last radio contact reported the plane on schedule with all operations normal. Brown's wife sued the airline for damages resulting from her husband's death. Also included in the action was a claim for $300, the value of luggage checked in by the husband before boarding the plane. Will a court permit recovery on both claims? Explain.• See also *Williams* v. *Illinois Central Railway Co.*, 229 S.W.2d 1.

2. Strawberries were shipped in Skyway Truck Company's refrigerated truck from Fruitland, Maryland, to Boston. One hour out of Fruitland, the driver joined other drivers in a "wildcat" strike against the company. The refrigeration unit was shut off, and the strawberries were ruined after two days of sitting in the sun. Does the shipper have any rights against Skyway? Explain.• See also *Akerly* v. *Railway Express Agency*, 96 N.H. 396.

3. Rodenheiser, a bus passenger, was critically injured when a tire blew, sending the bus careening out of control into a culvert. Careful inspection proved that the tire that blew was a new one and had been run only 557 miles. It was properly mounted and inflated. The blowout was caused by a sharp object that had been dropped to the road by a careless motorist. Will Rodenheiser recover damages from the bus company if he decides to sue? Explain.• See also *Delta Airlines Inc.* v. *Millirons*, 73 S.E.2d 598.

4. Van Cleaf Movers contracted to move a piano from Randall's home to a nearby church. The piano was destroyed when the moving van was struck by a tractor-trailer rig that hit the rear of the van. The driver of the tractor-trailer accepted full responsibility for the accident. Randall demanded damages from Van Cleaf Movers for the value of the piano. Will Randall recover this loss from the moving company? Explain.• See also *Watson* v. *Jacksonville Bus Line Co.*, 349 Ill. App. 462.

5. Ohio Mining Company located a vein of coal a short distance from the lines of the New Castle and Southern Railroad, which was equipped to carry livestock only. The mining company requested a spur line into its mining area for shipment of coal mined. The railroad refused to carry Ohio's production. Charges of unfair discrimination were placed against the railroad. Will the Interstate Commerce Commission require New Castle and Southern to serve the mining company? Explain.• See also *Kansas Pacific Railway Co.* v. *Nichols*, 9 Kans. 235.

6. Hill purchased a ticket and waited for the arrival of the 6:49 express to San Diego. While sitting in the waiting room a large crate fell on Hill from an overhanging shelf. Hill was injured and is suing the carrier for medical and hospital bills related to the misadventure. The carrier denied responsibility, claiming that Hill was not a passenger. May the carrier be held responsible for Hill's claim? Explain.• See also *Fremont, E. & M. Railroad Company* v. *Hagblad*, 101 N.W. 1032.

Legal Reasoning and Business Judgment

Analyze the legal aspects of these business problems. Suggest possible solutions.

1. The shipping and receiving department has made a complaint to you. One of its trucks was at the freight depot when a shipment of twenty cases of machine parts arrived, consigned to your firm. Since the truck was returning empty to the plant, the freight clerk was asked to load the cartons on the truck. He refused to do so, because the driver of the truck did not have a copy of the bill of lading. How will you explain the carrier's decision to the receiving clerk in your company?

2. Reed, your sales manager, scheduled a meeting of regional sales representatives at the Clermont Hotel, in Baltimore. Reed attempted to board a train that would get him to Baltimore in time for the meeting. Unfortunately, it was crowded with a group of sympathizers going to Washington to protest a congressional decision against changes in the Taft-Hartley law. Reed was refused admission to the train. He could not

meet with his sales representatives in Baltimore and claimed damages against the railroad. Will Reed be awarded damages on this complaint?

3. Goods consigned to your firm awaited pickup at the freight depot in a nearby town. One of your truck drivers had been instructed to pick up the shipment shortly after the arrival notice had been received from the freight office. The driver forgot about the pickup until three days later. Hours before the driver planned to make the late pickup, the freight depot was destroyed by an incendiary bomb supposedly set by an arsonist. Will your company be reimbursed under the carrier's obligation as insurer? What instructions would you pass on to the receiving department and all drivers working in that area?

Part 6
Commercial Paper
Chapter 21
Kinds of Commercial Paper

Negotiable instruments which are used conveniently and safely as a substitute for money and to obtain credit are known as *commercial paper*. In the course of a year, many billions of dollars of these instruments circulate among business houses and individuals. They are usually *negotiable* because they can be transferred from one person to another by indorsement and delivery, or by delivery alone. Examples of negotiable instruments are checks, promissory notes, drafts, bills of exchange, and bonds.

Although negotiable instruments are payable in money, they are not money themselves. Where they are payable at a future date rather than on demand, negotiable instruments are, in effect, credit instruments since they extend credit. Whether commercial paper is payable on demand or at some future date, the person holding it always runs some risk that it is not genuine or that the party to it is or will become unable to pay the debt when it is due. For the most part, the rules governing commercial paper are found in Article 3 of the Uniform Commercial Code.

PARTIES TO COMMERCIAL PAPER

Commercial paper expresses the monetary rights and obligations of the parties involved in a transfer of money or extension of credit. These parties are the original drawer, drawee, and payee in a draft or check, and the maker and payee in a note. Other parties involved are the bearer, holder, indorser, and indorsee.

Drawer and Drawee

The person who creates a draft, check, or trade acceptance by writing it is known as the *drawer*. This party is the one who makes a demand on a bank or another person for the payment of money to a third person. The drawer does not have primary responsibility for payment of the instrument that he or she writes.

The person on whom a bill of exchange, such as a draft or check, is drawn is called the *drawee*. A bank is the drawee on all checks drawn on accounts held by the bank.

Maker and Payee

The person who makes and signs a promise instrument such as a promissory note, collateral note, or installment note is known as the *maker*. In contrast to the maker of a draft or check, the maker, in signing, accepts primary responsibility for the payment of the note.

The person to whom a negotiable instrument is made payable is the *payee*. In "Pay to the order of Jane Winn," Jane Winn is the payee and has no rights in the instrument until it is delivered to her. She is not liable in any way until she receives payment or transfers the instrument by indorsement. A payee can be a party to an *order instrument*, such as a check, or to a *promise instrument*, such as a promissory note.

Other Parties

The person in physical possession of a commercial paper that is payable to the person who holds it or is indorsed in blank is known as a *bearer*.

Any person to whom commercial paper is delivered is the *holder*. A holder may be a holder for value or a holder in due course. An employee who receives a check for services rendered is a *holder for value* of the check, having received it in payment of wages earned and due. Under certain circumstances, a person holding a commercial paper is treated as favored and is given immunity from certain defenses; he or she is termed a *holder in due course*. A detailed discussion of holders in due course can be found in Chapter 23.

The person who holds a commercial paper, transfers it to another person by signature on the back of the instrument, and delivers it to the other person is said to *indorse*[1] the instrument. The person who makes an indorsement is known as an *indorser*. The person to whom an indorsement is made is known as an *indorsee*.

Article 3 of the Uniform Commercial Code classifies all negotiable instruments or commercial paper as drafts, checks, notes, or certificates of deposit. A further subdivision of all instruments is that they are either "orders to pay," "promises to pay," or simply *order* or *promise* instruments.

ORDER INSTRUMENTS

Negotiable instruments containing the words "Pay to . . . " or their equivalent are *order instruments*. The purpose of the instrument is to order the drawee to pay money to the payee or the payee's order. Plain language must be used to show an intention to make an order and to signify more than a request or authorization. Order instruments involve parties in three capacities—drawer (creditor), drawee (debtor), and payee (third party). The same party may appear in more than one capacity (drawer and payee), and more than one payee may appear in a single capacity. Order paper requires an indorsement for negotiation, except if made payable to the bearer or to "cash."

---

[1]The spelling *indorse* is used in the UCC; *endorse* is acceptable in business correspondence.

Drafts

A ***draft*** is an order instrument through which the drawer-creditor orders the drawee-debtor to pay money to a third party who is the payee. Drafts may be either "time" or "sight." The former draft is payable at a specified future date; the latter is payable immediately upon presentation of the draft to the payee.

Time Drafts A ***time draft*** is frequently used when a manufacturer is shipping goods to a distributor who requires credit at the time of purchase. Upon receiving a signed acceptance of the debt from the customer, the seller may convert the draft into cash immediately by means of *discounting*. This simply means that through indorsement and delivery, the seller sells the draft to a bank for its value, less interest and risk charges. The bank then becomes the holder, entitled to payment on maturity of the draft. The customer (drawee), by acceptance of the draft, warrants that:

- ☐ The signature of the drawer is genuine.
- ☐ The drawer has the authority and the capacity to enter into such a contract.
- ☐ The payee, who indorsed the draft, was competent to do so.
- ☐ The acceptor will pay the draft at maturity, according to the terms of the acceptance.

There are two kinds of time drafts: (1) those payable after sight and (2) those payable after date. The time draft in Fig. 21-1 is an order on Carr to pay the purchase price of goods sold. The terms of this draft require that Carr pay it within 30 days after the draft has been presented "to sight"—that is, 30 days after Carr is shown the draft, is asked to agree to its terms, and has signified agreement by writing on the face of the draft "Accepted, Walter Carr, June 5, 19—." Carr must pay this draft on or before July 5, 19— (30 days after the date of acceptance). In a time draft payable after sight, the date of the draft is of no significance.

If the time draft just illustrated had been payable "30 days *after date*" instead of "30 days *after sight*," Carr would have been required to pay the draft 30 days after May 26, that is, on June 25. The fact that the draft was not accepted until June 5 had no bearing on the maturity date. In a time draft payable after date, the date of acceptance does not affect the date of maturity.

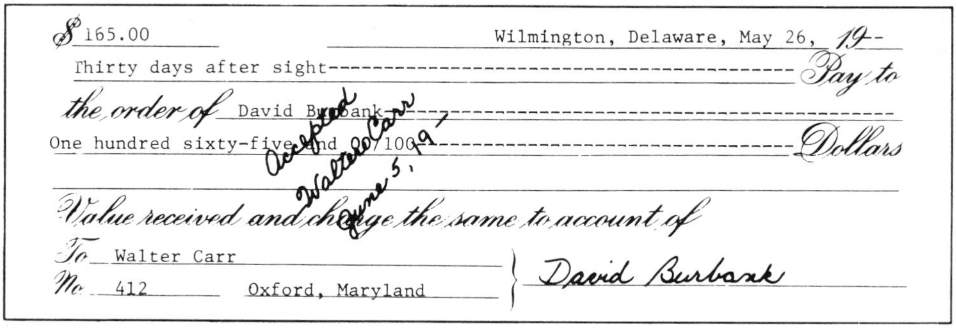
$165.00 Wilmington, Delaware, May 26, 19-
Thirty days after sight Pay to
the order of David Burbank
One hundred sixty-five and 00/100 Dollars
Value received and charge the same to account of
To Walter Carr
No. 412 Oxford, Maryland
David Burbank
Accepted Walter Carr June 5, 19-

Fig. 21-1. Accepted time draft

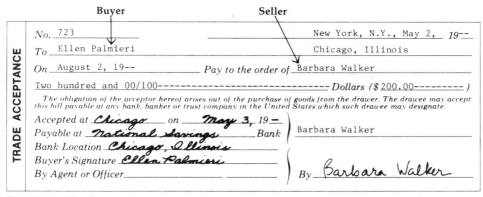

Fig. 21-2.   Trade acceptance

Trade Acceptances   A form of time draft known as a *trade acceptance* is used as a credit instrument. Trade acceptances are ordinary drafts, or bills of exchange, drawn on the purchaser by the seller and accepted by the purchaser. Trade acceptances result only from the purchase and sale of goods. As illustrated in Fig. 21-2, Walker is the seller and drawer of the trade acceptance. She sends it to Palmieri, the buyer and drawee, who "accepts" the draft by signing and dating it. Once returned to the drawer, the draft may be discounted at a bank for cash or used as collateral on a loan. Special provision is made in the Federal Reserve Act for the rediscount of trade acceptances.

Sight Drafts   A *sight draft* is a written order on the drawee to pay on demand the amount named in the draft. It is payable on presentation to the drawee. Sellers frequently use such instruments to collect money due from purchasers of goods. Sight drafts are also used to collect debts that are due or overdue. Drafts of this kind contain no legal obligation until accepted by the named drawee.

> Sirot, a Chicago distributor, wishes to purchase goods from Romano Brothers of Springfield, Illinois. Romano Brothers would ship the goods and then prepare a sight draft drawn on Sirot. It would be attached to the order bill of lading from the carrier selected to truck the goods and then would be sent to a Springfield bank for collection. The bank would forward the draft and the order bill of lading to its correspondent bank in Chicago for collection. The correspondent bank would present the draft to Sirot and, on receiving payment, would mark the draft "Paid" and deliver it to Sirot along with the order bill of lading, which entitles the distributor to claim the goods from the carrier.
>
> The Chicago bank would then notify the Springfield bank that the draft had been honored (paid) and the amount credited to the bank. The Springfield bank would notify Romano Brothers that the draft had been collected and that the manufacturer's account had been credited with the amount of the draft less the bank charges for collection. (See Fig. 21-3 for an illustration of a sight draft.)

Checks

A *check* is the most common form of a draft. It is drawn on a bank by the drawer, who has an account with the bank, to the order of a specified person named on

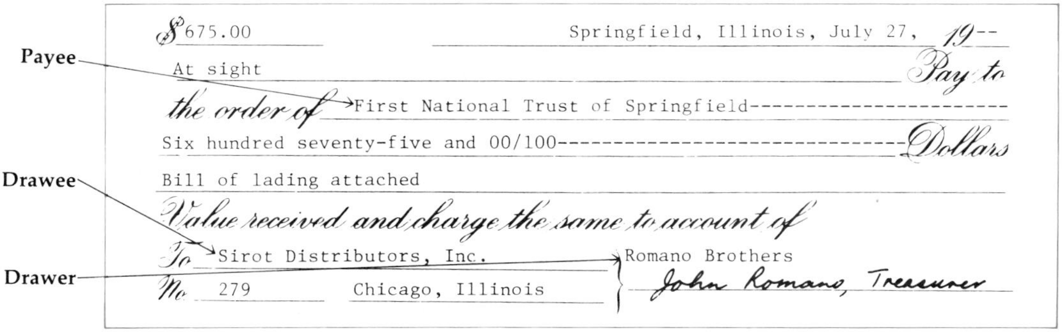

Fig. 21-3. *Sight draft*

the check, or to the bearer. A check is a safe means of transferring money, and it serves as a receipt after it has been paid and canceled by the bank. When properly drawn against a credit balance, a check must be paid by the bank when presented by the payee.

In the check shown in Fig. 21-4, Dewey is the drawer; he has an account in the County Trust Company. Security Loan Company is the payee. County Trust, on whom the check is drawn, is the drawee.

Ownership of a check may be transferred to another person by indorsement by the payee. In this manner, checks may circulate among several parties, taking the place of money. A bank must honor a check when it is properly drawn against a credit balance of the drawer. Failure to do so would make the bank liable to the drawer for resulting damages.

Check Form Requirements   Banks provide regular and special printed check forms. These display a series of numbers printed in magnetic ink, which makes it possible to process checks speedily and accurately by computers. The first set of figures is the bank's Federal Reserve number. This is followed by the bank's own number. The second set of numbers is the depositor's account number. The use

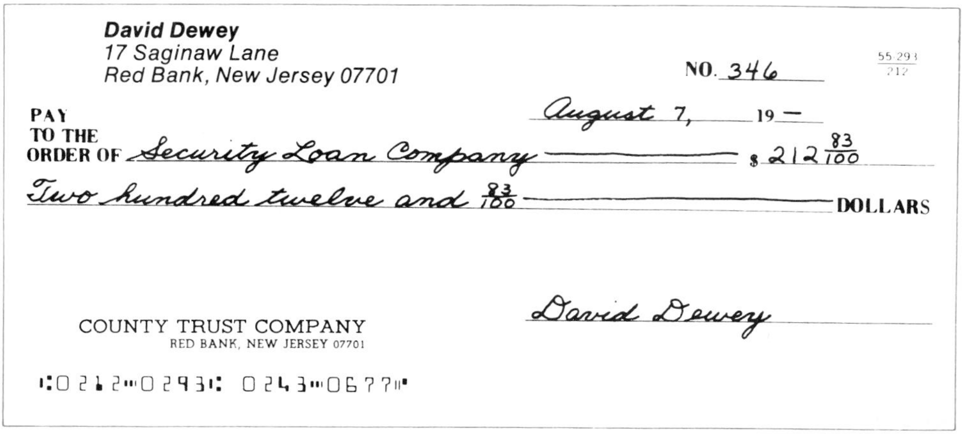

Fig. 21-4.   *Check*

of printed forms is not required. Any writing may become a negotiable check if it is a draft drawn on a bank and payable on demand.

> Martinez, when checking out of a motel, discovered she had lost her checkbook and credit cards, and there were no blank checks available. She wrote out a check on a 5- by 9-inch index card, taking care to comply with the requirements of negotiability. When signed by Martinez, this writing would constitute a valid check.

Certified Checks *Check certification* is an action of a bank in which, at the request of either the depositor or the holder, the bank acknowledges and guarantees that sufficient funds will be withheld from the drawer's account to pay the amount stated on the check. A prudent person would request a certified check when involved in a business transaction with a stranger rather than accept a personal check.

> For services rendered, Cerreta writes a $414 check payable to the order of Hydr-O-Matic Well Drilling and presents it to her bank for certification. The cashier checks the form of the check and verifies Cerreta's account balance. The cashier stamps the word "Certified," writes the date across the face of the check, and signs his or her name. An entry is then made in Cerreta's account, indicating that $414 has been set aside for payment when the check is presented. The bank thereupon assumes absolute liability for payment.

The *certification* of a check by the bank upon which it is drawn, at the request of a holder, amounts to an acceptance. The effect of such certification is similar to a payment by the bank and redeposit by the holder. On the other hand, when the drawer has a check certified, such a certification merely acts as additional security and does not relieve the drawer of any liability. A bank may refuse to certify a check at the request of a holder without dishonoring it. The bank has a duty to pay, but not necessarily the duty to certify checks which are drawn on it. A drawer cannot countermand a check after the bank has certified it (see Fig. 21-5).

Bank Drafts A *bank draft* is a check drawn by one bank on another bank in which it has funds on deposit, in favor of a third person, the payee. Many banks deposit money in banks in other areas for the convenience of depositors who

Fig. 21-5. Certified check

depend upon the transfer of funds when transacting business in distant places. When the buyer is unknown to the seller, such checks are more acceptable than personal checks are.

 Lomas, a resident of Hillside, Nevada, wished to conclude a $10,000 transaction with Heinz in San Francisco. Lomas could go to the National Bank of Hillside (with which she does business) and purchase a $10,000 bank draft drawn on the Commercial Trust Company in San Francisco, payable to the order of Heinz, the seller-payee. When Heinz cashed the check at the Commercial Trust Company, $10,000 would be deducted from the amount National Bank has on deposit.

Traveler's Checks *Traveler's checks* are similar to cashier's checks in that the issuing financial institution is both the drawer and the drawee. The purchaser signs the checks when they are purchased, in the presence of the issuer. To cash a check, the purchaser writes the name of the payee in the space provided and countersigns it in his or her presence. Only the purchaser can negotiate traveler's checks, and they are easily replaced by the issuing bank if they are stolen.

 In preparation for a business trip, Kolinski purchased $500 in traveler's checks in his name. En route to Greeley, Colorado, the checks were stolen. He reported the loss to the issuing institution, and the stolen checks were replaced without additional expense. Only Kolinski, the purchaser, can negotiate the stolen traveler's checks by countersigning them.

Traveler's checks are issued in denominations of $10 and up, and the purchaser of the checks pays a fixed fee to the issuer.

Cashier's Checks A *cashier's check* is a type of check whereby a bank lends its credit to the purchaser of the check. In its legal effect, a cashier's check is the same as a certificate of deposit, certified check, or draft. Cashier's checks are made payable either to the depositor, who purchases it from the bank, or to the person who is to cash it. If the check is made payable to the depositor, it must be indorsed to the order of the person to whom it is transferred.

 The Security Loan Company had checking accounts in several banks located throughout the state. When one of these accounts needed additional funds, the treasurer of the loan company would transfer funds from one of the banks to the other in need of funds by purchasing a cashier's check made payable to the loan company for the desired amount. The receiving bank would have no doubt of the validity of the check when returning it for payment to the bank that issued it.

If, on the other hand, the treasurer of Security Loan Company elected to use a bank draft to transfer the funds, the drawee bank would deduct the sum from the funds the drawer bank had on deposit with it. The drawer bank would simply deduct the amount of the bank draft from the loan company's account instead of returning it for payment to the bank that issued it. (A cashier's check is illustrated in Fig. 21-6.)

Domestic and International Bills of Exchange A draft that is drawn and payable in the same state or that is drawn in one state and payable in another is called a

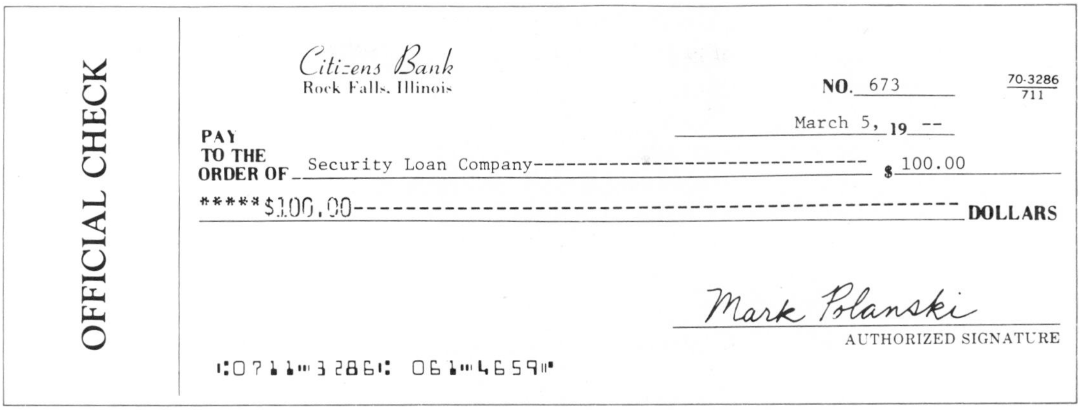
OFFICIAL CHECK

Citizens Bank
Rock Falls, Illinois

NO. 673 70-3286/711

March 5, 19 --

PAY TO THE ORDER OF Security Loan Company------------------------------- $ 100.00

*****$100.00-- DOLLARS

Mark Polanski
AUTHORIZED SIGNATURE

⑆0711⑈3286⑆ 061⑈4659⑈

Fig. 21-6. Cashier's check

domestic bill of exchange. A bill of exchange or draft that is drawn in one country but is payable in another is an ***international bill of exchange*** or a ***foreign draft***. This system of balanced payments enables business executives in one country or state to transact business in another country or state without the risk of an actual transfer of money (see Fig. 21-7).

Forged Checks and Depositor Protection A ***forgery*** is committed when a person fraudulently makes or alters a check or other form of commercial paper to the injury of another. The *intent to defraud* and the *creation of a liability* must be proved by the prosecutor.

Wheeler applied for a $400 loan from Home Finance Company and received its check for that amount. He painstakingly altered the amount to read $4,000. Later he presented the check, properly indorsed, to a building contractor in partial payment of an outstanding debt. In transferring the check, Wheeler was guilty of forgery; he had the intent to defraud Home Finance Company by making and creating for it a liability that had not previously existed.

The depositor is also protected against a signature's being forged. When a checking account is opened, the depositor must fill out a signature card, which is

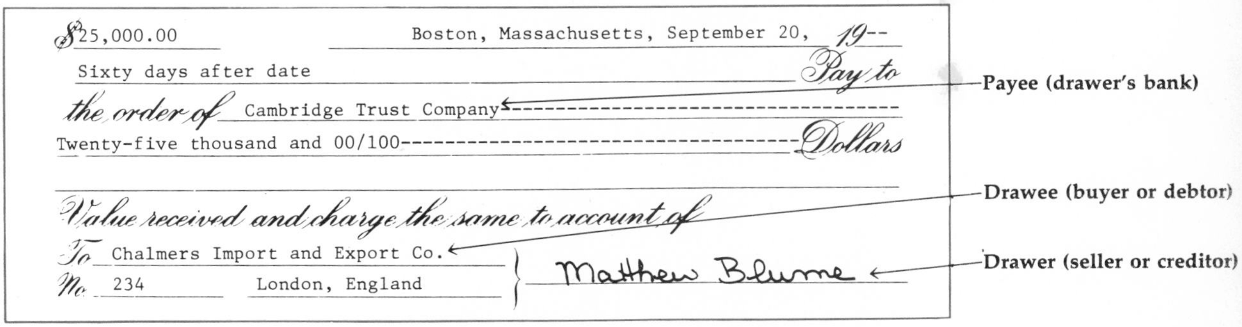
$25,000.00 Boston, Massachusetts, September 20, 19--

Sixty days after date Pay to

the order of Cambridge Trust Company--------------------------------

Twenty-five thousand and 00/100-------------------------------- Dollars

Value received and charge the same to account of

To Chalmers Import and Export Co.

No. 234 London, England

Matthew Blume

Fig. 21-7. International bill of exchange

permanently filed at the bank. Thereafter, the bank is held to know the depositor's signature. The bank is liable to the drawer if it pays any check to which the depositor's signature has been forged. The depositor has the responsibility of notifying the bank of a forgery within a reasonable time after receiving a bank statement accompanied by the forged check.

Because the bank alone has the opportunity of inspecting a check at the time of payment, it is liable for the payment of an altered check, unless the alteration was made possible through the depositor's own carelessness. Even so, if the bank could have reasonably detected the alteration, it may be held liable.

> A check received from Gertrude Gunnip by Union Finance Corporation was indorsed and transferred to Benvenuto for value. Benvenuto altered the check, not very skillfully. Although the alteration should have been obvious to anyone who inspected it, the bank teller cashed it without challenge. The maker, Gunnip, could hold the bank responsible for the loss, although she had been negligent in making out the check.

With respect to liability on forged and raised checks, one court ruled: "The maker of a check is obliged to use all diligence in protecting it. Failure to use the most effectual protection against alterations is evidence of neglect, which renders the maker responsible for the fraudulent amount, the bank being liable only for the genuineness of the signature and the ordinary care in paying checks."

Who bears the loss when a person poses as someone else and causes the drawer to issue a check payable to the order of the person being impersonated? In such cases, the indorsement by the impostor is effective, and the loss is on the drawer rather than the bank which honored it.

Bad-Check Laws   Most states have statutes making it a larceny for a person to issue a check drawn on a bank in which the person *has no funds*. Some states make it an offense to issue a check on a bank in which the person *has insufficient funds*. Such statutes usually have the following provisions, which must be observed in the prosecution of anyone issuing a bad check:

☐ The payee has the obligation of informing the drawer of the nonpayment of the check, together with notice of the provisions of the bad-check law and of the party's legal rights and obligations.
☐ After receiving notice of nonpayment, or dishonor, the drawer is given a specified number of days, usually five or ten, in which to make the check good, without fear of prosecution.
☐ Failure to make full payment of the check within the number of days allowed by statute serves as presumption of guilt that the drawer issued the check with full knowledge of the facts and with intent to defraud.

> State National Bank received Yoder's check for $120 due on an installment note it held. After it was deposited, the check was returned to State National with the notification "Insufficient Funds." The bank's collection department sent a registered letter to Yoder in which responsibility under the bad-check statute was explained. Failure on the part of Yoder to make the check good within the period of time indicated would result in a criminal complaint's being lodged against Yoder through the office of the state's prosecuting attorney.

Needless to say, bad-check statutes are effectively used as a means of collection. Most bad-check writers make an effort to make full payment of the check when advised that they are subject to prosecution.

Postdated Checks   A check may be *postdated* (dated ahead) when the drawer has insufficient funds in the bank at the time the check is drawn but expects to have sufficient funds to cover the amount of the check at a future date. Postdating is also practiced when some act or performance is to be completed before the date for payment of the check. Such a check, at the time it is drawn, has the effect of a promissory note inasmuch as it is a promise to pay a specified amount at a future date stated.

 Jaworski, an employee of Berk Associates, started a two-week vacation on August 2, five days before his weekly payday. The company gave Jaworski a salary check before he left on vacation but dated it August 7. Although the negotiability of this postdated check is not affected, the time when it is payable is determined by the stated date.

Stop-Payment Rights   A drawer may by order to a bank stop payment on any item payable on his or her account. The *stop-payment order* must be received in time and in such a manner as to afford the bank a reasonable opportunity to act on it before accepting it, paying the item in cash, settling for the item, or completing the process of posting the item to the drawer's account. An oral order is binding upon the bank for fourteen calendar days only, unless confirmed in writing within that period. A written order is effective for only six months, unless renewed in writing. The burden of establishing the fact and amount of loss resulting from the payment of an item contrary to a binding stop-payment order is on the customer.

 Chieco applied for an installment loan from People's Savings Bank, offering as credit reference a letter bearing the signature of a prominent business executive. People's Savings granted the loan and issued a check for the amount. A credit check revealed the reference letter to be a fraud. People's Savings issued a stop-payment order on Chieco's check. Since People's Savings had a good and valid reason for issuing the order, it will be free of liability in any action taken by Chieco.

PROMISE INSTRUMENTS

Promise instruments are commercial papers that contain the words *I* (or *we*) *promise to pay*—, or their equivalent. They create an obligation to pay on the part of the person signing the instrument. In the event the promise is conditional—where reference to some other agreement is required or where payment is subject to the terms of another contract—the instrument is not negotiable.

Notes

Notes are instruments whereby a person known as the maker promises to pay to the order of a second person called the payee, or to bearer, a stated sum of money on demand, sometimes in installments, and sometimes at a stated future date. In contrast with order instruments that involve three parties, notes embrace only two: the maker and the payee.

The purpose for which a note is used, and the nature of the security for the promise given by the maker to support the promise, are used to indicate the kind of note. One which carries on its face only the promise of the maker is limited to "personal security" and is called a simple *promissory note*. The personal promise of the maker, for business convenience, is often supported by other contracts which make property available as collateral security. The payee may require the obligation of another person, such as a cosigner or an accommodation party. Notes are frequently secured by personal property in the form of stock certificates, bonds, and other notes, temporarily placed in control of the payee. The security for a note may be a mortgage. Descriptions and examples of some notes follow.

Simple Promissory Notes   A *demand note* which carries interest at the rate stated until the amount is paid is a promissory note in its simplest form (see Fig. 21-8).

A simple promissory note may also take the form of a *time note*, payable at a fixed time following the date of issue at a stated interest rate. Another type is the *discount note*, which requires the repayment of the amount borrowed plus the interest payable to maturity. For example, if the borrower receives $2,500, payable in twelve months at 10.5 percent interest, he or she will sign a twelve-month note for $2,762.50. This sum represents the principal plus interest at the 10.5 percent rate.

Collateral Notes   A *collateral note* is generally a demand or time note which is secured by the pledging of personal property in the form of a mortgage, another note, a contract, a bank account passbook, a bill of lading, or stock certificates. The collateral is placed with the payee (holder) as security that the note will be paid at maturity. The note gives the payee the power to dispose of the property if the maker fails to pay the full amount when it falls due.

No. __381__	Boston, Massachusetts, October 1, 19--

On demand, the undersigned, for value received, promise(s) to pay to the order of
CAMBRIDGE TRUST COMPANY

Two thousand four hundred and 00/100-------------------- Dollars,
at its offices in Boston, Massachusetts, together with interest thereon from the date thereof until paid at the rate of __11__ percent per annum.

Address __100 Bedford Street__   *Victor Powell*

__Waltham, Massachusetts__

Fig. 21-8.   Demand note

The payee's rights to sell the collateral on default, according to the secured transactions provisions of Article 9 of the UCC, are detailed in the fine print of the collateral note. In a limited number of states, collateral notes may also contain a *confession of judgment* similar to that found in a judgment note. This amounts to an added power of attorney, enabling the payee's lawyer to request a court to have judgment entered without the formality of a trial if the note is not paid when due. The wording of a confession of judgment, also used extensively in the sale of articles on the installment plan, would be similar to the following:

> I hereby authorize any attorney at law in the United States to appear in any court of record in the state of _____, or in any other state in the United States, after the above obligation becomes due, and waive the issuing and service of process and confess a judgment against me in favor of the holder of this note, for the amount appearing due and the costs of suit; and thereupon to release all errors and waive all rights of appeal and stay of execution in my behalf, and I hereby waive all right to the appraisal of property on any execution issued on any judgment rendered on this note.

Installment Notes An *installment note* is an ordinary note in which the principal is payable in installments (series of payments) at specified times, together with interest on the unpaid balance, until the note is paid in full. It contains an "acceleration" provision, which permits the payee-holder to consider the principal amount and accrued interest payable immediately upon default by the maker in the payment of any installment. In the event the note is on a discounted basis, the acceleration payment would be of principal only. Such notes are used in the purchase of merchandise, and they enable the maker (buyer) to pay for purchases out of income. In the event of default, the payee may repossess the article sold. Nearly every installment note includes a power of attorney and confession of judgment in favor of the payee. An illustration of an installment note is provided in Fig. 21-9.

Certificate of Deposit

A *certificate of deposit* is an acknowledgment by a bank to a depositor, as a receipt for a deposit. The instrument is payable to the order of the depositor on demand or at a fixed date, and usually with interest. It is, in effect, a negotiable promissory note against which checks cannot be drawn. Special funds are frequently deposited in this way.

Other Negotiable Instruments

Instruments other than commercial paper may be negotiable but are not covered by the provisions of Article 3 of the UCC. Money is negotiable under separate statutes. Documents of title (such as bills of lading and warehouse receipts) are covered by Section 7, and investment securities (such as stock certificates and corporate bonds) are dealt with in Article 8. All these instruments have qualities of negotiability and thus have varying degrees of negotiability.

THE STATE TRUST COMPANY

INSTALLMENT NOTE

$ 3,000.00   Memphis, Tennessee

_____ March 1 , 19--

The undersigned, for value received, hereby promise(s) to pay to the order of THE STATE TRUST COMPANY (hereinafter called the "Bank") at its office in ___Memphis___ the sum of Three Thousand and 00/100--- Dollars in _36_ installments as follows: $ 125.00 _____ on ___April 1___ , 19--, and the same amount on the same day of each successive month thereafter (except that the last installment shall be the unpaid balance) until paid in full, together with interest after maturity on all unpaid principal amounts at the rate of seven per cent (7%) per annum.

At the option of the holder hereof, this note and all other liabilities of the undersigned (hereinafter called the "Maker") to the holder howsoever created, whether now existing or hereafter arising and whether due or to become due (this note and all such other liabilities being hereinafter called the "Obligations"), shall become immediately due and payable without notice or demand upon the occurrence of any of the following events of default:

(a) Failure of any Maker to comply with any of the promises contained in this note or to pay or perform any other Obligation of the Maker to the holder; or

(b) Death, dissolution, termination of existence, insolvency, failure to pay debts as they mature, business failure, appointment of a receiver of any part of the property of, assignment for the benefit of creditors by, or the commencement of any proceedings under any bankruptcy or insolvency laws by or against, any Maker indorser, or guarantor hereof; or

(c) Any warranty, representation or statement made or furnished to the Bank by or on behalf of the Maker in connection with this note or to induce the Bank to make a loan to the Maker proves to have been false in any material respect when made or furnished.

At any time any deposit or other indebtedness credited by or due from the holder to any Maker may be set off against and applied in payment of any Obligations, whether due or not, and such deposits or other indebtedness may at all times be held and treated as collateral security for the payment of the Obligations.

No delay or omission on the part of the holder in exercising any right hereunder shall operate as a waiver of such right or of any other right under this note. A waiver on any one occasion shall not be construed as a bar to or waiver of any such right and or remedy on any future occasion.

Every Maker, indorser and guarantor of this note, or the obligations represented hereby, expressly waives presentment, protest, demand, notice of dishonor or default, and notice of any kind with respect to this note or any guaranty of this note or the performance of the obligations under this note or any guaranty of this note. No renewal or extension of this note, no release or surrender of any collateral or other security for this note or any guaranty of this note, no release of any person, primarily or secondarily liable on this note (including any Maker, indorser or guarantor), no delay in the enforcement of payment of this note or any guaranty of this note, and no delay or omission in exercising any right or power under this note or any guaranty of this note shall affect the liability of any Maker, indorser or guarantor of this note.

Delinquency charges: The Maker agrees to pay a delinquency and collection charge on each installment in default for a period of more than 10 days in an amount equal to five per cent (5%) of the installment or five dollars ($5) whichever is less.

The Maker will pay on demand all costs of collection, legal expenses, and attorneys' fees incurred or paid by the holder in collecting and/or enforcing this note on default.

As herein used the word "holder" shall mean the payee or other indorsee of this note, who is in possession of it, or the bearer hereof, if this note is at the time payable to the bearer. As used herein the word "Maker" shall mean each of the undersigned. If this note is signed by more than one person, it shall be the joint and several liabilities of such persons.

On any loan of eight-hundred dollars or less, the undersigned agrees to pay a service charge of five dollars ($5) in addition to the interest, which will be collected when the loan is made.

ADDRESS   SIGNATURE

31 North Fern Street   _Larry Vargas, Jr._

Memphis, Tennessee 38117

Fig. 21-9.   Installment note

Bonds A negotiable bond is a promissory note, signed by the maker, and usually issued by corporations and governments for sale to investors. Corporate bonds secured only by the promise of the maker to pay are known as *debenture bonds*. Bonds secured by a mortgage on the property of the issuer are known as *mortgage bonds*. If other bonds or stocks are pledged as security for a bond issue, the bonds are known as *collateral trust bonds*. Bonds payable to bearer, to which are attached separate promissory notes for each interest period, are known as *coupon bonds*. Those payable to the order of a specified person whose name is registered in the books of a corporation are *registered bonds*.

Stocks The term *stock* refers to the ownership of right in a corporation. These rights include (1) the right to participate indirectly in the control of the corporation, (2) the right to share in profits, and (3) the right to receive a portion of the assets at time of dissolution. A stock is comparable to a promissory note of which the corporation is the maker. The owner of a share of stock has the right to transfer it, just as he or she may transfer any other personal property. A share may be transferred by the indorsement and the delivery of the certificate or by a bill of sale.

Warehouse Receipts and Bills of Lading The warehouse receipt and bill of lading are the two most common documents of title. Each document is negotiable if by its terms the goods are to be delivered to bearer or to the order of a named person. These documents are evidence that the person in possession has the legal right to receive, hold, and dispose of the document and the goods it covers.

A warehouse receipt need not be in any particular form, although it should embody within its written or printed terms each item listed below. If these essential terms are omitted, the person engaged in the business of storing goods for hire may be held liable for any damages stemming from their omission.

☐ Location of the warehouse where the goods are stored.
☐ Date of issue of the receipt.
☐ Consecutive number of the receipt.
☐ Statement whether the goods received will be delivered to bearer, to a specified person, or to a specified person on his or her order.
☐ Rate of storage charges.
☐ Description of the goods or of the packages in which they are contained.
☐ Signature of the person engaged in the business of storing goods.
☐ Statement of the amount of advances made and the liabilities incurred for which a lien or security interest is claimed.

The terms and form of a bill of lading are regulated by the Interstate Commerce Commission. A person entitled to delivery, to whom a negotiable bill has been duly negotiated, may rely upon the description therein of the goods and upon the date shown. He or she may recover from the issuer damages caused by any resulting loss. When goods are loaded by a carrier, the packages of goods or the kind and quantity of bulk freight must be determined. The shipper guarantees to the carrier the accuracy at the time of shipment of the description, marks, labels, kind, quantity, condition, and weight, and thereby indemnifies the carrier against damage caused by inaccuracies in such particulars. Damages may be limited by a provision that the carrier's liability shall not exceed a value stated in the document, if the shipper is afforded an opportunity to declare a higher value.

A bill of lading to the order of a named person is negotiated by indorsement and delivery. After an indorsement has been made in blank or to bearer, any person can negotiate the document by delivery alone. Indorsement of a non-negotiable bill neither makes it negotiable nor adds to the transferee's rights.

A holder to whom a negotiable bill of lading has been duly negotiated acquires

☐ title to the document and goods;

☐ all rights under the law of agency or estoppel, including rights to goods to the bailee after the document was issued; and

☐ the direct obligation of the common carrier to hold or deliver the goods according to the terms of the document.

Letters of Credit Although *letters of credit* are not classified as negotiable instruments, they are similar to commercial paper in that they have to do with issuing and honoring drafts. They are used in international trade to simplify the sales of goods and to afford protection to both seller and buyer. The buyer is protected because the bank with which the arrangements for the letter of credit are made will not honor drafts drawn against it by the seller, except upon the presentation of documents which designate the goods are available to the buyer. The seller is protected because the bank has obligated itself to honor drafts drawn by the seller for payment for the goods. If the documents are in order, the bank will pay the seller without regard to the condition of the goods.

▶ Chavis, an American importer, entered into a sales contract with Anton, a West German buyer, for the sale of heavy machinery. The contract called for credit in the form of a letter of credit. The German, Anton, went to his bank and made arrangements for the letter of credit authorizing Chavis to draw on the bank for account of Anton for $25,000, the amount of the sale. The German bank cabled the letter of credit to its correspondent bank in the United States. Chavis, upon shipment of the machinery, would present a sight draft and the necessary documents to the American bank. The bank would immediately give Chavis the cash or credit.

Questions for Review and Discussion

1. Identify the three parties involved in the transfer of negotiable "order" instruments, and describe their capacities.

2. Contrast the parties involved in the transfer of order instruments with those involved in the transfer of "promise" instruments. Describe the capacities of the latter parties.

3. In business transactions involving the sales of goods, explain the reason for using either a *time draft* or a *sight draft*.

4. Describe the primary characteristics that justify the use of checks, rather than any other negotiable instrument, as a means of making payments.

5. Explain the procedure whereby a check is certified.

6. Distinguish between a bank draft and a personal check. Explain why a bank draft is considered more acceptable in payment of a debt than a personal check.

7. What does the drawee warrant in the acceptance of a draft?

8. Define a simple negotiable promissory note. Indicate the manner in which it differs from (a) a collateral note, (b) an installment note.

9. Identify the two most common documents of title, and indicate what the person in possession of them is entitled to.

10. Although stock certificates and corporation bonds are classified as investment securities rather than commercial paper, explain why each is comparable to a promissory note.

Analyzing Cases

1. Before he set off on a business trip, Santo signed a check on which he left both the payee and amount blank. His secretary put it in the top drawer of her desk. It was to be used to pay for a c.o.d. delivery that was expected. Two days later, Santo learned that the delivery had arrived, but the check was missing. When Santo contacted his bank, he was told the check had already cleared in the amount of $500. It had been indorsed in the teller's presence in the same name as the payee on its face. Investigation revealed that one of the night cleaning crew had put her name on it as payee, filled in the $500, and cashed it. The office cleaner argued in court that she wasn't guilty of forgery because she had not passed a "false" instrument. Santo's signature was on the check as the drawer, and her name as the payee and indorser were truly genuine. How would the court hold? • See also *State* v. *Rovin*, 518 P.2d 579.

2. Reiner purchased a new Dodge Dart and gave a certified check for $5,140 in payment. When the automobile agency presented the check for payment the next day, it was discovered that the bank had failed that morning. Can the automobile agency look to Reiner for its money? Explain. • See also *Parker* v. *Walsh*, 205 N.W. 853; N.I.L. Sec. 187.

3. Moynahan drew a check in favor of Ludwig for $120 in payment of a personal debt. When Ludwig presented the check for payment during banking hours, the teller refused to accept it, although Moynahan had sufficient funds on deposit. (*a*) What are Ludwig's rights against the bank and against Moynahan? (*b*) What are Moynahan's rights against the bank for its failure to honor the check? • See also *Mieling* v. *Quasdord*, 68 Iowa 726.

4. Kranz requested in writing that his bank stop payment on a certified check previously drawn. The bank refused, even though the check had not been presented for payment at the time the notice was received. Was the bank liable for its refusal to stop payment? Explain. • See also *Young et al.* v. *Hembree*, 73 P.2d 393.

5. Ajemian executed and delivered to Alcott a note payable when Alcott reached the age of thirty-four. Would this be considered a negotiable instrument? Explain. • See also *Feeser* v. *Feeser*, 93 Md. 716, 50 A. 406.

6. Chan executed and delivered to Carlucci a promissory note in payment of a business debt. Carlucci indorsed the note to Pacelli. When the note became due, Chan refused to pay it, claiming that Pacelli had given no consideration for it and could not therefore enforce the claim. Pacelli sued. In whose favor would the case be judged? Why?• See also *Fehr* v. *Campbell*, 288 Pa. 549, 137 A. 113.

Legal Reasoning and Business Judgment

Analyze the legal aspects of these business problems. Suggest possible solutions.

1. The purchasing department of your company is getting ready to send a representative to South America to contract with several firms for raw materials needed by your company. It is considered too risky to carry cash for the anticipated purchases, and it is doubtful that checks drawn on the company bank would be acceptable there. How can this problem be handled?

2. An order for machinery is received from an out-of-state company. The customer has little or no credit standing. The credit manager decides not to accept the customer as a credit risk. How can the order be accepted under these conditions without subjecting your firm to the risk of loss?

3. A certified check was received by your firm in payment of a debt owed by an out-of-state company. The cashier deposited the check on the day it was received. However, when it reached the bank on which it had been drawn, it was found that the bank had closed because of insolvency. The customer who sent the check claims that because the payment was made by certified check, his company is released from all liability. What is the law as to the rights and obligations of your company, the customer, and the bank?

Chapter 22
Form, Transfer, and Negotiation

A written contract can also become a negotiable instrument if the person who is writing it includes the basic requirements of negotiability. Likewise, an individual can write something that appears to be a negotiable instrument but is really nothing more than a simple contract, because it lacks certain basic requirements which allow commercial paper to pass from hand to hand freely. Both conditions can be knowingly or unknowingly created, because negotiability of a commercial paper is wholly a matter of form. Within the borders of an instrument is the required information which determines whether an instrument is negotiable or simply a promise or order to pay money.

REQUIREMENTS OF NEGOTIABILITY

The form of negotiable instruments is explained in Section 3-104 of the Uniform Commercial Code. Any writing that is to be a negotiable instrument must include the following qualities:

- ☐ It must be in writing and have the signature of the maker or drawer.
- ☐ There must be an unconditional promise or order to pay.
- ☐ It must designate a sum certain in money.
- ☐ It must be payable on demand or at a definite time.
- ☐ It must be payable to order or bearer.

These essentials of negotiability, illustrated in Fig. 22-1, are discussed in the following paragraphs.

Written Instrument

An instrument must be in writing in order to circulate in the economy as freely as money. Writing is broadly understood to include printing, typewriting, pen or pencil writing, or even painting. A negotiable instrument written in pencil is, however, an invitation to alteration by forgery.

Most negotiable instruments are written on paper, but this is not a requirement. Oddly drawn checks, for example, are sometimes presented and paid by banks. Since a negotiable instrument must be capable of circulating, it should not

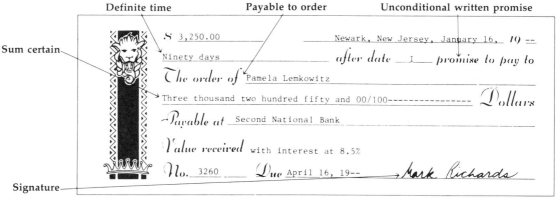

Fig. 22-1. Requisites of negotiability

be written on any nonmovable object. Neither should an instrument be written on anything unstable and unable to retain writing for a lasting period of time.

Signature of Maker or Drawer

To be negotiable, an instrument must be signed by the maker or drawer. Any writing or executed symbol is accepted as a signature. It may be handwritten, typewritten, printed, or produced in any way that will make a lasting impression. The writing can be done with ink or with anything that makes a mark. For proof of authority or genuineness, however, it is good judgment on the part of the receiver of an instrument to insist on a written signature.

A signature may be made by an *agent* (one who represents and acts for another) or other representative. No particular form of appointment is necessary to establish such authority. Agents who sign their own name to an instrument are personally obligated if the instrument neither names the person represented nor shows that the agent signed in a representative capacity.

Industrial Supply, Inc., held notes that were signed as follows: (*a*) John Spink, secretary; (*b*) Walter Hecht, agent; (*c*) Harry Licek, cashier, Delta Enviro Laboratories; (*d*) Smith-Holden, Inc., by Louis Boise, treasurer.

In (*a*) and (*b*), Spink and Hecht—not the firms or persons whom they represented—would be liable for the amounts involved. The words *secretary* and *agent* are mere terms of description. In (*c*) the Delta Enviro Laboratories was bound. In (*d*) Smith-Holden, Inc., was bound. Both Licek and Boise had clearly indicated that they had signed as agents of their respective employers.

The signature may be either subscribed (written at the bottom) or written into the body of the instrument, as, "I, Mel Purcell, promise to pay . . ." Any person who through negligence contributes to the making of an unauthorized signature may not assert the alteration against a drawee or other payor who pays the instrument in good faith or takes it for value. The party seeking collection on a note has the burden of proving the genuineness of the signature.

Unconditional Promise or Order to Pay

A *promise* is an undertaking to pay and must be more than the recognition of an obligation. An *order* is a direction to pay. It must be more than a request or an authorization, and it must identify the person with reasonable certainty. Thus, a writing that says "due Martha Charett $400" or "IOU Martha Charett $400" is not negotiable. In a similar manner, the signed request "Please let the bearer have $1,000 and charge it to my account with Putnam Trust Company" does not amount to an unconditional order. The instrument would not be negotiable.

The promise or order to pay in a negotiable instrument must be unconditional if the instrument is to be capable of rapid circulation at minimum risk. Obviously, if the holder of an instrument had to take it subject to certain conditions, the risk factor would be high, and the credit function of the instrument would be defeated. Section 3-105 of the UCC defines two provisions that can make a promise or order conditional, thereby destroying negotiability.

Subject to Other Agreements   A test of an unconditional promise or order is whether the holder of the instrument must look beyond the writing of the instrument to determine whether the person obligated is required to pay. Consider the following:

> I promise to pay to the order of Cycle Works, Inc., $750 for a Kawasaki motor scooter to be delivered one week from date in accordance with a sales contract between Cycle Works, Inc., and the undersigned.

This statement does not restrict negotiability. The reference to the sales contract does not condition the undersigner's obligation to pay. The note might have included either of the following statements:

> (1) In the event the motor scooter is not delivered, the undersigner's obligation shall be null and void *or* (2) and subject to the sales contract between Cycle Works, Inc., and the undersigned.

In these two cases, the negotiability would be affected. In the former case, the holder must be concerned with the question of whether Cycle Works, Inc., delivered the motor scooter on the date specified. In the latter case, a holder would find it necessary to examine the sales contract before knowing the extent of the undersigner's obligation.

Particular-Fund Doctrine   A promise or order is not unconditional if the instrument states that it is subject to or governed by any other agreement. A promise or order otherwise unconditional is made conditional if the instrument states that it is to be paid only out of a particular fund. Payment depends upon the terms of the specified agreement or the state of the particular fund.

> Eleanor Hess accepted a friend's note which read, "Ninety days after date, pay to the order of Eleanor Hess $150 out of the proceeds of a garage sale." The order is conditional since payment will be made only if the garage sale takes place and the proceeds of the sale are sufficient. Hess should insist on rewording the last part of the note to read, ". . . to be charged to the proceeds of a garage sale." This

wording does not affect negotiability, since the neighbor's general credit is relied upon and the reference to the garage sale is simply a recordkeeping instruction following payment.

Sum Certain in Money

The sum payable must be determinable from the instrument's face. Only in this way can the present and future value of the instrument be determined. A sum is considered certain even when payable with stated (1) interest or installments, (2) rates of interest based on payment before or after a specified date, (3) discounts or fees based on payment before or after the payment date, (4) exchange at a fixed or current rate, or (5) costs of collection or an attorney's fee.

> The note shown in Fig. 22-2 was received by Berk Associates from Leonard Sobek in return for a loan of $1,500 plus interest that the business had made to him. If Sobek refuses to pay the loan when it becomes due, can Berk Associates expect to recover the full amount? Probably not. Depending upon attorney fees and related collection costs, Berk Associates will recover less than the face value of the note. If the instrument had contained a promise to pay clause to the effect that Sobek would pay collection charges and attorney fees in the event of default, Berk Associates could recover the $1,500 sum certain.

Any promise to pay in addition to the sum certain in money in the event payment is not made at maturity is a collateral obligation. Although an uncertain sum is created after maturity, the negotiability of the note is not affected.

The term *money* is defined in Section 1-201 of the UCC as a medium of exchange adopted by a domestic or foreign government as part of its currency. Thus, a sum certain in money need not be money of the United States. Unless otherwise indicated, an instrument payable in Japanese yen, German marks, or other foreign currency would be satisfied by payment of the dollar equivalent of that currency—that is, the amount of dollars which the foreign currency would buy at the exchange rate on the date the instrument was due and payable.

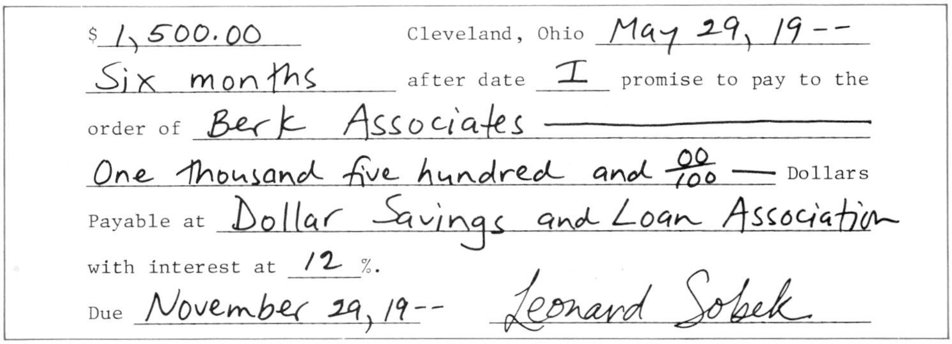

Fig. 22-2. *Promissory note without a collateral obligation.*

Security Loan held a note which they had received from a branch of the National Bank of France. The note specified payment in French francs. On the due date the note would probably be paid in dollars and cents according to the exchange rate of francs and dollars on the date of maturity and payment.

Payable on Demand or at a Definite Time

Negotiable instruments must be made payable on demand or at a definite time. This requirement makes it possible to determine when the debtor or promisor can be compelled to pay. Without this information, the present value of an instrument cannot be determined.

Demand Paper   An instrument is payable *on demand* when it so states, or when it is payable *on sight* or *on presentation*, or if, as in the case of a check, no time for payment is stated. The key characteristic of demand instruments is that the holder can require payment at any time by making the demand upon the obligated person.

Definite-Time Paper   Certainty as to the time of payment of an instrument is satisfied if it is payable on or before a definite date. Instruments payable at a fixed period after a stated date or at a fixed period after sight are also considered to be payable at a definite time. In each instance, a simple mathematical calculation makes the maturity date certain. The expressions *one year after date* and *thirty days after sight* are definite as to time. An undated instrument payable sixty days after date is not payable at a definite time. Since the date of payment cannot be figured from its face, the instrument would be incomplete. Although incomplete, the instrument is negotiable as a demand paper.

A promise to pay only upon an act or event, the time of whose occurrence is uncertain, is not payable at a definite time. Thus, an instrument payable when a person marries, reaches a certain age, or graduates from college, or one payable within a specific period of time after a named person's death, is not negotiable.

 Starr offered a note to a nephew which stated he would pay $500 thirty days after his nephew's graduation from college. Since graduation is an event the time of whose occurrence is uncertain, the note is not payable at a definite time (even though the event occurs) and is not negotiable.

Acceleration   An acceleration clause on the face of an instrument hastens the maturity date. For example: "In case of default in payments of interest (or of an installment of the principal), the entire note shall become due and payable." Instruments payable at a fixed time but subject to acceleration are negotiable.

Extension   Extension clauses give the maker of a note the opportunity to extend the payment date to a further definite time. For example, a maker may make a note payable in six months, but may include the right to extend it to one year without loss of negotiability.

Payable to Order or to Bearer

The chief characteristic of a negotiable instrument is its capacity to circulate freely as an instrument of credit. This function is achieved, and the intention of the maker (i.e., ease of transferability and payment of the amount indicated to any designated holder) is expressed, by the words "to the order of" or "to bearer."

Payable to Order An instrument is *payable to order* when by its terms it is payable to the order of any person with reasonable certainty. The maker or drawer may state, "Pay to the order of . . . ," "Pay to . . . or his (her) order," or "Pay to . . . or his (her) assigns." An instrument may be payable to the order of the maker or drawer; the drawee; a payee who is not the maker, drawer, or drawee; two or more payees; an estate, trust, or fund; an office or an officer by title; or a partnership or unincorporated association.

Payable to Bearer An instrument is *payable to bearer* when by its terms it is payable to bearer or the order of bearer; a specified person or bearer; cash or the order of cash; or another indication which does not designate a specific payee. An instrument made *payable to order and to bearer* is payable to order unless the bearer words are handwritten or typewritten. The omission of these or similar words destroys the negotiability of the instrument, making it a simple contract, valid only when legal consideration is present. The basic characteristic of bearer instruments compared with order instruments is that they can be negotiated by delivery without indorsement. Whether an instrument is a bearer instrument may be determined either by what appears on the face of the instrument or by the last indorsement. A special indorsement which designates the name of the indorsee ("Pay to Paul Minor") transforms a bearer instrument into an order instrument. A blank indorsement consisting of the indorser's signature transforms an order instrument into a bearer instrument. Thus, a check payable "to the order of Olga Pirina" becomes a bearer instrument if it is indorsed "Olga Pirina." Since bearer instruments are similar to cash and can be negotiated by delivery, caution in their handling is required.

 Pet 'n' Poodle received a check payable "to the order of cash. . . ." The proprietor indorsed it "Pay to Cedar Products, Inc., in partial payment of a shipment of red cedar shavings." Any further transfer of the check will require an indorsement by Cedar Products, Inc.

Omissions, Ambiguity, and Nonessentials

The omission of the date does not affect the negotiability of an instrument. When the date is omitted, the date on which the instrument is received is considered to be the date of issue. An instrument may be antedated or postdated. Any instrument lacking one or more elements of negotiability, however, cannot be enforced until it is completed. Handwritten terms control typewritten and printed terms, and typewritten ones control printed. Words control figures, except where words are ambiguous (capable of being understood in more than one way). The numbering of, or the failure to number, an instrument does not affect its negotiability.

The practice of placing the words *For value received* on an instrument is rapidly falling into disuse. As consideration is presumed, the use of the phrase does not strengthen or weaken the instrument in any way. This is not to say that actual consideration which supports the obligation on the instrument is not necessary.

If the place where the instrument is drawn or made is not stated, it is presumed to be the maker's place of business or home. If the place of payment is not stated on the instrument, it is likewise presumed to be the maker's place of business or home.

In some states and in some transactions, it is customary to require the seal beside the signature of the person responsible on an instrument. The presence of the seal will in no way alter the essentials of negotiability of an instrument. The presence of the seal, a facsimile of a seal, or the word SEAL, where used, characterizes the instrument as formal and often permits increased time under the state's statute of limitations for its collection.

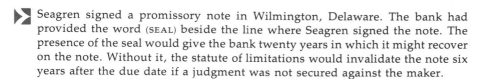

Seagren signed a promissory note in Wilmington, Delaware. The bank had provided the word (SEAL) beside the line where Seagren signed the note. The presence of the seal would give the bank twenty years in which it might recover on the note. Without it, the statute of limitations would invalidate the note six years after the due date if a judgment was not secured against the maker.

In some states, however, the presence of the seal serves as proof that there is consideration to support a promise.

TRANSFER

The rights which a person holds in commercial paper may be transferred by assignment or negotiation. *Transfer* is the act by which the owner of an instrument delivers it to another with the intention of passing rights in it to the other.

Assignment

A commercial paper is *assigned* when a person whose indorsement is required on an instrument transfers it without indorsing it. In all such transfers, the *transferee* (person to whom transfer is made) has only the rights of an assignee and is subject to all defenses existing against the assignor. If the *transferer* (one who transfers) indorses the instrument, the transferee becomes a holder, and defenses are cut off. An assignment of commercial paper also occurs by operation of law when the holder of an instrument dies or becomes a bankrupt. In such instances title to the instrument vests in a trustee or in the representative of the estate. (For a discussion of defenses, see Chapter 23.)

Negotiation

By definition, *negotiation* is a specific type of transfer in which the transferee is a holder—the person in possession of an instrument which is properly drawn, issued, indorsed or to the person's order or to bearer, or in blank. There are two ways of negotiating an instrument so that the transferee becomes a holder. If it is payable to the order of bearer or cash, it may be negotiated by delivery alone. If it is made out to a specified person, both indorsement and delivery are required. The finder of a lost or misplaced bearer instrument can transfer it, but an order instrument cannot be transferred.

 A check made payable to bearer and signed by Adolph Buttz was delivered to Reynold's Nurseries by Ralph Jessup as payment on an overdue invoice. Buttz's bank returned the check to Reynold's Nurseries because of insufficient funds in Buttz's checking account. Without indorsements on the check, the bank will be unable to trace previous holders of the check whom it might wish to hold liable. Had the check been made payable to the order of Jessup, it could have been transferred only by indorsement and delivery to Reynold's Nurseries.

NEGOTIATION BY INDORSEMENTS

An instrument is indorsed when the holder has written or printed his or her name or other pertinent matter on it or on a paper (rider or *allonge*) affixed firmly to it, so that it becomes part of the instrument. Indorsements may be written in ink, typewritten, or stamped with a rubber stamp. To be negotiable, however, indorsements must be made for the entire amount stated on the instrument. For convenience, indorsements are placed on the back of the instrument. The order in which the signatures appear determines the order of liability.

 Drive-In Cleaners received a check in payment of an account with the indorsement on the face of the check in such a position that it was impossible to tell with certainty the capacity in which it was made. In such an event, the signer of the check would be treated as an indorser.

The indorsement must be for the entire amount of the instrument. Hence, holder A may not indorse $40 of a $75 check to B. A holder may, however, negotiate the unpaid balance due on an instrument. If the name of the payee is misspelled, the instrument may be negotiated by indorsement in the name appearing on the instrument, or in a correctly spelled name, or, more desirably, in both names.

Types of Indorsement

Ordinary indorsements are either special or blank. When other terms are added to condition the indorsement, it is a restrictive indorsement. Qualified indorsements, on the other hand, limit the liability of the indorser. These indorsements are explained and illustrated in the following paragraphs.

Blank Indorsements In a *blank indorsement*, the payee's name is written exactly as it appears on the instrument. When the holder indorses an instrument in blank, it then becomes payable to bearer and may be transferred by delivery alone. Fig. 22-3 shows a blank indorsement.

 Ira Honig received a check from a client which he delivered to his bank and indorsed in blank. Use of the blank indorsement would be proper, since there is no likelihood the check would become lost or stolen. In the event the check is lost or stolen after being indorsed in blank and gets into the hands of another holder, the new holder can recover its face value by mere delivery.

Special Indorsements A *special indorsement* (or *full indorsement*) spells out the name of the person or firm to whom the instrument is being transferred immediately following the words *Pay to the order of . . .* or *Pay to . . . .* Indorsed in this manner, the instrument requires further indorsement by the indorsee for negotiation.

The holder of an instrument may convert a blank indorsement into a special indorsement by writing the same words (*Pay to the order of* or *Pay to*) over the transferee's signature.

 Suppose in the case of the full indorsement in Fig. 22-4 Fern Lowry had borrowed $1,200 from her bank to repay a debt owed to Charles Rutz. Fearful the check might get lost in the mail, Lowry indorsed it as shown. Since the check cannot be legally transferred or negotiated until Rutz indorses it, Fern Lowry is protected.

Restrictive Indorsements A *restrictive indorsement* limits the rights of the indorsee in some manner in order to protect the rights of the indorser. Indorsements of this type include (1) indorsements for deposit or collection, (2) conditional indorsements, (3) indorsements in trust, and (4) indorsements prohibiting further transfer.

Indorsements for deposit or collection are designed to get an instrument into the banking system for deposit or collection. By indorsing a check *For deposit only*, as in Fig. 22-5, the indorser is not negotiating it but is simply prohibiting any further use of the check other than to deposit it to his or her account. Retail stores often stamp each check "For deposit only" as it is received.

Conditional indorsements make the rights of the indorsee subject to the happening of a certain event or condition. Thus, an indorsement "Pay Michele Chirco only if Purchase Order 438 is received by September 20, 19—" is condi-

Fig. 22-3. *Blank indorsement*

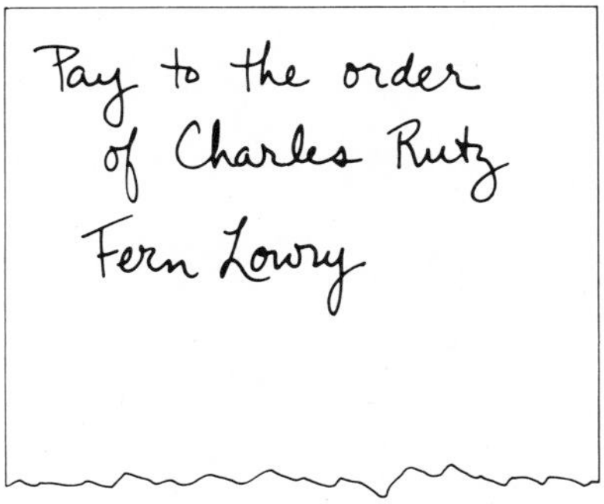

Fig. 22-4. *Full indorsement*

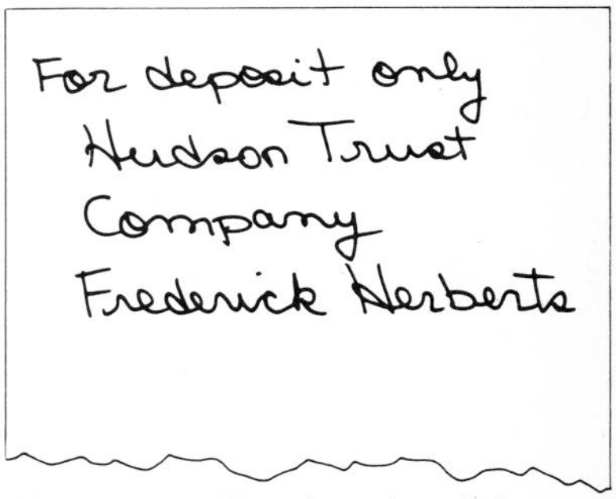

Fig. 22-5. *"For deposit only" indorsement*

tional, but it does not destroy negotiability. If the order is not received by September 20, the indorsee has no rights in the instrument; if it is presented to the maker or drawer for payment, it must be dishonored. A note is dishonored if it is not accepted by the party to whom it is presented.

▶ Ellison wished to transfer a check to her granddaughter, Doris Ross, as a birthday gift. Since Ellison did not want Ross to cash the check before her twenty-first birthday, a conditional indorsement such as the one illustrated in Fig. 22-6 was used. Until the condition presented in the indorsement has been satisfied, Ross has possession of the check, but she does not have full title or the right to cash it.

Trust indorsements state that the indorsement is for the benefit or use of the indorser or of another person. The trust indorsement designates the indorsee (person to whom the instrument is assigned), the agent of the person making the indorsement. For example, the indorsement "Pay Constance Canon in trust for Anthony Cusack" or "Pay Constance Canon for Anthony Cusack" is restrictive. The first taker (Canon) must pay or apply any value given consistently with the indorsement. Unless given notice, a later holder is not affected by the breach of duty of any such agent.

A *restrictive indorsement* does not prevent further transfer or negotiation of the instrument. Indorsements that purport to prohibit further transfer of the instrument have the same effect as unrestricted indorsements. "Pay Maurice Draper," "Pay Maurice Draper only," and similar indorsements are without exception indorsed as having satisfied the requirements of negotiability. A depository bank (the one with which the instrument is deposited), however, must apply any value given consistently with what the indorsement directs.

Qualified Indorsements In a *qualified indorsement*, the indorser disclaims (refuses to accept) liability for payment of an instrument should the maker fail to pay it. The manner of disclaiming the indorser's liability is to add the words *without recourse* before or after the signature, as shown in Fig. 22-7. Qualification of an indorsement limits the indorser's liability. It does not affect the transfer of title to the instrument or its negotiability.

▶ Chappell, a lawyer, receives a $10,000 check payable to his order in payment of a client's claim. Chappell indorses the check to the client "without recourse." In

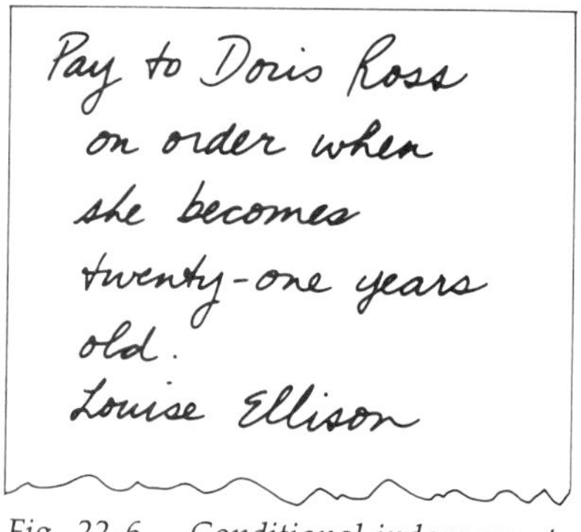

Fig. 22-6. Conditional indorsement 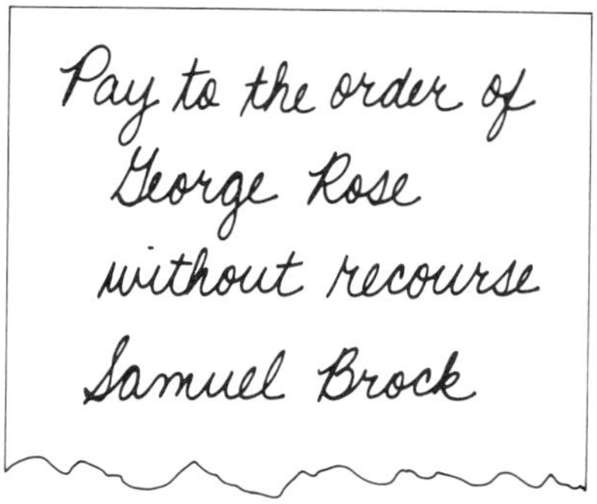   Fig. 22-7. Qualified indorsement

doing so Chappell disclaims liability as a guarantor of payment of the check. The qualified indorsement serves to move title from the drawer of the check through the attorney to the client.

Accommodation Party An *accommodation party* is one who signs an instrument in any capacity for the purpose of lending his or her name to another party to the instrument. An accommodation party is not liable to the party accommodated, but is liable to all subsequent holders of the instrument as a regular indorser.

Warranties of Indorsers

In making an indorsement, an indorser (with the exception of a qualified indorser) agrees to pay any subsequent holder the face amount of the instrument. To enforce this liability, the holder must present the instrument to the primary party when it is due. If payment is refused, the holder must give the indorser(s) notice of the default. The notice may be given orally or in writing before midnight of the third full business day after the day of the default.

By indorsement, the indorser of a negotiable instrument warrants to an indorsee the following:

☐ *The instrument, whether a check, note, or draft, is genuine and in every respect what it is represented to be.* The indorser warrants that there has been no forgery, alteration, or other irregularity. If the instrument is not as it is warranted to be, the indorser can be held responsible and can be sued by the subsequent holder for breach of warranty.

☐ *All prior parties had capacity to contract.* If the maker or a prior indorser of an instrument refuses to pay because he or she is a minor, a lunatic, or otherwise incompetent, the holder can collect from any indorser whose name follows that of the incompetent party. For instance, should the maker of a note avoid liability because of drunkenness at the time the note was signed, the indorser would have to reimburse the holder.

☐ *The indorser has good title to the instrument.* With this warranty, the new holder has assurance that the person indorsing the instrument did not find it, steal it, or come into possession of it in any unlawful manner.

State National Bank accepted a check from Lawless for deposit to her account. The check contained a blank indorsement by Anthony Fiore. The bank later discovered that Lawless had found the check in a supermarket. A stop payment order had been issued by the real owner, Anthony Fiore. Lawless, by her indorsement, had warranted that she was the true owner of the check. She would be held liable on this warranty for any loss suffered by the bank or by any previous indorser.

☐ *The instrument is a valid and existing obligation at the time it is indorsed.* This warranty protects the holder against illegal contracts, Sunday contracts, and those entered into by a mistake concerning the existence of the subject matter of the contract. The holder can also recover against the indorser when the instrument is usurious or when it is given in payment of a gambling debt.

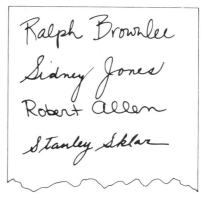

Fig. 22-8. Indorsers are liable to subsequent holders of the instrument

An exception to these warranties is provided the indorser who has used the qualified indorsement, having written the words *Without recourse* immediately before the signature. Qualified indorsers are not obligated to make good to a holder if the instrument is not paid at its source due to insufficient funds or refusal to pay. Other warranties, however, due any payor, acceptor, or indorser of an instrument (as listed on page 295) remain in effect.

Holder's Obligations to Indorsers

The holder of an instrument may hold the regular unqualified indorsers liable for payment only if:

- The instrument has been duly presented to the maker or acceptor for payment, or the instrument, if payable after sight, has been duly presented to the drawee for acceptance.
- The indorser is given notice of the fact that the instrument was dishonored.
- The dishonored instrument, if it is a foreign bill, has been duly protested.

> The Security Loan Company received a check indorsed and delivered to it by Stanley Sklar in payment of a loan. When presented for payment at the maker's bank, the check was returned for want of sufficient funds. Security Loan would have the right to demand payment from any or all of the indorsers shown on the back of the check (see Fig. 22-8), starting with Stanley Sklar. To be assured of maximum safety, the holder should demand payment from the indorsers in reverse of the order in which their names appear—Sklar, Allen, Jones, and Brownlee—until payment is received from one of them.

It would be Security Loan Company's obligation to satisfy the provisions listed above if its demand for payment against any one of the indorsers were to be successful.

Questions for Review and Discussion

1. Name the essential qualities that an instrument must include to be negotiable.

2. Explain the manner in which the maker or drawer of a negotiable instrument may sign it.

3. Why is it necessary that the holder of an instrument be able to determine from its face the amount to be received, even though it may be payable with stated interest, with discounts, or with costs of collection?

4. Identify two ways an instrument may be negotiated so that the transferee becomes a holder.

5. What must a holder of a dishonored negotiable instrument do to hold prior indorsers liable on the instrument?

6. What indorsement is used by a holder who wishes to be relieved of responsibility on a negotiable instrument in the event it is not paid when due because of insufficient funds? Explain.

7. May an instrument be transferred to another person after it has been negotiated with a restrictive indorsement? Explain.

8. What effect does a conditional indorsement have on the rights of the transferee of the instrument?

9. Is a blank indorsement unsafe when the instrument is being carried in the holder's pocket or sent by mail? Explain.

10. What does the indorser of a negotiable instrument warrant to an indorsee?

Analyzing Cases

1. Burton borrowed $300 from Roberts and in return signed a promissory note payable in one year with interest at 7.5 percent. Roberts later negotiated the note to Green, who was a friend of Burton. When the note became due, Green agreed to extend the time of the note for an additional three months, on the promise from Burton that the 7.5 percent interest would be paid during the extended period of time. At the end of the three months, Burton dishonored the note, claiming insufficient funds. Green proceeded to sue Roberts, the indorser. Is Roberts liable on the note? Explain. • See also *National Bank of Commerce* v. *Kenney,* 83 S.W. 368.

2. Jewell, Jennings, and Jaworoski were indorsers on a draft that had been accepted by Schwartz. When the draft was presented for payment, Schwartz claimed insolvency and refused to pay it. The holder took no action for three weeks, hoping that Schwartz's financial condition would improve. When payment was not forthcoming, the holder finally decided to notify Jewell, Jennings, and Jaworoski that they were being held responsible on the dishonored draft. They refused to pay, claiming the presentment and notice of dishonor were unnecessarily delayed beyond the time such presentment and notice are due. Were they liable on the draft? Explain. • See also *Myers* v. *Bibee Grocery Co.,* 148 Va. 282.

3. Romano indorsed a $950 monthly salary check in blank and put it in his coat pocket. Later, upon arrival at a bank, he discovered the check had been lost. He immediately asked his employer to initiate a stop payment order on it, but it was too late. The check had been found and transferred by the finder, for value, to an innocent rare-coin dealer, who had cashed it. The bank and Romano's employer brought suit against the coin dealer, demanding that the $950 be returned. In whose favor would judgment be given? Explain. • See also *Angus* v. *Douns,* 147 Pac. 630.

4. Vanech, a landscape contractor, received a $230 check for work done and indorsed it in blank, using a typewriter. When he presented it at his bank, the teller refused to cash it because the indorsement was not in his handwriting. Was the teller correct in refusing payment? Why? • See also *Farnsworth* v. *Burdick,* 147 Pac. 863.

5. Chaffee, the payee of a promissory note signed by VanNess, payable in sixty days, indorsed and delivered it to Bedwell for value. Before presenting the note to VanNess for payment, Bedwell struck out Chaffee's indorsement. When VanNess subsequently defaulted on the note, Bedwell sued Chaffee for the value of the note. For whom would judgment be given? Explain. • See also U.N.I.L., Art. III., Sec. 48.

6. Withrow agreed to indorse a personal check for a visiting business associate when he learned that the local bank with whom he had an account would not cash it because of the person's out-of-state address and credit references. The check was returned for lack of sufficient funds, and the bank charged Withrow's account for the amount. Withrow claimed that he was not liable on the check because he had received no consideration for his indorsement. For whom would the court find? Explain. • See also *Bank of California* v. *Starrett,* 9 A.L.R. 177.

Legal Reasoning and Business Judgment

Analyze the legal aspects of these business problems. Suggest possible solutions.

1. Aaron, a salesperson for Rettinger Importing, Inc., sold a shipment of rainsuits, parkas, and ponchos to a dealer whose credit rating was poor. The dealer gave Aaron a note, payable in sixty days. The credit manager for Rettinger returned the note to Aaron with instructions to get something further in the way of an assurance of payment on the note at maturity before authorizing and making shipment of the order. What assurance might Aaron request of the dealer?

2. Amalgamated Container, Inc., held a customer's note due October 4, 19—. The note was presented for payment on the due date, but payment was refused by the maker. On the reverse side of the note were the names of three indorsers. What action should Amalgamated Container take to recover the face value of the note? Explain.

3. Fernandes received a number of checks on Friday afternoon, too late to be delivered to the bank for deposit. It was the practice to mail such deposits rather than hold them until the following Monday. What indorsement should Fernandes use in negotiating these checks? For what reason?

Chapter 23
Holders, Defenses, and Discharge

A *holder* of commercial paper is a person in possession of an instrument drawn, issued, or indorsed to order, to bearer, or in blank. Value need not have been given for the instrument by a holder; he or she may transfer it, negotiate it, or enforce payment. Although a holder has the right to demand payment or to sue on an instrument, collection depends upon whether the person sued is liable and whether any defense may be stated against the holder.

> ►► United Wrecking indorsed a $1,000 note it held of Polymer Industries to Heires, its lawyer, for services to be rendered. Heires becomes a holder (assignee) of the note on the basis of the promise of services not yet performed. Heires is subject to all defenses to which an assignee would be subject. The defenses available to an assignee are the same that would be available to the original party in an action on a simple contract: lack of consideration, lack of mutual assent, fraud, alteration, and so forth. Thus, if Polymer had illegally altered the note that it gave to United Wrecking, it would be liable on a simple contract. Heires, as a holder or assignee, could therefore sue Polymer, just as United Wrecking could have were it still in possession of the note.

HOLDER IN DUE COURSE

A *holder in due course* is a person in possession of a bearer instrument or in possession of an order instrument that is made or issued to the holder or properly indorsed. The instrument must have been taken for value, in good faith, and without notice that it is overdue or has been dishonored. A holder in due course is entitled to all the rights and benefits under the instrument. He or she is also almost wholly free from the risk that the parties liable on the instrument may have a defense to an action for collection of the money. That is to say, a holder in due course has rights and title that are superior to those of a mere assignee or ordinary holder.

Value

A person must pay value for an instrument in order to qualify as a holder in due course. Thus, if an instrument is transferred to a person by legal process, through inheritance, or as a gift, that person would not qualify as a holder in due course.

▶ Daggett executed a note payable to the order of Cavanaugh in payment for goods to be delivered later. Cavanaugh failed to make delivery, but in the meantime he gave the note to his daughter. When the note became due, Daggett refused to pay, asserting the defense of failure of consideration. Since Cavanaugh's daughter had not given value for the note, she was not a holder in due course, so the defense would be allowed against her.

A holder who purchases an instrument for less than its *face value* can be a holder in due course only to the extent of the interest purchased.

▶ Cruz makes a $1,500 note payable to the order of Jessup. Jessup borrows $1,000 from Teal, who requests Cruz's note to secure repayment of the loan. Since Teal has advanced $1,000, she has given value to this extent and qualifies as a holder in due course to this extent. If Jessup cannot repay the loan, Teal can foreclose on the note by collecting it from Cruz. Should Cruz have a personal defense against Jessup, Teal is free and clear of the defense to the extent of $1,000. The defense may be asserted with respect to the $500 balance.

Good Faith

Good faith requires that the taker of a commercial instrument acted honestly in its acquisition. If the taker is negligent in not discovering that something was wrong with the paper, this does not establish lack of good faith. It is of no consequence whether the transferor of an instrument acts in good faith.

▶ Cesareo convinced Loyd that she could get him a new Volkswagen Rabbit for $3,500 from a local dealer. Loyd executed a promissory note for the amount, due in thirty days, payable to the order of the Volkswagen dealer. He delivered the note to Cesareo, who then delivered it to the Volkswagen dealer in payment of her own indebtedness. The dealer had no knowledge of Cesareo's fraudulent representation to Loyd and acted in good faith in acquiring the note. The dealer would satisfy the requirements of a holder in due course and be entitled to payment. Loyd's only recourse would be against Cesareo on the ground of being a bad-faith holder.

Without Notice or Dishonor

A taker must *not* have notice of any claim or defense to an instrument or have notice that an instrument is overdue or has been dishonored. The purchaser has notice of a claim or defense if the instrument bears visible evidence of forgery or alteration or is so incomplete or irregular as to make its legal acceptance doubtful. Notice of a claim or defense is also considered given if the purchaser notices that the obligation of any party is voidable in whole or in part. Thus, the maker of a note has the right to avoid an obligation on the instrument in the event of a fraud carried out by the payee.

▶ Hinkson gave Carlo $175 for a note signed by Lambert. A casual inspection of the note showed that the amount had been erased and altered. Hinkson would *not* be a holder in due course. It would be useless for her to argue that she did not see the obvious erasure and alteration.

A purchaser has notice of a claim against an instrument when someone such as an agent or trustee has negotiated the instrument in payment of or as security for a personal debt, personal benefit, or otherwise, in breach of duty.

The purchaser has notice that an instrument is overdue when there is reason to know that (1) any part of the principal amount is overdue, (2) an acceleration of the instrument has been made, or (3) an unreasonable length of time elapsed after demand for the payment had been made or after the instrument was issued. What is an "unreasonable time" is determined by a consideration of the nature of the instrument, the usage of the trade or business, and the circumstances and facts involved in each case. A reasonable time to negotiate a check drawn and payable within the states and territories of the United States is presumed to be thirty days.

▶▶ Travers received a check from Thawley, placed it in a desk drawer, and redis-
covered it three months later. Collins, a local merchant, offered to cash the check
for Travers for value. Collins is *on notice* that the check is overdue for an unreasonable time, and so he is not a holder in due course.

An instrument that is payable in installments may be transferred when one or more of the installments are past due. The purchaser with knowledge of an overdue installment on principal has notice that the instrument is overdue and therefore cannot be a holder in due course. Past-due interest, however, does not give notice of any defect in the instrument.

Shelter Provision

A holder who receives title to an instrument through one who is a holder in due course receives all the rights of the former party. This is called a *shelter provision*. It is designed to permit the holder in due course, who is free from personal defenses, to transfer all rights in the paper. However, should the transferee be party to a fraud or other illegal act which affects the instrument, he or she would not have the rights of a holder in due course.

▶▶ Riverbank Motors defrauded Ashwell in the sale of a used Toyota for which
Ashwell gave a note for $1,400. The note was transferred to Cerreta for value.
Cerreta had no knowledge of the fraudulent sale to Ashwell and became a holder
in due course. The note was later purchased by Sayer, a Riverbank Motors
salesperson who was involved in the fraudulent sale to Ashwell. Sayer would not
have the rights of a holder in due course, since he was party to fraud and thus not
allowed to improve his status by purchasing the note from a later holder in due
course.

The shelter provision is subject to the following limitation. A person who formerly held the paper cannot improve his or her position by later reacquiring it from a holder in due course. In taking title to an instrument a second time, the holder assumes the same legal position held previously. Thus, if a holder originally was a holder in due course and later received back the instrument from one who was not, he or she would nevertheless become a holder in due course again. A *reacquirer* may reissue or further negotiate the instrument but is not entitled to enforce payment against intervening persons to whom he or she was liable.

Neither may a person make clean a fraudulent instrument by passing it into the hands of a holder in due course and then repurchasing it.

> Greene fraudulently induces Stamm to execute a note payable to the order of Greene. Greene indorses it in blank and delivers it to Roman, who has notice of the fraud but did not participate in it. Roman indorses it to Griswold, who takes it in good faith and otherwise satisfies the requirements of a holder in due course. Greene repurchases the note from Griswold, but he remains subject to Stamm's defense of fraud and does not acquire Griswold's rights as a holder in due course.

Ineffective Notice of Defense or Claim

Knowledge of some facts does not of itself give the purchaser notice of a defense or claim. For example, the fact that an instrument is postdated or antedated does not prevent someone from being a holder in due course. Being aware that an instrument was issued or negotiated in return for an executory promise or that the instrument was accompanied by a separate agreement does not constitute having notice of a defense or claim; neither does completing an incomplete instrument constitute having such notice, unless the purchaser has notice of any improper completion. The filing or recording of a document does not of itself constitute notice to a person who would otherwise be a holder in due course. Obviously, instruments would not pass as freely as money if transferees were required to check public records to determine whether a defense existed. To be effective, notice must be received at such time and in such manner as to give a reasonable opportunity to act on it.

DEFENSES

A holder in due course takes an instrument free from all claims to it on the part of any person and free from almost all defenses of any party with whom the holder has not dealt. There are, however, a limited number of defenses that are available against everyone, including holders in due course, that will render an instrument null and void. These are known as *real defenses*. In contrast, defenses which may be cut off by a holder in due course are known as *personal defenses*.

Real Defenses

The defenses which are available against a holder in due course are those listed in Section 3-305(2) of the UCC. These are as follows.

Infancy or Mental Incompetence   A minor or anyone who has been found insane by a court does not have legal capacity to sign and become liable on a commercial instrument. All such instruments are invalid from their beginning and will not be collectible by anyone.

Illegality, Duress, or Other Incapacity   An instrument which is associated with an illegal act—such as gambling or smuggling—or which was obtained from someone under the influence of alcohol, drugs, or barbiturates—would be void from its beginning and would not be valid or collectible by anyone. This would be true even though the holder was unaware of the above acts or conditions.

> Crockett met with several people for the purpose of playing craps, a gambling game. After losing more money than he had in his wallet, Crockett borrowed $100, putting up a promissory note made out to bearer. The note was later negotiated to the holder's creditor, who had no knowledge of how it was obtained. Although a holder in due course, the holder of the note would not have any rights if the gambling occurred in a state that had a statute expressly declaring that commercial instruments given for gambling debts and the like were void.

Mere lack of consideration on a commercial paper given for gambling debts, or on an instrument carrying usurious interest charges, constitutes a personal rather than a real defense if state statute does not expressly declare such instruments to be void.

Misrepresentation in Making an Instrument Any action or misrepresentation that prompts a party to sign a commercial instrument without knowledge or reasonable opportunity to obtain required knowledge or essential terms will render the instrument void and uncollectible.

> Hartsook was asked to sign what his brother explained was a letter being sent to a close friend. Hartsook, who was extremely ill and had poor eyesight, signed the paper as instructed without reading it. The paper was actually a promissory note payable to the order of Hartsook's brother. Reasonable proof that the real nature of the paper signed was misrepresented and that Hartsook was not physically capable of reading it would invalidate the note.

Discharge in Insolvency Proceedings Anyone ruled a bankrupt is relieved of all obligations on a commercial instrument. The holder will receive equal treatment with other creditors when the assets of the bankrupt are collected and divided according to the bankruptcy law. An exception would be in those cases where the note is secured by a recorded mortgage on personal property (i.e., chattel mortgage). By taking physical possession of the collateral, by filing a financial statement, or by attachment, the secured party will continue to have a perfected security interest whenever the debtor is involved in insolvency proceedings.

Unauthorized Signatures Any unauthorized signature of another's name on a commercial instrument is totally inoperative unless approved by the person whose name is signed. An unauthorized signature, however, would operate as the signature of the unauthorized signer in favor of any person who in good faith pays the instrument or takes value for it.

> Ochoe paid value for a promissory note held by Baum, who was a holder in due course. Originally the instrument was drawn by Becwar, who forged the name of Fulmer to the note. When the note is presented for payment, Fulmer may refuse

to honor it, inasmuch as the forgery is an unauthorized signature and a real defense against all holders. Becwar would be liable in favor of any person who paid for the note or took value for it.

Material Alteration   Any alteration of an instrument is material if it changes the contract of any party thereto in any respect. Included are changes in the number or relations of the concerned parties, completion of an incomplete instrument, and the adding to or removal of any part of the writing as signed. Fraudulent and material alteration by the holder discharges any party whose contract is changed thereby, other than a subsequent holder in due course. No other alteration discharges any party, and the instrument may be enforced according to its original draft.

 McWalters wrote out a check for $175 and presented it to Eastman in payment of a used Canon AE-1 camera. Eastman altered the check to read $375, then presented it for payment at McWalters's bank. The bank honored the altered check. McWalters may demand that the bank reimburse his account for $200, the difference between the original and the altered amount.

Any person who negligently contributes to a material alteration of an instrument or an unauthorized signature may not exercise the defense of alteration of lack of authority against a holder in due course, a drawee, or other payor who pays the instrument in good faith. For example, using a pencil to write a check or not being careful to keep the figures compact and clear gives a dishonest holder an opportunity to alter the amount. The careless writer would be without defense.

Personal Defenses

Unless he or she is a holder in due course, any person takes a commercial instrument subject to numerous personal defenses. In general, these are defenses to liability on an instrument similar to those available in the case of a simple contract. They include (1) all valid claims to an instrument; (2) all defenses which would be available in any action on a simple contract; (3) defenses that the holder (or the person through whom the holder holds the instrument) acquired it by theft; and (4) defenses of want or failure of consideration, nonperformance, or nondelivery. The most common personal defenses are illustrated in the following paragraphs.

Lack of Consideration   Consideration makes a promise binding in a commercial instrument. Unlike the situation in contract law, however, consideration is not required with the issuance or transfer of a negotiable instrument when it is in payment of or as security for an existing debt. *Consideration* determines whether a binding obligation has been made; it shows what the maker has received for his or her obligation. It must be distinguished from *value*, which is used to determine whether a holder has given something in payment for an instrument in acquiring the status of a holder in due course.

▶ Gruel executes a note in favor of Searle in return for a shipment of plumbing supplies which is never delivered. Searle indorses the note to Chard in payment of an obligation. As against Searle, Gruel has a defense of lack of consideration. Chard has furnished value and can enforce the note against Gruel in spite of his defense.

Lack of Delivery   Every commercial instrument may be revoked by its maker or drawer until it has been delivered to the payee. *Delivery* means the transfer of possession from one person to another. If the transfer of possession is not intended to give the transferee rights, delivery is made in a physical sense but the instrument has not been "issued." Thus, in the event a payee forcibly, unlawfully, or conditionally takes an instrument from a drawer, the drawer has the defense of conditional delivery. The payee therefore may be denied the right to collect on the instrument. If the payee negotiates the instrument to a holder in due course, however, this defense is cut off.

▶ Castro drew a check in favor of Rush and delivered it with the express understanding that it was to be negotiated only on condition that Rush first paint her car. Rush negotiated the check to Bee-Line Auto Center in violation of this understanding. Only in the event that Bee-Line is not a holder in due course can Castro assert against Bee-Line a defense of conditional delivery and Rush's failure to perform.

Payment   When a commercial instrument is paid, its indebtedness is discharged. Payment of an instrument before maturity discharges the maker from further liability to immediate parties. The maker is not relieved, however, should the instrument come into the possession of a holder in due course. The maker or acceptor of an instrument should demand the return of the instrument when it has been paid. If the instrument is payable on demand, it should be marked *Paid*. Partial payments should be recorded on a note. Unless such precautions are taken, a defense of payment would not prevail against any subsequent holder in due course.

▶ Tropsa executed a promissory note on February 1 for $2,500 due October 1, with interest at 9 percent from date, payable to Ingersoll. On May 1, Tropsa paid $500 and obtained a receipt. On August 5, Ingersoll indorsed the note to Byram and received $2,300 in value. Byram, in taking the note in good faith, became a holder in due course and could recover $2,500 from Tropsa.

Counterclaim, or Setoff   The party obligated on an instrument may counterclaim, or setoff, against an immediate party's demand for payment any amounts owed to the obligated from the payee. A *counterclaim*, or *setoff*, is a cross-complaint by an obligated party usually seeking a reduction in the amount owed another party on a note.

▶ Guardian Insurance Company loaned Sclafani $800 on his personal note. Before the note matured, Sclafani performed carpentry work for Guardian Insurance but was not paid upon completion of the job. When Sclafani's note became due, he made payment of $200, the difference between the amount of the note and the amount owed by Guardian Insurance for the carpentry work. Sclafani is within his rights as an immediate party in making this counterclaim against the amount due and payable on the note.

Consumer Credit Protection

New Federal Trade Commission rules substantially limit the effects of the so-called "holder-in-due-course doctrine." This doctrine placed the person to whom an installment contract was assigned in a better position than the original seller. Under the doctrine, third parties (such as banks and finance companies) who purchased installment notes were formerly not obligated in any way to customers who had been sold shoddy merchandise. Thus, the holder-in-due-course doctrine allowed sellers a simple means to avoid accountability to consumers by separating a buyer's duty to pay for goods and services from the seller's comparable duty to perform as promised. This separation, forbidden under the new rules, was accomplished in three ways.

☐ The insertion of a promissory note in the installment contract, thereby making it an unqualified promise to pay the amount specified.
☐ The inclusion in the contract of a standard clause called "waiver of defenses," by which the buyer agreed to pay a credit company or other third party no matter what dispute might arise with the seller.
☐ The arrangement of loans by the seller for the buyer—or "vendor-related loans"—with the lender entitled to payment without regard to the seller's conduct or the seller's continuing relationship with the loan.

Installment Contract Protection   The new Federal Trade Commission rule states in effect that anyone who purchases an installment contract from a seller is equally responsible with the seller for any deception or misconduct. Thus, credit contracts used by sellers and transferred to holders in due course will retain their character as sales agreements. In addition, the rule expressly preserves the buyer's option of asserting legitimate claims against the seller by making it unlawful to include a waiver-of-defense clause. Finally, sellers may not accept the proceeds from a buyer's loan directly from a lender unless the contract authorizes the consumer to assert claims and defenses against the lender too.

⊳ Gruner bought a washing machine under an installment sales contract and found that it broke down repeatedly during the first two months. When the store that sold it refused to exchange it, Gruner refused to continue paying for it. Then the real troubles began. The store had already sold the sales contract to a financial institution which disclaimed any responsibility for the operation of the washing machine. It threatened to sue Gruner for nonpayment, with further threats of repossession and garnishment of salary. Previously, under the holder-in-due-course doctrine—which originated over two hundred years ago to serve the English banking system—Gruner had little practical alternative but to pay. Under the new FTC rule, however, such actions by sellers involving breach of contract and fraud are prohibited. Gruner may therefore successfully avoid payment to the financial institution in question.

Credit Card Transactions   The federal Fair Credit Billing Act further limits the holder-in-due-course doctrine by voiding waiver-of-defense clauses in certain credit card transactions. Although forty states already have laws containing restrictions on the doctrine, none is so far-reaching as the federal law.

Under the Fair Credit Billing Act, a credit card issuer is treated as a holder in due course. The card issuer is made responsible for settling disputes over which the cardholder and the merchant cannot agree. The cardholder or customer may cease further payment to the issuer for a specific transaction if his or her complaints with the merchant are not satisfied by the issuer. However, before this law can apply the following conditions must be met:

☐ The cardholder must make a good-faith effort to resolve the disagreement with the merchant honoring the card.
☐ The amount of the initial transaction must exceed $50.
☐ With certain exceptions, the place where the initial transaction in dispute was made must be in the same state as the address the cardholder has listed with the card issuer, or within a hundred miles of that address. Credit cards issued by nationwide chain operations such as Sears Roebuck or J. C. Penney are included in this condition regardless of the location of their stores or the place of residence of the cardholder.

A creditor may not penalize a credit card holder by impairing his or her credit rating because the customer asserts claims or rights under the act. If the merchant or the credit card issuer feels that the customer's complaints are not justified, he or she may take to court any customer who refuses to pay the outstanding debt.

 Van Voorhies purchased a record player with a credit card. A few weeks after purchase, the unit stopped working, and Van Voorhies returned it to the merchant. Should the merchant refuse to settle the issue, Van Voorhies has the right to advise the credit card issuer that the conditions of the Fair Credit Billing Act have been complied with and further payments on the transaction are ceasing. It would then be left to the credit card issuer and the merchant to resolve the matter by either writing off the transaction or taking the dispute to court.

PRESENTMENT

Presentment is a demand for acceptance or payment made upon the maker, acceptor, drawee, or other payor by or on behalf of the holder. It is needed to place liability on the drawer and indorsers of a negotiable instrument.

Presentment for Acceptance

A draft payable after date requires acceptance before anyone is absolutely liable. The drawee shows willingness to obey the order of the drawer and pay the time draft according to its terms and instructions by writing "Accepted" or "Presented" across the face of the draft. After the date and signature are added, the drawee becomes absolutely liable on the draft, and the drawer's liability becomes that of an indorser. The presentation of the draft for acceptance, however, does not discharge the drawer from liability. If the draft is refused, it is dishonored, and the drawee can demand payment from both drawer and indorsers.

Presentment for acceptance must be made (1) where the draft states that it must be presented for acceptance, (2) where the draft is payable elsewhere than at the residence or place of business of the drawee, and (3) where the date of payment depends upon presentment, as with a statement like: "Thirty days after sight pay to the order of...."

Presentment for Payment

If the holder fails to make a presentment for payment, this results in the complete discharge of indorsers. Failure to present for payment, however, does not discharge the drawer. An exception would be where there was unreasonable delay in presenting a draft to a bank where funds were available for its payment, and the bank became insolvent in the interim. The loss from such insolvency would fall upon the tardy holder.

Time of Presentment

When the specified date is not a full business day for either the person making the presentment or the party paying or accepting, presentment is due on the next following full business day for both parties. To be sufficient, presentment must be made at a reasonable hour. If presentment is made at a bank, it must take place during the banking day.

Unless expressed differently in the instrument, the time for any presentment is determined as follows:

☐ Where payable on or at a fixed period after a stated date, presentment for acceptance must be made on or before the date it is payable.
☐ Where payable after sight, it must either be presented for acceptance or negotiated within a reasonable time after date or issue, whichever is later.
☐ Where the date on which it is payable is shown, presentment for payment is due on that date.
☐ Where the instrument is accelerated, presentment for payment is due within a reasonable time after the acceleration.
☐ To fix liability upon all secondary parties, presentment must be made for acceptance or payment within a reasonable time after such secondary party became liable, e.g., after indorsement.

> Batchelder indorsed a note as an accommodation to a friend. When the note became due, the holder did not present it to the maker for payment. Two weeks after the date of maturity, when the note was dishonored, the holder attempted to hold Batchelder liable. Because the holder delayed presentment beyond the time when the note was due without excuse, Batchelder's liability as an indorser would be discharged.

A reasonable time for presentment is determined by the nature of the instrument, any practice of banking or trade, and the facts of the case. In the case of an uncertified check which is drawn and payable within the United States, the drawer would be free of liability thirty days after its date or issue, whichever is later. The indorser's liability ends seven days after his or her indorsement.

 A check was drawn by Sarr on June 15. It was indorsed and delivered to Stabler on June 22 by the payee. Stabler then indorsed it to Roche on June 28. When Roche presented the check to Sarr's bank for payment on July 18, he learned that the bank had been ordered closed by bank examiners. Should the bank be unable to pay off its depositors and other liabilities, Roche would have no recourse against either Sarr, the drawer, or Stabler, an indorser. A reasonable period of time within which to initiate bank collection had been exceeded.

How Presentment Is Made

Presentment may be made at the place of payment specified in the instrument. A draft accepted or a note made payable at a bank in the United States must be presented at that bank. When an instrument is not payable at a collecting bank, that bank can obtain acceptance or payment of the instrument by sending a written notice, however. If the place of acceptance is not specified in the instrument, presentment can be made at the place of business or residence of the acceptor or payor. If neither the acceptor or payor nor anyone authorized to act in their behalf is available, presentment is excused. In addition to face-to-face presentment, the mail or a bank clearinghouse may be used. The time of presentment by mail is determined by the time of receipt of the mail.

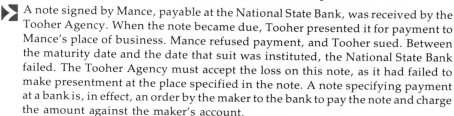 A note signed by Mance, payable at the National State Bank, was received by the Tooher Agency. When the note became due, Tooher presented it for payment to Mance's place of business. Mance refused payment, and Tooher sued. Between the maturity date and the date that suit was instituted, the National State Bank failed. The Tooher Agency must accept the loss on this note, as it had failed to make presentment at the place specified in the note. A note specifying payment at a bank is, in effect, an order by the maker to the bank to pay the note and charge the amount against the maker's account.

The party to whom presentment is made may without dishonor require display of the instrument and reasonable identification and evidence of authority of the person making the presentment. The payor may require that the instrument be produced at a specified place. A signed receipt on the instrument for partial payment and its surrender upon full payment may also be required.

Dishonor

An instrument is *dishonored* when presentment is duly made and acceptance or payment is refused or cannot be obtained within the prescribed time. Dishonor also occurs when presentment is excused and the instrument is past due and unpaid. The presenting party has recourse against indorsers or other secondary parties after notice of dishonor has been given.

A note was presented to Czarnecki for payment on the date specified. Czarnecki refused to honor it, claiming the note was a forgery. The holder would have to proceed against the indorsers on their implied warranties in order to obtain payment. The note was dishonored when Czarnecki refused to pay it.

Notice of dishonor may be given, by or on behalf of the holder, to any person who may be liable. It may also be given by any party who has received notice or by any other party who can be compelled to pay the instrument. Also, an agent or bank in whose hands the instrument is dishonored may give notice to the principal or customer or to another agent or bank from which the instrument was received. Necessary notice must be given by a bank before its *midnight deadline* and by any other person before midnight of the third business day after dishonor or receipt of notice of dishonor. These time provisions are viewed as adequate for making decisions and for sending notice.

Notice may be given in any reasonable manner that conveys the information to the liable parties. It may be given orally or in writing. Written notice is effective when properly *sent*, even though it is not received. In the event the party to be given notice is involved in insolvency proceedings, notice may be given either to the party or to the court-appointed representative of the estate. The banking practice of returning an instrument bearing a stamp to the effect that acceptance or payment has been refused is sufficient notice of dishonor.

Proper notice operates for the benefit of all parties who have rights on an instrument against the party notified.

 Karl, Kalish, Janik, and Kunes are indorsers of a dishonored note in that order. The holder gave notice only to Karl and Janik. Janik is not required to give additional notice to Karl. Should Janik be compelled to pay, he would have recourse against Karl. Both Kalish and Kunes are discharged if they are not notified by the holder or by one of the indorsers.

Delay in giving notice of dishonor or in making presentment is excused when the holder has acted carefully and the delay is due to circumstances beyond his or her control. The conditions of giving notice or making presentment must be complied with as soon as the cause of the delay ceases.

Protest A *protest* is a certificate of dishonor which states that a draft was presented for acceptance or payment and was dishonored. It also states the reasons given for refusal to accept or pay. It is *required* for drafts drawn or payable outside the United States and *optional* in all other cases with the holder. A protest is made under the hand and seal of a United States consul or vice consul, or of a notary public or other person authorized to certify dishonor by the law where dishonor occurs.

Protest Waiver An indorser who has written *Demand and notice waived* or *Protest waived* above his or her indorsement or across the face of the instrument is liable for payment without subsequent presentment or notice of dishonor. Prior indorsers are excused from their liability to such an indorser.

If a waiver of notice or protest is stated on the face of the instrument, it is binding upon all parties; when written above the signature of an indorser, it binds only the indorser.

DISCHARGE OF PARTIES

A holder in due course no longer has liability to the payor or acceptor once an instrument has been paid or accepted. Thus, the holder in due course is protected from any further liability and is entitled to retain the payment or to enforce the liability of the acceptor.

> Melsopp, a holder in due course, received payment through a bank before it discovered that the check in question was forged. Melsopp may keep the payment, since the bank cannot recover a payment made to a holder in due course.

In addition, no discharge of any party is effective against a subsequent holder in due course unless notice of it is received at the time the instrument is taken.

Any party may be discharged from liability on an instrument by any one of the following methods.

Payment or Satisfaction

The most frequent method of obtaining a discharge from liability is for the primary party to pay the amount of the instrument. This can be accomplished even though the payor knows that some third party has a claim on the instrument.

Tender of Payment

If the maker or acceptor is ready and able to pay at the place(s) specified in the instrument when it is due, an offer to pay has been made. This rule of tender gives a limited discharge to the obligor on an instrument, and he or she is discharged to the extent of subsequent liability for interest, costs, and legal fees. In this manner, makers and acceptors of notes and drafts payable at a bank have made a tender of payment if they maintain an adequate balance in the bank as of the due date of the instrument.

Cancellation and Renunciation

The holder of an instrument may discharge any party on the face of the instrument or an indorser even without consideration. This can be accomplished intentionally by striking out the party's signature. Renunciation of the holder's rights can also be achieved by a writing signed and delivered or by surrender of the instrument to the party being discharged.

Impairment of Recourse or Collateral

A party to an instrument is discharged to the extent the holder releases or agrees not to sue any person against whom the party has recourse. A similar discharge takes place when the holder agrees to suspend his or her rights in any collateral or impairs any collateral. *Impairment of recourse* takes place when the holder strikes out the name of one of the indorsers on an instrument. Such an act discharges not only that indorser, but also all parties who have a right to recourse against the discharged indorser.

Reacquisition of the Instrument

Where an instrument is returned to or reacquired by a prior party, any indorsement which is not necessary to the holder's title may be canceled. In any subsequent reissue or further negotiation of the instrument, any intervening party is discharged as against the reacquiring party.

Fraudulent and Material Alteration

Except for a subsequent holder in due course, any fraudulent and material alteration by the holder discharges any person whose contract is thereby changed.

Certification of a Check

Certification of a check is acceptance. Where a holder procures certification, the drawer and all prior indorsers are discharged.

Acceptance Varying Draft

Where the drawee's acceptance of tender in any manner varies the draft as presented, the holder may refuse the acceptance and treat the draft as dishonored. In such a case, the drawee is entitled to have his or her acceptance canceled. Where the holder assents to an acceptance varying the terms of the draft, each drawer and indorser who does not agree to the assent is discharged.

Unexcused Delay

Any indorser is discharged from an instrument when any necessary presentment or notice of dishonor is delayed beyond the time when it is due without excuse. Similarly, where without excuse a necessary protest is delayed beyond the time when it is due, any drawer or indorser is discharged.

Questions for Review and Discussion

1. What are the requisites that constitute a holder in due course?

2. What is the purpose of the shelter provision, and to what limitation is it subject?

3. (*a*) Identify the real defenses that are available against everyone, including a holder in due course, which may render an instrument null and void. (*b*) What are the personal defenses available to the maker or acceptor of a negotiable instrument?

4. What effect do new Federal Trade Commission rules have on the holder-in-due-course doctrine—that is, the doctrine placing the person to whom a negotiable instrument is assigned in a better position than the original seller?

5. To what extent does the Fair Credit Billing Act limit the effects of the holder-in-due-course doctrine?

6. Under what circumstances is presentment of an instrument for acceptance required?

7. Indicate the time for presentment of an instrument (*a*) payable at or a fixed period after a stated date, (*b*) payable after sight, (*c*) payable on a given date, (*d*) that is accelerated, and (*e*) to fix liability upon all secondary parties.

8. When is an instrument dishonored, and what is meant by prompt and proper notice of dishonor?

9. Explain the method of giving notice of dishonor of an instrument drawn or payable outside the United States. How is it accomplished?

10. Under what circumstances will the holder of an instrument be excused from giving notice of dishonor to prior indorsers or to a drawer?

Analyzing Cases

1. E&B Construction Corporation engaged in high-pressure door-to-door solicitation to secure the signatures of inner-city homeowners on home remodeling contracts. The price to the homeowners for the improvements ranged from two to three times the actual cost of remodeling work. Homeowners were under the false impression, deliberately created by E&B Construction sales agents, that the company's activities were government-sponsored. E&B Construction arranged loans to refinance the homeowners' prior mortgage payments plus the monthly charges due for the home improvement services with Home Financing Company. The loans were secured by liens on the homes. Biller, a homeowner, paid heavy monthly installments for several months and then brought an action in the U.S. District Court for rescission of the contract and restitution of money paid. Biller claimed fraud, unconscionability, usury, and illegal moneylending against Home Financing Company. The defendant denied all allegations and asserted its status as holder in due course. For whom should judgment be made?• See also *Slaughter et al.* v. *Jefferson Federal Savings and Loan Association,* 42 U.S.L.W. 2115.

2. Insell held a note, due on July 3, signed by Ulrich. Both lived in the same city. July 3 fell on a Sunday, and Insell did not present the instrument for payment on that day or the following day. When Insell presented the note for payment on July 5, Ulrich refused to honor it. Insell called upon Sandor, an indorser, for payment. Sandor claimed that she was discharged from liability on the note because of Insell's failure to present the note on July 3 when it was due. Whom should judgment favor? Why?• See also *Rosenbaum* v. *Hazard,* 82 At. 62.

3. (*a*) Slocum gave her daughter a $1,000 note payable on January 26, when the girl reached majority. On the specified date the daughter presented the note to her mother for payment, but the mother refused to pay it. What rights does the daughter have against the maker? (*b*) Suppose the daughter negotiated the note to Simmons for value. Simmons knew nothing of the circumstances under which the note had been issued. On the due date Simmons presents it to Slocum, who refuses to pay it. Is Slocum obligated to Simmons on the instrument? Explain.• See also *In re Smith's Estate,* 277 N.W. 141, and *Wheeler* v. *Alabama National Bank,* 76 So.2d 679; U.N.I.L. sec. 28.

4. Clemmens presented a note to Tucker for payment on the due date. Tucker had become insolvent and could not honor the note. There were four indorsers on the note, and Clemmens gave notice of dishonor to the indorser immediately ahead of him. That indorser failed to give notice to the other indorsers. If Clemmens fails to collect from the indorser to whom notice was given, may he then proceed against each of the other indorsers for payment? Explain. • See also *Von Blaine* v. *Sanders,* 80 At.2d 52.

5. Adams Interiors held a note signed by Cassano, payable on March 21. On March 28, the firm attempted to present the note for payment; they were unable to locate Cassano, who had moved away without leaving a forwarding address. Adams Interiors then notified Coppola, an accommodation indorser, of the default in an attempt to collect. Coppola claimed that he was relieved from liability owing to the lateness of the presentment of the note. What are the rights of Adams Interiors in this matter? • See also *Dana* v. *Sawyer,* 22 M. 244.

6. Gordon received a note from Leavitt and instructions to have it discounted for her at her bank. Instead, Gordon transferred the note to Thorne, in payment of merchandise purchased. When the note became due and was presented for payment, Leavitt refused to pay it, claiming that Gordon failed to follow her instructions. Thorne sued, claiming that he was a holder in due course and, as such, was entitled to payment. For whom should judgment be given? Why? • See also *Implement Credit Corporation* v. *Elsinger,* 268 Wis. 143, 67 N.W.2d 925.

Legal Reasoning and Business Judgment

Analyze the legal aspects of these business problems. Suggest possible solutions.

1. A note is handed to you by the cashier of your company with instructions that you present it for payment. You find that the note is signed by the American Nail and Wire Company, located in your city. The Allied Trust Company's name is indicated on the note as the place of payment. For the protection of your company from any loss on this note, where should presentment be made? Explain.

2. Your firm issued a note to an electrical contractor for work to be done in the plant. On the due date of the note, the work had not yet been started and there was no indication that it would be started within a reasonable time. The contractor presented the note for payment on the due date, and the cashier refused to honor it. Your firm is threatened with a suit on the note. What are the rights of your firm on this note?

3. A Chicago bank informed your firm that they held a $5,000 note, signed by an officer of your firm and made out to the Chicago Supply Company. The Chicago firm had shipped an order of materials to a company in Wisconsin. The latter concern had indorsed the note to the Chicago firm in payment. Upon examination of the note, your firm's treasurer discovers that it is a forgery. What is the responsibility of your firm to the bank holding the note? What should the bank do in this matter?

An automobile accident often involves loss of property and injuries to the passengers. Hospital care and medical treatment, replacement of the demolished cars, and long and expensive litigation are but a part of the aftermath of the accident. A devastating fire may result in extensive property damage to buildings and their contents, interruption of employment for those who work in the shops and offices destroyed, and the possible termination of a flourishing business through loss of income—or even bankruptcy.

It is impossible to escape the risks of life. The known hazards—such as accidents, fires, illness, and the like—pose a continual threat to our personal and business lives. The principal way of protecting ourselves against losses from such hazards is insurance.

Part 7 Insurance Chapter 24 Principles of Insurance

FUNCTION OF INSURANCE

Insurance is a contract by which an individual or business can pay for protection against the risk of loss arising from one or more specified hazards. The principle underlying insurance is the *distribution of risk*—that small contributions made by a large number of individuals can provide sufficient money to cover the losses suffered by the few as they occur each year. Thus the function of insurance is to distribute each person's risks among all others, who may or may not experience losses.

Because of the element of chance and risk involved, at one time insurance was considered a form of illegal wagering—with the insured party betting that a certain hazard, such as death, would occur, and the party offering the insurance betting it would not. Early in the history of insurance, for example, many churches refused to buy fire insurance mainly because of the strong belief that it was sinful. Insurance today, however, is considered a respectable social benefit to all. People recognize that only through the distribution of risk among the many are the benefits of insurance possible. Furthermore, we realize that the insurance contract is *not* a wagering contract. If the insured person were to suffer *no* loss because of a certain event, a wagering contract would, of course, result, and it would be unenforceable, since such contracts are illegal. But this is not the case with insurance, for the very purpose of insurance is the reimbursement of the holder for *actual loss* suffered due to a hazard such as fire, injury, or death.

PARTIES TO INSURANCE

The parties to an insurance contract are the insurer, or underwriter; the insured; and the beneficiary. The *insurer* accepts the risk of loss in return for a *premium* (the consideration paid for a policy) and agrees to indemnify the insured against the loss specified in the contract. The *insured* is the party (or parties) protected by the insurance contract. The contract of insurance is called the *policy*. The period of time during which the insurer assumes the risk of loss is known as the *life of the policy*. A third party, to whom payment of compensation is sometimes provided by the contract, is called the *beneficiary*.

As with other contracts, an insurance agreement is voidable if made by a party who does not have the capacity to contract. In most instances, insurance contracts are made with persons who have reached their legal age, or majority. It is common practice, however, that adult parents provide insurance coverage for minors and property owned by a minor.

 When Martinelli reached the age of sixteen, she took a driver education course in her high school. After she passed it, she was licensed to drive by her state. She did not own a car, but she was occasionally permitted the use of her parents' car. They paid the premiums for the automobile insurance policy, which provided identical coverage for personal injuries or property damage for any of the three drivers in the Martinelli family. Coverage for both parents alone would have cost $508 per annum. To cover their teenage daughter, even though she was only a part-time driver, the parents had to pay an annual premium of $940.

THE INSURANCE CONTRACT

Contracts of insurance are like other contracts in that they require mutual assent, capable parties, consideration, and valid subject matter. A life insurance contract written for someone whom the beneficiary intends to kill would never be honored if that person were killed. A fire insurance policy written on a building where the owners permitted the illegal manufacture of fireworks would be voided in the event of fire.

Unlike other contracts that you have studied previously, an insurance contract has additional unique characteristics and requirements, which will be discussed below.

Insurable Interest

A person or business applying for insurance must have an insurable interest in the subject matter of the policy, whether it is a person or property. One who might suffer financial loss through another's death is said to have an insurable interest in that life. Thus, a husband and wife have an insurable interest in each other's life. A creditor has an insurable interest in the life of a debtor. Each partner has an insurable interest in the lives of the other partners. Likewise, one who would suffer because of the destruction or loss of property has an insurable interest in that property. A secured creditor, for example, has an insurable interest in the secured property of a debtor. In each of these instances, the party seeking insurance would suffer a loss through death or destruction of the subject matter of the insurance policy. The qualifications of an insurable interest are different, however, in the case of life insurance and property insurance. (See pages 325 and 334.)

Premiums

An insurance contract differs from most other contracts in that it requires the payment of premiums. This, you will recall, is the consideration or payment an insured gives the insurer for its acceptance of risk. The amount of the premium is determined by the nature and character of the risk involved, and by its likelihood of occurring. The premium increases as the chance of loss increases. Thus, an insurance premium on a fireproof building in a city with an efficient fire department will be much lower than the premium on a barn and other buildings located on a farm where fire fighting equipment is not available and water supplies are not readily accessible.

Since the amount of a premium is greatly affected by the likelihood that a particular risk will occur, the role of *actuaries* is very important. They are professional experts who apply mathematical principles to determine as accurately as possible the amount of losses that might occur from a given category of risk. Based on their calculations, premium rates for any given amount of insurance coverage can be determined.

Form of Contract

Insurance contracts in which performance will take less than one year may be oral agreements. When performance takes more than a year, the contract must be in writing to be valid and enforceable.

In most states, contracts of insurance come in a prescribed form. These standard forms are carefully drafted by an insurance commissioner with help from the state's legal advisers (for example, the attorney general or state's attorney). In this way the consumer-buyer is protected from deception or fraud. Approval of a standard contract is a public trust. Most people buying insurance do not read, and probably would not understand, all the provisions of such a complicated written document. As an additional protection to consumers, some states now require that, to the greatest extent possible, insurance contracts must be written in clear, understandable language and printed in a readable type face. Courts also give protection to the insured by broadly interpreting the terms of an insurance contract in favor of the one who was *not* responsible for its writing, especially when the terms of the contract come into dispute or are ambiguous. In other words, the courts tend to rule against the insurer whenever there are "gray areas" involving the contract's interpretation. Matters of dispute and questions arising from the ambiguity of the contract terms are most likely to result from the addition of *riders* to the contract of insurance. These are special provisions not contained in the basic policy contract but added to it. Another term for these added clauses is *indorsements*. Either party may add a rider, or indorsement, to the contract, but it is usually the insurer who takes the initiative in drafting them.

Binders

Between the time an individual's application for insurance is received and either approved or rejected, an insurer or an insurance agent may issue a *binder*, or *binding slip*. These are brief legal memorandums providing temporary insurance coverage until a policy can be written. In life insurance, this memorandum is referred to as a *conditional receipt*. Whether a binder, binding slip, or conditional receipt, such a document should (1) be in writing; (2) contain a definite time limit; (3) specify the insurance company which is bound thereby; (4) stipulate the amount of insurance; (5) set down the hazards insured against; and (6) designate the type of insurance involved. This information will protect the parties to the agreement if questions later arise. Again, if matters of dispute arise involving the binder, the courts tend to interpret the terms against the insurer.

> The owners of Brittingham's department store signed an application for a fire insurance policy covering both building and contents. The agent accepted the application and issued a binder for the insurance. Before the policy was issued, the insured property burned to the ground. The insurance company is fully liable on the contract and must reimburse Brittingham's for the loss up to the face value of the policy.

If insured personal property is moved to a new location, the consent of the insurance company for the protection at the new location must first be obtained. Failure to obtain this permission from the insurer deprives the insured of the protection of the policy. Binders are not necessary in such cases; insurance companies usually require the filing of special consent forms by the parties involved.

Limitations on Powers of Insurance Agents

An agreement or promise by an agent to change or modify in any way the contract of insurance does not bind the company the agent represents.

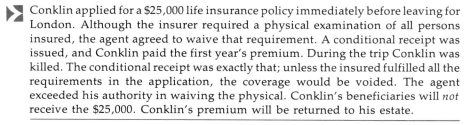

> Conklin applied for a $25,000 life insurance policy immediately before leaving for London. Although the insurer required a physical examination of all persons insured, the agent agreed to waive that requirement. A conditional receipt was issued, and Conklin paid the first year's premium. During the trip Conklin was killed. The conditional receipt was exactly that; unless the insured fulfilled all the requirements in the application, the coverage would be voided. The agent exceeded his authority in waiving the physical. Conklin's beneficiaries will *not* receive the $25,000. Conklin's premium will be returned to his estate.

Lapse of Contract and Grace Periods

When premium payments cease and the insured is in default, an insurance contract becomes void, and it is said to *lapse*. This does not mean, however, that the contract will terminate automatically on the date that the last premium is paid. Nor will it lapse automatically if the insured makes a delayed payment. Most contracts allow for a *grace period* of thirty or thirty-one days in which the insured may make payments so the policy can remain in force. Beyond this period, however, the insurance contract will lapse and the policy terminate.

KINDS OF POLICIES

There are two general types of personal and property insurance policies—open policies and valued policies.

Open Policy

A contract of insurance in which the amount recoverable is determined by the amount of the loss is an *open policy*. Although the amount recoverable for any loss is left "open," the maximum amount that can be recovered for that loss is stated in the face of the contract.

 Nugent insured a power boat for $2,500. The insurer issued an open policy that would reimburse Nugent for losses resulting from fire, explosion, or damage from storms and submerged and uncharted navigation hazards. The boat sank during a storm and was completely ruined. A claims agent confirmed that the boat could be replaced for $1,500. That is the amount the insurer is bound to pay Nugent.

Valued Policy

A *valued policy* is one in which the insurer puts a definite value on the subject matter of the insurance. The figure is conclusive in the event of loss.

 Suppose in the previous example that Nugent had requested a valued policy for the power boat. On proof that the boat was completely ruined, the insurer would have paid Nugent the value of the policy, or $2,500.

Valued policies are issued in life insurance and in health and accident liability. In fire insurance, such policies are illegal in most states. Some, however, have so-called "valued-policy laws" requiring that fire insurance policies on buildings be treated as valued policies in the event of "total loss by certain perils." But in most cases property insurance is written as an open policy.

ADVANCE OR FORFEITURE OF INSURANCE

Under certain conditions the insurer is given a legal right to forfeit, or cancel, an insurance policy. Proof of forfeiture permits cancellation either before a loss or at the time the claim is made on a policy. Among grounds permitting forfeiture are a lack of contract essentials in the insurance agreement; a policy that is improper in form; a breach of warranty; or a concealment of some material fact by the insured. Neither the insured nor the insurer may deny statements or acts previously made or committed that might affect the validity of the policy.

Warranties

In insurance, a *warranty* is an insured's guaranty of facts, statements, or promises contained in an application. It may also be an insured's promise to abide by restrictions especially written into a policy. An insured's warranty must be literally true, otherwise it gives the insurer in some jurisdictions the right to void the policy. By statute in many states, an insurance company has the burden of proof in establishing that a warranty was fraudulently made. If this is proved, the insurer may refuse payment of loss to the insured or to a beneficiary.

 Sexton applied for life insurance after having had two serious accidents while mountain climbing. The insurer was aware of Sexton's climbing experiences. On instructions from the insurer, Sexton promised to do no more climbing while the policy remained in force. Sexton was killed during an especially difficult expedition in the Andes Mountains. The insurer may rescind any obligation to pay Sexton's beneficiary.

Concealment

Fraudulent concealment is any intentional withholding of a fact that would be of material importance in the insurer's decision to issue a policy. The applicant need only give answers to questions asked. However, by act or statement the insured may not conceal facts that would be material in acceptance of a risk.

 Evans applied for car insurance with a company that did not accept drivers who were habitual drinkers. When questioned about drinking, he answered, "I never take a drop." The policy was issued. Evans was later charged in a civil action for damages resulting from a serious accident which he had caused. The insurer learned that Evans was a heavy drinker and was intoxicated at the time of the accident.

The insurer would be permitted to forfeit Evans's policy. The insured intentionally withheld information about his drinking habits, knowing that if the truth were told the application would be rejected. Any judgment levied against Evans in this action would be paid out of Evans's own assets, with no assistance from the insurance company.

Representations and Misrepresentations

A *representation* is a factual statement given by an applicant as part of the process of securing insurance. To justify the voiding of a policy, a representation must be false and made with intent that the insurer rely on the statement. But there is more. The representation must also concern a material fact before it will be sufficient to void a policy. It makes no difference whether such false representation was knowingly or innocently made. Representations may be either oral or written.

> Brezhinski applied to Guaranty Insurance Company for a liability policy on a new car. When questioned as to age, Brezhinski said she was twenty-six. In fact, she was only twenty-four at the time. Premiums for persons twenty-five and above were less than for younger drivers. Brezhinski's representation was false, so Guaranty Insurance Company may void the already issued policy.

If an insured's false representation is willing and knowingly made, with intent to falsify facts, it is a ***misrepresentation***. The insurer may use it as grounds not only to void the policy but also to sue the insured for any damages that may have resulted from the wrongdoing.

> Suppose that, in reply to the question "How many miles do you drive each year?" Brezhinski had answered 5,000. In fact, as field auditor for a large corporation, she drove approximately 20,000 miles each year. Thus, Brezhinski managed to get a smaller premium charge in recognition of a risk 75 percent less than it actually was. Brezhinski's policy may be voided. If her misrepresentation had resulted in proven damage to the insurer, the latter could have sued her for these damages.

Estoppel

An insurer may not deny acts, statements, or promises that are relevant and material to the validity of an insurance policy. This is called an *estoppel*. The insurer is said to be *estopped* from denying its liability under a policy. A *waiver* is one type of estoppel. For example, when the insurer agrees to rescind one of its customary rights for the benefit of the insured, it may not later deny its waiver; it will be estopped from using that waived right to its advantage.

> Farmers Insurance Company insured Snaveley's house and barn against fire, water, and windstorm damage. All of Farmers' policies contained a condition that insured properties must be within 300 feet of a fire plug, with water tested at 50 pounds of pressure. The house and barn were a mile from a water main, but less than 300 feet from the property was a farm pond containing approximately 100,000 gallons of water. Farmers waived the fire-plug requirement in view of the water available in the event of fire. Farmers would be estopped from denying that the waiver had been made in the event of a reported fire loss by the insured.

In most states, however, insurers simply may not waive certain rights. For instance, an insurer cannot waive the necessity of having an insurable interest. The reason is that most legislatures strongly believe that lack of an insurable interest would promote fraud and crime by persons buying a policy. When a waiver refers to a rule or regulation of the insurance company itself, the courts will usually hold the insurer liable for a loss. Acceptance of an insured's application, with knowledge that its information would ordinarily reject the application, makes the insurer liable.

▶▶ Apex Insurance Company sold fire and burglary insurance to the owners of the Baumann Building even though it was located in an area designated "high risk." The home office had issued instructions that no buildings in that area would be issued fire and burglary coverage. Once it was issued, however, Apex would be liable on the Baumann policy. The insurer would be *estopped* from denying liability because its agents and employees violated company policy and rules in issuing the policy.

SUBROGATION

Subrogation is the right of an insurer to claim damages from third parties through whose fault, negligence, or intentional wrongdoing the insurer has been required to pay a claim. The insurer may subpoena all evidence and may summon all witnesses to its case who might have been available to the insured. Persons responsible for damage are not, therefore, released from responsibility merely because benefits have been paid by the insurance company to the injured party.

▶▶ Struther's house was set afire by the gross negligence of a guest. (The guest violated local laws by smoking in bed.) Struther's house was insured for $80,000. Most of the loss was covered by insurance, and the house was restored to its original condition. The insurer is subrogated to all rights Struther had with respect to the guest. The company may bring suit, in Struther's name, against the guest, and Struther will have to cooperate fully or lose the right to recover. Being a guest in another's home does not permit the breaking of a law and the commission of a tort.

Questions for Review and Discussion

1. How do open policies differ from valued policies?

2. Discuss the early concept of insurance as a wagering contract. Is this concept or view given any validity today?

3. Distinguish between requirements of insurable interest in property insurance as compared with life insurance.

4. What is a binder, or binding slip, in property insurance? What is the term used in life insurance that means the same thing?

5. Explain the term *warranty*, as applied to insurance.

6. How does subrogation work to the disadvantage of third parties who have been responsible for damages caused insured persons or their property?

7. List the grounds whereby an insurer may forfeit an insured's insurance policy.

8. Discuss the function of insurance.

9. Discuss the limitations that the law places on the powers of insurance agents.

10. Name and explain the three parties associated with a life insurance contract.

Analyzing Cases

1. Vajda was one of Wright's best customers. When he fell behind in paying for his purchases, Wright would "carry" his valued customer. Vajda always made good on his arrears. But as Vajda began to get older, Wright worried. Over the past three years, Vajda's average account balance with Wright was $45,000. Not wanting to take any more chances, Wright applied to Mutual Benefit Association, a life insurance company, for $75,000 of life insurance on Vajda. A year later Vajda died, owing Wright $41,800. The insurance company paid only that amount to Wright, saying that the $75,000 face amount of the policy exceeded Wright's insurable interest in his customer. Wright sued the company for the $33,200 difference. What would the result be? • See *Wright* v. *Mutual Benefit Association,* 118 N.Y. 237.

2. Bollin sold a house and garage to Post. Bollin's insurance was paid up for six months. Relying on Bollin's policy, Post did not apply for fire and windstorm insurance on the house. A fire loss gave rise to a claim made to Bollin's insurance company. Will Post recover the loss? Explain. • See *Bullman* v. *Commercial Union Assurance Co.,* 159 Mass. 118.

3. Kalman and Harper were partners in a contracting business. Kalman, with Harper's knowledge, insured Harper's life for $50,000. Five years later Harper died. The insurance company denied any obligation to Kalman, arguing that Kalman had no insurable interest in Harper's life. Will Kalman collect as beneficiary of the $50,000 policy? Explain. • See *Chapman* v. *Lipscomb-Ellis Co.,* 22 S.E.2d 393.

4. In a written application for fire insurance, Dasch stated that the building being insured was eight years old, although it was actually twenty years old. After a fire loss, the insurer refused to acknowledge Dasch's claim. The insurer argued that Dasch's statement as to the age of the building was a warranty, the falsity of which had voided the policy. Was the company correct? Explain. • See *Virginia Fire and Marine Insurance Co.* v. *Morgan,* 90 V. 290, 18 S.E. 191.

5. Bates purchased an insurance policy on the life of his very good friend, wishing to provide the protection to have funds available for the family in event of his friend's untimely death. The insurance company subsequently canceled the policy and returned the premium. The insurer claimed that Bates had no insurable interest in the friend's life. Was Bates qualified to take out this policy? Explain. • See *Chapman* v. *Mutual L & I Association,* 131 Ga. 82, 61 S.E. 1036.

6. Atlantic Mutual Life Insurance Company issued a policy of insurance on Burke's life. The company's agent had asked Burke whether any previous applications for insurance had been rejected by other companies. Burke replied that this was the first time he had submitted an application to any company. Burke died several months later. Atlantic refused to honor the beneficiary's claim after learning that Burke had applied to five other companies and had been rejected by each one. Was Atlantic justified in rescinding the policy? Explain. • See *Flannigan* v. *Sunshine Mutual Insurance Company,* 73 S.D. 256.

Legal Reasoning and Business Judgment

Analyze the legal aspects of these business problems. Suggest possible solutions.

1. Your company is expanding its plant facilities to include an old factory building previously owned by a neighboring industry. The old buildings will require much restoration before they can be used. The seller had recently paid a $2,500 premium covering fire insurance on the buildings. By the terms of the sale, this policy was assigned to your company upon payment of a proportional amount of the $2,500 premium. Your opinion is sought in this matter. What would you suggest to your company's property manager?

2. One of the executives of your firm owns a boat which is kept at a nearby marina. An insurance broker has been talking to the executive about insuring the boat for $1,000. A competing broker offered this person a policy of the very same face value for only $400. You have been asked to explain, if you can, why the great difference in premiums exists for two policies with the very same face value. In tackling this problem, what would you first look for?

3. The executive in charge of purchasing insurance has a problem to talk over with you. An application was made for fire coverage on one of the firm's older buildings. The insurer was told that the building had recently been surveyed by a fire protection firm and that many changes had been made to assure the owners of less risk of fire. Now it develops that a mistake was made. It was another building that had been inspected and in which the changes had been made. What might be the results of this mistake, and what would you suggest be done for the best protection of your firm's interests?

Chapter 25
Major Kinds
of
Insurance

It is possible to obtain insurance against almost any risk if one is willing to pay the price (premium). The premium charged will depend on the risk involved. Insurance is available to cover the risk of loss or damage to realty or personal property. This is *property insurance*. The premiums charged, again, will be in proportion to the risk to be assumed by the insurer; if the risk is small, the premium is low; if the risk is great, the premium is high.

Insurance is obtainable to provide indemnity for losses suffered by reason of death, accident, or ill health. This is *life insurance* and *personal insurance* and includes hospital insurance, accident insurance, medical insurance, and workers' compensation.

In this section, however, the discussion is of the most common kinds of insurance: life, automobile, and fire. Workers' compensation and another type of insurance, social security, are covered in a discussion of agency and employment in Part 8.

LIFE INSURANCE

A *life insurance policy* is a contract whereby the insurer promises, for a stipulated premium, to pay a specified sum of money to the beneficiary on the death of the person insured. The subject matter of a life insurance contract, though speculative in nature, is made legal because the contract is considered beneficial to the public welfare. The statutes in many states provide that standard clauses must be inserted in all life insurance policies.

Principles of Life Insurance

Regardless of who insures a life and why, a number of the same considerations always apply. These concern insurable interest and premiums.

Insurable Interest The person who insures the life of another must have an interest in the person insured such that a financial loss will occur if that person dies. Thus, a person has an insurable interest in the life of another if he or she is dependent on that person for education, support, aid in business (partners), collection of debt (interest of creditor in debtor's life), and the like.

> The Security Loan Company introduced the practice of insuring all persons to whom they granted loans on notes not secured by collateral. The cost of the insurance was added to the debtor's loan charges. The loan company was, of course, made beneficiary of each policy, whose face value equaled the amount of the loan. In this way, the company was assured that the loan would be repaid, even if the debtor died.

A life insurance policy will remain valid and enforceable even if the insurable interest terminates. It is necessary only that the insurable interest exist at the time the policy was issued. Thus, if a debtor whose life was insured by a creditor subsequently pays the debt, the life insurance policy continues in force provided the former creditor pays the premiums.

Payment of Premium   A life insurance policy usually is delivered and becomes effective when the first premium has been paid. All subsequent premiums must be paid when due or within a *grace period* of thirty or thirty-one days thereafter; otherwise, the policy will lapse.

Standard Clauses

By statute or by custom, life insurance contracts usually contain standard clauses. The five most common of these standard clauses are described briefly.

Change of Beneficiary   Policies today usually grant the insured the right to make a change of beneficiary. If this is not a condition to the policy, the insured may ask it to be included. Some policies, written as collateral for a debt, make a creditor the beneficiary subject to repayment of the debt. The insured may not change the beneficiary in such an insurance contract.

 Holstein borrowed $10,000 from Beneficial Trust Company. Holstein's house was used as a mortgage to secure payment. Due to Holstein's advanced age at the time of the loan, a term insurance policy for $10,000 was also required by the bank. Holstein was barred from changing the beneficiary until the $10,000 loan was repaid.

Misrepresentation of Age   If a claim is made on a life policy on whose application the insured misstated the age of the person whose life is covered, the insurance company need pay only the amount of insurance that could have been purchased by the premium paid, based on the decedent's true age.

 Larkins applied for a $25,000 life insurance policy. She had been raised by a relative and was never sure about her correct age. At age twenty-one, by her reckoning, she purchased the policy. Prior to death, the insured discovered that she was actually twenty-three when she had applied for the policy. Her beneficiary will not be paid $25,000, but a lesser amount equal to what the premiums actually paid would have purchased if her correct age had been utilized.

Suicide of Insured   Most states have laws barring recovery of any life insurance policy within two years of issuance where the cause of death is suicide. After two years, death by suicide will not bar payment of a claim. Other states vary the prescribed period.

Incontestability Clause   A life insurance policy usually contains a clause stating that the policy shall be incontestable except for nonpayment of premiums after a period of one or two years following its issuance.

> Roman applied for a life insurance policy. When questioned about his prior medical history, Roman did not mention a heart attack he had experienced twenty years earlier. Five years later Roman died of a heart attack. The insurance company tried to suspend the policy because of Roman's concealment. A court disallowed this attempt because of the incontestability clause in the policy.

War Activities   Life insurance policies usually include an exemption of liability in time of war. The exemption states that the insurer will not be liable on the policy if the insured is killed (1) while a member of the Armed Forces, generally outside the continental United States, and (2) from service-connected causes.

Kinds of Life Insurance Policies

The most common types of life insurance policies are straight life; limited payment; endowment; and term insurance. Annuity contracts are also offered by life insurance companies.

Straight Life Policy   An *ordinary, whole*, or *straight life* insurance policy is one for which the insured pays premiums at fixed dates until the policy is terminated by death or discontinuance. The face value of the policy is to be paid to the beneficiary or to the estate of the insured on the death of the insured. Most companies consider an ordinary life policy to be paid up when the insured reaches the age of one hundred. At either that age or at death, the full face value of the policy will be paid.

> At age twenty-two, LaFarge purchased a straight life insurance policy with a face value of $10,000. The premiums were quite modest. At some later time he could trade in the policy for a flat payment, called the *cash surrender value*. Or, LaFarge may elect to continue premium payments until death or age one hundred.

The statutes in most states provide for a minimum *cash surrender value* for a life insurance policy after the policy has been in force for two or three years. Contracts of insurance usually provide that the insured may borrow, at a specified rate of interest, an amount equal to the cash surrender value of the policy.

> Dugan took out a $10,000 ordinary life insurance policy ten years ago and paid premiums regularly. A family emergency required $1,500 immediate cash. Dugan was able to borrow the money on her policy at the legal rate of interest, as the policy had an immediate cash value of more than $1,700. Borrowing on the

policy would keep it in force, and her beneficiary would receive the face amount of $10,000 less the amount of the loan should Dugan die before repaying the loan.

Limited Payment Policy A *limited payment life insurance policy* is one for which the insured makes a specified number of periodic premium payments. When these payments have been made, the insurance is fully paid for, and on the death of the insured the amount of the policy will be paid to the beneficiary. Thus, a twenty-payment life policy is one for which twenty equal annual payments must be made. Because of the limited number of payments made by the insured on this type of policy, the premiums are proportionately higher.

Term Insurance *Term insurance* is similar to a straight life policy, but it is written to expire after only one, two, five, ten, or more years. Premiums are smaller than with any other type of life insurance. This is because term policies have no cash (or loan) value, as others do. In most cases, term insurance is written for some special purpose—such as to secure a loan, mortgage, or other indebtedness.

▶ Dennis bought a new car, financing $4,500 over a three-year period. The bank approved the loan only after Dennis purchased a three-year term insurance policy for the amount of the loan. The car, of course, represented some security to the bank. But if it were demolished and Dennis killed, the term policy would be necessary to clear the indebtedness.

Endowment Policy An *endowment policy* assures the insured of a cash payment of the face amount of the policy at the expiration of a prescribed number of years. Should the insured die before the end of that period, a beneficiary is paid the full amount of the policy. Because this type of policy builds up a cash value more rapidly than other policies, the premium is higher.

▶ Sutton, aged twenty-one, purchased a $10,000 face value, twenty-year endowment policy. His beneficiary will get $10,000 if he dies before age forty-one. If he survives, he gets a check for $10,000. His annual premium is $461.

Annuity Contract An *annuity contract* provides the insured with a monthly, quarterly, or annual income when he or she reaches a specified age written into the policy. For example, an annual premium of $100, on a policy purchased at age twenty-one, might pay the insured an income of $32 a month for life, with payments beginning at age sixty. Multiples of the $100 annual premium could assure the person of a specific income to be added to social security or pension benefits.

To take a similar example, a *joint annuity contract* might be employed to provide a husband or wife with fixed monthly benefits commencing at the death of the spouse and lasting until his or her own death. Premium payments for such a policy are based on the ages of both husband and wife.

Termination of Life Insurance

Life insurance policies are terminated by expiration, as in term policies; by nonpayment of premiums; by cancellation for cause; or by payment of the policy at death or when specified in an endowment policy.

AUTOMOBILE INSURANCE

The millions of cars, trucks, and buses in operation on our streets and highways represent a multibillion-dollar investment by their owners. The operation of these vehicles imposes a liability upon the owners in the event of accident involving others and their property. Automobile insurance provides indemnification against losses incidental to the ownership or operation of all types of motor vehicles.

Among other coverage, automobile insurance provides for indemnity against (1) losses resulting from fire, theft, or collision of motor vehicles and (2) damages arising out of injury by motor vehicles to the person or the property of another.

Principles of Automobile Insurance

Two concerns predominate in automobile insurance. They are the question of insurable interest and the issue of warranties.

Insurable Interest To secure any type of automobile insurance, the insured must own the automobile in question or operate it regularly. Once the insurable interest ends, the insurance cannot continue. Automobile insurance policies are not assignable.

▶ Koget selected a used car in Maurice's Used Car Lot. Agreement was made for the car's delivery the next day, at which time Koget would pay the $1,800 promised. Koget called an insurance agent immediately and covered the car with a fire and theft policy. The car was stolen from Maurice's lot that night. Koget did not have an insurable interest at the time, thus he could not recover for the loss.

Warranties A *warranty* in an automobile insurance policy may be either affirmative or promissory. An *affirmative warranty* is a statement as to an existing or past fact concerning the insured or risk involved.

▶ Doberstein made application for automobile insurance. Among the questions asked was one seeking information about any arrests made during the past two years for careless or inattentive driving. Doberstein denied having ever been arrested. If this were later discovered to be false, the policy could be voided by the insurer. This is an affirmative warranty.

A *promissory warranty* is one where the insured promises to perform or refrain from a specific act in the future. A promissory warranty cannot be used to void an insurance policy unless the breach of the warranty either is persistent or has materially increased the risk of loss at the time of the loss.

▶▶ Phillips promised his insurer that he would never allow his car to be driven by anyone under the influence of alcohol. One night, Phillips's drunken brother borrowed the car. When Phillips found out, he immediately went to his brother's apartment and retrieved the car. On the way home, he was in an accident and his car suffered some $600 in damage. The insurer had to pay the claim because Phillips's brother had not increased the risk of loss at the time of the accident. The insurer could void the policy if episodes such as this occurred frequently.

Kinds of Automobile Insurance

The most common types of automobile insurance are collision insurance; theft, pilferage, and robbery insurance; liability insurance; no-fault insurance; and comprehensive insurance.

Collision Policy   This policy provides against any loss arising from damage to the insured's automobile caused by accidental collision with another object or with any part of the roadbed, or by an upset. Liability under collision insurance is limited to the insured's car. The policy does not cover damage to any trailer drawn by the car or damage to another person's automobile. The property damage insurance policy covers losses of this type.

Unless there is a provision in the policy to the contrary, the company is still liable even when the collision that caused the loss occurred while the insured was violating the law, for example, driving recklessly, driving inattentively, or speeding. Although the insured may be found guilty of such charges, this will not necessarily relieve the insurer of liability for damages claimed.

In determining the amount of an insurance company's liability for damage to an automobile, the maximum liability is the cash value of the car before the collision. Quite often, to obtain lower-premium insurance, the owner of the car will buy *deductible collision insurance*. Under this policy, the insured person pays the first $50 or $100 of the loss, and the insurer is liable only for the remainder up to the amount specified in the policy. Some policies include *coinsurance clauses*, whereby the insured person bears a certain proportion of each loss, such as 20 or 25 percent, and the insurer pays the difference up to the maximum liability indicated in the policy.

Theft, Robbery, and Pilferage Policy   This type of policy covers losses arising from theft, robbery, or pilferage of an automobile or its equipment. It also covers damage or destruction of the insured's property when damage is related to theft, robbery, or pilferage. Theft insurance does not cover losses of personal property left in a car. Only if the entire vehicle is stolen will it cover loss of tools and repair equipment.

The insurance company becomes liable on a theft policy only if the car or its equipment is taken with the intent of stealing it; that is, larceny must be committed. The car must be taken without permission and unlawfully. Wrongful conversion, such as borrowing a car and then selling it without the owner's permission, or taking the car for a joyride with the intention of returning it, is not considered larceny and hence is not theft within the meaning of the provisions of this type of policy.

Automobile Liability Insurance Bodily injury and property damage liability insurance covers the risk of bodily injury or property loss to the insured's passengers, to pedestrians, or to the occupants of other cars. This type of insurance does not cover any injury to either the person or the property of the insured. Loss through accident to the insured is covered under other types of policies.

> In parking her car on a hill in the center of Duluth, Hortin failed to engage the emergency brake. The car rolled down the hill, hitting a passing car, wrecking both cars, and injuring the occupants of the other car. Hortin's liability insurance would cover claims made by the injured persons and damages to the other car. Hortin's own car is not covered by the liability policy.

Under liability insurance the insurer is liable for damages up to the limit of the insurance purchased. The insurance company also must provide attorneys for the insured's defense in any civil court action. Obviously, the company hopes to introduce a good defense for the insured, since they will have to pay any final judgment handed down by the jury or judge.

Injury and damage caused by the negligent driving of someone other than the owner may make the driver responsible. Statutes in many states provide that the owner be responsible no matter who is driving a car. The owner is always liable for damages resulting from negligent driving by the owner, a member of the owner's family, or other persons who are driving with the owner's consent. The insured is released from liability when a car is being driven without the owner's knowledge or consent.

> Demming left the keys to the family car on the living room table. One of his teenage children found the keys, took off in the car, and had a serious accident. Demming may be held responsible. Negligence in leaving the car keys, making them easily available to anyone, could be used as a charge against the owner. The same would be true even though the one taking the keys was not a member of the family.

Many liability insurance policies disclaim liability for bodily injury and/or property damage if the accident is caused by a driver under the legal age limit for driving; if the car is rented or leased or used to transport passengers for hire, or for purposes not specified in the policy; or if a trailer is attached to the car. Liability may also be disclaimed if the insured voluntarily assumes liability or incurred an expense in connection with the accident (unless instructed by the insurer).

> Haggerty's car ran into the rear of another car, causing considerable damage. Without consulting the insurer, Haggerty instructed the other driver to repair the car and submit a bill. The insurer denied liability owing to Haggerty's unauthorized acceptance of liability.

An insurer will often disclaim liability if the insured causes damage to property he or she owns, leases, or is transporting.

> DeFren moved furniture to her new apartment. While she was unloading the car, the safety brake became unhinged, and the car rolled down an incline onto the

unloaded furniture, crushing much of it. DeFren's insurance company is not liable for damages to the furniture.

Comprehensive Policy   A comprehensive automobile insurance policy includes coverage for personal injury to the insured as well as for the risks outlined above in collision, theft, and liability policies. Because of the wide scope of this policy, the premiums are relatively high.

"No-Fault" Insurance   A dramatic change in insurance protection has been legislated in several states recently and is known as *no-fault insurance*. Simply stated, no-fault insurance provides that drivers collect damages and medical expenses from their own insurance carriers regardless of responsibility. This eliminates the costly and time-consuming litigation in which it must be determined which of two or more drivers has been negligent and caused an accident.

> Porter collided with a car driven by Reed, causing a great deal of damage to both cars and physical injuries to Reed. It was very difficult to determine who was at fault in this accident. Under no-fault insurance, both Porter and Reed would recover damages from their own insurers. In states without this legislation, no recovery would be allowed either driver until responsibility was determined by court action or out-of-court agreement.

Financial Responsibility Laws   Some states have enacted laws that either require all automobiles to be covered by bodily injury liability and property damage liability insurance or provide penalties for drivers who are not financially responsible. These laws are made necessary by the great increase in accidents involving motor vehicles, often caused not only by negligent drivers but also by financially irresponsible ones.

Insured's Obligation to Give Notice

An insured is obligated by the terms of the policy to give notice of loss to the insurer. Statutes in force in most states also require that notice be given to state and local authorities in cases involving personal injury and property damage by operation of a motor vehicle.

Notice to the Insurer   In case of a loss, notice must be given to the insurer as soon as possible after the accident, usually on a form provided by the insurance company. The notice must include the name and address of the insured; the time, place, and circumstances of the accident; and the name and address of the owner of the damaged property and of any witnesses. If a suit is filed against the insured on account of an accident, the insurer must be notified immediately. Most property damage policies provide that the insurer will defend any suits against the insured involving property damage caused by the operation of the motor vehicle.

If a claim is made or a suit is brought against the persons insured, they must promptly forward to the insurer any legal papers or summonses served on them.

The insured must not settle claims or incur any expenses except those for immediate medical attention, unless authorized to do so by the insurer. If the insurance company pays a claim, under the law of subrogation it is entitled to step into the shoes of the insured and acquire any rights that the insured had against others because of such claims (see the discussion of subrogation in Chapter 24).

Notice to Public Authorities   Nearly all states and many local communities have laws requiring that notice of accidents involving damage over a specified amount be given to the police within a certain time. Failure to make such a report subjects the driver of the car involved to a fine. Failure to report an accident is considered a misdemeanor. The laws require that a report be filed whenever there is injury to either a passenger or a pedestrian, regardless of whether there was any resulting damage to the cars or other property.

 DiAngelo parked her car in the downtown area during rush hour. A pedestrian stepped behind the car, and DiAngelo accidentally struck this person while backing the car into place. The pedestrian received slight injuries but refused medical attention. Should DiAngelo fail to report the accident, she would be subject to arrest and fine.

FIRE INSURANCE

A fire insurance policy is a contract whereby the insurer promises, for a stipulated premium, to pay the insured a sum not exceeding the face amount of the policy if a particular piece of real or personal property is damaged or destroyed by fire.

A fire insurance policy or a binder is effective as soon as it is unconditionally delivered to the insured, even though the premium has not yet been paid. Even an oral binder is valid and may make fire insurance effective.

Although fire insurance contracts may be made orally, they are usually in writing. Since 1943, the New York Standard Fire Insurance Policy has been adopted, with slight variations, by all states with the exception of New Hampshire. Special provisions, called *riders*, may be added to the policy by the insurer, but only if the riders are approved by the state insurance commissioner. These special provisions supersede any part of the policy in conflict with them.

 Haskell insured a house that was located in an area not served by a paid or volunteer fire company. The standard policy issued to Haskell contained a condition that reduced the insurer's liability in cases of this kind. After charging an additional premium, the insurer included a rider in the policy. The rider removed the condition of reduced liability.

Losses

The insurer's liability under a fire policy usually covers losses other than those directly attributed to fire. Under most policies, claims may also be made for losses from (1) water used to fight the fire, (2) scorching, (3) smoke damage to goods, (4) deliberate destruction of property as a means of controlling a spreading fire, (5) lightning, even if there is no resultant fire, (6) riot or explosion, if a fire does result, and (7) losses through theft or exposure of goods removed from a burning building.

Principles of Fire Insurance

In most states, the following factors are pertinent to analysis of coverage under a fire insurance policy.

Insurable Interest   To enforce a claim through fire insurance the insured must have had an insurable interest in the covered property at the time of securing the policy, and at the time of a reported loss. Any attempt to assign a fire insurance policy to a new owner is void. By agreement with the insurer a novation may be made—that is, a provision whereby the new owner takes over the policy and the insurer issues a new policy in the new owner's name.

Vacancy Clause   Fire insurance may be voided by the insurer when insured property is left vacant or unoccupied for more than sixty days. An insurer may accept the risk through agreement with the insured and the paying of an added premium. A building is vacant when it is empty. If goods or furniture are left in a building, it is not said to be vacant, even though it is not occupied by the owner or others by permission. If an owner or tenant is absent but has every intention of returning, the insurance company cannot claim that insured premises are vacant or unoccupied.

Double Insurance   Double insurance occurs when two or more policies provide protection or coverage for the same risk. In the event of a reported loss, each company would pay the insured only a proportional amount of the claim. The insured is barred from making two complete recoveries through a single loss.

 Hampden owned a house which was insured against fire by Mutual of New Holland. As a double assurance of protection, Hampden took out another policy with Fire Writers of America. Each policy was written with a face value of $25,000. Hampden's house was completely destroyed by fire. Instead of receiving $25,000 from each insurer, he would receive only half of the claim from each.

Hostile Fires   Fire insurance covers losses resulting only from *hostile fires*. A hostile fire is a fire outside the control of the insured. It may be a fire resulting from the insured's, or another's, negligent handling of any fire or ignitable product. Of course, not even all hostile fires will be covered. A hostile fire intentionally set by the insured or an agent of the insured is arson and will void the policy.

 Julian permitted waste paper and old newspapers to accumulate in the basement of the Julian Building. The piles of combustible materials presented a real fire hazard. Fire resulting from a smoldering cigarette started a blaze that caused $35,000 damage. Julian's poor housekeeping methods were a prime reason for the loss. The insurer, however, was liable for the loss from this hostile fire.

Friendly Fires   Fire insurance does not cover *friendly fires*. A friendly fire is one created for some useful purpose and is under the control of the one who started it. A fire in the furnace or a fireplace would illustrate a friendly fire. However, a friendly fire can become a hostile fire, as when escaping sparks from a fireplace cause nearby dangerous goods to explode. In that event, a fire insurance policy may cover the resulting losses, depending on the circumstances.

Alienation Clause   An *alienation clause*, contained in standard fire policies, voids a policy when property is transferred to another owner. Transfer may be by sale, gift, or loss through a judgment against the owner. An exception to this rule is when the insurer agrees to the substitution of a new owner.

> Juhl owned a house insured by Fire Mutual Insurance Company. In default of a judgment made to a plaintiff in a tort action against Juhl, the house was transferred by court order to the plaintiff in that case. Juhl's insurance was paid up for several months. The judgment creditor did not confer with the insurer about the transfer. Any fire loss experienced by the new owner would not be covered by the policy.

When a policy is assigned, with consent of the insurer, the original policy is canceled and a new policy is issued to the new owner. An insured may, without consent of the insurance carrier, assign a claim under the policy without the insurer's consent.

> Roland owed Contractor's Lumber Company $5,000 for lumber that had been delivered to the building site for a new house. Vandals set fire to the lumber, destroying all of it. Roland had covered the building materials under a special contractor's risk policy. Roland assigned the $5,000 claim to Contractor's Lumber Company, who had not yet been paid for the lumber.

Extended Coverage Indorsement   The original intent of a fire policy, historically, was to cover losses directly traceable to fire or lightning. Other policies were available for risks such as windstorm, explosion, riot, or water damage. Issuance of five or more separate policies covering the same property resulted in confusion and misunderstanding between insurer and insured. *Indorsements* to the fire policy have now been developed. These cover all related risks outlined here and are obtained by payment of a relatively small additional premium.

> Pell owned a large home in Allentown. It was covered by a policy written with indorsements for extended coverage. A fire was discovered in his home, and because of its stubborn nature, thousands of gallons of water were used to keep it from spreading. While some loss was attributed to fire, greater losses resulted from water damage to plastered walls, lighting fixtures, woodwork, and tiled floors. A claim for all damages would be enforceable because of the extended coverage indorsement in Pell's policy.

Kinds of Fire Insurance Policies

The most common fire policies are the ordinary policy, the policy containing a coinsurance clause, and the one containing an 80 percent average clause.

Ordinary Policy   Under the *ordinary fire insurance* policy, the insurance company will compensate the insured for any fire losses up to the amount of insurance carried, but never more than the actual loss suffered by the insured nor more than the amount of insurance carried.

> ▶ Watson insured his $60,000 house for only $30,000. A fire broke out, causing damages amounting to $25,000. Under an ordinary fire insurance policy, Watson would recover the entire loss of $25,000. However, if the house had been insured for $20,000, that would be the limit of any recovery.

Coinsurance Clause Policy   Under a *coinsurance clause* policy, that part of the loss is paid by the insurance company that the insurance carried bears to the value of the property. Thus, if a house valued at $50,000 is insured for $40,000, only 40,000/50,000, or four-fifths, of the loss can be recovered by the insured, since only four-fifths of the value was insured.

> ▶ Suppose Watson's home, valued at $60,000 and insured for only $30,000, as above, had a fire loss of $30,000. Under the provisions of the coinsurance clause policy, Watson would receive only $15,000 as full payment of any claim.
>
> $$\frac{30{,}000}{60{,}000} \text{ of } \$30{,}000 = \$15{,}000, \text{ the amount recoverable}$$

This type of policy is based on the premise that the insured is a coinsurer with the insurance company if the property is insured for less than its actual value. The difference between the value of the property and the amount of insurance is assumed to be the personal risk of the insured. Of course, if the insurance carried is more than the value of the property, only the actual fire loss will be paid.

Eighty Percent Coinsurance Clause Policy   Under an *80 percent coinsurance clause* policy, the insurance company will pay that part of a loss that the insurance carried bears to 80 percent of the value of the property. Thus, if a house valued at $50,000 is insured for $30,000, only

$$\frac{\$30{,}000}{80\% \text{ of } \$50{,}000} \quad \text{or} \quad \frac{\$30{,}000}{\$40{,}000} \quad \text{or} \quad \frac{3}{4}$$

of the loss can be recovered by the insured, since only three-fourths of the 80 percent value was insured. If, on the other hand, $40,000 of insurance had been carried, the full loss up to $40,000 could have been collected from the insurance company, since this amount is 80 percent of the value of the property.

> ▶ Watson insured his $50,000 summer home for $30,000 under an 80 percent average clause policy. A fire loss was determined to be $20,000 by an insurance adjuster. Under the formula shown above, Watson would recover three-fourths of his claim, or $15,000.

The 80 percent clause in a policy does not mean that only 80 percent of the value of the property is the maximum amount collectible. If the property is insured for its full value, the full amount would be collected in case of a total loss.

Homeowner's Policy   Many of the leading insurance companies offer a new combination policy known as the *homeowner's policy*. This gives protection for all types of losses and liabilities related to home ownership. Among the items covered are losses from fire, windstorm, and related damage; burglary; vandalism; and injuries suffered by other persons while on the property. These policies usually contain deductible clauses for some of the protection given. The rates are much lower than if each protection offered were covered by a separate policy.

All homeowner's policies are based on the 80 percent coinsurance clause, although more or less than 80 percent can, of course, be purchased.

> ▶ Andrews insured her house under a homeowner's policy. One evening, two children went into Andrews' yard and were injured when they fell into a hole being excavated for a swimming pool. Under the doctrine of *attractive nuisance*, their parents were permitted to sue for all costs relating to the injuries. The homeowner's policy covered Andrews' liability for injuries to persons on the property.

Other Classifications   Policies may be classified as specific, blanket, or floating policies.

A *specific policy* applies to one item only. Thus, the policy of fire insurance on Watson's home mentioned earlier would be a specific policy in that it included only one property. A *blanket policy* is one that provides protection for several single items of the same kind located in different places. The owners of several resort cottages would be charged a lower premium if they bought a blanket policy to cover their property risks. *Floater policies* cover fire risks for property being moved from one place to another. Circus and carnival goods, theatrical effects, and the like are often covered by floater policies.

Merchandise Inventory Policy   Another policy is a great advantage to merchants whose inventories fluctuate greatly from month to month or season to season. This type permits a change of premium based upon the value of inventory reported to the insurer. Premium payments are reduced during periods of low inventory, which means a savings for the insured.

SHORT-RATE CANCELLATION

Insurance policies are often canceled either by the insurer or by the insured before the expiration of the policy.

If a policy on which the premiums have been paid for a year is canceled by the insurance company before the expiration of the year, the company retains only the proportion of the annual premium that corresponds to the expired time as related to the entire time. The exact-time method on the basis of a 365-day year is used in computing the expired time on the policy.

> ▶ Central Fire Insurance Company canceled a policy on Parrish's house when it was learned that gasoline in large quantities was being stored in the basement. The

annual premium of $60 had been paid. The policy had been in force only 73 days when canceled. Parrish received a check for $48, that is, the $60 premium less $12; the amount deducted was equal to 73/365, or 1/5, of the premium.

A different method is followed when insurance is canceled by the insured. On a one-year paid-up premium, the amount returned would be the difference between the premium paid and the amount allowed the insurer according to a special short-rate scale.

Questions for Review and Discussion

1. Name the five most common types of life insurance policies, and briefly describe each type.

2. Discuss the advantages of term insurance over other kinds of life insurance.

3. How does misrepresentation of age affect a life insurance policy?

4. Discuss the incontestability clause in life insurance policies.

5. Name five kinds of automobile insurance, and discuss the risks covered by each of these policies.

6. How does a collision policy differ from a liability policy in automobile insurance? Give an example.

7. Distinguish between hostile and friendly fires. May a hostile fire result from a friendly fire? Give an example.

8. In what ways are life insurance policies usually terminated?

9. Explain the alienation clause contained in standard fire policies.

10. Distinguish between an ordinary fire insurance policy and a homeowner's policy.

Analyzing Cases

1. Balter gave an agent false information concerning a heart condition. The policy was issued, and a year later Balter died of a heart attack. May the insurer void the obligation to honor the claim of the beneficiary because of a misrepresentation? Explain. Suppose Balter died ten years later? • See *Alabama Gold Life Insurance Co.* v. *Johnson*, 2 S. 125.

2. Kalb insured a house worth only $40,000 for $50,000. Premiums were paid regularly. Fire totally destroyed the house. Will Kalb collect the face value of the $50,000 policy? Explain. • See *Commonwealth Insurance Co.* v. *Sennett*, 37 Pa. 205.

3. A fifteen-year-old girl drove the family car with her parents' permission. She did not have a

driver's license, which the state would not issue to anyone below the age of sixteen. An accident occurred, causing both property damage and personal injury to other persons. What is the liability of the insurance company? Explain. • See *Firkins* v. *Zurich General Accident and Liability Insurance Co.*, 111 Cal. App. 655.

4. Driscoll permitted Doyle to test drive a car which Doyle showed an interest in buying. Doyle never returned, and the car was never recovered by the owner. May Driscoll collect a claim under a theft, robbery, and pilferage policy? Explain. • See *Ledvinka* v. *Home Insurance Co.*, 138 Md. 434.

5. Reginald made premium payments for six years on a ten-year term insurance policy. In need of money, Reginald contacted the insurer and asked for the payment of the cash value of the policy. How much, if anything, will Reginald receive? Explain.

Legal Reasoning and Business Judgment

Analyze the legal aspects of these business problems. Suggest possible solutions.

1. Your employer invited the office staff to an outing at the company's recreational camp. One cold evening, a fire was started in a fireplace in the large game room. Sparks escaped from the fireplace, landed on combustible materials, and started a fire. No fire equipment could reach the scene in time to save any of the buildings. The fire insurance company refused to accept a claim of loss, claiming that the fire started from a friendly fire. How would you defend your employer's rights for reimbursement for this loss?

2. Your company provides several automobiles for use by outside sales representatives. Territories are located in all parts of the United States. You are asked to make a survey of insurance coverage that should be purchased to cover the firm's risks as related to these vehicles and their use. What coverage would you recommend in your survey?

3. One of your employees has a home valued at $50,000 which is fully protected by insurance. A friend of the employee, an insurance agent, has suggested that a second policy be taken on the house that would double the owner's protection in the event of a loss. What advice would you give this employee? Would the agent's suggestion be a good idea if the premium were reasonable?

Part 8
Agency and Employment
Chapter 26
Creation of Agency

The job placement agent, the service station attendant, the attorney—all represent someone else in their business dealings with third parties. The complexities of business today often cause us to delegate to others the things we cannot conveniently do for ourselves. In this way, the agent-principal relationship is created. Even someone operating a small business has to delegate authority to other people at times. In doing so, he or she is regulated by the law of agency.

THE AGENT-PRINCIPAL RELATIONSHIP

Generally, an *agency* is a relationship between one party, known as the *principal*, who authorizes another, known as the *agent*, to represent him or her in commercial or business dealings with third persons. Specifically, the term *agency* is defined as the legal relationship that exists when the principal authorizes the agent to create, modify, or end contractual arrangements involving the principal and third parties. The agency relationship is created by the conduct of two parties. The principal must show in some way that the agent is to act for him or her; and the agent must agree to act on the principal's behalf and subject to the principal's control.

Agency relationships greatly influence the size and operation of every business unit. One principal, by using agents, may complete many business transactions in the same amount of time needed to personally conduct a single transaction. Thus, without agency, it would not be possible for a corporation, which acts only through its agents, officers, and employees, to conduct business. And without agency, the law of partnership, whereby every partner is both an agent and a principal of his or her copartners, would also require radical change.

The law of agency and employment, in the areas of contracts and torts, is based on case law. Statutes provide the basic legal principles in the areas of civil rights, minimum wages, and labor-management relations. Agency issues are usually settled within the framework of three parties: the principal, the agent, and the third

340

party with whom the agent contracts or against whom the agent commits a tort while in the principal's control or employ.

 Berk Associates, Inc., an employment agency, hired three salespersons to recruit top-flight employees for client companies. The three agents screened and tested job applicants for nationwide placement. They arranged interviews between job applicants and potential employers, which frequently resulted in employment agreements. The relationship between Berk Associates, Inc., and the three salespersons was one of agency; the principal was liable for the acts of the agents in their dealings with the third-party job applicants and the client companies seeking qualified employees.

CREATING AN AGENCY

An agency is usually created by appointment or mutual agreement. It may also be created by law, necessity, estoppel, and ratification.

Agency by Appointment or Mutual Agreement

Anyone appointed by a principal through contract or by conduct and acts may be an agent. Even a minor or one who is mentally ill may be an agent, because the acts of such persons are judged to be those of the principal. Thus the principal should exercise care in the appointment of an agent, as he or she may be held responsible for an agent's acts. The appointment of an agent may be oral, written, implied, or apparent. When the agency is created to dispose of or acquire land, most states have laws requiring the appointment to be in writing. In some states, appointments in writing must be under seal—an impression or mark used for authenticating documents and records. A written authorization of agency is called a *power of attorney*—an instrument authorizing another to act as one's agent or attorney in fact (see Fig. 26-1).

The Equal-Dignities Rule   The statute of frauds specifies that certain contracts must be in writing if they are to be enforceable. The *equal-dignities rule* specifies that a contract of agency must be in writing if the contracts that the agent is to make with third parties in behalf of the principal are required to be in writing. Likewise, if the agent is to enter into contracts under seal, his or her agency must be created by authority under seal.

 Reynolds designated Ruben as an agent to sign a contract guaranteeing the payment of rent by a friend who was about to be ejected from an apartment. Since contracts guaranteeing the debt or the performance of another must be in writing according to the statute of frauds, the agency agreement between Reynolds and Ruben must also be in writing and signed by Reynolds if it is to be valid under the equal-dignities rule.

Power of Attorney
Know all Men by these Presents:

That I, Thomas Conklin--

residing at 404 Bolton Road
in the City   of   East Windsor   in the County of
Mercer   and State of   New Jersey   as Principal(s),
do make, constitute and appoint   Margaret Kleinberg--------------------------------

residing or located at   25 Montgomery Street
in the City   of   Hightstown   in the County of
Mercer   and State of   New Jersey   , as   my   true and
lawful attorney   for   me   and in   my   name, place and stead, for the following uses and
purposes: to represent me in the disposition of my property located at
33 Claiborne Street, Hightstown, New Jersey--

giving and granting unto   my   said attorney   full power and authority to do and perform all
and every act and thing whatsoever requisite and necessary to be done in and about the premises,
as fully to all intents and purposes as   I   might or could do if personally present, with full
power of substitution and revocation, hereby ratifying and confirming all that   my   said attorney
or   his   substitute   shall lawfully do or cause to be done by virtue hereof.

In Witness Whereof,   I   have hereunto set   my   hand   and seal
the   fifteenth   day of   July   19 --   .

Signed, Sealed and Delivered   )
                                    }
in the Presence of   )

.... Thomas Conklin .... (L.S.)

Arlene Pastorini   .... (L.S.)

Fig. 26-1.   Power of Attorney

Another section of the statute of frauds specifies that all contracts that cannot be completed within one year of the date of the making of the contract must be in writing to be enforceable.

> The Builders and Contractors Association retained an attorney as legal aide for a period of two years. A written contract was not entered into for the creation of this agency agreement. Any attempt by either party to enforce the agreement would fail because the parties had not complied with the provision of the statute of frauds.

Agency by Operation of Law or Necessity

Certain relationships that are influenced by necessity or social desirability create agency rights, although in fact they may not actually exist. The wife and children of a man who fails to provide essentials of life may be declared agents of the husband by the court for the purpose of purchasing such necessaries. The husband is responsible for the contracts made in his name as long as the purchases are reasonable.

> Gustavson, the father of three children, abandoned his family after placing an advertisement in the classified section of the local newspaper stating that he would no longer be responsible for any bills unless contracted by himself. Mrs. Gustavson bought food, clothing, and medical care for the children and herself, charging everything to her husband. Mrs. Gustavson is an agent by necessity, and her husband is responsible for contracts made by her for all reasonable necessaries of life.

An emergency power of an agent to act under conditions not covered by granted authority would be recognized when communication with the principal is not possible and failure to act will result in a loss to the principal.

> On a snowy day, the driver of a rental car, who was carrying several business associates as passengers, purchased a set of skid chains for the car. The chains provided by the car rental company had disintegrated en route. The driver, although not ordinarily authorized to buy skid chains, would receive authority by operation of law. The rental car company would be required to reimburse him for the cost of the chains.

Agency by operation of law is often authorized by statute. An example is the nonresident motorist statute. Under its provisions, the secretary of each state is appointed the agent of a nonresident for the purpose of serving legal papers in any action arising from the operation of a motor vehicle by the nonresident within the state.

Agency by Estoppel or Conduct

When a principal's actions are misleading and cause others to believe that another person is an agent, the principal is generally barred from denying the apparent agency. This is called *agency by estoppel*. For example, if the owner of an electric appliance shop places another person in complete charge, third parties may assume that the person in charge is the agent of the owner. Failure to object to acts performed by an apparent agent over a period of time would also be viewed by the court as assent on the part of the principal.

> ▶ Franco, manager of the Devon Apartments, permitted her nephew to use the apartment office, typewriter, and telephone, thus leading the tenants to believe that the nephew was an employee. Several tenants paid their rent to the nephew. Should the latter fail to turn the money over to Franco, the tenants could maintain that the rent had been paid. The nephew appears to be authorized and would therefore be said to have apparent authority. Franco is estopped, or prevented, from denying an agency that one would reasonably conclude existed from another's actions and performance.

Agency by Ratification

When the principal approves of an unauthorized act performed by an agent or approves of an act performed in his or her name by a person without authority to act as an agent, this results in an *agency by ratification*. The ratification may be expressed or may be implied by the principal's conduct. By accepting the benefits of an unauthorized agreement, a principal approves the means used in obtaining the agreement unless steps are taken within a reasonable time to return such benefits. Therefore, when an unauthorized agent commits fraud in obtaining a contract with the knowledge and intent of the principal, the principal's acceptance of the contract's benefits confirms the contract and also confirms the fraudulent acts. The principal is liable.

> ▶ Cerone applied to the Fidelity Trust Company for a four-year automobile loan. He signed the note in blank. When the loan officer found that a four-year loan could not be obtained, she filled in the instrument Cerone had signed to show a one-year loan. When the loan was due at the end of the year, Cerone gave Fidelity a renewal note for the amount of the debt. Later, when Fidelity sued on the loan, Cerone claimed that the loan officer did not have authority to negotiate a one-year loan. Cerone's signing of a renewal note with the knowledge that the loan was a short-term loan ratified the act of the loan officer in filling in the instrument to show a one-year loan.

CAPACITY OF PRINCIPAL

Whatever a principal may do personally, he or she may do through an agent. Similarly, whatever a principal cannot do legally cannot be delegated to an agent to do. Simply stated, the capacity to act through an agent depends on the capacity of the principal to act.

Insane Persons as Principals

Persons who have been declared insane by the courts lose their legal capacity and may not thereafter make valid contracts. The appointment of an agent by such a person is void. State-appointed guardians act as agents of the state in the protection of the insane person's rights. They are qualified to make contracts deemed necessary for the health and welfare of their ward. Acts not necessary, reasonable, and advisable for the preservation of a mentally incompetent person's property, business, and person would become the personal responsibility of the guardian.

Persons who may be irrational but have not been declared insane as well as those who have lucid periods are not classified as insane. Such persons have responsibilities like those of minors and may themselves appoint agents to do those things that they may legally do for themselves.

> Bradshaw, a "neighborhood character," was irrational at times but he was able to function safely and competently in ordinary human relations. He asked a friend to purchase medication for him to treat an infected foot. Such purchases on Bradshaw's behalf would constitute necessaries for which Bradshaw could be made personally liable, although he was occasionally unstable emotionally.

Minors as Principals

Under common law, persons under the age of twenty-one are minors or infants. Over thirty states now have statutes making eighteen the age of majority; in several others it is nineteen. Marriage terminates minority in a few states. (See Chapter 8, "Capacity of Parties.")

Contracts entered into by a minor and appointments of an agent by a minor are voidable, unless the agency was necessary to the minor's health or welfare. A minor may also void agreements with third parties made on his or her behalf unless the agreements are enforceable under the *rule of necessaries*.

Originally, necessaries were limited to things absolutely required for the sustenance and shelter of a minor—food, clothing, and lodging. The rule was extended to include items relating to the health, education, and comfort of the minor. Although property used for pleasure by a minor is generally not regarded as a necessity, property used by a minor for support has been ruled so in recent court decisions. It appears that the courts will in time judge necessaries to be whatever is important by contemporary standards. When this occurs, television sets, stoves, refrigerators, sewing machines, and furniture of all kinds will be considered akin to necessities of life. Necessaries are also interpreted with a view to each person's wealth and position in society.

> Chanko, aged seventeen, purchased a used car on credit. When she stopped making payments, American Auto Sales sued for the purchase price. Chanko argued that she was not liable because she was a minor when the contract was signed. It was shown that Chanko used the car for transportation to and from her place of employment and that her job was her only means of support. The court required her to pay for the value of the car because it was necessary for transportation to her job.

Partners as Principals

Each partner in a business is a principal. At the same time, each partner is implied to be the agent for the other partners in matters related to the partnership business. The appointment of an agent by one partner is binding on all other partners. Likewise, partners are considered agents of the partnership, making all partners liable for contracts each makes in behalf of the business.

 Bianco and Gilman operated the Polka Dot Shop as partners. During Bianco's vacation, Gilman ordered a large selection of pantsuits, skirts, coordinated separates, and blouses for the spring selling season. Although Bianco was not present and might disagree with the selection, she will be liable for her share of the expense. Gilman was acting as agent for the partnership, representing both herself and Bianco.

Corporations as Principals

A corporation, which is created by an act of a state legislature, is an artificial "person" for purposes of tort, contract, and criminal law. It can act only through its board of directors, officers, and employees, who are considered agents of the corporation. The corporation is subject to the doctrine that the principal is liable for the acts of agents and may be punished for their criminal acts. All aspects of agency law relating to wrongful acts committed by agents against third persons or their property also apply to corporations. Corporate liability also includes actions against fraud committed by officers or agents within their actual or apparent authority.

 Sanchez claimed that Chou, president of Haase Equipment, Inc., made an oral contract appointing Sanchez the national sales manager of the corporation. His compensation was to be based on a straight salary and a percentage of any increased volume of sales. The corporation directors later refused to pay the percentage of compensation based on increased sales volume and argued that Chou had no authority to make such an agreement. The agreement would be binding on the corporation, however; Sanchez would not be expected to know that Chou's agreement with him required approval by the board of directors. Thus, the corporation is liable for the acts of its president within the scope of the business it is empowered to engage in.

Public Corporations as Principals

The agents for cities, towns, school districts, and other municipal corporations, known as public corporations, are not authorized to contract in excess of the power granted them by their parent state. Although redress is possible against a private corporation which acts beyond its powers, there is no recovery against a public corporation which exceeds its legal limitations. Thus, third parties should exercise caution when contracting with public corporations. It is wise to examine carefully the regulations governing the terms of authorization and to make sure that those acting on its behalf have the lawful authority to bind the public corporation.

Nondelegable Acts

A principal may not delegate certain acts to an agent. For example, a principal cannot act through an agent in performing military service, voting in an election, serving a jail sentence, and taking an oath. In addition, an agent may not appoint a subagent unless the subagent's duties are mechanical in nature.

CLASSES AND KINDS OF AGENTS

An *agent* is one employed by and under the control of another, known as the principal, to represent the principal in business and legal dealings with third persons. This definition does not distinguish the relationship of agent and principal from that of servant and master or employee and employer. In both latter relationships, the servant or employee does what he or she is instructed to do, usually does not deal with third persons in any authorized capacity, and is generally not required to use discretion and judgment in protecting or promoting the interests of the principal. In many instances, a person may function alternately as an employee and as an agent, but not at the same time during the same work period. The salesperson in a department store, for example, acts in the capacity of an employee while stocking shelves and checking inventory. When waiting on customers, however, this same person becomes an agent. In tort law when the issue is whether the person committing the tort was acting within the scope of employment, the terms *servant* and *master* and *employee* and *employer* are commonly used.

Agents are generally classified according to scope of authority or manner of appointment.

General Agents

A *general agent* is one given broad authority to act on behalf of a principal in a number of acts. Furthermore, in the exercise of the authority, the agent is expected to use discretion and judgment in protecting and promoting the interests of the principal.

 Semlak, manager of a Reliable Oil Company service station, hired A-1 Painting Company to paint the interior office and work areas. Semlak also employed two extra attendants to monitor the self-service pumps. As a general agent for Reliable Oil Company, Semlak has the authority to take these independent actions which protect and promote the interests of Reliable Oil Company. He thereby binds his employer.

Special Agents

A *special agent* is one whose authority to act is restricted to a particular job or a specific task. For example, a real estate broker employed to sell a house is a special agent in that authority and is restricted to those acts necessary to sell the principal's property. When such agents act outside the scope of their specific authority, they become personally liable for their acts.

Factors and *Del Credere* Agents

Agents working independently, for example as intermediaries or commission merchants with whom customers deal directly and to whom they look for satisfaction, are known as *factors*. When the factor guarantees the credit of a third person to a principal, such a factor is operating under a *del credere agency* or commission.

 Lutz employed Saverine to act as her agent in selling merchandise. The contract of agency was for one year, and it included a guaranty by Saverine that Lutz would not suffer loss because of sales on credit that Saverine made with third persons. Merchandise valued at $1,200 was delivered to Malloy, who presented $200 in down payment and signed a promissory note for $1,000, payable in 90 days at 8 percent interest. Malloy declared bankruptcy fifteen days after the sale. Lutz sued Saverine. As a *del credere* agent, Saverine guaranteed the credit of Malloy and is liable to Lutz for the $1,000 balance.

Actual Agent Versus Ostensible Agent

An *actual agent* is a person acting under a contractual agreement with a principal. A person may also become an actual agent under the rules of implied agency. This occurs if a person by his or acts or conduct does things incidental to the implied authority granted by a principal (see the discussion of implied authority later in this chapter). An *ostensible agent* is one acting under the apparent authority of a principal.

 Semlak, manager of the Reliable Oil Company service station, permitted the painter to use one of the uniforms worn by the station attendants. Without authority, the painter sold a new car battery to a customer at a reduced price that was excessively low. Since he had let the painter give customers the impression that he was a regular employee, Semlak would be estopped from denying that the service station was liable on the contract for the battery or its replacement warranty.

Independent Contractors

A person may, in contracting for the services of another, ask only that the second person accomplish a certain result. If the second party also has the freedom to choose the manner and methods to be used in obtaining the result, he or she is considered an *independent contractor*. The principal receiving the benefit of the contractor's services is not responsible to third persons for the independent contractor's contract or tort actions. Construction contracts used in the building trades are the most frequent application of this type of relationship. Thus, when such contracts are awarded, it is important to make sure that the contractor is protected by insurance (to cover possible injuries to third persons) and by indemnity bond (giving assurance that the work will be completed according to the agreement).

 National Development Corporation awarded a contract to Case Utility Equipment to transport four temporary structures and erect them on a new building site. One of the trailers broke loose in transit and crashed into a passenger bus.

The bus was heavily damaged, and a number of passengers were injured. Since Case Utility Equipment was operating as an independent contractor, all damages awarded as a result of the accident would be charged to it rather than to National Development Corporation.

AUTHORITY OF AGENT

The authority of an agent is limited to those acts authorized by the principal. When an agent performs such acts, he or she is acting within the scope of the agent's authority. Unauthorized acts or acts outside the scope of an agent's authority become the agent's sole responsibility unless the third person might reasonably believe that the agent is acting within the scope of authority. An agent's authority may be (1) express, (2) implied, or (3) apparent.

Express Authority

Express authority refers to that authority which is clearly set forth by the principal as instructions in the agency agreement. It is voluntarily conferred on the agent by the principal, and it binds the principal both as to third persons and as to the agent.

 Sabo's employment agreement with Ring's End Supply Company stated that he was to pay all bills, hire necessary personnel, make all building product purchases, and in general, manage the operation of the business. Contracts made by Sabo within the actual authority set forth in these instructions will be binding upon the principal, Ring's End Supply Company.

Implied Authority

Implied authority is additional authority required by an agent to carry out the express authority. It is also authority arising out of business custom and usage. All such incidental authority binds the principal as to third parties and as to the principal's agent as well.

 Merritt, a real estate broker and general agent for Ventura Realty Company, has the express authority to represent property owners in contractual relations with potential buyers. Merritt then delegates this authority to three full-time and one part-time subagents, or salespersons. Although an agent generally does not have the authority to delegate authority to subagents, the custom and nature of the real estate business are such that the seller is presumed to expect that the authority given to Merritt will be exercised through salespersons.

Apparent Authority

Apparent authority is the appearance of authority that is not actual authority. It is communicated to an agent by the acts or words of the principal. It extends to all acts which a person of ordinary prudence, familiar with business usage, would be justified in assuming that the agent has authority to perform. It binds the principal only as to third parties. In other words, the principal is liable for acts and words communicating apparent authority to an agent and is responsible to third parties even if the actual intent of the communication was that the agent act in exactly the opposite way.

> ▶▶ Jurkops wrote a letter to Wheeler authorizing her to sell his BMW and sent a copy of the letter to prospective purchasers. Before the car was sold, Jurkops wrote another letter to Wheeler revoking the authority to sell the car, but this time he failed to notify the prospective purchasers. Wheeler retained apparent authority to sell the BMW; Jurkops would be bound to a third person should the car be sold.

Two kinds of conduct by the principal may give rise to an agent's authority. These are passive assent and failure to object to acts performed by an apparent agent over a period of time. For example, if an employee draws checks made out to herself for over a year which are debited to her employer's account, and no complaint is made, the lack of objection is ample communication to the bank that the employee had the authority to draw the checks.

Questions for Review and Discussion

1. Name four ways in which an agency may be created.

2. What is the scope of the agency relationship?

3. Who may be an agent? Must an agent have the capacity to contract? Explain.

4. When is an agent said to be acting within the scope of authority?

5. Distinguish between express, implied, and apparent authority.

6. What is the equal-dignities rule?

7. Contrast the authority of private and public corporations in acting through their agents.

8. What is (a) a general agent, (b) a special agent?

9. What is the principal's liability on contracts made with independent contractors? What precautions should be taken with respect to such contracts?

10. What is the agent's liability on contracts in which (a) a special agent, in dealing with third parties, acts outside the scope of the job, and (b) a principal refuses to ratify the unauthorized act of an agent?

Analyzing Cases

1. Wallmark, who was under the age of legal competence, owned a restaurant and employed Keafer, an adult, to manage the business. Keafer contracted with Savage Refrigeration, Inc., for the purchase of a new refrigerator for the restaurant. When the refrigerator was delivered, Wallmark refused to accept and pay for it. Can Savage Refrigeration enforce the contract? Ex-

plain. • See also *Lyon* v. *Kent*, 45 Ala. 656, and *Wickham* v. *Torley*, 136 Ga. 594, 71 S.E. 881.

2. Tugman appointed Fitzmaurice as an agent to manage the National Television Service Company. On display was a special Sony TV model which Fitzmaurice was instructed not to sell. Crabtree, a customer, unaware of these instructions, offered to purchase the TV set. Fitzmaurice sold the set to Crabtree, promising delivery the following afternoon. Tugman refused to deliver the set, and Crabtree sued for breach of contract. For whom should judgment be made? Explain. • See also *T. S. McShane* v. *Great Lakes Pipe Line Co.*, 57 N.W.2d 778.

3. The sales manager of Mohawk Service Company agreed to sell Montessori one of the company's power lifts. Although the sales manager had no authority to sell the company's equipment, the proprietor accepted Montessori's check, which he had already given to the sales manager for the equipment. Mohawk Service Company began one court action to get back the power lift and another against its agent for selling company equipment. What will be the outcome of these two actions? Explain. • See also *Davison* v. *Varr*, 273 S.W.2d 500.

4. Jarombek, owner of Eagle's Lair Antiques, asked Seabron to contact the owners of a rare old blanket chest and to purchase it. Seabron was instructed not to divulge that she was representing an antique dealer, inasmuch as they might be tempted to increase the asking price of the chest. Seabron was successful in making an agreement with the owners of the chest to purchase it for $75. Jarombek thought the price was excessive and informed Seabron he did not want the chest. What rights do the owners of the chest have against Seabron? Explain. • See also *Camp* v. *Barber*, 88 At. 812.

5. Engineering Associates, Inc., accepted a contract to construct an addition to a condominium community. The investors supplied all blueprints and gave instructions to Engineering Associates to begin work. During construction, a steel beam fell and seriously injured a pedestrian. Suit was brought by the pedestrian against the investors in the condominium for all damages incurred. Will the injured person recover from the investors? Explain the rights of the injured party. • See also *Dean* v. *Ketter*, 65, N.E.2d 572.

6. Nadro authorized her office manager to employ an additional data processing clerk. The office manager did so, and also hired a correspondence secretary. Nadro refused to pay the salary of the correspondence secretary, claiming that the office manager had exceeded her authority and that she (Nadro) was therefore not liable. Was this a correct claim? Why? • See also *T. S. McShane Co.* v. *Great Lakes Pipe Line Co.*, 156 Neb. 766, 57 N.W.2d 778; *Continental Oil Co.* v. *Baxter*, 59 S.W.2d 463.

Legal Reasoning and Business Judgment

Analyze the legal aspects of these business problems. Suggest possible solutions.

1. The shipping and receiving manager of Plastic Products, Inc., learned that a company driver had struck a pedestrian with a company truck while transporting furniture from his home to that of a friend. The driver was using the truck without authority and contrary to company policy. The injured pedestrian, who had to be hospitalized, was now inquiring what Plastic Products would do to remedy the situation. What is the company's legal responsibility?

2. A small group of students from a nearby university visited a plant to observe the operation of a newly installed computer. An operator of an electric truck was carrying materials from the supply room and moving at an excessive rate of speed in violation of plant safety rules. He struck and injured one of the students. What action would be proper in this case, taking into consideration the rights and responsibilities of the driver, the student, and company management?

3. The research and development director needed a new vacuum pump that would aid the department in carrying out experiments related to a new process. Without conferring with the manager of the purchasing department, the director placed an order for a pump costing $2,575. Confirmation of the order was received from the supplier by the purchasing department, which refused to issue a purchase order. The director lacked authority to place an order exceeding $500 without the signature of the purchasing manager. What would be the correct disposition of this case?

Chapter 27

Obligations, Rights, and Liability of Agency

When an agency relationship is created, obligations, rights, and liabilities emerge which relate to the principal, the agent, and the person with whom the agent deals. These obligations, rights, and liabilities are special to the principal-agent relationship.

AGENT'S DUTIES AND LIABILITIES

Among the duties that an agent has to a principal are obedience to instructions; loyalty and good faith; skill, judgment, and discretion; an obligation to account for actions; personal performance; and an obligation to relay information.

Obedience to Instructions

An agent must obey all reasonable instructions issued by the principal that fall within the contract of agency. Failure to do so may make the agent liable to a principal for any loss resulting from violations of instructions. Even a *gratuitous agent* (one not legally obligated to fulfill a performance promise) must follow instructions or become responsible for any loss resulting from failure to do so.

▶▶ Datapro instructed one of its representatives to meet with the officers of New Castle Foundry Castings and to explain its services. The Datapro agent decided to take a roundabout route in order to visit at the home of a friend. During this unauthorized excursion, the agent's company car was involved in a serious accident. The agent had exceeded the instructions given and thereby became liable to Datapro for damages to the company car.

Loyalty and Good Faith

An agent may not engage in any activity that interferes or competes in any way with the business interests of a principal. Loyalty requires that information acquired by an agent may not be used to profit the agent at the expense of the principal.

▶ The manager of National Products offered Misra, the sales manager of Precision Industries, $100 in return for unauthorized price quotations and special discounts on a new equipment installation. Acceptance of the $100 would place Misra in a position where he was representing both the seller and the buyer in the same transaction without the consent of both.

The relationship between an agent and principal is one of highest trust and confidence. Thus the selling of a principal's property for a lower or higher price than that authorized by the principal would be a breach of good faith.

▶ With his own personal funds, Yeager, manager of Compudata's service department, purchased 10,000 jumper wires (used for wiring panels) from Page Wire Products at a special discounted price. Each time Compudata replenished their inventory of jumper wires, Yeager accounted for the jumpers at the regular price and indicated that they were purchased from an acceptable supplier. This practice is a breach of the fiduciary relationship (of loyalty and trust) between agent and principal. Discovery of Yeager's bad faith could result in his discharge by Compudata and a damage suit for recovery of profits earned at the principal's expense.

Skill, Judgment, and Discretion

An agent must exercise reasonable judgment, discretion, and skill in performing duties. In addition, within the terms of the agency, the agent implies that he or she possesses the necessary training, knowledge, and skill to carry out the work of the agency in a professional manner. The agent is liable to the principal for losses resulting from personal neglect or incompetence.

▶ Thermotec sent a fractional horsepower motor to Delco Motors for repair. When the motor was returned and installed on a plastic fabricating machine, it was discovered that the motor's rpm had been reduced from 3,000 to 1,500. A number of acrylic sheets were damaged before the error was discovered. The shop supervisor for Delco Motors had miscalculated and could be held responsible to the principal for failure to use ordinary prudence, skill, care, and diligence in performing the necessary repair to the motor.

Obligation to Account

An agent must keep proper and accurate records so that all money or property entrusted by the principal may be accounted for. Money collected by the agent must not be combined with his or her own money. When funds that belong to a principal are deposited in a bank, they must be deposited in a separate account so that a trust is apparent. If an agent keeps a trust account in a careless way and it is impossible to tell what belongs to the agent and what belongs to the principal, the agent loses all claim to the money. Failure to keep funds separate is known as confusion, or *commingling* (see the discussion of confusion in Chapter 15, "Title and Risk").

Moffat made c.o.d. deliveries for Taylor Rental Service. Each time a cash collection was made, Moffat would mix the money with his own. Should he fail to keep an accurate record of customers' c.o.d. payments or be unable to account for all money collected during the working day, Taylor Rental Service would have a right to demand all of Moffat's commingled money.

Personal Performance

In the absence of authority to do so, an agent may not delegate duties unless such duties are purely mechanical in nature, requiring no particular knowledge, training, skill, or responsibility.

If an agent is permitted to assign subagents to perform designated duties, all possible care, skill, and judgment must be exercised in selecting the subagents. By doing so, the agent will be free of liability for any acts of the subagents. If the principal has not authorized the agent to make such appointments, the agent must assume responsibility for the subagents' act.

 Executive Tax Service employed Watkins to prepare tax returns for a number of its clients. During the peak season when the work load was extremely heavy, Watkins, without authority, turned over a number of the accounts to a niece who was a business administration student. Because tax return preparation requires special knowledge and skill, Watkins would be liable to Executive Tax Service for any loss it sustains stemming from the unauthorized performance of the niece.

Obligation to Relay Information

An agent is duty bound to inform the principal of all facts affecting the agency that come to the agent's attention within the scope of employment. In other words, the agent is responsible for communicating all information which might affect the interest of the principal.

 Ludder, in her capacity of real estate broker for Seymour, learned that the principal's property was to be rezoned from single-family residential to commercial. Ludder did not share this information, which would increase the value of the property, with Seymour. Instead, she arranged the sale of the property to a friend at the asked-for price, with the understanding that she would share in the profits when the property was subsequently sold for commercial use. Ludder would be liable to Seymour in a suit for such profits made at the principal's expense.

AGENT'S LIABILITY TO THIRD PERSON

When an agent informs a third person that he or she is acting as an agent and names the principal, there is no liability as to future contractual obligations as long as the agent acts within the scope of delegated authority.

Undisclosed Principal

For personal or business reasons, a principal may instruct an agent to enter into contracts with a third person without divulging the fact that an agency relationship exists. Under such circumstances, the agent becomes personally liable on contracts with the third persons *until* the undisclosed principal is identified. A similar situation arises when the agent contracts with a third person for a fictitious or nonexistent principal, except that here the agent alone is liable.

An agent who signs as maker or drawer will be held liable on a negotiable instrument to a third person unless the principal's name appears somewhere on the instrument. The agent's signature, followed by the descriptive title "Agent," is not sufficient protection. It must be preceded by the identifying name of the principal.

Warranties of Agent

In every business relationship between agent and third persons, it is important to determine the agent's warranties. When acting in a representative capacity for a principal with a third person, the agent warrants an authority to so act. If the agent knows he or she has no authority when dealing with a third person, the agent is guilty of fraud. Similarly, an agent who exceeds his or her authority becomes personally liable for damages to a third person who suffers injury. An agent also warrants that his or her principal is capable of being bound. Thus, an agent representing a principal who is under the age of legal competence may be held liable for nonperformance by the principal.

The authority of public officials is part of the public record. Their contractual powers are clear and limited. Thus, they generally assume no personal contractual liability when acting as agents of the government.

PRINCIPAL'S OBLIGATIONS

The principal's obligations to agents and to third persons, if not specifically mentioned in the agency contract, are implied by law.

Obligations to Agents

The principal is obligated to compensate, to reimburse, and to indemnify an agent.

Compensation for Services The principal is obligated to pay an agent for all services rendered unless the agent agrees to perform duties gratuitously. The amount of compensation is usually set forth in the agency agreement. If no specific amount has been stated, a reasonable sum of money must be paid for authorized acts performed by the agent on behalf of the principal. An agent cannot recover compensation for illegal services, even though they were rendered at the request of the principal. The principal's duty to pay the agent exists whether the services rendered were authorized by an agency contract or by the principal's approval (ratification) of previously unauthorized acts of the agent. A person who acts as agent for two parties to a contract *with their knowledge* is entitled to receive compensation from each. When there is a so-called "secret agreement," the principal is not obligated to pay the agency fee.

▶ Fidelity Trust Company agreed to act as agents for Fabrizio for the purpose of procuring a loan. Without the knowledge or consent of Fabrizio, Fidelity Trust entered into an agreement with AMICA whereby AMICA would pay Fidelity Trust a finder's fee and a servicing fee in the event the loan was made. Fabrizio refused to pay the agreed fee for obtaining the loan commitment, claiming an unauthorized duality of agency. Judgment would be entered for Fabrizio. Contracts of dual agency are void because the agent represented both parties, and this was not known to each. The biblical expression applies: "No man can serve two masters; for either he will hate the one and love the other, or he will hold to the one and despise the other."

Reimbursement for Expenses The principal is obligated to reimburse the agent for expenses incurred while acting on behalf of the principal and within the agent's scope of authority and employment.

▶ Starrett, the credit manager of Bicor Machinery, Inc., attended a company-approved meeting in Houston. He submitted an expense account listing amounts advanced for plane fare, hotel room, food, and gratuities. Should Bicor Machinery question any of these expenses, Starrett would be justified in demanding full reimbursement as long as the amounts indicated were supported by a receipt for payments of $25 or more and were reasonable for amounts less than $25.

Agents have an obligation to limit expenses to items necessary to act on the principal's behalf and within the scope of their authority. Expenses resulting from personal pleasure, carelessness, neglect, or passing fancy will not be reimbursed by the principal.

▶ Suppose that Starrett, while in Houston on company business, decided to attend a professional football game. Although his attendance at the game was made possible by the business trip for Bicor Machinery, Inc., the expense was of a personal nature and would not be considered reimbursable.

Indemnification for Losses The principal is obligated to make good a loss or damage an agent suffers while following the principal's instructions under the agency relationship. If the character of the duties requires the agent to assume personal liability, the principal usually secures the agent against loss by indemnity bond or by some other means, such as insurance. An agent may presume that instructions given by the principal are lawfully given and that performance resulting from such instructions will not damage third persons. If this is not the case, and the agent incurs a liability to a third person for an act such as trespass, the principal must indemnify the agent against loss.

▶ While making repairs on a high-voltage circuit breaker, Kilbane received second-degree burns which required intensive medical care and a long period of rehabilitation. Since Kilbane was performing an authorized task on behalf of the principal, the employer would be responsible for all losses suffered and for all medical expenses resulting from the accident. Workers' compensation statutes in most states provide for fixed awards to employees or their dependents in case of industrial accidents. This dispenses with legal actions and the need to prove negligence.

Right of Lien An agent may retain possession of property belonging to a principal if the principal refuses to compensate the agent appropriately for authorized services. The right of lien terminates when the agent has been paid.

> Volpe, a salesperson for Flemming-Rutledge Industries, used a company-owned car for business travel. When Volpe quit, the employer failed to compensate him for commissions earned during the previous month. Volpe would have the right to hold the car as security until Flemming-Rutledge Industries paid the earned commissions.

Protection from Injury A principal has a duty to provide reasonably safe conditions of work for an agent. Agents must be notified of any unusual risk involved in the employment, if that risk is known and if it is unlikely that the agent would become aware of it. The duty of a principal concerning working conditions extends to the maintenance, inspection, and repair of the area of employment under the principal's control and the tools, equipment, and supplies the agents use. Principals must also provide competent supervisors where this is reasonably necessary to prevent undue risk of harm to agents or employees. Where work is dangerous to agents, unless rules are made governing its conduct, the principal must make known and enforce suitable rules.

Obligations to Third Persons

The principal is obligated to honor all contractual agreements entered into by the agent with a third person while the agent is acting within the scope of either express or implied authority. It is not necessary that the third person knows he or she is dealing with an agent. An agent with actual authority is authorized to make a binding contract in the principal's name. If a principal ratifies an unauthorized act of an agent, the principal becomes liable to the third person. A determination must be made, in the case of apparent agency, whether or not the principal clothed the agent with apparent authority to so act.

> Kaufman Instrument Labs sent Bauer to Sterling Electronics with instructions to purchase testing equipment. Bauer was told to act in his own behalf and not disclose that Kaufman Labs was the principal. After signing a purchase order, Bauer inadvertently revealed that he was representing Kaufman Instrument Labs. In the event of a dispute, either Bauer or the previously undisclosed principal might bring suit, but the right of Kaufman Instrument Labs is superior.

A principal is liable for an agent's torts if they are committed while the agent is working within the scope of his or her employment, even though they are not authorized. The third person may seek damages from either the principal or the agent. The liability of the principal and the agent is thus joint and several—the third party may sue them separately or jointly.

> Urban Electric Company, a retail appliance dealer, instructed Romanos to repossess a TV set from Washburne, who purchased it on an installment contract. Urban Electric informed Romanos that Washburne was in arrears with her payments, when actually her payments were current. (A recordkeeping error had

been made by Urban Electric.) Following instructions, Romanos made the repossession over the protest of Washburne. Romanos has committed a tort, but Urban Electric must indemnify him and satisfy Washburne's claim if she attempts to collect from Romanos.

Respondeat Superior   The liability imposed on principals and employers which makes them pay for the wrongs they have not actually committed is frequently referred to as *respondeat superior* ("let the master respond"). In addition to negligence of an agent, the doctrine also applies to intentional torts such as fraud, libel, assault, and trespass. It applies even though the principal or employer did not direct the willful act or agree to it. The theory here is that injuries to persons and property are hazards of doing business, the cost of which the business should bear; the loss should not be borne by the victim of the tort or by society as a whole.

 Garcia, a passenger in a taxicab owned by LaPenna Company, brought a suit for damages suffered when the driver assaulted, raped, and robbed her. Garcia argued that a common carrier is liable to a passenger who is assaulted by one of its employees before the transportation has been completed, whether or not the employee was acting within the scope of employment. The court would support Garcia's position. A taxicab is a common carrier, and the operator is duty bound to deliver passengers to their destination as promptly, efficiently, and safely as possible.

Governmental Bodies   Some employers are immune from legal action brought by an injured third person. There is some question about how to resolve liability when an agent or civil servant commits a tort while serving such an employer. For example, in some states a town or city is immune from legal action when a police officer or other public official commits a tort. The common view is that government employees are *not* protected by such immunities, however, and the police officer would be liable. In recent years, immunity granted to governmental and other administrative bodies has been greatly reduced in scope.

In respect to contracts, the authority vested in public officials is clearly set forth in public records which are open to public inspection. If, while acting as an agent, a public official exceeds his or her authority in dealing with third persons, the contract is void. Public officials, unlike private agents, assume no personal liability on contracts made outside their vested authority. Such contracts are void and unenforceable against either the agent or the represented government body.

 The chief of police of the town of Centreville entered into a contract with Dataline Corporation for the installation of a $9,000 information processing system. After it had been installed, the town's treasurer refused to honor the contract. The treasurer pointed out that all town purchases of materials and services amounting to $500 and over had to be made through a central purchasing department. The contract with Dataline would be unenforceable, and the chief of police would be protected from any personal actions that might be brought against him by third persons.

THIRD PARTY'S OBLIGATIONS AND LIABILITIES

The third party who is dealing through an agent is contracting with the principal, the agent being recognized just as a go-between. Once the contract has been entered into, however, the agent is no longer involved. The obligations which follow are those of the principal and the third party.

Contractual Liability to Principal

Once an agent contracts with a third party *for the principal,* it is the obligation of the third person to live up to the terms of the agreement. The principal may recover from third persons all property wrongfully disposed of by the agent or that he or she had no right to sell. Third persons who willfully interfere with the duties of the agent, to the injury of the principal, or who maliciously cause the agent to give up the work the agent is under contract to do for the principal, become liable to the principal. A third person who, by false representations or other fraud, causes an agent to make a contract for the principal, may be held liable for damages.

Contractual Liability to Agent

The third person ordinarily owes no contractual duty to the agent representing a disclosed principal. The agreement exists only between the third person and the principal. In contrast, the third person is liable for suit by the agent of an undisclosed principal. In these contractual agreements, the agent is bound to the third person. Torts committed by third persons generally result in an action by the agent, regardless of the type of agency.

An agent of an undisclosed principal may be bound to a third person because of commission rights. Factors, who buy and sell in their own name without disclosing their principals, may sue third persons to recover goods sold.

 Broderick contracted, on a commission arrangement, for the services of Computer Sciences Corporation. He was acting for an undisclosed principal, Die-Craft Tool Company. When Computer Sciences refused to carry out the terms of the contract, which called for the remote application of computers to improve payroll, accounts receivable, and accounts payable for Die-Craft, Broderick would be permitted to sue as though he were the principal.

Tort Liability

Any party to an agency transaction, whose person or property is damaged by the reckless misconduct of one of the others, can bring tort action against the offender. The violation of a legal duty owed by one party to another may manifest itself in reckless misconduct or negligence.

An agent who is injured because of the *malfeasance* (commission of an unlawful act) of a third person would be awarded compensatory damages in a court action. A third person who intentionally interferes with the wages or commissions to which an agent is entitled is also liable to the agent for the loss of any and all such potential earnings. Any third person who influences another to break a contract in which the agent is interested is liable to the agent as well as to the principal.

 Slaight, a neighbor of Lovato, discouraged him from continuing his building contract with EPB Construction Company. If the words or deeds of Slaight result in a breach of the contract in force between the building contractor and Lovato, EPB or its agent may seek damages from Slaight, who would be judged a *third-person intermeddler* (one who meddles with the affairs of others).

TERMINATION OF AGENCY

The methods of ending the agency relationship may be grouped according to the acts of the parties and the operation of the law. Among the factors that influence the termination of the contract of agency are provisions of collective bargaining contracts and of the Civil Rights Act that deal with employment, promotion, tenure, and termination. Both profoundly influence and limit the employer's right to end the agent's employment contract.

Termination of Agency by Acts of the Parties

Termination of an agency by acts of the parties can derive from (1) the terms of the original agreement (performance), (2) mutual agreement, (3) discharge by principal or breach by agent, and (4) wrongful termination by agent.

Performance   An agency is a contract and hence may be terminated by agreement and by performance, like any other contract. Termination of an agency may be predetermined by the passing of a specified period of time or the completion of designated tasks. In short, when the purpose of the contract has been served, the agency ends. When several agents have the capability of performing, as when a house is offered for sale on an open listing (a listing with a broker by the owner that permits other brokers to sell the property), the performance of one agent ends the authority of the others. In such terminations, notice to third persons who were aware of the agency relationship is advised.

Mutual Agreement   Any agency contract or relationship may be canceled and thus terminated by mutual agreement.

Discharge by Principal or Breach by Agent   If either the principal or the agent breaches the agency agreement, the agency will have been terminated. The principal or the agent has the power (not necessarily the right) at any time to terminate the agency. If such discharge is in violation of the agency contract, the principal or agent will be liable. Regardless of what may follow as the result of legal action, the principal-agency relationship is terminated. The agent may simply quit, thereby ending the agency. Wrongful termination, however, may subject the agent to a suit for damages by the principal. In any event, the agent cannot be forced to work against his or her will.

▶▶ Ziegler, an engineer-designer employed as an agent by Otto Foundry, Inc., quit the job without notice and without a company release. The corporation could hold the engineer liable for any damages suffered as a result of this impulsive termination of the agency contract.

Wrongful Termination Should the principal breach the agency relationship without just cause, the action may subject the principal to a suit for damages by the agent. A discharge of an agent for incompetence, disloyalty, or similar shortcomings, in other words, "for cause," would not enable the agent to recover damages under the law of agency.

Unwritten contracts between a worker and an employer cannot be terminated easily. Employers learned years ago that dismissing a unionized hourly worker almost always causes trouble, often a prolonged grievance procedure. Nonunion employees used to feel that they served at the pleasure of management. Most of them departed as quickly and quietly as possible when their services were no longer wanted. As a general rule, this is no longer the case.

Terminated employees may file charges under the National Labor Relations Act, the Civil Rights Act, or other regulations pertaining to age, sex, race, and religious discrimination. Some discharged employees sue former employers for damages to their professional reputation. Even people fired for stealing from the company or other crimes may fight to get their jobs back. Hard-pressed cities, states, schools, hospitals, and other public employers, including federal agencies, also are targets for a growing number of formal complaints.

A key reason for protests by fired employees is that few companies discharge white-collar employees on the basis of seniority. Instead, employers try to weed out the poorer performers and keep the better people, regardless of length of service. It is often hard, however, to convince the person fired that merit was the only consideration. Even poor attendance, long lunch hours, and shortened hours may be difficult to prove. Few salaried employees punch a time clock, and frequently their jobs are not strictly nine-to-five.

▶▶ Fidelie, a young computer programmer, was fired for allegedly keeping a tryst with her boss instead of going to work. She filed sex discrimination charges against the company, stating that any time off she and her boss took while on out-of-town assignments was to compensate for extra hours they worked on other days. She insisted that had two men taken such compensatory time off, nothing would have been said. The burden of proof would fall on the company to support its claim that the two employees were "fooling around" on company time.

Employers can avoid such problems by making sure that the termination of an employee can be justified. The worker's file must contain records—such as annual performance reviews and written reprimands—that prove the person was advised in advance that he or she was not performing satisfactorily.

When the employment relationship is unfairly terminated by the employer, the agent must be paid any amount due under the employment agreement for work performed and, in addition, money damages.

Agency Coupled With an Interest   An agency agreement in which the agent is given an interest in the substance of the agency in addition to the amount of compensation for services is said to be an *agency coupled with an interest*. A principal lacks power to revoke agencies of this kind without the consent of the agent. Such agencies, sometimes called *irrevocable agencies*, arise in situations where a principal allows an agent to sell property or collect rent as a means of liquidating a debt to the agent. The agent deducts commission and applies the proceeds to the credit of a debt that is owed by the principal.

> Wong contracted with Economy Sales Company, on a 30 percent commission arrangement, for an exclusive five-year agency in a designated area for the sale of vacuum cleaners. A $1,000 check was deposited with Economy Sales as evidence of Wong's good faith. The money was to be returned to Wong from the proceeds of sales of the vacuum cleaners. Economy Sales attempted to revoke the agency, claiming dissatisfaction with the sales effort made by Wong. Since Wong, in addition to his interest as agent, had an interest in getting back the $1,000 advance from the proceeds of the sales, Economy Sales could not revoke the agency.

Termination of Agencies by Operation of the Law

An agency is terminated by operation of law when events make the continuance of the agency impossible or impractical. The most common of these events are death, insanity, bankruptcy, and destruction of the agency.

Death   The death of the principal or the agent generally will cancel the agency relationship. Notice of the death need not be given, as the law assumes constructive notice to all concerned at the time of death.

Insanity   The insanity of either the principal or the agent terminates the agency. If the principal becomes insane, however, and the agent makes a valid agreement with a third person who has no knowledge of the insanity, the contract will be allowed to stand.

Bankruptcy   The bankruptcy of either party ends the agency. In case of the bankruptcy of the principal, the agency is ended because title to the principal's property is vested in a trustee for the benefit of creditors. An exception would be a doctor or attorney who has been acting for a principal prior to bankruptcy, or an artist who has completed 75 percent of a painting for the principal.

Destruction of Subject Matter   The destruction or loss of the subject matter of the agency automatically ends the agency. Thus, destruction of a house by fire ends the real estate broker's agency to sell the property. The imprisonment of the agent makes performance impossible and terminates the agency. In such cases, the agent is not relieved of an action on the agency contract for damages to the principal. In addition, the statute of limitations against such actions will not be in force while the agent is confined to prison.

▶ Helwig was hired by Contoura Business Products to photograph a new minicomputer. Before Helwig could take the pictures, he was arrested for involvement in the production of a pornographic film. He could not secure bail and was imprisoned. Inability to perform because of Helwig's imprisonment would terminate the agency agreement with Contoura Business Products.

Notice of Termination to Third Persons

When the termination of an agency results from the operation of law, notice of its termination need not be given to third persons. The courts rule that events such as death, insanity, or bankruptcy receive adequate publicity through newspapers and public records. As stated previously, however, notice of an agency termination by the parties is given to everyone affected. Principals who fail to provide notice may be estopped from denying a continuing agency should a third person believing that the agency still exists, contract with an agent.

▶ Spitzer, a buyer for Fox Department Store, was discharged. Lerner had never sold to Spitzer but knew that Spitzer was a buyer for Fox. After Spitzer was discharged, an article about her changing jobs was in the local newspaper, but Lerner did not read it. If Spitzer should purchase goods on credit from Lerner and charge them to Fox, the department store would not be liable for the cost of the goods. The newspaper publicity on Spitzer's job change would be adequate notice of agency termination. Lerner would have no cause of action against Fox.

The above incident illustrates that, although Spitzer had been known to be an agent for Fox, the power to bind the principal by estoppel was lost when the publicity relating to Spitzer's departure from Fox and her job change appeared in the newspaper.

Questions for Review and Discussion

1. What are the duties of an agent to his or her principal?

2. May an agent delegate his or her duties to a subagent? Explain.

3. When the principal is undisclosed, to what extent is an agent liable to third parties (a) on contracts, (b) on negotiable instruments, (c) for money received, and (d) in tort?

4. What are the agent's warranties when acting in a representative capacity for a principal with a third party? Explain.

5. Identify the principal's three primary obligations to an agent while the agent acts within the scope of actual or apparent authority.

6. What are the principal's obligations to third parties for acts of an agent and for torts of an agent? Explain.

7. Explain the extent of liability imposed on employers, principals, or masters by the doctrine of *respondeat superior*.

8. What are the third party's obligations and liabilities to the principal? Explain.

9. In what ways may an agency be terminated?

10. What is meant by an agency coupled with an interest?

Analyzing Cases

1. Hardee agreed to act as agent for Realtech Corporation in the purchase of acreage on which Realtech planned to construct a shopping mall. Realtech instructed Hardee to keep her identity secret. Its management felt that the landowners would inflate the price of their land if they knew of Realtech's intentions. Hardee contracted to buy the acreage, but Realtech refused to honor its agreement with Hardee and to advance her the money needed to complete the purchases. Hardee is sued for damages by the owners of the acreage. For whom would the court decide? Why?• See also *Meyer* v. *Redmond,* 205 N.Y. 478.

2. Knickerbocker Aviation Company hired Pinkham as its pilot to deliver planes to purchasers. While delivering a plane to a buyer, Pinkham decided to dive and fly low and fast over the home of an acquaintance. He lost control of the plane and crashed into the house. Although no one was hurt, a fire started which destroyed the house. Knickerbocker Aviation was sued for damages to the house. Its defense was that, at the time of the accident, Pinkham was flying in a manner prohibited by the company, and therefore it was not responsible. How will the court rule? Explain.• See also *Missouri R. Co.* v. *Raney,* 4 Texas Civ. A. 517.

3. Associated Properties, Inc., was engaged by Rosett to locate a $76,000 house. After locating the house, Associated Properties learned that the property was in the center of an area that a power and light company planned to purchase for expansion of its operations. Instead of transferring interest in the property to Rosett, Associated Properties purchased the house and placed it in the name of one of its agents. They subsequently sold the property to the power and light company for $250,000. Rosett sued Associated Properties for the difference between $76,000 and the $250,000, claiming lack of good faith on the part of the realty company. Will Rosett recover in this action? Why? • See also *Utlant* v. *Glick Real Estate,* 246 S.W.2d 760.

4. Finocchio worked as a driver-salesperson, making sales and deliveries in a suburban area. While making a delivery, Finocchio was attacked by a vicious dog and was hospitalized for a week. Finocchio sued her employer for damages for injuries received while working within the scope of employment. The employer denied responsibility, claiming that the owner of the dog was the only one responsible. For whom should judgment be made? Explain. • See also *Maggon* v. *Cahoon,* 26 Utah 444.

5. During a serious illness, Roeder was attended by a physician who advised an operation. Roeder consented, and the operation was performed. Following recovery, Roeder received the physician's bill for $990 and refused to pay it. Roeder claimed that no agreement concerning payment had been made prior to the operation. Would the physician be successful in an action against Roeder to enforce payment? Explain. • See also *Albert Steinfeld and Co.* v. *Broxholme,* 211 Pac. 473.

6. Kaplan instructed Coster, her banker, to invest $15,000 for her. Coster purchased speculative mining stock, which proved to be worthless. Kaplan sued Coster for her loss. Who should win the case? Why?• See also *Isham* v. *Post,* 35 N.E. 1084.

Legal Reasoning and Business Judgment

Analyze the legal aspects of these business problems. Suggest possible solutions.
1. You are a purchasing manager, and it has come to your attention that one of the assistant purchasing agents has been accepting money from vendors who have sold quantities of raw

material to your company. What are the rights of your company against this employee? What would you suggest your company do?

2. Guido, a sales representative, submitted the following expense report:

Luncheon, Roof Garden Cafe $ 18.00
Cleaning of suit and overcoat   6.75
Repair of car radio   21.00
Entertainment of purchasing
   agent and wife and three of
   Guido's acquaintances—
   designated as a sales expense   120.00

Would Guido's manager approve the payment of these items? Explain.

3. A company sales representative sold a large shipment of merchandise to a dealer in the Midwest. The dealer's check was enclosed with the order and was deposited to the company's account. It was subsequently discovered that the sales representative had given the dealer an unauthorized discount. Must the company accept and ship the order at the unauthorized discounted price arranged by the company sales representative? Explain.

Chapter 28
Law
of
Employment

The law of agency governs the rights and duties of principals and agents and the rights and duties of each with respect to third persons in contract and in tort. The law of agency is closely related to the law of employment on the state and federal levels, which includes numerous statutes regulating business and labor. State legislation controls such matters as hours of work and wages, workers' compensation, occupational safety and health, unemployment compensation, fair employment practices, social security, and pension reform. Federal legislation deals with hours and wages, liability for injuries to employees, civil rights, social security, and pension reform.

WAGES AND HOURS

Early efforts by lawmakers to regulate wages earned by employees and their hours of work were held by the courts to violate the employers' right to make contracts free of limitations. Gradually, the idea that employment contracts should be subject to reasonable restrictions gained support. The areas of employment that received early attention concerned women and children. The first shift in thinking came in 1936, when the U.S. Supreme Court upheld the right of the state governments to set minimum conditions of employment for women and children. The ruling went even further, however. The Court declared that "Freedom of contract is a qualified, and not an absolute, right." Freedom to contract, it said, is subject to the restraints of due process as guaranteed under the Fourteenth Amendment and to reasonable regulation. State governments may interfere with freedom of contract in order to set minimum standards of employment if such standards are needed to prevent injury to an employee's health or safety and to avoid harm to the public welfare. These standards may apply to most workers, not just women and children. This historic case upheld the regulation of the minimum employment contract and effectively eliminated most constitutional objections to social legislation regulating employment. One important result is that today about 70 percent of the states have passed minimum-wage laws. The path was also cleared for the federal government to begin to regulate hours and wages for workers engaged in interstate commerce.

The Fair Labor Standards Act

Congress passed the Fair Labor Standards Act (FLSA) in 1938 to correct conditions fostered by low wages, long work hours, and the exploitation of child labor.

Its purpose was to bar from interstate commerce goods produced under conditions harmful to minimum standards of living necessary for health and general well-being. The Fair Labor Standards Act was amended in 1977 to raise the minimum wage for most workers in a series of steps to $2.65 from $2.30 an hour; this minimum hourly rate will also be increased, in stages, to $3.35 by January 1, 1981. The workweek for covered employees must not be longer than forty hours, unless each employee receives compensation for overtime at a rate not less than one and one-half times the regular rate. Excesses in the maximum workweek are not violations, however, if the employee is hired subject to the terms of an individual contract or as the result of collective bargaining by employee representatives. The amendment also allowed employers to pay lower than minimum rates to full-time students in part-time jobs, as long as the students did not displace adults.

 Cusack's hourly rate as an employee of Cole's Food Store is $4.75 an hour, which is $2.10 over the minimum hourly wage. Cusack's overtime rate would be $7.125. Wages received for a forty-six-hour week would be $232.75, $42.75 of which represents work performed over the standard forty-hour week.

Exemptions to Act   The FLSA and its amendments specify those workers who are protected by and those who are exempt from its provisions. Not covered are persons employed in executive, administrative, or professional capacities. Others not covered by the provisions of the act include:

☐ Outside salespeople.
☐ Retail and service workers employed in establishments with an annual dollar volume of sales less than $250,000.
☐ Persons employed aboard a ship.
☐ Workers employed in the catching, taking, propagating, or harvesting of any kind of fish.
☐ Workers employed by small farms or engaged in agricultural processing.
☐ Domestic service workers.

Automatically excluded from FLSA coverage is nearly a third of the labor force—state, local, and federal employees, self-employed persons, and members of the armed forces. Also excluded are handicapped workers, messengers, and apprentices. Workers in these categories may be paid less than minimum wages, provided the employer obtains a certificate of approval from the Wage and Hour Division of the Department of Labor.

Minimum Age for Employment   The FLSA imposed an indirect prohibition on child labor in most private businesses. The act defined *oppressive child labor* as employment of a child of sixteen to eighteen in a hazardous occupation or the employment of any child under sixteen. A child of fourteen or fifteen can work for anyone, provided Labor Department permission is obtained and provided the job is not hazardous and does not interfere with schooling and well-being.
   Subsequent changes in the act broadened the prohibition against oppressive

child labor to include any aspect of interstate commerce. The agricultural provision was changed to bar child labor during school hours. Exempt from these regulations are the following:

- [ ] Children employed by parents, except in mining or manufacturing jobs.
- [ ] Newspaper deliverers.
- [ ] Children employed as actors or performers in the theater, motion pictures, radio, or television.
- [ ] Children working on farms outside school hours.
- [ ] Children working in local retail and service firms which make no deliveries across state lines.

> Ansley, a fifteen-year-old, was employed as a newspaper deliverer by Chase News Service. She worked four hours a day, six days a week and was paid $18. A school official challenged the News Service for employing a fifteen-year-old and paying only 75 cents an hour. The Attorney General advised the official that Ansley was exempt from the provisions of the Fair Labor Standards Act. Neither the minimum-wage provision nor the provision governing the maximum number of hours employed was operative in this case.

Equal Pay Act Federal legislation aimed at ending the traditional low-wage status of women in private industry was passed in 1963. The Equal Pay Act provided that no employer subject to the provisions of the FLSA is to discriminate on the basis of sex in payment of wages when the skill, effort, and responsibility required are equal for both sexes. Wage differences based on seniority, merit, rate of production, and similar factors other than sex are allowed. Payment of different wage rates to permanent employees and temporary employees also does not violate the equal pay provisions. According to the provisions of the act, state laws or other laws regarding hours of work, jobs requiring physical strength, rest periods, and the like do not make work "unequal."

As a result of several well-publicized court cases, a number of employers (notably the American Telephone & Telegraph Company) have been compelled to make substantial back-pay awards to women who were found to have been discriminated against in violation of this act.

> A review of the salary structure in a state university was ordered to determine whether inequities existed. Average salaries paid to male employees were compared with those paid to female employees for comparable jobs, using a formula based on levels of education, specialization, experience, and merit. It was found that thirty female faculty members were being underpaid, so the university raised the minimum pay of the females to the formula level. Approximately ninety male faculty members also discovered that they were receiving salaries below the average. The men claimed that the university's attempt to equalize male and female pay discriminated unlawfully against the lower-paid males. The U.S. Eighth Circuit Court of Appeals found the university in violation of the Equal Pay Act and ruled that the same formula must be applied to raise the minimum pay of the lower-paid males to the formula level.

From 1964 to 1972 the Equal Pay Act did not apply to exempt workers—to executives and to administrative and professional employees. But included in the 1972 amendments to the Higher Education Act was an amendment to the Equal Pay Act, making its provisions applicable to exempt workers of any employer subject to the federal Wage-Hour Law. The Equal Pay Act also prohibits labor unions and their agents from influencing any employer, whose employees they represent, to discriminate on the basis of sex.

Equal Rights Amendment

An equal rights amendment, guaranteeing equal rights to men and women, will be added to the U.S. Constitution on March 22, 1979, if three-fourths (thirty-eight) of the states ratify it. The proposed amendment states that "Equality of rights under the law shall not be denied or abridged by the United States or by any state on account of sex."

Supporters believe that the amendment will strengthen sex discrimination laws and bolster specific struggles for equal rights. Opponents argue that women would lose more rights than they would gain; i.e., labor laws giving special protection to women would be negated, and special widows' insurance and pension benefits would be eliminated. By the end of 1977, thirty-four states had ratified the amendment. Tennessee and Nebraska subsequently rescinded their ratifications but will probably face a court challenge if another four states ratify the amendment.

WORKERS' COMPENSATION

Workers' compensation statutes, sometimes called *employers' liability insurance laws,* are in force in all states. Under these statutes, workers injured in the course of employment are guaranteed indemnity for medical expenses, time lost from gainful employment, and permanent injury. **Indemnity** is security against hurt, loss, or damage. A covered worker is compensated for all expenses incurred in the treatment of the injury received. When a worker's death is attributed to injuries received on the job, benefits are provided the surviving members of the family. Schedules stating the amount of compensation granted under all covered claims are provided. Specific amounts are awarded for permanent partial disabilities such as the loss of an eye.

Some state laws provide compensatory payments for occupational diseases such as poisoning from lead and mercury. Individual states provide coverage for anticipated loss caused by the work and health hazards involved in mining.

Coverage Exclusions

The scope of the workers' compensation statutes differs in the various states. In some states, the laws apply to all industries; in others, to all work except agriculture and domestic services. In some states, specified kinds of accidents and diseases are not covered.

Workers' compensation statutes are mandatory in most states. In the remaining states, employers can usually elect to accept the provisions of the compensation statutes or the results of a suit brought by the injured employee or his or her survivors. In all such lawsuits, the employer may not rely on the common-law defenses which formerly prevented workers from recovering for almost any type of injury. These defenses were:

☐ Assumption of risk rule—inability to recover damages because the employee knowingly assumed the risk of such dangers.
☐ Fellow-servant rule—the injury resulted from the acts of a fellow worker.
☐ Contributory negligence rule—the injury was due partly to the negligence of both employee and employer.

Administering Workers' Compensation

Most states use a form such as the Universal Standard Workers' Compensation and Employers' Liability Policy to determine a company's liability. The premium paid by the employer is based on the size of the company's payroll and the kind of work performed. A commission usually administers the provisions of the statute. It has authority to direct payments of claims and to hear appeals.

An appeal to the courts may be made if the commission's ruling seems unfair. Courts have become liberal in upholding awards questioned on the grounds that an injury did not arise in the course of the employee's work.

In many states, an employee who brings suit for injuries is required by law to accept the court's decision and may not thereafter decide to accept the grant provided under workers' compensation. Likewise, if a compensation award is accepted, a worker is usually barred from later court action for further damages.

Most state statutes which establish rights related to employment forbid retaliation against an employee who tries to use such rights Even when a statute does not specifically say so, any attempt to block the broad corrective purpose of such a law usually gives the employee a cause of action for damages.

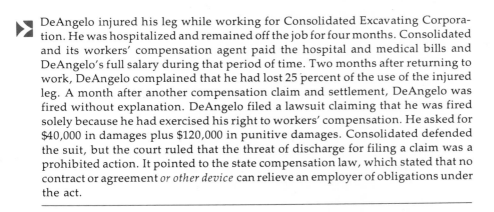 DeAngelo injured his leg while working for Consolidated Excavating Corporation. He was hospitalized and remained off the job for four months. Consolidated and its workers' compensation agent paid the hospital and medical bills and DeAngelo's full salary during that period of time. Two months after returning to work, DeAngelo complained that he had lost 25 percent of the use of the injured leg. A month after another compensation claim and settlement, DeAngelo was fired without explanation. DeAngelo filed a lawsuit claiming that he was fired solely because he had exercised his right to workers' compensation. He asked for $40,000 in damages plus $120,000 in punitive damages. Consolidated defended the suit, but the court ruled that the threat of discharge for filing a claim was a prohibited action. It pointed to the state compensation law, which stated that no contract or agreement *or other device* can relieve an employer of obligations under the act.

Federal Employer's Liability Act

At the national level, the Federal Employer's Liability Act (FELA) covers certain kinds of employees, such as railroad workers, for injuries, disease, and deaths arising out of the course of employment. The FELA, unlike workers' compensation, requires proof of employer negligence, but it does not limit the amount of recovery. By eliminating the defenses the employer would have at common law, however, the act greatly increases the chances of a worker's winning a lawsuit.

The original act has been amended several times. In its present form it has the following provisions:

☐ Employees of common carriers engaged in interstate and foreign commerce may claim damages for injuries caused by the negligence of the officers, agents, or employees of a carrier. Damages may also be claimed for injuries caused by equipment that has become defective through the employer's negligence.

☐ Contributory negligence of the injured employee may lessen the amount of damages owed to the employee, but it will not bar the employee from collecting on a claim.

☐ Any term in the contract of employment which attempts to exempt a carrier from liability or prevent enforcement of the FELA is void.

☐ A deceased employee's legal rights created by the act are transferred to the next of kin (persons who are most nearly related to the deceased by blood).

> Fabeck signed an employment contract with P&G Motor Freight, Inc., which included the following liability paragraph: "If injured in any accident caused by another vehicle while operating a P&G vehicle, I will not seek damages from P&G but from the owner and operator of the other vehicle." After he was in a collision with another tractor-trailer and was seriously injured, Fabeck sued P&G, who denied liability. It was held that P&G Motor Freight was fully liable. The disclaimer in Fabeck's contract was ruled invalid.

The Jones Act gives maritime employees the same rights aginst their employers as employees of carriers have under the FELA. Covered employees include those whose work involves (1) the navigation of the sea, Great Lakes, and rivers or (2) commerce conducted by navigation or done upon the sea or in ports. Another such statute is the Longshoremen's and Harbor Workers' Compensation Act. The Defense Bases Act extends the latter act's coverage to workers for private employers on U.S. defense bases.

THE OCCUPATIONAL SAFETY AND HEALTH ACT

The Occupational Safety and Health Act (OSHA) of 1970 covers more than 55 million industrial, farm, and construction workers employed by firms engaged in interstate commerce. Under the provisions of this on-the-job safety program, employers are required to furnish a workplace free from recognized hazards that have caused or are likely to cause death or serious injury to employees.

▶▶ A construction crane manned by an operator and an oiler went out of control, causing a fatal injury to another worker. The oiler had put the crane through a test run by raising and lowering the boom. It was revealed, however, that the boom brake bands were covered with grease and the backup brake system was not operating because of a missing part. OSHA regulations require the employer to designate a competent person to inspect cranes both before and during use. Neither the operator nor the oiler knew he had been designated to carry out such inspections. The court of appeals would rule that *designate* means that an employee must be informed of the existence and nature of his or her inspection duties. In short, that means formal selection and notification.

Safety and Health Standards and Hearings

The Secretary of Labor is required by OSHA to establish federal safety standards. Hearings on objections to a proposed safety and health standard are also authorized. A standard may be revised or revoked within sixty days after a hearing has been completed. Exemptions from standards are permitted any employer who applies for an exemption and meets certain OSHA commission standards. Warnings to inform employers and employees of safety and health hazards to which they are exposed are required. Any person may file for a judicial review of a standard within sixty days after it is officially announced or *promulgated*.

Inspection and Enforcement Procedures

OSHA provisions authorize periodic federal inspections of all working conditions. The inspections may be unannounced, and employers must permit federal inspectors to enter their plants without delay and at any reasonable time. The employer and employee representatives are permitted to accompany the federal official during the inspection. Employees are permitted to request an inspection if they believe that a safety or health violation exists. An OSHA Review Commission, with responsibility to review reported violations of a standard, has been established. The commission members are appointed by the President with Senate consent.

When a violation of a standard is observed, the federal inspector issues a citation. A posting of the citation near the violation site is required. If an employer contests the citation, a hearing is conducted by the commission. The basic function of the commission is to review the facts involved in the violation, recommend changes, or, if it is appropriate to do so, void the citation or penalty entirely. If the employer does not give notice that the citation is being contested, the citation and penalty are considered final and not subject to review by the commission. Persons affected by a commission order can obtain review in a U.S. Court of Appeals within sixty days after receiving the order.

The Secretary of Labor is also required to petition a U.S. district court to issue an order restraining any practices in a plant that pose an "imminent danger" to employees. In each case, the inspector must notify the affected employees and employer of the danger. In effect, an OSHA inspector has the power to close a plant when a standard violation threatens lives.

Penalties

The OSHA Review Commission may assess a civil penalty of not more than $10,000 for each willful or repeated violation of its standards. It may also assess a civil penalty of not more than $1,000 for each nonserious violation and up to $1,000 for each day a serious violation remains uncorrected. A criminal penalty of not more than $10,000 or six months' imprisonment or both may be assessed if a willful violation causes the death of an employee. If that violation is repeated and again results in the death of an employee, the $10,000 penalty is increased to $20,000.

EQUAL EMPLOYMENT OPPORTUNITY

A variety of federal, state, and local laws, executive orders, and federal guidelines, as well as court decisions and rulings, have been issued dealing with discrimination in employment. While there is still some confusion on several key issues awaiting final court clarification, the greater part of the equal employment opportunity area is now clear. It is illegal to discriminate on the basis of race, color, religion, sex, age, or national origin in all employment practices relating to hiring, discharging, promotion, and compensation, as well as in all other terms, privileges, and conditions of employment.

Civil Rights and Equal Employment Opportunity Acts

The Civil Rights Act of 1964, as amended by the Equal Employment Opportunity Act of 1972 (EEOA), carries blanket provisions prohibiting any manner of job discrimination on the basis of race, color, religion, sex, or national origin. To come under the law, a company must be doing work *affecting commerce*, and it must employ at least fifteen persons during each working day for at least twenty weeks in either the current or previous calendar year. This means an employer is subject if, either this year or last, he or she had fifteen or more employees on the payroll during twenty complete calendar weeks. Those weeks need not be consecutive, and it is calendar weeks and calendar years that count (i.e., Sunday through Saturday and January through December).

 Hayden Machinery Company has a labor force which fluctuated during the past eighteen months because some contracts were lost and later regained. Since the beginning of the calendar year, Hayden Machinery never had fifteen employees on the payroll; but it did have fifteen during the first nineteen weeks of the previous calendar year. The total labor force also rose to fifteen for four days during one week in August and then sixteen for a full week in September (both were busy periods which required temporary office help). Is Hayden Machinery subject to the EEOA, since its average number of employees for the previous year was well under fifteen? Yes, it is. For twenty normal five-day weeks Hayden had fifteen or more employees. It makes no difference that some were temporary, or that the firm did not have fifteen or more employees during any week of the present calendar year.

The provisions of these acts apply to the following organizations:

- ☐ All private employers of fifteen or more persons.
- ☐ Private and public educational institutions with respect to persons whose work involves educational activities.
- ☐ All state and local governments, governmental agencies, political subdivisions and departments. Exempted, however, are state and local elected officials and their personal assistants and advisers.
- ☐ Public and private employment agencies.
- ☐ Labor unions with fifteen or more members, and all unions which operate a hiring hall.
- ☐ Joint labor-management committees for apprenticeship and training.

The provisions of the acts do not apply to the employment of aliens outside of any state. Also exempt are religious organizations, Indian tribes, employees of private-membership clubs, and personnel of the federal government. United States government personnel, although excluded from protection under the acts, look to the Civil Service Commission, which is charged with the responsibility to enforce equal employment opportunity in federal agencies.

Equal Employment Opportunity Commission

Under the Civil Rights Act, the Equal Employment Opportunity Commission (EEOC) was established to receive and, on its own initiative, to investigate job discrimination complaints and to reach agreement through reconciliation. Should it fail in its efforts, however, the EEOC has the power to go directly into federal court to enforce the law. In addition, interested organizations may also bring class actions on behalf of individuals who feel that they have been discriminated against by their employers. In this connection the employee can claim back pay and damages as well as legal fees. Aggrieved persons can also go into court directly to sue an employer for alleged discriminatory practices.

If the court finds that an employer, employment agency, or labor organization has been or is intentionally engaged in an unlawful employment practice, it may enjoin the accused party from such practice. It may order affirmative action, including the reinstatement or hiring of employees, with or without back pay. Employees may not recover more than two years' back pay, calculated from the date the charge was filed.

Federal Contract Compliance

Contractors or subcontractors on a contract from the federal government are subject to the requirements of Executive Order 11246, which places them under the Office of Federal Contract Compliance (OFCC) regardless of how many employees they have. The orders prohibit discrimination because of race, color, religion, sex, or national origin in all employment practices including hiring, firing, promotion, and compensation. In addition, the orders require that each organization develop and implement an *affirmative action program* to encourage the employment of minority workers. Failure to comply may prompt the OFCC to cancel existing federal contracts and forbid the granting of future contracts to the blacklisted company.

Affirmative Action Programs

An *affirmative action program* details present employment policy. It also outlines what management intends to do about hiring, compensating, and promoting women, blacks, Hispanics, and other minorities to correct imbalance between minority employees and white male employees. The plan shows goals and timetables in problem areas that reflect *underutilization*—a lower number of minority persons than could be expected from the labor market drawn upon—and *concentration*, a preponderance of minority-group members in a low-paying job category. The major problem areas are:

- [ ] Recruitment and hiring policies which keep minority employment at low levels.
- [ ] Compensation programs which do not give equal pay for equal work.
- [ ] Promotion policies which keep qualified minority members in low-paying jobs.
- [ ] Benefit programs which discriminate against minority groups.

Application Forms   The law includes blanket provisions against questions on employment application forms that could be used to discriminate against an applicant. The form should include a statement that the questions are not designed to secure racial, religious, or other personal data and that the applicant should feel free not to answer a specific question if he or she feels it conveys such information. The following requests are potentially hazardous, unless they relate in some way to a sincere employment objective. They should be eliminated from employment applications.

- [ ] State race or color of skin.
- [ ] State religion, parish, or church.
- [ ] State whether applicant is a naturalized citizen or native-born.
- [ ] Give birthplace of applicant, applicant's spouse, or parents.
- [ ] Give national origin of applicant, spouse, or applicant's parents.
- [ ] Give names of relatives other than husband, wife, minor children, father, or mother.
- [ ] List organizations, clubs, lodges, and societies of which applicant is a member.
- [ ] Give applicant's original name, if it has been changed by court order.

The EEO Commission also advises against requesting the following information:

- [ ] Applicant's service in the armed forces.
- [ ] Applicant's maiden name, if she is a married female.
- [ ] Applicant's length of residence in a location.

Remedial Affirmative Action When there is a finding of discrimination through investigation or through employer self-audit, remedies and requirements are outlined by the federal courts. Courts have ordered numerical hiring and promotion when these are necessary to correct the effects of past discrimination. It is important, therefore, to know what the courts have identified as discrimination prohibited by law and what remedies have been ordered.

☐ Where *class-wide discrimination* is found to exist, action to eliminate it must apply to all members of the affected class.

☐ The *consequences* of employment practices, *not the intent*, determine whether discrimination exists and requires remedial action.

☐ Any employment practice or policy which has an unequal effect on members of a protected class—those groups specified in the law—or which continues the effect of prior discriminatory practices amounts to unlawful discrimination. To justify any such practice or policy, an employer must prove that the policy is required by business necessity. Courts interpret business necessity very narrowly, requiring convincing evidence that a discriminatory practice is essential to safe and efficient operation of the business and/or a demonstration of extreme adverse financial results.

Courts have required basic changes in all aspects of employment systems. They have specified numbers or percentages of minorities and females to be hired, trained, or promoted in job categories, until certain goals are reached. They usually require an employer to take action quickly, with follow-up checking by the court.

▶ Household Finance Corporation paid more than $125,000 to its female employees, who charged that they were denied promotion because of sex. Under terms of the consent decree, HFC agreed to hire 20 percent females for branch representatives' openings until such representatives were 20 percent female. HFC also agreed to train female and minority employees to help them qualify for better jobs where they are underrepresented.

Sardis Luggage Company was ordered to pay $120,000 in back wages to black plaintiffs, plus $25,000 in attorney fees and court costs. The company was ordered to hire black workers in a 2:1 ratio for four years, until the combined production and clerical work force had a ratio of blacks proportionate with the nonwhite work force in the company's labor area.

The extent of legally required affirmative action to correct the effects of discrimination is reflected in the major agreement signed by American Telephone & Telegraph Company after more than two years of court action. In addition to a $15 million back-pay award and $50 million in yearly payments for promotion and wage adjustments to minority and female employees, specific affirmative actions were decreed by the court:

☐ Specific hiring and promotion targets, including goals to increase use of women and minorities at every job level.

☐ Goals for employing males in previous all-female jobs.

☐ Women and minorities now in nonmanagement, noncraft jobs will be able to compete for craft jobs based on their qualifications and company seniority.
☐ Promoted employees will be paid, generally, based on length of service.
☐ Female college graduates hired in eight prior years will be assessed to determine interest and potential for higher-level jobs, and a specific development program will prepare these women for promotion.

Ban on Wage Discrimination

The coverage of the Equal Pay Act, which amended the FLSA, was extended in 1972 to many additional exempt workers and to outside salespeople. Its provisions require that equal wages be paid for substantially similar work performed by men and women, regardless of race, national origin, religion, or sex. Equal pay is required for jobs of equal skill, effort, and responsibility. This means the same base pay, opportunity for overtime, raises, bonuses, and commissions. The act is also concerned with the more subtle kind of discrimination where a wage rate is depressed because only women or minorities traditionally have been employed in a job category.

 Anaconda Aluminum Company was ordered to pay $190,000 in back wages and court costs to 276 women who charged that the company had sex-segregated job categories. Jobs classified "female" and "male" had been reclassified as "light" and "heavy," but women were prevented from transferring to heavy jobs. After layoffs, the company hired new male employees for heavy jobs rather than recalling females with seniority in light jobs. The company was ordered to assure opportunity for all jobs to anyone who could qualify.

Age Discrimination

The Age Discrimination in Employment Act of 1967 and the 1974 amendments to the Fair Labor Standards Act make it illegal for firms employing twenty or more persons to discriminate against present employees or job applicants solely because they are between forty and sixty-five years of age. Included are state and local government employees, but not elected officials. Under the terms of this legislation, an employer may not:

☐ Advertise for job applicants in such a way as to indicate or suggest a preference, specification, or limitation on age.
☐ Discriminate in any way, including refusing to hire and discharging an employee or applicant because of age. This provision prohibits discrimination in matters of pay, working conditions, and privileges of employment.
☐ Put limits on an older employee so as to deprive him or her of employment opportunities equal to those of younger employees.

Employment agencies are subject to the Age Act in most of their functions. Want ads that express age preference are outlawed. Phrases, such as "prefer recent graduate," "25 to 35," "young girl," or "young boy," that imply an age preference are forbidden. Stress on age in interviews with clients and failure or refusal to refer persons in the protected age bracket for jobs may expose an employment agency to challenge.

Unions must look closely at the provisions of this act. Canceling memberships, failing to refer for jobs, or dropping from the active list are outlawed practices when based on age. Writing discriminatory clauses in a negotiated contract can cause trouble for a union. Since neither the employer nor the union may bargain away an employee's inherent rights, illegal age clauses would be struck down by the courts.

The Age Act requires that employers keep all personnel records for three years, including name, address, birthdate, occupation, pay rate, and weekly amount of pay. Records of job applicants must be kept for one year.

Training and apprenticeship programs are exempt under the act, since these are offered to help youth enter the work force. In all other areas of employment, however, the only exceptions to the terms of the act are government-funded projects and *bona fide occupational qualifications*. Both are arguable. Although government-funded projects are not covered, the agencies handling the funding probably are. And, of course, federal contractors and subcontractors are covered.

Claiming that a bona fide occupational qualification is the reason for not hiring above a certain age is risky. Should anyone challenge the business necessity for not hiring older workers to do a certain job, proving that age was a legitimate occupational qualification under the law would be difficult.

 In an effort to save labor costs, Standard Oil of Ohio decided to clear out the ranks of older, more experienced, and higher-paid employees. When challenged, Standard Oil signed a consent decree in a federal court, and the cost to the company was approximately $2 million. Some of the workers who had been fired were not ordered reinstated. They were tested and found unable to perform their jobs properly. But they had to be paid back wages in the settlement. Had the company fired only for incompetency, rather than attempting to clear out older employees, there would have been no suit, or the costs would have been less.

Employment Testing

Shortly after the Equal Employment Act was passed, the Supreme Court ruled (*Griggs* v. *Duke Power Company*, 401 U.S. 424) that tests may not be used as a cover-up for discriminatory tactics in employment, for hiring, promotion, or other personnel actions. It is not enough that employment tests be given uniformly to both majority and minority applicants. The tests must be fair and impartial; that is, test questions must not be stated in such a way that it is easier for a member of one ethnic group to answer than another. For example, blacks and some members of other ethnic groups often speak less formal English than the majority of whites. Therefore, a question about English grammar would usually be easier for a white applicant than a black one. The bias becomes more evident when the questions about English grammar have little relevance to actual job qualifications.

The Supreme Court did not outlaw employment tests. It did, however, set standards which tests must measure up to. An employment test must have a clear and obvious relationship to job requirements, such as an office worker's filing or typing skill and a taxicab driver's knowledge of streets. Tests must also be validated by the EEOC. This involves a review of the employer's entire employment procedure and the test data to determine whether the test is a reliable indicator for success on the job and whether it is discriminatory in any way.

Employee Record Retention Requirements

The Labor Department requires employers to maintain certain records for a minimum of three years for every employee hired. Those that must be maintained are the employee's name, address, date of birth, occupation, rate of pay, and pay earned each week. Employers must also keep records of all job or promotion interviews and copies of advertisements used to recruit applicants.

The following records must be kept for one year:

- ☐ Employment applications.
- ☐ Résumés submitted in response to advertisements.
- ☐ Copies of instructions given to employment agencies or unions to hire people.
- ☐ Copies of all notices advertising to the public or staff the existence of job or promotion possibilities, overtime opportunities, or training program openings.
- ☐ Records showing why an applicant was hired, promoted, or rejected.

SOCIAL SECURITY

The Social Security Act was enacted by Congress in 1935. Since then a number of amendments have increased the kind of benefit coverage and the dollar amounts. The social security law requires that during their working years, covered employees, their employers, and self-employed persons pay taxes to the federal government in anticipation of benefits when a family's earnings are reduced or stopped because of retirement, disability, or death. Under social security's Medicare provisions, hospital and medical insurance helps protect persons who are sixty-five and older from high health care costs.

Protection Under Social Security

Under the Social Security Act, over 32 million persons receive regular monthly sums for old age, survivor's, and disability benefits. About 10 million persons a year have some of their medical bills paid under Medicare; and 25 million poor persons are helped under Medicaid. During the 1974–1975 recession, over 10 million persons drew benefits under the unemployment insurance features of the law. Supplemental security income payments are being drawn by over 4 million aged, blind, and disabled persons. Some 11 million draw aid for dependent children, and thousands of parents and children receive maternal and child health, crippled children's, and child welfare services under the act. Over $100 billion is being paid out under the Social Security Act annually. Along with other

federal, state, and private pension and social welfare programs, the total amount
being disbursed exceeds $15 billion a month. This represents a significant vol-
ume of purchasing power that has set a floor below which consumer income will
not fall and that reduces the harmful effects of recession on families and the
economy.

Social Security Tax Contribution Procedures

The wage base upon which social security taxes are levied is adjusted each year
according to a formula written by Congress. The rate of tax imposed by law is 5.85
percent through 1977, 6.05 percent through 1980, 6.30 percent through 1985, 6.45
percent through the year 2010, and 7.45 percent thereafter. Employers must
deduct their employees' share of the contribution to the social security system
from their wages, match those payments, and send the combined amount to the
Internal Revenue Service. Self-employed persons who net $400 or more a year in
wages pay their tax each year when filing their individual income tax return.
Employers file an Employer's Quarterly Tax Return with the IRS and deposit
social security taxes with an authorized federal reserve or commercial bank at
various times. Employers are also required to keep records pertaining to employment taxes for a period of at least four years after they are due or are paid. The
records must include such information as the names, addresses, occupations,
and social security numbers of all employees paid; the amounts and dates of
payments; the period of employment; duplicate copies of tax returns; and the
dates and amounts of deposits.

The income base for social security has gone up every year since 1971, and it
will probably go up annually from now on to keep ahead of inflation. Congress
voted in 1972 to make social security benefits "inflation proof." The law provides
that benefits—and the income base on which taxes must be paid—shall go up
every year in which the cost of living rises 3 percent or more.

UNEMPLOYMENT COMPENSATION

The 1935 Social Security Act provided the legal framework for the federal-state
unemployment insurance system. The act made use of a tax-offset device which
encouraged the states to set up their own unemployment programs. As amended,
the act requires all covered employers of four or more persons engaged in
interstate commerce and industry to pay a federal payroll tax of 3.2 percent of the
first $4,200 of covered wages. Employers participating in a state-approved pro-
gram are entitled to a federal tax credit (offset) of 2.7 percent. States are required
to place their tax revenue in a trust fund managed by the Secretary of the
Treasury.

Each state is responsible for administering its own program and for determining coverage benefits, tax rates, and eligibility. States are not required to hold to
the same coverage, wage base, or tax rates used for computing federal unemployment tax. Most do, however, in order to gain maximum advantage from the
federal tax offset. A portion of the state tax (0.5 percent) is retained by the federal
government and is used to finance administration of the program at the federal

and state levels. The retained funds are also used to offset the federal share of extended and emergency benefits during periods of high unemployment. The retained tax also serves as a loan fund from which states may borrow when their state benefit fund account is overdrawn.

Benefit Structure and Additional Insurance Programs

Although benefits and other features of the insurance system vary considerably according to state, most states pay eligible workers a maximum of twenty-six weeks of benefits under the regular program. In an effort to cope with economic downturns, Congress has provided for additional benefits. Whenever the national unemployment rate reaches 4.5 percent, the benefit period is lengthened by thirteen weeks. The cost of the extra weeks of insurance is borne equally by state and federal trust funds. A supplemental benefit which pays up to twenty-six additional weeks of compensation to those who have used up regular and extended benefits has been authorized during times of high unemployment.

Qualifications for Compensation Payments

To qualify for unemployment compensation payments, a covered employee must register for employment at the state employment office. The worker must meet state requirements regarding length of time employed and amount of wages. The worker must be physically and mentally capable of accepting employment and must not refuse an offer of suitable employment.

 Wilkins, a machinist, was furloughed from his job with Hughes Helicopters because of economic conditions. He registered with the state employment agency and requested unemployment compensation. The interviewing official told him about a job opening for a machinist with United Technologies. Wilkins refused it on the grounds that he needed a rest before accepting another job. Wilkins would be ineligible for compensation for any week in which his unemployment resulted from failure to accept suitable work offered to him by the employment office or by any employer.

Additional permanent unemployment insurance programs have been established by federal legislation. Railroad workers are covered by an independent unemployment insurance program that is financed by a payroll tax which is administered by the Railroad Retirement Board. A separate program for federal civilian employees is financed by annual federal appropriations and is administered by the state unemployment insurance agencies, acting as federal agents. An extension of the federal employees' program covers veterans who have served in the U.S. armed forces after January 31, 1955.

Rights to Jobless Benefits During Strike Period

Generally, a worker is disqualified from receiving unemployment benefits when he or she quits work voluntarily or is discharged for proper cause. Thus, in most states, when unemployment is the result of a strike or other labor dispute, the worker's disqualification from jobless pay lasts as long as the dispute.

▶▶ Employees of Buffalo Forge went on strike when the contract between their union
and the company expired. Several workers made application for unemployment
compensation after the strike was in effect for a week. The Unemployment
Compensation Board would deny their request for benefits because they had left
their jobs voluntarily.

The court has held, however, that workers who are on layoff at the time a
strike is called and who are not notified to return to work during the strike period
are still on layoff under the law and qualify for unemployment benefits. Those
who disregard recall notices while on layoff would be disqualified from receiving
benefits.

▶▶ Madrone Excavating, Inc., began a layoff of its employees during the coldest
winter months, when construction work was halted. During the layoff, the labor
contract with the operating engineers expired. When the bargaining deadlocked,
the union declared a strike to be in effect. Madrone Excavating filed protests
against granting unemployment benefits to any of the employees during the
strike period. The unions argued that none should be disqualified by the strike.
The appeal court held that the workers on layoff at strike time who were not
notified to return to work during the strike period were still on layoff and thus
qualified for unemployment benefits.

"Floaters," who linger on a job just long enough to qualify for unemployment
pay and then plot for dismissal, risk forfeiting all benefits.

▶▶ Rimland performed well for five months and then suddenly made mistakes in her
work, arrived late, was often absent, developed a sullen attitude, and became
sloppy in appearance. She boasted to a co-worker that this behavior would result
in dismissal and unemployment compensation. Most state unemployment agencies would rule such conduct improper and would deny Rimland benefits.

Exemptions From Unemployment Insurance

The Social Security Act exempts certain employees from the unemployment
insurance provision. Those are federal and state government workers; religious,
charitable, and educational workers; agricultural workers; and family workers.
Benefits to federal government workers, similar to those granted by the states, are
provided from a separate fund supervised by a federal agency known as the
Unemployment Compensation for Federal Employees.

PENSION REFORM

The Employees' Retirement Income Security Act of 1974—better known as the
Pension Reform Act—affects an estimated 30 to 35 million employees under
private pension plans. It includes a number of conditions affecting the management of funds supporting private pension systems. Highly detailed, the act has
considerable impact on company benefit policy.

Benefit Provisions

The following paragraphs describe the general effects of the provisions of the Pension Reform Act.

Eligibility   An employee in a group covered by a qualified pension plan must be eligible to participate in the plan after age twenty-five and after one year of employment. Participation must begin within six months after these requirements are satisfied or on the first day of the next plan year, whichever is the earlier.

Maximum age exclusions are forbidden with one exception: a pension plan may bar an employee hired within five years of normal retirement age. Union employees may be excluded from a plan if there is evidence that retirement benefits have been the subject of good-faith bargaining.

Service   For purposes of eligibility and vesting, 1,000 hours of work determines a year of service. This hour standard is used to determine whether an employee may be excluded from a plan as a seasonal or part-time worker. All service with an employer must be counted, subject to certain rules regarding breaks in service. An employee has a one-year break in service, for example, if he or she fails to work at least 500 hours in a twelve-month period. In the event of a break in service, the plan may require employment for up to one year following the return to work before prebreak service is counted.

Vesting   *Vesting* is the term applied to the set of conditions (such as length of service and age) that gives a worker a nonforfeitable right to a pension before retirement. Under the law's terms, workers for companies with pension plans must be given vesting rights—accrued retirement credits that the company cannot take away. Employers have the following three vesting options:

☐ A worker is vested for at least 25 percent of his or her accrued benefit from the employer's contribution after five years of service, plus an additional 5 percent for each of the next five years of service and an additional 10 percent for each succeeding year.

☐ A worker is provided with 100 percent vesting—full pension rights—after not more than ten years of service.

☐ A worker is entitled to at least 50 percent vesting when the sum of his or her years of service and age totals forty-five. Vesting would increase by 10 percent for each additional year. This "rule of forty-five" applies only after an initial five-year period of service, but full vesting is assured after fifteen years of employment regardless of age.

Benefits   For most workers, the maximum annual employer-provided pension is 100 percent of the average salary during the highest three consecutive years of compensation (but not less than $10,000) or $75,000, whichever is the smaller. Cost-of-living increases or retirement before age fifty-five would of course require an annual or an actuarial adjustment.

A worker's pension must begin within sixty days after normal retirement age.

A vested worker who ends employment after satisfying the service requirement for early retirement must be given the right to receive a reduced pension when the early retirement age is reached. A worker may be given a cash payment at termination instead of a deferred vested pension if the vested benefit is less than $1,750. If the value is greater, a cash payment may be given if the worker agrees. Former employees who return to an employer may reinstate their past service credit by repaying the amount received plus 5 percent interest. A pension plan must include a 50 percent spouse's survivor provision for retiring workers who have been married for at least one year, unless the worker elects against it.

Vested benefits may be used as collateral for reasonable loans from a pension plan. Otherwise, benefits are nonassignable and nontransferable.

Pension Insurance

The Pension Reform Act establishes an independent *Pension Benefit Guaranty Corporation* under the joint direction of the Secretaries of Labor, Treasury, and Commerce to insure unfunded vested pension benefits in the event of a pension plan failure. Pension plans must purchase insurance from the agency to cover both persons already retired and workers with vested benefits. The agency is empowered to pay as much as $750 monthly in retirement benefits to each worker should his or her pension plan collapse. Companies and unions pay premiums of from $.50 to $1 per worker per year. An employer is liable for repaying the agency for any insurance benefits paid because of a plan failure. Maximum liability is 30 percent of the employer's net worth as valued within 120 days before the plan is ended.

Reporting and Disclosure

Employers must give annual pension plan accountings to their covered employees, the Department of Labor, and in some cases the Social Security Administration. Annual reports also must be audited by independent accountants. A worker must be given a summary of the pension plan's major provisions, written so as to be understandable by the average plan member. At the worker's request, he or she must also be given an accounting of the plan's financial condition. Every worker covered by a pension plan is entitled to notice in writing if a claim for benefits is denied, with reasons for the denial included. Workers also have the right to bring suit in a federal court to recover benefits wrongfully denied.

Individual Retirement Account

Workers at companies that do not offer pension plans can establish what are called *individual retirement accounts* (IRA). These are domestic trusts organized for the exclusive benefit of an individual or beneficiaries. Employees can set up their own accounts with a bank or insurance company, or can have the employer or the union set up accounts. Persons can contribute 15 percent of annual earned income into an IRA, up to a maximum of $1,500. The amount is deductible from gross income for federal income tax purposes, whether itemized or by standard deduction. Taxes on these contributions and on money earned by the account are deferred until the funds are withdrawn on retirement, which can be no earlier than age 59½ and no later than age 70½.

 Van Ness, who earns $15,000 a year, is in the 22 percent tax bracket. If she makes the maximum contribution of $1,500 to a retirement annuity, her annual tax saving will be approximately $330. The annuity is tax-sheltered until she retires, when her overall income presumably will be lower than it is at present.

Premature distribution of money from the retirement account before reaching age 59½ will be penalized by a 10 percent nondeductible excise tax on the amount. Withdrawals because of death or disability are not considered premature. The tax-free rollover of amounts from one individual retirement account to another or from an employer-operated plan to an individual plan are also not premature if made within a prescribed period of time.

Contributions from the employer to an employee's account are allowed. In such cases, however, the total of contributions cannot exceed $1,500 annually. A spouse can also set up a separate retirement account. His or her earned income is treated individually, and the total contribution of both to the plan can amount to as much as $3,000.

Persons can set up a retirement account by establishing a special trust or custodial account in a bank, savings and loan association, or credit union in which the funds would remain at the prevailing rate of interest. A simple savings account from which money can be withdrawn at any time would not qualify. Another alternative would be to invest in shares of a mutual fund, in securities, or in a special type of United States Treasury bond that currently pays 6 percent interest annually on redemption. There is also the option of selecting a retirement annuity or endowment contract issued by an insurance company. This contract must be nonforfeitable, nontransferable, and have no life insurance element in it. The option is usually the most advantageous, because it guarantees a life income of a fixed amount determined when the plan begins.

In the period when withdrawals from an IRA are permitted—ages 59½ through 70½—a person can take the money either in the form of a full distribution, a lump sum, or an individual or joint-and-survivor annuity. This decision is an important one, with many tax implications; it should usually be made with the benefit of professional advice.

Keogh Plans for Self-Employed Individuals

Retirement plans for self-employed persons, which are known as *Keogh plans*, were introduced after passage of the Self-Employed Individuals Tax Retirement Act of 1962. Physicians, salespersons, authors, shopkeepers, and owners and partners of full-time or part-time businesses may set up such plans.

Currently the self-employed are permitted to set aside, on a tax-free basis, as much as 15 percent of earned income each year, up to a ceiling of $7,500. A provision of the Keogh law restricts annual additions to an account to the lesser of 25 percent of earned income or $25,000. Thus, the top minimum deduction of $750 is available only to persons whose earned income amounts to at least $3,000.

For example, an artist or author who free-lances at home in addition to his or her regular job and earns $2,000 a year for supplementary work cannot put more than $500 into a plan.

Questions for Review and Discussion

1. What is the purpose of the Fair Labor Standards Act? Explain.

2. What is the primary provision of the Equal Pay Act of 1963, and who is covered by its provisions?

3. Who administers workers' compensation statutes? Contrast the protection afforded employees from the hazards of their work under these statutes with those provided under common law.

4. In what manner does the Federal Employer's Liability Act differ from the protection offered by the workers' compensation statutes?

5. What is the purpose of the Occupational Safety and Health Act? What is the most significant aspect of the act?

6. What are the key factors that determine whether or not a company is subject under the job discrimination provisions of the Equal Opportunity Act of 1972?

7. What is the scope of an affirmative action program and the nature of the four major problem categories?

8. Two applicants, one aged forty-nine and the other aged sixty-one, applied for the same job. The senior applicant had more experience and a better validated test score, but the younger applicant was hired. The older applicant sued, but the company argued that the Age Discrimination in Employment Act did not apply because both men were over forty. Who has the better case? Explain.

9. Outline the duties imposed by the Social Security Act on (*a*) employers and (*b*) self-employed persons.

10. What are the minimal requirements set by an employer before an employee can participate in a pension plan?

Analyzing Cases

1. Chang, a special agent in the Federal Bureau of Narcotics and Dangerous Drugs, received several grade promotions, commendations, and awards. Rather than accept a transfer from Boston to Chicago, Chang resigned from the drug bureau. He applied to various public and private law enforcement agencies but was refused because the prospective employers received a report from the bureau stating that his performance was substandard or he had been terminated for misconduct. Chang sued the federal government for damages, claiming that the government had been negligent in failing to maintain complete and accurate records of his performance and employment history. Who should win the case? Explain. • See also *Quinones* v. *U.S.*, 492 F.2d 1269.

2. Superior Drug Company employed women in its warehouse as order clerks. Their principal duties were to arrange merchandise on warehouse shelves, gather stock from shelves to fill customer orders, and replenish the stock. Superior Drug also employed men to perform similar functions, but referred to them as sales trainees. They filled orders and replenished stock as part of a program designed to familiarize them with the products before beginning actual sales work. The trainees were paid substantially higher wages than the women. When

the disparity came to the attention of the women, they brought a suit against Superior Drug for an injunction and two years' back pay. Superior Drug argued that the higher wages for the men were justified because they were enrolled in a training program—a factor other than sex. For whom should the court decide? Explain.
• See also *Hodgson* v. *Behrens Drug Company*, 475 F.2d 1041, cert. denied, 414 U.S. 822.

3. Lazarus was a product manager for a business machine company located in a multistoried building. One day he had lunch with several co-workers in the lunchroom on the second floor, then took the elevator to his twelfth-floor office. Feeling in good spirits because things were going well, Lazarus tried a dance step in the rising elevator, fell, and broke his leg. The Workers' Compensation Board ruled that Lazarus's dance step was not an unreasonable activity. The employer argued that it did not pay Lazarus to dance, and that the injury resulted from a personal act which was not connected with the job in any way. Who should be awarded judgment? Explain.• See also *Bletter* v. *Harcourt, Brace & World*, 303 N.Y.S.2d 510.

4. In 1975 Smythe had gone to work for Jet Industries, Inc., where she met Allen Jarrett, an employee of Jet Industries since 1971. They married in June 1977, and she was terminated by the company in July. Jet Industries had a policy barring employment of employees' wives. Smythe brought a sex discrimination suit against Jet Industries. She argued that the policy was not neutral and penalized women. Should she win the case? Explain. • See also *Harper* v. *Trans World Airlines, Inc.*, CA-8, 11/18/75.

5. Sandor Construction Company was the general contractor for a multistory building. T&M Electric was a subcontractor installing electrical and sheet-metal work. OSHA inspectors came to the site and found an open stairway running from the basement to the top floor and an opening for an elevator shaft on each floor—all with inadequate guardrails. Both the general contractor and the subcontractor had employees on the site. The OSHA inspector handed citations for violations to both Sandor Construction and T&M Electric. The total fine amounted to $450, but T&M Electric contested its citation. It argued that the safety measures on the site were the work of the general contractor's employees. OSHA held that safety obligations fall equally upon every employer whose employees are working at a particular location. How should the case be decided? Explain. • See also *Anning-Johnson Co.* v. *Occupational Safety and Health Review Commission*, 516 F.2d 1081.

6. Yenco was hired by Spruce Ridge Farm as a trail guide trainee. One of the horses on the farm, a very spirited animal, had thrown two other employees who attempted to ride it. Yenco asked several times if she could try. Each time the answer was no, because Yenco was too inexperienced to handle such a horse. When the manager left the area, Yenco did try. She was thrown off and seriously hurt. Spruce Ridge Farm contested the award of workers' compensation on the grounds that Yenco had disobeyed the instruction not to mount the horse. Therefore, the activity that resulted in Yenco's injury was outside the scope of her employment. Who should win this case? Explain.• See also *Bartley* v. *C-H Riding Stables, Inc.*, 206 N.W.2d 660.

Legal Reasoning and Business Judgment

Analyze the legal aspects of these business problems. Suggest possible solutions.

1. The medical department of your company received a request from one of the workers in the shipping department for sick leave and medical coverage for a hernia operation. The worker claimed that the hernia resulted from the lifting of a large crate several months earlier. When asked why the incident was not reported promptly, the employee stated that he felt the condition would improve without surgery. The company doctor, in questioning the worker, discovered he was a member of an athletic club and had been an active wrestler during the past year. The doctor wondered whether the company was responsible for providing compensation for the worker's alleged employment-connected injury. What are the company's rights in this matter?

2. Your insurance agency has four major departments—fire, casualty, claims, and accounting. Bybee, a woman, is a vice president and head of accounting. The man in charge of claims is the president of a wholly owned subsidiary. The head of fire is a vice president. The top person in casualty is not an officer of the company. At one point, Bybee's salary was equal to that of the vice president in fire and higher than that of the other two men. But in three years Bybee has seen the officers in fire and claims pull way ahead in salary and the non-officer draw even with her. Bybee threatens to take legal action, claiming that it is discriminatory for the company to pay the head of accounting less than the male heads of claims and fire, and no more than the head of casualty. What course of action should your company follow?

3. Your company faces a dilemma. An Equal Employment Opportunity Commission affirmative action agreement requires that your company increase its minority-group employment through preferential hiring. A union contract provision, however, requires layoffs on a last hired, first fired basis. EEOC argued that the last hired, first fired layoff procedure, unless modified, would frustrate the proportional employment objective. Caught in the middle, how would you advise your company with respect to priority in layoffs?

Chapter 29
Labor-Management Relations

Employer and employees are in a sense partners in a common cause. Each is important to the other, and each makes a material and necessary contribution to the economic well-being of all. Nevertheless, they are hostile parties with respect to the share each takes from the business enterprise. One of the employer's primary objectives is to keep costs down. Labor unions, on the other hand, seek the highest wages and benefits possible.

Corporations are the employers of most organized workers. The representatives of corporations are management personnel whose aim is to provide dividends for shareholders. Employees, on the other hand, are represented by union leaders who are responsible to the membership. Both are often professional negotiators, with a mission to gain the best bargain possible. Although they occasionally achieve results agreeable to both parties, a gain for one cause is usually a loss for the other. Like competing teams, employer and union representatives are constantly on guard against the moves of the other. Each seeks advantages for use in bargaining.

Employers rely on certain resources to strengthen their bargaining position. The most obvious is a superior knowledge of the condition of the business. Another is that they are generally in a better position than unions are to release information so as to gain the ear of the public. The most effective weapon available to workers is the strike. An employer whose business is closed by strike action until employee demands are met may be forced to come to terms. Unionized workers also have the ability to exert pressure on elected officials.

EARLY LABOR-MANAGEMENT RELATIONS EFFORTS

Over a span of some sixty or more years a group of labor-management relations laws emerged. The first federal statute was the Clayton Act in 1914. Besides its antitrust provisions, it contained two sections relating to labor. The first attempted to prohibit federal courts from forbidding activities such as strikes and picketing in a dispute over terms or conditions of employment. The second stated that the antitrust laws did not apply to labor unions or their members in carrying out their lawful objectives.

Congress passed the Railway Labor Act in 1926. This law provided machinery for dealing with labor disputes in the railroad industry. Its provisions were later extended to airlines, so that collective bargaining could be encouraged for both air and rail transportation. Also established was a three-member National Mediation Board with the duty to appoint bargaining representatives for employees in railway and air transportation industries. The board has no judicial power to hold hearings or to issue cease and desist orders. Violations of the Railway Labor Act are punishable through criminal proceedings in the federal court system.

The Norris-La Guardia Act was passed by Congress in 1932. Often referred to as the Anti-Injunction Statute, this law was a further attempt to limit the authority of federal courts in prohibiting union activity. It did nothing, however, to impose any duty on employers to deal with or even recognize unions.

With the passage of the Wagner Act or National Labor Relations Act, in 1935, the door was opened for the rapid growth of the union movement. The act outlawed unfair labor practices by employers which either prevented the organization of employees or destroyed their unions where they existed. Provision was made for the selection by employees of a union with exclusive power to act as their collective-bargaining representative. Also created was a three-member National Labor Relations Board (NLRB) to administer the act. The board was given broad powers to prevent employers from using unfair labor practices by holding hearings and issuing cease and desist orders.

Five practices by employers were declared to be unfair to labor in Section 7 of the Wagner Act:

☐ Interference with efforts of employees to form, join, or assist labor organizations, or to engage in common activities for mutual aid or protection.

The employees of the Penn Coal Company were required by the company to purchase all food, clothing, and other supplies at designated company stores. When a group of workers decided to trade at other stores in their communities, they were discharged from their jobs. The NLRB would rule that the company had violated the provisions of the Wagner Act and would require Penn Coal to rehire the fired workers and award them back pay for the period of their improper discharge.

☐ Domination of a labor organization or contribution of financial or other support to it.

The personnel director of West Coast Poultry Company demanded the right to attend the membership meetings of the union representing company employees. Also demanded was a voice in union proposals involving working conditions. The Wagner Act bars any such effort on the part of an employer to dominate union operations. The demands of the personnel director would be refused by the union membership without fear of reprisal.

☐ Discrimination in hiring or tenure of employees for reason of union membership or for union activities.

Draper was selected by the union membership to serve as their representative in collective-bargaining meetings with Detroit White Line Company. After his selection, Draper was harassed by the production manager and the general manager for trivial matters concerning work schedules and productivity. Draper has the right to file a complaint with the NLRB for the discriminatory practices against him.

☐ Discrimination against employees for filing charges or giving testimony under the act.

☐ Refusal to bargain collectively with a duly designated representative of the employees.

> Knickerbocker Aviation, Inc., learned that its employees were planning to organize into a labor union. The management felt it had been fair in its treatment of the workers and resented the move to have a union certified. Notices were placed in each employee's pay envelope stating that anyone joining the proposed union would be fired. The organizers filed a complaint with the NLRB, and the company action was ruled an unfair practice. A cease and desist order was issued to Knickerbocker Aviation.

Unions and employers are entitled to cease and desist orders, injunctions, and awards for damages if any of the declared unfair labor practices are found to have occurred.

> ▶▶ The NLRB held an election by secret ballot among the employees of Technical Instruments Inc., at the request of the union. The union won the election by a vote of 45 to 43. Technical Instruments Inc. filed objections to the election. Before it was held, "recognition slips" had been given to employees by several employees picked by union officials. The workers were told that there would be no initiation fee charged to those who signed the slip before the election. The NLRB would deny certification of the union, finding that a fair election must honor the right of those who oppose a union as well as those who favor it. It would hold another election, free of such improper pressure on employees.

LABOR-MANAGEMENT RELATIONS ACT

The Labor-Management Relations Act, popularly known as the Taft-Hartley Act, was passed by Congress in 1947. It amended the National Labor Relations Act and added certain new provisions. Its purposes were (1) the protection of both parties to collective bargaining from wrongful interference by the other and (2) the protection of employees from the union itself.

The Taft-Hartley Act added a section concerning union practices that were outlawed as unfair labor practices.

☐ Preventing an employee from joining or forcing an employee to join a union; forcing an employer to choose particular representatives to bargain with the union.

☐ Causing the employer to discriminate against an employee who is not a union member, unless there is a legal union-shop agreement in effect. This provision outlaws the *closed shop* (in which none but members of the union are engaged as workers) in all states and the *union shop* (where a worker is required to join a union after a specified period of time) only in states with "right-to-work" laws. Such laws prohibit agreements requiring membership in a union as a condition of employment. About twenty states have right-to-work laws.

> Midland International hired two new turbine operators. Neither was a member of a labor union, and the union representative objected to having them start work

in the power plant. The provisions of the Taft-Hartley Act give Midland the right
to hire nonunion employees. After a trial period of not less than thirty days,
however, the new employees must join the union if they are to keep their jobs.

☐ Refusing to bargain with the employer or the NLRB-recognized representative of the employer.

☐ Striking, picketing, and engaging in a secondary boycott for illegal
purposes—that is, conspiring to cause the customers or suppliers of an
employer to cease doing business with that employer.

> Steel Specialists, Inc., sells strip steel to Thomas Spring Company. The steel is
> transported by Roadway Express, Inc., whose employees are nonunion. The
> union representing Steel Specialists instructs its employees to refuse to load
> Roadway Express trucks with steel in order to force Steel Specialists to stop using
> Roadway Express. This form of secondary boycott is an unfair labor practice and a
> violation of the Taft-Hartley Act.

☐ Charging new union members excessive initiation fees where there is a
union-shop agreement.

☐ Causing an employer to pay for work not performed.

In the event of certain unfair labor practices, the injured party was given the
right to sue the labor union.

> ▶ Kelly Asphalt Block negotiated a two-year contract with its union. Wages and
> fringe benefits were agreed upon by both the employer and the union. Six
> months before the contract would have ended, the union called a strike which
> caused Kelly Asphalt Block heavy financial loss because of uncompleted contract
> obligations. In a suit against the union, Kelly Asphalt Block would recover for its
> losses resulting from the wildcat strike.

The Taft-Hartley Act also permitted the use of an injunction, upon application
to the United States Attorney General, to forbid for a period of eighty days a
threatened strike or lockout in a major industry if the national health or safety
would be harmed. During the eighty-day period, a Federal Mediation and
Conciliation Service created by the act works with the parties to try to reach
agreement. If reconciliation fails, the employer's final offer is presented to the
members of the union. Should they vote against this final proposal, the strike
may continue until collective bargaining or congressional legislation solves the
dispute.

Unions were required to furnish detailed information about their organization and financial condition. Union leaders were also required to take affidavits
that they were not communists or advocating the forcible overthrow of the
government. The act further limited labor unions by restricting the use of union
funds for political activities and regulating the setting up and control of union
welfare funds.

> ▶ An officer of Pacific Gamble Corporation, after meeting with the president of the
> local union, contributed $5,000 of the company's money to the union's welfare
> fund. In consideration of the gift, the union official agreed to drop the union's
> current demand for a wage increase. This agreement would be judged illegal by
> the National Labor Relations Board.

NATIONAL LABOR RELATIONS BOARD

The National Labor Relations Board (NLRB) created by the Wagner Act was increased to five members by the Taft-Hartley Act. The members of this administrative agency are appointed by the President in staggered terms of five years each. Once appointed, members may be removed from office only after notice and hearing for neglect of duty or misconduct in office.

The NLRB has the exclusive power to prevent any person from engaging in any unfair labor practices affecting commerce.

Prevention of Unfair Labor Practices

Whenever it is charged that a person has or is engaged in an unfair labor practice, the NLRB issues a complaint stating the charges. A notice of a hearing before the NLRB is served on the person. It fixes a place and designates a time which may not be less than five days after the serving of the complaint. The person charged has the right to file an answer to the complaint and to appear in person (or to send a representative) and give testimony at the specified place and time. At the discretion of the NLRB member or agent conducting the hearing, any other person may be allowed to intervene and to present testimony. The rules of evidence that prevail in courts of law or equity, however, are not enforced.

Written testimony is taken by the NLRB. If it is concluded that the person named in the complaint has or is engaged in an unfair labor practice, the NLRB issues and serves its findings. The order requires the person charged to cease and desist from such practice and to take appropriate corrective action. The offender may also be required to make periodic reports showing the extent to which the order has been complied with. If the testimony reveals that the person named in the complaint has not engaged in any unfair labor practice, the NLRB states its findings and issues an order dismissing the complaint.

Enforcement of NLRB Orders

The NLRB has the power to petition for enforcement of its order any U.S. Circuit Court of Appeals within whose jurisdiction an unfair labor practice has occurred. Upon receipt of a transcript of the entire record of the NLRB proceedings and the findings and order of the NLRB, the court serves notice upon the person named. In so doing, the court takes over jurisdiction of the case. The court has the power to grant temporary relief or a restraining order as it deems just and proper. It can introduce a decree enforcing, modifying, or setting aside in whole or in part the order of the NLRB. The court considers the original findings of the NLRB to be conclusive. Additional material evidence is considered only when one of the parties shows to the satisfaction of the court that there were reasonable grounds for failure to present such evidence in the original hearing. The jurisdiction of the court is exclusive, and its judgment and decree are final, subject to review by the appropriate district court.

Any person aggrieved by a final order of the NLRB may also seek relief in any Circuit Court of Appeals. A copy of the petition must be served upon the NLRB.

The aggrieved person must also file with the court a transcript of the entire record of the proceedings, certified by the NLRB. Included must be the pleading and testimony upon which the disputed order was entered. Petitions are generally heard promptly, if possible within ten days after being docketed.

LABOR-MANAGEMENT REPORTING AND DISCLOSURE ACT

The Labor-Management Reporting and Disclosure Act (Landrum-Griffin Act) of 1959 contained a number of amendments to the Taft-Hartley Act, but its provisions for the most part dealt with union reform. It provided that nothing in the Wagner Act, as amended by the Taft-Hartley Act, prevents the courts of any state from dealing with labor disputes which the NLRB will not hear. Although this reinstated the power of state courts to apply common-law doctrines in dealing with labor disputes, only about seventeen state legislatures have taken advantage of this privilege.

The primary thrust of the Landrum-Griffin Act was to eliminate corruption in labor unions. The act provides for (1) the reporting and disclosure of certain financial transactions and practices of union officials, (2) the prevention of abuses in the supervision or control of union membership, and (3) standards with respect to the election of officers.

Section 101 of the act is a bill of rights of the members of labor organizations. Members are given specific rights, subject to reasonable rules and regulations, in the union's constitution and bylaws:

- ☐ To nominate candidates, vote in elections, and attend and participate in membership meetings.
- ☐ To meet and assemble freely with other members and to express views.
- ☐ To vote on dues, initiation fees, and assessments by secret ballot.
- ☐ To institute action in court against the organization or its officers.
- ☐ To be safeguarded against disciplinary action (except for nonpayment of dues), without written notice, time to prepare a defense, and a fair hearing.

> Gilfeather was charged with working against the interest and harmony of the union and using force against an officer of the union in order to prevent the proper discharge of the duties of the officer. Gilfeather was tried by the union, found guilty as charged, and expelled for an indefinite period. He then brought suit for damages in District Court, claiming that he had been denied a full and fair hearing. A notice of charges was provided containing a statement of the facts relating to the fight Gilfeather had had with the union official. This fight was the basis for the disciplinary action, and the fact that Gilfeather admitted having struck the first blow indicated the charges were supported by evidence. The District Court would hold that Gilfeather had not been deprived of the full and fair hearing guaranteed by the Landrum-Griffin Act.

The Landrum-Griffin Act also establishes the right of any employee to receive on request a copy of each collective bargaining agreement made by the labor organization with any employer.

Reports by Unions, Their Officers, and Their Employees

Every labor organization must file a copy of its constitution and bylaws with the Secretary of Labor, together with a report signed by its president and secretary. The report contains the following statements:

- ☐ Name of the labor organization, its mailing address, and the location of its main office or the office at which records referred to in the act are kept.
- ☐ Name and title of each officer.
- ☐ Initiation fees required from new members and fees for work permits.
- ☐ Regular dues or fees or other periodic payments required to maintain membership in the labor organization.
- ☐ Provisions made and procedures followed with respect to qualifications or restrictions on membership; levying of assessments; participation in insurance or other benefit plans; authorization for disbursement of funds; audit of financial transactions; calling of regular and special meetings; selection of officers and stewards; discipline or removal of officers or agents for breaches of trust; imposition of fines; suspensions and expulsions of members; ratification of contract terms; strike authorization; and issuance of work permits.

Labor organizations must also file an annual financial report with the Secretary of Labor. The union's financial condition and operations for the preceding fiscal year must be accurately disclosed, as follows:

- ☐ Assets and liabilities at the beginning and end of the fiscal year.
- ☐ Receipts of any kind and their source.
- ☐ Salary, allowances, and other disbursements to each officer and employee who received more than $10,000 during the fiscal year.
- ☐ Loans made to any officer or employee which amounted to more than $250, together with a statement of purpose, security, and repayment arrangements.
- ☐ Loans to any business enterprise, together with a statement of purpose.

RESTRICTIONS ON EMPLOYER CONDUCT

Under current labor legislation, employers are forbidden to engage in the several unfair labor practices.

Obstructing Employees' Efforts to Unionize or to Conduct Mutual Protection Activities

These practices include the use of *yellow-dog contracts,* in which workers agreed that they would not join a union and that they could be fired if they did. This practice included the circulation of blacklists among employers and the use of employees as labor spies in the plants and shops of employers. Also prohibited are tactics by employers involving threats to fire those involved in efforts to organize employees or to reduce employee benefits if they succeed in unionizing.

Another employer practice that is often ruled unfair is the discharge of workers for breaking company rules, such as "a worker may not leave work without permission." The NLRB has ruled that workers do not necessarily lose their right to take the most direct course of action available to them in order to correct an objectionable working condition, merely because they do not make a specific demand on their employer to correct the condition. Recently, however, the courts have read new meaning into this broad interpretation.

▶ Pochel's Construction Company fired an ironworker who left his post on the fifteenth story of a new building, where he was connecting steel beams. The ironworker refused to return to work because of high winds. The NLRB argued that a worker cannot be fired for refusing to work when there is a real danger of death or serious injury. The judges, however, read that language as merely permitting a worker to make a complaint about unsafe working conditions.

In making their ruling, the judges pointed to the congressional rejection, during consideration of the legislation, of a provision much like the rule that a worker cannot be fired for exercising his or her rights under the law. Congress feared that workers might abuse the rights granted and, for purposes of intimidation, disrupt or end their employers' business operations.

Another sensitive situation arises when employers are accused of interfering with, restraining, or coercing employees, by means of the written or spoken word, in the exercise of their right to form, join, or assist labor organizations. Employers are free to express or publicize any views or arguments in any printed or broadcast form, provided such expression contains no threat of reprisal or force or promise of benefit.

Domination of a Labor Union

Any organization of employees must be completely independent of the employer. Employers may not interfere with the formation or administration of any labor organization or contribute financial or other support to it.

Discrimination in Regard to Hire or Tenure

An employer may not discriminate in regard to hire or tenure of employment or use any term or condition of employment to encourage or discourage membership in any labor organization. However, in the several states that have enacted right-to-work laws, the employer may require, as a condition of employment, membership in a certified labor organization on or after the thirtieth day following the beginning of a worker's employment.

Discrimination Due to Filing Charges

An employer may not discharge or discriminate against an employee because he or she has filed charges with or given testimony to the NLRB. Accused employers must prove that the true reason for a course of action against a worker was misconduct, low production, or a necessary personnel cutback, and not the employee's filing of charges or giving of testimony.

> Wilshire was fired by Old Colony Transportation, Inc., after giving a written, sworn statement to an NLRB examiner who was investigating an unfair labor practice charge filed against the employer by other workers. Old Colony argued that labor law protected employees against employer reprisal only for filing an unfair labor practice charge or for giving testimony at a formal hearing. The NLRB ruled that the intent of the law was to give broad rather than narrow protection to the worker. It said that all persons with information about unfair labor practices must be completely free from retaliatory acts against them because they reported to the NLRB. It issued cease and desist orders to Old Colony Transportation and required the rehiring of Wilshire with back pay.

Refusal to Bargain Collectively in Good Faith

It is an unfair labor practice for an employer to refuse to bargain collectively and in good faith with the employee representatives who are selected by the majority of workers. An employer with reasonable cause to question whether the unit designated by the employees is qualified for recognition may petition the NLRB for relief. The Board has the authority to direct an election by secret ballot and to certify its results.

> The union obtained authorization cards from a majority of Caterpillar Diesel, Inc., workers and demanded that it be recognized as the collective-bargaining representative. Caterpillar Diesel doubted the majority that was claimed and insisted that the union petition the NLRB for a secret-ballot election. The union struck for recognition as the bargaining representative and filed a charge of unfair labor practice against Caterpillar Diesel based on its refusal to bargain. The NLRB held that unless Caterpillar Diesel interfered with the union's organizational campaign efforts, the union had the burden of taking the next step in obtaining an NLRB election, even though it held authorization cards supposedly representing a majority of the workers. The law did not intend to place the burden of getting a secret election on the employer.

Engagement in Secondary Boycotts

It is unlawful, in an industry affecting commerce, for any labor organization to encourage employees to engage in a secondary boycott with the purpose of forcing an employer to cease using, selling, or transporting the products of any other producer or processor. Anyone injured in business as the result of such a boycott may sue in a U.S. District Court and recover damages and court costs.

PROHIBITIONS ON UNION CONDUCT

Certain conduct or activities by labor unions are recognized as unfair labor practices and thus are illegal.

Hindering Workers From Joining or Forcing Workers to Join a Union

A labor organization or its agents may not restrain or coerce employees in the use of rights to self-organization, i.e., their rights to form or join a labor organization, to bargain collectively through their chosen representatives, and to engage in activities for the purpose of mutual aid or protection.

 The union levied a $200 fine on Coker and McKeown because of their strike-breaking activities after they had resigned from the union. In the hearing before the NLRB, the union argued that their constitution expressly prohibited members from strike-breaking. The NLRB found that the union restrained both Coker and McKeown in this exercise of their right to bargain collectively by seeking to enforce the fines.

Influencing Employer Discrimination Against Nonunion Workers

An unfair labor practice results when a labor organization or its agents cause or attempt to cause an employer to discriminate against an employee whose membership in the union has been denied or terminated. Failure to tender the dues and initiation fees uniformly required as a condition of acquiring or retaining membership is considered to be an exception to this rule. Thus, employees who object to the activities of a labor organization are protected from reprisal on the part of union officials.

 Colton was a member of the union representing Delmar Ken Films, Inc. She learned that another union member was stealing blank tape and reels from the company warehouse. She warned the person that the theft would be reported. When informed of the warning, the union representative revoked Colton's membership and asked the company personnel officer to have her fired. Colton filed a complaint with the NLRB, charging the union with illegal restraint in the exercise of her legal rights. The NLRB ruled that Colton's union membership could not be withdrawn for the reasons indicated and ordered the union to restore her membership.

Requiring Employees to Pay Excessive Fees

It is an unfair labor practice for a union to require employees to pay excessive or discriminatory membership fees. In judging such fees, the NLRB considers factors such as the practices and customs in the industry and employee wages.

Featherbedding

A make-work rule or *featherbedding* (forcing an employer to pay for work not performed) is sometimes included in union contracts. Sometimes, this practice is designed to increase safety or to reduce unemployment. Featherbedding is not illegal if the employer receives value or service owing to its practice.

Illegal Picketing

The Labor-Management Reporting and Disclosure Act of 1959 made it an unfair labor practice for any labor organization to picket any employer with the object of obtaining recognition of an uncertified union. It is also unlawful to picket for purposes of extortion, that is, to attempt to enrich any person, whether or not he or she is a member of the union, by taking money from an employer. Not prohibited is picketing for the purpose of informing the public that an employer does not employ members of a labor organization. Such picketing must not prevent other employed persons from receiving, delivering, or transporting goods to or from the employer being picketed.

Labor-Management Agreements

In signing an agreement with a union, the employer recognizes the union as the bargaining representative of a specified group of workers. Although such agreements do not contain all the characteristics of a legal contract, they are in essence a contract and are often so identified. The possible subjects comprising such agreements are numerous. They tend to explain the general principles according to which the employer and union are to operate together.

Typically, an agreement contains clauses dealing with dues collection; rights of unions to conduct business on employer time; working hours; seniority; promotions; layoffs; and grievance procedures. Many agreements provide that if a dispute cannot be resolved, it is turned over to a third party for arbitration. Every agreement contains a duration clause. The meaning of every word is important; misunderstandings over language can trigger grievances.

> In its collective-bargaining contract with Wilke Iron and Steel Company, the union had agreed to a clause which prohibited workers and union officials from distributing union literature in its work and nonwork areas. Later, the union challenged the rule. When Wilke Iron and Steel refused to negotiate a change, the union filed a charge of unfair labor practice with the NLRB, claiming interference with the rights of employees to form, join, or assist labor unions. Wilke Iron and Steel would be found guilty of a violation inasmuch as the place of work is considered to be a unique and proper place to distribute collective-bargaining information, provided it is done on nonworking time.

Negotiation Options

Labor disputes do arise over the meaning and the act of applying the clauses contained in the collective-bargaining contract. Sometimes employers and unions settle their differences by themselves. When the issue is too complex, a settlement is sought through mediation. In this procedure, a designated third party assists the employer and union representatives in seeking a compromise. But the mediator lacks authority to impose a binding solution. When such efforts to get unbiased input into the negotiations and to encourage conciliation fail, arbitration is considered.

The purpose of arbitration is the final solution of an employer-worker dispute. There is agreement in advance to accept the arbitrator's decision as final and binding. The parties involved are given notice of the time and place of the hearing; at the hearing, testimony is received from both sides; then the arbitrator considers the facts and renders a decision. There are several advantages to using arbitration instead of the courts in settling employer-worker controversies. It is a much quicker and far less expensive procedure. In addition, arbitration creates less hostility than does a court action, and it allows the employer to continue its business operations while the dispute is being decided.

If arbitration is not used and agreement cannot be reached, a strike may result. When the public interest is involved, the dispute may be resolved by government intervention. In that event, an injunction forbidding the strike for the statutory eighty-day cooling-off period could be invoked.

Questions for Review and Discussion

1. What resources and weapons do employers and employees use to strengthen their respective bargaining positions?

2. Besides its antitrust provisions, what was the effect of the Clayton Act on labor-management relations?

3. Discuss the purpose and state the major provisions of the National Labor Relations Act, known as the Wagner Act.

4. What five practices by employers were declared to be unfair to labor in Section 7 of the Wagner Act and are subject to cease and desist orders, injunctions, and awards for damages?

5. State the reasons for passage of the Taft-Hartley Act, and indicate the nature of its major provisions.

6. What union practices were outlawed as unfair labor practices by the Taft-Hartley Act?

7. State the primary thrust of the Landrum-Griffin Act and the specific rights it gave to union members.

8. For the purpose of revealing practices which may not be in the best interests of union members, what reports must unions and their officers file with the Secretary of Labor?

9. Identify the typical contract clauses contained in a collective-bargaining agreement.

10. How may the employer and the union who are parties to a collective-bargaining contract proceed to enforce a clause over which there is disagreement? Which procedure is binding on each?

Analyzing Cases

1. Workers employed by the Southern Textile Mills elected Jaworoski as their representative to negotiate with management regarding improvements in wages and working conditions. Upon learning of Jaworoski's appointment, the textile mill manager fired him immediately. He was told never again to come upon company property. Does Jaworoski have a remedy under the Wagner or National Labor Relations Acts?

Explain. • See also *Matter of Container Corp. of America*, 61 NLRB 823.

2. The *Greenville Times,* a daily newspaper which used syndicated features and advertised nationally, employed twenty persons in its newsroom who wrote copy and headlines and performed general editorial work. These workers were poorly paid, considering the education and skills required of them. Dougherty, a copy editor, called a meeting at her apartment for the purpose of discussing salaries and benefits. The group designated Dougherty as their representative to meet with the publisher of the *Greenville Times* and discuss possible improvements in wages and benefits. When the publisher heard about the meeting, Dougherty was discharged for insubordination. She filed a charge of unfair labor practices with the National Labor Relations Board. Should she win her case? Why?• See also *Goldfield Consolidated Mines Co.* v. *Goldfield*, M.U. No. 20, 159 Fed.

3. The management of Technical Instruments, Inc., refused to enter into contract negotiations with its employees as long as they were represented by Danzberger, whose reputation as a union organizer and spokesperson was well known. The union employees refused to replace Danzberger with another representative, and all efforts to bargain collectively stopped. What are the rights of the union members employed by Technical Instruments? Explain.• See also *Matter of American News Company*, 55 NLRB 1302.

4. Crockett joined the other workers at Engineered Components Company in a strike against the employer for a wage increase and a cost-of-living clause. After being off the job for two weeks, Crockett applied to the State Unemployment Compensation Office for unemployment insurance payments. Will Crockett qualify for unemployment insurance? Explain.• See also

Tri-County Trade Council v. *American Steel Foundries*, 238 Fed. 728.

5. Romanos, a subcontractor, installed an electric welding machine on the site of a construction job and gave the job of operating it to a member of the Ironworkers' Union. The job steward for the operating engineers threatened Romanos with a strike if the operating engineers were not given the work. When Romanos refused to agree to the demand, the job steward met with Westcott, the general contractor, informing him that the members of the operating engineers' local working at the job site had voted to strike unless Westcott gave them jurisdiction over the electric welding machine. When Westcott refused to accede to the demand, the operating engineers walked off the job. Does the action of the operating engineers represent an unfair labor practice? Explain.• See also *NLRB* v. *Local 825, International Union of Operating Engineers*, 400 U.S. 297.

6. March, an unsuccessful candidate for president of the local union, protested the election. He charged that union facilities had been used to promote the candidacy of the incumbent president and objected to the meeting attendance requirement as a condition of candidacy for union office. After failing to obtain relief through the internal procedure of the union local, March filed a complaint with the Secretary of Labor. In whose favor should judgment be made? Explain.
• See also *Hodgson* v. *Local Union 6799, United Steelworkers of America*, 403 U.S. 333.

Legal Reasoning and Business Judgment

Analyze the legal aspects of these business problems. Suggest possible solutions.

1. Your company has an employees' union not affiliated with any other union or national group. Several members of this union have petitioned a large national union for permission to affiliate with it. The personnel manager has information supporting the undesirable reputa-

tion of the national union officials, and he wants to warn the involved workers of the possible risks should an affiliation succeed. What rights does your company's management have under the provisions of the Taft-Hartley Act?

2. The office workers in your company have been dissatisfied with working conditions and salaries. They argue that employees doing the same type of work in competing companies are being paid more and are receiving more and better benefits. A young woman in the accounting department is spending much of her lunch period seeking the support of co-workers in forming a union that would represent the office workers in collective bargaining to remedy their dissatisfaction. The office manager is determined to discharge this worker because of her union interests. What are the worker's and the manager's rights in this matter?

3. The union has filed charges of unfair labor practices against your employer. A field examiner from the NLRB's regional office meets with your employer and the employees and discusses the charges. The day after the examiner's visit, your employer discharges two employees who gave statements. The reason given for the dismissals is that there is no work for them to do. The union files an amendment to their earlier complaint, charging that your employer dismissed the two employees because they gave statements to the examiner in connection with the earlier charge. To what extent is an employee protected from being discharged for participating in proceedings before the NLRB?

Part 9
Business Organizations
Chapter 30
Characteristics of Sole Proprietorships and Partnerships

Partnership operations, discussed in this chapter, are governed by the provisions of the firm's partnership agreement and by statutory law, which in most states is the Uniform Partnership Act (UPA). The rights, duties, and powers of partners are expressed in the agreement and implied by the statutes.

Those who plan to form a new business should first seek the advice of attorneys, accountants, and bankers. These experts have the ability and experience needed to weigh the risks and the costs involved. They can simplify the difficult task of deciding which form of organization is most suited to the needs of the intended business. All forms of business organization have advantages and disadvantages. The choice must be made on the basis of which one is least objectionable with respect to such factors as liability, control of the business, taxation, and duration. These key factors and others are highlighted and compared in Table 30-1. Business organizations are discussed in more detail in the four chapters that follow.

SOLE PROPRIETORSHIP

It is not unusual for a business to have a small beginning as a sole proprietorship. There are definite advantages in being a sole proprietor, such as being one's own boss. The owner alone decides the duration of the business. He or she controls the operations and makes all decisions. All property, real or personal, that is part of the business, belongs to the owner and may be sold, exchanged, or altered without consultation with others.

These advantages should be weighed against several disadvantages. The illness or death of the owner would reduce or end his or her control over the operation of the business. Business growth would eventually tax the owner's ability to make every decision personally and to take responsibility for every business transaction. Credit for increased inventory and plant expansion would be limited. Creditors are often unwilling to give too much credit to a sole proprietor who has only personal funds and property to secure a business loan.

TABLE 30-1.   COMPARISON OF TYPES OF BUSINESS ORGANIZATIONS

Factor	Sole Proprietorship	Partnership	Corporation
Creation	By owner.	By agreement of parties.	By state charter.
Liability	Owner has unlimited liability.	Partners have unlimited liability.	Shareholders have limited liability.
Control	Owner makes all decisions.	All partners, in absence of agreement, have equal voice.	Shareholders control through board of directors, which elects officers and hires agents.
Taxation	Owner pays income tax on profits or losses from operations.	Partnership not subject to federal income tax. Partners taxed on their share of profits or losses.	Corporation pays income tax; shareholders pay taxes on dividends.
Agency	Owner is the principal.	Each partner is both principal and agent of the copartners.	Shareholders are not agents of the corporation.
Duration	Terminated by owner's decision, death, or bankruptcy.	Terminated by agreement, death, bankruptcy, or withdrawal of a partner.	May be perpetual.
Transferability	Freely transferable.	Not transferable.	Freely transferable.

 After operating Marine Electronics for several months, Ballou discovered he had little time or energy for home and family. There weren't enough hours in the day for him to keep the customers satisfied. He realized that more space and additional employees were needed, which would probably leave him even less time to spend with his family. When Ballou went to the bank to discuss more credit, the manager suggested he talk to a lawyer about other forms of business organization.

Sole Proprietor as Principal

Sole proprietors perform as principals when they employ other persons as agents or employees. All contracts of employment are with the proprietor, who has the sole right to set wages and to prescribe the duties and obligations of those hired. Because sole proprietorships are usually small and have a limited number of employees, labor unions are rarely involved in their management-labor negotiations. The proprietor alone is responsible for all business transactions carried out by employees with third persons. He or she is likewise solely responsible for damages resulting from torts arising within the scope of each employee's duties.

> Baptist, proprietor of Westair Aviation, accepted a contract to service two light, twin-turboprop STOL (short takeoff and landing) airplanes owned by National Gas Pipeline Company. The new contract created the need for additional help, and Baptist employed Tipke, a licensed pilot and mechanic. While servicing one of the STOLs, Tipke damaged its digital computerized navigation unit. Baptist, as proprietor and principal, would be liable for the repair or replacement of the navigation unit.

GENERAL PARTNERSHIPS

A *partnership* (or *copartnership*, as it is sometimes called) is best defined by the Uniform Partnership Act (UPA): an association of two or more persons to carry on as co-owners a business for profit. It may result from an oral or written agreement between the parties. It may even be an informal arrangement in which the terms are not definitely expressed. However, in the interest of better understanding between partners, the terms and scope of the partnership agreement should be in writing.

Uniform Partnership Act

To a great extent, partnership law is now governed by the Uniform Partnership Act, which has been adopted in most states, the District of Columbia, Guam, and the Virgin Islands. Only Georgia, Louisiana and Mississippi are not governed by the UPA, but they have statutes which embody its major features. The act makes uniform the law relating to partnership including:

- ☐ Relations of partners to persons dealing with the partnership.
- ☐ Relations of partners to one another.
- ☐ Property rights of a partner.
- ☐ Dissolution and winding up of a partnership.

Articles of Partnership

A written agreement establishing the association of partners is called the *articles of partnership*. Several important items are usually included:

- ☐ The partnership's name and the identity of each partner.
- ☐ The nature of the partnership business.
- ☐ The duration of the partnership.
- ☐ The financial contributions of each partner.
- ☐ The division of profits and sharing of losses.
- ☐ The amount of time each partner agrees to devote to the business and the duties of each partner.

☐ Statement of salaries. (Unless specifically stated, partners only share in profits.)
☐ Authority of partners to bind the partnership.
☐ The right of a partner to withdraw from the partnership and the procedure in the event of such withdrawal.
☐ Conditions for continuing the partnership by the remaining partners in the event of death or withdrawal of a partner.

Although articles of partnership are not *required* in forming a partnership, they serve to reduce disputes regarding the intended terms of the agreement between the partners.

Kinds of Partners

Partners are classified according to their interests in the business or their obligations to the partnership. Partners may be general; special, or limited; silent; secret; dormant; or nominal.

General Partners   One who in law and in fact is a co-owner of a business for profit in association with one or more other persons is known as a *general partner*. General partners have unlimited liability for partnership debts, and they publicly and actively engage in the transaction of partnership business.

▶ Clark and King discussed the formation of a partnership to which each would contribute $12,000. Their attorney advised them that each would have unlimited liability in respect to contract and tort claims. In addition, each would be taxed on his share of the profits of the partnership, whether distributed or not. The attorney prepared the articles of partnership shown in Fig. 30-1.

Special, or Limited, Partners   A *special*, or *limited, partner* is one who does not share in the management of the partnership business. The contribution of a limited partner may be in cash or other property, but not in services. Limited partnerships are recognized under the Uniform Limited Partnership Act, which has been adopted in all states except Delaware and Louisiana.

A limited partnership is made up of one or more general partners and one or more limited partners. Limited partnerships may be formed only when permitted by statute, and the liability of the limited partners for debts is limited to the extent of the capital they contribute. Persons desiring to form such a partnership must sign and swear to a certificate which states:

☐ The name of the partnership.
☐ The character of the business.
☐ The location of the principal place of business.
☐ The name and address of each member—general and limited partners being designated.
☐ The term for which the partnership is to exist.
☐ The amount of cash and other property contributed by each limited partner.
☐ The additional contributions, if any, to be made by each limited partner.

ARTICLES OF PARTNERSHIP

Date ——————————→ This agreement made and entered into this eighth day of August, 19--,
Identity of partners ═══→ between Steven Clark, of the City of Jersey City, County of Hudson, State of
→ New Jersey, and Allan King, of the City of Elizabeth, County of Union, State of
New Jersey.

WITNESSETH:

Nature of the business ——→ ONE.   The parties, Steven Clark and Allan King, agree to become partners
in the aircraft maintenance and operation business.

Name and location of ——→ TWO.   The business of the partnership shall be conducted under the firm
firm   name, Clark & King, Aircraft Specialists, at 100 Journal Square, Jersey City,
New Jersey.

Duration of ——————→ THREE.   The partnership shall begin on the date that this agreement is
partnership   executed and shall continue for a term of five years thereafter.

Investments of ————→ FOUR.   Each partner shall contribute to the capital of the partnership the
partners   sum of Twelve Thousand Dollars ($12,000).   These contributions shall be without
interest.

Sharing of profits and ——→ FIVE.   All profits resulting from the business shall be divided equally
losses   between the partners, and all losses incurred by the business also shall be
borne equally by them.

Accounts of business ——→ SIX.   Proper books of account shall be kept of all transactions relating
to the business of the partnership.
    At the end of each calendar year, a full inventory shall be prepared; a
statement of the business made; the books closed; and the account of each partner credited or debited, as the case may be, with his proportionate share of
the net loss.   A statement of the business may be made at such other times as
the partners agree on.

Partners' drawings ——→ SEVEN.   Each partner may draw from the business, for his own use, a sum
not to exceed One Thousand Dollars ($1,000) a month, to be withdrawn at such
times as he may choose.

Duties of partners ———→ EIGHT.   During the continuance of this partnership, each partner agrees to
devote his entire time and attention to the business and to engage in no other
business enterprise without the written consent of the other.

Restraints on partners ——→ NINE.   Neither party shall, without the written consent of the other,
become surety or bondsman for anyone.

Termination of ————→ TEN.   At the termination of this partnership, a full inventory and balance
partnership   sheet shall be prepared; the debts of the business shall be discharged; and all
property then remaining shall be divided equally between the partners.

    In witness whereof, the parties have hereunto set their hands and seals
the day and year first above written.

In the presence of   *Steven Clark*   L.S.

Roberta Mays
Irving Pastori   *Allan King*   L.S.

Fig. 30-1.   Articles of partnership

- ☐ The time, if agreed upon, when the contribution of each limited partner is to be returned.
- ☐ The share of the profits or other income that each limited partner will receive.
- ☐ The right, if given, of a limited partner to substitute an assignee as contributor in his or her place, and the conditions of the substitution.
- ☐ The right, if given, of the partners to admit additional limited partners.
- ☐ The priority, if given, of one or more limited partners over other limited partners as to contributions or compensation.
- ☐ The right, if given, of the remaining general partner or partners to continue the business in the event of death, retirement, or insanity of a general partner.
- ☐ The right, if given, of a limited partner to demand and receive property other than cash in return for his or her contribution.

This certificate must be filed in the office of a designated public official in the county in which the principal office of the limited partnership is located. The use of the surname of a limited partner in the partnership name is not permitted unless it is also the name of a general partner. Upon the death of a limited partner, the executor of the estate has all the rights of the partner for the purpose of settling the estate.

In some respects, a limited partner occupies a position similar to that of a corporate shareholder. He or she is primarily an investor and cannot take part in the management or operation of the business unless he or she is also a general partner. The limited partner is not an agent of the partnership.

> Fenton, a design engineer, offered to join the partnership of Bunn and Humphrey as a limited partner. He agreed to lend the firm $10,000 and take 12 percent of the profits in lieu of interest. The general partners requested that Fenton also contribute design services in return for the percentage of profits requested. As a limited partner, however, Fenton's contribution may be cash or property but not services.

Silent Partners   An actual partner who has no voice or active part in the business management or operations is a *silent partner*.

> Schilling, a retired government worker, offered to join the partnership of Wenzel and Morris. He would make an equal contribution of cash and receive a proportionate share of the partnership profits but would take no active part in the management or operations of the business. If accepted as a silent partner by Wenzel and Morris, Schilling would have the status of an actual partner, with unlimited liability for partnership debts and an equal share in profits.

Secret Partners   An actual partner who takes an active part in the management of the partnership business but is not known to parties outside the partnership is a *secret partner*.

> Ballard and Lance frequently used the services of Post, a certified public accountant. Post offered to handle all the partnership's tax work if Ballard and Lance would make her a partner with a 3 percent share of the profits. Because of her tax work with other clients, however, she insisted that she did not want her associa-

tion with the partnership publicly known. If accepted as a secret partner, Post would have the legal status of a real partner and be a co-owner of the business for profit.

Dormant Partners *Dormant partners* are actual partners who are both silent and secret. They do not take an active part in the management or operation of the business, and they are not known publicly as partners.

 Warren and Wellington needed additional capital and agreed to admit McLeod, a wealthy acquaintance, to the partnership. McLeod's contribution to the business was the $20,000 he invested. McLeod received no rights to participate in the management of the firm. Neither was he publicly identified with the partnership. McLeod was a dormant partner.

Nominal Partners A *nominal*, or *apparent, partner* is a partner by estoppel—that is, one who is not an actual partner but who by his or her actions can be reasonably believed to be a partner. A nominal partner is as liable as an actual partner to anyone who extends credit in good faith on the assumption that the person is an actual partner both in law and in fact.

If a partnership liability results, the nominal partner is as liable as though he or she were an actual member of the partnership.

 Hopwell and Horne sought permission of a former government official to use her name in the title of their partnership business. They felt that the addition of the name would add prestige and result in more business. The official refused, knowing that she would be only a nominal partner and might be held liable for some of the debts and obligations of Hopwell and Horne.

Partnership Name

The name of a partnership should not be the same as any other existing business. (This avoids confusion and possible legal complications.) It may consist of the names of the partners, as *Wellington & Albrecht*, or of one partner's name followed by the words *and Company*.

The partners may elect to operate under a coined name, such as *The Fashion Conspiracy* or *Cove Pizza*. However, nearly all states have statutes that require persons conducting a business under an assumed or fictitious name to file a certificate designating the actual names and addresses of all persons conducting the business as partners or proprietors. In some states it is illegal for individuals to conduct a business under a name ending with the word *Company* unless there is some indication that the business is not a corporation. Terms such as *Unincorporated* or *Not Inc.* must follow, so that the name used would not represent the business as being a true corporation.

Partnership Capital

Partnership capital is the total of the money and property contributed by the partners for use in the business endeavor. By the terms of the partnership agreement, a partner may contribute his or her skills and services instead of capital. In other agreements, a partner may contribute the use of property rather than the property itself.

Tenancy in Partnership

A partner is a co-owner, with his or her partners, of partnership property. Simply stated, a partner's ownership interests in any item of partnership property is not that of an outright owner, joint tenant, or tenant in common, but is that of a *tenant in partnership.* The characteristics of this tenancy are such that:

☐ Partners have an equal right with their copartners to use partnership property for partnership purposes. Such property cannot be possessed for other purposes without the consent of the other partners.

☐ Partners may not transfer to another their rights in specific partnership property. Any sale of partnership property by a partner acting as an individual does not result in the passing of title.

☐ A partner's individual interest in partnership property is not subject to attachment—being taken to furnish security for debts or costs—by a partner's personal creditors. It is subject to attachment only on a claim against the total partnership.

☐ Upon the death of a partner, rights in partnership property remain with the other partners, who possess the property only for partnership purposes subject to the partnership agreement and the rights of the estate of the deceased partner.

☐ A deceased partner's rights in partnership property are not subject to any rights of a surviving spouse or other next of kin.

When an individual partner owned realty before the partnership was formed and subsequently it is used in the partnership business, it is not always clear whether the realty is a capital contribution of the partnership. If the partnership agreement fails to resolve this issue, one must look to certain objective factors; for example, (1) Is the realty being carried on the books as a partnership asset? (2) Are taxes, maintenance, and insurance being paid by the partnership or the individual partner? (3) Is the income generated by the realty being deposited in a partnership account?

> When Wisecarver and Woodcock formed the Wisecarver and Woodcock Electronics partnership, they located their shop in a garage owned by Woodcock. Although the electric, oil, and water services used in the business were billed to the partnership and paid with partnership funds, the taxes and insurance on the property were paid by Woodcock. If the partnership were ever dissolved, ownership of the garage would remain with Woodcock and would not be considered a part of Woodcock's capital contribution to the partnership.

Duties and Rights of Partners to One Another

The duties and rights of partners with respect to one another are much the same as in the relationship of principal and agents, and they are governed by law or agreement.

Right to Participate in Management   Although each partner may perform different duties within the business, all partners have equal rights in the management and conduct of the partnership business. Any difference of opinion that involves ordinary matters connected with the business may be decided by a majority of the partners. For example, increasing employees' salaries, modernizing the firm, or launching an advertising campaign, when decided by a majority of the partners, are valid and binding on the partnership. But any unauthorized act by one partner that violates any agreement between the partners makes the wrongdoer liable to the others, unless the act is affirmed by them.

If there is an equal division of opinion on any action, a stalemate results. If the disagreement is important enough to affect the successful operation of the business and there is no way to settle the issue, the only recourse a partner has is to petition the court for an order of partnership dissolution.

> Gomez argued with his partner Sudol that their business operations should be expanded to several neighboring states for increased income and profit. Sudol disagreed, insisting that the increased overhead of expansion would cancel out any net profit. When their discussion of the matter became bitter, Gomez petitioned the court to render a decision on dissolution based upon the disagreement. The court could issue a dissolution decree after trying unsuccessfully to resolve the issue by reaching a compromise between the partners.

Stalemates can be avoided by setting forth, in the articles of partnership, the responsibilities and authority of each partner in management.

Right to Share in Profits   Unless the partnership agreement provides otherwise, partners share the profits equally regardless of the amounts of their financial contributions or the value of each partner's participation in the business. Partners bear losses in the same proportion in which they share profits, unless the agreement provides for a different ratio.

> Illness required McDougal to be hospitalized for six weeks. Her partner in McDougal & Rockwell Antiques had to work long hours to keep the business operating. In spite of her extra effort, Rockwell would not be entitled to a greater share of the profits than that established in the partnership agreement.

Right to Compensation   Unless there are agreements to the contrary, no partner is entitled to a salary for services rendered in the partnership business. Even when the services are unusual or specialized, the partner rendering them is not entitled to more than his or her share of the profits. There is a single exception: A surviving partner may receive compensation for his or her services in winding up partnership affairs.

Right to Return of Capital Investment   Subject to partnership creditor rights, each partner is entitled to repayment without interest of his or her capital contribution. Each partner's share of the partnership profits is that partner's earnings on his or her capital investment.

A partner's advances of money to the partnership business, beyond the capital contribution, are loans. The partner making the loan becomes a creditor of the business and has a right to recover the loan with interest. If the partnership is terminated, *nonpartner* creditors must be paid before partner creditors.

 The partnership of Wyman and Wurst was terminated before Wyman had recovered $1,200 spent on behalf of the partnership in the ordinary and proper conduct of the business. Wyman is entitled to repayment after claims of the partnership's creditors have been satisfied and before the capital investment of the partners is distributed.

Right to Inspect Accounts and Records   Complete information on partnership transactions must be available to each partner. The books of the partnership must be kept at the principal place of business. At all times, each partner should have the right to have access to them, to inspect them, and to copy them. This right may be exercised by a partner's authorized lawyer, accountant, or other agent.

 After an extended business trip, Sykes returned to his office and discovered that the firm's records of receipts and expenses kept by his partner had been removed from the office. His partner had taken them home, explaining that it was more convenient to record an accumulation of transactions in the privacy of his home. This unauthorized removal of the firm's records and accounts could be considered a breach of the partnership agreement.

Fiduciary Relationship   Each partner has a duty to act primarily for the other's benefit in matters connected with a partnership. This fiduciary relationship between copartners is based upon a high standard of mutual trust and confidence. A partner may not do anything that would interfere with the best interest of the partnership. Any profits resulting from a partner's involvement in other business ventures that compete with the business of the partnership would revert to the partnership.

 O'Keefe discovered that her partner Mays was servicing several clients and pocketing the fees collected. O'Keefe demanded a full accounting of these transactions and requested that all such fees be deposited in the partnership account. If Mays failed to do so, she would be giving evidence of bad faith, which constitutes a breach of the partnership agreement.

Right to Choose Associates   No person can become a member of a partnership without the consent of all the partners. If a partner sells or transfers an interest to another party, the new owner may not take part in managing the business without the assent of the other partners. If the new owner is accepted, the partnership is terminated and replaced by a new one.

Although a partner need not merely accept the efforts of other partners to bring a new partner into the business, the partners have no way of preventing a partner from withdrawing. Courts will not order a partner who has wrongfully withdrawn to return to the partnership. A wrongfully withdrawing partner would be held responsible in an action brought by copartners for breach of the partnership agreement and for damages which the copartners may have sustained.

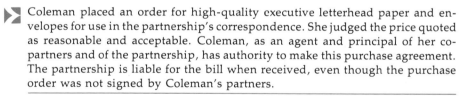 Epstein and Rappaport, law partners of Pettengill, were convinced that the firm would benefit if the partnership was enlarged. They proposed to Pettengill that a new partner be brought in to handle the increased caseload. Pettengill disagreed and threatened to dissolve the partnership, if necessary, and seek an accounting against them. Pettengill is acting within his rights. He can bring about the dissolution of the partnership if his partners insist upon taking in a new partner.

Right to an Accounting   A partner is entitled to an accounting and may petition a court of equity to order a formal accounting whenever wrongfully excluded from the partnership business or from possession of its property by copartners. Although a partner cannot sue the partnership itself, he or she may sue the copartners individually to force them to give an accounting of any individual profits that should have gone to the partnership.

RELATION OF PARTNERS TO THIRD PERSONS

When the relationship between partners and third persons is analyzed, it is usually necessary to look to one or more principles of agency law.

Partners as Agents

Every partner acts as the agent of the partnership and of every other partner. Thus, the acts of every partner carried out within the scope of the partnership business bind all the other partners.

Coleman placed an order for high-quality executive letterhead paper and envelopes for use in the partnership's correspondence. She judged the price quoted as reasonable and acceptable. Coleman, as an agent and principal of her copartners and of the partnership, has authority to make this purchase agreement. The partnership is liable for the bill when received, even though the purchase order was not signed by Coleman's partners.

Partners' Authority

In relations with third persons, a partner's authority to act for the partnership is similar to that of an agent to act for his or her principal. Each partner may have express authority to perform certain acts, inasmuch as the partnership agreement so specifies or a sufficient number of partners have agreed to the acts.

By virtue of being comanager of the partnership business, a partner has the necessary authority to carry out certain business, even in the absence of express authority. The scope of such implied authority varies with business custom and usage in the area where the partnership operates.

▶▶ Bowers and Maus opened an aircraft-engine repair shop after completing an apprenticeship. They accepted a contract for the maintenance and repair of six Piper Cherokees owned by a local flight-training school. Although Bowers and Maus had not entered into a formal partnership agreement, by their actions and the manner in which they were doing business it would be assumed that a partnership existed and that both had implied authority to bind the other.

The following authority is implied by the circumstances, the general language, or the conduct of the partners:

☐ The authority to hire employees and agents needed for the conduct of the partnership business.
☐ The authority to receive money due the partnership and to issue receipts. A third party who makes a proper payment is protected even though the partner receiving the payment fails to account to the partnership for it.
☐ The authority to make any contract necessary to the transaction of partnership business.
☐ The authority to purchase goods and services normally handled by the firm, and for this purpose, to pledge the credit of the partnership.
☐ The right to make, accept, and indorse negotiable instruments issued in the name of the partnership if it is a trading firm. If the third party acts in good faith, such transactions are binding, even though the partner misappropriates the money.
☐ The authority to sell the partnership's goods or services in the regular course of business and to make the usual warranties incidental to such sales.
☐ The authority to compromise, adjust, and pay claims against the partnership. Although a partner lacks authority to pay personal debts from partnership assets, a creditor receiving such payment in good faith and without the knowledge that it came from partnership assets is protected.
☐ The authority to insure the partnership's property, to cancel a policy of insurance, and to make proof and accept settlement of a loss.
☐ The authority to borrow money on the partnership's credit and to secure the loan by a pledge or a mortgage on the partnership's property. This provision is contained in Section 11 of the Uniform Partnership Act.
☐ The authority to receive notice of matters affecting partnership affairs. Such notice, in the absence of fraud, is binding on the other partners.

Limitations of Partners' Authority

Certain acts do not bind a partnership unless they are authorized by all the partners. These are:

☐ Assignment of partnership property for the benefit of creditors.
☐ Disposition of the goodwill of the business.

After an extended period of excellent service to customers, the name "McKinsey & Company" became a synonym for dependable, competent work in the home construction industry. Any agreement made with some, but not all, of the partners to buy the trade name would be unenforceable. The name represents the goodwill of the firm, and its sale would require the consent of all partners.

☐ Payment of individual debts out of partnership assets.

Lash owed Combustion Engineering $350 for services rendered prior to the formation of the partnership of Lash, Finney, and Filardo. Combustion Engineering owed the partnership $750 on its account. Lash agreed to cancel his personal debt with them by setting off the $350 against the $750 owed the partnership. Unless this arrangement was agreed to by Finney and Filardo, Lash's agreement would not bind his partners.

☐ Confession of judgment or admission to a charge against the partnership before trial of the charges by a court or a jury.

Keeler, a partner in an automobile sales agency, was accused of negligence in the theft of a customer's new automobile that had been returned for scheduled service. A suit was brought against the partnership. Without consulting his partner, Keeler signed a confession of judgment, admitting the partnership's liability for the financial loss suffered by the customer. By giving the plaintiff a written confession of negligence, Keeler permitted judgment to be entered against the partnership without the institution of legal proceedings of any kind. Since Keeler had acted outside the scope of his powers as a partner, the confession of judgment could be voided by his partner.

In addition to the foregoing, a partner who does not have actual authority from each copartner may not bind the partnership by the sale of partnership property, unless it is for sale in the usual course of business. As an example, one partner could not sell the partnership's office furniture without the approval of the other partners.

Liability of Partners

Insofar as partnership debts and contractual obligations are concerned, partners have *joint liability*. If suit is brought against any partner, all other partners are named as parties to the action, and a judgment must be rendered against all partners or none. A release of one joint-liability partner releases all.

 Wait disagreed with Ernst on the need for a new chain hoist used in lifting aircraft engines that they were servicing. Without Wait's agreement, Ernst placed an order for the hoist in the name of Wait, Ernst, and Company. The seller may hold both Wait and Ernst jointly liable for the cost of the hoist.

The personal property of a partner may be seized and sold under law for the satisfaction of debt when a judgment is obtained against a partnership. However, the creditors of an individual partner have first claim to such property.

Tort Liability   Respecting liability for torts—a partner's wrongful act or omission in the course of partnership business—each partner is *jointly and severally liable*. That is, all partners may be sued jointly, or each may be sued separately, with separate judgments being obtained against each partner. Payment of any one of the judgments, however, satisfies all.

▶ Bean was employed as a sales representative for the partnership of Bishop and Ellsworth. In a sales transaction, Bean intentionally and knowingly made false statements regarding the cooling capacity of a room air conditioner. After it had been installed, the customers discovered the unit was too small. A close examination of the manufacturer's manual revealed that the unit's BTU (British thermal unit) rating was inadequate for the area to be cooled. Inasmuch as the customer had relied upon the false statement of Bean, both Bishop and Ellsworth could be held liable collectively and individually for damages.

Incoming Partner A person admitted as a partner into an existing partnership is liable for all partnership obligations arising prior to his or her admission. All such liability, however, is limited to the incoming partner's capital contribution.

▶ Havemeyer was offered an active partnership in the firm of Belovsky and Tilley. She hired an accountant to examine the records and accounts of the partnership and was advised that its liabilities exceeded available assets. Havemeyer would be wise to reject the partnership offer. She would be liable for all obligations of the partnership arising before she became a partner, but only up to the amount of her contribution to partnership property.

Questions for Review and Discussion

1. What are the advantages of being a sole proprietor? The disadvantages?

2. How is a partnership defined in the Uniform Partnership Act?

3. What is the extent of a partner's role in a partnership business in respect to (a) creation, (b) liability, (c) control, (d) taxation, (e) agency, (f) duration, and (g) transferability?

4. Identify at least ten items of information usually expressed in the articles of partnership.

5. Compare silent, secret, dormant, and nominal partners in respect to management and involvement in the operation of a partnership business.

6. Explain the partnership property rights of partners and the meaning of tenancy in partnership.

7. What are the rights and duties of partners with respect to one another?

8. Identify four acts of a partner that do not bind a partnership unless they are authorized by all of the partners.

9. What is a partner's liability for (a) contracts entered into by copartners and (b) torts committed by copartners while acting within the actual or apparent scope of the business of the partnership?

10. Explain what is meant by partnership capital in terms of a partnership agreement. What forms may the partnership capital take?

Analyzing Cases

1. Mather employed Stark as a sales representative, agreeing to pay her as salary 33⅓ percent of the profits of the business. The business showed a loss of $3,500 at the end of the year. Mather argued that since Stark was to receive one-third of any profits earned, she was also liable for one-third of any losses suffered by the firm. Was Mather correct? Explain. • See also *Swanson* v. *Swanson,* 124 Cal. App. 519.

2. Seaman and Lyman were partners. The articles of partnership provided that Lyman was to receive half the profits but was not be be responsible for any losses. What is the effect of this provision (*a*) on Seaman and (*b*) on third parties doing business with the partnership? • See also Uniform Partnership Act, Sec. 15.

3. Paulson and Carter were partners in Monaplastics, a manufacturing business. The articles of partnership provided that Carter was a special, or limited, partner. The articles further specified that Carter was to make his capital contribution in services. Does this agreement have the legal effect of limiting Carter's liability for the debts and obligations of the partnership? Explain. • See also *Fletcher* v. *Pullen*, 70 Md. 205.

4. American Deli, a partnership, had a checking account agreement with Universal Savings Bank requiring that any two of its three general partners had to sign checks drawn on the partnership account. Over a period of twenty-one months, twenty-four checks with only one signature were drawn on the American Deli account and paid by the bank, for a total of $15,450. Since the charges to its account were not questioned for over a year and a half, the bank refused to accept responsibility or make good. American Deli sued, and the bank based its de-fense on the section of the Uniform Commercial Code which imposes a duty on the customer to "exercise reasonable care and promptness" in examining the monthly bank statement and canceled checks to discover any unauthorized signatures. The code also provides that failure to notify the bank of an unauthorized signature within a year after receiving the statement precludes the assertion of a claim against the bank for such unauthorized signatures. For whom would the court decide? Explain. • See also *Wolfe et al.* v. *University National Bank*, 310 A.2d 558.

5. Calloway and Gordy are partners in the operation of Ice Machine Rentals. During Calloway's absence, Gordy employed an extra helper at a salary of $122.50 a week. When Calloway returned, he refused to pay the new employee, claiming that Gordy had no authority to hire the helper without his permission. Is the partnership liable to the helper for the wages? Why? • See also *Corley* v. *Jenkins*, 46 Vt. 721.

6. Rugg and Horney entered into an oral agreement to operate Research & Development Laboratories for a period of two years. Continuance beyond this period would depend upon the success of the venture. A short time after the business was launched, Rugg withdrew. Horney sued for losses resulting from Rugg's action. Will Horney recover the damages sought? Explain. • See also *Sanger* v. *French*, 157 N.Y. 213, 51 N.E. 979.

Legal Reasoning and Business Judgment

Analyze the legal aspects of these business problems. Suggest possible solutions.

1. Your sales representative has forwarded an order for art and craft supplies from Jones, Green, and Allison Studio. Although it is a new account, you know that Allison is a prominent commercial artist. The credit manager cannot find the firm listed in Dun & Bradstreet but recommends accepting the account because of Allison's interest in the firm. What should you do before extending credit?

2. Kolbe and Kryger, two former shop supervisors of Straton Tool & Die Company, seek your advice about the advisability of opening a machine tool repair venture. Both are capable machinists and have saved sufficient money to establish the business. What guidance and direction should you give the pair?

3. Your company is limited in the number of new accounts that it may open during the next quarter. The owner of a patent development, an individual with an excellent financial rating and several successful inventions to his credit, has placed an order for supplies on account. Another order has arrived from a new firm of five partners, each with limited resources but with recognized (though untested) competence in their line of business. Your company can accept only one account. Which account should you accept? Explain.

Chapter 31
Partnership Dissolution and New Ventures

Three formal steps are involved when a partnership comes to an end: (1) The partnership is dissolved; (2) the partnership's business affairs are wound up; and (3) the partnership is terminated.

DISSOLUTION OF A PARTNERSHIP

According to the Uniform Partnership Act, a *partnership dissolution* occurs when any partner stops carrying on the partnership business. However, although any partner has the power to dissolve a partnership, that power is by no means absolute. When other partners resist, the partner's rights are weighed against those of his or her fellow partners; ultimately, the court may have to decide. A partnership dissolution can come about by the act of one or more partners, by operation of law, or following a court decree.

Dissolution by Acts of the Partners

A partnership is dissolved by the acts of the parties when the purpose for which the partnership was formed has been served, or the agreed upon term of the partnership has expired.

> Spratlin and Thomas specified in their articles of partnership that the partnership would be dissolved after three years of operation or after its operation netted each partner a profit equal to his initial capital investment of $25,000, whichever occurred first. After one year of business operations, Spratlin and Thomas shared equally a net profit of $54,000. The business would be dissolved at that point by the terms of the agreement.

A partnership is dissolved by the acts of the parties when a partner decides to withdraw; whenever its membership changes; or when there is mutual agreement to dissolve.

> Christoffersen, a partner, suffered heavy personal losses which exceeded his personal cash reserves and other property assets. He decided to sell his interest in the partnership of Christoffersen and Murray to Guarino in order to pay off this

debt. Guarino, as purchaser of Christoffersen's interest, does not become a partner. If Murray agrees to admit Guarino to the partnership, the old partnership ends and a new one will be formed.

A partnership is dissolved by the acts of the parties when a partner is expelled for misconduct, failure to act, or violations of the partnership agreement. If there are more than two partners and one is expelled, the remaining partners may form a new partnership and continue the business.

 The partnership of Gregory, Belovsky, and West suffered serious losses because of West's damaging conduct, which violated their partnership agreement. Gregory and Belovsky served notice expelling West from the partnership, relying on authority provided in the articles of partnership. Gregory and Belovsky may form a new partnership and continue the business either alone or with others. The partnership affairs need not be liquidated; the creditors of the dissolved partnership remain creditors in the continuing business.

Dissolution by Operation of Law

When it becomes unlawful for a business to be conducted in a partnership consisting of the specific partners, the partnership is said to be dissolved by operation of law. For example, the disbarment of a law partner would trigger the dissolution of a law partnership. Dissolution by operation of law also occurs when a partner dies or becomes bankrupt.

It should be noted that dissolution does not mean the immediate termination of a partnership. On the contrary, the surviving partner or partners (and they alone) are obliged to complete the unfinished business of the partnership. This is called *winding up* the partnership affairs.

When a partner's death causes dissolution, the surviving partner or partners continue to hold title to the partnership property, both real and personal. What is more, it may be necessary to sell or mortgage the property to raise funds to satisfy the claims of creditors. Ultimately, the surviving partner or partners give an accounting to the deceased partner's legal representative and pay the estate the appropriate share of the partnership's net assets after satisfying all partnership debts. However, the deceased partner's estate is not liable for contracts unrelated to the winding-up process that are entered into by the surviving partners. To avoid a hasty winding up, a partnership may be extended beyond the partner's death, say, for a three-year period, if the partnership agreement so stipulates.

The bankruptcy of a partner causes a dissolution of the partnership. The bankrupt partner's interest passes to a trustee appointed by the bankruptcy court to protect the interests of creditors. The mere insolvency of a partner, however, does not lead to a dissolution of a partnership.

If the partnership itself becomes bankrupt, dissolution results. In this situation, each partner is personally liable for the debts of the partnership that cannot be satisfied out of its assets. Conversely, a partner's personal creditors cannot levy on or sell the partner's interest in specific partnership property. But the claim of a partner's personal creditor takes priority over that of a partnership creditor who seeks to collect on the debt from the partner.

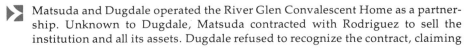 Kirby and Lilly were forced to dissolve their partnership when the partnership became bankrupt. The personal assets of Kirby and Lilly, including their homes, cars, and other property, would be subject to the partnership's debts only after their personal debts had been satisfied. In short, a court gives priority to partnership creditors in partnership assets and priority to private creditors in personal assets.

Dissolution by Court Order

When partners cannot work out their differences by agreement, one or more of them usually petitions a chancery court for a dissolution. Usually, the form of the proceeding is an action for an accounting. If the court agrees with the petitioning partner or partners that the partnership should be dissolved, it enters an order to that effect. A court-supervised liquidation of and accounting for partnership assets follow. Courts in most states order a dissolution under the following circumstances:

- ☐ A partner's gross misconduct, irresponsibility, or neglect so extreme that profitable partnership operations are impossible. (Mere bad judgment or differences of opinions are insufficient.)
- ☐ A partner's misappropriation of funds, a fraudulent act or acts, or other breach of the partnership agreement.
- ☐ A partner's inability to perform duties assigned in the partnership agreement.
- ☐ A partner's being declared insane or incompetent.

> The Davis Brothers Hardware Store appeared to operate smoothly until one brother discovered that the other was selling items from stock and pocketing the receipts. An inventory revealed that approximately $10,000 had been taken from the business in this manner. The defrauded brother can petition a court of equity for an accounting and dissolution of the partnership.

WINDING UP A PARTNERSHIP'S AFFAIRS

Unless otherwise agreed, the partners who have not wrongfully dissolved the partnership have the right to wind up (liquidate) the partnership affairs.

Rights of Partners

All partners, including a withdrawing partner, are usually entitled to take part in the winding-up process. In most dissolutions, the partnership property is used to satisfy partnership debts, with any surplus applied to the net amounts owed each partner, including the withdrawing partner. When a dissolution is caused by a partner's breach of the partnership agreement, each "innocent" partner may be entitled to damages for breach of contract.

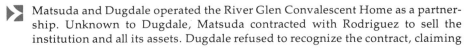 Matsuda and Dugdale operated the River Glen Convalescent Home as a partnership. Unknown to Dugdale, Matsuda contracted with Rodriguez to sell the institution and all its assets. Dugdale refused to recognize the contract, claiming

that is was not binding, since the sale was not authorized by both partners; if the contract of sale were enforced, it would make it impossible for the partnership to continue in business. Had such a breach of the partnership agreement caused a dissolution of the partnership, Dugdale would have the right to receive damages.

Partners who have not wrongfully caused the dissolution may continue the business in the same name, either by themselves or with others, during the term of the partnership. For this purpose, the continuing partners may possess the partnership property provided they pay the errant partner the value of his or her interest in the partnership at dissolution, less any damages recoverable. In the calculation of the errant partner's share, the goodwill of the business is not taken into consideration.

▶▶ Ostriker and Oviatt formed a partnership to operate a restaurant. Ostriker obtained a dissolution of the business on account of Oviatt's wrongful withholding of the former's share of the profits. After dissolution, but before final judgment on the accounting and termination of the partnership, Ostriker formed another partnership with Fuchs and Flores, and the new partnership made a profit operating the restaurant. Ostriker, Fuchs, and Flores have the right to continue the restaurant's operation during the term of the original partnership. They can possess the restaurant property provided they pay Oviatt the value of his interest at dissolution.

If one or more of the partners is insolvent, bankrupt, or out of reach of the law or refuses to contribute a share of the losses, the other partners are obliged to pay the additional amount.

▶▶ Krucker, Kennedy, and Fisher were partners. They shared business profits in the proportion of one-sixth, one-third, and one-half, respectively. The business failed, and the partnership was dissolved. At the time of dissolution, the liabilities owed to creditors were $36,000 greater than assets. Kennedy moved to South America, where she was out of reach of the law. Krucker and Fisher would be obliged to pay the full $36,000 liability in the relative proportions in which they were to share the profits: Krucker, $9,044; Fisher, $26,956.

TERMINATION

Normally, dissolution terminates the actual authority of any partner to act for the partnership. Although partners have no authority after dissolution to create new obligations, they retain authority for acts necessary to wind up partnership affairs, liquidate the assets of the business, or complete transactions begun but not then finished.

Notice to Third Parties

Notice of partnership dissolution must be given to third parties when it is caused by an act of the partners. Such notice is not required when dissolution has been caused by operation of law. Between partners, however, the Uniform Partnership Act requires knowledge or notice of dissolution by death or bankruptcy.

NOTICE IS HEREBY GIVEN that the partnership of Steven Clark and Allan King, doing business at 100 Journal Square, Jersey City, New Jersey, under the firm name of Clark & King, Aircraft Specialists, has this day been dissolved by the retirement of Allan King from said firm. Steven Clark will continue the business at the same address, under the name of Steven Clark, Aircraft Specialist.

Fig. 31-1. Notice of partnership dissolution in a newspaper

When a partner dies, immediate notice must be given by the executor in order to avoid further liability. Unless notice of dissolution is given when caused by an act of the partners, liability to all persons who formerly dealt with the partnership will continue. Actual notice of dissolution must be given to persons who have dealt with the partnership. Notice of dissolution in a newspaper in the area where the partnership business was transacted or by a typed or printed notice posted in a public place is sufficient for persons who have had no dealings with the partnership. A sample of such a notice is given in Fig. 31-1.

Distribution of Partnership Assets

After a partnership agreement has been dissolved and the assets sold, the order in which the liabilities of the partnership are ranked for payment is as follows:

- Liabilities owed to creditors other than partners.
- Money owed to partners for personal loans advanced to the partnership.
- Money owed to partners, in proportion to their capital investments.
- Money owed to partners as profits.

Each of the foregoing liabilities must be paid in full in the order listed. If the liquidation of the assets was not sufficient to repay the capital investments of each partner, profits would not be distributed to partners and losses in respect to their capital investments would be borne by the partners in the same ratio as for the division of profits.

▶▶ The lawyer handling the dissolution of the Losner and Wilshire partnership submitted the following report to the partners summarizing how the assets of the partnership had been distributed:

Realized from liquidation		$125,000
Owed creditors	$15,000	
Employees' salaries	10,000	
Owed Wilshire on personal note	5,000	
Capital investment of partners:		
Losner	12,000	
Wilshire	12,000	54,000
Profit to partners		$ 71,000

Partnership Insolvency

A court of equity acquires jurisdiction when a partnership is insolvent. Its assets, both those of the partnership and those of the individual partners, are distributed in accordance with a rule known as *marshaling of assets.* Hence, the court in distributing these assets gives priority to partnership creditors in the firm's assets as against the separate creditors of the individual partners. The court also gives priority to private creditors of individual partners in the separate assets of the partners as against the firm's creditors. Each class of creditor is not permitted to make demands on the funds belonging to the other until the claims of the other have been satisfied. Therefore, the firm's creditors are not entitled to payments out of the individual assets of the partners until the individual creditors have been paid. The rule of marshaling of assets is not applicable to tort claims. The liability is joint and several, and the injured person may sue the partners individually or as a partnership.

Partnership Continuation

The operation of a partnership is commonly continued after dissolution and winding up. If the business continues, with the remaining partners alone or joined by new partners, it is a new partnership. The liquidation of the old partnership may be accomplished by little more that the making of accounting entries. All parties merely recontribute to the new partnership any payments obtained from the liquidation of the original partnership. Technically, however, the original partnership ceases to exist, and there is a new partnership agreement.

NEW BUSINESS VENTURES

Modern business and investment needs have given rise to new arrangements and types of business organizations. Each arrangement meets a specific requirement not adequately fulfilled by traditional proprietorship, partnership, or corporate forms.

Franchises

In a *franchise* arrangement, the owner of a trademark or trade name (the *franchisor*) licenses a franchise holder (the *franchisee*) to use the trademark or trade name in providing goods or services to the public. In this fashion, the franchisor can expand the number of outlets offering its goods or services and keep overall control of operations while leaving to franchisees the everyday problems of operating the business. The franchisee can be a proprietorship, a partnership, or a corporation. The franchisee's chief advantages are national advertising or promotion and training by the franchisor. Also, the franchisor sometimes provides assistance to a franchisee in selecting a business site and may offer some start-up capital to launch the franchise.

The Franchisor-Franchisee Relationship   The franchisor and franchisee deal with each other at arm's length, as any two parties to a contract might. A franchisor generally tries to maintain uniform standards throughout the chain. Sometimes, this involves imposing certain price standards upon the franchisee. However, a franchisor may run afoul of antitrust laws if he or she adopts a policy tantamount to price-fixing with the aim of eliminating competition. To avoid this, most franchisors establish a price range for the goods and services they provide to franchisees, and then allow franchisees to set their own prices in dealing with customers.

> Simpson was lessee and operator of a retail filling station owned by Union Oil Company. The agreement between them permitted Union Oil to set the prices at which Simpson sold the gasoline. During a local "gas war," Simpson sold gasoline at two cents below the price set by Union Oil. Because of this action, Union Oil refused to renew Simpson's lease when it expired. Simpson sued for treble damages. The Supreme Court ruled that an agreement which allows a supplier to impose noncompetitive prices on many persons whose prices otherwise might be competitive is illegal under the antitrust laws.

Virtually all franchise agreements require *exclusivity*; that is, the franchisee must agree to deal only with the franchisor as the source for the goods and services it offers to the public. Financial arrangements vary substantially, but the most typical situation involves the payment of an initial license fee for the granting of the franchise and regular monthly or quarterly payments on the basis of a percentage of gross sales volume or some other measure. In recent years, there have been complaints that some franchisors have acted in an arbitrary manner or have made unreasonable demands upon their franchises. Thus, franchise arrangements are being subjected to closer scrutiny by the courts. A common complaint is that the restrictions imposed by the franchise agreement are unduly burdensome. When the charge involves possible antitrust violations, the courts are often quick to respond.

> American Motor Inns (AMI) operated a number of franchised motor hotels for Holiday Inns, Inc. When AMI applied for another franchise to construct an additional Holiday Inn near a large airport, the application was rejected. Holiday Inn had sent letters on this matter to the three franchises nearest the proposed location, and they had strong objections. AMI brought an antitrust action against Holiday Inn, claiming that Holiday Inn's practice of allowing existing franchisees to deny the application of a possible competitor was unduly burdensome and a violation of the Sherman Act. The U.S. Third Circuit Court of Appeals agreed. Had Holiday Inn used its own business judgment as to whether the area could support another franchise, its rejection would have been perfectly legal.

There is no such thing as a "typical franchise period." The term of the agreement can range from one year to ten years. Often the agreements allow a franchisor to terminate the arrangement upon thirty days' notice or less. However, courts often refuse to allow the franchisor a sudden termination on the grounds that it is unconscionable, particularly when a franchise has failed to earn back its initial investment. Concern for owners of small businesses has prompted some states, including Connecticut, Delaware, Hawaii, New Jersey, Puerto Rico, Virginia, Washington, and Wisconsin, to pass laws protecting the franchisee or distributor or both from a sudden termination without cause.

 Mariniello operated a gas station as a franchisee of Shell Oil under a three-year lease and dealership contract. The lease permitted Shell to terminate at the end of the term upon thirty days' notice. The dealer contract allowed termination at any time upon ten days' notice. When notified by Shell that it would not renew either agreement, Mariniello appealed to the New Jersey Supreme Court to continue his franchise. The state's high court ruled for Mariniello. It based its ruling on New Jersey's common law which barred unilateral termination without good cause, even though a federally registered trademark was involved.

Liability to Third Parties   As a general rule, a franchisor is not held liable to third parties who deal with the franchisee. This is because the franchisee is an independent contractor and does not bind the franchisor. But the current trend in the law has seen some erosion of this general rule.

Under the modern concept of product liability, a franchisor can usually be held liable if the product injures a third party. This is the case, even if the injured party dealt only with the franchisee, when the product was unsafe and the franchisor can be shown to have known (or it can be shown that the franchisor should have known) that its product line would be sold by the franchisees to the public. A franchisor can also be held liable for claims other than those concerning product liability if it controls the daily operations of the franchise. In determining whether such control exists, courts ask questions such as these: (1) Does the franchisor hire and fire the franchisee's employees? (2) Does the franchisor adjust consumer complaints? (3) Does the franchisee make contracts in the franchisor's name?

Pyramid Sales Franchises

There has been a rapid growth of franchise businesses which involve *pyramid selling* and multilevel distribution schemes, especially in the cosmetics business. The strategy in this form of business is recruitment. Each recruited "distributor" receives a commission not only on the products sold but also for recruiting other sellers. The problem with these schemes is that (by simple mathematical progression) unless the distributor is near the beginning of the recruitment chain, the entire population of the covered area becomes involved. The Attorney General of Pennsylvania summed up this point in referring to one such scheme.

Should each associate distributor recruit only one associate distributor per month (for which he would receive a $50 referral fee each time) and each newly recruited associate distributor in turn recruit only one associate distributor per month, the entire population of Allegheny County would be recruited within 21 months, the entire population of the United States would be recruited within 28 months, and the entire population of the world would be recruited within 32 months.

Persons caught up in these schemes are usually not very well informed about business; they are easily influenced by high-pressure tactics and dramatic sales meetings.

Laws regulating and controlling this type of sales and distribution business are emerging. At the federal level, all such interstate schemes must be registered with the Securities and Exchange Commission. The Federal Trade Commission is prepared to take action against pyramid sales franchise companies when they engage in misleading advertising in respect to recruiting new distributors and the likelihood of earnings. Action is also taken on the premises that (1) pyramid sales are illegal lotteries, (2) they violate federal antitrust regulations by limiting territorial customer allocations, and (3) they involve illegal price discrimination in violation of the Robinson-Patman Act.

Some states have passed laws completely prohibiting pyramid schemes. Others impose strict regulations and limit certain practices.

The regulatory statutes generally require repurchase by the seller of inventory purchased by the distributor. They also give the distributor the right to cancel the purchasing contract. The most encouraging success on the state level is the Iowa Supreme Court decision in *State of Iowa* v. *Koscot Interplanetary, Inc.,* which upheld the Iowa Consumer Fraud Act. The act contains the following provision:

> The advertisement for sale, lease, or rent, or the actual sale, lease, or rental of any merchandise at a price or with a rebate or payment or other consideration to the purchaser which is contingent upon the procurement of purchaser, or the procurement of sales, leases, or rentals to persons suggested by the purchaser, is declared to be an unlawful practice rendering any obligation incurred by the buyer in connection therewith, completely void and a nullity.

Joint Ventures

A *joint venture* is an association of two or more people, partnerships, or corporations who combine their property and skills in order to carry out a single business transaction. Although a joint venture is similar to a partnership and, in fact, is governed by most of the same rules affecting partnerships, a distinction exists in terms of duration and effect: A partnership carries on many activities for an indefinite or extended period of time; a joint venture is limited in scope and time. What is more, because of the limited scope, a joint venture normally cannot bind the co-venturers, whereas a partner *can* bind fellow partners. Usually, each co-venturer has joint and several liability for all joint venture obligations. The management and operation of a joint venture are shared equally by all co-venturers. The death of one co-venturer does not automatically dissolve the joint venture.

In determining whether a business relationship is a joint venture, it is necessary to show the absence of an employer-employee relationship. The withholding of social security and payroll taxes and the payment of premiums for workers' compensation coverage can signify an employment situation. But the absence of these factors indicates that a joint venture probably exists.

 Chandler held a fried-chicken franchise. He had several employees, but in addition to them, Chandler's son and daughter helped out by serving customers.

Chandler paid each of them but kept no record on the company books and did not make deductions for tax purposes. If the son or daughter were hurt in the course of their work, they would not be covered by state workers' compensation. Neither would be recognized as an employee of the business, which was in fact being operated as a joint venture, with the family members acting as co-venturers.

Except for the indicated differences between a joint venture and a partnership, a joint venture is generally governed by the law of partnership.

Mining Partnerships

A *mining partnership* is a special type of partnership. The individual partners form an association for the purpose of operating a mine and extracting minerals to which they own rights. Although a mining partnership is similar to a general partnership, it differs in that any partner may sell his or her interest in the partnership to anyone without the approval of the other partners. Thus, transfer of a partner's interest in a mine by sale or by death to a purchaser or heir carries with it a membership in the firm. Neither event operates to end a mining partnership.

Mining partners do not ordinarily have actual or apparent authority to represent or legally bind the partnership. One partner is usually appointed manager of the operation, and he or she has sole authority to bind the partnership on contracts. Mining partners have unlimited liability for partnership debts and obligations resulting from the usual and ordinary operations of the business.

In some Western states, mining partnerships are regulated by special statutes. In all other areas, the formation of such partnerships is a matter of intention, and, like general partnerships, such concerns may be established by words or conduct of the parties.

Unincorporated Associations

Voluntary associations of two or more persons for common but nonprofit social, political, or trade association purposes are not partnerships; rather, they are *unincorporated associations*. The property rights and legal liabilities of the members depend upon the association's constitution and bylaws. Members are liable to third persons as though they were partners. Every member is regarded by law as approving whatever action is taken by the majority of the members. Absence when a vote is taken or a contrary vote is not an escape from liability. Unlimited liability can be avoided by prompt protest of an action of the members and termination of membership.

Cooperatives

The sale of certain kinds of products and certain techniques by which such products are sold have been exempted from the federal antitrust laws by special legislation. An example of such legislation is the Capper-Volstead Act of 1922, which permits farmers to act together in associations or cooperatives to process and market their agricultural products. The Fishermen's Collective Marketing Act of 1934 permits associations of fishermen to meet together to permit more equitable bargaining in their selling to dealers and processors.

There is also a growing interest in cooperatives and buying clubs as a means of helping low-income consumers to increase their spending power. Typically, *consumer cooperatives* buy goods at wholesale, resell them to members at a reasonable market price, and return the profits pro rata to members in the form of refunds. Some of the more common types of cooperatives are (1) food stores, (2) credit unions, (3) hospital and medical services groups, (4) housing, (5) nursery schools, and (6) insurance groups.

Statutes usually govern the operation of incorporated cooperatives, ruling upon such matters as the refund of any excess of member payments over the costs of operation.

Business Trusts

A *business trust* is essentially a voluntary agreement whereby owners of property transfer legal title to one or more persons (trustees) so that the property can be managed for the benefit of the original owners. An early form known as a Massachusetts trust was established to avoid a former prohibition that denied corporations the authority to own and deal in real estate.

Certain key features distinguish the business trust. Each grantor, by the terms of the agreement, is entitled to a trust certificate showing his or her ownership of a stated interest in the trust. The grantor's interest can be sold or otherwise transferred. Trustees have the sole right to manage and control the business free of the control of the grantors. Shares in a business trust may be transferred. The trust agreement usually sets forth the property being transferred, the life of the trust, and the duties of the trustees in respect to the management of the property. It may also state the persons to whom the income of the trust is to be paid, the share to be received by each grantor, the method of winding up the trust, and the number of shares to be left in the trust property when it is terminated.

> The partnership of Shaw, Mudge & Company transferred its capital contribution to McKeown, Minkler, and Buhl to hold and manage as a business trust for their benefit. The trust agreement specified that the trust was to continue for eight years. Toward the end of the eight-year period, the trustees decided to continue the business by transferring the trust's assets to a new business trust. Since the intention of the original partners to end the trust in eight years was clear, the court would rule that any move to evade this intention by transferring trust shares to another trust would be illegal.

The trustees are personally liable for the debts of the business, since they are its legal owners. To escape liability on contracts of the business, trustees must obtain agreement with the grantors that all such obligations rest with the assets of the trust. All personal responsibility for trustee torts or torts of their agents and employees cannot be avoided, although it can be offset by insurance.

Joint Stock Companies

A *joint stock company* or association is a form of general partnership with some characteristics of a corporation. It is different from a partnership in that its capital is represented by certificate shares, which may be transferred by its members. The business affairs of the joint stock company are conducted by managers or directors elected by the members. An elected officer has sole authority to represent and bind the members who are not agents of the company. A member's death or other incapacity, or a transfer of a member's shares, does not dissolve the company. Unlike members of a corporation, the joint stock company's members have unlimited liability for the debts and obligations of the company during the period of their membership.

Questions for Review and Discussion

1. What are the three steps that lead to the abolition of a partnership? Explain each step.

2. How may partnerships be dissolved by acts of the parties?

3. Explain the various ways a partnership may be dissolved by operation of law.

4. What are the rights of partners when a partnership dissolution is caused by something other than a breach of the articles of partnership? When dissolution is caused by breach of the partnership agreement?

5. Indicate the order of distribution of the amount realized from the marshaling of assets of a partnership. What change, if any, is there in this order when a partner becomes bankrupt?

6. When is notice of dissolution of partnership required? When is it not required?

7. Define a franchise, and explain why its form of business organization has expanded rapidly as a desirable method of controlling and financing a business operation.

8. What is the liability of the franchisor in respect to third persons when the franchisee is an independent contractor? Does liability in respect to injured third persons change when the franchisor sets the manufacturing standards under which the franchise holder makes products?

9. Describe how pyramid selling operates. Explain why there are state and federal laws regulating, controlling, and prohibiting such schemes.

10. Contrast a joint venture with an ordinary partnership. How does one determine whether a business relationship is a joint venture or one of employment?

Analyzing Cases

1. When Romanello died, his two sons, Charles and Roger, entered into a partnership to carry on the family insurance business. Among the provisions of the articles of partnership were: (*a*) the partnership would terminate upon the death of either partner, and (*b*) any dispute over operation of the partnership would be submitted to arbitration. Charles became dissatisfied with Roger's failure to attend to business and wanted to dissolve the partnership. When Roger insisted upon arbitration, Charles went to court for dissolution, claiming the unqualified right to dissolve the partnership. Roger argued that the provision for termination "upon the death of either partner" made the agreement one of *limited duration*, and that Charles would have to establish just cause. How would the court rule? Explain. • See also *Lawrence A. Stone II* v. *Langdon Stone*, 292 So.2d 686.

2. Eskin withdrew as a partner from the firm of Sloan and Eskin. At the time of withdrawal, Sloan agreed to pay all the debts of the firm. Eskin so informed all the partnership creditors. (*a*) Is this agreement binding on the creditors, and is Eskin released from all liability? Explain. (*b*) Suppose that a creditor of the firm to whom notice of Eskin's withdrawal had not been given sold additional goods to Sloan, believing the transaction to be with the partnership of Sloan and Eskin. Could the creditor sue Eskin in case of nonpayment? Explain. • See also *Engle* v. *Bucher*, 6 Ohio St. 295.

3. Hartman, a partner in Hartman and Chester, made an agreement with Lamb in relation to partnership business. The agreement was a fraudulent one, and Lamb was not aware of the false representation. Lamb sued Hartman and Chester. Is the partnership liable? Explain.• See also *Hobbs* v. *Chicago Packing Co.*, 98 Ga. 576.

4. Young and O'Neill were partners in Pack-Roads, a men's clothing and tailoring outlet. O'Neill personally was adjudicated a bankrupt. What effect, if any, would O'Neill's bankruptcy have on the partnership? Explain. What effect would there be on the partnership if O'Neill was personally insolvent rather than legally bankrupt?• See also *Lesser* v. *Gray*, 8 Ga. A. 605.

5. The Fidelity Bank was the lease holder of which the partnership of Greenedge, DeVane and Company was the lessee. Drake was taken in as a partner, and the new partnership paid the rent due prior to the new partnership. The bank brought an action to recover rent due for a twelve-month period commencing with the date of the new partnership. Drake contended that the lease was executed before she became a partner and that the obligation of the lease arose prior to her admission. Therefore, she contended, her liability can only be satisfied out of partnership property. Since the second partnership did not expressly assume the obligations of the lease but had occupied the premises, would Drake as well as the old partnership members be joint and severally liable for the rent?

6. Leonard, Lohman, and Armstrong, certified public accountants, organized a partnership business to be operated for their mutual profit in the auditing of corporation books and the preparation of income tax statements. After three months of operation, it was found that Armstrong was devoting most of her time to activities outside the business. Leonard and Lohman protested, arguing that Armstrong did not have a right to full benefits in the division of profits gained through their work. Is Armstrong entitled to her agreed-upon share in the profits? Explain.• See also *Wisner* v. *Field*, 11 N.D. 257, 91 N.W. 67.

Legal Reasoning and Business Judgment

Analyze the legal aspects of these business problems. Suggest possible solutions.

1. The firm of Van Brunt and DuBiago was engaged by your company to audit the books and to prepare an annual report to the shareholders. One of the partners of the accounting firm certified the report, which was later found to be in error, to the embarrassment and expense of your company. The other partner of the accounting firm denied responsibility for the certifying partner's negligence. What action, if any, can your company take in this matter?

2. Your company made a loan to Vann and Wiler, Contractors, for the purpose of building a new garage for equipment. In a Dun & Bradstreet report, you learn that the partnership plans a complete dissolution because of the death of Wiler, one of the general partners. It is generally known that the partnership owed Vann a large amount that he had once loaned it. Can your company obtain repayment of its loan by filing a claim for a share of the money realized by Vann from the liquidation of the partnership's assets? Explain.

3. Johnson, of the partnership of Johnson, McKay & Brown, electronic specialists, called at your office and demanded payment for work that had been done. Johnson presented a correct statement, and payment was made. Several weeks later, an attorney telephoned and stated that at the time your payment was made to Johnson, he was no longer a partner; he had in fact absconded with the money you had paid to satisfy the statement. The attorney requested that the bill be paid a second time, threatening legal action if it were not taken care of within a reasonable period. What are your obligations in this matter?

Chapter 32
Types and Formation of Corporations

The corporation is one of the most important forms of business organization. It came into being to meet the economic needs of an expanding and capital-hungry business economy. It offers a convenient and efficient way to finance a large-scale business operation by dividing its ownership into many units; these units can be sold easily to a large number of investors. The corporate form also offers limited liability to those who share its ownership. Unlike the legal status of the sole proprietorship and partnership, the legal status of the corporation is not affected by the death, incapacity, or bankruptcy of an officer or shareholder. And since a corporation is an artificial person created by law, it can own property and can sue or be sued just as an individual can.

TYPES OF CORPORATIONS

Corporations may be classified as public, private, and quasi-public; domestic and foreign; close and open; professional; and special service.

Public, Private, and Quasi-Public Corporations

A federal, state, or municipal government may establish a *public corporation* to carry on activities considered to be in the public interest. School systems, transportation systems, and sanitation facilities are types of enterprises undertaken by public corporations. Notable examples of public corporations are the Tennessee Valley Authority (TVA) and the U.S. Postal Service.

> The statute establishing the Tennessee Valley Authority created a corporation of which the U.S. government is the sole shareholder. The TVA is managed by three directors, who are appointed by the President of the United States. The purpose of the corporation is the control of floods, conservation, and elimination of soil erosion; the improvement of river navigation; the manufacture and sale of nitrate for fertilizer; and the production of electrical power in surplus quantities for sale to political subdivisions, corporations, and individuals.

A *private corporation,* also referred to as a business corporation, is a state-licensed corporation established by private individuals, usually for purposes of engaging in business activities. Sometimes a private corporation is designed to carry on charitable activities. In such cases, it is known as a *nonprofit corporation*. Examples of this type of corporation are the National Red Cross, the Salvation Army, hospitals, homes for orphans and the aged, certain recreational clubs, and many educational institutions.

A *public-service corporation* is a quasi-public corporation providing a service on which the public is dependent. Such a corporation is often referred to as a public utility or a public-service corporation. Examples of quasi-public corporations are those supplying gas, electricity, and water and those operating railroads and bridges.

 An incorporated town lacked sufficient funds for creating an adequate water supply by means of a watershed. It granted a special franchise to a group of area residents who agreed to form a corporation for the purpose of supplying water to homes, industry, and commerce and for fire protection. Customers would pay according to an approved rate schedule. The new corporation would be a quasi-public corporation whose ultimate purpose was supplying a required service for a profit. It would be subject to government regulation.

Domestic and Foreign Corporations

A corporation is said to be a *domestic corporation* when it has been created under the laws of a particular state; it is a *foreign corporation* in all other states. For instance, a corporation holding a Pennsylvania charter is a domestic corporation in Pennsylvania but a foreign corporation in Texas or Massachusetts. Any lawsuit involving $10,000 or more brought against a Pennsylvania corporation by anyone not a citizen of that state must be brought in a federal court in any federal district in which a summons may be served upon the corporation.

Close and Open Corporations

A number of states, such as Delaware, have *close corporation* codes. Small corporations that qualify under such statutes are permitted to have a simpler structure than that of big corporations. Such small corporations often have a small number of outstanding shares of stock, which are closely held by one person or a small group of family or friends and not traded publicly. Special allowances are made, including incorporation by a small number of persons, a one-person "board of directors," and the elimination of shareholder meetings. In contrast, an *open corporation* is one in which all the shareholders have a vote in the election of the directors and other officers.

Professional Associations

A corporation is not regarded as a person in the case of statutes which license persons to practice professions (e.g., medicine, dentistry, and law) and which require personal competency qualifications. By statute in a few states, optometry, chiropody, architecture, engineering, and auditing are professions that are prohibited from certification as corporations.

In recent years, however, almost every state has passed laws permitting professional associations. These are given a legal status similar to corporations for tax purposes. Persons interested in forming and operating a professional association should first study the law of their particular state.

Special Service Corporations

Certain types of corporations that are subject to state or federal regulation because of the types of activities they conduct are known as *special service corporations.* State- or federally-regulated banks or credit unions, transportation companies, and insurance companies are typical examples.

CREATION OF THE CORPORATION

The creation of a corporation requires that certain actions be taken by several interested persons and groups—promoters, subscribers, incorporators, and government officials. Initially, there must be a state statute authorizing the issuing of a charter to a group of persons who satisfy the requirements of the statute. *Promoters* carry out much of the preliminary detail work and preparation of legal papers for presentation to state officials for examination and approval. Promoters also seek and obtain offers from interested persons, known as *subscribers*, to buy stock in the corporation when it is created. *Incorporators*—often subscribers—prepare the *articles of incorporation*. The secretary of state issues the *charter* or *certificate of incorporation* after acceptable incorporation papers have been filed. An organization meeting of incorporators and shareholders is held after the charter has been issued. Finally, the certificate of incorporation is recorded in the public recorder's office and with the Securities and Exchange Commission.

After incorporation, the promoters' work is completed, and the subscribers become shareholders. After participation in the incorporators' meeting, the incorporators cease to function. At this point, the corporation's existence begins.

Articles of Incorporation

The incorporators are required to prepare the articles of incorporation. Most states have a general corporation code that outlines the requirements. The Model Business Corporation Act calls for the following information:

- ☐ Name of the corporation.
- ☐ Address of the corporation's initial registered office and its registered agent.
- ☐ Life span of the corporation, either limited or unlimited.
- ☐ Names and addresses of the incorporators.
- ☐ Purpose for which the corporation is formed, excluding banking or insurance.
- ☐ Number and kinds of shares of stock and the *par value* of each share, which is the face value printed on the stock certificate.
- ☐ The provisions for the issuance of preferred or special stock.

☐ The number of directors, with their names and addresses, who are to serve until the first annual meeting of shareholders or until successors are elected and qualify.

☐ Provisions which the incorporators choose to include for the regulation of the internal affairs of the corporation.

The articles of incorporation are signed by the incorporators and sent to the secretary of state and other designated public officials for approval and filing. There are legal firms that specialize in the preparation of articles of incorporation. (For an illustration of such articles, see Fig. 32-1.)

Name

Name requirements for corporations vary widely according to state. Every state will refuse to grant a corporate charter for a corporate name already in use (or too similar to one in use). Virtually all states insist that a corporate name be set forth only in English. Many states insist that the corporate title include one or more of the following words or abbreviations to indicate corporate status: *Corporation (Corp.), Incorporated (Inc.), Limited (Ltd.), Company (Co.),* and, sometimes, *Institute, Society, Association, Syndicate,* or *Club.* In a few states the term *Company* may not be preceded by the word *and.* Names such as *Bank* or *Trust* are also barred under general corporation statutes.

Corporate Charter

Once the new corporation is properly named and its articles of incorporation are in order, the next step is the issuance of a corporate charter. One should realize that corporations are formed by provisions of a general statute, not by special acts of the legislature. In effect, the legislature passes a general law, and the secretary of state or other designated official issues a charter or certificate of incorporation to individuals who conform to its provisions. The charter is thus a contract between the corporation and the state. Once approved, the certificate of incorporation becomes the charter or the corporate franchise. The corporation is then said to be in existence, and it is authorized to begin operations.

▶▶ Before the corporate charter for Recycle Material, Inc., was approved by the secretary of state, the incorporators made contracts with Criscuolo Trucking in the name of their new corporation. The incorporators may be held personally liable for any damages to Criscuolo Trucking unless they can show that a de facto corporation existed. (This is discussed below.) The state, of course, may bring an independent suit for the purpose of challenging the corporation's existence.

De Facto and de Jure Corporations

A *de jure corporation* is one that has received its state charter after satisfying all requirements for the formation of a corporation under the statutes of the state. It is entitled to exist and operate for the period named in its charter—or perpetually, if so provided. A *de facto corporation*, on the other hand, is an organization

```
                        Articles of Incorporation

                                   of

                   MIDLAND AIRCRAFT COMPANY, INC.


        We, the undersigned, desiring to form a corporation, for profit, under the
   general corporation laws of the State of California, do hereby make, subscribe,
   acknowledge, and file this certificate for that purpose, as follows:

        FIRST.  The name of the proposed corporation is:  the Midland Aircraft
   Company, Inc.

        SECOND.  The principal office of the corporation is to be located in the
   City of Salinas, County of Monterey.

        THIRD.  Ralph Lodge, with offices located at 370 Broad Street, Salinas,
   California, is the registered agent on whom process may be served.

        FOURTH.  The purposes for which the corporation is to be formed are:  the
   manufacture of aircraft parts and research into scientific navigational equip-
   ment.

        FIFTH.  The amount of capital stock of the corporation shall be Two Hun-
   dred Thousand Dollars ($200,000) divided into 1,000 shares of preferred stock,
   par value $100 per share, and 10,000 shares of common stock, par value $10 per
   share.

        SIXTH.  The names and the post office addresses of the three directors of
   the corporation who are also subscribers to this Certificate of Incorporation,
   and the number of shares of common stock that each agrees to subscribe for,
   are:

            Alfred Colleto, 174 Broad Street, Salinas, 2,000 shares
            Dawn Scott, 732 Renner Avenue, Salinas, 2,000 shares
            Philip Wooters, 211 Park Place, Salinas, 2,000 shares

        SEVENTH.  All the subscribers to this certificate are of full age; a
   majority of them are citizens of the United States, and at least one of them
   is a resident of the State of California.

        In witness whereof, we have made, signed, and acknowledged this certifi-
   cate this fifth day of July, 19--.

        (Signed)  Alfred Colleto
        (Signed)  Dawn Scott
        (Signed)  Philip Wooters
```

Fig. 32-1. Articles of incorporation

operating as a corporation and in most, but not all, ways satisfying the requirements for formation of a corporation. Usually, it has not fulfilled some minor
requirement of the statute governing the formation of corporations. Only the
state can directly challenge the existence of a de facto corporation. Thus, a de facto
corporation has the same rights and privileges as a de jure corporation insofar as
any person other than the state is concerned.

▶▶ Mohawk Motors, Inc., in securing its charter, failed to have it recorded. Although this means that the company is not in compliance with the state statute, only the state has the right to challenge Mohawk Motors' corporate existence. Until the state brings an independent action, the de facto corporation may sue and be sued, make contracts, and perform every other act which a de jure corporation may perform.

Subscribers and Subscriptions

A *subscription* is an offer to purchase stock in a corporation yet to be formed; the offeror is known as a subscriber. The subscriber is not liable unless the corporation is completely organized as a de jure corporation and the full amount of the stock has been subscribed.

A distinction must be made between a subscription and a contract to purchase stock in an existing corporation. A subscriber becomes a shareholder as soon as his or her offer is accepted. A purchaser of stock, however, does not become a shareholder until the certificate of stock is issued.

▶▶ Tower-Olschan, Inc., became insolvent, and its assets were delivered into the hands of a trustee in bankruptcy. The trustee could not collect the consideration for unpaid stock purchased by Wetzel, who had not received the certificate of stock prior to the bankruptcy. But had Wetzel been a subscriber, she would be liable for payment of the stock with the acceptance of her subscription, even though the stock certificate had not been delivered.

The statutes generally set forth requirements as to the consideration for the shares of stock which a subscriber is to receive. Usually, shares having a par value (equality between the face value of a share of stock and its actual selling price) may not be issued for less than par. Shares without par value may be issued for consideration as determined by the board of directors or shareholders. Payment for shares must be made either in money, in other property, or in services actually performed. Neither promissory notes nor future services are acceptable in payment for shares of stock.

Bylaws

The *bylaws* of a corporation are the rules and regulations adopted by the corporation for its internal management. They may contain any provisions for the regulation of affairs of the corporation, but they must be consistent with state laws and the articles of incorporation. Generally, the power to change or repeal the bylaws or adopt new ones is held by the board of directors of the corporation or its shareholders.

CORPORATE POWERS

A corporation obtains all its powers from the state. Therefore, it has only powers that the state gives under statute or that are expressed in the corporation's articles of incorporation.

Powers Granted by Statute

A corporation organized under state statute usually is empowered as follows:

- ☐ To have perpetual life, unless a limited period is stated in its certificate of incorporation.
- ☐ To sue and be sued.
- ☐ To have a corporate seal.
- ☐ To purchase, lease, acquire, hold, and deal in real or personal property.
- ☐ To sell, convey, mortgage, or own interests and shares in other domestic or foreign corporations, associations, or partnerships.
- ☐ To make contracts and guarantees and incur liabilities, borrow money, issue bonds, and secure obligations by mortgage of, or creation of a security interest in, all or any of its property, franchises, and income.
- ☐ To lend money and to invest and reinvest funds.
- ☐ To conduct its business, carry on its operations, and have offices and exercise its corporate powers anywhere.
- ☐ To elect and appoint officers, employees, and agents of the corporation and to define their duties and fix their compensation.
- ☐ To make and alter bylaws for the administration and regulation of its affairs.
- ☐ To establish pension, profit-sharing, stock-option, stock-purchase, and incentive plans and to offer fringe benefits to any or all of its directors, officers, employees, their families, dependents, or beneficiaries.
- ☐ To declare and pay dividends.
- ☐ To effect and implement a merger with one or more other corporations.
- ☐ To create and issue shares of stock as provided in the articles of incorporation.
- ☐ To acquire its own shares.
- ☐ To participate with other corporations, partnerships, or associations of any kind in any legal transaction, undertaking, or arrangement.
- ☐ To transact, at the request of the federal government, any lawful business in time of war or other national emergency, notwithstanding the purpose or purposes set forth in its certificate of incorporation.
- ☐ To make donations for charitable, educational, or public welfare purposes.
- ☐ To have and exercise all other powers necessary or convenient to effect any or all of the purposes for which the corporation is organized.

Express and Implied Powers

The articles of incorporation list the express powers of the corporation. They relate to the specific business activities to be carried on by the corporation. Special service corporations usually cannot be chartered under a general corporation statute. Therefore, a corporation that intends to engage in banking, insurance, or the railroad industry must incorporate under separate statutes that apply to such activities.

In addition to its express powers, a corporation can perform unspecified acts that are consistent with its express powers. This power is said to exist "by implication." A general statement of corporate purpose is sufficient to establish all of the implied powers of a corporation.

 The articles of incorporation for Rocliff Corporation state that it is organized for the purpose of buying and selling goods, wares, and merchandise. From this express language, one may safely conclude that the corporation has implied power to purchase or lease stores, employ sales personnel, and buy or rent delivery trucks. Also implied would be the authority to spend money for advertising, open a bank account, and perform many other acts closely akin to the express powers from which they are derived by implication.

Ultra Vires Acts

If a corporation performs any acts or enters into any contracts that go beyond the express and implied authority found in the articles of incorporation, the corporation is said to be acting *ultra vires,* that is, beyond its authority. In such cases, the state has the authority to take away the charter of the corporation or fine the corporation.

This does not mean that an *ultra vires* act is automatically void. On the contrary, an *ultra vires* contract is enforceable, and neither the corporation nor its directors may use excess of authority as a defense. Individual shareholders may bring suit to block performance of an *ultra vires* contract, and the corporation itself can hold its directors liable for any losses resulting from such acts which they authorized.

 Amtrak directors signed contracts for the construction of inns at several of its major junctions. The railroad's charter did not expressly state that one of its purposes was to build, own, and manage inns. Shareholders or the state may challenge this action by the directors. The action may be declared *ultra vires* by the court, unless Amtrak can show that it has the implied power authorizing it to build, own, and manage inns to accommodate its passengers.

Corporation Tort and Crime Liability

A corporation may be held liable for any torts or crimes it commits. The fact that the action on constituting the tort or crime was itself *ultra vires* is no defense. Corporations are liable for fraud committed by officers or agents within the scope of their actual or apparent authority. Corporations are also liable for acts committed by their agents in the conduct of corporate business as well as for injury caused by failure of agents to perform corporate duties. Examples of the latter include failure to keep corporate property in safe condition or to install safety equipment required by statute.

A corporation may knowingly or unknowingly commit a crime. Punishment is commonly a fine. Many criminal actions involving corporations result from antitrust violations. Another type of violation, known as a *quasi-criminal act,* occurs when a corporation fails to comply with a state reporting requirement. The usual punishment is a small fine.

REGULATION OF SALE OF SECURITIES

Because of the ease with which corporations may be formed and the possibility of fraud in the sale of securities in corporations now in existence, strict regulations have been introduced regarding the sale and announcement of new stock issues. Both state and federal regulatory acts protect the investor in today's market.

Blue-Sky Laws

The so-called *blue-sky laws* regulate the issuance and sale of stock of *intrastate* corporations. Under these laws, which vary only slightly from state to state, the seller must make a public statement of responsibility, disclose the general financial condition of the corporation, and make a full accounting of the use to which the proceeds of the new stock issue are to be put by the corporation. These facts are registered with a designated state official or security commission. Both criminal and civil penalties are provided if a violation of the law is uncovered. Liability to refund money is placed not only on the issuer of the security but also on anyone who assists in the sale. You should always obtain legal advice as to the requirements of the blue-sky laws before selling any investment.

 A corporation was formed for the purpose of selling stock in a new venture. The new corporation planned to prospect for oil and to sink oil wells in certain marshes where the organizers' engineers indicated oil might be found. The information upon which the reports were based was later found to be fraudulent. The officers of the corporation were charged with criminal fraud, and the investors received judgments in civil actions for the return of money they used to purchase stock.

Federal Securities Act

To regulate the sale of securities in *interstate* commerce, Congress passed the Federal Securities Act in 1933. The act applies to the sale of securities totaling more than $100,000 in public issues. It does not apply to sales between individuals. Under the act, a prospectus of any new issue must be filed with the Securities and Exchange Commission for examination before the actual sale of the securities. Information submitted must include types of securities already outstanding, terms of sale, bonus and profit-sharing arrangements, options to be created in connection with the issue, and other information which the commission may consider necessary.

A registration statement is made to the commission and signed by the company, its principal officers, and a majority of the board of directors. The commission will not certify and permit the sale of the securities if there are any misstatements or omissions in either the registration statement or the prospectus. Any sale considered improper because of false information, fraud, or the like gives the investor the right to sue the persons who have signed the registration statement for all resulting damages. Failure to comply with the law subjects the responsible officials to criminal prosecution.

Federal Securities Exchange Act

In 1934, a Federal Securities Exchange Act was passed by Congress. Under this act, all stock exchanges dealing in the sale and transfer of securities are required to register with the Securities and Exchange Commission. If an exchange fails to register, it is prohibited from using the mails to transact its business.

No exchange is permitted to sell securities that have not been registered with the commission. An exchange must also set up strict rules for the operation and disciplining of its own officers and members in the event of misconduct in relation to the operation of the exchange.

 A new corporation was created for the purpose of operating a communications system between two towns located directly across state lines. The stock issue had never been presented or approved by the Securities and Exchange Commission. The board of managers of an exchange agreed to list the new corporation on its stock board and handle transactions involving the public sale and transfer of the issue. This was in violation of the Federal Securities Exchange Act, and the exchange was subject to discipline or loss of license.

Federal Reserve Control of Margin Sales

Purchase of stock *on margin* consists of an arrangement whereby a broker permits the investor to make only part payment for his or her shares, the balance being secured by the certificates held by the broker. Strict regulation of the amount of margin permitted is under the jurisdiction of the Federal Reserve Board. The board is given discretionary powers in this matter and raises and lowers the margin required according to its interpretation of current economic conditions and the position of the market at any time.

 The Board of Governors of the Federal Reserve System felt that business conditions indicated a recession in the near future. As a means of reversing the trend of sales of stock on the exchange, the Federal Reserve announced a more liberal margin. This brought hundreds of new buyers into the market and was a factor in averting the threatened business recession.

CAPITAL STOCK

The term *capital stock* is often misunderstood and confused with other terms, such as *capital*, *stock*, and *shares*. A number of states have discarded the term altogether and have adopted *stated capital* in its place. Both terms accurately designate property or consideration obtained by the corporation from its shareholders. The capital stock is used in the business and is represented by outstanding certificates for a specified number of shares. It may be in the form of cash, property, or services rendered. The term has little practical importance except as it relates to the number of shares of stock which have been sold and issued.

The value of a corporation's assets changes constantly, as does the total number of shares outstanding. Thus the market value of the corporation's shares has the capacity to change from moment to moment. But capital stock has a fixed, predetermined value, set by the corporation's charter or by action of the board of directors or the corporate shareholders or both. This value cannot be changed except in the manner established by state law. Shares of capital stock are property that designates a certain interest in the corporation but does not give the holder any claim or right to any specific property that is owned by the corporation.

 Abco Wholesaler, Inc., stated its total capital stock value in its corporate charter to be $60,000. Its three subscribers—Osgood, Farwell, and Matzen—each received one thousand shares of stock in return for their know-how, time, and effort and two thousand additional shares for cash payments of $15,000 that were dedicated for use in the business. The $60,000 stated capital is the aggregate value of all the issued shares.

TYPES OF CORPORATE SHARES

Corporations can issue two types of shares. The legal and financial rights they carry can vary substantially, and investors whose needs are met by one kind may find little merit in the same corporation's other class of stock.

Common Stock

The most usual kind of corporate security is *common stock*. It carries with it all the risks of the business, inasmuch as it does not guarantee to its holder the right to profits. The return, if any, is based on the earnings of the venture. If the business is successful, the holders may receive the largest share of the profits. If the business fails, the holders must accept the heaviest losses. In return, they generally have the controlling voice in management.

Common-Stock Voting Power   Ordinarily, each share of common stock has one vote. In this manner, a majority group of shareholders can elect all the directors and gain control of the affairs of the corporation. To give the minority shareholders an opportunity to elect one or more directors, the laws of some states permit *cumulative voting*. In these states, each share of stock has as many votes as there are directors to be elected. These votes may be cast for one director or may be distributed.

Logue, Griffith, Harris, and Kline were presented to the shareholders as directorship candidates of Market Rubber Company, Inc. Three of the four were to be chosen. Since cumulative voting was authorized, the minority shareholders cast all of their weighted votes for Logue, who had promised to represent the minority voice in corporation affairs. Had the minority voters been allowed only one vote for each share instead of three, they might have failed in their effort to elect a favored director.

Preferred Stock

Capital stock other than common is usually referred to as *preferred stock*. Within this broad classification, there is a great variety of contract rights between the corporation and the preferred shareholder. Preferred rights generally give the holder a priority claim of some kind over the holder of common stock. These preferences are either dividends or the assets of the corporation on liquidation. The extent of the preferences can only be determined by the terms stated in the contract (certificate), by the corporate charter, by the bylaws of the corporation, or by the provisions of the state statute.

There are two common contract rights of preferred shareholders. The first is the right to receive dividends at stated intervals and at fixed rates before any dividends are paid to the common shareholders. The second is the right to receive a specific sum of money upon liquidation before any assets are distributed to the common shareholders. After the preferred shareholders have received the dividends guaranteed to them in their certificates, any profits remaining may be apportioned among the common shareholders.

> Dividends were distributed to holders of shares in National Stores, Inc., for the current period. Ellis received 75 cents per share for one hundred shares of preferred stock. The remaining profits, amounting to $1.90 per share, were apportioned among the common shareholders. Although unhappy with the uneven division of profits, the holders of preferred-stock shares could do nothing about it. They had received their dividend at the rate fixed in their certificate.

Preferred-stock certificates often provide for *cumulative dividends*. This means that if a preferred dividend for one or more years is not paid, no dividend on the common stock may be paid until the past dividends have been paid. If the certificate does not contain this expressed right, the preferred shareholders lose their right to the past dividends.

> Wisnieski purchased three hundred shares in Elmrite Fuel Corporation of 7-percent cumulative preferred stock at par value of $50 a share. After the first year of operation, the business failed to show a profit. The directors voted not to pay a dividend to all shareholders for the year. The $1,050 in unpaid dividends must be paid to the preferred shareholders before any dividends are paid to owners of common stock.

The terms of the contract (certificate) between the corporation and the preferred shareholder often include a provision to the effect that preferred shares will be *participating*. This means that the owner of preferred shares of stock may share with another class of stock beyond the stipulated dividend. For example, in the same year, suppose that participating preferred shareholders were paid a regular 8-percent dividend and common shareholders received a specified annual dividend of 5½ percent. If there is a surplus remaining for dividends, both the preferred and the common shareholders would participate proportionately in the remaining surplus.

> Laslo purchased one hundred shares of Kohler, Inc., participating preferred stock. When Kohler profits brought a surplus for dividend payments to all shareholders, Laslo would receive both the guaranteed amount for the hundred shares held and an amount equal to that received by each common shareholder. Obviously, Laslo is assured a greater return on investment than are the holders of common-stock shares.

The holders of preferred stock do not have voting power. As with common stock, preferred stock represents a contribution of capital. Until a dividend is declared, the holder of shares is not a creditor of the corporation. Also, preferred shareholders do not have rights to specific corporate assets. They also have rights subordinate to those of all creditors of the corporation.

Par Value–No Par Value Stock

The value that the incorporators place on the shares of stock issued by a corporation must be stated in the corporation's charter. This value, which is the same for each share of stock of the same issue, is referred to as the par value. In the case of par value shares, the amount of the capital stock or stated capital is the total par value of all the issued stock.

Should stock shares sell for less than par, the corporation or its creditors, in the event of insolvency or bankruptcy, may sue the purchaser for the difference between the sales price of the stock and its face, or par, value. The shareholder who purchases stock from a corporation and pays full par value for it may subsequently dispose of it at any price.

The practice of placing a par value on a share of stock has been criticized as misleading. Uninformed buyers often interpret the par value printed on the face of the certificate as the actual *market value* of the shares. To correct this condition, New York and many other states have authorized the issuance of *no par value stock*. The advantage of stock without par value has been outlined in a Delaware court ruling: "If the assets received are $1,000 in money, it is of no consequence whether five shares or ten shares, or one thousand shares are given for it. Each share has its one-fifth, or one-tenth, or one one-thousandth part of the $1,000 as the case may be, and no one is damaged. Everyone knows that under each share is simply its proportionate part of the total assets, unexpressed in terms of money."

Watered Stock

Stock issued as fully paid when, in fact, its full par value has not been paid in money, property, or services is known as *watered stock*. The original holders of such stock are liable to corporate creditors for differences between its par value and the amount they actually paid for the stock.

 A director of Steel Specialists, Inc., suggested that the officers of the business be given a bonus of five hundred shares of the corporation's common stock for the loyalty shown during the first year of operations. A bonus such as this, unless rightfully earned and owed to the officers, would be considered watered stock.

Treasury Shares

Shares of its own stock lawfully acquired by a corporation and not canceled are called *treasury shares*. A corporation may acquire its own shares by purchase, gift, or otherwise. The stock may be resold at a below-par price agreed upon by the board of directors. Shares acquired by purchase or by donation may be canceled or retired in the manner provided by law. The effect is to reduce the stated capital stock to the extent of the shares canceled.

Only surplus funds may be used for the purchase of treasury shares. Treasury shares cannot be voted, and no dividends of any kind are payable upon them.

 Metal Aire, Inc., was faced with financial difficulties, and its directors encouraged several shareholders to donate a portion of their shares as treasury shares. The directors proposed to resell the returned shares below par and to return the proceeds to the treasury of the corporation for working capital. In taking this action, the cooperating shareholders were assuring the continuance of the troubled corporation and raising the possibility of an ultimate return on their investment.

Dividends

The most common type of dividend is the *cash dividend* declared and paid out of current corporate earnings or accumulated surplus at regular intervals. A corporation's board of directors has the sole authority to determine the amount, time, place, and manner of dividend payment. Typically, the director's declaration of a dividend sets a cutoff date—the date by which a shareholder must hold corporate stock of record in order to receive payment.

 Employee productivity and effective management returned substantial profits to Industrial Packaging, Inc. The board of directors declared a dividend to all shareholders of record on June 30. All persons owning shares as of June 30 will share in the dividend, even though they may sell their shares before the actual distribution of the dividend.

Stock Dividends In a few instances, a distribution of earnings is made to shareholders in the form of shares of the capital stock. This is called a *stock dividend.* Payment of a stock dividend is shown on the corporate books by a reduction in the surplus account equal in value to the dividend. The capital account is increased by the same amount. After a stock dividend is paid, the corporate assets are identical to what they were before. However, each share constitutes a smaller proportionate interest in these assets. But, because the number of shares has been increased, the value of each shareholder's holdings remains the same. One situation does not remain the same: Surplus previously available for other uses becomes frozen in the capital account.

Stock Split In a *stock split,* each outstanding share of stock is broken up into a greater number of shares, each representing a lesser value in the corporation. Usually, the purpose of a stock split is to lower the unit price of a share in an effort to stimulate sales interest and increase the number of shareholders. The stated, or par, value of each share is reduced after splitting, but no change occurs in the actual total value of stock outstanding or in the surplus account.

Transfer and Registration

Ownership of a stock certificate is essential to owning an interest in the corporation. To transfer the shareholder's interest, there must be a transfer of the stock certificate.

The statutory rules that apply to the transfer of shares of stock, bonds, or other securities for value are contained in Article 8, Investment Securities, of the Uniform Commercial Code. Under the code, a transfer of shares of stock is made by delivery of the certificate alone if it is in bearer form or indorsed in blank. If the certificate is in registered form, the transfer is made by delivery, with either indorsement by the person entitled to it or a separate document of assignment and transfer signed by the appropriate person.

Stock Registration   The transfer of a registered stock or security is complete when indorsement and delivery take place. But the transfer must be registered; that is, the new owner's name must be placed on the stock register, and the previous owner's name must be removed. When a registered security is presented to the corporation that issued it, and instructions are given to register the transfer, the corporation must do so promptly, after ascertaining that the transfer was legitimate in all respects.

Lost Stock Certificates   It is the obligation of the owner to notify the issuing corporation that a stock certificate has been lost, stolen, or destroyed. This notice must be given within a reasonable time after the loss occurs. If the issuer registers the transfer of the lost certificate prior to receiving notice of loss, the original owner has a right against the corporation to receive a new certificate for the same number of shares. If newly issued shares are not available, the original owner may recover from the issuer the price he or she or the last purchaser paid for the certificate, plus interest as of the date of the demand.

 Donovan lost by theft an unindorsed certificate of stock. Mooney, the thief, signed Donovan's name as his agent. Mooney then sold and delivered the certificate to Rojas, a bona fide transferee, who paid value and took the certificate without knowledge of the theft or of the unauthorized indorsement. Donovan is still the owner of the shares, and Mooney is liable to him for their value. However, if Mooney surrenders the certificate to the issuing corporation and the corporation recognizes him as the owner, cancels the certificate, and issues a new one in Mooney's name, Mooney is then the owner of the shares represented by the new certificate registered in his name. However, Donovan has a right against the issuer to receive a new certificate for the same number of shares.

Corporate Bonds

Another method of corporate financing is the issuance and sale of bonds. This common method of long-term borrowing is known as *creditor*, or *debt, financing*. A usual type of corporate bond is a written promise to pay a designated sum of money at a specified date with interest at a stated rate. Such bonds are usually offered in series and secured by a deed of trust or mortgage. Property of the corporation is mortgaged to a trustee for the benefit of all the bondholders. Thus, bondholders are secured creditors who have lent money to the corporation but hold a special assurance of payment of the debt. However, they do not have the right to vote or participate in the management and control of the corporation.

Questions for Review and Discussion

1. Why is the corporation the most important form of business organization?

2. What actions are required, and by whom, to create a corporation?

3. What is the certificate of incorporation, often referred to as the corporation charter? How is it obtained?

4. In what ways does a de jure corporation differ from a de facto corporation? Who can challenge the existence of a de facto corporation?

5. (*a*) What is the function of the corporation's bylaws and their relationship to the articles of incorporation? (*b*) Are they of significant importance to the board of directors, officers, and shareholders? Explain.

6. (*a*) What is the purpose of blue-sky laws? (*b*) Who may be held liable under the blue-sky laws?

7. In what manner does the corporation obtain its power to conduct its usual business?

8. What effect do the *ultra vires* acts of a corporation have on the enforcement of contracts in respect to (*a*) third parties, (*b*) shareholders, and (*c*) the state?

9. Compare the ownership rights of a holder of a certificate of stock with those of a holder of a corporate bond. Which of the holders is a creditor of the corporation?

10. What are the two common contract rights of preferred shareholders that give them superior standing over holders of common stock?

Analyzing Cases

1. Hamilton held 500 shares of 5-percent cumulative participating preferred stock issued by the Logan Manufacturing Corporation. The stock also carried a preference as to dividends and a preference in the distribution of assets. Discuss Hamilton's rights in each of the following situations: (*a*) If the earnings of the corporation were not sufficient in any one year to pay the 5-percent dividend on the preferred stock; (*b*) if the earnings of the corporation were sufficient to pay a 10-percent dividend on all stock issued, both common and preferred (assume that there were an equal number of $100 par value shares of preferred and common stock issued); (*c*) if the corporation dissolved. • See also *Arizona Power Co. v. Stuart,* 212 Fed.2d 535.

2. Harvard owned one hundred shares in String Instrument Manufacturing, Inc. He bought a large supply of raw materials at an auction sale for the company, paying cash for them. The company refused to accept the goods or to reimburse Harvard for them. Harvard sued. Who will win the case? Why? • See also *Grand Truck W.K. Co. v. H. W. Nelson Co.,* 116 Fed.2d 823.

3. Budd contracted to buy stock in an existing corporation but failed to pay the entire amount due. A dividend was declared after she purchased the stock. The corporation refused to pay the dividend to Budd, claiming that she was not entitled to it because she was not a shareholder.

Budd sued. Will she be successful? Why? • See also *U.S.* v. *White Sulphur Springs*, 57 Fed. Supp. 48, 52.

4. Drewen, a majority stockholder, designated his son as treasurer of the corporation. Certain minority stockholders objected, claiming that Drewen did not have the authority to make the appointment. They took court action to enforce their objections. What should the court decide? Why? • See also *Abrams* v. *Allen*, 173 A.L.R. 671.

5. Warren owns securities in many corporations and keeps the stock certificates in a strongbox in her home. After studying market trends, she decides to sell seven hundred shares of stock of a company which she notes is using outmoded merchandising methods. Warren cannot locate her stock certificate for the shares in question. She realizes that time is of the essence and that some action must be taken in a short time to avoid loss of this investment. What may Warren do, having lost or misplaced the certificate which she must have in order to make the sale? • See also *Cecil National Bank* v. *Watsontown Bank*, 105 U.S. 217.

6. Evans owned five thousand shares of stock in a corporation that had issued only fifteen thousand shares, and she was the largest stockholder. During a visit to one of the company's plants, she directed the plant manager to suspend operations and redesign the production line being used in one of the plant areas. The general manager refused to follow the instructions, and Evans ordered his dismissal on grounds of insubordination. Was the manager correct in refusing to follow Evans's directions? Explain. • See also *Jones* v. *Williams*, 139 Mo. 1, 39 S.W. 486.

Legal Reasoning and Business Judgment

Analyze the legal aspects of these business problems. Suggest possible solutions.

1. The owner of a small manufacturing plant is aware of her responsibility and liability as sole proprietor. She knows that any suit or tort action against the business might lead to a levy on her home and personal estate. She decides to protect herself by incorporating the business. At the same time, she plans to offer stock for public sale to increase her capital. Must any state laws be observed in respect to issuance of this stock for public sale? Explain.

2. Your company's research and development department has discovered a new process for making steel castings which will increase shareholders' profits. To put the new process into operation, your company will need $500,000. The board of directors is not willing to borrow the amount from banks or to issue bonds. The corporation's stock has all been issued, and there is no authority for the issuance of additional stock in order to finance the new process. What would you recommend as the proper method of raising the required capital?

3. Your company is sponsoring a television series as a means of promoting goodwill among consumers. The board of directors approved the program's objectives, and arrangements for the series were made by officers of the corporation through employees of the promotion and advertising department. After one of the programs, a member of the board of directors contacted the producer and demanded that the series be terminated immediately, since he personally did not like the way the corporation's objectives were being presented. Must the producer submit to the demand of the board member?

Chapter 33
Operations and Dissolution of Corporations

Both state statutes and the influential Model Business Corporation Act provide that a corporation's business and affairs are to be "managed under the direction of a board of directors." This wording makes it clear that the duty of directors to manage the corporation may be carried out by officers and employees under the direction of the board. Thus the board of directors is the appropriate unit for the establishment of board policies and procedures and for reviewing performance. Management is the agency delegated by the board to make these policies and procedures effective, subject to board review.

How to keep the role of the board separate and independent from executive management is related to the challenge of how best to organize the board and select its members. The issues to be resolved are the size of the board; criteria for selecting directors; time commitments; directors' fees; relationship among board members, the chairperson, and the company's president; and retirement policies.

BOARD OF DIRECTORS

The business and affairs of a corporation are managed by a board of directors elected by the shareholders. The board's responsibility is to take whatever actions are appropriate, in conformity with the corporate charter, to further the corporation's business. Individual board members are supposed to use their own judgment in the corporate decision-making process. Shareholders cannot usurp the management function. If directors are inept, dull, and lazy, the shareholders have only themselves to blame. In short, directors are not legally liable for losses to the corporation resulting from poor business judgment or honest mistakes.

Qualifications of Directors

The statute of the state plus the corporation's articles of incorporation and bylaws determine the qualifications which a person must possess in order to serve as a corporation's director. Unless prohibited by the charter, membership on the board of directors may be extended to anyone, including aliens, minors, women, and persons who are not shareholders. Often it is stipulated that at least one director be a resident of the state of incorporation. A primary consideration in selecting an individual as a director or officer of the board is his or her ability to bring to the board a calm and objective view of corporate operations.

Time Commitment of Directors

General directors are elected at the annual meeting of the shareholders to hold office for one year. A board of directors consists of as many members as are stated by resolution of the board in accordance with the corporation's bylaws. The number usually ranges between eight and twelve. Boards are normally elected as a group for the purpose of obtaining continuity; this procedure permits one-third of the board to be elected annually for a two-year term. The basic time commitment for a director is approximately thirty days per year, but depending upon need, availability, and interest, it can be forty, sixty, eighty or even more days.

Meetings of Directors

The board of directors of most large corporations meet on a regular basis, at a precise time and place chosen by the directors. But the directors of many smaller corporations meet only when specific items are to be considered. Some statutes require board meetings to be held within the state; most do not.

The directors must be given notice of meetings and must be present at meetings to vote. They may not vote by proxy, that is, specify another person to vote in their place. The quorum, or minimum number of directors necessary to conduct business, is usually one more than half the number of directors. But the bylaws may require more than a quorum, say 80 percent of the directors in attendance, to conduct certain types of business. Generally, however, the act of the quorum constitutes the official action of the board.

 The board of directors of Cleanmark Service, Inc., was made up of five persons. At a properly called meeting, a motion was presented by which the salaries of the president, secretary, and treasurer of the corporation were to be increased by 15 percent for the coming year. The attendance of any three directors would constitute a quorum, and the vote of two of them would be the act of the board.

Responsibility of Directors

The responsibility of directors is to perform their role "in good faith, in a manner they reasonably believe to be in the best interests of the corporation, and with such care as an ordinarily prudent person in like position would use under similar circumstances." This standard of care, embodied in the newly amended Model Business Corporation Act, is a well-established principle of common law and is incorporated expressly, in various forms, in a growing number of state statutes.

The use of the phrase *ordinarily prudent person* focuses on the director's basic common sense, practical wisdom, and informed judgment. Understood in the phrase *under similar circumstances* is the fact that the responsibility and attendant liability of a director may vary according to his or her background and the particular problems involved. The duty of a director to act as a prudent person, that is, to act reasonably, is taken into consideration in determining a director's responsibility and liability in a given situation.

Should a director fail to exercise the degree of care and skill attributable to an ordinarily prudent person, the corporation can bring an action against the director. Two factors should be borne in mind: First, the corporation has the burden of proof in demonstrating actual negligence on the part of the director. Mere faulty judgment or an accident will not do if a director has acted in good faith and if it can be shown that a person of ordinary prudence might have made the same blunder. And this burden of proof is especially difficult to establish in large corporations, in which careful directors often have no choice but to delegate to others a wide variety of tasks. Second, and more important, it should be noted that proving actual damages is often quite difficult.

A director can also be held liable to his or her corporation for torts more serious than negligence. For example, a director who participates in fraudulent activities is personally liable to the corporation.

Nowadays, most corporate directors insist that their corporations provide and pay for policies of indemnity insurance covering their actions as directors. This is the norm in most large corporations; the policies are regarded as fringe benefits for directors. The costs of legal defense and of a resultant judgment against a director accused of negligent actions are covered by these policies. However, such policies usually do not indemnify against criminal activities or intentional torts.

The Securities and Exchange Commission (SEC) has struggled unsuccessfully to develop guidelines with respect to the responsibilities and liabilities of corporate directors. The SEC finally noted that too much clarity and too many specifics in laws covering the personal liability of directors can result in irrational decisions in individual cases. The commission indicated that the basic guideline should be the legal concept of negligence—in other words, reasonable care must be taken in executing one's responsibilities. In short, the SEC expects every corporate director to do his or her duty without being told exactly what that duty is in every situation. The SEC does, however, expect directors to take seriously what the law has in fact long required of them: that they give their primary duty and loyalty to investors. They must overcome the traditional and very human tendency to be compliant "good guys" and make the job of management more pleasant. Instead, directors must take reasonable measures to protect the interests of investors. The applicable standard of care provides that duties are to be discharged with the same skill, prudence, and diligence that a sensible person acting in a like capacity and familiar with such matters would use in the conduct of a similar enterprise.

▶▶ Jensen, a director of Woundy & Company, Inc., for six years, had never attended a board meeting or made an examination of the corporation's books and records. The corporation suffered a severe loss when the unsupervised cashier made improper loans to several business friends. Jensen pointed out that she lived 460 miles away and could not be expected to attend board meetings. The court would hold that she and the other board members would have to answer for the losses that resulted because of neglect of duty. A director must show an active interest in the affairs of the corporation and keep abreast of the general condition of its operations.

OFFICERS OF THE CORPORATION

Directors are not expected to spend all their time and energy attending to the management of the corporation. They have authority given by the bylaws to assign power to appoint officers and agents. By statute, the usual officers are a president, several vice presidents, a secretary, and a treasurer. Other officers, such as a comptroller, cashier, and general counsel, are often provided. The bylaws of the corporation describe the duties of each officer responsible for carrying out the policies laid down by the directors. Officers have the authority of general agents for the operation of the normal business of the corporation. They, in turn, delegate duties to various department heads.

Directors do not necessarily receive salaries for their services. To retain and attract competent directors, however, a number of corporations are providing compensation beyond the conventional fee per meeting (a few hundred dollars) that most directors receive. When a director receives other than nominal fees for service, he or she inevitably feels a true sense of responsibility which enhances the commitment and does not infringe upon his or her independence. Often, a director holds the position of an officer, however, and is paid the salary approved for such an officer by the board of directors.

 Respass, a director of Crothers Transport, Inc., was appointed traffic consultant by the board, but no salary was fixed. Respass was later elected treasurer of the corporation, while continuing to serve as the traffic consultant. Although an officer, Respass could recover salary for services provided as traffic consultant. The court would hold that being both a director and an officer was insufficient grounds for not being paid for the consulting services provided to Crothers Transport.

Responsibility of Managers

Corporate managers at several levels—from chief executive officers to plant managers—are "feeling the heat" as new regulatory laws are placed on the books and established regulatory agencies take a harder line toward those who err. There are signs that more prosecutions, accompanied by fines and even jail sentences, may be in the offing.

New regulations are being enforced by traditional agencies, such as the Justice Department and the Securities Exchange Commission. And new federal standards of care are applicable to managers as well as to directors with respect to their authority and responsibility under rules of newer agencies, such as the Environmental Protection Agency (EPA), the Consumer Product Safety Commission (CPSC), and the Equal Employment Opportunity Commission (EEOC).

There are new laws, such as the Employee Retirement Income Security Act
(ERISA) and the Occupational Safety and Health Act (OSHA). The new laws and
mandates are often vague, and the body of legal opinion not yet adequate, but the
potential penalties for offenders are heavy (see Table 33-1).

 The Illinois-based Lloyd A. Fry Roofing Company was ordered by a Minneapolis
municipal judge to select one of its executives to serve a thirty-day jail term after it
was ruled that odors coming from the company's plant violated the city's air
pollution standards. The action was later set aside only because of a legal techni-
cality. The company, but not the individual officers, had actually been indicted.

The manager at an H. J. Heinz Company plant in Tracy, California, received a
suspended six-month sentence and summary probation after being cited by
California state food and drug officials for unsanitary conditions in the plant.

Reckless Default

More punitive legislation may be enacted in the wake of corporate payoff
scandals—the use of company resources to influence the outcome of an election
or government actions. Pending in the U.S. Senate is a bill codifying federal
criminal laws which would subject business executives to criminal penalties for a
new offense called *reckless default* (in supervising an organization's activities). A
corporate officer would be personally subject to prosecution for not properly
supervising employees who violated federal regulations. If this bill passes with
the reckless default provision unchanged, executive officers of companies
charged with price fixing would not be able to escape personal liability with the
"I didn't know" excuse.

The Supreme Court ruled (in a case involving Acme Markets, Inc., and its
president) that an executive's liability for criminal conduct can extend to a
business unit far below his or her direct supervision. In this case, the president of
the food chain was personally fined for failing to ensure that the company kept
rats out of a Baltimore warehouse, as required by law.

SHAREHOLDERS' RIGHTS

The shareholders of a corporation are its primary reason for existence, and they
have certain established rights.

Right to a Stock Certificate

The stock certificate is tangible evidence of ownership of shares in a corporation.
A shareholder must have possession of the certificate and must indorse and
deliver it to the person to whom title is transferred (the transferee) when selling or
pledging shares. Loss of a certificate does not take away the owner's title to the
shares of stock represented by the certificate. The shareholder's name and address are shown on the books of the corporation, and he or she will receive
dividends, notices of meetings, and any distribution of shareholder reports
prepared by the board.

TABLE 33-1. THE RISKS EXECUTIVES FACE UNDER FEDERAL LAW

Agency	Year Enforcement Began	Complaint May Name Individual	Maximum Individual Penalty	Maximum Corporate Penalty	Private Suit Allowed Under Applicable Statute
Internal Revenue Service	1862	Yes	$5,000, three years, or both	$10,000, 50% assessment, prosecution costs	No
Antitrust Div. (Justice Dept.)	1890	Yes	$100,000, three years, or both	$1 million, injunction, divestiture	Yes
Food & Drug Administration	1907	Yes	$1,000, one year, or both for first offense; $10,000, three years, or both thereafter	$1,000 for first offense; $10,000 thereafter; seizure of condemned products	No
Federal Trade Commission	1914	Yes	Restitution, injunction	Restitution, injunction, divestiture, $10,000 per day for violation of rules, orders	No
Securities & Exchange Commission	1934	Yes	$10,000, two years, or both	$10,000, injunction	Yes
Equal Employment Opportunity Commission	1965	No		Injunction, back pay award, reinstatement	Yes
Office of Federal Contract Compliance	1965	No		Suspension, cancellation of contract	Yes
Environmental Protection Agency	1970	Yes	$25,000 per day, one year, or both for first offense; $50,000 per day, two years, or both thereafter	$25,000 per day, first offense; $50,000 per day thereafter; injunction	Yes
Occupational Safety & Health Administration	1970	No*	$10,000, six months, or both	$10,000	No
Consumer Product Safety Commission	1972	Yes	$50,000, one year, or both	$500,000	Yes
Office of Employee Benefits Security (Labor Dept.)	1975	Yes	$10,000, one year, or both; barring from future employment with plan; reimbursement	$100,000, reimbursement	Yes

*Except sole proprietorship.

▶ Craig purchased six hundred shares of stock of American Pictures, Inc., and placed the certificate in his office safe. He reported it stolen following an office burglary. Craig is entitled to have a new certificate issued to him by the corporation. He must furnish a bond, however, to protect the corporation against possible loss should the stolen certificate reappear later in the hands of a legal holder.

Right to Vote

Shareholders usually get one vote per share of common stock held. Stockholders who have preferred stock usually cannot vote those shares, although they have the limited right to vote on proposals governing certain types of corporate organizations. And, as stated previously, some state statutes allow for the election of directors by cumulative voting. When this is the case, shareholders may give one candidate as many votes as the number of directors to be elected multiplied by the number of shares that the shareholder owns.

The method of voting is carefully defined under most state laws. A shareholder has the right to designate another to vote his or her shares. This arrangement is known as *proxy voting.* Most states provide that a proxy authorization can be withdrawn by the shareholder at any time up to the time of the vote.

▶ Lummis found that she could not attend a scheduled shareholders' meeting. Accordingly, she drew up a power of attorney appointing a business associate as her agent to vote on all matters to be brought before the shareholders. The agent, of course, does not have title to the stock or possession of the stock certificates. And unless ended sooner by Lummis, the proxy terminates automatically at the end of eleven months.

Right to Examine Corporate Books and Records

A shareholder's right by statute to inspect the books and records of the corporation is usually limited to inspections for proper purposes at the proper time and the proper place. Idle curiosity and purposes that interfere with or embarrass corporate management would prompt officers or directors to refuse requests to examine corporate accounts, minutes, and records of shareholders. Where the purpose of inspection is not improper, it may be enforced by a *writ of mandamus*. This is an order by a court directing a public officer to perform a particular act. This writ would compel the corporation to make its books and records available for inspection.

▶ In an effort to determine whether a certain company officer was actually a holder of voting stock in the Tucson Power & Light Company, Burke, a shareholder, retained an attorney to examine the records of shareholders. Burke has the right to appoint a competent agent to make this inspection provided his purpose is not to make improper use of the information. Refusal by an officer or agent of Tucson Power & Light Company would result in a penalty recoverable by Burke in a civil action.

Right to Dividends

Shareholders have the right to share in dividends after they have been declared by the board of directors. Once declared, a dividend becomes a debt of the corporation and enforceable at law, as is any other debt. The shareholders cannot force the directors to declare a dividend, however, unless it can be shown that the directors are not acting in good faith in refusing to do so. Courts are not inclined to order directors to meet and declare a dividend if it involves substituting the court's business judgment for that of the directors.

> Uhle, the chairman of the board and controlling shareholder of Lund Realty Corporation, had stated that she would never pay a dividend as long as she lived. In a suit of equity brought against the directors of Lund Realty, the court would probably grant an injunction and require Uhle to declare a dividend. Uhle appears to have other than proper business reasons for keeping all the earnings of Lund Realty.

Unlawful Dividends Many states hold directors personally liable to creditors for improperly declared dividends. The statutes may further require repayment of such amounts by the shareholders receiving the improper dividends, although repayment is often impossible with out-of-state shareholders. Often, dividends can be declared only out of net profits. In most states, though, the legitimacy of a dividend is determined by whether its payment would impair net assets to such an extent that they would fall below the figure set for the corporation's outstanding capital stock.

Right to Transfer Shares of Stock

A shareholder has the right to sell or transfer his or her stock. The person to whom stock shares are transferred has the right to have the stock transfer entered on the corporate books. The transferee becomes a *shareholder of record* and is entitled to vote, receive dividends, and enjoy all other shareholder privileges.

> Chatlos made a move to take over the control of General Cigar Company. He made an offer of $12 a share to shareholders, payable in a matter of seven days. Although a number of shareholders feel victimized by the offer (which they believe did not truly reflect their company's worth), those shareholders who find the offer acceptable have the right to transfer their shares to Chatlos.

Rights Upon Dissolution

When a corporation is dissolved and the claims of all its creditors are satisfied, the shareholders share proportionately in the distribution of the remaining assets. The holders of preferred stock have priority to the extent of their contractual rights.

Shareholders need not sit idly by and suffer the actions of directors who waste the assets of the corporation or threaten injury to the corporation through illegal, oppressive, or fraudulent acts. They may apply to the court of equity for relief in the form of a receiver to liquidate the assets and business of the corporation.

Right to Buy Newly Issued Stock

Unless the right is denied or limited by the articles of incorporation, shareholders have the right to purchase a proportionate share of every offering of stock by the corporation.

 Mills owns 400 shares of stock of PPG Industries, Inc., which has 1,200 shares outstanding. The corporation decides to increase its capital stock to 2,400 shares. Mills has the right to protect his proportionate interest in PPG Industries. He and every other shareholder will be offered one share of the newly issued stock for every share they own. If Mills accepts the offer and buys, he will have 800 shares out of the total 2,400 outstanding. Thus his relative interest in the corporation will remain unchanged.

CREDITOR RIGHTS

All persons who have advanced money, property, or services to a corporation are its creditors. Included are those who have unpaid wages due from it, purchasers of its bonds and notes, and the government, to the extent of unpaid taxes. The rights of creditors of a corporation are essentially the same as those of creditors of individuals.

Participation in Management

Creditors have no voice in the management of a corporation and may not interfere with its operation. The only right of creditors is to have their claims paid out of corporate assets.

Employee Rights to Unpaid Wages

In some states, the largest shareholders are jointly and severally personally liable for wages or salaries due employees for work performed by them for the corporation. In several states, employees must be legally unsuccessful in collecting the owed wages from the corporation and must give proper notice to the specified number of largest shareholders before they may be held personally liable. In New York, shareholders whose shares are listed on a national securities exchange are free from this liability.

Unlawful Distribution of Assets

Unlawful distribution of any assets of a corporation makes each shareholder liable to the corporation's creditors for the amount involved. For instance, if a dividend was declared and distributed out of capital because no surplus profits were available, the shareholders would be liable to the creditors for the dividend received.

A transfer of the corporation's assets for insufficient value would not serve the claims of creditors and would be considered a fraudulent action. Payments made by an insolvent corporation to one of its creditors are also unlawful. All such payments are voidable if made within four months prior to the filing of a bankruptcy petition by or against the corporation.

Unpaid Stock Subscriptions

A subscription of stock of an existing corporation is a contract between the person subscribing and the corporation. Such a contract results from an offer either made by the corporation and accepted by the subscriber or made by the subscriber and accepted by the corporation. If the contract is for the purchase of shares, the purchaser becomes a shareholder when a certificate of stock is delivered. A shareholder is liable to the corporation and its creditors for any unpaid portion of the stock subscription.

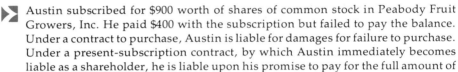

Austin subscribed for $900 worth of shares of common stock in Peabody Fruit Growers, Inc. He paid $400 with the subscription but failed to pay the balance. Under a contract to purchase, Austin is liable for damages for failure to purchase. Under a present-subscription contract, by which Austin immediately becomes liable as a shareholder, he is liable upon his promise to pay for the full amount of the stock. Should Peabody Fruit Growers become insolvent, the creditors of the corporation could recover the $500 balance plus interest for the period Austin has been in default on the balance due.

CONSOLIDATIONS AND MERGERS

A corporation sometimes decides to acquire the assets of another business enterprise and combine it with its own. This is accomplished by purchase or lease of such assets; merger; consolidation; or purchase of controlling interest in the stock of another corporation.

The procedure is outlined in each state's general corporation statutes. The usual procedure is for the directors of each company to approve the plan. The plan is then submitted to the shareholders, who must approve it by a two-thirds vote of all shares. If the plan is approved by the shareholders of both companies, articles of consolidation or merger are prepared and filed with the state. If they are in order, a certificate of consolidation or merger is issued.

Consolidation of Corporations

A *consolidation* of two or more corporations involves the combining of their total assets. Title to the assets is taken by a newly created corporation. Each of the original corporations ceases to exist, and all debts and liabilities are assumed by the new one. A shareholder who objects to a consolidation may demand that the corporation purchase his or her stock at the fair market value on the day prior to the vote on the consolidation action.

Merger of Corporations

A *merger* of two or more corporations also involves the combining of their total assets. However, one corporation preserves its original charter and identity and continues to exist. The absorbed companies cease to exist, and their debts and other liabilities become those of the surviving corporation. Objecting shareholders of corporations involved in the merger may demand from the surviving corporation a fair value for their stock shares.

> The directors of Fried Provisions Company and those of Farmers' Packing Company agreed upon a merger plan under which Farmers' Packing Company would transfer all its assets to Fried Provisions and cease using its name. But the directors failed to obtain approval of the plan by a two-thirds vote of the shareholders, and the minority shareholders of Farmers' Company brought an action in equity to stop the merger. The court would hold that a merger of the two companies without the approval of holders of two-thirds of its outstanding stock was in violation of the merger provisions of the state statute.

Purchase of All Assets or Stock of Another Corporation

A corporation can purchase or lease another corporation's assets without changing the legal status of either. Each corporation continues its separate existence, with the purchaser (lessee) acquiring ownership or control of the assets and the seller (lessor) receiving money. Such a sale or lease, however, must be approved by the majority of the shareholders and directors of the selling corporation.

No change is made in the legal existence of either corporation when one obtains a full or controlling interest in the stock of another. There is no legal procedure to be followed, inasmuch as the sale of stock is by the corporation's shareholders, and the action to purchase is taken by the acquiring corporation's directors.

FOREIGN CORPORATIONS

Corporations cannot conduct business in a state other than the one in which they are incorporated without first receiving the "foreign" state's permission in the form of an appropriate certificate. In order for such a certificate to be issued, the foreign corporation must agree to obey the local regulations. Generally, these rules do not deny a foreign corporation any rights extended to a domestic corporation. As a further prerequisite of doing business in a state, a foreign corporation must file annual reports and usually pay an annual fee. It is usually required that the foreign corporation obtain a local registered agent within the state, so that the foreign corporation can be made susceptible to litigation within the state. A foreign corporation may also be required to deposit a bond or security with an official of the state as a means of protecting local policyholders and shareholders.

Although a state may indirectly force a corporation to incorporate if it wants to do business in the state, it may not deny a foreign corporation the constitutional right of due process and equal protection under the law.

 The Diamond Mining Company, a West Virginia corporation, was owner of a mineral lease in Pennsylvania. Diamond Mining hired a local drilling company to sink a mine shaft by boring. During the operation the shaft collapsed, causing considerable damage. Suit was brought, charging the drilling company with negligence. In its defense, the drilling company contended that Diamond Mining Company was a foreign corporation conducting business in Pennsylvania without having qualified to do so. As such, Diamond Mining did not have a right to sue. The court would rule that if Diamond Mining Company wished to qualify to do business in Pennsylvania, it could proceed with the suit.

Gaining Jurisdiction Over a Foreign Corporation

A state or litigant within that state can usually gain jurisdiction over a foreign corporation for purposes of starting litigation if it can be shown that the foreign corporation was *doing business within the state*. Although this is a common phrase, its definition is not an easy one. It is usually agreed, though, that it refers to activity of a foreign corporation within a state for the purpose of seeking a profit.

Certain types of activities related to corporate affairs usually fall outside the definition. For instance, corporate activities carried on merely to wind up a corporation's business do not constitute doing business. And certain activities, such as the holding of realty, may not have the effect of doing business. But a group of acts, any one of which would be insufficient to establish that a foreign corporation was doing business, may combine to prove just the opposite. For example, maintenance of warehouse and shipping facilities, sales staff, and consumer relations offices within a state would probably constitute doing business.

Interference With Internal Affairs

Most state courts do not interfere with the internal functioning of a foreign corporation. For example, they will not assume jurisdiction over or decide disputes concerning shareholder rights. Such questions are left to the scrutiny of an appropriate court in the state in which the corporation is incorporated.

DISSOLUTION OF A CORPORATION

The life of a corporation may be brought to an end in a number of ways. As previously stated, its life technically ends with a consolidation of one or more corporations; in a merger, it ends for one of the involved corporations. All other methods of corporate dissolution are set forth in the charter or come about by the voluntary or involuntary act of the corporation.

Dissolution by Charter

A corporate charter may provide that the corporation will "self-destruct," that is, cease to exist after a specified period of time. In such cases, the termination is automatic, unless the state of incorporation grants a request to continue. Most corporate charters provide for perpetual life.

> The Carbon Products Company owned a controlling interest in the stock of a subsidiary product-development corporation that had been chartered to carry on five years of research in connection with rocket propulsion. Six months before its specified expiration, the directors of Carbon Products petitioned the appropriate state official for authority to continue the corporate operation for five additional years.

Voluntary Dissolutions

A corporation can be dissolved voluntarily by the unanimous approval of the shareholders or by a positive vote of the directors with the approval of two-thirds of the shareholders. Then, a statement of intent to dissolve must be filed with the state of incorporation; the corporation must actually cease business; and notices must be given to the public (by publication) and to all creditors (by certified mail). After all claims have been received, corporate assets will be used first to pay creditors, with the surplus going to shareholders. If the existing assets cannot meet all claims, a receiver may divide available assets fairly among the creditors.

Following the distribution of all assets, the corporation must prepare articles of dissolution and present them to the secretary of state for signature.

Involuntary Dissolutions

Action by the state to cancel a corporation's charter may be taken by the attorney general, at the request of the secretary of state, by *quo warranto* proceedings. The usual grounds for such action are that the corporation was organized through fraud, has repeatedly exceeded its authority, or has repeatedly conducted business in an unlawful manner. The list of illegal acts is lengthy, but failure to file annual reports, to pay franchise taxes, or to maintain a registered agent to receive legal process are among the more common examples.

In most states, shareholders may bring an action seeking a dissolution if they can demonstrate that a deadlock exists in the management or that the management is acting illegally to waste corporate assets. Such actions are rarely brought and are rarely successful, for the tough burden of proving waste of corporate assets rests upon the shareholders. In addition, with the full resources of the corporation behind them, corporate managements are well organized and able to meet such challenges.

> Minority shareholders of United Credit Bureau, Inc., brought suit to compel dissolution of the corporation on the grounds of waste. It was charged that Le Gros, who dominated and controlled the affairs of the corporation, was taking salary and bonuses in such amounts as to leave little net profit annually for

dividend payments. No evidence was found that there was any looting of assets or manipulation of corporate affairs for special benefit at the expense of the other shareholders. The court would not decree a dissolution of a corporation on such meager charges. It would require proof that Le Gros acted illegally, oppressively, or fraudulently and that corporate assets were being wasted or looted.

Procedures After Dissolution

The dissolution of a corporation renders it legally nonexistent and no longer capable of carrying on the activities a corporation has the right by charter to perform. But a court has a wide range of discretionary powers that enable it to take over the business the corporation can no longer administer. For example, it can appoint receivers to collect and preserve or to sell and distribute corporation assets. Also, it can enjoin third parties from acting to impair the corporation in any way, thus further protecting shareholders.

After corporate assets are sold and debts are paid, the remaining funds are applied to pay the following items in the order of preference shown here:

1. Payment of all federal, state, and local taxes.
2. Full payment of all secured liabilities, such as mortgages and liens.
3. Payment of unsecured debts.
4. Payment to preferred shareholders.
5. Payment to common shareholders.

Failure to follow the order of preference makes the directors and shareholders liable for any losses that might result. However, a lack of sufficient assets to satisfy all creditors does not place a further liability upon the shareholders. No judgments may be placed against their personal estates.

 American Motel, Inc., forfeited its charter and ceased operations. Its assets were liquidated and distributed by the court-appointed receiver. Taxes owed to the federal and state governments took all the cash obtained from the converted assets. The shareholders would not be liable for the personal claims of other preferred creditors. In a case like this, they would receive nothing in payment of their own claims.

After all money in the hands of the receiver is paid out, the court issues a decree of dissolution that is filed with the secretary of state.

INSOLVENCY AND BANKRUPTCY

A corporation or other business entity lacking sufficient assets may file for bankruptcy or be declared bankrupt by the courts on petition of the corporation's or entity's creditors. Contrary to popular belief, however, the insolvency or bankruptcy of a corporation does not lead automatically to its liquidation, although as a practical matter such proceedings may have that very effect. A distinction must be made between proceedings for dissolution and proceedings for bankruptcy. The forum for dissolving a corporation is, in most cases, a state court of equity, whereas the forum for bankruptcy proceedings is, more often than not, a federal bankruptcy court.

Insolvency

Insolvency under the National Bankruptcy Act—today's prevailing bankruptcy law—is the condition whereby the liabilities of a person or business exceed the assets of that person or business. This is not the same as the definition or concept of insolvency in equity law, however, which describes it as the condition of one who is unable to pay his or her debts when they become due. Obviously, there is a conflict between these two meanings.

▶ Raymond Manufacturing Corporation owned its plants and machinery and had outstanding accounts payable of $85,000. Because of an economic downturn and a temporary cessation of orders, the corporation was not able to pay its current bills. The firm's assets were more than $750,000. Raymond Manufacturing Corporation is far from insolvent by definition of the National Bankruptcy Act.

As stated previously, insolvency of a corporation will not in and of itself result in the dissolution of the corporation. Some states will allow the continued legal existence of the corporate entity, while others provide for *de facto dissolution*. This simply means that the corporation will be considered dissolved as far as its creditors are concerned, provided that the latter initiate an action for dissolution. It must be stressed, however, that dissolution in this case applies *only to the corporation's creditors*, not to others with whom the corporation may have had dealings.

Voluntary and Involuntary Bankruptcy

Bankruptcy may be declared when the debts of any corporation, partnership, or other business entity are greater than its assets. Bankruptcy may be declared voluntarily by the debtor, or it may be declared by the creditors without agreement from the debtor.

Any corporation or partnership—except banking, insurance, railroad, and municipal corporations—has the right to file a voluntary petition in bankruptcy with the proper court, regardless of how much it owes and how many creditors it has. Such a corporation or business entity is known as a *voluntary bankrupt*. Through the voluntary acknowledgment of financial difficulties, it is possible to make an equitable distribution of the corporation's remaining assets among the creditors. While this is far less desirable than receiving full payment of an account, a creditor at least is assured a fair and just share of what remains from an unsuccessful venture.

An unincorporated company, financial business, or commercial corporation (with the exceptions noted above) may also be adjudged an *involuntary bankrupt* if it owes debts above a given limit. Thus a debtor may be judged an involuntary bankrupt on a motion filed by three or more creditors with provable claims totaling $500 or more. And a debtor having fewer than twelve creditors may be adjudged an involuntary bankrupt on a petition filed by a single creditor, provided the petition shows that the debtor owes $1,000 or more, is insolvent, and has committed an *act of bankruptcy* (discussed below).

Proceedings in bankruptcy, as mentioned, will not necessarily result in the liquidation of the business enterprise. Two actions generally follow when an entity such as a corporation is adjudged bankrupt: (1) the sale of the corporation's or entity's assets or (2) the attempted reorganization of the enterprise. If corporate assets are sold, the corporation usually will lack the means to carry on; in that case, it may *then* formally seek dissolution. If reorganization is ordered under federal law, the legal existence of the corporation is not terminated. However, if reorganization is ordered under state law, a bankrupt corporation may be dissolved and a new one formed. State bankruptcy laws usually operate only in special cases, and they are designed to supply additional legislation that will better regulate situations created by individual geographic differences. In most circumstances, however, federal law operates.

Acts of Bankruptcy

Any acts committed by a debtor that prevent creditors from obtaining their fair share of the assets are considered *acts of bankruptcy*. According to the National Bankruptcy Act, a company or company officer who commits any of the following acts while insolvent may have the business declared bankrupt:

☐ Conveying, transferring, or concealing property with intent to hinder, delay, or defraud creditors.

> Claybourne owned and operated Margaret's Beauty Salon, Inc. The business was in serious financial difficulties and on the brink of bankruptcy. For a consideration of $50, she had her corporation transfer ownership of the dryers and all other salon equipment to her sister. Certain of the beauty salon's creditors learned of the transfer and submitted a petition to have the business declared bankrupt. The court accepted the petition and simultaneously ordered the sister to return title and possession of all the shop equipment that had been sold to her.

☐ Transferring a portion of property to one or more creditors with intent to prefer such creditors over others.
☐ Giving any creditor preference over others through legal proceedings.
☐ Making a general assignment of property for the benefit of creditors or, because of insolvency, applying for a trustee or receiver of the property.

Bankruptcy Proceedings

The U.S. district courts are the bankruptcy courts, and they have jurisdiction over all petitions within each court's geographical borders. In certain situations involving involuntary bankruptcy, the bankrupt may be entitled to a jury to determine the answers to specific questions of fact. In all other cases and in all other matters, final judgment and decision is made by the court judges.

Every participant in a bankruptcy proceeding has duties specifically defined by the Bankruptcy Act. The participants and their roles are described below.

The Bankrupt   The bankrupt, corporate or otherwise, must attend the first meeting of the creditors. At the hearing for discharge for bankruptcy, the bankrupt must prepare and file schedules showing the amount, kind, and location of its property, must list all creditors, and must indicate the amount due each one. The bankrupt must examine and check the correctness of proofs of claims filed by creditors and must submit to whatever examinations are required at various meetings of the creditors. In general, the bankrupt must aid the creditors and the receiver or trustee in bankruptcy.

The Creditors   The persons seeking involuntary bankruptcy proceedings against a debtor are known as the *petitioning creditors*. It is their duty to make a petition to the court on the grounds of their rights, listing the facts which prove one or more of the acts of bankruptcy. In order to be acceptable, the petition must be filed within four months of the act or acts complained about.

Each creditor must file a separate proof of claim with the bankruptcy court within six months of adjudication, or the claim will be barred. A *proof of claim* consists of a written statement setting forth the claims made under oath, prepared on forms prescribed by the bankruptcy court, and signed by the creditors. If the claim is proved, it will be allowed and the creditor will share in the distribution of the bankrupt's estate or remaining assets.

Court Officers   During the time when the bankruptcy proceedings are under the control of a district court judge, officers are appointed for the administration of the bankrupt's estate or property. The officers appointed are the referee, the trustee, the receiver, and the appraiser.

The Referee   Appointed by the court for a period of six years, the *referee* is in almost complete charge of the bankruptcy proceedings in any particular case. The referee must be an attorney in good standing in the area where the court is located, must act with absolute impartiality in all cases before him or her, must not be related to the judge, and must not act in any cases in which there is a personal interest. It is the duty of the referee to send out all notices to creditors advising them of the time and place of the first meeting of the creditors.

The Trustee   The *trustee* is the person appointed by the court to take possession of all the property of the petitioner. He or she has the responsibility of actual physical administration of the bankrupt's property. It is his or her duty to collect and convert to money all property of the bankrupt's estate. Trustees must keep accurate records of all monies received, with disposition of the same. They must make final reports to the court as to all monies, records, and liquidation of the petitioner's estate or remaining assets.

The Receiver   The *receiver* is a temporary officer appointed by the court to preserve the assets for the creditors until a trustee is elected and qualified. In certain circumstances, the receiver may be given the authority to operate the business for a limited period.

The Appraiser   The *appraiser* is appointed by the court to appraise and give an approximate valuation of the property. In some cases, three appraisers are appointed. They establish standards that will help determine the reasonableness of bids received in the sale of the bankrupt's property or estate.

Distribution of Property

When all the evidence is before the court, the bankrupt's property may be sold to settle the debts. In special circumstances, some creditors' claims will be given priority over others.

Reclamation   If a bankrupt has possession of property belonging to others, the latter may file reclamation claims for the specific property. This is not considered a creditor's claim. Should these owners submit a proof of claim together with the other creditors, they should no longer have the right to demand the return of the specific property but would merely be listed with the other creditors.

> Sanderson Paper Supply Corporation was declared bankrupt by the U.S. district court. In listing the assets of the corporation, a trustee listed a Xerox copying machine. The Xerox Corporation claimed title to this piece of equipment, claiming that it had been rented to Sanderson Paper Supply. Upon proof of this assertion, Xerox Corporation would be permitted to reclaim the property.

A seller of goods is permitted to reclaim the goods from a buyer who was insolvent at the time of delivery. The demand by the seller must be made within ten days of the date the goods were received. Furthermore, if the buyer made false statements as to his or her solvency on which the seller relied, the ten-day rule does not apply. The buyer's statements must be in writing and must be made within three months of the date of delivery of the goods.

> On January 10, Stewart Corporation provided Hollingsworth Manufacturing Company with fraudulent financial statements supporting their allegedly strong financial condition. In March of the same year, Hollingsworth accepted an order for $5,800 worth of tools and shipped them to the Stewart Corporation on a generous credit arrangement based on the financial information provided. Hollingsworth would be permitted to reclaim the goods shipped, as long as they were still in the buyer's possession, without regard to the ten-day limitation specified in the bankruptcy code.

Priorities   The bankruptcy statute recognizes certain priorities in the distribution of a bankrupt's assets and requires payment in full of these debts, provided the assets (or security held by creditors) are sufficient. Debts having such priority and the order of their payments are as follows:

1. Secured claims, such as those secured by chattel mortgages, mortgages on real estate, or recorded liens.

   When the Merson Corporation filed for bankruptcy, the building and all assets were sold to pay off the creditors. First, however, a lien of $11,600, upheld in a lawsuit several years previously and never collected, was paid.

2. The cost of preserving the estate (or assets of a business entity) after the filing of the petition and the expenses of administration of the bankruptcy and liquidation of assets.

   Carton Building Corporation had partly finished construction of four new houses when adjudged bankrupt. The court ruled that the houses were to be finished and placed on the market for sale. Income from the sale of the finished houses would far exceed what they would bring in their present state of completion.

3. Wages due employees that have been earned within three months prior to filing the bankruptcy petition. The wages paid to each employee making a claim may not exceed $600.

Browning had worked for Carton Building Corporation for several years. The
firm owed him $2,800 in back wages, going back three months prior to the date of
filing the bankruptcy petition. Only $600 of that amount would be given priority
over other claims. The $2,200 unpaid balance could be listed with other creditors'
claims to share in the distribution of the bankrupt corporation's final remaining
assets, if any.

4. Taxes due the city, county, state, and federal government.
5. Debts due anyone entitled to priority under state or federal laws.

The ordinary creditors receive only what remains after all the foregoing have
been paid. Secured creditors are paid first. If the security, when sold, does not
satisfy the secured debt, the remaining balance is listed among the claims of
ordinary creditors.

Composition With Creditors   After a bankruptcy petition has been filed and the
bankrupt has been examined, the bankrupt may offer to pay a certain percentage
of the debts in full satisfaction. A composition may be offered by a bankrupt
either before or after adjudication, but it can be confirmed by the court only after
(1) a majority of creditors in number and amount of claims have accepted in
writing, and (2) the bankrupt has filed the required schedules of all property and
debts. After the settlement has been confirmed by the court, it becomes binding
on all the creditors, whether or not they had agreed to the composition.

Discharge in Bankruptcy

After a month has passed and within twelve months after being adjudged
bankrupt, a person or business may, upon application, be granted a discharge
from the debts listed in the schedule of liabilities.

A discharge in bankruptcy frees the debtor from all liabilities listed in the
schedule, except for (1) taxes and wages earned within three months before the
beginning of bankruptcy proceedings; (2) money deposited by employees or
retained by the employer as security for the faithful performance by such employees of the terms of their contracts of employment; (3) debts tinged with fraud
or wrong, such as property obtained under false pretenses; and (4) liabilities
incurred by reason of willful and malicious injuries to the person or property of
another.

A discharge in bankruptcy may be refused by the court if the debtor (1) has
gotten a discharge in the past six years in voluntary proceedings; (2) has failed to
explain the losses satisfactorily; (3) has used a false statement as a basis for credit;
(4) has, within a year immediately preceding the filing of the petition, transferred, destroyed, or concealed property with intent to defraud the creditors;
(5) has destroyed, falsified, concealed, or failed to keep books of account or
records; (6) has refused to answer questions approved by the courts.

> Martin's Refinishing, having been adjudged a bankrupt, applied for discharge of
> debts listed in the schedule of liabilities. Before the court granted the application,
> it was discovered that Martin's Refinishing had received a discharge five years

earlier after successfully petitioning for voluntary bankruptcy. Since the application occurred within a six-year period of a previous discharge, the new application will not be granted.

Kinds of Bankruptcy

The Bankruptcy Act defines several kinds of bankruptcy. Each kind is commonly known by the number of the chapter in which it appears in the act.

Straight Bankruptcy   Also known as Chapter X, straight bankruptcy is available only to corporations, and it may be either voluntary or involuntary. If a corporation is declared bankrupt under Chapter X, there is a provision allowing the court to completely dissolve the corporation to pay its creditors, if that proves necessary.

Reorganization Under Trustee   Chapters XI and XII of the Bankruptcy Act allow for a voluntary bankrupt to pay off all debts and reorganize the business entity. The act provides plans for debtors which are in the nature of compositions. These are devised to help the debtor and at the same time protect the interests of creditors. They are known as (1) corporate reorganizations, (2) arrangements involving unsecured creditors, and (3) arrangements involving creditors secured by real property.

Under this legislation, a corporation is turned over to a trustee, not for the purpose of liquidation, but for the purpose of operating and reorganizing the corporation. If it is restored to a sound operating position through this measure, the business is subsequently returned to the control of the stockholders. Through this relief, failing corporations are often returned to full operation with no loss experienced by either the creditors or the owners. If the trustee's efforts fail, the corporation then faces final bankruptcy proceedings and liquidation, as described earlier in this chapter.

Questions for Review and Discussion

1. What is meant by the fundamental notion that a corporation's business and affairs are to be "managed under the direction of a board of directors"?

2. What is the broad power of directors in the business and affairs of the corporation? What are the consequences of this power with respect to the shareholders who appoint them?

3. To what extent is a board of directors legally liable for losses to the corporation resulting from (a) poor business judgment or honest mistakes, (b) negligence?

4. Name six rights that a shareholder has against a corporation.

5. (a) Who are the creditors of the corporation? (b)What are the creditors' rights with respect to participation in the management of the corporation?

6. If a dividend is declared and distributed out of capital because no surplus profits were available, who is liable? Explain.

7. Compare a consolidation of two or more corporations and their total assets with a merger. In which case may a shareholder demand that the corporation purchase his or her shares at a fair market value on the day prior to the vote on the action?

8. What are the common grounds upon which a state may demand the involuntary dissolution of a corporation?

9. After a corporation has been dissolved, what is the order of preference in the distribution of corporate assets?

10. What debts in a bankruptcy settlement may be considered to have priority over the debts owed to ordinary creditors?

Analyzing Cases

1. Rivera, a vice president for Real Property Development, Inc., was in charge of an operation that involved readying a tract of land next to a river for development. Fill was needed, so Rivera obtained a state dredging permit in order to dredge it from the riverbed. The permit specified how much material could be removed. When the limits had been reached and the project's needs still had not been met, Rivera ordered the dredging contractor to continue removing material. Neither the president nor the board of directors of Real Property Development knew of this action. The state prosecuted the firm for dredging beyond the limits of its permit. Real Property Development contended that Rivera, though a vice president, was really just a salaried employee, and as such he could not bind the corporation by his unauthorized criminal act. How would the court rule? Explain. • See also *West Valley Estates, Inc. v. State of Florida*, 286 So.2d 208.

2. Drury was the controlling shareholder and president of Genovese Sand and Stone, Inc. A fifty-acre tract of land adjacent to the corporation's present operations came up for sale. Drury tried to obtain financing for the corporation to buy it. The banks turned Drury down, since the firm was $500,000 in debt and was delinquent on some accounts. Drury got together with the corporation's lawyer and its accountant, borrowed the money personally from another bank, and purchased the tract of land in the name of a corporation owned by the three. After the acquisition, the group rented the tract to Genovese Sand and Stone at a reasonable rate, which allowed Genovese to make a profit. Minority shareholders brought suit in the name of Genovese Sand and Stone against the three for misappropriating the corporate opportunity for a "bargain" to themselves. Who should win this case? Why? • See also *A. C. Petters Co. v. St. Cloud Enterprises, Inc.*, 222 N.W.2d 83.

3. Yankee Lumber, Inc., supplied Bucher, a residential building contractor, with construction materials. When he failed to pay, Yankee Lumber sued him. Bucher argued that the obligation was not his but that of Bucher Development and Construction, Inc. During the lawsuit, it developed that Bucher was the secretary, treasurer, and principal shareholder of Bucher Development and Construction and that the corporation had not filed its annual report as required by the state corporation law. Who is entitled to a judgment? Explain. • See also *Glaser's Elevator & Lumber Co. v. Perry*, 212 N.W.2d 617.

4. Patients of a charitable hospital brought a class action against certain of its directors for breach of trust. They demanded appropriate injunctive relief and an award of damages to be paid into the hospital's funds. The principal charge against the defendants was that, through their lack of due diligence, the treasurer was permitted to maintain unnecessarily large amounts of money in a non-interest-bearing checking account. In whose favor would judgment be given? Explain. • See also *Stern* v. *Lucy Webb Hoyer National Training School for Deaconesses and Missionaries*, 381 F. Supp. 1003.

5. Watson purchased fully paid-up stock from the Nelson Construction Company at a price less than its par value. Subsequently the corporation became insolvent, and its creditors sued Watson for the difference between the amount paid for the shares and their par value. Was Watson liable? Explain. • See also *Central Fiber Products Co. v. Lorenz*, 66 N.W.2d 30.

6. The Driggs Office Furniture Company, Inc., was incorporated to manufacture and sell office furniture and equipment. Without amending its charter, the directors expanded its manufacturing facilities to include household furniture. The state, on petition of the secretary of state, took action to forfeit the charter. How would the court rule? Explain. • See also *Pittsburgh, Cincinnati & St. Louis Railway Co. v. Keokuk & Hamilton Bridge Co.*, 131 U.S. 371.

Legal Reasoning and Business Judgment

Analyze the legal aspects of these business problems. Suggest possible solutions.

1. A plan is ready for presentation to the shareholders at their regular meeting. It proposes the purchase of a large block of real estate that the company might need for expansion in the near future. Certain shareholders are opposed to the plan and have threatened to have the board of directors charged with mismanagement if they carry it through. The right to buy real estate is not one of the rights given the company in its charter. What are the company's legal rights in this matter under the charter?

2. New members are to be elected to your company's board of directors this year, and the present members are anxious to continue in their positions. As the year has not been a profitable one, the board is groping for some means of paying a dividend in order to win reelection. One of the board members suggested that some old properties owned by the company be sold and the money used to declare a dividend. Could such a plan lead to any difficulties? Explain.

3. You are employed by a corporation engaged in the publication of several magazines which specialize in articles relating to the design of clothing for young men and women. The business department realizes that, with the reputation it has achieved as a leader in this field, the company might realize a sizable profit through selling products which it could manufacture itself, advertise in its own pages, and sell through direct mail. As a junior executive in the firm, you are asked for suggestions. What encouragement or warning would be proper at this point?

The term *property* is broadly interpreted. It includes everything that one might own—for example, a car, a shirt, a building, and the land on which a building is built. There are other types of property that one cannot see, such as a patent for an invention, a franchise to sell something, and the goodwill of a brand name. Property is more than ownership. It includes the *legal right* to use and enjoy, to dispose of, and to bestow property in the event of death.

The Fifth and Fourteenth Amendments to the U.S. Constitution protect the individual's right to *life*, *liberty*, and *property*. The legal protection of the rights of property and the related rights of freedom of contract are essential to our private enterprise system. Only in rare cases may the individual's property rights be invaded or reduced. These cases occur most commonly when, for the public good, it becomes necessary for the government to take private property required for the safety, welfare, or betterment of the populace as a whole. This is the right of **eminent domain**. Even in these cases, the property owner is compensated by the government for any loss resulting from such lawful denial of ownership rights.

KINDS OF PROPERTY

All property (things and rights) is generally divided into two classes: personal property and real property. The terms *personalty* and *realty* may also be used. In certain legal documents, lawyers may use the words *mixed property* when they foresee a possibility of misunderstanding the intents of a seller and a buyer of property.

> Martinez sold a house and contents to Woodring Realty Company. The house, garage, and land would be classified as real property. The contents would in most cases be defined as personal property. To eliminate any misunderstandings related to items that either party might question, the attorney used the phrase *real, personal, and mixed property* in drawing up the sales agreement.

Personal Property

Personal property includes all property that is movable. Known also as *chattels*, personal property embraces such items as automobiles, furniture, animals, clothing, aircraft, and boats. Personal property which may be seen or touched and which may be given an actual physical description is known as *tangible property*.

> ►◄ Snyder sold to Acme Athletic Club a building which previously had been rented as a meeting place for community and political clubs. The building contained 175 folding chairs when sold. Acme Athletic Club claimed title to the chairs, arguing that they "went with the building." It would be difficult to prove that chairs were included in Acme's purchase of Snyder's real property. Snyder had no intention of making the chairs a permanent addition to the building. The 175 chairs were personal property.

On the other hand, certain other types of property are valued for the *rights* they assure their owners. Thus a document of title guarantees the right of ownership. The document is not valued for itself, but for what it represents. Such rights are defined as *intangible property*. Stock certificates, the deed to a house, a bond and mortgage, even a dollar bill are examples of intangible personal property. The value of the dollar bill is not the dollar itself, but what it might buy for the owner in the marketplace.

Real Property

Real property embraces all land extending downward to the center of the globe and items intended to be permanent improvements to the land. Houses, buildings, trees, shrubbery, and permanent fixtures installed in houses and buildings are real property. Also included in real property is a right-of-way over someone else's property and the air space over land.

Personal property becomes real property when attached to or made a permanent part of land or buildings. Bricks, lumber, concrete, and other building materials are personal property when delivered to a building site. When these materials are combined with others in the creation of a permanent building, they become real property.

Real property, likewise, becomes personal property when separated from land or from houses or other buildings. When a tree is cut down, it becomes personal property. Fruit harvested from trees loses its identity as real property when detached from the tree and placed in a waiting basket.

> ►◄ Minton paid real property taxes on a house and small barn built on a five-acre tract of land. The barn was of no further use to Minton, and it was taken down. Having reverted to personal property, the materials were sold to a firm that dealt in used building materials. Minton's real property taxes would be reduced, reflecting the reduction in the value of the remaining real property.

Trees and Perennials   Trees, shrubs, vineyards, and field crops which are harvested each year without replanting (perennials) are included in real property. These plants have been planted and cultivated with the intention that they remain as a part of the realty. Once planted and growing, such improvements to the land are defined as the *fruit of nature*.

> The graduating class of '78 planted a grove of copper beech trees on the campus of Oldman College. Members of the class, dissatisfied with the college, dug up and removed three of the trees. If they had been stealing personal property, they would have been subject to arrest on a charge of larceny. But the trees, being the fruit of nature, were real property. Thus a more proper charge would be one of criminal trespass or malicious destruction to real property.

Crops or garden plantings that produce flowers, vegetables, or other harvest only for the year in which they are planted are defined as the *fruit of industry*. The fruit of industry constitutes personal, not real, property.

> When the Woodring farm was sold early in the spring, the new owner was deeded "all the real property consisting of what is known as the Woodring Farm." A 25-acre section of winter wheat had been planted the fall prior to the sale. Woodring, in July, demanded the right to come into the farm and harvest the wheat. The wheat crop is the fruit of industry, that is, personal property. The buyer did not receive title to personal property on the farm, so Woodring would be permitted the right to enter the farm and remove the wheat.

Chattels Real   An interest in the real property of another which is limited in its duration through the decision of the owner of the property is known as a **chattel real**. The right to use another's land or to live in another's house at the will of the owner are illustrations of this classification of property, which, of course, covers the ordinary lease between a landlord and a tenant. Blackstone termed these rights chattels real because "they have the immobility of things real and the precarious duration of things personal." Chattels real also include such items as house keys, which although usually treated as personal property, have such a close relationship to the real property that they are said to be a part of it.

> Hastings rented an apartment to two students under a ten-month lease. Would the lease include the keys to the apartment? Although the keys are movable and not intended to be a permanent addition to the realty, the keys are said to be chattels real. At the termination of the lease, the students would be obliged to return the keys to Hastings when giving up possession of the apartment itself.

Fixtures   Chattels lose their identity as personal property when attached to the real property with the apparent intent that they are not to be detached at some later time and removed. When so attached, chattels become fixtures and are considered part of the real property, or realty. Arguments often arise between landlords and tenants about the rightful ownership of such items at the end of the tenant's lease. The following questions are useful in determining whether a chattel is personal property belonging to the tenant or is real property subject to the landlord's demand of ownership.

☐ Has there been a *temporary* or *permanent* installation of the chattel?
☐ Has the chattel been *adapted* to the intended use of the real property?

☐ What was the apparent *intent* of the party at the time of affixing the chattel to the real property?

> Frazer occupied rented space that she and a partner operated as a combined beauty and barber shop. New lighting fixtures of modern design were installed; mirrors were permanently attached by lagscrews to studs in the walls; stereo speakers were hung from convenient places to provide soft music for clients. It is obvious that the lighting fixtures and mirrors are permanently fixed to the building and thus become real property belonging to the landlord. The stereo equipment is not permanently installed and remained the tenant's property.

By agreement between landlord and tenant, fixtures may be installed with permission for their removal at the end of the lease period. Arguments and misunderstandings result from a tenant's failure to include this right in the written lease. When such arrangements are made, it is the expressed or implied obligation of the tenant to leave the premises without damage caused by removal of fixtures. In the previous illustration, if Frazer is permitted to remove the lighting fixtures, the older fixtures previously removed would have to be replaced and rewired. If the mirrors are removed, by conditions in the lease, any holes in the wall or discoloration would have to be taken care of at Frazer's expense.

LIMITATIONS ON OWNERSHIP AND USE OF PROPERTY

Owners of both real and personal property are severely limited and restricted in the use of such property, either by agreement with the previous owner, by restrictions already in a deed, or by law. The ancient concept whereby an owner might use property in any way he or she desired is far from current today. Society has demanded changes, and they have been provided by state and local legislation.

Limitations in Use of Personal Property

Use of personal property is restricted and limited by law, by contract, and by copyright and patent.

Limitation by Law   Laws for the protection of the health, safety, and welfare of the owners of personal property and others that might be affected are enforced under federal, state, and local statutes. Owners of motor vehicles must offer such vehicles for inspection and licensing and must operate them in accordance with the laws of areas in which they are driven. They may not be used for illegal purposes. Aircraft must be licensed and operated only by certified pilots. Alcoholic beverages, drugs, and certain other consumer goods may be used only as permitted by law.

Limitation by Contract   Personal property is often sold with restrictions on use through agreement with the seller. Records and tape recordings sold to consumers often contain restrictions against using them for any commercial purposes.

Rubbing alcohol is sold with the understanding that it is to be used only for external purposes. Dynamite and other explosives used in construction are sold with limitations of use imposed both by law and contract.

Limitation by Copyright and Patent   The owner of a patent or copyright may restrict the buyer of artistic and literary creations and inventions from making duplications either in part or in full. These restrictions apply worldwide, not only within the United States.

 Rogers, a college instructor, made twenty copies of a copyrighted publication and sold them to members of a chemistry class. No permission had been secured from the author and publisher for the duplication and sale of this publication. Rogers may be prosecuted under copyright laws and ordered to pay damages to both author and publisher.

Limitations on Ownership of Real Property

Use of real property is even more carefully restricted and limited than use of personal property. Unrestricted uses of real property may create severe financial losses to adjoining property owners, make living conditions unhealthy and unbearable to others, and infringe upon the rights of others in the same community. Restrictions and limitations may originate from conditions contained in the property deed or conditions imposed by law.

Restrictions by Deed   The buyer of real property is almost always restricted in its use by conditions contained in the deed. The restrictions may be created by the seller before giving up title. They may also be restrictions that have been inserted by former owners of the property. If the restrictions are unreasonable, they may be removed through an order given by a court of equity on petition by the new owner. Thus a restriction that limits the occupancy of a ten-room house to no more than three people may be removed on the grounds that such a restriction is unreasonable. On the other hand, restricting the use of a house as a hotel might be considered reasonable depending on the circumstances. Such a restriction would be deemed reasonable, for example, if imposed in order to protect neighbors from the undesirable conditions that a hotel might bring to a residential neighborhood. Hence, it is important to be familiar with the restrictions in a deed before taking title to real property.

 Harper bought a house in Cooper Village. All deeds issued by the developer contained a restriction against owners' having dogs and cats. Harper owned two collie dogs that had always been regarded as part of the family. Unless he succeeded in getting a court to remove this restriction, the residents of Cooper Village would be within their rights in making Harper get rid of the dogs.

Historically, deeds to properties in certain geographic regions restricted sale to anyone other than a member of the white race. These restrictions, known as *restrictive covenants*, have been declared invalid by decision of the U.S. Supreme Court.

Easements An *easement* is the right of one owner of real property to make legal and beneficial use of the real property of another. It is a right that "runs with the land"; it is not a personal right conferred upon an individual or a family as such. The property to which the right or privilege of easement attaches is known as the *dominant tenement*. By contrast, the property through which the easement is created or extends is known as the *serviant tenement*.

> The Harrises bought a property from the Sendaks, who for many years had used a path across a neighboring property as a shortcut to the local school. Through continued use, an easement had developed in favor of the Sendaks. This easement was now extended to the Harris property by virtue of their purchase of the property from the former owners. In this case, the Harrises' property was the dominant tenement. The neighbor's property was the serviant tenement.

Easements may consist of a right-of-way over another's land; the right to take water from another's well; use of a party wall, a driveway, a stairway, or almost anything related to another's land. Easements may arise through contract and may be recorded in the deeds of both the dominant and serviant lands. They may also be created through adverse use, as discussed in the following chapter. Easements, however created, may not be disregarded by subsequent purchasers of the serviant property at the expense of the one being served. They may be terminated only by mutual agreement or by abandonment of use by the owners of a dominant tenement. An order of a court of equity may also terminate an easement.

> Donaldson, Inc., developed a residential area, laying out streets, building houses, and providing deeds to buyers. Each deed provided for a common driveway between any two homes. One half of each driveway was constructed on each adjoining property. The deed contained easement rights covering this situation. Thus each property was both a dominant and a serviant tenement. The owners would be barred from denying a neighbor the use of their portion of the common driveway.

Easements in deeds may make provision for wires, cables, water lines, and other necessary items that go under or above ground. Utilities may enforce this right even though subsequent owners demand the removal of unsightly wires and cables from their property.

Profits a Prendre **Profits a prendre** are a special type of easement with the added privilege of removing something of value from the serviant property. For example, the right to enter another's property and remove sand, gravel, soil, or the like is a profit a prendre. A profit a prendre may be created by deed, will, or adverse use.

Restrictions Imposed by Law State and local laws provide restrictions against particular uses of real property. The law serves to protect the value and enjoyment of real property ownership. Uses that make living unbearable in a residential community or undesirable in a commercial area may be outlawed.

Zoning **Zoning** is the practice of regulating the uses that may be made of properties within specified geographic areas or districts. Residential zoning prohibits properties from being used for commercial purposes within a given area. Multifamily zoning permits construction of apartment buildings. Limited-commercial zoning allows the construction of small stores but restricts the building of large department stores and commercial centers. Industrial zoning allows the building of factories and industries within a particular area. Zoning laws tend to protect property values and permit property owners to make improvements with some certainty that the comforts and value enjoyed as a result will not be threatened by construction of undesirable buildings or by offensive use being made of existing properties.

Zoning is usually designed to preserve the status quo, although provision for change is made under the so-called *change-of-neighborhood doctrine*. This gives recognition to the fact that economic changes and the gradual depreciation of properties through the passing of time or through failure to provide upkeep tend to bring change to neighborhoods. Over a period of years, a previously attractive residential area may lose its value as residential property. Zoning designed to maintain the status quo might stifle the use and development of an area that may now be better suited to industry or commercial uses. Under the change-of-neighborhood doctrine, zoning boards may rezone an area to conform with practical use.

> Several families in the Hampstead area moved to new suburban homes being developed by enterprising builders. Their former dwellings were no longer attractive to buyers who could afford the prices at which they were offered for sale. Many neighboring houses were boarded up and became fire hazards. The land was valuable for industrial use, however. When the area was rezoned, owners were able to sell their properties for industrial and commercial use.

Zoning is generally a function of local government. It is an exercise of *police power* as long as the regulations bear a reasonable relation to health, safety, morals, or general welfare. Zoning powers are delegated to localities under authority of the state constitution or by an act of the state legislature. A locality appoints or elects a zoning board or commission to study the land-use needs of the community and to make zoning regulations accordingly. Zoning laws are not enforced arbitrarily. By appeal to the local zoning board, variances may be permitted to individuals or businesses when justified and reasonable. A *variance* is an exemption or an exception permitting a nonconforming use—that is, a use that differs from those permitted under the existing ordinance. Variances are granted in special circumstances to protect citizens who might otherwise suffer if zoning laws were applied and enforced arbitrarily.

> Brewer owned a corner lot with a 100-foot frontage on two main traffic arteries in an area zoned for residential use only. The nearest gasoline station was two miles away. Brewer secured a petition with the signatures of all property owners within a four-block radius of his property, favoring construction of a service station there. A review of the petition by the zoning commission resulted in a variance giving Brewer the right to build a service station on his property.

Decisions of a local zoning commission may be appealed to county commissioners, a county court, and to the highest court in the state. In rendering a

decision, the court may not discriminate in favor of any race, religion, sex, or
ethnic group. The federal courts will not hear a local zoning case on appeal unless
it is tinged with federal issues or involves alleged violations of the U.S. Constitution.

A decision to purchase real property may be influenced by the absence or
enforcement of zoning regulations. A prospective buyer would hesitate to build
an expensive home in an area that is unzoned, since adjoining lands might one
day be used for commercial or industrial purposes. Consequently, a person
intending to buy real estate should be aware of the zoned or regulated uses to
which real property may be put in the area concerned.

Nuisances   Loud noises, constant vibration, smoke, dust, obnoxious odors,
offensive lighting, and the like may be termed *nuisances* by those who are
subjected to them. Conditions which unreasonably interfere with the enjoyment
of life and property may be declared nuisances. When the annoyance affects only
one or two owners or people, it is a *private nuisance*. When conditions arise that
affect an entire community, the condition is a *public nuisance*. Public nuisances
today usually come within the jurisdiction of public authorities responsible for
environmental control.

In determining whether a complaint satisfies the requisites of a nuisance, a
court will apply the test of reasonableness. If the matter complained of would not
be a nuisance to the *ordinary person of ordinary prudence*, the court will not act on
the complaint.

> Churches in Ellsworth had for years pealed their bells each Sunday morning
> before the beginning of services. To most people, this was a pleasing and
> acceptable routine, but Sanders entered a complaint against the ringing of the
> bells. An attempt was made to silence them on grounds that they represented a
> nuisance to persons who wished to sleep late on Sunday mornings. Weighing
> both sides of the case, the court ruled that the bells could continue to ring, as they
> were not a nuisance to the general population of the town of Ellsworth.

Air Rights   One who owns land owns the air space above that land. Common
law interpreted this right to include all the air above the land. Commercial
aviation interests asked for interpretation of this right in a case decided by the
Supreme Court in the early 1920s. The court confined ownership to a point above
the land over which the owner might be said to have reasonable control. This
decision removed the possibility of charging pilots with trespassing when flying
even at great heights. Present interpretation allows the owner of land to claim
property rights in an area defined as being a reasonable height over the highest
structure on the land.

Federal agencies require the owners of structures that are over a prescribed
height and are within the flight pattern of aircraft to install lights for the purpose
of warning pilots of their presence. Other laws prohibit construction of signs or
buildings above a certain height when adjacent to public airports. State and
federal laws regulating aircraft and altitudes at which they may fly have little
bearing on the rights of property owners over whose lands aircraft may operate.

Air rights are often valuable and may be sold to interested buyers, particularly
in land-depleted metropolitan areas. Developers purchased air rights over a

railroad terminal in New York City, using the space for construction of the new Madison Square Garden. Other developers bought air rights over the access to the George Washington Bridge and constructed multistory buildings. Use of air rights becomes important when land is no longer available for new buildings.

Subterranean Rights   The owner of land has exclusive title to the earth below the land. The right extends to a point determined to be the exact center of the earth. These *subterranean rights* are at times sold to corporations exploring for coal, oil, or other mineral deposits. Taking out oil or minerals from below the surface would constitute trespass if such rights were not obtained from their owners.

 McGee's house and lot were adjacent to land on which a small industrial plant had been built. McGee discovered that the plant owners had driven drainage pipes underground from the plant into her land. She may charge the plant with trespass. She can also sell this right to the plant or demand that the practice be stopped and the pipes removed.

Utilities, pipeline companies, and the like purchase easement rights for the construction of underground pipelines through private property. These easement rights are written into the deeds of property owners and become an obligation for all subsequent owners of the serviant properties.

Riparian Rights   The rights that a landowner has in a flowing stream are known as *riparian rights*. The owner of lands through which flows a stream, creek, or other body of water owns the soil beneath the water. The landowner does not own water in the stream, but he or she may draw from it whatever might be needed for domestic purposes, watering of animals, bathing, and other ordinary uses. The owner also has the right to construct and use a dock out to a navigable point in the stream. A landowner may not use the watercourse in any way that would damage the rights of others further downstream. Water may not be drawn for sale or use on another property if this might injure the riparian rights of others. Interestingly, riparian rights give owners title to ice in the stream, but not to the waters therein.

Percolating Waters   **Percolating waters** are the waters running below ground in springs, underground streams, and other bodies. They serve property owners when brought to the surface through the convenience of dug or artesian wells. Common law gave property owners absolute right to percolating waters below the titled land. Under modern statutes, property owners may draw only the water that is reasonably required to satisfy their needs. Other property owners damaged by unreasonable and excess use may seek an injunction against such use by petitioning a court of equity.

 Valleybrook Swim Club drilled a deep well from which water was pumped to fill an Olympic-size pool. The pool water was changed periodically. Adjacent property owners complained that their wells ran dry during the periods when Valleybrook's pumps were running round the clock. The club was enjoined from this excessive pumping to the damage of others who depended on the same water source.

Suburban water companies supply thousands of families with water pumped from artesian wells. Persons depending on water from the same underground streams are at times deprived of their supply because of excessive pumping by the water companies. The latter have been ordered to reduce pumping in favor of those whose supplies have been depleted.

Surface Waters   Runoff water resulting from rain and drainage may not be diverted by a property owner to the damage of a neighbor. Such water must be left to its natural watercourse. Filling in the land with soil or building up one's own land as a means of interfering with the natural flow of water from another's land may be halted by a complaining property owner. The law *does* permit a property owner to install pipes or other such devices to carry the water through the land, even beneath the surface. Here again, however, the normal course of water may not be changed to another's injury.

> Quinlan's house and yard were located in an area historically known to become flooded during periods of heavy rainfall. Quinlan was not aware of this condition when she purchased the property during a dry season. She bought enough topsoil to build up her plot, thus creating undesirable conditions for adjacent properties. Quinlan may be enjoined from this practice and ordered to remove the barriers which changed the natural course of the runoff.

Excavations   A landowner must not dig a cellar or other excavation so close to the boundary between his or her land and that of a neighbor as to cause the neighbor's land to cave in or the neighbor's building to be damaged. If the person excavating fails to shore up the adjoining land, he or she is liable in damages for negligence.

> Downie Community Club owned an unimproved lot adjacent to the Darlington Apartments. Excavations were started on the Downie lot in preparation for building a clubhouse. No effort was made to shore up the side of the excavation bordering on the Darlington Apartment site. The Darlington property suffered serious damage. Downie Community Club or the independent contractor doing the work would be responsible for money damages and the repair of the Darlington Apartments.

Eminent Domain   All ownership of private property is subject to the government's superior rights if property is needed for purposes of the public good. In times of national emergency, this right relates to both real and personal property. The right is usually confined to the taking of real property through eminent domain proceedings. Historically, under common law, all persons who owned real property were subservient to the king in such ownership. The property could be taken from the owner if needed for reasons that would benefit the people. Under today's law, property may be taken by the federal, state, or local government for new highway construction, public parks, state hospitals, and other facilities.

The right of eminent domain is not available to persons or businesses when taken for private profit. In such situations, property may be acquired only through mutual agreement and for consideration acceptable to the owner. Eminent domain is at times extended to public utilities when it can be shown that denial of a right-of-way for electric, telephone, gas, or other lines may interrupt construction of installations providing needed services to an entire community.

When private property is taken by eminent domain proceedings, the owner is compensated for the fair value of what has been taken. The owner is not required to accept an amount offered by those assessing the value of the property. But if an offer is refused, the owner must then defend his or her demand for greater compensation through action in the state or federal courts.

> Interstate 95 was designed to cut a swath through a residential section of Chester. Hundreds of homes, businesses, and churches lay in the path of the new highway. Kovach refused to accept the $9,500 offered by assessors for his property. An appeal was made through the county court, with Kovach claiming a fair value of $15,000; this amount would provide the family with a similar home in a comparable neighborhood of the same city. The court might accept the assessors' figure as final; might increase the amount offered; or, in some instances, might reduce the $9,500 if it was considered excessive when reviewed.

Liens on Realty   Mortgages, unpaid taxes, or artisans' (mechanics') liens may be entered against real property. The liens are for work and materials furnished in the repair and improvement of real property. Liens are filed in a public office for inspection of those who may be buying the property. Court judgments for the payment of money to creditors may also be filed as liens against real property. Real property sold to a new owner is subject to all liens recorded against the property. The buyer takes the property with the responsibility of clearing all presently recorded liens. In researching title to property for sale, the buyer's attorney reviews all recorded liens, giving the information to the buyer. The expressed warranties in the deed signed by the seller assure the buyer of no other claims other than those properly recorded.

> Taylor purchased the Summers Hardware Store and the building that contained it. His attorney discovered an $11,000 lien against the building, covering bills owed contractors for improvements made two years before. Taylor purchased the building and business against the advice of his attorney. He is now responsible for the payment of the lien if title to the property is to be cleared.

Taxes and Assessments   Unless it is owned by a nonprofit quasi-public corporation, real property is taxed for the support of state, county, or local government operation and improvements. The owner of realty, whether an individual, partnership, or corporation, is liable for legally approved taxes and assessments. Failure to make payment within a specified period results in the creation of a tax lien against the property. Penalties and interest are included in the lien. The continued disregard of demands for payment will give the taxing authority the right to sell the property at public sale in order to collect the taxes or assessments owed.

> The town of Seaford voted for installation of new street lights throughout the business and residential areas of the incorporated town. Each property owner was assessed $12 a year over a period of five years to defray the installation costs.

Disapproval of the street lights by any property owners would not permit such persons the right to refuse payment of the $12 annual assessment. Over the five-year period, a $60 lien would be placed against the properties of owners who refuse to pay the assessment, together with added fees and interest.

Questions for Review and Discussion

1. How does one distinguish real property from personal property?

2. Which of the following are real property, and which are personal property? (*a*) Fruit of industry, (*b*) fixtures, (*c*) chattels real, (*d*) trees and perennials.

3. In what ways may one develop an easement in another's property? Explain the terms *serviant tenement* and *dominant tenement*.

4. In what way does intangible property differ from tangible personal property?

5. Explain eminent domain. When and by whom may it be applied?

6. Distinguish between private and public nuisances. Give an example of each.

7. What are riparian rights? Discuss the rights of a property owner who has them.

8. Explain each of the following: (*a*) zoning, (*b*) variance in zoning, (*c*) change-of-neighborhood doctrine.

9. Enumerate the three rules that assist a jury in determining whether an object is personal property or has become a fixture in real property.

10. Discuss the obligation of property owners to those who have liens on realty.

Analyzing Cases

1. Richards sold Stein a lot on which the latter planned to build a frame house. After buying the land, Stein discovered that zoning laws in the city prohibited property owners from building frame houses or frame additions to already-existing buildings. He went ahead with the building despite this regulation. May Stein complete and live in the house under construction? Explain. • See also *Euclid* v. *Ambler Realty Co.*, 276 U.S. 365.

2. Acme Realty opened a new development in which it planned to build five hundred medium-priced homes. In order to supply city water to these homes, it was necessary to construct an underground waterline that would go beneath property belonging to King. King refused to give permission for the laying of the water main beneath her property. May the city bring any action that will grant the right of construction of the waterline? Explain. • See also *People* v. *City of Chicago*, 66 N.E.2d 761.

3. Rinaldo owned property adjacent to the National Airport. He bought a sign 110 feet high that was to advertise a motel he had built on the land. The sign would be in the direct path of a much-used flight pattern into the airport. The building inspector refused to issue a permit for the erection of the already-delivered sign. May Rinaldo secure permission to erect the sign by appeal to the county court? Explain. • See also *Windsor* v. *Whitney*, 95 Conn. 357.

4. Jones, a resident of Kingston, fell ill from a highly contagious and dangerous disease. The doctor referred the case to the local health board. A health inspector visited the Jones residence, quarantined the family, and gave strict orders that no one was to enter or leave the house until the quarantine had been lifted. Members of the family refused to obey the order, claiming that they had to report to school, work, and other appointments. Did the health authorities have the power to quarantine the Jones residence? Explain. • See also *Bryan* v. *City of Chester,* 212 Pa. 259.

5. Henley Shoe Store terminated its present lease and made plans to move to another nearby building. Preparations were made to remove shelving and other fixtures that had been built into the store when Henley's lease first started. The landlord warned Henley to desist in any act

of removing these things from the property. May Henley remove the shelves that were paid for and installed by him during his tenancy? Explain. • See also *Derner* v. *Faunce,* 191 Md. 495, 62 A.2d 304.

6. Valdez owned a farm, and the Savage Creek ran through one of his fields. Cows, horses, sheep, and other animals belonging to him depended on this freshwater stream for water. A neighbor upstream dammed up the creek and cut off the supply of water to Valdez, running irrigation pipes to an adjacent farm that agreed to pay for water delivered. Valdez objected to this unfair use at the expense of his own farm operation. May he enjoin the neighbor from cutting off the water for this reason? Explain.

Legal Reasoning and Business Judgment

Analyze the legal aspects of these business problems. Suggest possible solutions.

1. A new building is being constructed next to your suburban office building. You have noticed that a huge quantity of soil is being brought in to build up the surface ground on all sides of the new building. It appears that this will change the flow of surface waters, and your company's lawn areas may suffer during times of heavy rain and thawing snow. What suggestions would you make to the management concerning this problem?

2. During the past twenty-five years, water from boilers operating in the company's plant has drained out over an open field between the plant and the river. Owners of the property

never objected, but they never actually gave your company the right to send the waste water in that direction. Now you receive a notice that the practice must stop. There is no other way to dispose of the waste water without causing great expense to the firm. Do you have any suggestions for resolving this problem to the benefit of the company?

3. Your company has always taken pride in the appearance of its buildings, lawns, and gardens. An open lot opposite the main entrance to the building has not been cleared of weeds, high grass, rubble, and rotting garbage for many months. Appeal to the owners has brought no response. How would you go about getting some action to clear up this distasteful situation?

Chapter 35
Acquiring Title to Real Property

The common belief that the only ways to obtain title to real property are to buy it or have it come to you by inheritance is not entirely true. The law has long acknowledged other means. The basic ways of securing ownership are derived from English common law. However, some states have passed legislation that has modified the common law or supplanted it entirely.

Title to, or ownership of, real property may be bestowed or acquired in one of several ways: through mutual assent, by marriage, by separation or divorce, by will, or by operation of the law. In a larger sense, title to real property has even been acquired by the conquests of armies and the discoveries of explorers.

TITLE BY MARRIAGE

Title to real property is bestowed upon a husband or a wife, one to the other, at the moment of marriage. No contract or agreement is necessary, as the law provides both husband and wife with certain rights in each other's real property. By common law, a wife received a *dower right* in the real property of the husband at the time of marriage and thereafter.

Dower Right

By common law, the dower right of a wife in her husband's property amounted to a one-third interest and extended during the wife's lifetime. A number of states still respect this right. Statutes in these states vary regarding the property interest given the wife, some allowing a surviving wife a one-third interest, others allowing one-half. In states which recognize the common-law dower right, a husband cannot convey by sale or gift any real property owned by him without the wife's written permission. This is true even though the wife's name does not appear on the deed along with her husband's name. In the event of her death, the dower right is lost, and the heirs of the husband then have final and complete ownership of what had been the wife's interest.

▶▶ Jarvis owned three parcels of real property at the time of marriage. During their married years, his wife's name never appeared on the three deeds. Jarvis's will

486

left the properties to a son by a previous marriage. The surviving widow has a superior claim and may exert her dower right during her own lifetime.

Curtesy Right

Under the common law, *curtesy* is a life interest that the husband acquires in all the inheritable realty of his wife provided children have been born alive to them, even though they may have died before the mother. In most states, the wife has the right to defeat the right of curtesy by selling the land during her lifetime or by willing it away at her death.

▶ Before her marriage, Clark received title to an old house through a will left by her grandfather. While her husband had no rights in this property at the time of their marriage, such rights arose at the birth of their first child. Her husband thereafter had the right of curtesy should Clark die while she was still married to him.

A husband or a wife sometimes leaves a will in which a bequest is made to the survivor *in lieu of dower*. This means that if the will is accepted, the surviving spouse will give up the common-law right in the other's real property. The husband or the wife has the right of decision in determining whether to accept the bequest named in the will or to claim his or her dower or curtesy rights.

Legislation in many states has removed the common-law rights of dower and curtesy, replacing them with what seem to be more equitable rights. The new statutes give the surviving spouse an entire rather than a life interest in a fractional part of the other's real and personal property. Both husband and wife are treated alike under most of these new laws. Some states have passed *community property laws*. Community property assures both the wife and the husband a one-half interest in the property of the other both during their lifetimes and at the death of one of them. Of course, a husband or a wife may provide more in a will for the surviving spouse than is guaranteed by law.

Community Property

States which came under Spanish influence at their origin and colonization have recognized community property. Included in this group are Arizona, California, Idaho, Louisiana, Nevada, New Mexico, Pennsylvania, Texas, and Washington. Certain other states have adopted a system of community property with some changes. In general, under community property rules, the property that the husband and wife individually own at the time of marriage is considered separate property, wholly free of any interest or claim of the other spouse. All property acquired subsequent to the marriage is community property. This concept provides that the husband and wife share equally all property acquired by their joint efforts during marriage. Various interpretations of this rule are found in those states embracing community property ownership.

▶ Bennett and Miller married on February 2, 1974. Both husband and wife owned a great deal of property in their own names prior to marriage. Two days after their marriage, Miller fell heir to the estate of a wealthy aunt. The married couple take equal shares in this legacy.

Contracts in Consideration of Marriage

It is customary, in anticipation of marriage between persons who own much real and personal property in their own right, to create a *contract in consideration of marriage*. Such a contract specifically identifies the property rights of each marriage partner to the property each contributes to the marriage. In anticipation of the possibility of a later separation or divorce, the parties agree to the manner in which a settlement of the property will be made. The statute of frauds requires that all such contracts must be in writing to be valid. In respect to state statutes and their requirements, skillful attorneys are retained to create such agreements.

Homestead Estate

A *homestead estate* is a statutory life estate in the realty of the deceased spouse granted to the surviving spouse or to the children during their minority. It is the right to enjoy, free from liability for debts and exempt from tax levy, a fixed amount of the real property that is being occupied as a residence. The amount of land exempted under the right of homestead varies in the different states: in some, the amount is fixed by area; in others, by value; and in still others, by both area and value.

TITLE BY DESCENT

When an owner of real property dies without leaving a will (intestate), his or her property is distributed according to statute. The property will descend to the heirs, with certain rights providing for the surviving spouse, as previously explained. Heirs are children, grandchildren, parents, grandparents, or collateral relations—brothers, sisters, aunts, uncles, cousins, nieces, nephews. It should be noted that a wife or a husband is never an heir of the other. They are related by marriage, not by blood lines, as required of heirs. Real property and personal property are often treated differently under these statutes.

TITLE BY WILL

The owner of real and personal property is permitted by law to designate the person or persons who are to share in the distribution of his or her property at death. A surviving spouse, however, may always enforce his or her rights guaranteed by law rather than accept the will's provisions.

TITLE BY OCCUPANCY

Title by occupancy includes ownership secured through conquest, discovery, and other means in which no consideration is given to the rights of former owners.

 A Coast Guard vessel discovered an uncharted island that had erupted in the wastes of the Arctic Ocean. After a study of the island's location and description and a radio consultation with the State Department in Washington, a landing party claimed the island as a U.S. possession. The island now is the property of the United States, as recognized by international law.

Adverse Possession

Rights in the lands of another, known as *easements*, may be secured through what is known as *adverse possession*. These rights arise under circumstances in which neither mutual agreement nor consideration is given for ownership of another's lands. To establish ownership rights through adverse possession, a claimant must prove (1) that he or she has had continuous use of the property for twenty-one years or a period set by state statute, which in some cases may be as short as ten years, and (2) that this use has been without interruption by the owner, without the owner's permission, and with the owner's knowledge.

Proof of these facts will give a person superior rights over the one in whose name a legal deed is recorded. In some cases, a court of equity will declare the one claiming under adverse possession to be the new owner and will order that a new deed be issued and recorded in his or her name.

 For many years, on their way to the railroad station, commuters took a shortcut across the property of Midland & New England Aircraft Corporation. The company was aware of the practice although it had never granted permission for such trespassing, and it had never constructed a fence or other obstruction around the property. Should Midland & New England now attempt to close off the path to the station, the users could demand that it be reopened, owing to their superior rights arising through adverse possession or use.

TITLE BY SALE OR GIFT

Ownership and title to real property are most frequently transferred from one owner to another by sale or by gift. This is done by means of transferring a written instrument called a *deed*. The person transferring the title to the realty in the deed is the *grantor*. The person to whom the title is transferred is the *grantee*. A deed becomes effective when it is delivered to the grantee or his or her agent. A deed to real property may be bestowed as a gift from the owner or through a sale. In either case, it is given with the consent of the owner.

PROPERTY AND OUTER SPACE

Laws relating to property rights in outer space have not yet been either fully clarified or tested in litigation, but in December 1963 the United Nations General Assembly adopted a declaration of legal principles to govern the behavior of human beings in space, as follows:

☐ Exploration and use of outer space shall be carried on for the benefit of all persons.
☐ Celestial bodies and outer space will not be subject to appropriation by individual nations.

☐ Before carrying out space projects that can harm other states, a nation should undertake international consultations for approval.

☐ A nation launching an object into space will retain jurisdiction over the object even though the object falls to earth in another state. It is also entitled to have said object returned.

☐ The nation launching an object into space will be liable to any nation or person that might be injured by reason of the object falling at any unpredicted place. This principle follows long legal precedents which hold that the malfunction of a device creating a hazard or causing injury makes the owner liable for damages.

☐ States should render assistance to astronauts in the event of accident, distress, or emergency landing on the territory of a foreign state or on the high seas.

This declaration of legal principles is in direct conflict with the older principles of title by occupancy, discovery, and conquest. The United States, however, in the successful space flights to the moon, has observed the first two principles of the declaration of the United Nations. Discoveries made during the moon flights and landings have been shared with other nations, and at no time was there any indication of the United States' intent to declare the moon as one of its territorial possessions.

ESTATES IN REAL PROPERTY

An *estate* is the interest or right that a person has in land. Estates in land are of two kinds: (1) freehold estates and (2) less than freehold estates.

Freehold Estates

A *freehold estate* is an estate in which the holder owns the land for life or forever. A person having a freehold estate may transfer his or her interest to another by sale, by gift, or by will. Freehold estates are either (1) freehold estates of inheritance or (2) freehold estates of less than inheritance.

Freehold Estates of Inheritance   A person who owns land outright—that is, forever—is said to have a freehold estate of inheritance. Such estates are also known as *estates in fee simple*. This is the kind of estate that descends, on the death of the owner, to one's heirs if one has left no will. The holder of an estate in fee simple has *absolute ownership* in the real estate, with the right to use it or to dispose of it as he or she pleases, so long as the use of it does not interfere with the rights of others.

 When the Gerlachs bought the land on which to build their house, they received an estate in fee simple from the former owners. They thus received full rights to the property. They may sell it, give it away, or use it as they wish. The only restrictions are those contained in the deed or required of them by law.

Freehold Estates of Less Than Inheritance   One who owns a freehold estate of less than inheritance does not have absolute and final ownership. Ownership is limited and continues only for the time stated in the deed. Estates that terminate on the death of the owner or on the death of another are called *life estates*. The one to whom the life estate passes is said to have an *estate in remainder*. The title and possession of the property are postponed until the death of the holder of the life estate.

 Kirkorian's grandmother received a life estate in the real property of her husband by the terms of his will. The will further provided that, on the death of his wife, his estate should descend to his granddaughter, that is, to Kirkorian. The latter would receive an estate in remainder on her grandmother's death.

One who holds an estate of less than inheritance is not permitted to depreciate the property to the extent that its value will be substantially decreased. Neither may the holder of such an estate sell standing timber or other assets belonging to the estate. A person who buys property from someone having this type of estate takes the property subject to the same restrictions and for the limited time extended to the original grantee.

 Jordan died, leaving a wife and four small children. Jordan's will provided that the house and land (which he owned in fee simple) would pass to his wife for her lifetime. After her death, it was to be sold, and the money was to be divided equally among the children still living. Although Jordan provided his wife with a house and land, he also imposed upon her an obligation to maintain the property for the benefit of their minor children, who would receive their rights years later.

Less Than Freehold Estates

An estate which does not bestow the right of ownership to real property is less than a freehold estate. Estates of this kind are also called *leaseholds*. The holder of such an estate has the right of enjoyment only for a fixed or determinable period, but not for a lifetime.

Conditional Estates

When the duration of an estate is dependent upon a condition in a will or a deed, the estate is a *conditional estate*. The condition determines the right of the one named to continue as owner of the property. This condition may be (1) a *condition precedent* or (2) a *condition subsequent*. A property that is leased for ten years with a condition that the tenant is to have absolute ownership upon payment of $120,000 is an estate on condition precedent. Property granted to a minor provided he or she earns a college degree before reaching the age of twenty-eight is an estate on condition precedent. If the condition were not filled in these examples, the estate could be terminated.

FUTURE INTEREST OR ESTATES IN LAND

As to time of enjoyment, estates are either present estates (estates in possession) or future estates (estates in expectancy). A *present estate* is an estate in land that the owner is immediately entitled to possess. A *future estate* is an estate that the true owner is prevented from possessing and enjoying until some future time. A future estate in land is either a *reversion estate* or a *remainder estate*.

Reversion Estates

When the terms of a deed or a will state that land is to *return* to the grantor or to the grantor's heirs at the expiration of a conditional or life estate, the future interest is a *reversion estate*.

 Hardesty deeded ten acres of prime land to the Community Church. The deed contained a condition providing that if at any future time the church was disbanded, the property would revert to Hardesty's granddaughters, or to their heirs living at the time. Hardesty thereby created a reversion estate.

Remainder Estates

When the terms of a deed or a will state that the land is to pass, upon the termination of a life or a conditional estate, to someone other than the grantor or the grantor's heirs, the future interest is a *remainder estate*.

 Suppose Hardesty, in the previous illustration, had stated that the church property would be passed on to any other religious group that would continue services in the church, were Community Church to disband. Such a provision would become the basis of a remainder estate. In this case, the land would not revert to Hardesty's heirs.

ESTATES OWNED BY ONE OR MORE PERSONS

Real property may be held by one or more persons and represents either (1) *estates in severalty*, (2) *estates in common*, or (3) *joint estates*.

Estates in Severalty

An estate in land that is owned by one person alone is said to be an *estate in severalty*.

Estates in Common

An *estate in common*, also called a *tenancy in common*, exists when two or more co-owners have equal rights in the possession and use of property. The co-owners need not have equal ownership, but they must have *unity of possession* (possession and enjoyment). A tenant in common has the right to sell or deed away as a gift his or her share in the property. By will, co-owners may bequeath their share of the property to their heirs. The share of a co-owner who dies without leaving a will goes to such persons as are provided in the statutes of the state where the property is located.

 Coleman, Lank, and Caulk owned a suburban mart as tenants in common. Coleman's will provided that her one-third share go to her husband at death. Lank and Caulk objected to this agreement. They preferred that each partner's share go to the remaining partners in event of death. Coleman's decision, however, created an estate in common favoring her husband as the surviving owner.

Joint Estates

A *joint tenancy*, or *estate*, is one in which the right of survivorship is to the still-living survivor rather than to a co-owner's heirs, as is the case with an estate in common. Whereas an estate in common requires only a unity of possession, a joint estate requires (1) unity of interest, whereby each co-owner has an equal share in the property; (2) unity of title, evidenced by the names of all co-owners in the same instrument or deed; (3) unity of time, requiring that the co-ownership of all commenced at the same time; and (4) unity of possession, giving the equal right of possession and enjoyment to all co-owners.

Partners owning property in this way usually provide life insurance on the life of each partner. A surviving spouse would in each case be named as beneficiary to an amount equal to the value of the deceased partner's share in the estate. In this way, the surviving partners may reorganize and continue the business without the possibility of interruption by an outside party (who might demand the sale or division of the property).

> In the interest of continuing their partnership business, Coleman, Lank, and Caulk proposed that the suburban mart be owned by them as joint tenants. Insurance policies were purchased by the partnership. These would provide monetary payments to the partners' spouses in order to prevent new persons from entering the picture as possible co-owners.

By statute in most states, estates held by two or more persons are considered to be tenancies, or estates, in common, unless they are expressly indicated as joint estates.

Estate by the Entireties

A joint estate held by a husband and wife is an *estate*, or *tenancy, by the entireties*. In addition to the unity requirements of a joint estate, an estate by the entireties requires that there must be a fifth unity, a unity of person. Under this arrangement the survivor takes the entire estate as an estate in severalty, providing nothing for any remaining heirs. Advantages of this type of estate are that both parties must agree to any sale or conveyance of the property; and an execution by a judgment-creditor resulting from an action against a husband or wife alone may not be placed against the property.

> The DeVoes owned their home together as an estate by the entireties. While driving a car titled in her name alone, Mrs. DeVoe caused an accident. A judgment far exceeded insurance covering the owner's liability. The house owned jointly by the DeVoes would not be subject to sale to cover the judgment.

Another important aspect of an estate by the entireties is that no administration of the estate is necessary upon the death of one of the parties. This eliminates the costly and time-consuming details of making a settlement of the property, as required in the probate of a will.

In the event that husband and wife are separated by a divorce, the estate by the entireties no longer exists and they then become tenants in common, with separate and equal rights in the property.

COOPERATIVES AND CONDOMINIUMS

Less than one hundred years ago there appeared in this country a system of cooperative ownership of apartment residences. The demand for cooperatives waned during the 1930s, but in recent years they have again become popular in certain metropolitan areas where apartments represent a sizable part of all available residential housing.

Cooperatives

The cooperative begins with the formation of a corporation which builds an apartment building containing a number of living units. The corporation usually places a mortgage on the land for the purpose of constructing the building. Prospective tenants purchase shares of stock in the cooperative to bring in the necessary capital to complete the apartment building. The purchase of a specified number of shares gives a prospective tenant the right to a *proprietary lease*, which is a long-term lease issued by the corporation. Such a lease gives the tenant all the usual rights of ownership. He or she has the right of possession of his or her apartment, for which regular payments are made to the corporation for the tenant's share of operating expenses, mortgage debt and reduction, and taxes. The amount levied against each tenant is determined by the number of shares of stock held. The larger apartments are held by those owning a greater number of shares. Tenants provide their own electrical appliances, floor coverings, and interior maintenance.

The disadvantage of cooperatives is the possibility of a mortgage foreclosure, in which case the tenant may lose his or her rights. In such a case, a receiver would be appointed for the operation of the apartment project for the benefit of the mortgagee, and each tenant would then be required to pay either a proportionate share of the mortgage or full rental for his or her apartment as a means of liquidating the mortgage.

Condominiums

A *condominium* is a more recent legal invention which gives the purchaser of an apartment or household unit a freehold estate of inheritance in the unit that is purchased. The buyer's property becomes separate and distinct from the corporation or business enterprise that developed the project. After all apartment or household units have been sold, the original corporation or entity that developed the project is dissolved, and ownership is vested entirely with those who have deeds to the units sold.

Condominium Deeds   A condominium, in effect, grants to its owner two deeds:(1) a freehold estate of inheritance in the apartment or household itself, and (2) co-ownership with all other owners in those parts of the grounds and structure that are not under the supervision or care of one individual.

Freehold Estate of Inheritance   The owners of a condominium have absolute rights in the unit they purchase, the same rights as are guaranteed the owner of a house or other type of premises. At the option of the buyer, the deed may confer upon the owners a severalty estate, joint estate, estate in common, or estate by the entireties. All repairs, interior decoration, improvements, and additions are made at the owner's expense. In most cases, an owner is restricted from making improvements and additions that might interfere with the rights of other owners. Changes that might depreciate the value of adjoining units or of the entire project are not permitted. In some condominium projects, an administrative board selected by the owners must review and approve any changes that an individual wishes to make.

> Craven owned a condominium apartment in the Pacific Shore project. Five years after moving in, the Craven family decided to partition off a section of a large living room as a means of providing an extra bedroom. Details of Craven's construction plan would be reviewed by the project's administrative board. If the alterations were deemed undesirable in view of the rights of all other owners, Craven would be barred from proceeding with his plans.

Deed in Co-Ownership   A condominium deed makes the owner of an individual apartment or household a co-owner with all other owners in what are known as *common areas*. Hallways, driveways, stairways, lobbies, elevators, the roof, and walls and the land on which the building rests, the yard and garden areas, tennis courts, swimming pools, laundry and storage rooms—all may be considered common areas. Each owner has an undivided interest in these common areas. In addition, all are co-owners of the heating, air-conditioning, plumbing, and electrical systems that support or maintain the project and its units.

Each owner is assessed an equitable share toward maintenance, repair, and replacement of all co-owned areas and facilities. Painting, janitor service, lawn and garden care, security guards, and common-area utilities must be proportionally paid by each of the co-owners. Many states have passed legislation that defines the responsibilities of management in the control of condominiums. Some states have given each owner a voice in management decisions. By statute, expenses are divided equally among all owners or in proportion to the size and value of each unit.

> Ross sold her house and bought a condominium apartment, for which she paid $42,500. The management board assessed Ross $350 a month as her proportionate share of maintenance and operating costs of the condominium building. Five years later, the heating and air conditioning system broke down and had to be replaced with an entirely new unit. Ross was assessed an additional $975 as her share of this necessary and emergency expense.

Assessments made against owners parallel those levied against property owners of an incorporated city or town. Failure by the condominium's management committee to pay the assessments can result in the placing of a tax lien on each unit in a condominium project. Some state statutes permit the cutting off of all utilities (heat, water, electricity, and the like) until the assessments, if overdue, are paid. Continued nonpayment permits the management to sell the owner's unit after judgment has been handed down by a court against the owner.

Tort Liability   Condominium and cooperative owners are liable for injuries that befall guests and licensees in the same way that liability attaches to other types of home ownership. Sales agreements for condominium dwellings generally do not stipulate who has liability for injuries to third parties due to accidents occurring in common areas. Some states have dealt with this problem by making all co-owners equally liable, together, for damages in third-party tort actions.

> Hawkins delivered groceries three times each week to apartments in the Seaside Condominium. During one of these deliveries, Hawkins slipped and fell. Investigation showed that water from a leaking faucet had been trickling across an entranceway for several days. Hawkins sued the condominium and received a final judgment of $23,000. Each owner will be required to pay a proportionate share of this judgment.

Questions for Review and Discussion

1. Distinguish between a freehold estate of inheritance and a freehold estate of less than inheritance.

2. What type of estate is confined to persons legally accepted as one person? As husband and wife?

3. Discuss the principal advantage of condominium ownership over having a proprietary lease in a cooperative.

4. Explain each of the following: (*a*) dower right, (*b*) curtesy right, and (*c*) community property.

5. May the terms of a will supersede the rights of a spouse in the real property of the other? Explain.

6. Discuss tort liability of owners of condominium units for injuries to third parties in common areas.

7. In each of the following estates, who succeeds to the deceased's title interest? (*a*) Estate in common, (*b*) joint estate, and (*c*) estate by the entireties.

8. Describe the two qualifications that permit one to claim ownership by adverse possession.

9. How does one determine who takes title to the real property of a person who dies without a will?

10. What special qualification distinguishes an estate by the entireties from a joint estate?

Analyzing Cases

1. Johnson, by a will, left property to Kelleher. By a condition in the will, the property was to go to the Eastern Guards Lodge after Kelleher's death. Kelleher's children claimed the property at the time of Kelleher's death. To whom will Johnson's property finally go? Explain.• See also *Thompson* v. *Baxter*, 119 N.W. 797.

2. Cantini and some friends, who liked to go hunting, built a cabin on little-used land owned by the Northern Lumber Company. Inspectors for the lumber company were aware that the party used the site several weeks out of each year. Permission had never been given to use the area. Neither had the hunters ever been denied the right to come in when it suited them. After more than twenty years, Cantini was told that use of the land must stop. What are the rights of the parties in this matter? Explain.• See also *Larsen* v. *Peterson*, 30 A. 1094.

3. Cover and Canaris owned a store, which they had deeded to themselves as a joint estate. Over the years, much money was invested in improvements of the building and surrounding land. After Cover's death it was learned that she had left her one-half interest to a son. Canaris contended that this part of Cover's will was in error. Who will receive Cover's share of the business property, Canaris or Cover's son? Explain. • See also *Case v. Owens,* 139 Ind. 22.

4. An estate was left to Ballard, Hall, and Wright as tenants in common. Hall died, and the interest in the estate was claimed by his heirs. Ballard and Wright claimed Hall's interest as survivors to the estate. Who were correct in their claims to the share owned by Hall? Explain. • See also *Earp v. Mid-Continent Petroleum Corp.,* 167 Okla. 86, 27 P.2d 855.

5. Schumann owned a condominium apartment located in New York City. Guests entered the building's elevator to visit her and were injured when it accidentally dropped two floors to the basement. Medical, hospital, and other expenses resulting from the accident amounted to $19,000. Is Schumann personally liable to the guests for damages claimed? Explain.

6. Overton had a life estate in forest lands left by an admiring relative. The relative's will stated that the properties were to go to Overton's son and daughter if they survived their father. During his lifetime, Overton began selling off young timber from the woodland. May Overton's children object to this practice? Explain. • See also *Brokaw v. Fairchild,* 165 Misc. Rep. 70, 237 N.Y.S. 6.

Legal Reasoning and Business Judgment

Analyze the legal aspects of these business problems. Suggest possible solutions.

1. Your firm needs space for a regional office in the center of Chicago. Property is too valuable to plan a new building, and real estate brokers have suggested renting the floor space available in the Illinois Building. You understand that space is also available in a newly constructed condominium office building and in a cooperative building nearby. Your advice is sought as to the best decision to make in this pressing matter. What report would you make to your management division?

2. The board of directors would like to give a plot of ground to the city to be used as a public park. At present the land is used for sandlot baseball, but it has greater possibilities if the city were to use available funds for improvements. The board fears that if conditions in the area change and the park is abandoned, the property might be sold by the city to someone that the company found unacceptable. How would you ease the board's worry and at the same time promote the idea of a public park?

3. Your firm was asked to bid on a contract for renovation of a factory building owned by Rhone, Parker, & Burns, Printers and Binders. Inquiry disclosed that the building was owned by the three partners as tenants in common. Two of the partners were of advanced age, and one of them faced serious surgery in two months. What suggestions would you make to your credit and contracting supervisors that might be important to the development of this proposition?

Chapter 36
Sale
of
Real Property

The largest investment most families make is the buying of real property such as a home. This often involves financial obligations over a period of twenty or more years. In the transaction, the property purchased becomes security for a loan. This chapter deals with matters related to the purchase and financing of real property: purchase and sale agreement, property survey, protection of title, deed preparation, escrow, and recording the deed.

PURCHASE AND SALE AGREEMENT

The purchase and sale agreement is probably the most important document in a real property sales transaction. A poorly drawn agreement may lead to disagreement between the parties involved, open controversy, failure to perform, and expensive court action. The purchase and sale agreement (often referred to as an offer to purchase or a binder contract) must include all the essentials of a contract to be valid.

Mutual Assent

Mutual assent is comprised of an *offer* and *acceptance*, which are contained in the statement of the purchase and sale agreement that identifies the parties. An example is *Beatty, hereinafter called the Seller, agrees to sell, and Root, hereinafter called the Buyer, agrees to buy, according to the terms set forth....* The offer must be intentional and definite. To be definite, the description should identify the precise location, shape, and size of the property.

Acceptance

Acceptance in the purchase and sale agreement includes *consideration*, *competent parties*, *legal purpose*, and *legal form*. Consideration may involve the payment of a token sum, depending upon the size of the purchase. There is no requirement under the law that the considerations exchanged be of equal value or of even approximately equal value. All persons are presumed to be competent to contract without restriction except infants, insane persons, convicts, and those incapacitated by intoxication. The agreement must be legal in its purpose. It cannot violate any law or infringe upon the legal rights of others. Under the statute of frauds, the agreement must be in writing to be enforceable.

498

Equitable Interest

Once the contract to convey has been signed, the buyer receives an *equitable interest* in the property purchased. This is more than a mere contractual interest. By virtue of his or her equitable interest, the buyer has a financial or *insurable interest* in the property. In many ways, the buyer might be considered the owner without legal title. He or she may then complain of any acts by the seller or outside parties that may in any way damage, depreciate, or change the property or its value. The purchaser may seek help from courts of equity in enforcing the right of equitable title.

 Kerchek contracted to buy Homestead Estates from Larkin Realty Company. The purchase price was to be paid and deed delivered on November 25. Larkin Company failed to deliver the deed, although Kerchek stood ready to pay for the property. A court of equity would issue a decree of specific performance on behalf of Kerchek, demanding that Larkin deliver a good and proper deed to Homestead Estates to Kerchek.

PROPERTY SURVEY

To assure the purchaser that the property itself conforms to the dimensions and acreage defined in the contract or in the seller's deed, a survey of the land should be made by a competent surveyor or civil engineer. Differences between the surveyor's findings and the description in the deed should be settled before proceeding further with the purchase.

 The seller's deed stated that the land totaled 22 acres, designating in feet and inches the measurements of its perimeter and the angles at the corners. However, Rezk's surveyor reported that the tract contained only 21.5 acres. The seller would be expected to make an adjustment in the contract price to compensate for the 0.5-acre difference.

PROTECTION OF TITLE

The buyer of real property may obtain an *abstract of title* as a result of a *title search*, a policy of *title insurance*, or a *Torrens system registration* to guard against the claims of others to the land.

Title Search

Careful and prudent buyers of real estate insist upon a *title search*, an investigation of the legal history of the property and the seller's rights and interest in the property. A title search requires the professional scrutiny of a lawyer who understands the importance of details which might have little meaning to the average buyer. Conditions looked for in the search include unpaid taxes and other liens against the property, assessments, easements and restrictions placed on the property by previous owners or by adverse use, cases pending in the courts against the seller or members of the seller's family, unpaid judgments against the owner or the owner's family, the seller's marital status, the rights of the present owner as defined by former deeds or wills, and numerous other matters disclosed only through the careful inspection of records in the county courthouse and other state and federal offices.

In most large real estate developments, the seller provides an attorney who draws up all legal instruments and does the title search for a set fee included in the settlement costs of the house and lot. While there is no objection to such practice, a buyer may be better served by retaining an attorney of his or her own selection. The attorney will be very careful to investigate anything suggesting that the purchase will not be satisfactory—for example, restrictions imposed upon the purchaser or other matters that only one's own attorney can suggest.

 Walther retained an attorney to do a title search on a suburban property on which she had already made a down payment of $500. The search disclosed that the buyer would not be permitted to make alterations or changes in the exterior of the house without approval by the commissioners of the incorporated village. While such a restriction might be valuable in protecting a neighbor's investment, it might also be a deterrent to Walther's decision to go through with the contract. She might lose the $500 by breaching the sales agreement at this time without reasonable cause, but she would then be relieved of buying a property with restrictions that might interfere with her plans.

Abstract of Title   The attorney making the title search provides the buyer with a statement of the result of the search, known as an *abstract of title*. The abstract contains a complete history of the property—a summary of all conveyances, recorded liens or encumbrances, unpaid taxes, and other matters of importance to the security of the buyer. Based upon information contained in the abstract of title, the attorney advises the client whether to accept the deed to the property.

 Polk, an attorney, made a title search in connection with a tract of real property being purchased by Hurka. He delivered an abstract of title to Hurka, indicating no unpaid liens, judgments, or other deficiencies. Six months after taking a deed to the property, Hurka was sued for $2,500, the amount of an unpaid lien against the property. The lien had been recorded, but it was not discovered by the attorney. Hurka may demand damages if she can prove the attorney was negligent in preparing the abstract of title.

Title Insurance

Policies guaranteeing that one's title to real estate is good are available through companies specializing in this type of insurance. Should the purchaser of a title policy ever be called upon to answer for any liabilities created through another's ownership, the insurance company will indemnify the insured against all damages suffered because of errors in the public records, incompetency of grantors, or lack of delivery in the chain of title over the years.

In many states, corporations have been chartered to make title searches and sell title policies. The advantage of this type of service by such corporations is the continuing liability of the corporation for any damages that the insured may suffer due to a defective title. If a buyer discovers in later years that the search was not competently made and suffers a financial loss as a result, the buyer could seek damages from the corporation that searched the title.

DEED PREPARATION

Following the title search, the attorney or the title company may issue a *warranty of title* guaranteeing the accuracy and thoroughness of the search. A *deed* is then prepared, indicating the sale of the property to the buyer and the obligations of the seller in the matter of the buyer's future rights.

Types of Deeds

Four types of deeds are in general use: (1) *quitclaim deed*; (2) *bargain and sale deed*; (3) *special warranty deed*; (4) *full covenant and warranty deed*.

Quitclaim Deed A *quitclaim deed* is one that transfers to the buyer only the interest that the seller may have in a property. This type of deed merely releases a party's rights to the property. It is used when one gives up some right in property, such as an easement, a dower right, or right of curtesy.

> Pacific Power Company discontinued operation of an electric railway between Ocean Shores and New Britain. The vacated right-of-way was offered to property owners whose lands abutted the former railway line. They were not charged for this addition to their own land. Quitclaim deeds were issued to all takers. Thus, Pacific Power Company did nothing more and nothing less than grant whatever title they had.

Tax Sale Deeds This is a special type of quitclaim deed. The **tax sale deed** is given by a sheriff or other public official when there is a forced sale of a property to recover unpaid taxes against the property. It is also used when property is sold by the court to enforce a judgment against a defendant in a tort or contract action. No warranties are included in the deed. The grantee takes the property subject to any claims that may exist against it.

Bargain and Sale Deed A *bargain and sale deed* is very similar to a quitclaim deed. It is a simple form of deed containing no warranties. It differs from a quitclaim in that there is a recital of the consideration given by the buyer in exchange for the property. Whereas the quitclaim deed is not used in a sale, the bargain and sale deed is. In today's real estate market, it would be rare to find a buyer willing to accept this deed. It might be used in selling land between members of a family, or in cases where the sale price was so small as not to warrant a deed containing the grantor's guarantee of title. Another name used for this deed is a *deed without covenants*, meaning a deed without promises.

> Shapiro bought a seashore property from a close friend. Trusting each other's honesty and integrity, they prepared a bargain and sale deed without the assistance of an attorney or a title search. The seller's wife later asked Shapiro for

damages, because the property had been sold without the wife's having given up her dower right. The deed contained no warranties that would now protect Shapiro from these unexpected claims.

Special Warranty Deed A *special warranty deed* guarantees that the buyer will not be interrupted in "quiet enjoyment" of the property by claims for which the seller might have been responsible. This means that the buyer will not be dispossessed because of defects in the title or because someone else has superior title. The warranty does not extend beyond the seller, and it does not guarantee the title against claims arising from situations existing prior to the seller's title interest. This deed is preferred over the bargain and sale deed in that it does give the buyer some limited assurance of title. A claim against the property, such as one established by a contractor's lien for work done and not paid for, may be charged against the seller who created the debt. However, if such a claim existed before the seller's ownership, there is no warranty protecting the buyer. This type of deed would not be acceptable in most commercial and residential real estate transfers and under Federal Housing Administration and Veterans Administration mortgaging. Again, it might be used by parties who mutually agree to dispense with the usual title searches and land surveys accompanying a property sale.

> Harkness sold a vacant lot to Grahm. The lot had been left to Harkness through the will of a distant relative. Harkness had never had the title searched, but she could guarantee Grahm that no liens or claims against the property had been created since the execution of the will. Harkness would be safe in granting title under this special warranty deed. Likewise, the buyer would be protected, but only by making a title search that would disclose claims not covered by the seller's warranty.

Full Covenant and Warranty Deed A *full covenant and warranty deed* contains express warranties whereby the grantor guarantees the property to be free of encumbrances created by the grantor or by others who had title previously. This is the deed that is standard in the transfer of residential and business properties, when transfer is accomplished through professional real estate offices and by attorneys (see Fig. 36-1). Covenants (that is, promises) in the full covenant deed may vary by mutual assent of seller and buyer. The standard full covenant and warranty deed contains the following warranties, or covenants.

☐ *Covenant of Seizen.* The grantor (seller) guarantees that he or she is the owner of the property in fee simple (freehold estate of inheritance), with the right to convey title.
☐ *Covenant Against Encumbrances.* The grantor guarantees that there are no liens, mortgages, or other encumbrances against the property other than those recorded in a public office or disclosed in other ways to the grantee.
☐ *Covenant for Quiet Enjoyment.* The grantor guarantees present and succeeding grantees that they will not be evicted and that their quiet legal enjoyment will never be disturbed by third parties who may prove a better title or claim.

P 1678—Warranty Deed, Short Form with Lien Covenant,
Ind. or Corp.: One Side Recording

JULIUS BLUMBERG, INC., LAW BLANK PUBLISHERS
80 EXCHANGE PL. AT BROADWAY, N. Y. C. 10004

THIS IS A LEGAL INSTRUMENT AND SHOULD BE EXECUTED UNDER SUPERVISION OF AN ATTORNEY.

THIS INDENTURE, made the 31st day of July 19-- .

BETWEEN Ira Berlin, New York------------------------------------

--- grantor

and Pamela Clark, New York------------------------------------

--- grantee

WITNESSETH, that the grantor, in consideration of Two Thousand (2,000)--------------------
-- Dollars,
paid by the grantee, hereby grants and releases unto the grantee, the heirs or successors and assigns of the grantee forever.

    ALL that certain parcel of land, situated and described as Lot 23, Block 17 of development shown on map filed with the Office of the Clerk of the County of Westchester, State of New York, on the 25th day of July, 19--, entitled, "Map of Lake Carter, George Resch, Civil Engineer."------------------------------

TOGETHER with the appurtenances and all the estate and rights of the grantor in and to said premises.
TO HAVE AND TO HOLD the premises herein granted unto the grantee, the heirs or successors and assigns of the grantee forever. **AND** the grantor covenants as follows:
FIRST. The grantee shall quietly enjoy the said premises:
SECOND. The grantor will forever warrant the title to said premises:
This deed is subject to the trust provisions of Section 13 of the Lien Law. The words "grantor" and "grantee" shall be construed to read in the plural whenever the sense of this deed so requires.
IN WITNESS WHEREOF, the grantor has executed this deed the day and year first above written.
In presence of:

Christine Belovsky
Mark Hellerman

Ira Berlin .... L. S.
.... L. S.

Fig. 36-1. A warranty deed states that certain facts are true

    By virtue of the warranty of quiet enjoyment, the seller may be required to procure and deliver to the buyer those legal documents necessary to perfect title. The grantor must also defend the buyer's rights in event of unexpected claims.

    A breach of any or all of the warranties makes the seller liable in damages for the full value of the real estate at the time of the sale. The value of title insurance becomes evident when one realizes that the seller may not be available for suit or may be insolvent or deceased without any remaining esate available to cover the buyer's damages.

Statutory Requirements of a Deed

The execution and transfer of title must follow the requirements set forth in the laws of the state in which the property is located. Although the grantor and grantee may live in other states, laws of those states are not applicable to the transfer of ownership. Generally, all states require the following procedures.

☐ Deeds must be in writing and must be signed by owners who transfer title. Many states require both the signature and seal of the grantors.

☐ Deeds must contain words that show the grantor's intention to transfer title.

☐ A deed must contain sufficient description of the realty to identify it unmistakably.

> Henshaw prepared a deed to property being sold to Reuther. In describing the perimeters of the tract, Henshaw wrote: "Thence along an old stone wall to an old oak tree; from that point in a northerly direction to the middle of the Mispillion creek," and so on. Such a description would be questionable, since the points chosen were not permanent. Future surveys of the property would be unacceptable and difficult if the tree were to die and fall or if the creek changed its course.

☐ The signatures on the deed must be witnessed.

☐ The deed must be *acknowledged* before being recorded in the books of the registrar or other public office recording deeds to real estate. A deed is acknowledged by being signed in the presence of a notary public or other authorized official whose signature and seal are then affixed to the deed.

☐ The deed must be delivered to the grantee and accepted by him or her. In the event of the buyer's absence at settlement, the buyer's attorney may act as his or her agent.

Tender and Performance

On the date of final settlement specified in the sales contract, the grantor (seller) must show readiness to deliver a proper deed to the buyer, and the buyer must make tender of the purchase price named in the contract. If it is impossible or inconvenient for either party to be present at the settlement, he or she may be represented by an agent who has power of attorney. Failure of either party to perform results in a breach, permitting the injured party to sue for damages or to rescind the contract.

Money Damages When the injured party will accept money as damages, an action is brought in the lawcourts for breach of contract.

 Turner contracted to buy Jordan's store building as an investment. Her actions were prompted by an agreement that she had made with a grocery chain whereby she would renovate the building and rent it to the chain for $12,000 a year on a fifteen-year lease. Jordan's failure to carry out the contract of sale could be satisfied by a judgment against him for the money that Turner would obviously lose through the breach.

Specific Performance   When money damages do not satisfy, the buyer may seek a decree of specific performance in a court of equity. Through the award of this decree, the seller will be required to carry out the agreement of sale. A buyer may always seek such a decree on the strength of the principle of equity, which holds that all parcels of real estate are unique as to location and other characteristics. Money damages would not permit a buyer to seek out another property exactly like the one in the breached agreement.

> Marketing surveys satisfied Turk Brothers that the corner of Limestone Road and Kirkwood Highway would be a profitable location for one of their service stations. Sales contracts were written and signed by all parties for sale of the corner lot for $225,000. The seller then received a better proposition from another interested buyer and informed Turk Brothers of intention to cancel their agreement. Turk Brothers could seek a decree of specific performance, with a directive from the court requiring the owner to carry out the initial agreement.

Escrow

While delivery of a deed, in most states, is made to the buyer or one appointed by the buyer, some states require delivery in *escrow*. This is accomplished by delivery of the deed to a disinterested third party who has been accepted as the escrow agent by both parties. Delivery is made with a condition that the deed will be given to the grantee only on payment of the purchase price (or other conditions). The escrow agent may not return the deed to the grantor, except after a stated period of time during which the buyer has agreed to comply with the condition of payment. Delivery in escrow eliminates the possibility of the new deed's being delivered and recorded in the new owner's name before the buyer has made full performance.

Recording the Deed

It is the obligation of the grantee and the grantee's attorney to have the new deed recorded in a county office maintained for that purpose. Recording the deed is public notice to all that the property has been transferred to a new owner. Records are available for inspection by attorneys and others who, in good faith, have reason to inspect them. One whose name appears on the deed is known as the *owner of record*. All mortgages, liens of any kind, and unsatisfied judgments are likewise recorded in the same office.

Title by Estoppel   Failure to record the deed of a new owner may result in another's superior claim of ownership. A second sale by the owner of record before the first sale has been recorded may defeat the original buyer's claim of title. A search of the deed by the second buyer will fail to show that there has been a previous deed issued if it has not been recorded, and the second buyer will receive *title by estoppel*.

Simpson, at settlement, gave Harvey a certified check for $55,000 in return for which Harvey delivered a good deed to Simpson. Harvey later discovered that Simpson had delayed the recording of the deed, so she made a second sale to Burgess, giving him a similar deed in return for $60,000. Burgess's attorney found Harvey to be the owner of record. Simpson is estopped from enforcing his prior title rights. Because of Simpson's negligence, Burgess has been permitted to respect Harvey as the owner.

Torrens System

Where available, a Torrens system public registration may replace the usual method of conveyance. After public notice, a court examines the title. It directs that a certificate of title be issued and filed when it finds a title to be valid. Anyone suffering a loss because of errors made is reimbursed from a fund collected from registration fees. The system has not proved popular even though attorney's fees are not required and the cost of transfer is not as great as in the ordinary title transfer.

REAL ESTATE MORTGAGE

In purchasing a dwelling or other real estate, the buyer may use the property as security for a loan. When this is done, the property owner gives the lender a document, known as a real estate *mortgage*, as evidence of such security. The person who signs and gives the mortgage is the *mortgagor*, or debtor. The one to whom the mortgage is given is the *mortgagee*, or creditor.

Accompanying a mortgage is a bond, or note, executed by the mortgagor to the lender, making himself or herself personally liable for the debt.

A mortgage on real estate creates a lien on the property and gives the lender the right to have the property sold if the debt is not paid. It does not transfer title to the property. The mortgage usually provides that, in the event of default in the payment of any installment of principal or interest, the entire amount of the debt shall become immediately due and payable. It also provides for payment by the mortgagor of taxes, assessments, insurance, and other expenses.

 Morea bought a house in Pendleton Acres. Purchase price was $55,000, toward which Morea used his savings of $20,000. Home Savings and Loan Association loaned the buyer $35,000 on a note secured by a mortgage on the house. Morea defaulted on the mortgage, and the house was sold to cover the loan. The house actually brought $4,850 less than Morea owed. Morea will be held personally liable for the $4,850, with interest, until the debt is cleared.

Recording the Mortgage

Like a deed, the mortgage must be in writing; must be under seal; and must be executed, acknowledged, and recorded. Recording a mortgage has the effect of serving notice on any third parties who may be interested in purchasing the property or in lending money to the owner that the mortgagee has an interest in the realty covered by the mortgage. (See Fig. 36-2.)

REAL ESTATE MORTGAGE

THIS MORTGAGE, made the 6th day of April , nineteen hundred and --
BETWEEEN Allen Blake,

herein referred to as the mortgagor,

and Peter Casler,

herein referred to as the mortgagee,

WITNESSETH, that to secure the payment of an indebtedness in the sum of Twenty Thousand

(20,000)-- dollars,

lawful money of the United States, to be paid on the 6th day of April, 19--,

with interest thereon to be computed from 6th day of April , 19-- , at

the rate of nine per centum per annum, and to be paid---------------------------------

--- according to a certain bond,

note or obligation bearing even date herewith, the mortgagor hereby mortgages to the mortgagee

ALL The two-story and basement dwelling located at 306 Madison Street,
Town of Bethpage, State of New York.---

AND the mortgagor covenants with the mortgagee as follows:

1. That the mortgagor will pay the indebtedness as hereinbefore provided.
2. That the mortgagor will keep the buildings on the premises insured against loss by fire for the benefit of the
mortgagee; that he will assign and deliver the policies to the mortgagee; and that he will reimburse the mortgagee
for any premiums paid for insurance made by the mortgagee on the mortgagor's default in so insuring the buildings
or in so assigning and delivering the policies.
3. That no building on the premises shall be removed or demolished without the consent of the mortgagee.
4. That the whole of said principal sum and interest shall become due at the option of the mortgagee:
after default in the payment of any instalment of principal or of interest for twenty days; or after default in
the payment of any tax, water rate, sewer rent or assessment for thirty days after notice and demand; or after
default after notice and demand either in assigning and delivering the policies insuring the buildings against loss
by fire or in reimbursing the mortgagee for premiums paid on such insurance, as hereinbefore provided; or after
default upon request in furnishing a statement of the amount due on the mortgage and whether any offsets or
defenses exist against the mortgage debt, as hereinafter provided.
5. That the holder of this mortgage, in any action to foreclose it, shall be entitled to the appointment of a
receiver.
6. That the mortgagor will pay all taxes, assessments, sewer rents or water rates, and in default thereof, the
mortgagee may pay the same.
7. That the mortgagor within six days upon request in person or within fifteen days upon request by mail will
furnish a written statement duly acknowledged of the amount due on this mortgage and whether any offsets or defenses exist against the mortgage debt.
8. That notice and demand or request may be in writing and may be served in person or by mail.
9. That the mortgagor warrants the title to the premises.

This mortgage may not be changed orally.

IN WITNESS WHEREOF, this mortgage has been duly executed by the mortgagor.

In presence of

Paul Hass

Sandra Wolff

Allen Blake

Fig. 36-2. Real estate mortgage

If the mortgage is not recorded and a subsequent mortgage is given on the same property, the new mortgage would be superior to the first one, provided the second mortgagee paid value, had no knowledge of the first mortgage, and recorded the mortgage first.

> ▶ Lacey borrowed $5,000 from First Savings and Loan. She gave a first mortgage as security. First Savings neglected to have the mortgage recorded in the county recorder's office. Lacey later sold the house to Samuels, whose attorney found no mortgage recorded against the property. Samuels will take the property, free of the mortgage. First Savings, of course, may collect the $5,000, with interest, by enforcing Lacey's note.

Sometimes an owner of realty may execute a second mortgage and subsequent mortgages on the property. If all the mortgages are recorded, the holders of second and subsequent mortgages may exercise their rights against the property only after the first or prior mortgages have been satisfied. Thus, if the first mortgagee causes the property to be sold and is paid off in full, the second and subsequent mortgagees take such rights in the proceeds of the sale as remain.

> ▶ Holden borrowed $10,000 from Central Savings Bank, giving a first mortgage on a business property as security. Five years later, he needed additional cash for alterations and improvements to the building. Marshallton Building and Loan took a second mortgage on the property and loaned Holden another $2,500. In the event of default and sale, Central Savings Bank will be paid any balance owed on the $10,000 mortgage. Any money remaining will be available for satisfying the $2,500 second mortgage.

Both state and federal legislation prohibits lenders from discriminating against borrowers because of race, creed, color, sex, or ethnic background. Thus, a lender may not refuse a mortgage to a woman making application for a loan under a real estate mortgage. While the loan may be refused for reasons other than sex, basing rejection on sex alone subjects the lending institution to a heavy fine.

Rights and Duties of the Mortgagor

By law and by agreement, the mortgagor has the following rights and duties in conjunction with a mortgage.

- ☐ The right to the possession of the mortgaged property. The mortgagor continues to be the owner of the property, with right of possession.
- ☐ The right to sell, lease, or assign the mortgaged property.

> Bankers Trust Company held a mortgage on a house owned by Hanscomb. Hanscomb rented the house to a tenant of whom the mortgagee disapproved. There were no restrictions in the mortgage or deed that restricted Hanscomb's right to rent the house to a tenant of her own choice.

Mortgage terms usually prohibit the owner of the property from assigning or transferring the mortgage to a third party without the consent of the creditor. A creditor has the right to select the risks accepted in the repayment of money loaned to anyone.

☐ The right to use the same property as security for second or third mortgages.

☐ The duty to insure the premises for the benefit of the mortgagee, to the amount of the mortgaged debt.

☐ The duty to preserve and maintain the mortgaged property for the benefit of the mortgagee's interest and security.

☐ The duty to pay interest and payments on the principal according to the conditions of the bond or note.

☐ The duty to make repairs and pay all taxes and assessments that may be levied against the property.

Mortgage Insurance   The mortgagor often protects his or her spouse and children by taking out what is known as *mortgage insurance*. This is nothing more than a term insurance policy which will pay off any of the remaining mortgage debt in the event of the mortgagor's death. Such policies are recommended not only as a benefit to the mortgagor's estate but as security to the mortgagee as well.

 The Padgetts lived in a house on which they had a $20,000 mortgage. The monthly payments to a home savings and loan society reduced the amount of the debt monthly. The couple purchased a term insurance policy that was written to pay the savings and loan association any remaining balance owed on the mortgage in the event of the insured's death.

Equity of Redemption   By statute law in many states, a mortgagor who has defaulted on his or her payments to the mortgagee is given a certain period in which to redeem property by paying the amount due with interest. This right to redeem is known as the mortgagor's *equity of redemption*.

If the property is sold as a result of *foreclosure*, the statute provides that a deed is not to be executed to the purchaser immediately after the sale. It also provides that the mortgagor may recover the property within a certain period if he or she pays the total debt plus the costs of sale. If the mortgagor fails to redeem the property within the allotted time, it becomes the absolute property of the purchaser.

 After defaulting on the mortgage, Benson lost his house through foreclosure and sale by the bank that held the mortgage and bond. The property brought $18,000 at public auction. Benson's fortunes changed during the ensuing eight months. Before the end of the year, Benson succeeded in having the house returned by paying the purchaser $18,000 plus the interest accrued over the eight-month period.

Rights and Duties of the Mortgagee

The mortgagee has the unrestricted right to sell, assign, or transfer the bond and mortgage to a third party. Whatever rights the mortgagee had in the mortgage are then the rights of the assignee. The only way the mortgagor may bar such an assignment would be to make full payment of the mortgage debt. By its terms, this is not permitted in the majority of mortgages issued today unless the mortgagor pays a specified penalty.

Foreclosure If the debt is not paid by the mortgagor when due, the mortgagee has the right to apply to a court to have the property sold and the proceeds applied to the payment of the debt for which the mortgage was given as security. This is known as the *right of foreclosure*.

A mortgage is foreclosed when the creditor (mortgagee) proves the amount of the unpaid debt (including interest and other charges), and the property is sold by and under the direction of a court of equity. The proceeds realized from the sale are then applied to the payment of the debt. Any money remaining after the claims of the mortgagee have been satisfied goes to the mortgagor or to the second and subsequent mortgagees.

Frequently, a mortgage contains a provision giving the mortgagee a power of sale without requiring him or her to bring an action of foreclosure.

If the amount realized at the sale is less than the amount due on the foreclosed mortgage, a *deficiency decree* or a *deficiency judgment* is entered against the mortgagor for the remainder. If the mortgagor does not or cannot pay the judgment, the court may garnishee the borrower's salary; that is, it may order an amount to be taken regularly from salary or wages until the amount of the judgment is fully paid.

Federal Housing Administration and Veterans Administration Mortgages The Federal Housing Administration (FHA) and the Veterans Administration (VA) are responsible to the lending institution in the event of a mortgagor's default and foreclosure on an FHA or VA mortgage. The U.S. government, through these agencies, reimburses the mortgagee for any loss and takes over the property. Such properties are then offered for sale to interested buyers to recover the loss that had been sustained by the government.

Federal Real Estate Settlement Procedures Act The Federal Real Estate Settlement Procedures Act, passed in 1974 and amended in 1975, gives greater protection to consumers. It requires that mortgage lenders enumerate to home buyers the fees they will face when the purchase of a home is consummated. The law also forbids a variety of practices which can run up settlement costs. It requires the federal government to offer a booklet that explains the home buyer's new rights. The booklet can usually be obtained from the mortgage lender, which in most cases is a bank.

The Real Estate Settlement Procedures Act sets forth the following provisions:

☐ Lenders must fill out a form designed by the Department of Housing and Urban Development to spell out the settlement costs of any prospective home purchase. The form is in the nature of a disclosure statement to the potential home buyer.
☐ If the lender fails to disclose all fees at least twelve days before settlement, he or she must give the buyer $500 and pay the buyer's legal fees and court costs.
☐ Sellers may not require that, as a condition of sale, the buyer purchase title insurance from a company specified by the seller.
☐ The lender may not collect from the buyer and hold in escrow more than one month's advance payment on taxes and property insurance.

☐ The lender must guarantee that the seller will disclose to the buyer the
previous purchase price of a home if the home was not the seller's place of
residence for at least two years.

☐ Anyone connected with the settlement may be fined up to $10,000 if found
guilty of participating in a scheme to kick back fees collected in the settlement
process. This sometimes occurred when the seller required the buyer to
purchase title insurance from a title company which the seller specified, a
practice now banned.

☐ Lenders must comply with state consumer protection laws whenever these
are more stringent than the Real Estate Settlement Procedures Act.

The importance of this act to home buyers is evident when one realizes that
settlement fees for home purchases average $3,000, according to the Senate
Banking Committee which helped draft the new law. These costs are expected to
keep increasing in the near future.

Purchase by Mortgage Takeover

By consent of both the mortgagee and the purchaser of mortgaged property,
existing mortgages are often permitted to remain on properties being sold. In
such takeovers, the transfer of title to a new buyer is subject to the buyer's
payment of the seller's mortgage at the existing rate of interest.

In purchasing a property already mortgaged, the buyer will either *assume the
mortgage* or take the property *subject to the mortgage*. When the buyer decides to
assume the mortgage, he or she assumes full and complete responsibility as
though he or she were the original mortgagor. On foreclosure, the buyer will be
subject to loss of the premises and also liable for any deficiency or difference
between the indebtedness and the amount secured from sale of the property.

▶❯ The Blakes offered their new home for sale. A mortgage debt remained in the
amount of $17,500. Hoffman agreed to purchase the property under the condition
that the mortgage be transferred to him. The bank which held the Blakes'
mortgage agreed to the transfer only if Hoffman agreed to assume the mortgage.
In event of a great reduction in property values in the area, Hoffman would be
subject to a personal judgment against him should the property ever be foreclosed and bring less than the amount of indebtedness at the time of sale.

A more favorable arrangement to the buyer is provided when he or she
purchases the property subject to the mortgage. Under these conditions, the
purchaser is not liable for any deficiency in the event of foreclosure. The most the
purchaser can lose is any equity he or she may have built up in the property. The
seller remains primarily liable to the mortgage.

▶❯ Suppose, in the previous case, Hoffman had insisted on terms whereby he would
purchase the property subject to the mortgage. Even though real estate values in
the neighborhood depreciated to the point where the property would bring no
more than one-half of the indebtedness, Hoffman would be under no obligation
to make up the mortgagee's loss.

It should be observed that a lawyer representing the mortgagee usually seeks an agreement whereby the buyer assumes the mortgage. The purchaser's attorney would prefer that his or her client take the property subject to the mortgage.

Satisfaction

A mortgage becomes void on payment of the entire debt or on performance of the obligation. When the debt is paid, the mortgagee, on demand of the mortgagor, must execute and deliver to him or her a certificate that the mortgage has been discharged or satisfied and may be so recorded.

Trust Deed

When an indebtedness consists not of a single but of a multiple series of notes or bonds, it is more convenient and practical to use a *trust deed*, or a *deed of trust*. Under a **trust deed**, the secured property is conveyed to a disinterested third party, known as the *trustee*, who holds the property for the benefit of a creditor or creditors. In the event of default, it is the duty of the trustee to foreclose upon the property. Proceedings are the same as with an ordinary mortgage as far as foreclosure and equity of redemption rights are concerned.

Corporations issuing mortgage bonds use this arrangement, since it would be impractical to divide real estate into many small parts, each section securing a particular bond. The trustee holds the property in common for the benefit of all purchasers of the mortgage bonds.

 Ferber & Gross Aircraft Corporation needed $300,000 to be used in improvements to its buildings and in installation of radar devices on approaches to its landing field. Mortgage bonds in denominations of $1,000 were approved, issued, and secured by a trust deed to all existing real estate. The trustee appointed was one of the large bank and trust companies in the area. In this way, each bond issued was secured by the one mortgage.

Questions for Review and Discussion

1. Must a contract for the sale of real property be in writing and under seal in all states? Explain.

2. Discuss the importance of recording a mortgage in a public office in the county where a property is located.

3. Give several reasons why it is recommended that an attorney make a title search before one accepts the deed to a property.

4. Discuss the mortgagor's obligations when, in a foreclosure sale, the property is sold for less than the existing debt.

5. How does equity of redemption provide relief to a mortgagor whose property is sold through foreclosure of the mortgage?

6. Discuss delivery in escrow. What are the obligations of the third party in such delivery?

7. Under what conditions would a wronged buyer seek assistance from a court of equity? How does a decision in equity differ from a judgment given in a court of law?

8. Name the three covenants, or warranties, included in a full covenant and warranty deed.

9. For what reasons would a buyer of real property purchase title insurance on the new property?

10. Distinguish between a buyer's equitable interest and a title interest.

Analyzing Cases

1. Alexander loaned $15,000 to Staley, secured by Staley's note and mortgage for that amount. The note was not paid at maturity, and Alexander foreclosed on the mortgage. When sold at public sale, the property brought only $11,000. (*a*) What may Alexander do to collect the $4,000 still due on the note? Explain. (*b*) If Staley's property, when sold, brought more than $15,000, what would be done with the balance remaining after satisfying the mortgage? • See also *Gelfert* v. *National City Bank*, 313 U.S. 221; *Reichert* v. *Stillwell*, 172 N.Y. 83.

2. Montalvo executed a deed, giving it to Mahan, an attorney, to deliver to the buyer. The attorney was bound by promise not to deliver the deed to the buyer until the buyer tendered a certified check for $18,000, the purchase price of the sale. Did this constitute a valid delivery of the new deed? What kind of delivery was made here? Explain. • See also *Boger* v. *Hadley*, 66 N.E.2d 903.

3. Byrne agreed to sell a 100-acre farm to Fields for $85,000. Contracts were signed, a deposit paid, and a deed prepared. Before delivering the deed, Byrne discovered that the land was extremely valuable to oil companies, who would pay $400,000 for the same 100 acres, with royalties promised Byrne if oil were found. He therefore refused to deliver the deed to Fields when the latter tendered the $85,000. What action would best benefit Fields in this situation? Explain. • See also *Graves* v. *Carlin*, 107 S.W.2d 542.

4. Steinberg sold a property to Quillan, giving Quillan a special warranty deed on delivery of the $9,500 purchase price. Two years later, Quillan sought to hold Steinberg responsible for difficulties that arose between Quillan and the party from whom Steinberg had bought the property many years before. What are Steinberg's obligations arising from warranties in the special warranty deed? Explain. • See also *Ripley* v. *Trask*, 100 Me. 547, 76 A. 951.

5. Krinski borrowed a total of $45,000, giving a first, second, and third mortgage on the Hotel Krinski. The first mortgage secured a note of $30,000; the second mortgage, $10,000; and the third mortgage, $5,000. Krinski's default in mortgage payments ended in a foreclosure sale. The property brought $35,000. How will this money be divided among the three mortgagees? Explain. • See also *Lincoln N.L.I.* v. *Freudstein*, 87 S.W.2d 810.

6. Steffens borrowed $12,000 from Bergen and gave Bergen a mortgage on real property covering the loan. Bergen delayed recording the mortgage in the county recorder's office. Steffens then borrowed an additional $10,000 from County Trust Company, offering a first mortgage on the same property to the bank. In searching for mortgages against Steffens's property, the bank found nothing recorded. Discuss Bergen's rights and the rights of County Trust Company should there be a foreclosure on Steffens's property. • See also *McBrayer* v. *Harrill*, 152 N.C. 712.

Legal Reasoning and Business Judgment

Analyze the legal aspects of these business problems. Suggest possible solutions.

1. A new building is needed to increase production facilities at your company's Red River plant

location. The board of directors is not willing to sell treasury stock or issue bonds to cover the $500,000 that will be needed to finance the project. What suggestion would you offer that might make the financing of the new building feasible?

2. Your firm's real estate department is about to accept title to a property owned by a family which experienced legal difficulties for years in connection with claims against the property. Attorneys have researched the title and have found no defects, but they are cautious in advising acceptance of the deed, fearing that some claimant may establish a right through an old deed of a former owner. Your company will be protected by the three general warranties to be included in the full covenant and warranty deed. What additional steps would you suggest be taken that would further assure your firm's rights to the property?

3. A company employee has had financial difficulties, requiring him to borrow $12,500 for a mortgage. Local banks are unwilling to make him a loan, and you have been asked to see what might be done to help. The employee's work record goes back many years and has always been good. Personnel records indicate that he is thirty-five and in good health and has had good credit experience in the community for many years. Your company's credit union has $85,000 available for loans and mortgage financing for employees. What would you suggest as a means of assisting this individual? How would the loan be secured if it is agreed to?

Chapter 37
Leasing Real Property and Owning Mobile Homes

Does home ownership always serve the best interests of a family? Why do so many people find it more desirable to live in rented houses or apartments or to buy mobile homes? Are the legal rights and obligations of these people more favorable than those enjoyed by the homeowner?

Although many families are turning to home ownership, there is a definite trend toward the construction of apartment buildings and other rental units. So great is the demand for these conveniences in some areas that one must wait several months or more before a dwelling is available for occupancy under a lease. Nevertheless, there is a lively debate over whether renting or leasing real property is more or less advantageous than owning the property. This chapter considers the issue and reviews other questions regarding the leasing of real property and the ownership of a mobile home.

LEASING VERSUS OWNERSHIP

The decision whether to own or lease real estate is usually based on a number of practical considerations. Most observers agree that, in the long run, owning property will prove to be more economical than renting it. But many other factors play a part, especially the specific needs of the would-be tenant or property owner.

Advantages of Renting Real Property

Important advantages of renting real property are as follows:

Cost Management   Whether a family or a business, the renter can control monthly expenses by choosing a rental within a budget. Furthermore, the tenant may move a home or business from one location to another in times of either decreased or increased income or profit. The owner of residential or business property may not so easily be relieved of mortgage payments, taxes, assessments, maintenance costs, and the other financial obligations of operating real property. Proponents of renting feel that it is cheaper than ownership. They contend that the same money which would be tied up in a home or business building could be soundly invested to reduce the costs of renting.

Freedom of Movement   Members of a household may have to move to take
advantage of job opportunities elsewhere or for reasons of health. A business
may have to move to be nearer to important customers, suppliers, or a population
from which it will draw its employees. A neighborhood may decay, causing
property values to plummet. Emergency moving without the opportunity to
carefully market a residential or business property may result in unexpected
financial losses not experienced by one who rents.

No Fear of Eminent Domain   Should the government take a leased property
through condemnation or some other form of eminent domain proceedings, the
tenant need only seek out other available property to rent. The renter will not
suffer the losses a property owner might face in such situations.

Advantages of Owning Real Property

Proponents of property ownership acknowledge some of the drawbacks presented but regard them as either unlikely to occur or insignificant when compared with the advantages of ownership. The two primary advantages are as
follows:

Property Appreciation   Tenants never share in the appreciation of the property
they rent. But homeowners may watch the value of the residence they own
increase dramatically.

Tax Breaks   Both business and residential owners of property realize significant
federal and local income tax relief from being able to deduct mortgage interest
payments and real estate taxes. Tenants cannot deduct the portion of their rent
that is used for either of these expenses incurred by their landlords, even where,
under the terms of their lease, they must pay a specific portion of the realty taxes.

THE LEASE AGREEMENT

The agreement between a landlord and a tenant governing the rental of real estate
is a contract called a *lease*. The landlord is called the *lessor*, and the tenant is
referred to as the *lessee*. The lease creates the relationship of bailment and
provides the tenant with exclusive possession and control of the real property of
the landlord. Rent is the consideration given by the tenant. A lease may be oral
but should be in writing if it extends for more than a year.

Parties to a Lease

A lease contract must be entered into by the property's owner or agent and the
tenant who will actually occupy the leased premises. Often the property owner
delegates the authority to execute leases to a rental or management agent. Typically, the management company collects all rents and performs all building
services for the property owner. It collects a percentage of the gross rents (usually
5 to 8 percent) for its efforts.

An agent may execute the lease for the lessee, but he or she must disclose who the actual tenant will be. That is because the landlord will usually ask for references, that is, a list of the prospective tenant's business contacts or former landlords. The purpose is to help in deciding whether the prospective lessee would be a responsible tenant.

Voidable Leases   Since a lease is a contract, it may be voided by a party who did not have the capacity to execute the contract when it was entered into (see Chapter 8). Similarly, if a person adjudged to be incompetent has entered into a lease, that lease may be voided by someone who has the authority to govern the affairs of the incompetent. A minor may also void his or her lease, unless it is shown to be a necessity. Minors who are married are *emancipated* from this right, however, and may be held responsible by the lessor for all unpaid rents and any damages inflicted upon the rented premises.

 Seward, seventeen years old, attended Central College. She rented a one-bedroom apartment for the college year. To assure an enforceable lease, the landlord required that Seward's parents sign the lease as guarantors of the terms of the contract. Although living quarters might be termed a necessity, would they still be considered so if Seward vacated the premises? Had she been married and living with her husband, also a minor, the landlord's precautions might not have been warranted.

Oral and Written Leases

A lease may be oral if the term is shorter than one year. All leases of longer duration must be in writing. Because of misunderstanding and possible troubles between landlord and tenant, it is advisable that even a short-term lease be put in writing, to spell out all the conditions of the lease in regard to the tenant and the landlord.

 Chapman rented an apartment for six months under an oral lease. At the end of the leasehold, the landlord demanded $150 for repairs that Chapman claimed were not discussed when the lease was entered into. (In general, written leases indicate who will bear the costs of certain repairs.) A magistrate or small-claims court might have to determine Chapman's rights and obligations in the oral lease.

An example of a written lease is shown in Fig. 37-1.

Interpretation of Leases

If a landlord and tenant disagree over the interpretation of their lease, they may find themselves arguing over their differences in court. The usual rules for interpretation of contracts would come into play. As a result, one very important rule might favor a tenant. That rule says that, in an ***adhesion contract***, any ambiguities or doubts as to interpretation are resolved in favor of the party who did not prepare the contract. An adhesion contract is an agreement drawn

LEASE made September 15, 19-- whereby WE, REGAL ARMS CORPORATION, the landlord, lease and YOU, Bruce Jay Jonson, the tenant, take Apartment 5F in building 3 at 112 Michael Street, Franklin Square, New York, for a period of two years from the date the apartment is ready for occupancy, at a rent of $250 a month, payable in advance, without demand, on the first day of each month.

SECURITY AGREEMENT

We have received $250 security for your performance of this lease

1. Which we will return if
   a. You cancel BEFORE notice of occupancy date is mailed, or
   b. We cancel because the Government takes the building or any part of it, or
   c. We cancel because the building is damaged and we decide not to repair it, or
   d. This lease remains in effect for the full two year period:

2. Which we will keep if
   a. You cancel AFTER notice of occupancy date is mailed and before the lease begins, or
   b. We cancel because YOU DO NOT OBSERVE this lease and the regulations which are a part of this lease, or
   c. You do not leave the apartment in good condition, regardless of how or when the lease ends or is canceled

If you cancel after the lease begins, we will return $10.50 for each full month's rent paid, and keep the balance.

WE AGREE TO:

3. Give you thirty days notice by registered mail of the date the apartment will be ready for occupancy;

4. Deliver the apartment in good condition;

5. Supply at no extra charge the following:

Gas
Electricity
Heat as required by law
Hot water
Cold water
A refrigerator
A gas range
A sink and laundry tub
Kitchen floor linoleum

Venetian blinds
Window screens
Use of:
Washing machines
Drying machines
Television antenna
Incinerators
Parking areas
Playgrounds
Storage & Carriage rooms

YOU AGREE TO:

6. Pay all RENT at our office or other place we specify;

7. Observe the regulations which are part of this lease;

8. Leave the apartment in good condition when you move out.

BOTH OF US AGREE:

9. We may repair any damage caused by you and charge the cost to you as ADDITIONAL RENT;

10. You will receive no rent reduction or compensation for inconvenience due to repairs or interruption of service unless caused by our negligence.

YOU MAY CANCEL THIS LEASE ANY TIME:

11. BEFORE the lease begins by delivering in person to our office your signed copy of this lease. If notice of occupancy date has been mailed, we will keep the security.

12. AFTER the lease begins, if your rent is paid, by sending a signed notice by registered mail, postmarked thirty days before the day you select.

WE MAY CANCEL THIS LEASE BY GIVING YOU:

13. THREE DAYS' NOTICE if the building is damaged and we decide not to repair it;

14. FIVE DAYS' NOTICE if you do not observe this lease and the regulations which are part of this lease. In this case we will keep the security;

15. Whatever notice we receive if the building, or any part of it, is taken by the Government for any reason.

BOTH OF US ALSO AGREE:

16. If you do not move out when this lease ends or is canceled we may
    a. Bring dispossess proceedings, or

Fig. 37-1. A lease

b. Charge you DOUBLE RENT;

17. If you do not leave the apartment in good condition when you move out
    a. We will keep your security, and
    b. You will pay on demand as damages all costs of cleaning and repairing the apartment;

18. If you do not pay the RENT, ADDITIONAL RENT or DOUBLE RENT
    a. We may bring dispossess proceedings, or
    b. Sue you for the unpaid rent;

19. If we bring dispossess proceedings you will pay on demand as damages
    a. All costs of summary proceedings and other legal actions including attorney's fees;
    b. All other expense of removing you;
    c. The cost of redecorating and repairing the apartment.

BOTH OF US SPECIALLY AGREE:

20. We have not guaranteed a specific delivery date for the apartment.

21. You will not assign this lease.

22. You will not sublet your apartment or any part of it.

23. We have made no promises except those in this lease.

24. This lease can be changed in writing only, signed by both of us.

25. This lease is subject to all land leases or mortgages now or hereafter placed on the property.

REGAL ARMS CORPORATION (WE)

By: *Michael Alan Edward*

(X) *Bruce Jay Jonson* (YOU)
(Sign Your Name Here)

YOU AGREE TO COOPERATE WITH US BY OBSERVING THE FOLLOWING REGULATIONS:

You Will Not:
1. Leave any personal belongings on lawns, walks, driveways or in public halls;
2. Do anything to disturb your neighbors;
3. Overload the electric system or use the kitchen sink or the toilet for garbage or waste disposal;
4. Erect any window or door signs or private radio or television aerials;
5. Interfere with the operation of the elevator;
6. Change the lock on your apartment door;
7. Store furniture, bedding or highly inflammable material in the storeroom;
8. Litter the public halls or grounds;
9. Do anything that will violate any law or increase the insurance rates on the building.

You Will:
10. Place your garbage for disposal as we direct;
11. Use the laundry and drying machines in the manner and at the times we direct;
12. Encourage your children to use the playgrounds instead of the open areas around, and the public halls in, the buildings;
13. Use the apartment only as a residence for the persons listed in your application;
14. Take good care of the apartment and the equipment we supply;
15. Permit us to enter the apartment during reasonable hours to
    a. inspect for or make necessary repairs, or
    b. show the apartment to future tenants.

YOU AGREE that we may change these regulations from time to time as may be required to protect the property or add to your enjoyment of it.

I have read the above regulations.   Initial Here

entirely by one party and presented to the other party for agreement or rejection. Typically, prospective residential tenants are presented with a proposed lease which they can either sign or reject; they are not given an opportunity to modify the landlord's terms. Business tenants, on the other hand, usually play an active part in negotiating lease terms with a landlord. Any vagueness in a tenant's adhesion lease, then, will usually be interpreted in the tenant's favor.

> Allen's lease provided for a $500 security deposit, which the landlord could apply at the expiration of the lease to the cost of any damages to the apartment or to the amount of any rent not paid by the tenant over the term of the lease. Another clause in the lease provided that Allen had to pay a "tax surcharge" of 2 percent of any increase in the landlord's taxes. The landlord's tax increase for that year came to $7,600. Allen did not pay his $152 tax surcharge obligation. When he moved out of his damage-free apartment on December 31, the landlord withheld the tax surcharge from the security deposit, paying Allen only $348. Allen sued for the rest in small-claims court. Since it is not clear whether the tax surcharge is considered rent under the lease, and since Allen's lease was an adhesion lease, that issue had to be resolved in Allen's favor. Thus the unpaid amount was not considered rent, and the landlord should not have used it to offset Allen's security deposit. Allen recovered the $152.

Leasehold Duration

The property rights given to a tenant when he enters into a lease contract are commonly referred to as a *tenancy*. Most states recognize four distinct durations for tenancies.

Tenancy for a Definite Period   When the lease prescribes a stated time—one month, one year, or some other definite period—there is a *tenancy for years*. The lease is automatically terminated at the expiration of the time stated.

> Gonella was due to graduate from law school in January 1978. In September 1976 she took $3,400 she had managed to save from a summer job and rented a one-bedroom apartment from Brown Management Company for the period September 15, 1976, to January 15, 1978. The landlord's initial reluctance to rent her an apartment for such an odd term was overcome by her willingness to pay the entire rental for the apartment in advance.

Leases of this type often include a condition requiring the tenants to inform the landlord of their intention to vacate the premises at the end of the period of tenancy. Such notice, by terms of the condition, usually must be communicated to the landlord two or three months prior to the expiration of the lease. This gives the landlord the opportunity to offer the rental property to new prospective tenants. Failure to give the required notice may make the tenant a *tenant at sufferance* (see page 521).

A landlord who accepts additional rent from a tenant after the expiration of the leasehold enters into an implied agreement for the renewal of the present lease on its present terms. The landlord is bound by this renewal, even though acceptance of the rent was inadvertent and the property was already rented to another party under a valid written lease.

▶ Young's lease on offices in the Harmon Building was written for one year, terminating on June 25. Young did not notify his landlord that he intended to renew the lease. On June 15 the landlord mistakenly accepted Young's check for $275 rental for the month June 25 through July 25. Even though the landlord had acted unintentionally, acceptance of the check renewed Young's lease for another year.

Periodic Tenancy A *periodic tenancy* is governed by a lease that provides for rent payments at stated intervals such as a week, month, or year. When a periodic tenancy is from year to year, the tenant is usually given the option of making monthly rent payments. A periodic tenancy continues until one of the parties gives proper notice of termination.

▶ Feinstein's lease in Presidential Towers is on a year-to-year basis at an annual rental of $3,900. However, his lease calls for him to pay the rent in monthly installments of $325.

Unless the landlord or the tenant gives advance notice of an intention to terminate the lease, it will be automatically renewed at the end of each period for the same term. Advance notice varies from state to state, but it generally is defined as a period of three months for periodic tenancies of one year or longer and "one period" for periodic terms of less than a year.

▶ Orsini's year-to-year lease expires on December 21. On November 1 she gave her landlord notice of her intention to terminate the lease. In her state, three months' notice is necessary to terminate a year-to-year tenancy. Orsini's landlord can hold her to an additional year.

Tenancy at Will When no specific term of lease is agreed upon, the relationship is called a *tenancy at will*. It continues indefinitely until terminated. Notice is not usually required to terminate a tenancy at will. Some states, however, require thirty days' notice in writing from the landlord before a tenant can be forced to give up a leasehold under a tenancy at will.

▶ Kenton had a permanent residence in Smithville, but his company assigned him for an indefinite period to its plant in Jonesboro, eighty miles away. Rather than commute, Kenton rented an apartment in Atlantic Arms Apartments under an agreement of a tenancy at will. He paid rent on a weekly basis and could terminate the lease at any time merely by leaving.

Tenancy at Sufferance A tenant who fails to leave leased premises after the lease expires creates a *tenancy at sufferance*. The landlord may deal with such a tenant as a trespasser. In most states, a holdover tenant is bound under a tenancy at sufferance for the period of the expired lease, not to exceed one year. By allowing continued occupancy and accepting additional rent, the landlord creates a new tenancy from year to year.

▶ Berzin leased his apartment from Briarcliff Towers on a year-to-year basis. His lease was due to expire on December 31. On September 29 he gave his building's management notice of his intention to terminate at the end of the period. He arranged with a local moving company to move his effects across town to a garden apartment on Saturday, December 30. Unfortunately, the movers went on a wildcat strike the day before. The strike was not settled, and Berzin's belongings were not moved, until Tuesday, January 2. Briarcliff Towers could treat Berzin as a holdover tenant at sufferance and force him to pay an additional year's rent.

In some states, a tenant who fails to give the landlord notice of intent to vacate at the end of the term of a tenancy for a definite period can be treated as a tenant at sufferance. The landlord may then treat the lease as renewed for the original term (or for one year in the case of long leases). The tenant has no option in the matter once he or she has failed to give notice at the time specified in the lease.

Mortimer and his family occupied a ten-room house under a two-year lease. In the middle of the leasehold, Mortimer decided to purchase a house for the family, to be ready for occupancy at the end of the present lease. Mortimer did not give his landlord notice of intention to vacate. The landlord elected to hold Mortimer for an additional year as a tenant at sufferance.

Security Deposit

Traditionally, leases have required security deposits to protect landlords against damages to their apartments as well as nonpayment of rent. In recent years, consumer groups have brought to public attention landlord abuses in improperly holding onto a security deposit when a tenancy ends. Some landlords deducted charges for ordinary wear and tear, rather than for actual damages to their premises. Others charged amounts for unnecessary cleaning expenses. Still others gave no accounting at all.

While tenants have always had the right to take a landlord to court to get back an improperly withheld security deposit, most state legislatures have now passed statutes governing security deposits for residential tenants. Such laws spell out tenant rights and make it easier for tenants to prevail in court. While these laws differ from state to state, certain characteristics are commonly found.

Amount Most states limit security deposits to 1½, 2, or 2½ months' rent.

Interest Most states require that security deposits be placed in interest-bearing accounts. The interest is either paid to tenants on an annual basis or accrued in their favor.

Accounting The landlord is given a specific period, usually thirty days after the lease ends, to account for the security deposit and return the balance due to a tenant.

Damages Many states have now put "teeth" into the law by providing for double damages, court costs, and attorney's fees for tenants whose security deposits were wrongfully withheld.

Santos rented a $300-per-month apartment from Hollis for a term of two years. When Santos's tenancy ended, Hollis refused to return any of the $450 security deposit to Santos, claiming that the damages to the apartment fully offset the amount of the deposit. Santos hired a lawyer, who brought suit against Hollis. The landlord was able to demonstrate only $70 in damages to Santos's apartment. The court found that Hollis had wrongfully withheld $380 of Santos's security deposit. The court awarded Santos a judgment for double damages of $760 plus attorney's fees of $200. With court costs, the landlord was forced to pay over $1,000.

Termination of the Lease

Leases are terminated in much the same way as other contracts (see Chapter 13). Most leases terminate upon their expiration. Other circumstances may lead to termination.

Mutual Agreement   The landlord and tenant may agree to terminate their lease before the stated end of the leasehold. Sometimes a landlord will demand one month's rent (or more) or other payment as a concession in order to agree to terminate a lease.

 Sandlofer purchased a house and arranged to take title on May 15. Her apartment lease ran through August 31. Her landlord agreed to terminate the lease on May 30, provided Sandlofer would pay an extra month's rent. Sandlofer agreed.

Landlord's Loss of Title   Leases usually contain a provision allowing a tenant to remain in possession if the landlord sells the property during the leasehold. (Purchasers sometimes offer to *buy back* a tenant's remaining leasehold for a cash consideration.) But this right to possession is extinguished if the landlord loses title through eminent domain action.

 Lodge Servicenter rented an area at the corner of King and Duke Streets under a ten-year lease. The state took the property through condemnation proceedings directed against Lodge Servicenter's landlord, in order to construct a new right-hand turn lane from King into Duke Street. Lodge must lose his lease.

Eviction   One of a landlord's remedies in the event of nonpayment of rent is to sue for *eviction*, that is, to remove the tenant from the leased premises. Landlords who succeed in eviction actions succeed, too, in terminating their defaulting tenants' leases.

Yellin was three months behind in his rent. On April 9 his landlord sued for eviction. On April 21 the landlord-tenant court ordered Yellin evicted from the apartment by April 26. Yellin's leasehold agreement is terminated as of that date. While the landlord may sue for back rent, he can sue only for the period through April 26.

RIGHTS AND DUTIES OF LANDLORDS AND TENANTS

A good lease agreement will carefully spell out the respective rights and duties of landlord and tenant. However, appropriate laws may restrict or expand upon what is set forth in the lease.

The standard lease at Helmsly Arms provides that residential tenants may renew automatically after expiration of their standard two-year leases at a new rental rate 12 percent higher than the previous rental. A local "rent-leveling" ordinance limits rent increases in such circumstances to 8 percent. When the ordinance was first passed, a group of landlords brought suit to attack its constitutionality. The matter went all the way to the highest court in the state, where the ordinance was upheld. Helmsly cannot impose its terms despite the clear language of the lease.

Landlord's Duty to Lease Property

A landlord may not discriminate in selecting tenants on the grounds of race, creed, color, or sex. A landlord may restrict rentals to persons without children, but may not restrict a married couple's freedom to bear children during the leasehold.

The Stimsons, a married couple, rented a luxury apartment from Chester Realty Associates. A condition inserted in the lease read, "The lessee agrees that if a child or children are born to the tenants during the period of the lease, the lease will be automatically terminated without the necessity of notice from the landlord." This condition is not enforceable against the Stimsons. Persons may not be denied the freedom of bearing children through contracts made with a landlord or others.

Landlord's Rights Under Lease

Under most leases, a landlord has the following rights.

Right to Rent The landlord has the right to collect rent from the tenant.

Right to Possession The landlord has the right to recover possession of the rental premises, in good condition, at the expiration of the lease. The tenant must keep the property in good repair, unless the landlord has accepted that obligation.

O'Neal Music Center rented a store under a lease in which nothing was said about obligations of either landlord or tenant in the matter of repairs. A plate glass window was destroyed by high winds and required immediate replacement. The music center would be responsible for the replacement.

Right to Evict The landlord has the right to evict a tenant for nonpayment of rent, disorderliness, or illegal or unpermitted use of the premises.

Dr. Hembly rented a house as a residence. Her office was located in the Physicians' and Surgeons' Professional Building. When Hembly's office lease expired, she moved her office to her home. Hembly would be subject to eviction if, after a warning, she continued to practice medicine in the leased residence.

Right to Retain Permanent Improvements   The landlord has the right to keep fixtures that have been made a permanent part of the real property by the tenant during the leasehold.

 Dr. Hembly installed partitions in the rented house, dividing the living room for consultation offices. New lighting fixtures were installed, as well as a built-in air-conditioning system. Hembly would be barred from removing the additions at the expiration of her lease or upon her eviction.

Tenant's Rights Under Lease

Under most leases, a tenant has the following rights.

Right to Possession   The tenant is entitled to the peaceful possession and quiet enjoyment of the rental premises. This includes both the physical and legal rights of possession. The landlord may not interrupt the tenant's rights of possession as long as the tenant abides by the conditions of the lease and those imposed by law. The right to exclusive possession by the tenant makes the landlord a trespasser should there be any unauthorized entry by the landlord into the rented premises.

 Benson & Childs rented a skylight suite for their architecture offices. The lease gave the owner permission to enter only when request had been made or in the event of extreme emergency. The landlord entered the offices late one evening for what he termed his regular safety and fire inspection. Benson & Childs may treat the landlord's trespass as a breach of their right to sole possession, giving them the right to terminate the lease or charge the landlord in either a civil or criminal complaint.

A tenant does have the duty to observe the restrictions contained in the lease. Leases may impose duties of all kinds as long as they are legal and do not deny a tenant's constitutional rights. Failure to abide by the restrictions agreed to at the time of the signing of the lease gives the landlord the right to seek eviction of the tenant.

 Boggs's lease states that he cannot paint any exterior woodwork or walls without first getting written permission from the landlord. Painting these surfaces, even though doing so improves the property, gives the landlord the right to terminate Boggs's lease.

Assignment of a Lease   A tenant often has the right to sublet, or assign, the rental contract. A *sublet* creates a new tenancy in which the tenant moves out and gives possession to a new tenant, called the *sublessee*. The sublessee is liable for payment of a rental to the old tenant, called the *sublessor*. The old tenant, meanwhile, is still liable to the lessor for payment of the rental obligation. An *assignment of a lease* is an arrangement in which a new party, called the *assignee*, steps into the shoes of the tenant, or *assignor*, and is liable for all the old tenant's obligations and entitled to all the old tenant's rights under the lease. Virtually all leases require landlord approval for an assignment; many require landlord approval for a sublet as well.

Right to Renew   Many leases give the tenant the right to renew his or her lease, subject to a formula or the reaching of an agreement with the landlord as to a new rental rate.

Responsibility for Repairs

The obligation for repairs to rental property has been the subject of much legislation over the past decade. What was formerly regulated by common-law practices and court decisions is now under the supervision of public housing authorities in many states and municipalities.

Obligations of Tenants   At common law, a tenant was obligated to return premises to the owner in the same condition as when delivered to the tenant. Normal wear and tear and depreciation is not included in this definition. Some states have in the past interpreted this duty in the strictest way, requiring tenants to rebuild structures that have been destroyed for whatever reason during the leasehold. Other states have taken a milder view of the tenant's obligations through judicial interpretation or the passing of laws that limit the tenant's obligations. A lease may be written to contain a more thorough description of the tenant's obligations in the matter of repairs, rather than leaving decisions to judicial decision and statute. In any case, the tenant will be held responsible for all repairs resulting from his or her negligence, illegal use, or uses not described and permitted by the lease.

 Turner rented a house in Westminster. The lease contained the usual statements covering repairs by tenant and landlord. When Turner negligently plugged in an electric space heater with a defective thermostat and left the house, a serious fire resulted. Turner is responsible for all repairs necessary because of his negligent act.

Obligations of the Landlord   Traditionally, a landlord needed to make only those repairs detailed in the terms of the lease contract. But certain parts of a structure have also been considered the landlord's responsibility. Outside walls, foundations, and structural parts of a building are examples. Most leases for apartments or office suites require the landlord to make all repairs to stairways, halls, outside walls, roof, heating and air-conditioning systems, plumbing, and the like. The tenant's obligations would be confined to the areas assigned to the tenant under the lease.

 Daniels and Cohen, attorneys, rented a suite of offices in the Farmers Bank Building. Excellent management kept the offices clean, well decorated, and comfortable. But leaking water from the roof was reported to the bank manage-

ment, which made no effort to remedy the situation. A heavy storm resulted in
serious water damage to the office, ruining $4,000 worth of valuable law books.
The landlord, not the tenant, is responsible for this loss.

Many municipalities have adopted ordinances to protect tenants from unsafe
or unhealthy conditions created by a landlord's refusal to make necessary repairs.
Building inspectors, health authorities, and other public officials are empowered
to make inspections and demand improvements when they are contacted by
dissatisfied tenants. In many cases, ordinances permit the tenant to cease payment of rent for the period during which the landlord fails to make the repairs or
improvements ordered.

> Huggins lived in a run-down apartment building. Other tenants complained
> about conditions to the local building inspector, who came and investigated. He
> issued a report noting the following defects, which Huggins's landlord was
> required to repair: (1) windows, window frames, doors, and door frames were so
> badly worn and rotted that water leakage, excessive drafts, heat loss, and infesta-
> tion resulted; (2) railings on the balconies, landings, porches, and steps were
> dilapidated and unsafe; and (3) none of the pedestrian walkways or other por-
> tions of the premises regularly used by occupants were illuminated. After thirty
> days, nothing had been done. The building inspector served a notice on Huggins
> to withhold rental payments until the repairs were made.

MOBILE HOMES

Mobile homes, sometimes called *trailers*, are becoming increasingly popular and
represent a sizable segment of dwellings in this country. They offer certain
advantages which have made them desirable in many areas and to many people.

Advantages of Mobile Homes

Among the advantages of a mobile home are freedom from assessments and
real-property taxes, efficiency living, and mobility, making possible a change of
location.

☐ Mobile homes, unless placed on permanent foundations and given other
special treatment, are said to be personal property and therefore do not come
within the jurisdiction of real estate tax boards. However, most states have
passed legislation requiring special fees to be paid by trailer residents. These
fees, in addition to the usual highway license, provide income from the
mobile-home owners for use in providing schools and other services enjoyed
by all citizens.

The Popoviches purchased a mobile home for $17,500 and parked it on a desig-
nated site in compliance with zoning regulations. A small house nearby was
assessed by the local tax office at a valuation of $18,000, which included the land.
The Popovich children attended public school, and the family received the
benefits provided those living in the area; but, unlike their neighbor, they did

not have to pay property taxes. Their only expense was a small annual registration fee charged mobile-home owners, plus a small rental for their parking privileges.

In most cases, the fees levied on mobile homes are not proportionate to those levied on real property or in consideration of the benefits received. This condition creates dissension and hostility at times between homeowners and those who occupy mobile homes.

☐ Because of the efficient construction and utilization of space, owners of mobile homes find that less time is needed in maintenance and care than is required of the ordinary dwelling. This is a saving in both cost and time.

The Morses, who had formerly occupied a rented house, now lived in a mobile home and found that they had no responsibilities in the maintenance and care of the parking area. All expenses of lawn care, driveways, outside lighting, and the like were borne by the owner of the mobile-home park. An additional benefit included free use of a spacious swimming pool.

☐ At a minimum of cost, mobile homes may be moved from place to place either by the owner or through the services of trailer-moving specialists. Persons engaged in work that requires frequent changes of residence find that the convenience and saving offered by a mobile home are great.

Jackson worked as an engineer for an automobile manufacturer with assembly plants in many parts of the country. His special talents required that he change his location several times each year. The company paid for the moving of his mobile home each time to its new location, relieving the family of the responsibility of selling or terminating a lease and the added difficulty of finding a new home.

Disadvantages of Mobile Homes

There are certain disadvantages to mobile-home living, such as possible community disapproval, depreciation, and unsatisfactory family living.

☐ Residents of mobile homes are not considered by other citizens as stable members of the community. Although this objection is gradually being overcome, some property owners are reluctant to accept mobile-home owners as contributing members of a community.

Bell had a background of experience in educational matters and felt that he should place his name in nomination for membership on the local school board. Although he had three children in school, was an active member of the PTA, and had many of the qualifications required of a board member, he received very few votes in the election. His defeat was attributed to his family's occupancy of a mobile home, reflecting a lack of stability in the community.

☐ Mobile homes depreciate in value much more rapidly than ordinary dwellings. The resale value of such an investment is not nearly as high as the same amount invested in real estate.

Although Fera had made an investment of $15,500 in her mobile home, she found that after ten years' use it would bring less than half that amount if sold or traded on a new model. The same amount of money invested in properly chosen real estate could have shown an increase in valuation over the same ten years.

☐ The space limitations of mobile homes present difficulties in the raising of a family. Insufficient storage space for children's toys, seasonal clothing, and other family possessions results in great inconvenience to all members of the family.

Sammler enjoyed efficiency living, as was possible in her family's mobile home. She found, however, that it was impossible to entertain members of the family or put them up for an extended visit. As the children grew older, they also realized that space limitations made it very difficult to entertain their friends.

Obligations of Mobile-Home Owners

Owners of mobile homes are required to observe many statutes adopted in most states for the regulation of mobile homes, both as dwellings and as moving vehicles. The states are gradually adding more restrictions and obligations each year for the regulation of mobile homes.

When mobile homes are moved from one state to another, special fees must be paid by the owners, and inspections must be made by the authorities. Failure to obtain permission to transport such vehicles before passing through a state can lead to arrest and fines. The fees charged are determined by the size of the home being transported. Because of their small size, certain types used as vacation trailers are accorded special privileges in this respect. Complying with the laws of the states traversed while the mobile home is being moved from state to state can be expensive.

 Pratt accepted a position with a new firm in a city 1,200 miles from his present location. He contacted a company which specialized in the transport of mobile homes and was told that the usual charge for moving a unit the size of his was approximately 34 cents per mile. This did not include special licenses, tolls for bridges, throughways, and other added fees. Pratt would have to decide whether it would be to his advantage to move the mobile home to the new location or sell it and make other provisions for his family after the move.

Questions for Review and Discussion

1. Define or explain each of the following legal terms or phrases: (*a*) lease, (*b*) tenancy at will, (*c*) periodic tenancy, (*d*) tenancy at sufferance, (*e*) peaceful possession, and (*f*) normal wear and tear.

2. How are leasehold estates created?

3. Name five ways in which leases are terminated.

4. List and explain a landlord's rights under a lease.

5. List and explain a tenant's rights under a lease.

6. Discuss the obligations of the tenant and the landlord in the matter of repairs to rented premises.

7. Distinguish between a tenancy for years and a periodic tenancy.

8. Are oral leases enforceable? Explain.

9. Is a lease signed by a minor enforceable? Explain.

10. Discuss the comparative advantages and disadvantages of mobile-home ownership.

Analyzing Cases

1. Gomez rented a house to Burroughs for one year at a monthly rental of $400. After three months, Burroughs moved, claiming that he had never signed a written lease and was not, therefore, liable to Gomez. Gomez sued for the rent for the remaining nine months, during which the house remained unoccupied. How would the court rule? Why? • See also *Warner* v. *Frey*, 228 S.W.2d 729.

2. Shin Lee signed a one-year lease for an apartment in the Wilshire Arms. During the winter, ice and snow piled up over the front entrance to the building, and the janitor made no effort to remove it. Shin Lee slipped and fell on the ice, suffering serious injury to her back. She sued the landlord for her injuries. The landlord defended himself, saying that he had no responsibility to clear ice and snow from the premises. What will be the final outcome of this case? Explain. • See also *Kline* v. *Rider*, 73 N.E.2d 378.

3. Cleaver, a construction engineer, lived with his wife and one child in a mobile home, which he transported from one job to another throughout the United States. In one state his home was assessed by the state tax department, and he was billed for the state's real estate tax. Cleaver refused to pay the tax. Will he have to do so? Explain. • See also *Atlantic Safe Dep. Co.* v. *Atlantic City Laundry Co.*, 64 N.J. Eq. 140.

4. Vogel, a chemist, rented a house from Davis in a rural area. He carried on experiments in the development of a new rocket fuel that he planned to patent. Because of an ignition failure during an experiment, an explosion wrecked the house. Davis sued Vogel for the cost of rebuilding and refitting the house. In defense, Vogel claimed that a tenant was protected by law from the liability of rebuilding premises that are destroyed. What are Davis's rights in this case? Explain. • See also *Roberts* v. *Cottey*, 100 Mo. App. 500.

5. In a lease signed by Fowler, the following term was included: "The tenant agrees to inform the lessor by registered mail three months prior to the expiration of this lease if he intends to vacate the premises at the end of the lease period." Fowler had not read his lease and therefore never informed the owner that he planned to move at the end of the lease period. The landlord sued Fowler for another year's rent. Who is entitled to judgment, the landlord or Fowler? Why? • See also *Welcome* v. *Hess*, 90 Cal. 507.

6. O'Brian rented a house from the American Fruit Farms Company during his employment as a seasonal worker with the company. After two months, his employment with the company was terminated, and the American Fruit Farms Company requested him to move out of the house immediately. O'Brian did not comply with the request, and the company sought to have him removed by court order. What are O'Brian's rights in this matter? Explain. • See also *Levering Investment Co.* v. *Lewis*, 20 Mo. App. 679.

Legal Reasoning and Business Judgment

Analyze the legal aspects of these business problems. Suggest possible solutions.

1. A small percentage of the workers in your plant are seasonal employees, brought into the area at certain times of the year when production is at its peak. The workers usually bring their families and must make arrangements for renting houses and apartments nearby. As the duration of the work is uncertain, what advice regarding rentals should the company give these employees?

2. Your firm is contemplating the purchase of a 42-foot mobile home to be fitted out as a display room for the firm's products. The advertising department plans to send the trailer into all parts of the United States, Canada, and Mexico as a goodwill and advertising venture. What investigation should be made before the advertising department goes too far with its plans?

3. As a stopgap measure while awaiting the construction of a new building, your firm is considering the rental of a factory building not too far from the plant site. Extensive alterations will have to be made, and boilers and other expensive equipment will have to be installed in the building. What kind of lease should the firm request, and what provisions should be included regarding the alterations and equipment installed?

Chapter 38
Transfer of Property Through Wills

After years of study, hard work, and careful investment, nearly 70 percent of Americans die *intestate*—without making any provision for the distribution of their property. Untold millions of dollars in real and personal property are at this moment unclaimed in our courts because people neglected to make wills. Endless litigation and family argument often follow the death of a person who has not made a will. In some cases, an entire estate dwindles to nothing because of such litigation. Often the estate *escheats* to (becomes the property of) the state when property remains unclaimed for a number of years (specified by statute). By means of a document known as a *will*, a person may determine the distribution of his or her property after death.

WILL PREPARATION

A *will* is a legal document which takes effect upon the death of the will's maker, who is known as the *testator* (male) or *testatrix* (female).[1] After death, the will's maker is often called the *decedent*. It directs an *executor* (male) or *executrix* (female) as to the manner in which the decedent's property is to be distributed. A will may be changed or canceled at any time during the maker's life.

Personal property that is left by will is a *bequest*, or legacy; real property, a *devise*. Those who receive the property by testacy are referred to as *beneficiaries* or *heirs* (when related by blood or marriage).

Wills are distinguished from deeds in that a deed takes effect during the grantor's lifetime. A gift given during one's lifetime, in contemplation of death from a known cause, is a *gift in causa mortis* and is not to be confused with property received through a will. Gifts *in causa mortis* are conditional. The donor may reclaim the property if death does not come as expected or is caused by circumstances other than those feared.

> Hopkins was seriously ill following an abdominal operation. Realizing that death might be near, Hopkins signed over a savings account to Hill, giving Hill the

---

[1]In this chapter the masculine form of terms like *testator* is used for purposes of discussion. It refers to people of either sex.

savings book with necessary notations of assignment. Hopkins did die three
weeks later, not because of the surgery but because of pneumonia. Hopkins's
executor may declare the gift *in causa mortis* void and demand the return of
Hopkins's savings for benefit of the estate.

Testamentary Capacity

Anyone may make a will, but all persons do not have what is called ***testamentary
capacity***. Testamentary capacity relates to a person's age, mental ability to comprehend the meaning of what is written in the instrument, and intent, as expressed by the testator. Without capacity the instrument is void.

Persons of legal age and sound mind generally may make a valid will. There is
no real conformity among the states as to the age requirements. Statutes often
permit younger persons to make bequests of personal property, while restricting
them from devising any interest in real property. Sometimes females may write
valid wills at an earlier age than males. Physical incapacity at the time of drawing
an instrument will not invalidate a will if such physical debility has not had an
effect upon the testator's mental competence.

A person need not possess superior or even average intelligence as long as he
or she is capable of understanding (1) the nature and extent of the property he or
she owns, (2) the persons who would be the most natural recipients of his or her
estate, and (3) the disposition being made of the property. He or she must also (4)
have the intelligence and understanding to relate each of the foregoing with one
another, resulting in (5) the ability to come to an orderly understanding of how he
or she intends to leave the property.

 Salvido had very little formal education and understood only a smattering of
English. Despite these handicaps, he had been able to build a large estate during
the forty years he had lived in the United States. Salvido had an attorney prepare
a will which he signed after having its terms carefully explained. There is no
reason to question Salvido's mental capacity in probating this will.

Legal Restrictions   A will does not take precedence over the rights of persons to
whom the testator had obligations or in whose favor the law guarantees a right in
the estate. For instance, a widow may enforce her dower right even though her
husband left her little or nothing in the will. Creditors and those with other
contract rights may also enforce claims against the estate prior to the distribution
of the assets.

Undue Influence   A will may be attacked and held invalid if a probate court
finds that the testator made his or her will under circumstances of undue influence. When a person comes under the influence of another to the degree that
the testator is unable to express his or her real intentions in a will, the will may be
declared invalid. The court must distinguish between undue influence and the
kindnesses, attention, advice, guidance, and friendliness shown toward the
testator by the one named in the will.

Heid suffered a disabling illness, which confined her to the hospital for several weeks before her death. Heid's older sister, who had greatly influenced her life since childhood, persuaded her to draw up a new will, making the sister sole heir to Heid's estate. Circumstances surrounding the execution and signing of this will were investigated by the probate court. The will was declared void on the grounds that the sister had exerted undue influence on Heid because of the latter's physical condition and their close relationship.

TYPES OF WILLS

Three types of wills—*holographic*, *nuncupative*, and *formal*—are recognized by law. They are discussed here.

Holographic Wills

A *holographic will* is one written entirely in the handwriting of the testator. No formalities are followed; it is important only that the document be proved to be that of the testator and that the testator was of legal age and of sound mind when the will was made. Care must be taken to distinguish a holographic will from a letter in which a person expresses a desire to make a gift during his or her lifetime.

 Mrs. Garrett was left $17 million when her husband died. For the rest of her lifetime she lived frugally, and she left no formal will. An attorney located writings by Mrs. Garrett that some claimed were her holographic will. Failure to substantiate the claim, however, resulted in Mrs. Garrett's fortune being distributed to distant heirs.

Holographic wills are not recognized as valid in all states. The requisites of execution of this type of will vary from state to state; and unless the statutes are carefully followed, the instrument will not be declared valid.

Nuncupative Wills

An oral will made by a person in his or her last illness or by soldiers and sailors in actual combat is a *nuncupative will*. Nuncupative wills are not valid in all states, and usually they are restricted to the bequest of personal property only. The testator must make statements to indicate his or her bequests. The testator must also state that those hearing the statements are to be considered witnesses to the oral will. A nuncupative will is difficult to prove, is subject to deception, and is not desirable in the distribution of a testator's property.

Formal Wills

A *formal will* is a written document prepared according to statute and common law. It must be signed by the testator and witnessed. Formal wills are valid in all states. (See Fig. 38-1.)

P 1682—Will

JULIUS BLUMBERG, INC., LAW BLANK PUBLISHERS
80 EXCHANGE PL. AT BROADWAY, N. Y. C. 10004

𝕷𝖆𝖘𝖙 𝖂𝖎𝖑𝖑 𝖆𝖓𝖉 𝕿𝖊𝖘𝖙𝖆𝖒𝖊𝖓𝖙

I, William E. Paxton *of the*
Town *of* River Forest *in the County of* Cook
and State of Illinois *being of sound mind and memory, do make, publish and declare
this my last* **Will and Testament***, in manner following that is to say:*

First. *I direct that all of my debts and funeral expenses be paid as soon after my death as may
be practicable.*

Second, after my lawful debts are paid, I give to my wife Anne M. Paxton, all
my real property, to have and to hold as she sees fit, and in addition, Forty-five
Thousand Dollars ($45,000) in cash.
Third, to my son Patrick, Fifteen Thousand Dollars ($15,000) in cash.
Fourth, to the Hospital for the Blind, the balance of my estate remaining
after the above bequests have been distributed.

Lastly *I hereby appoint* Robert Anderson, 406 Franklin Street, River Forest,
Illinois

*executor of this, my last Will and Testament, with full power and authority to sell and convey, lease
or mortgage real estate, hereby revoking all former wills by me made.*

In Witness Whereof *I have hereunto subscribed my name the* fourth *day
of* February *in the year Ninteen Hundred and* --.

William E. Paxton [L. S.]

We, whose names are hereunto subscribed, **Do Certify** *that on* February 4, 19--

*the testator above named, subscribed his name to this instrument in our presence and in the presence
of each of us, and at the same time, in our presence and hearing, declared the same to be his last
Will and Testament*, and requested us, and each of us, to sign our names thereto as witnesses to the
execution thereof, which we hereby do in the presence of the testator and of each other, on the day of
the date of the said Will, and write opposite our names our respective place of residence.*

Myra Evans *.....residing at* 121 Lake Street, River Forest, Illinois
Andrew Youngman *.....residing at* 231 Chicago Avenue, River Forest, Illinois

Fig. 38-1.   A formal will

Written Instrument   A formal will *may be handwritten or typewritten.* The will
offered for probate must be the original copy, not a carbon. It must not be torn or
mutilated or show any signs of burning, as such conditions may be accepted as
evidence of the testator's intent to revoke the instrument.

Signature of the Testator   A will must be signed by the testator. If the document covers more than one page, the signature should be placed at the bottom of each page. It must be signed in the presence of the witnesses, and the usual signature should be used in anticipation of any later dispute as to the genuineness of the will or the signature. A testator who is not able to write may make his or her mark, attested to by at least two witnesses. If the testator's condition makes movement impossible, as in paralysis, another may sign for him or her. This must be done in the testator's presence and in the presence of the witnesses.

> Damian, a successful farmer, amassed much wealth during his working years. He had no formal education and could not read or write. His will was prepared by an attorney after his wishes in the matter had been fully discussed. The will was signed in the presence of witnesses, as shown in Fig. 38-2.

Witnesses   The number of witnesses varies according to local statutes. Usually two or three are required. Since the witnesses will be called upon to attest to the genuineness of the testator's signature, it is advisable that witnesses be young persons but not minors. The law usually states that *persons named as beneficiaries in a will may not be witnesses*. The failure to observe this provision may result in their being disinherited.

> Johnstone lived in a state whose laws required two witnesses to a will. She owned real property located in another state whose laws required three witnesses to a formal will. Following her own state law, Johnstone asked two young friends to witness the document. When Johnstone died, the will was accepted as sufficient for distribution of property in Johnstone's own state. The will was not acceptable for distribution of the real estate located in another state that required three witnesses.

Accuracy   Certain words often used in wills may have a legal interpretation that is different from their everyday meaning. Care should be taken to describe each bequest and devise in a manner that will satisfy the legal definition. For instance, a testator may use the word *heirs* when really meaning *children*. The difference in the meaning of the two words could result in much dispute and expensive litigation.

It is better to express gifts as fractional parts of an estate rather than as fixed amounts.

> Alberts left a will in which he distributed his estate in the following manner: "First, $25,000 to Community Charities; second, $15,000 to the Memorial Hospital; and the entire remaining estate to be divided equally among my three sons, Ralph, Robert, and James." When Alberts died and the estate was settled, only $25,000 was available for distribution after all Alberts' creditors were paid. The bequest to Community Charities took the remainder of Alberts' estate, leaving nothing for the hospital or his three sons. Had Alberts provided for the distribution of fractional shares rather than of fixed amounts, his wishes could have been carried out.

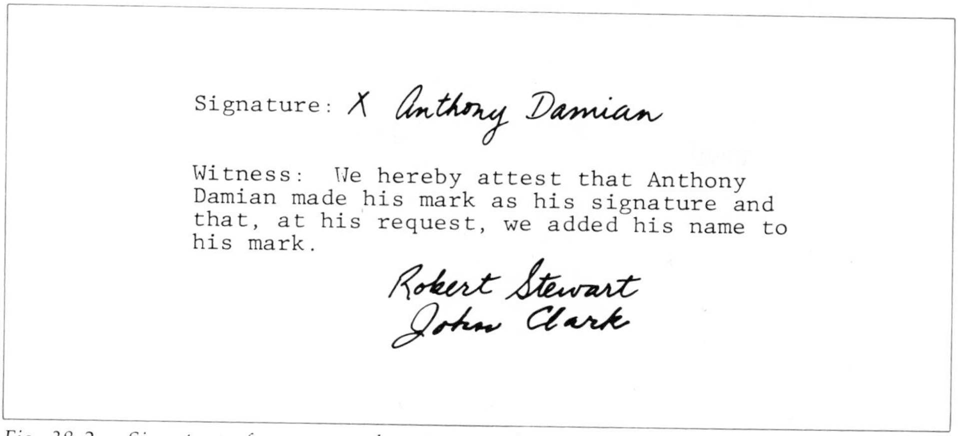

Signature: X *Anthony Damian*

Witness: We hereby attest that Anthony
Damian made his mark as his signature and
that, at his request, we added his name to
his mark.

Robert Stewart
John Clark

Fig. 38-2. Signature of a person who cannot write

Many states have passed legislation restricting the percentage of an estate that may be left to charities. This has been done to protect those who might have justifiably received a greater share if the testator had not been emotionally motivated by appeals for charitable bequests.

Omitting Names of Children From the Will Some states have passed laws to protect children whose names have been unintentionally left out of a will. By these laws, a forgotten child will receive the same share that he or she would have received had the parent died intestate.

These laws do not imply that a parent may not disinherit a child. A parent is not obliged to leave children anything at all. If the testator intends to disinherit a child, he or she should mention the child's name, leaving the child $1, or stating that the child is to receive nothing.

Subsequent Children State laws have generally protected children born after a will has been drawn, in the same way that forgotten children are protected. Exceptions to this rule would be cases in which the testator expressly excluded unborn children from any distribution of the estate.

Adopted Children Only children who have been *legally adopted* by the testator can share in the estate if not mentioned in the will. Children who have been taken into the family for one reason or another, but never legally adopted, are not protected by the provisions described in the previous two situations. This rule extends to children of a wife by previous marriage in cases where they have not been formally adopted by the second husband.

▶▶ The Hartleys took into their home three preschool children whose parents had been killed in an accident. The couple developed a strong love for one of the children, adopting her through proper legal proceedings. Only the adopted child would have any rights equal to those of the Hartleys' own children.

Alterations and Codicils Alterations, write-overs, erasures, and the like serve to invalidate an otherwise valid will. Alterations, additions, or changes may be made, however, but only through a *codicil*, or *supplement*. Adding a codicil requires the same formalities as the creation of the will itself. The codicil must be written, signed, and witnessed. The document should be incorporated into the will in such a way as to leave no doubt that it is a part of the will.

> Rabel's will provided that his entire estate would pass to his wife at the time of his death. Rabel later enjoyed unusual financial success and felt inclined to leave $100,000 toward a new church building under construction in his parish. Rabel's attorney prepared a codicil which, when signed and witnessed, was attached to the original will. The conditions contained in the codicil became an integral part of the will itself.

Revoking and Rewriting Wills   Because of changes in economic conditions, family responsibility, and many other reasons, testators often rewrite wills. Divorce, remarriage, birth of children, death of persons named as beneficiaries—all may lead to changes in wills. *Before the new will can be valid, the old one must be destroyed or revoked by a statement in the new will.*

> Clark's company prospered, and he became a very wealthy man. He felt that the will he had once prepared was outdated. His attorney prepared a new will, which Clark signed and witnessed, at the same time destroying the old will by burning it. The new will contained the customary phrase *my last will and testament, all others having been revoked.* By these acts Clark now replaced the older will with the new will.

ADMINISTRATION OF THE ESTATE

After the death of the testator, the rules controlling the management of the estate are statutory and vary from state to state. In all states, however, the estate is managed and finally disposed of under the supervision of a court. The procedure is known as **probate**. The court which supervises the procedure is usually called a *probate court*, but in some states it is known as a *surrogate court*, or an *orphan's court*. The system of administration under the Uniform Probate Code (UPC) is highly flexible.

Executor and Administrator

The first step after death of the testator is to determine whether or not the deceased left a will. The testator's personal attorney may have the will on file. Sometimes a careful search of the safe deposit box and personal papers of the deceased is necessary.

If a valid will exists, it names the executor or executrix (usually the spouse, a friend, or a trust company). If there is no will, the court will upon petition appoint an *administrator* (male) or *administratrix* (female) to take charge of the estate in accordance with statutes. The closest adult relative who is a resident of the state of the deceased is usually appointed.

> Worthy died, leaving a will in which DeMarco was named as executor. Worthy had also named Blevin to take DeMarco's place if the latter could not serve. DeMarco died before Worthy, and Blevin had too many other responsibilities to be able to serve. The probate court, therefore, appointed an administrator.

Bond Requirement To insure faithful performance, the executor or administrator is required to post a bond unless the deceased indicates that the executor need not post bond. Once approved or appointed by the court, the executor or administrator holds title to all the personal property of the deceased and accounts to the creditors and the beneficiaries.

Steps in Probate

A will must be proved before the court by those who witnessed the signing. The witnesses must also testify to the mental condition of the testator at the time the will was executed. In the event the witnesses are dead, proof of their handwriting is necessary. When satisfied that the will is proved, the court enters a formal decree admitting the will to probate.

By the admission of the will to probate or the issuance of *letters of administration*, the executor or administrator is authorized to proceed. He or she must file an inventory of the estate. A bank account is opened in the name of the estate, and the executor or administrator begins the process of collecting assets, paying outstanding debts and taxes, and disbursing the remaining assets in accordance with the will.

Assets

Securities and items of personal use are part of the estate of the deceased. The executor or administrator exercises the same powers in the handling of such property as the deceased exercised during his or her life. Insurance on the life of the deceased passes directly to the named beneficiary. Taxes are imposed by both the federal and state governments. It is the responsibility of the executor or administrator to pay these taxes. An income tax return must be filed on income received during the partial year preceding the death of the testator or intestate and also on income received during the administration of the estate.

Federal Estate Tax A tax is levied upon the total value of the deceased's estate by the federal government through the Internal Revenue Service. By 1980, $250,000 will be exempted from taxation. Also permitted as deductions are the debts and expenses to be paid out of the estate and expenses involved in the final settlement.

State Inheritance Tax The state imposes an inheritance tax upon the beneficiaries or heirs of a bequest or legacy and not upon the estate. The exemption and the tax rate are graduated according to the relationship of the recipients to the decedent. Thus, a member of the deceased's family pays less tax than a stranger.

LETTERS OF LAST INSTRUCTION

The testator often prepares an informal, nonlegal instrument known as a *letter of last instruction*. Such a letter gives much valuable information to the executor, such as the exact location of the will, burial instructions, location of safe deposit boxes and keys, names of insurance companies and insurance brokers, names of lodges and other organizations to which the testator belonged, and other information of value in carrying out the duties of the executor.

INTESTACY

Intestacy is a term given to the estate of one who dies without having prepared a valid will. Real property left by one without a will is distributed to blood relatives according to a chart prepared by each state. Personal property is kept separate and goes to the next of kin, another designation that varies with state laws. A surviving spouse may not be listed as an heir, the latter being someone related by blood. The surviving spouse's share is guaranteed under the wife's dower right and the husband's right of curtesy.

> Stevens died, leaving a large estate but no will. She was survived by her husband and three children. According to state law, the husband was awarded a curtesy right to all the real property of the wife during his lifetime. At death the real property would go to the surviving children. Stevens's personal property would be divided among the next of kin, as provided for under state law. No distribution would be made until all creditors' claims had been liquidated out of the estate.

Many states have made specific provisions in their decedent estate laws for the distribution of property when the intestate is survived only by husband or wife and children and parents, or any of them. Thus, the decedent estate law of one state provides that:

- ☐ If only the husband or the wife survives, the surviving spouse shall receive the entire estate.
- ☐ If the husband or the wife and children survive, the surviving spouse shall receive one-third of the estate, and the children shall receive two-thirds of the estate.
- ☐ If the husband or the wife and parents survive, the surviving spouse shall receive $5,000 and one-half the remainder of the estate and the parents shall each receive one-fourth of the remaining estate.

TRUSTS

A *trust agreement* is one in which title to either real or personal property or both is held by one party while another party is designated to receive the benefits accruing from the property *in trust*.

For many and diverse reasons, a trust agreement may be preferable to a formal will because it provides for the distribution of property in a more satisfactory manner. As a means of protecting an estate from the anticipated habits of those who may squander a hard-earned fortune, whether large or small; to assure a continued income to those who survive; to provide dividend or interest income for the education of younger children; or for any other purpose, the owner of property may wish to create a *trust estate*. It may also be to the advantage of the survivors in consideration of taxes that might be saved through the use of a trust.

The person, bank, attorney, or fiduciary organization to which title of the property is given is called the *trustee*. The person or persons for whom the trust is created are the *beneficiaries*, or the *cestui que trust*. There must be an intent, with exceptions, to have the trust terminated at some time in the foreseeable future. Otherwise the trust violates what is known as the *rule against perpetuities* and may be declared unenforceable. Most agreements of this kind are made for the protection of family members until they have reached the age of caution and maturity, at which time it is stated that the trust will go to them or will go on to others named in the agreement.

> Urie died, leaving four grown sons and daughters. His children had never demonstrated any real ambition and had depended heavily on prospects of receiving large legacies from the estate. Urie feared that his heirs would quickly spend their inheritances and have nothing to support them in the years ahead. He therefore provided for this possibility by assigning all assets to a trust arranged by an attorney. The assets would remain intact, safely invested, and a small income would be paid from the trust income to the children. Urie's purpose was realized in that the estate would be preserved and the surviving children would not squander their inheritance.

In a trust such as the one illustrated, provision must be made for final distribution of the trust assets when the purpose of the trust has been served. For example, Urie could have the trust property go to a church, college, or some other worthy nonprofit organization on the death of the last surviving child.

Obligations of the Trustee

The trustee is obligated by law to use reasonable care and prudence in the investment of funds allocated to the trust. If real property is held in trust, it is the trustee's obligation to supervise and care for the property. When economic and other reasons indicate the need to shift trust assets to safer areas of investment, it becomes the duty of the trustee to make such changes. If investments selected by the trustee fail, he or she is held liable unless a court rules that the action was taken with reasonable prudence and caution.

The trustee relationship is one of great and continuing responsibility. Appointment as a trustee should not be accepted by those without the knowledge and background that would afford prudent and good management. Banks, trust companies, and other kinds of fiduciary corporations offer professional services in the administration of trusts. They provide professional investment services and generally give maximum security and benefit for the fees charged.

ESTATE PROBLEMS

So complex are the laws related to estates that it has become necessary to place estate planning in the hands of those who have professional training and experience. Federal and state laws must be respected if the owner of real property, personal property, and investments wants to realize the maximum value for his or her survivors. Although laws are written to protect the rights of survivors, professional advice is needed in determining the best way to achieve the testator's objectives and intentions. Attorneys, investment counselors, professional insurance planners, and the like all provide expert guidance in these matters. It would be quite risky for an individual even to attempt to plan or arrange his or her own estate given the complex nature of the law in this area.

Questions for Review and Discussion

1. Discuss the advantages of establishing a trust for the administration of property after death.

2. Explain some of the advantages of preparing a will rather than accepting the risk of dying intestate.

3. How important are the letters of last instruction? Is a letter of last instruction a legal document requiring survivors to follow its commands?

4. Distinguish the difference between a will and a gift *in causa mortis*. When does a will become a legally enforceable document?

5. Name three types of wills and the outstanding characteristics of each.

6. Generally, to whom does the property of the deceased descend when there is no will?

7. Discuss procedures and requirements to be observed in signing and witnessing a will.

8. How does an administrator differ from an executor in duties to be performed?

9. Summarize the duties and obligations of a trustee. What type of person or agency is best fitted for this responsibility?

10. Discuss the steps required in the probate of a will.

Analyzing Cases

1. Hall prepared a holographic will naming Johnson as sole beneficiary to all of her real and personal property. Before putting the will away for safekeeping, Hall typed in the date. The will was found after her death and was presented for probate. Will the holographic will be accepted as valid? Explain. • See also *In re Billings,* 64 Cal. 427.

2. Kellum left a will designating Jarvis as recipient of a bank account and all of his real property. Many creditors presented claims when the will was offered for probate. Money owed for debts incurred over the past several months amounted to more than the balance of the bank account and the value of the real property. Jarvis claimed prior rights over the creditors as sole beneficiary

of the will. Will Jarvis succeed in this claim? Explain. • See also *Tinan* v. *Lee,* 65 S.D. 208.

3. A short time before his death, Holsinger decided to remove the name of a former friend from among those to benefit from his estate. Holsinger blanked out the name, inserting another name in its place. When the will was offered for probate, an interested heir asked that the will be declared unenforceable. What will be the decision of the probate court? Explain. • See also *Trotter* v. *Van Pelt,* 144 Fla. 517, 198 So. 215.

4. King agreed to take the responsibility of rearing the daughter of a friend whose untimely death made the child an orphan. The youngster was made to feel like a member of the family and grew up with King's own children. King died intestate. When the estate was settled, the friend's daughter sought to claim an equal interest in King's real property along with the other four children. Will she succeed in this claim? Explain.• See also *Scott* v. *Scott*, 238 Ind. 474, 105 N.E.2d 740.

5. Williams made a new will at age sixty. The name of a brother to whom half the estate had been left in the former will was removed, leaving him only a bequest of $1. The new will was valid in all respects, signed and witnessed. Williams placed it in a safety deposit box together with the earlier will. On Williams's death the brother ar-

gued that the first be admitted to probate rather than the one recently executed. Will the probate court agree with this petition? Explain.• See also *Ewell* v. *Sneed*, 191 S.W. 131.

6. Kogat was named executor of Lambert's will. Kogat lived on the Eastern Shore in Maryland. Lambert lived several hundred miles away in western Pennsylvania. Kogat considered the time, expense, and inconvenience that would be entailed in carrying out the duties of executor. May he reject the deceased's wishes and refuse to assume these duties? Explain. • See also *Adams* v. *Readnour*, 134 Ky. 230.

Legal Reasoning and Business Judgment

A meeting of company employees was called to discuss the importance of the older employees' preparing wills to cover future distribution of their property. An attorney was invited to be present to answer questions. The following questions came up during the meeting. Suggest possible solutions.

1. One employee stated that all his property was being held jointly by himself and his wife. The wife was the older of the two. They had no children. This employee saw no advantage in having a will, considering each one's right of survival in what they owned together. All their assets would total $75,000. Was the employee correct, or would it be best to have wills prepared by both husband and wife?

2. One of the employees explained that five years earlier, she and her husband had prepared a will stating that after they both died, their property would be divided equally among the three surviving children. Since that time, two of

the children had been very successful and had amassed sizable fortunes. The other child had married, had four children, and was employed, but he was struggling financially. The costs involved in raising a large family were substantial. The employee wondered whether the will might be changed to give the greater part of the estate to the child who needed financial assistance. How could this be done?

3. A third employee had a difficult problem. He had been approached by a nonprofit charitable organization that suggested he leave his entire estate to their group. The organization promised to look after his widow for the rest of her life at a rest home to which she would be admitted. Pictures and brochures of the rest home showed a beautiful and comfortable retirement facility. The employee feared that if such a will were written, and it was later discovered that the beneficiaries were frauds, his wife would receive nothing. What advice would the attorney give?

Law Dictionary

A

Abandonment   In the law of property, the voluntary relinquishment of personal or real property, with the intention of terminating ownership.

Abstract of title   A document, issued by one who has searched title to real property, describing the grantor's title and all existing encumbrances and including a warranty to the buyer against flaws in the title.

Acceleration   The hastening or advancement in the time for payment of a debt because of breach of some condition, such as failure to pay interest when due.

Acceptance   The act or promise of an offeree indicating compliance with terms and conditions of an offer; a drawee's act acknowledging the obligation cited in a draft.

Accession   The right to all which one's own property produces, whether that property be movable or immovable, and the right to that which is united to it either naturally or artificially, such as a button that is sewed on a person's coat.

Accommodation party   A person who signs an instrument as a maker, acceptor, or endorser without receiving value therefore, and for the purpose of lending his or her name to some other person as a means of guaranteeing payment on the due date.

Accord and satisfaction   An agreement between two or more persons, one of whom has a right of action against the other, that the latter should do or give, and the former accept, something in satisfaction that is less than what might be legally enforced.

Acknowledgment   A statement made by a person before an authorized public officer, such as a notary public, that the person making the statement has signed a certain legal paper.

Act of God   An act occasioned exclusively by violence of nature without the interference of any human agency.

Adjective law   The rules of procedure used by and in courts for enforcing the duties and maintaining the rights defined by the substantive law. Matters of evidence, procedure, and appeals are involved. Also called *remedial law*.

Administrative agency   An agency of the sovereign power charged with administering particular legislation.

Administrative law   The branch of public law that deals with the various governmental agencies, prescribing their procedures.

Administrator   A party chosen to carry out the terms of a will in cases where an executor was not appointed, or where one who was appointed refused or did not have the capacity to carry out the obligations of the appointment.

Adverse possession   Possession not granted by the owner but not legally objected to by the owner over a lengthy period of time. Usually associated with easements derived in real property; may also apply to personal property.

Affirmance   An act or expression of a previously incompetent party, by which a contract is confirmed after the party acquires qualifications of capacity to contract. Affirmance makes an otherwise voidable agreement valid and enforceable.

Affirmative action program   A program designed actively to promote the position of minority workers and women with regard to hiring and advancement.

After sight   A term used in a bill payable after legal presentment for acceptance. Often called *legal sight*.

Agency   The relationship existing between two persons, one identified as the principal and the other as the agent, by virtue of which the agent may make contracts with third persons on behalf of the principal.

Agency by estoppel The relationship that exists when a principal, by negligence in supervising an agent's affairs, allows the agent to exercise powers that were not granted, thus justifying others in believing the agent possesses the requisite authority.

Agent A person authorized to act for another person.

Agreement A meeting of the minds between two parties, necessary to a contract obligation.

Air rights The exclusive right to space above land to a height over which the owner has reasonable control.

Alienation clause In an insurance policy, a restriction against the assignment of the policy to another party by the insured.

Alteration Any unauthorized change by a party to a written document which changes the meaning or language of the document and affects the rights of any other person who has an interest in the instrument.

Annual percentage rate The relative annual cost of the credit that is extended in a credit transaction.

Anticipatory breach of contract The express or implied communication of intent to abandon a contract obligation prior to the date that performance would commence.

Apparent authority Power which has not been actually granted but which a principal knowingly permits an agent to exercise or which the principal presents the agent as possessing.

Appeal The proceeding by which a case is brought from an inferior court to a higher court for reexamination, review, reversal, or modification.

Appellant A party seeking appellate review of a lower court decision.

Appellate court A court having jurisdiction of appeal and review.

Appellee A party responding to an appeal; a respondent.

Apportionment The division, partition, or distribution of subject matter into proportionate parts.

Arbitration Submission of a dispute to an extrajudicial authority for resolution.

Arson The malicious burning of real property.

Articles of incorporation Articles of association, subscribed by the incorporators of a corporation, which create the corporate union between them and which specify the form of organization, amount of capital, kind of business to be pursued, location of the company, etc.

Articles of partnership An agreement by which the parties enter into a copartnership upon the terms and conditions stipulated in the agreement.

As is An expression in a sales agreement which implies that the buyer accepts delivery of goods that may or may not be defective and which includes the express condition that the buyer must trust such goods to his or her own examination.

Assault An attempt to do harm to another by physical violence; a threat to do physical harm to another person.

Assignee A person to whom an assignment has been made. Also called *assign*.

Assignment A transfer to another person of the whole of any property, real or personal, or of a contract right.

Assumption of risk A common-law doctrine that an employee accepts the chances of injury when working in a hazardous occupation, without obligation to the employer.

Attorney-at-law An advocate, counsel, or official agent employed in preparing, managing, and trying cases in court.

Attorney-in-fact An agent authorized by another, through a written power of attorney, to act in his or her place for the transaction of business in general, not of a legal character. See also *Power of attorney*.

Auction   A public sale of land or goods at public outcry and to the highest bidder.

B

Bailee   A person into whose possession personal property is delivered; a person who by bill of lading or some other document acknowledges possession of goods and contracts to deliver them.

Bailment   Possession of the personal property of another without ownership and for a special purpose, under the express or implied contract that it be redelivered to the bailor.

Bailor   One who delivers personal property into the possession of another.

Balloon payment   Any installment payment that is more than twice the amount of a regularly scheduled payment.

Bank draft   A check drawn by one bank on another bank and payable to a third party, the payee.

Bankrupt   A person who by formal decree of a court has been declared subject to be proceeded against under bankruptcy laws, or to receive the benefit of such laws.

Bankruptcy law   A law for benefit and relief of creditors and their debtors in cases in which the latter are unable or unwilling to pay their debts.

Bargain and sale deed   An instrument similar to a quitclaim deed but including information about the consideration given in exchange for the property transferred. Such a deed contains no warranties to the grantee.

Barren promise   A promise to do or not do that which has already been made enforceable either by previous agreement or by law. Not valid as consideration.

Battery   The unlawful use of force against another.

Bearer   The person in possession of an instrument, document of title, or security payable to bearer or endorsed in blank.

Bequest   A gift by will of personal property; a legacy.

Beneficiary   A party named in an insurance policy to receive benefits paid by the insurer in event of a claim.

Bilateral contract   A contract in which two parties are bound to fulfill obligations reciprocally toward each other, as where one is bound to deliver the thing sold and the other to pay the price of it. See also *Unilateral contract*.

Bill of lading   A document evidencing the receipt of goods for shipment and issued by a person engaged in the business of transporting or forwarding goods.

Binder   A verbal or written memorandum of an agreement for insurance, intended to give temporary protection pending investigation of the risk and issuance of a formal policy.

Blank indorsement   An indorsement in which the holder or payee does no more than sign his or her name on the instrument.

Blue laws   Nineteenth-century statutes, still in force in many states, regulating and prohibiting the creation of business agreements and the operation of businesses on Sunday.

Blue-sky laws   Popular name for acts providing for the regulation and supervision of investment securities.

Board of directors   The body responsible for setting policies or directing the business of a corporation.

Breach   A break, infraction, or violation, as of a contract.

Bribery   The offering, giving, receiving, or soliciting of something of value with the purpose of influencing the action of another person in an official position or in the discharge of legal or public duty.

Bucket-shop transaction   A stock or commodity sale in which there is no intent of delivering a stock certificate or the commodity. Classed as a wagering contract.

Burglary   By common law, breaking and entering the dwelling of another, at night and with intent to commit a felony therein, whether or not it is actually committed. By statute today, in most states, burglary includes breaking and entering during the day, and the crime is not confined to private dwellings.

Business trust   A form of organization in which the owners of the property to be used in the business transfer the title of the property to trustees together with full power to operate the business.

Buyer   A person who contracts to take little to goods or rights in consideration for an agreed price.

By-bidding   In a sale by auction, the practice of making fictitious bids for property under secret arrangement with the owner or auctioneer for the purpose of misleading and stimulating other persons who are bidding in good faith.

Bylaws   The rules adopted by the members of the board of directors of a corporation. These rules affect only the rights and duties of the members of the corporation.

C

Cancellation   Abandonment of a contract, other than a breach.

Capital   The net assets of a sole proprietorship, partnership, or corporation, including not only the original investment but also all gains and profits realized from the conduct of the business.

Capital investment   Capital stock, surplus, and undivided profits.

Capital stock   Amount fixed by charter to be subscribed and paid in or secured to be paid in by shareholders; amount of stock that corporation may issue; amount subscribed, contributed, or secured to be paid in by shareholders.

Carrier   A transporter of passengers or freight.

Cashier's check   A bill of exchange drawn by the cashier of a bank, for the bank, upon the bank for delivery or issue to a payee or holder.

Causa mortis ['kau-ˌzä 'mȯrd-ˈəs]   Made in contemplation of approaching death from a known or feared cause.

Cause of action   Invasion of a person's legal rights either by breach of contract or by breach of a legal duty toward the person or his or her property. Grounds for a lawsuit.

Caveat emptor ['ka-vē-ˌat 'em(p)-tər]   "Let the buyer beware"; a rule that a purchaser is responsible for examining, judging, and testing a product before contracting to buy.

Caveat venditor ['ka-vē-ˌat 'ven-di-tər]   "Let the seller beware"; a rule casting the responsibility for defects or deficiencies upon the seller of goods.

Cease and desist order   A decree by an administrative agency or court directing a party to refrain from committing a specified act.

Certificate of deposit   Written acknowledgment by a bank or banker of a deposit, with promise to pay to the depositor, to order, or to some other person the order of the depositor.

Certificate of incorporation   The instrument by which a private corporation is formed, under general statutes. The instrument is executed by persons as incorporators and is filled in a designated public office as evidence of corporate existence.

Certificate of stock   A certificate issued by a corporation which designates a named person as the owner of a specified number of shares of stock.

Certified check   A check that has been "accepted" by the bank on which it was drawn and has been marked, or certified, thus guaranteeing payment to the holder.

Chattel An article of personal property; a thing personal and movable. Also called *chose in being*.

Chattel mortgage An instrument used prior to the Uniform Commercial Code which was executed by a debtor (called the *mortgagor*) and which transferred an interest in personal properties to a creditor (called the *mortgagee*), for the purpose of security for a debt.

Civil law The Roman law; the body of law dealing with the rights and duties of private citizens among one another, as distinguished from criminal law.

Civil rights acts Statutes prohibiting the denial of equal rights in employment and other matters on the basis of race, religion, sex, or national origin.

Close corporation A corporation in which the directors and officers have the power to fill vacancies from among their own number, without allowing the general body of shareholders any choice or vote in their election; a corporation in which power of voting is held through manipulation under fixed and perpetual proxies.

Closed shop A place of employment in which a worker must be a member of the union as a condition of employment.

Closed shop contract A contract requiring an employer to hire only union members and to discharge nonunion members, and requiring that employees, as a condition of employment, remain union members.

Codicil An addition to or change in an existing will, with the same requisites as in creation of a formal will.

Codification Process of collecting and arranging the laws of a country or state into a code.

Collateral Property subject to a security interest, including accounts, contract rights, and chattel papers which have been sold.

Collective bargaining A good-faith meeting between representatives of employees and employer for purposes of discussing the terms and conditions of employment.

Commerce Trade, traffic, buying and selling, transportation, transmission, or communication within the states or between a state and any place outside itself.

Commerce Clause Article I, Section 8, Clause 3 of the Constitution of the United States, granting Congress the authority to regulate commerce with foreign nations and among the states.

Commercial law The body of substantive law applicable to the rights, dealings, and relations of persons engaged in commerce, trade, or mercantile pursuits.

Commingle To put together in one mass, as property or money. See also *Confusion of goods*.

Common carrier A transportation company that offers its facilities to the general public for compensation and without discrimination.

Common law The great body of unwritten law, founded upon general custom, usage, or common consent and upon natural justice or reason.

Common stock Stock which has no right or priority over any other stock of the corporation with respect to dividends or distribution of assets upon dissolution.

Communication The oral, written, or implied response by one party to another, in an offer, acceptance, rejection, or revocation; the act of transmitting, imparting, or disclosing one's intentions or some information to another.

Community property A statutory right giving each spouse a one-half title right in the personal and real property of the other. Applicable only to property acquired after marriage.

Company An association of persons, for business or other purposes, which may or may not be incorporated.

Competent Duly qualified; having adequate mental competence or authority; possessing the natural or legal qualifications required in a given situation; legally fit.

Complaint The first paper a plaintiff files to initiate a lawsuit, stating who the parties are, describing the nature of the charge, and requesting relief.

Concealment Withholding known material facts that would affect the decision of a party in making a purchase or entering into a contract.

Concentration The presence of a larger number of employees from a particular group in a specific job category or department of an organization than would reasonably be expected on the basis of the composition of the local work force; the monopolizing, dominating, or gaining control of a resource, product, or market.

Conciliation Settling a case by resolution of charges without a trial.

Condition precedent In a sale, a condition that must be fulfilled before the title may be passed to the buyer.

Condition subsequent In a sale, a condition arising after title has passed, affecting the rights of seller and buyer as agreed to in a sales contract.

Conditional indorsement An indorsement by which the indorser annexes a condition which must be fulfilled before the indorsee obtains title to the instrument.

Conditional sale A sale in which the transfer of title is made to depend on the fulfillment of a condition, usually the payment of the price.

Condominium A freehold estate of inheritance in an apartment or office suite, with a deed of co-ownership to areas of common use and convenience in the building housing the apartment or office suite.

Confession of judgment The act of a debtor in permitting judgment to be entered against him or her by a creditor, for a specific sum, by a written statement, without legal proceedings of any kind. Usually a cognovit note. It is illegal in some states.

Conflict of laws A body of law that determines which state's law applies when two or more states are involved in a given case.

Confusion of goods The blending or intermingling of property belonging to different owners, making it impossible to determine what each one owns. See also *Commingle*.

Consent decree A means of settling court or administrative agency cases by agreement of the parties, having the binding effect of a judicial decree.

Consideration The inducement to a contract; the cause, motive, or impelling influence which induces a contracting party to enter into a contract.

Consolidation of corporations A combining of two or more corporations in which the corporate existence of each one ceases and a new corporation is created.

Constitution The Constitution of the United States contains the rules of organization of the United States and enumerates the powers and duties of the federal government thereby created. The constitutions of the several states prescribe the organization of each of the states and in general enumerate those powers that are not specifically reserved for the federal government.

Constitutional law A law which is consonant to and agrees with the constitution; a law which is not in violation of any provision of the constitution of the particular state. The fundamental organic law of a state or nation.

Constructive delivery Symbolic delivery of the subject matter of a sale by the delivery of something which is representative of it, which renders access to it possible, or which is evidence of the purchaser's title to it, as the key to a warehouse or a bill of lading of goods on shipboard.

Consumer Credit Protection Act An act of Congress regulating the disclosure of credit terms by a creditor to one borrowing money or making a purchase on credit.

Consumer Product Safety Commission An independent administrative agency set up by

Congress in the Consumer Product Safety Act to carry out the terms of that act.

Contract   An agreement between two competent parties binding them to legally enforceable obligations. The total obligation which results from the agreement of two or more parties as affected by the Uniform Commercial Code and any other applicable rules of law.

Contract of sale   An agreement about goods in existence, whereby both title and right of possession are transferred from seller to buyer at the time of the sale.

Contract to sell   A sales agreement in which, for any reason, title to goods does not pass at the time of the sale.

Contributory negligence   The failure of a plaintiff to have used reasonable care, which will bar the plaintiff from recovering from the defendant.

Conversion   Unlawful assumption and exercise of ownership over property belonging to another.

Cooling-off period   A procedure designed to avoid strikes by requiring a period of delay before the strike may begin, during which negotiations for a settlement must continue; a three-day period under the Truth-in-Lending Law and the Uniform Commercial Code, during which time a promissor may rescind certain agreements that were previously made.

Cooperative   A group of two or more persons or enterprises that act through a common agent with respect to a common objective, as buying or selling.

Cooperative apartment   In real property, a dwelling unit with a proprietary lease giving the tenant the rights of ownership and use. Not a freehold estate of inheritance as in condominiums.

Copyright   Exclusive right of ownership of literary, musical, or artistic creations, granted by the government for a limited period of time, with right of renewal.

Corporate bond   A written promise by a corporation under seal to pay a fixed sum of money at some future time named, with stated interest payable at some fixed time or intervals in return for money received by the corporation.

Corporate franchise   The right or privilege granted by a state or government to the persons forming an aggregate private corporation, and their successors, to exist and do business and to exercise the rights and powers incidental to that form of organization or implied in the grant.

Corporation   A legal entity created by statute and vested with powers and capacity to contract, own, control, and convey property and to transact business within the limits of the powers granted.

Counterclaim   Any claim filed by the defendant in a lawsuit against the plaintiff in the same suit which is permissible under the court's rules of practice.

Countermand   A change or revocation of orders, authority, or instructions previously issued, either express or implied.

Course of employment   In reference to compensation for injuries within the purview of Workers' Compensation Acts, the time, place, and circumstances under which an accident takes place.

Court of appeals   An appellate tribunal, in some states the court of last resort and in others the supreme court of appeals; one of eleven judicial circuit United States Courts of Appeals. In the federal judicial system, the court of last resort is the U.S. Supreme Court.

Court of Claims   A court of the United States with jurisdiction over claims against the United States arising out of any contracts with the government.

Court of Customs and Patent Appeals   A court of the United States with appellate jurisdiction in patent and trademark cases.

Court of equity   A court in which rules of equity, rather than rules of law, are supplied, giving relief in situations where money damages are not adequate; a tribunal empowered to exercise equitable jurisdiction by issuing injunctions and demanding performance or by barring obnoxious performance.

Court of law A court in which the rules of common law, statute law, and the law extracted from decided cases apply in court proceedings.

Credit The right granted by a creditor to a customer to defer payment of debt, to incur debt and defer its payment, or to purchase property or services and defer payment therefor.

Creditor A person who in the ordinary course of business regularly extends or arranges for the extension of credit.

Crime A wrong against society which has elements of evil that affect the public as a whole and not merely the person whose property or person has been invaded.

Criminal law The body of law dealing with wrongs against the state as representative of the community at large, to be distinguished from civil law. See also *Civil law.*

Cumulative dividend A preferred dividend, which if not earned or paid pursuant to agreement, must be paid at some subsequent date.

Cumulative voting A system of voting for directors in which each shareholder has as many votes as the number of voting shares owned multiplied by the number of directors to be elected.

D

De facto corporation [(')dē 'fak-,tō] A corporation existing under color of law and in pursuance of an effort made in good faith to organize a corporation under the statute; an association of persons claiming to be a legally incorporated company and exercising the powers and functions of a corporation, but without actual lawful authority to do so.

De jure corporation [(')dē 'jŭ-rē] A corporation existing by reason of full compliance by incorporators with requirements of an existing law permitting organization of such a corporation.

Deceit Conduct in a business transaction in which one person, through fraudulent representations, misleads another who has a right to rely on such representatives as the truth. A tort similar to fraud in contract law.

Decree An order of a court of equity determining some right or adjudicating some matter affecting the case; an order or judgment of the court, corresponding to the judgment of a court of law.

Deed (Noun) A written instrument in a special form signed, sealed, and delivered, that is used to pass legal title of real property from one person to another; a conveyance.

Deed (Verb) To transfer ownership of real property.

Deed in co-ownership A deed to a condominium, giving the owner an undivided interest, with others, in the common areas of a condominium project.

Defamation Injury of the name or reputation of another person by slander or libel.

Default Omission or neglect of duty; failure to meet a legal obligation.

Defendant A person sued in a court of law; a person who answers the plaintiff's complaint in civil actions; a respondent.

Del credere **agency** [(')del, 'kra-də-rē] An agent, factor, or broker who undertakes to guarantee to a principal the payment of a debt due from a buyer of goods.

Delivery Voluntary transfer of possession of instruments, documents of title, chattel papers, securities, or personal property.

Demand note A note which states that it is payable on demand, on presentation, or at sight, and in which no specific time for payment is expressed.

Disaffirmance An act or expression of one without capacity to contract, indicating the intention of disavowing any obligation under a voidable agreement.

Discharge A release from legal obligation.

Disclaimer The disavowal, denial, or renunciation of an interest, right, property, or power vested in a person.

Disclosure A revelation; the imparting of information, knowledge, or facts that were previously hidden, withheld, or kept secret from parties having an interest.

Discount A drawback or deduction made upon an advance or loan of money, upon negotiable paper payable at a future date.

Discovery procedure Disclosure by defendant or plaintiff of facts, titles, documents, or other things which are in their knowledge or possession and which are necessary to either party in a pending cause or action. Used in pretrial motions and procedures.

Discrimination Treating persons unequally because of their race, sex, color, national origin, or religion.

Dishonor To refuse to accept or pay a negotiable instrument when it is presented.

Dissolution Termination of a corporation at the expiration of its charter, by proper statutory authority, by consolidation, or by action of the shareholders.

District courts The trial courts in the federal court system which have original jurisdiction over civil and criminal cases at the federal level.

Divestiture An antitrust remedy which forces a company to rid itself of assets acquired through illegal mergers or monopolistic practices.

Dividend A shareholder's share in the profits of a corporation, payable in cash, scrip, property, or stock.

Divisible contract A contract containing two or more separate and distinct obligations, each

of which could stand alone without weakening or interfering with the other obligations.

Doing business in the state Transaction within the state of some substantial part of a person's ordinary business, which must be continuous and which creates some form of legal obligation.

Domestic bill of exchange A bill of exchange drawn on a person residing in the same state as the drawer; also, a bill of exchange dated at a place in the state and drawn on a person living within the state.

Domestic corporation A corporation created by or organized under the laws of a state.

Domicile The place where a person or business has a true, fixed, and permanent home and principal establishment.

Dominant tenement Real property in whose favor there exists an easement in another property.

Dormant partner An actual partner who is silent, secret, and passive in the conduct of the business of the firm.

Dower By common law, the vested right of the wife to a one-third lifetime interest in the real property owned by her spouse.

Draft A written order drawn upon one person by another, ordering payment of money to a designated third party.

Drawee A party named in a draft on whom demand for payment is to be made.

Drawer A party who creates a draft, check, or trade acceptance.

Duress Conduct that deprives a victim of free will at the time of entering into or discharging a legal obligation. The use or the threat of force is involved.

E

Earnest money Money given to an offeror by an offeree, in return for the offeror's promise to keep an offer open for a stated or reasonable length of time.

Easement   In equity and in law, a special right to use real property owned by another person.

Emancipated   Set free; said of a minor who has been given parental authority to act on his or her own before reaching majority, when it is proved that the relationship with the parents has been severed without intention of renewal.

Embezzlement   Fraudulent appropriation, for personal use or benefit, of property or money entrusted to a clerk, agent, trustee, public officer, or other person.

Eminent domain   The right of federal, state, and local governments, or other public bodies, to take private lands, with compensation to their owners, for public use.

Enjoin   To require performance of or abstention from some act through issuance of an injunction.

Equity   A body of law which seeks to adjust conflicting rights on the basis of fairness and which may require or prohibit specific acts where monetary damages will not afford complete relief.

Equity of redemption   The right of a mortgagor of an estate to redeem the estate after it has been forfeited at law by a breach of the condition of the mortgage, upon paying the amount of debt, interest, and cost.

Escheat   The right of the state to title to property when no legal owner may be found. Usually allowed after the passing of a period of years set by law.

Escrow   A deed, bond, or deposit which one party places in the keeping of a second party who is obligated to deliver it to a third party upon fulfillment of some condition.

Espionage   The practice of spying; the secret observation of words and conduct.

Estate   All the property of a living, deceased, bankrupt, or insane person.

Estate in remainder   An estate which cannot take effect and be enjoyed until after the death of the holder of a life estate.

Estate of inheritance   An estate which may descend to heirs; an estate limited absolutely to a person and his or her heirs and assigns forever, without limitation or condition. Also called an *estate in fee simple*.

Estoppel   A legal bar to alleging or denying a fact because of one's own previous actions or words to the contrary, or because of one's silence which induced another person to believe something which was not true.

Excise tax   A tax imposed by a legislature which is a fixed, absolute, and direct charge laid on merchandise, products, or commodities without regard to an individual's income or assets.

Execution   A remedy in the form of a writ for the enforcement of a judgment.

Executor   A person who by authority of a will has the power to administer the estate upon the death of the testator and to dispose of it according to the intention of the deceased; called *executrix* if a female.

Express authority   Power delegated to an agent by oral or written words which specifically allows the agent to do a delegable act.

Express warranty   A guarantee, either oral or written, made to a buyer of goods by the seller.

Extension   An allowance of additional time for the payment of debts; a renewal of commercial paper.

F

Face value   The nominal or par value of an instrument as expressed on its face.

Factor   An agent for the sale of merchandise who may hold possession of the goods and is authorized to sell and to receive payment for the goods.

Fair Credit Reporting Act Federal legislation regulating the operation of and information available from retail credit reporting agencies and bureaus.

Fair Labor Standards Act A statute designed to prevent excessive hours of work, low pay, the employment of young children, and other unsound practices.

False imprisonment Restricting the freedom of movement of a person other than one lawfully detained.

False pretenses Designed misrepresentation of existing fact or condition which enables a person to obtain another's money or goods.

Featherbedding In labor relations, demand for the payment of wages for a particular service not actually rendered.

Federal Real Estate Settlement Procedures Act A federal law that requires mortgage lenders to disclose most fees and settlement costs related to the placing of a mortgage on real property.

Federal Register The official publication containing executive orders and rules and regulations of all federal departments and agencies.

Federal Securities Act A statute designed to protect the public from fraudulent securities.

Federal Securities Exchange Act A statute enacted by Congress in 1934 to control and regulate securities transactions in securities exchanges and over-the-counter markets.

Federal Trade Commission A federal authority with powers to regulate advertising and trade practices between businesses and consumers. Created to watchdog deceptive advertising and sales practices.

Fellow servant rule A common-law doctrine stating that an employer who has provided safe and suitable tools, machinery, and appliances is not to be held accountable for an injury to an employee resulting from the carelessness of other employees.

Felony A crime of a graver or more atrocious nature than those designated as misdemeanors; a crime punishable by imprisonment or death rather than by fine.

Fiduciary relation An informal relation which exists when one partner or person trusts and relies upon another.

Finance charge The sum of all charges payable directly or indirectly by the customer and imposed directly or indirectly by the creditor.

Financial statement A formal statement to corporation shareholders showing in reasonable detail its assets, liabilities, and the results of its operation.

Flood insurance Insurance available through application to the office of the Secretary of Housing and Urban Development. Flood risks to real and personal property are covered in states operating approved land-control programs.

Foreclosure The right given a mortgagee to take and sell the property of a mortgagor who has defaulted in payments on a secured note or bond.

Foreign corporation A corporation created by or under the laws of another state, government, or country.

Forgery The false writing or alteration of an instrument with the fraudulent intent of deceiving and injuring another.

Franchise An arrangement in which the owner of a trademark, trade name, or copyright licenses others to use the device in purveying goods or services. Also a special right given public service corporations to operate free of competition.

Franchise tax A tax on the right and privilege of carrying on the business of a corporation.

Fraud False statements or concealment of factual information made with the intention of inducing another person to rely upon the false information.

Freedom of Information Act A statute passed by Congress to permit individuals to inspect records maintained on them by an administrative or executive agency or a cabinet department.

Freehold   An estate in land or other real property, of uncertain duration.

Friendly fire   A fire created for some useful purpose and under the control of the person who started it.

Full covenant and warranty deed   A deed in which the seller conveys property to a buyer, while giving special warranties, known as covenants.

Fully insured   Under social security, the status of a person who made contributory payments for a required period, thereby giving the person full coverage under the social security regulations.

Fungible goods   Movable goods which may be estimated, sold, or replaced according to weight, measure, and number.

G

Garnishment   A writ from a court ordering the employer of a person owing money to a judgment creditor to pay it out of the debtor's salary or wages for the benefit of such a creditor.

General agent   A person who is authorized by a principal to execute all deeds, sign all contracts, or purchase all goods required in a particular trade, business, or employment.

General partner   A partner who is active in the management of the business and who shares in its gains and losses. Also called a *real partner*.

Good faith   An honest intention to abstain from taking any unfair advantage of another.

Gratuitous agent   An agent working without compensation.

Gratuitous bailment   A bailment for the sole benefit of either the bailor or the bailee, in which the other party receives no considerations for benefits bestowed.

Grievance   An injury, injustice, or wrong which gives ground for complaint because it is unjust and oppressive.

Guaranty   A promise to answer for the debts, defaults, or wrongdoings of another person. Must be in writing to be enforceable.

H

Holder   A person who is in possession of a document of title or an instrument or investment security that is either blank or is drawn, issued, or indorsed to the holder, to the holder's order, or to bearer.

Holder in due course   A person who has acquired possession of a negotiable instrument through proper negotiation for value, in good faith, and without notice of any defense to it, i.e., without notice of anything irregular about the instrument.

Holographic will   An informal will written entirely in the handwriting of the testator.

Homeowner's policy   A single insurance policy covering the majority of known risks associated with the ownership and operation of a home.

Homestead estate   A statutory life estate in the realty of the deceased spouse guaranteed to the widow or to the surviving children during their minority.

Homicide   The killing of any human with or without intent. Homicide in the first degree requires malice aforethought (intent); lesser degrees of homicide do not all require malice aforethought.

Hostile fire   A destructive fire not under the control of the insured or anyone else.

I

Illegal   Contrary to common law, statutes, constitutions, and public policy.

Illegal consideration An act which if done, or a promise which if enforced, would be prejudicial to the public interest or would disregard the law.

Implied authority Actual authority circumstantially proved; that which the principal intends an agent to possess and which is inferred from the principal's conduct.

Implied contract A contract inferred by the law as a matter of reason and justice from the parties' acts or conduct, making it a reasonable assumption that a contract existed between them by tacit understanding.

Implied warranties The seller's warranties of title and quality, imposed by law rather than by agreement between seller and buyer.

Income tax A tax on a party's yearly income and profits arising from property, professions, trades, offices, or employment.

Incontestibility clause In a life insurance policy, a condition that bars the insurer's right to contest the validity of a policy after it has been in force for two years.

Indemnify To save from harm; to compensate another person for losses incurred.

Independent contractor A person who, exercising an independent employment, contracts to do a piece of work according to his or her own methods and without being subject to the control of an employer except with respect to the result of the work done.

Indorsee A person to whom a bill of exchange, promissory note, etc., is negotiated or assigned by indorsement.

Indorsement Writing one's name upon a paper for the purpose of transferring title.

Indorser A person who writes his or her name on the instrument to transfer title.

Infant Synonymous in contract law with *minor*. See *Minor*.

Inheritance Property received from a deceased person either by terms of a will or through state intestacy laws.

Injunction A court order or decree, often issued by a court of equity, directing a party to perform or to refrain from performing some act.

In pari delicto [ən 'pä-rē də-'lik-(,)tō] Equally at fault in the creation and operation of an illegal agreement; used in describing both parties to the illegal contract.

Insolvency In bankruptcy, the situation in which one's liabilities exceed all known assets.

Instrument A negotiable paper, a security, or any other writing which evidences a right to the payment of money to be transferred by delivery with necessary indorsement or assignment.

Insurable interest Evidence that shows an insured person would lose some financial benefit through the death of another, through destruction of property, or through some other insured risk.

Insurance A contract whereby, for consideration known as a *premium*, one party undertakes to compensate another for losses resulting from risks or perils specified in the contract.

Insured A person whose risks are covered by an insurance policy.

Insurer A party that issues an insurance policy protecting the insured against specified risks.

Intangible property Property consisting of rights rather than goods and chattels. Evidenced by documents in some cases.

Intent A state of mind that exists prior to or at the same time as an act; closely related to but not the same as *motive*. See also *Motive*.

International bill of exchange A bill of exchange drawn in one country or state and payable in another.

Interstate commerce Commerce or the transportation of persons or property from points in one state to points in another state, or between points in the two states.

Interstate Commerce Commission An administrative agency created by Congress to carry out the terms of the Interstate Commerce Act, which regulates interstate commerce.

Interstate shipment   A shipment of goods between points not located in the same state.

Intestate   Dying without having made a valid will.

Intrastate shipment   The shipment of goods between points located in the same state.

Invitation to trade   An advertisement or announcement of any kind made for the purpose of attracting buyers who may make valid offers. Not an offer.

Involuntary bailment   A gratuitous bailment implied by law; a bailment arising from the leaving of personal property in the possession of a bailee through an act of God, accident, or other uncontrolled phenomenon.

Involuntary bankruptcy   Bankruptcy originating from the petition of three or more of the bankrupt's creditors.

J

Joint and several obligation   An obligation binding two or more persons individually as well as jointly. The obligation can be enforced either by joint action against all the persons or by separate actions against one or more.

Joint liability   A liability which arises when two or more persons act as one in accepting a contract obligation. Persons involved in a joint liability are usually sued together, or they may be sued individually by some state laws.

Joint-stock company   An association in which the shares of the members are transferable and control is delegated to a group or board.

Joint tenancy   Ownership of property by two or more persons, wherein the right of any deceased owner is automatically transferred to other surviving owners.

Joint venture   A relationship in which two or more persons combine their labor or property for a single undertaking and share profits and losses equally, unless otherwise agreed.

Judgment   The sentence of the law upon the record; the application of the law to the facts and the pleadings.

Jurisdiction   The right of a court to adjudicate the subject matter in a given case.

Jury   A group of persons sworn to declare the facts of a case as they are proved from the evidence presented and to find a verdict in the cause before them.

Justice   The ultimate goal of the rules which civilized people adopt and enforce in order to operate in harmony.

K

Kidnapping   Forcible abduction and carrying away of a person to some other place to exact money or for other unlawful end.

Knowingly   Consciously; intelligently; willfully; intentionally.

L

Labor-Management Relations Act   Legislation, passed by Congress in 1947, providing for mediation of labor-management disputes. Known also as the *Taft-Hartley Act*.

Labor-Management Reporting and Disclosure Act   A law, passed by Congress in 1959, regulating certain aspects of internal union affairs. It requires unions to give to the government reports and detailed disclosures of union activities and finances. Popularly known as the *Landrum-Griffin Act*.

Landlord   A party, usually the owner or the owner's agent, renting premises to a tenant.

Larceny The wrongful taking and carrying away of the property of another, without consent and with intent to keep it.

Last clear chance The rule that if a complainant had a last clear chance to avoid being injured, damages will not be allowed to the complainant.

Lawsuit An action or a proceeding in a court.

Lawyer A person licensed to practice the profession of law; an attorney.

Layoff The cessation of employment of an employee or a work force.

Lease The oral or written contract between landlord and tenant providing terms and conditions under which real property is rented.

Legal birthday By common law, 12:01 A.M. of the day prior to the anniversary of birth. Affirmed in most states by judicial decision or by statute.

Legal tender Coin and currency issued by a government and declared valid for payment of all debts, both public and private.

Legacy In a will, a bequest of money or personal property.

Legatee One to whom, by terms of a will, a legacy of personal property is left.

Lessee The party to whom premises are rented under a lease.

Lessor The party, usually the owner or the owner's agent, who rents premises to a tenant (lessee).

Libel A defamatory statement communicated to a third party.

License A personal privilege, given by the owner to another party and revocable at will, to perform designated acts upon the land of the owner; a privilege, granted by a state or city upon payment of a fee, which is not a contract and may be revoked for cause, conferring authority to perform a designated act.

License fee A charge for a privilege, imposed by a state or local government with the purpose of regulation or protection, or to discourage dangerous employments.

Licensee A person to whom a license is given; a social guest; a person entering or using premises by permission or by operation of the law but without express or implied invitation; a person entering premises by permission only; a person on another's premises solely in pursuit or furtherance of his or her own business, pleasure, or convenience.

Liquidation The process of winding up the affairs of a firm or corporation for the purpose of paying its debts and disposing of its assets.

Litigation A contest in a court of justice for the purpose of enforcing a right; a lawsuit.

Lockout An attempt by an employer in a labor dispute to pressure employees by closing the work site.

Locus sigili ['lō-kəs sə-'ji,-lī] "Place of the seal." Designated by the initials *L.S.*, which may be used in place of a seal on a written, formal agreement.

M

Magistrate The judge in a lower court, such as a justice of the peace or a police judge.

Magistrate's court In most states, a court of original jurisdiction in criminal and civil cases.

Maim To cripple or mutilate; to inflict upon a person any injury which deprives the person of the use of any limb or member of the body; to seriously wound or disfigure; to disable.

Maker The party obligated as the payor on a promissory note; the one promising to pay.

Malice aforethought A predetermination to commit an act without legal justification or excuse. Must be proved in order to establish criminal homicide in the first degree.

Malicious act A wrongful act intentionally done without legal justification or excuse; an unlawful act done willfully or purposely to injure another.

Malpractice In medicine, improper and negligent treatment resulting in injuries or physical discomfort to a patient under a physician's care. Also, a tort against lawyers and other professional persons.

Manslaughter The unlawful killing of another without malice, voluntarily or involuntarily, in the commission of some unlawful act.

Market value A price which an item or stock might be expected to bring if offered for sale in a fair market.

Master An employer-principal who employs another to perform service in his or her affairs and who controls the conduct of the other in the performance of the service.

Maxim A truth or rule that needs no proof or argument.

Mediation A procedure for settling disputes, whereby parties bring their case before a board that makes nonbinding recommendations.

Medicare Hospital and voluntary medical insurance available to nearly all Americans who are sixty-five or over.

Merger of corporations A combining of two corporations by which one absorbs the other and continues to exist, preserving its original charter and identity, while the other corporation ceases to exist.

Midnight deadline In banking, midnight on the next banking day following the banking day on which the bank receives a relevant item or notice, or following the banking day on time for taking action commences, whichever is later.

Minimum wage An amount, specified by federal or state statute, that will maintain a normal standard of living and preserve the health and efficiency of a worker.

Minor An infant or person who is below the age of legal competence as determined by state law.

Misdemeanor An offense lower than a felony; generally an offense punishable by fine or imprisonment other than in a penitentiary.

Misrepresentation An innocent and unintended misstatement of fact, which if accepted by another leads to his or her injury.

Money A medium of exchange authorized or adopted by a domestic or foreign government as a part of its currency.

Monopoly Any combination or organization which is so extensive, exclusive, and unified that its tendency is to prevent competition, and which has the power to control prices and cause the public harm.

Monthly tenancy A lease in which rent is paid monthly. Notice of termination must be equal to the lease period. When no definite period is expressed between the parties, the period is presumed to be for one month.

Mortality table A statistical table that shows the life expectancy of males and females at given ages.

Mortgage A conveyance or transfer of an interest in property for the purpose of creating a security for a debt.

Mortgagee A lender, or creditor, whose loan is secured by a mortgage on the borrower's real property.

Mortgagor The owner of real property given as security for a loan.

Motive A purpose or design to perform or refrain from performing an act.

Mutual assent A meeting of the minds between two or more parties in agreement on rights and obligations.

N

National Bankruptcy Act A federal law outlining rights and obligations in petitions of bankruptcy, and giving the U.S. District Courts jurisdiction over bankruptcy cases.

National Labor Relations Act A law, passed in 1935, encouraging collective bargaining and protecting the rights of workers in organizing and negotiating the terms and conditions of their employment. Popularly known as the *Wagner Act*.

Necessaries Articles or things required to maintain human life; such things as are suited to the condition and station in life of a person and his or her family, to satisfy their needs and wants. Food, clothing, medical and dental care, and shelter are generally classified as necessaries.

Negligence Failure to exercise reasonable care, which foreseeably causes injury to another person.

Negotiable instrument Any written document which may be transferred by indorsement and delivery or by delivery, so as to vest in the indorsee the legal title.

Negotiation The transfer of an instrument in such form that the transferee becomes a holder; transfer of a negotiable instrument from one person to another.

Nexus A logical connection.

No-fault insurance Motor vehicle insurance, enacted and in force in many states, whereby claims for accidents are paid by the insurer without the necessity of submitting proof of responsibility or fault for any loss.

Nominal damages Token damages permitted by a court against a defendant who has intruded on another's legal rights but who did not, thereby, cause actual damage. In England, 6 pence; in most U.S. courts, $1.

Nominal partner A person who appears to the world to be a partner or who is held out to all persons having dealings with a firm in the character of a partner, whether or not he or she has any real interest in the firm; a partner by estoppel. Also called *apparent partner*.

Nonperformance Neglect, failure, or refusal to do or perform a stipulated act; failure to keep the terms of a contract in respect to acts or doings agreed upon.

Notice Actual knowledge of a fact; receipt or notification of a fact; reason to know that a fact exists from all the facts and circumstances known at the time in question.

Notice of protest A notice given by the holder of a bill or note to the drawer or indorser that the bill or note has been protested for refusal of payment or acceptance.

Novation A substitution, by mutual consent, of new terms, conditions, or a party to an original agreement; a new agreement originating from one already in existence.

Nuisance A condition which annoys and disturbs one in possession of property, rendering its ordinary use or occupation unbearable.

Nuncupative will A will dictated to witnesses while the testator lies dying with no immediate possibility of writing and signing a written will.

O

Offer A proposal by one person to another, oral, written, or implied, which is intended to create a legal duty on its acceptance by the person to whom it is made. A requisite of a valid contract.

Offeree The party to whom an offeror makes and directs an offer.

Offeror The party who makes an offer.

Open-end credit Consumer credit which allows a customer to make purchases from time to time with the privilege of paying the balance in full or in installments, and in which a finance charge must be paid on any outstanding balance.

Open policy An insurance policy in which the value of the subject insured is not fixed or agreed upon in the policy between the insured and the underwriter, but is to be estimated in case of loss.

Operation of law The devolving of rights and sometimes liabilities upon a person by the mere application to a transaction of the established rules of law, without any act of the person other than making the transaction.

Option A contract whereby an offeror, in return for receiving something of value, agrees to hold an offer open for an offeree for a reasonable or specific length of time.

Order A direction to pay. An order must be more than an authorization or request and must identify the person to be paid with reasonable certainty.

Order bill of lading A negotiable bill of lading, containing words of negotiability.

Ordinance A rule established by authority; a permanent rule of action; a law or statute.

Ostensible agent One whom the principal, either intentionally or by lack of ordinary care, induces third persons to believe to be an agent, though the principal has not conferred authority on the agent; an apparent agent.

P

Par value The face value of common stock as assigned by the company's charter. On the date of issuance the par value of stocks and bonds is the principal; at a later date it is the principal plus interest.

Parol evidence rule A rule that bars a party from either changing or adding oral promises to a written contract. Only that which has been accepted as the written agreement will be enforceable.

Partnership A combination by two or more persons of their capital, labor, or skill for the purpose of their commercial benefit.

Passbook A book in which a bank or banker enters the deposits and withdrawals made by a customer, and which is retained by the latter.

Patent An exclusive property right in an invention, granted to the inventor by the government, to make, use, and sell an invention for a term of years.

Pawn The act of giving up personal property as security for performance of a promise or future payment of a debt, usually associated with a loan made by a pawnbroker; a pledge.

Pawnbroker One whose usual business is to loan money, taking the borrower's personal property as security for repayment of any loan made.

Payee The party named in a commercial paper to whom payment is to be made.

Percolating waters Water flowing below the surface in underground streams and rivers, and in surfacing springs.

Performance The fulfillment or accomplishment of a contract, promise, or other obligation, according to its terms.

Performance bond A promise, usually by a bonding or insurance company, to underwrite any damages resulting from nonperformance of contract obligations.

Performance certificate A certificate issued by an architect, or other third-party referee, approving work done and giving authorization for payment.

Perpetrator The person who commits a crime.

Personal defense As applied to commercial paper, a limited defense which cannot be used against a holder in due course.

Picketing Stationing persons for observation, patrol, and demonstration at a work site as part of employee pressure on an employer to meet a demand.

Plaintiff A complaining party; a person who commences an action in a court of law.

Pleading The process by which the parties in a lawsuit define and clarify the issues that divide them through pretrial written arguments filed with the court.

Pledge In bailments, the giving up of personal property as security for performance of an act or repayment of a debt.

Police power The power incident to state and local governments to impose those restrictions upon private rights which are reasonably related to the promotion and maintenance of the health, safety, morals, and general welfare of the public.

Possession The actual physical control of personal property, with or without the right of ownership, but with power and responsibility of care.

Postdated check A check delivered prior to its date, payable at sight or upon presentation on or after the day of its date.

Power of attorney An instrument authorizing another person to act as one's agent or attorney in fact.

Precedent A prior judicial decision relied upon as an example of a rule of law.

Preferred stock A class of corporate stock which is accorded, by charter or bylaws, a preference or priority in respect to dividends over the remainder of the stock of the corporation.

Premiums In insurance, the consideration paid by the insured for protection afforded by an insurer.

Presentment A demand for acceptance or payment made upon the maker, acceptor, drawee, or other payor by or on behalf of the holder.

Presumption In a suit, a fact accepted as truthful and binding but with a right granted to the other party to present evidence that might prove otherwise.

Principal A person who appoints and directs the activities of an agent.

Private accommodations Shelter provided persons by lodging houses and dormitories, as contrasted with accommodations offered by hotels and motels.

Private carrier A carrier of goods or persons, working under individual contract with those seeking its services. A private carrier is not required to serve all who apply, as contrasted with a public carrier.

Private corporation A corporation which is founded by and composed of private individuals, for private purposes.

Privity Mutuality of contract interest (i.e., offeror with offeree); mutual or successive relationships to the same rights in property (i.e., executor with testator, assignee with assignor, donee with donor, and lessee with lessor).

Probate The process of proving a will to the satisfaction of public authorities and carrying out the terms of such a will by the executor or administrator.

Product liability The obligation of a manufacturer or seller of goods to provide goods which are safe and free from defects that might in any way cause injury or harm to the buyer or others.

Profit An increase in wealth resulting from the operation of a business.

Profit a prendre ['prä-fəd-ə 'prän-dr(ə)] An easement that gives its owner the right to remove something of value from another's property, as the right to enter lands of another for the purpose of cutting hay, harvesting wheat, and the like.

Promise An undertaking to pay, which must be more than an acknowledgment of an obligation.

Promissory note A written promise to pay a specified sum at a designated time, or on demand, to a person named, to order, or to bearer.

Promoters Persons who, for themselves or others, take the preliminary steps in organization of a corporation.

Property That which is peculiar or proper to any person; that which belongs exclusively to a person; an aggregate of rights which are guaranteed and protected by the government.

Property tax A tax that is imposed on real or personal property.

Protest waiver The act of dispensing with formal protest as well as demand and notice of nonpayment which ordinarily precede protest.

Proxy An authorization to one person to act for another in transacting some business.

Public accommodations Shelter made available to all transients, with the right of exception, by hotels, motels, and other public houses. Regulated under the ancient innkeepers' laws.

Public corporation A corporation created by the state for political purposes and to act as an agency in the administration of civil government, with subordinate and local powers of legislation.

Public offer A valid offer made through public media but intended for only one person whose identity or address is unknown to the offeror, as an advertisement in a lost-and-found column of a newspaper.

Public-service corporation A quasi-public corporation or venture whose operations serve the needs of the general public; a private corporation which has been given certain powers of a public nature, such as the power of eminent domain, in order to discharge its duties for the public interest.

Puffing Exaggerated statements of a seller that are permitted by law and not considered to be fraudulent statements.

Punitive damages Damages, in excess of actual damages incurred by the plaintiff, awarded as a measure of punishment for the defendant's wrongful and malicious acts.

Pyramid sales A multilevel distribution plan in which recruited distributors receive commissions not only on products sold but also for recruiting other sellers.

Q

Qualified indorsement An indorsement in which words have been added to the signature that limit or qualify the liability of the indorser.

Quasi-contract A contract implied by law, not by fact. Actually not a contract in the true sense, lacking the element of mutual assent.

Quitclaim deed A deed to real property in which the grantor transfers only what rights he or she may have, and gives no warranties of quiet enjoyment or other such benefits.

Quorum The number necessary to lawfully transact business at a meeting.

Quo warranto [ˌkwō wə-ˈrän-(ˌ)tō] An action by the government to test the validity of some franchise, such as the privilege of doing business as a corporation.

R

Ratification The confirmation of one's own previous act or an act of another.

Real defense A defense inherent in the thing (*res*) and therefore good against anyone seeking to enforce a negotiable instrument, even a holder in due course (i.e., forgery, material alteration, and fraud in the inception).

Real property Land, buildings, and those things permanently attached to the realty or intended to be so attached.

Realty Real property as distinguished from personal property, as land and anything permanently attached thereto.

Reasonable care The care that prudent persons would exercise under the same circumstances; care which is not immoderate or excessive but suitable, fair, or rational.

Recover To be successful in a suit; to collect or obtain an amount; to receive judgment; to obtain a favorable or final judgment.

Registration of stock A record in the official books of a corporation of the name and address of the holder of each certificate of stock with the date of its issue; and, in a stock transfer, the names of both parties.

Regulation The act of control; a rule of order prescribed by superior or competent authority relating to the actions of those under its control.

Regulation Z Regulations prescribed by the Board of Directors of the Federal Reserve System that describe what must be done to comply with the Truth-in-Lending Law.

Release The relinquishment, concession, or giving up of a right, claim, or privilege, by the person to whom it belongs or to whom it accrues, to the person against whom it might be demanded or enforced.

Remedy The judicial means or court procedure by which legal and equitable rights are enforced; the right to obtain damages, restitution, specific performance, or an injunction for a wrong.

Renunciation Act of the holder of an instrument, whereby he or she expresses the intention of abandoning rights to an instrument or claims against one or more parties thereto.

Replevin A writ by which a party seeks the recovery of personal property wrongfully held by another.

Rescission The right to cancel any transaction and escape from all liability that one had become obligated in writing to perform.

Respondeat superior [ri-'spän-dē-ət sū̇-'pir-ē-ər] A phrase meaning "the master is liable for the acts of his or her agent."

Respondent A person against whom an administrative charge of discrimination is filed. In a civil action or action in a court of equity, the party against whom a motion is filed; a defendant; an appellee.

Restraining order In equity practice, an order forbidding a defendant to perform a threatened act until a hearing on an application for an injunction can be had.

Restraint of trade Combinations and arrangements for the creation of a monopoly, the control of prices, and the suppression of competition.

Restrictive indorsement An indorsement in which words have been added to the signature of the indorser, restricting the further indorsement of the instrument.

Revocation The withdrawal of an existing offer by the offeror's communication, by lapse of time, or by action or operation of law.

Riparian rights Rights of an owner whose land is situated beside a stream of water flowing either through or along the border of the land.

Robbery Felonious taking of personal property from another person by immediate pressure and against the person's will, using force or intimidation.

Royalty A payment that is reserved, as by the grantor of a patent or the leaser of a mine, and is payable proportionately to the use made of the right by the grantee.

S

Sale and return A contract of sale in which title to goods passes at the time of the sale, giving the buyer the right to return the goods at his or her own risk and expense.

Sale on approval A conditional sale which becomes absolute only if the buyer approves or is satisfied with the article sold.

Satisfactory performance The performance expected by each party in the execution of contract promises.

Scope of authority All authority held by an agent, both that which has been actually conferred and that which has been delegated either apparently or by implication.

Scope of employment Any act that can fairly and reasonably be deemed to be an ordinary and natural incident or attribute of employment or a natural and logical result of it.

Seal A device used to attest the execution of a written contract in the most formal manner.

Secondary boycott A conspiracy or combination to cause the customer or suppliers of an employer to cease doing business with that employer.

Secret partner A partner whose connection with the firm is really or professionally concealed from the public but who partakes of the profits.

Security An instrument which is issued in bearer form or registered form and which is issued or dealt in as a medium for investment; a share, participation, or other interest in an enterprise.

Security agreement As provided in Section 9 of the Uniform Commercial Code, a signed agreement protecting a seller on credit by pledge of the buyer's goods or rights as security of payment. An agreement which gives the seller-creditor an interest in any property which secures payment or performance of an obligation by the buyer-debtor.

Security interest Any interest in property which secures payment or performance of an obligation.

Sedition An insurrectionary movement tending toward treason, but in which no overt act has occurred; attempts by meetings, speeches, or publications to disturb the tranquility of the state.

Seniority A person's length of service in a place of employment.

Serious intent A requisite of a valid offer; a requirement that an offer be made seriously, and not under emotional stress or distress or in a spirit of frolic, jest, or fun.

Servant A person employed by another and subject to the direction and control of the employer in performance of duties.

Serviant tenement In an easement, the property over which a dominant property has an easement right.

Setoff A cross-complaint used by a defendant in making a demand on a plaintiff, which is independent of and unconnected with the cause of action set out in the original complaint.

Several liability A liability in which two or more persons accept contract obligations, agreeing to be held individually liable for performance.

Severance pay An allowance based on length of service of an employee and payable on termination of employment, except in cases of disciplinary discharge.

Shareholder A person whose name appears on the books of a corporation as the owner of shares of stock and who is entitled to participate in the management and control of the corporation.

Sherman Antitrust Act An act passed by Congress in 1890 to prohibit combinations in restraint of trade.

Sight draft A written order on a drawee to pay on demand the amount named in the instrument.

Silent partner An actual partner who has no voice or active part in the business management or operations of a partnership.

Slander The speaking of false, defamatory words tending to harm another's reputation.

Small claims court   A court established for the purpose of bringing equal justice for rich and poor in the handling of cases that have personal importance but involve little money.

Social Security Act   A federal act providing financial assistance to retired workers at ages sixty-two and sixty-five, to widows at age sixty, and to insured workers who are totally disabled at any age.

Sole proprietorship   A form of business organization in which one person owns and manages an enterprise and assumes all risks.

Special agent   A person employed to conduct a particular transaction or piece of business, or authorized to perform a specified act, for a principal.

Special indorsement   An indorsement which includes the name of the party to whom title of the instrument is being transferred and to whom payment is to be made.

Special partner (limited)   A member of a partnership who furnishes certain funds to the common stock, and whose liability extends no further than the fund furnished.

Specific performance   An equity court order compelling a defendant to carry out a contract obligation.

Speculative damages   Prospective or anticipated damages from the same acts or facts constituting the present cause of action, but which depend upon future developments which are without real proof.

Stare decisis [ˌ'sta-rē dǎ-'sī-sǎs]   A traditional doctrine which indicates that a court should follow prior decisions in all cases based on substantially similar facts.

Statute   A law passed by the legislative branch of a state.

Statute of frauds   A provision that no suit or action shall be maintained on certain classes of contracts unless there is a note in writing signed by the party to be charged.

Statute of limitations   A state or federal law that limits the time in which court action and complaint may be made in criminal, tort, and contract actions, and in collection of debts.

Stock   A written instrument giving its owner the right to participate in the management and ownership of a corporation.

Stock split   A readjustment of the financial plan of a corporation whereby each existing share of stock is split into such number of new shares as may be determined by the managers of the corporation.

Stoppage in transit   An unpaid seller's right to stop delivery of goods before they come into the possession of a buyer who has become insolvent or bankrupt.

Straight bill of lading   A nonnegotiable bill of lading; a bill of lading that does not contain words of negotiability. May not be negotiated but may be assigned.

Strike   A concerted stoppage of work by employees as a means of enforcing a demand made on their employer.

Subrogation   The right of an insurer to recover money paid to an insured, from a party that may be held accountable for the loss.

Subscriber   A person who becomes bound by a subscription to the capital stock of a corporation; or, an employer who has become a member or is insured under a workers' compensation act.

Subscription   A written contract by which one engages to take and pay for capital stock of a corporation; a promise or pledge to contribute money.

Substantial performance   The performance and completion of all contract obligations with the possible exception of certain unimportant and minor details.

Substantive law   The part of the law which the courts are established to administer; laws which create, define, and regulate legal rights and obligations.

Subterranean rights The right of the owner of land to the exclusive use of all below-surface ground to the middle of the earth. Subterranean rights are sometimes sold to mining and oil companies.

Summary judgment A judgment issued by a court when no facts are offered by the defense which need to be disproved, and hence there is no need for a trial.

Summons A writ issued by a court to a sheriff directing the notification of a defendant that a plaintiff claims to have a cause of action that must be answered.

Supreme Court A court of high powers and extensive jurisdiction, existing in most of the states; the court of last resort in the federal judicial system.

Surety A person who may be held primarily responsible for the debts, defaults, or wrong-doings of another. (A surety differs from a guarantor, who is only secondarily liable.)

Survey Verification of the boundaries of real property by a civil engineer or surveyor; a statement of the results of such a survey.

T

Tax sale deed A special type of quitclaim deed issued as a result of a forced sale by a sheriff or other public official in order to recover unpaid taxes against property sold.

Taxing power A power inherent in government to raise revenues.

Tenancy The property rights given a tenant under a lease.

Tenancy at will A leasehold estate, or tenancy, that continues for as long as both parties desire. Notice of intent to terminate may be dispensed with, or may be of one month, depending on local statutes.

Tenancy by the entireties Ownership by husband and wife, considered by law as one, with full ownership surviving to the living spouse on the death of the other.

Tenancy from year to year A lease providing for payment of an annual rent without specifying a definite period over which the lease will be in force.

Tenancy in common Ownership of an undivided interest in property by two or more persons, with each owner's rights going to his or her heirs rather than surviving to the other co-owners.

Tenancy in partnership The ownership relation that exists between partners under the Uniform Partnership Act.

Tenant A party who has a leasehold estate, granted by a landlord, in consideration of payment of rent.

Tenant by sufferance A tenant who fails to inform the landlord of intention of vacating, as required by the lease. Such a tenant may either be evicted at the end of the leasehold or be held obligated to a renewal of the present lease.

Tender An indication of readiness and willingness to carry out a contract obligation; an offer of money or other form of payment.

Tenure A status granted to an employee as protection from dismissal except for serious misconduct or incompetence determined by formal hearings; a means by which title is held to real property.

Terminate To discharge contract obligations either by satisfactory performance or by mutual agreement.

Testamentary capacity In wills, the proof of sufficient age and mental capacity required of a testator to a will.

Testate Having made a valid will.

Testator A person who dies, leaving property through a valid will.

Third party A person or persons who are neither offeror or offeree of a contract with which they have some relationship. In negotiable instruments, those persons, indorsers and holders, whose names do not appear on the face of an instrument.

Third-party beneficiary   A person who is not a party to a contract but for whose benefit the contract was made.

Third-party referee   An impartial party selected by both parties to an executory contract to make all decisions about the satisfactory performance and completion of all contract terms and conditions.

Time is of the essence   An expression denoting the importance of time of performance in an executory contract. When this term is applied, a party may be charged with a breach if performance is not completed at the time stated in the agreement.

Title   The intangible right of ownership.

Title by estoppel   The superior right of ownership of a buyer who has recorded a new deed, as opposing a prior buyer whose deed has not been recorded. The first buyer is estopped from claiming title due to failure to properly record the deed from the grantor.

Title certificate   A written document that gives evidence of ownership; a bill of sale, a motor vehicle registration certificate, or the like.

Title insurance   Insurance available through title insurance companies, guaranteeing a buyer's quiet ownership of real property. Preferred over the usual abstract of title guaranteed only by one individual's promise.

Title search   An investigation of title rights to real property, conducted by a lawyer who scrutinizes all recorded evidence of ownership, encumbrances, and other legal and equitable claims against a parcel of real estate.

Torrens system   A simplified system of transferring and recording titles to real estate, which originated in Australia and is now used in some states of the United States.

Tort   A civil wrong, other than one arising from breach of contract, for which a law court will grant damage.

Tortious bailee   Any party having wrongful possession of another's personal property.

Trade acceptance   A draft or bill of exchange drawn by a seller on the purchaser, to be accepted by the purchaser.

Trade name   A name under which a person, firm, or corporation carries on a business, trade, or occupation.

Trademark   A sign, device, or symbol by which the articles produced or dealt in by a person or firm are distinguishable from those produced or dealt in by rival producers.

Transcript   A copy of a court record.

Transient   A hotel guest; a person who accepts the services of a hotel or other public accommodation without obligation to remain a specified length of time.

Traveler's check   A bill of exchange drawn by the issuing bank upon itself, accepted by the act of issuance, and without the right of countermand.

Treason   Breach of allegiance to one's government, specifically by levying war against the government or by giving aid and comfort to the enemy.

Treasury shares   Ordinary stock which has been issued as fully paid to shareholders and subsequently acquired by the corporation to be used in furtherance of corporate purposes.

Treaty   A compact made between two or more independent nations.

Trespass   An unlawful act causing injury to the person, property, or relative rights of another.

Trial   Examination before a competent tribunal, according to the law of the land, for the purpose of determining the issues.

Trover   A common-law writ by which one party, the owner, demands the value of personal property wrongfully held and retained by another.

Trust deed A deed conveying secured property, such as notes and bonds, to a disinterested third party who holds the property as trustee for the benefit of the owner.

Trustee A person who is entrusted with the management and control of another's property; an agent of the court who is authorized to liquidate the assets of a bankrupt for the benefit of the bankrupt and all creditors.

Truth-in-Lending Law A federal law which requires disclosure of total finance charges and the annual percentage rate for credit in order that borrowers may be able to shop for credit; Regulation Z.

U

Ultra vires ['əl-trə 'vī-(,)rēz] Beyond the scope of the expressed or implied powers of a corporate charter or act of incorporation.

Unconditional Not limited or affected by any circumstances or stipulations.

Unconscionable Contract provisions or acts which are oppressive, overreaching, or shocking to the conscience.

Underutilization Employing fewer workers from minority groups, or fewer female or male employees, in a given job category than would reasonably be expected on the basis of the relevant local labor market.

Undivided right A title to an undivided portion of an estate; a title owned by one of two or more tenants in common, or by joint tenants before partition, as joint ownership of a car or airplane.

Undue influence Use of a position of superiority to induce a weaker party to enter into a contractual agreement which he or she might not enter into if left to act freely.

Unfair labor practice An improper employment practice by either an employer or a union; a practice prohibited by the Labor Management Relations Act.

Unfair methods of competition Acts determined, on a case-by-case basis and in the light of particular competitive conditions, to be contrary to the public interest.

Uniform Bulk Sales Law A uniform state law that protects creditors from a retailer making a sale of goods in bulk, as selling the entire inventory of certain stocked goods. Seller and buyer may effect such a sale but only by following the provisions of the law.

Uniform Commercial Code A law formulated by the National Conference on Uniform State Laws and the American Law Institute dealing with most aspects of commercial transactions.

Unilateral contract A contract formed by an offer or a promise from one party concerning an act to be done by another.

Unincorporated association A combination of two or more persons for the furtherance of a common nonprofit purpose.

Union An organization of employees to act on behalf of all employees in negotiations with the employer regarding terms of their employment contract.

Union shop A place of employment where nonunion workers may be employed for a trial period of not more than thirty days after which the nonunion worker must join the union or be discharged.

Usury A percentage rate of interest higher than that permitted by state law.

V

Vacancy clause In fire insurance, the insurer's exemption from claims when premises are vacant and unoccupied for a period in excess of sixty days.

Valid   Good; legal; enforceable by contracting parties.

Valid subject matter   Subject matter of a contract that conforms to federal and state law, and public policy.

Value   Something given in return for rights acquired in negotiable instruments and bank collections.

Valued policy   An insurance policy in which the insurer is obligated to pay the face value of the policy in the event of a total loss.

Variance   An exception allowed by public authorities in the enforcement of zoning regulations when deemed unfair and unreasonable in a singular situation.

Verdict   The answer of a jury given to the court concerning the matters of fact committed to them.

Vested   Accrued; fixed; settled; having the character or giving the rights of absolute ownership.

Void   Having no legal effect or binding obligation to anyone.

Voluntary bankruptcy   Bankruptcy originating from the petition of the bankrupt.

W

Wager   A contract in which one party stands to gain on the unpredictable outcome of some specific event. Contracts associated with gambling and wagers are illegal and unenforceable.

Waiver   The intentional or voluntary relinquishment of a known right.

Warehouse receipt   A receipt issued by a person engaged in the business of storing goods; an instrument showing that the signer is in possession of described goods for storage and obligating the signer to deliver the goods to a specified person or to order or bearer upon presentation of the instrument.

Warrant (Noun)   A court order authorizing an arrest.

Warrant (Verb)   To guarantee; to answer for; to assure that facts exist.

Warranty   A promise by a seller to a buyer about the nature of the property sold.

Warranty deed   A deed which contains an assurance by a seller of an estate that a buyer shall enjoy the same without interruption caused by flaws in the title.

Watered stock   Stock issued by a corporation as fully paid-up stock, when in fact the whole amount of the par value thereof has not been paid in.

Will   A legal document, not valid until the testator's death, expressing his or her intent in distribution of all real and personal property.

Winding up   Settling the accounts and liquidating the assets of a partnership or corporation for the purpose of making a distribution and dissolving the concern.

Workers' compensation   A state statute providing for payment of money to workers injured in the scope of their employment. Also called *workmen's compensation*.

Writ of attachment   A civil process allowing property to be attached in order to enforce a judgment or in order to bar transfer of property that might secure a pending judgment.

Writ of certiorari [ˌsər-sh(ē)ə-ˈrär-e]   A writ issued by a superior court ordering appellate review of the record of a case tried in a lower court.

Writ of mandamus [man-ˈdā-məs]   A court order that orders a public officer to carry out the official duties of his or her office.

Written law   The body of law which is passed by legislatures as statutes, ordinances, laws, treaties, and constitutions; statutory law.

Y

Yellow dog contract A contract by which an employer requires an employee to promise not to join a union during the course of employment, with the provision that he or she will be discharged upon joining.

Z

Zoning law A local regulation or ordinance which restricts the use of certain areas to specific uses; as in the case of areas zoned for residential, commercial, agricultural, industrial, or other uses.

Index